D1480511

A TREASURY OF FRIENDSHIP

A Treasury of Friendship

SENTIMENT, PHILOSOPHY, HUMOR,
INSPIRATION, OBSERVATION,
COUNSEL, ANALYSIS, IDEALISM,
AND FRIENDSHIP IN ACTION

Gathered from

*Memoirs, Essays, Letters, Poetry,
Legend, Fiction, Epics, and History,
from Ancient Times to Today.*

Compiled and Edited

by

RALPH L. WOODS

DAVID McKAY COMPANY, INC.

New York

LIBRARY OF CONGRESS CATALOG CARD NO.: 57-11078

MANUFACTURED IN THE UNITED STATES OF AMERICA

VAN REES PRESS • NEW YORK

ACKNOWLEDGMENTS

The editor and the publisher gratefully thank the following publishers, authors, copyright owners, and agents for their cooperation in granting permission to use material from
the works indicated below:

THE ABINGDON PRESS: Leslie D. Weatherhead's *Prescription for Anxiety,* copyright, 1956,
by Pierce and Washabaugh.

GEORGE ALLEN AND UNWIN, LTD.: Bailey Saunder's translation of Schopenhauer's *Counsels
and Maxims.*

APPLETON-CENTURY-CROFTS, INC.: Anne Douglas Sedgwicke's *A Childhood in Brittany
Eighty Years Ago,* copyright, 1918, 1919, The Century Co.; Richard Burton's *Little Essays
in Literature and Life,* copyright, 1914, by The Century Co.

ERNEST BENN, LTD.: *Private Letters, Pagan and Christian,* edited by Dorothy Brooke.

THE BOBBS-MERRILL CO., INC.: Irvin S. Cobb's *Exit Laughing,* copyright, 1941, by Irvin
S. Cobb, used by special permission of the publishers, The Bobbs-Merrill Co.

THE BODLEY HEAD, LTD.: "My Old Friend" from A. C. Benson's *Collected Poems.*

CURTIS BROWN, LTD.: André Maurois's *The Art of Living,* copyright, 1940, by André
Maurois, reprinted by permission of the author.

MARGARET E. BRUNER: "The Monk and the Peasant" from her *The Hill Road,* copyright,
1932, by Margaret E. Bruner.

JONATHAN CAPE, LTD.: Séan O'Faoláin's *Bird Alone.*

THE CLARENDON PRESS, OXFORD: *Epicurus, The Extant Remains of,* translated by Cyril
Bailey; Robert Bridges' "The Unillumined Verge" from *Poetical Works of Robert Bridges,*
1929.

THE JOHN DAY CO.: Lin Yutang's *With Love and Irony,* copyright, 1934, 1936, 1937,
1938, 1940, by Lin Yutang.

J. M. DENT AND SONS, LTD.: Clara Bell's translation of Balzac's "The Atheist's Mass," in
The Everyman Library edition.

THE DIAL PRESS, INC.: Pierre van Paassen's *Days of Our Years,* copyright, 1940, by The
Dial Press, Inc., used by permission of The Dial Press, Inc.

DODD, MEAD AND CO.: Kenneth Grahame's *The Golden Age;* Nancy Byrd Turner's "To
Our Guest" from her *Star in a Well,* copyright, 1935, by Dodd, Mead and Co.; *Scott's
Last Expedition,* copyright, 1913, 1941, by Dodd, Mead and Co.; all reprinted by per-
mission of Dodd, Mead and Co., Inc.

DOUBLEDAY AND CO., INC.: O. Henry's *Roads of Destiny,* copyright, 1903, by Doubleday
and Co., Inc.; Burton Rascoe's *Before I Forget,* copyright, 1937, by Burton Rascoe, reprinted by permission of Doubleday and Co., Inc.; Fulton Oursler's *Modern Parables,*
copyright 1950, 1951, by Grace Perkins Oursler and Albert L. Cole, executors of the estate
of Fulton Oursler, deceased; W. Somerset Maugham's *A Writer's Notebook,* copyright,
1949, by W. Somerset Maugham, reprinted by permission of Doubleday and Co., Inc.;

iv

ACKNOWLEDGMENTS v

Helen Keller's *The Story of My Life,* copyright, 1902, 1903, 1905, by Helen Keller, reprinted by permission of Doubleday and Co., Inc.

LOUISE DRISCOLL: "The Banquet" from her *The Garden of the West,* copyright, 1922, by The Macmillan Co.

WILL DURANT: H. L. Mencken's contribution to *On the Meaning of Life,* edited by Will Durant, copyright, 1932, by Will Durant.

E. P. DUTTON AND CO. INC.: *Private Letters, Pagan and Christian,* edited by Dorothy Brooke, copyright, 1936, by E. P. Dutton and Co. Inc.; Clara Bell's translation of Balzac's "The Atheist's Mass."

BERNICE WILLIAMS FOLEY: B. Y. Williams' poem "The Friend Who Just Stands By," copyright, 1928, by Sully and Co.

W. AND G. FOYLE, LTD.: *Christian Friendship,* by St. Aelred of Rievaulx, translated by Revd. Hugh Cabot, O. Cist., 1942.

WILFRED FUNK, INC.: Lowell Thomas's *Pageant of Adventure,* copyright, 1940.

HARPER AND BROTHERS: *Mark Twain's Letters,* edited by Alfred Bigelow Paine, copyright, 1907, by The Mark Twain Co.; Robert E. Sherwood's *Roosevelt and Hopkins,* copyright, 1948, by Robert E. Sherwood.

WILLIAM E. HEINEMANN, LTD.: two poems by Algernon Charles Swinburne.

HODDER AND STOUGHTON, LTD.: Leslie D. Weatherhead's *Prescription for Anxiety.*

HOUGHTON MIFFLIN CO.: Kate Douglas Wiggins's *My Garden of Memory,* copyright, 1923; Agnes Repplier's *Eight Decades,* copyright, 1937; Winston Churchill's *The Second World War* (vol. 6), copyright, 1953, by Houghton Mifflin Co.; Frances Lester Warner's *To the People We Like,* copyright, 1929, by Frances Lester Warner; Randolph S. Bourne's *Youth and Life,* copyright, 1911, 1912, 1913, by The Atlantic Monthly Co., copyright, 1929, by Randolph S. Bourne.

DOUGLAS J. JOHNSON: Clara Barrus's *Whitman and Burroughs, Comrades,* copyright, 1931, by Houghton Mifflin Co.

DONALD S. KING: Henry Churchill King's *The Laws of Friendship,* copyright, 1909, by The Macmillan Co.

FRANCES KIRKLAND: Winifred Kirkland's *The Joys of Being a Woman,* copyright, 1918, by Winifred Kirkland.

KNAPP-FISHER, WARTNABY AND BLUNT: E. V. Lucas's poem "Friends."

ALFRED A. KNOPF, INC.: Eunice Tietjens' "Old Friendship" from her *Leaves in Windy Weather,* copyright, 1929, by Alfred A. Knopf, Inc.; *Dostoevsky: His Life and Letters,* translated by Koteliansky and Murray, copyright by Alfred A. Knopf, Inc.

J. B. LIPPINCOTT COMPANY: Damon Runyon's "For a Pal" from his *Blue Plate Special,* copyright, 1929, 1930, 1931, by Damon Runyon, published by J. B. Lippincott Co.

LITTLE, BROWN AND CO.: Jacques Barzun's *Teacher in America,* copyright, 1944, 1945, by Jacques Barzun.

McGRAW-HILL BOOK CO., INC.: Jesse Stuart's *The Years of My Rebirth,* copyright, 1956, by Jesse Stuart, published by McGraw-Hill Book Co., Inc.

THE MACMILLAN COMPANY: Vera Brittain's *Testament of Friendship,* copyright, 1940, by Vera Brittain; Henry van Dyke's *The Gospel for a World of Sin;* William Allen White's *The Changing West;* Robert P. T. Coffin's *Book of Uncles,* copyright, 1942, by The Macmillan Co.; Rufus M. Jones' *New Eyes for Invisibles,* copyright, 1943, by The Macmillan Co.; C. T. Winchester's *A Group of English Essayists of the Nineteenth Century,* copyright, 1910, 1938, by The Macmillan Co.

MACMILLAN AND COMPANY, LTD.: Pierre Loti's *A Child's Romance,* translated by Clara Bell; Mrs. Humphry Ward's translation of *Amiel's Journal;* Joseph Jacob's translation of Gracian's *Worldly Wisdom;* J. E. C. Welldon's translation of Aristotle's *Nicomachean Ethics;* Vera Brittain's *Testament of Friendship.*

MAJORIE CONNOR MURPHEY: *Letters to Children,* edited by Eva G. Connor, copyright, 1938, by The Macmillan Co.

JOHN MURRAY (PUBLISHER), LTD.: A. C. Benson's *From a College Window* and from his *At Large; Scott's Last Expedition.*

RACHEL BAKER NAPIER: David Grayson's (Ray Stannard Baker) *Adventures in Friendship,* copyright, 1910, by Doubleday, Page and Co.

NATIONAL PROVINCIAL BANK LTD.: J. E. C. Welldon's translation of Aristotle's *Nicomachean Ethics.*

New Directions: passage from the Antoine de St. Exupéry's story in *Modern French Short Stories*, edited by John Lehmann, all rights reserved, reprinted by permission of John Lehmann and New Direction Books.

Oxford University Press: two poems by Austin Dobson.

Pantheon Books, Inc.: *Goethe: Wisdom and Experience*, selected by Ludwig Curtius, edited and translated by Herman J. Weigand.

G. P. Putnam's Sons: A. C. Benson's *At Large*, copyright, 1908, by G. P. Putnam's Sons, and A. C. Benson's *From a College Window*, 1906.

Dorothy Quick: for her "A Little Girl's Mark Twain," *North American Review*, September, 1935.

Reader's Digest: Henry Morton Robinson's "You Won't Be Snubbed," copyright, 1935, by The Reader's Digest Association, Inc., reprinted with permission.

Paul R. Reynolds and Son: *Letters of William James*, edited by his son, Henry James, Little, Brown–Atlantic Monthly Press, 1920, copyright, 1920, by Henry James.

Henry Morton Robinson: his "You Won't Be Snubbed," *Reader's Digest*, September, 1935.

Charles Scribner's Sons: George Santayana's *Persons and Places*, copyright, 1944, by Charles Scribner's Sons; George Santayana's *The Middle Span*, copyright, 1945, by Charles Scribner's Sons; George Santayana's *The Life of Reason: Reason in Society*, copyright, 1905, 1933, by Charles Scribner's Sons; *Theodore Roosevelt: An Autobiography*, copyright, 1913, by Charles Scribner's Sons, copyright, 1941, by Edith K. Carow; William Archer's translation of Henrik Ibsen's *John Gabriel Borkman;* all published by Charles Scribner's Sons and reprinted with their permission.

Ora Searler: Charles Hanson Towne's poem "Around the Corner," from *Selected Poems*, copyright, 1925, by Appleton-Century Co.

Odell Shepard: *The Journal of Bronson Alcott*, edited by Odell Shepard, published by Little, Brown and Co., copyright, 1938, by Odell Shepard.

Simon and Schuster, Inc.: Ben Hecht's *A Child of the Century*, copyright, 1954, by Ben Hecht; Joshua Loth Liebman's *Peace of Mind*, copyright, 1946, by Joshua Loth Liebman.

Mrs. George W. Stark: Anne Campbell's poem "To My Friend."

Viking Press, Inc.: Sean O'Faoláin's *Bird Alone*, copyright, 1936, by The Viking Press, Inc., New York; *The Portable Woollcott*, by Alexander Woollcott, copyright, 1946, by The Viking Press, Inc., New York; Irwin Edman's *Philosopher's Holiday*, copyright, 1938, by Irwin Edman, reprinted by permission of The Viking Press, Inc., New York; John Steinbeck's *Tortilla Flat*, copyright, 1935, by John Steinbeck, reprinted by permission of The Viking Press, Inc., New York.

Dorothy Ward: Mrs. Humphry Ward's translation of *Amiel's Journal*.

A. P. Watt and Son and The Lewis Carroll Estate, and Macmillan and Company, Ltd.: *Letters from Lewis Carroll to His Child Friends*, edited by Evelyn Hatch, published 1933. And A. P. Watt and Son, W. Somerset Maugham, and William Heinemann, Ltd.: W. Somerset Maugham's *A Writer's Notebook*.

Mrs. M. Wells: S. S. Kotelansky's translation of *Dostoevsky: His Life and Letters*.

It is a pleasure to acknowledge the expert typing done by Mrs. Jean Meeker and Miss Antoinette D'Annibale. John Scott Mabon, Managing Editor of the David McKay Company, Inc., has been unfailingly helpful and understanding from the very beginning. Lillias Watt Woods did a great deal of checking of typescript, and helped with the indexes.

R. L. W.

Ridgewood, N. J.

To ROBERT LEIGHTON BARRET

Friendship is a word the very sight of which in print makes the heart warm.

—Augustine Birrell

CONTENTS

NOTE: Since the selections in this book are arranged for reading pleasure, the customary chronological form of Contents has been omitted in favor of the following more useful classified arrangement.

SHORT STORIES, PASSAGES FROM NOVELS, PLAYS, AND EPICS

REMINISCENCES

POEMS

TRIBUTES

CONTENTS

REFLECTIONS AND OPINIONS

LEGENDS AND FABLES

LETTERS

BIBLICAL AND OTHER SPIRITUAL QUOTATIONS

BIOGRAPHY

PHILOSOPHICAL COMMENTS

EPISODES AND ANECDOTES

PROSE QUOTATIONS (UNTITLED)

A TREASURY OF FRIENDSHIP

TESTAMENT OF FRIENDSHIP
Vera Brittain

Between 1922 and 1925, Winifred [Holtby] and I first occupied a ground-floor studio and then a top-floor flat in Doughty Street, the long straight road not far from the British Museum which links Theobald Road with Mecklenburg Square.

In the autumn of 1923 we moved into a spacious mansion flat in Maida Vale, without in the least realizing that we were exchanging the choice habitation of intellectual Bloomsbury for a district with quite another reputation. Winifred was always gaily indifferent to the peculiar snobbery which attaches importance to "good" note-paper and a "good" address....

We were ... glad of our strenuous, independent, enthralling London existence. Neither of us had ever known any pleasure quite equal to the joy of coming home at the end of the day after a series of separate and varied experiences, and each recounting these incidents to the other over late biscuits and tea. Our conversations were irradiated by Winifred's delight in small, absurd trifles. She used to sit on the floor in front of the tiny gas-fire, the light on her hair and her blue eyes sparkling with enjoyment, eagerly imploring: "Tell me some more!"

Those years with Winifred taught me that the type of friendship which reaches its apotheosis in the story of David and Jonathan is not a monopoly of the masculine sex. Hitherto, perhaps owing to a lack of women recorders, this fact has been found difficult to accept by men, and even by other women. Some feminine individualists believe that they flatter men by fostering the fiction of women's jealous inability to love and respect one another. Other skeptics are roused by any record of affection between women to suspicions habitual among the over-sophisticated.

"Too, too Chelsea!" Winifred would comment amiably in after years when some zealous friend related the newest legend current about us in the neighborhood.

After a year or two of constant companionship, our response to each other's needs and emotions had become so instinctive that in our correspondence one of us often replied to some statement or request made by the other before the letter which contained it had arrived. When I wrote Winifred from America at the beginning of May 1927 that I thought I was going to have a child, she replied that during the pre-

3

vious week she remembered having an unusually vivid dream about a baby of mine. She called it "the beloved and lovely child"—a sentiment which she always felt for my son John Edward from the time that he was born at the end of that year.

The only personal experience of telepathy that I have ever known occurred in connection with Winifred. One day in 1923, when I was out of London on a periodic teaching expedition, a class was cancelled and I arrived back at our Doughty Street flat before tea-time instead of the usual supper-time. Not knowing that Winifred was out, I ran up the stairs and called gaily, "Hullo, my dear!" as I opened the door.

Shortly before supper Winifred returned from an afternoon's shopping in the West End. As soon as she saw me she inquired rather oddly: "Look here—did you come back to-day at the usual time?"

I explained that I had been early, and she then asked:

"Well, did you go straight to the flat?"

"Yes," I replied. "I came back on the 'bus from London Bridge as usual. Why do you ask?"

"Because," she said, "I had the queerest experience this afternoon. I was in Berkley Street, going to Piccadilly, and suddenly I heard your voice just behind me calling. 'Hullo, my dear!' I turned around quite startled—and found you weren't there."

"When exactly did that happen?" I asked.

"It was about four o'clock," she said.

I then told her precisely at that hour I had run up the stairs and called my greeting to the empty flat.

Passionately as I desired Winifred's friendship, deeply as I needed it with the starving need of an individual whose earlier loves had been prematurely and violently shattered, the building of it was her achievement rather than mine. In the years which followed the war I was not easy to live with, and I often wondered even then why Winifred showed no sign of wanting to leave me. The heredity inconsiderately bequeathed me by nervous irritable ancestors, combined with the loss of every person for whose life I feared during the war, had implanted a habit of apprehension which I now accept as a lifelong burden, since twenty years have not sufficed to remove it. Today I can conceal and sometimes forget it, but in the nineteen-twenties it was perpetual and acute. Every hour of suspense, however slight its cause, meant unmitigated agony. Every minor set-back, criticism or disappointment upset me at least twice as much as any sane person. Our stimulating life in London, with its constant surprises and excitements, was probably the worst that I could then have lived, for whenever we spent a country holiday together at Whipsnade or Cornwall or Burgh Head, the sense of strain began to disappear. But that London life was inevitable if a beginning was ever to be made with the writer's career that I had already postponed for seven interminable years, and Winifred, realizing this, resolved that since the surroundings could not be changed the companion chosen must act as compensation.

Her own capacity for swift exasperation was not negligible; I once saw her take an inefficient secretary, who had bungled an important telephone message, firmly by the shoulders and shake her like a child. But it was chiefly fools whom she could not suffer; provided that intelligence and goodwill existed, she was ready to forgive every accompanying disadvantage. With me her generosity and forbearance were unfailing; patiently she consoled my lunatic anxiety over adverse reviews, rejected manuscripts, family ailments, and other minor everyday annoyances which to her must have seemed absurdly trivial. Sometimes, ruefully seeing myself as others saw me, I asked her half sadly and half amusedly why she put up with it. She would then answer quite seriously that she was a debtor to life, and therefore felt under an obligation to repay with love and service a friend whose personal history had given less reason for gaiety and confidence than her own.

"I didn't have to fight to go to college like you," she would explain. "Mother just sent me and everything came of its own accord. And then I didn't lose anyone in the war who was really necessary to my happiness."

When I asked her if she did not regard Bill and her comfortless relationship with him as a species of wartime tragedy, she would reply that at any rate he wasn't dead, or even any longer missing in South America. Soon, now, he would be back in London, and if she found that after all she had lost him, she had only herself to thank....

* * * * *

The day before I was married, Winifred gave me as her wedding gift a long fine platinum chain studded with small seed-pearls. With my wedding dress and for years afterwards I wore it as a necklace, but later, twisted two or three times round my wrist, it looked more effective as a bracelet. Two days before Winifred died I took the chain to the nursing home, twined as usual round my arm. Her illness had already made her blind, but I closed her fingers over it. Recognizing her gift, she smiled. "It was too little," she said characteristically. "It ought to have been bigger...."

* * * * *

I was due back from the United States in mid-August.... G. had agreed that I should spend the next half year in London to recover the lost contacts at home. Thanks to one of those idiotic misgivings which long separation provokes, I had found—Heaven knows how or where—some imaginary lack of response in Winifred's vivid, delightful letters, and had written suggesting a little sadly that perhaps she might not want to share the flat again during my six months in England.

She sought to dismiss these unworthy suspicions by an eager attempt to explain her own psychology.

"In one way I am self-sufficient; I can live; I can enjoy my life; see colors; hear music and voices; conceive ideas, taste new experiences, all with true zest and all alone!...You must remember that, though superficially affectionate, my real nature is cold. I do not find demonstrative intimacy an easy thing....This is probably a mean and ungenerous spirit which hesitates to surrender an iota of selfish integrity. I do not excuse it. I am only trying to explain. But this inarticulateness, this inhibition against the expression of love, is always ready to rise up in me....I wish that it were otherwise. I wish that I had not this subconscious desire to possess myself completely....I think that all love is gain. Only at times, an instinct beyond thought comes between me and the expression of love."

To her final reassurance, no word could have been added. "It is true that I love other people...that I find interest in almost every chance acquaintance—the people whom I met in Africa, or on the boat. But you are you. And because you are you, there is part of me with which, in Marguerite's words to Faust, 'I need thee every hour.'... Nothing could change me except your changing. Not your attitude towards me, I mean, but towards life....I have gained more from your companionship than I shall ever tell or know. What you mean to me I can never make you see, for you are too humble beneath your thousand vanities."

Whether this was really true, I do not know; I only record it because she said it. No one, least of all myself, is worth such pure rarity of devoted love. No treasure in heaven or earth can replace it or atone for its loss.

NEW FRIENDS AND OLD FRIENDS

Joseph Parry

Make new friends, but keep the old;
Those are silver, these are gold.
New-made friendships, like new wine,
Age will mellow and refine.

Friendships that have stood the test—
Time and change—are surely best;
Brow may wrinkle, hair grow gray;
Friendship never knows decay.
For 'mid old friends, tried and true,
Once more we our youth renew.
But old friends, alas! may die;
New friends must their place supply;
Cherish friendship in your breast—
New is good, but old is best;
Make new friends, but keep the old;
Those are silver, these are gold.

". . . the only release from the cave of loneliness . . ."

THE BEGINNING OF FRIENDSHIP
Séan O'Faoláin

They came in, and her wide smile and her blush did not make it easy to tell her why I came: it was a greeting for myself alone. And when we sat before the fire I felt immediately a live thread begin to spin itself between us, just as it did one night in Youghal, like a cobweb spinning across the road of a spring day. This was something I had not foreseen, and what with, in her, a shyness she could not conceal and, in me, that sense of the night outside, suddenly becoming vast and multitudinous, pitying to no one, according as the warmth of the room and her companionship came stealing over me; what, too, with the memory of the summer that had been so solitary and calm, I felt about us and our talk an atmosphere quite new to me.

It was akin to benevolence and far more deep and mysterious than friendship, because it was friendship in its first stage when one is giving all, spreading out all one's little riches, not yet having discovered either how much it is vain to offer or expect. That I knew now, who have for years tried to live alone, is how people do meet and join: a first slight bridge, a wavering feeler out of the shell of self; then a gush of willingness, giving with both hands; then, when all is given, the secret measuring by each of what—not of what the other has given but of what each has taken. The end and measure of utter friendship, the only release from the cave of loneliness, is with him who knows how to accept most. That discovery has meant everything to me. For as it is with men, so it is with life which we understand and love in proportion as we accept without question what it gives, without question as to whether we need it, nor even questioning whether its gift seems cruel or kind. It is the supreme generosity because we do not even know who the Giver is; why He has given; or what.

~~~~~~~

There may be moments in friendship, as in love, when silence is beyond words. The faults of our friend may be clear to us, but it is well to seem to shut our eyes to them. Friendship is usually treated by the majority of mankind as a tough and everlasting thing which will survive all manner of bad treatment. But this is an exceedingly great and foolish error; it may die in an hour of a single unwise word; its conditions of existence are that it should be dealt with delicately and tenderly, being as it is a sensible plant and not a roadside thistle. We must not expect our friend to be above humanity.

—OUIDA

~~~~~~~

"... distract his mind, cheer him up ..."

MARJORIE DAW

Thomas Bailey Aldrich

Dr. Dillon to Edward Delaney, Esq., at The Pines, near Rye, N. H.

August 8, 187—.

My dear Sir: I am happy to assure you that your anxiety is without reason. Flemming will be confined to the sofa for three or four weeks, and will have to be careful at first how he uses his legs. A fracture of this kind is always a tedious affair. Fortunately, the bone was very skillfully set by the surgeon who chanced to be in the drug-store where Flemming was brought after his fall, and I apprehend no permanent inconvenience from the accident. *Flemming is doing perfectly well physically;* but I must confess that the irritable and morbid state of mind into which he has fallen causes me a great deal of uneasiness. You know how impetuous and energetic our friend is ordinarily, never content unless he is rushing at some object, like a sportive bull at a red shawl; but amiable withal. He is no longer amiable. He sits with bowed head regarding his splintered limb, silent, sullen, despairing. Nothing can distract his melancholy. He refuses to eat, does not even read the newspapers, books have no charms for him. His state is truly pitiable.

Now, if he were a poor man, with a family depending on his daily labor, this despondency would be natural enough. But in a young fellow of twenty-four, with plenty of money and seemingly not a care in the world, the thing is monstrous. I have anaesthetics and lotions, to make people sleep and soothe pain; but I've no medicine that will make a man have a little common-sense. That is beyond my skill, but maybe it is not beyond yours. You are Flemming's intimate friend. Write to him frequently, distract his mind, cheer him up, and prevent him from becoming a confirmed case of melancholia. I am, my dear sir, with great respect, etc.

Edward Delaney to John Flemming, West 38th Street, New York

August 9.

My dear Jack: I had a line from Dillon this morning, and was re-joiced to learn that your hurt is not so bad as reported. Dillon will put you on your pins again in two or three weeks, if you will only follow his counsel.

I can imagine how tranquil and saintly you are with your leg in a trough! It is deuced awkward, to be sure, just as we had promised ourselves a glorious month together at the seaside; but we must make the best of it. It is unfortunate, too, that my father's health renders it impossible for me to leave him. I think he has much improved; the sea air is his native element; but he still needs my arm to lean upon in his walks, and requires some one more careful than a servant to look after him. I cannot come to you, dear Jack, but I have hours of unemployed time on my hands, and I will write you a whole post-office full of letters if that will divert you.

I wish I were a novelist. This old house, with its sanded floors and high wainscots, and its narrow windows looking out upon a cluster of pines would be the place in which to write a summer romance. It should be a novel like one of that Russian fellow's—what's his name?—Tourgenieff, Turguenef, Turgenif, Toorguniff, Turgenjew—nobody knows how to spell him. Yet I wonder if even a Liza or an Alexandra Paulovna could stir the heart of a man who has constant twinges in his leg. I wonder if one of our own Yankee girls of the best type, haughty and *spirituelle,* would be of any comfort to you in your present deplorable condition. If I thought so, I would hasten to find you one.

Picture to yourself a large white mansion just across the road, nearly opposite our cottage. It is built, perhaps, in the colonial period, with rambling extensions, and gambrel roof, and a wide piazza on three sides. Sometimes in the morning, and oftener in the afternoon, a young woman appears on the piazza with some mysterious Penelope web of embroidery in her hand, or a book. There is a hammock over there—very becoming when one is eighteen and has golden hair, and dark eyes and an emerald-colored illusion dress looped up after the fashion of a Dresden china shepherdess. All this splendor goes into that hammock, and sways there like a pond-lily in the golden afternoon. The window of my bed-room looks down on that piazza—and so do I.

But enough of this nonsense, which ill becomes a sedate young attorney taking his vacation with an invalid father. Drop me a line, dear Jack, and tell me how you really are.

John Flemming to Edward Delaney

August 11.

Your letter, dear Ned, was a godsend. My left leg weighs three tons. It is embalmed in spices and smothered in layers of fine linen, like a mummy. I lie from morning till night on a lounge, staring into the hot street. All is silence and dust and desolation.

Your letter really cheered me up. Send me a screed, Ned, as often as you can. Write me more about that little girl in the hammock. That was very pretty, all that about the Dresden china shepherdess and the pond-lily; the imagery a little mixed, perhaps, but very pretty. Tell me, what is her name? Who is her father? Where's her mother? Who's her lover? You cannot imagine how this will occupy me. The more trifling, the better. My imprisonment has weakened me intellectually to such a degree that I find your epistolary gifts quite considerable.

Edward Delaney to John Flemming

August 12.

The sick pasha shall be amused. *Bismillah!* he wills it so. But, truly, Jack, I have a hard task. There is literally nothing here—except the little girl over the way. She is swinging in the hammock at this moment. Who is she, and what is her name? Her name is Daw. Only daughter of Mr. Richard W. Daw, ex-colonel and banker. Mother dead. Brother at Harvard. Old, rich family, the Daws. This is the homestead, where father and daughter pass eight months of the twelve; the rest of the year in Baltimore and Washington. The daughter is called Marjorie— Marjorie Daw. Sounds odd at first, doesn't it? But after you say it over to yourself half a dozen times, you like it.

... How oddly things fall out! Ten minutes ago I was called down to the parlor, where I found my father and Mr. Daw doing the antique polite to each other. He had come to pay his respects to his new neighbors. Mr. Daw is a tall, slim gentleman of about fifty-five, with a florid face and snow-white mustache and side-whiskers. Was a colonel in the late war. Plucky old boy, backbone of New Hampshire granite. Before taking his leave, the colonel delivered himself of an invitation as if he were issuing a general order. Miss Daw has a few friends coming, at 4 P.M., to play croquet on the lawn (parade grounds) and have tea (cold rations) on the piazza. Will we honor them with our company? (or be sent to the guard-house.) My father declines on the plea of ill-health. My father's son bows with as much suavity as he knows, and accepts.

In my next I shall have something to tell you. I shall have seen the little beauty face to face. Keep up your spirits, my boy, until I write you another letter.

Edward Delaney to John Flemming

August 13.

The party, my dear Jack, was as dreary as possible. A lieutenant of the navy, the rector of the Episcopal church at Stillwater, and a society swell from Nahant. The women were much better, the two Miss Kingsburys of Philadelphia, staying at the Sea-shell House, two bright and engaging girls. But Marjorie Daw!

The company broke up soon after tea, and I remained to smoke a cigar with the colonel on the piazza. It was like seeing a picture to see Miss Marjorie hovering around the old soldier, and doing a hundred little things for him. She brought the cigars and lighted the tapers with her own delicate fingers, in the most enchanting fashion. As we sat there, she came and went in the summer twilight, with her white dress and pale gold hair, like some lovely phantom that had sprung into existence out of the smoke-wreaths. If she had melted into air, like the statue of Galatea in the play, I should have been more sorry than surprised.

I sat with the Daws until half past ten, and saw the moon rise on the sea. What did we talk about? We talked about the weather—and *you!* The weather has been disagreeable for several days past—and so have you. I glided from one topic to the other very naturally. I told my friend of your accident; how it has frustrated all our summer plans, and what our plans were. I described you; or, rather, I didn't. I spoke of your amiability, of your patience under this severe affliction. If you had been there, Jack, you wouldn't have known yourself.

Miss Marjorie asked all manner of leading questions concerning you. It did not occur to me then, but it struck me forcibly afterwards, that she evinced a singular interest in the conversation. When I got back to my room, I recalled how eagerly she leaned forward, with her full, snowy throat in strong moonlight, listening to what I said. Positively, I think I made her like you!

John Flemming to Edward Delaney

August 17.

You may abuse me as much as you like, and I'll not complain; for I don't know what I should do without your letters. They are curing me.

Ned, that Miss Daw must be a charming person. I should certainly like her. I like her already. When you spoke in your first letter of seeing a young girl swinging in a hammock under your chamber window, I was somehow strangely drawn to her. What you have subsequently written of Miss Daw has strengthened the impression. You seem to be describing a woman I have known in some previous state of existence, or dreamed of in this. Upon my word, if you were to send me her photograph, I believe I should recognize her at a glance.

You would laugh in your sleeve, you wretched old cynic, if you knew how I lie awake nights, with my gas turned down to a star, thinking of The Pines and the house across the road. Have you noticed anything in the shape of a lover hanging around the colonial mansion? Does that lieutenant of the horse-marines or that young Stillwater parson visit the house much? I wonder, Ned, you don't fall in love with Miss Daw. I am ripe to do it myself. Speaking of photographs, couldn't you manage to slip one of her *cartes-de visite* from her album—she must have an album, you know—and send it to me? I will return it before it could be missed. That's a good fellow.

O— my leg? I forgot about my leg. It's better.

Edward Delaney to John Flemming

August 20.

You ask me why I do not fall in love with Miss Daw. I will be frank, Jack: I have thought of that. She is young, rich, accomplished; but she lacks the something that would be necessary to inspire in me that kind of interest. Flemming, I am about to make a revelation that will astonish you. I may be all wrong in my premises and consequently in my conclusions; but you shall judge.

I think I mentioned to you the air of eager attention with which Miss Daw followed my account of your accident after the croquet party. Well, the next morning, as I went to the post-office to mail my letter, I overtook Miss Daw and accompanied her thither and back, an hour's walk. The conversation again turned on you, and again I remarked that inexplicable look of interest which had lighted upon her face the previous evening. Since then, I have seen Miss Daw perhaps ten times and on each occasion I found that when I was not speaking of you or some person or place associated with you, I was not holding her attention. She would be absent-minded, her eyes would wander away from me to some distant object in the landscape. If I abruptly dropped some remark about my friend Flemming, then the sombre blue eyes would come back to me instantly.

The effect which you tell me was produced on you by my casual mention of an unknown girl swinging in a hammock is certainly as strange. Is it possible, then, that two people who have never met, and who are hundreds of miles apart, can exert a magnetic influence on each other? As for myself, it would be impossible for me to fall in love with a woman who listens to me only when I am talking of my friend!

I am not aware that any one is paying marked attention to my fair neighbor. The lieutenant of the navy—he is stationed at Rivermouth—sometimes drops in of an evening and sometimes the rector from Stillwater; the lieutenant the oftener. He was there last night. I would not be surprised if he had an eye to the heiress; but he is not formidable. Mistress Daw carries a neat little spear of irony, and the honest lieutenant seems to have a particular facility for impaling himself on the point of it. He is not dangerous, I should say; though I have known a woman to satirize a man for years, and marry him after all. Decidedly, the lowly rector is not dangerous; yet, again, who has not seen the Cloth of Frieze victorious in the lists where Cloth of Gold went down?

As to the photograph. There is an exquisite ivorytype of Marjorie on the drawing-room mantelpiece. It would be missed at once, if taken. I would do anything reasonable for you, Jack, but I've no burning desire to be hauled up before the local justice of the peace, on a charge of petty larceny.

Edward Delaney to John Flemming

August 22.

Your letter in reply to my last has occupied my thoughts all the morning. I do not know what to think. Do you mean to say that you are seriously half in love with a woman whom you have never seen,—with a shadow, a chimera? I understand neither you nor her.

Yesterday afternoon my father and myself rode over to Rivermouth with the Daws. It is a drive of eight miles, along a winding road lined all the way with brilliant wild barberry-bushes. The colonel drove, with my father in front, Miss Daw and I on the back seat. I resolved that for the first five miles your name should not pass my lips. I was amused by the artful attempts she made, at the start, to break through my reticence. Then a silence fell upon her; and then she became suddenly gay. The keenness which I enjoyed so much when it was exercised on the lieutenant was not so satisfactory directed against myself.

By the by, I nearly forgot to say Miss Daw sat for a picture yesterday to a Rivermouth artist. If the negative turns out well, I am to have a copy. So our ends will be accomplished without crime.

Edward Delaney to John Flemming

August 23.

I have just returned from the strangest interview with Marjorie. She has all but confessed to me her interest in you. But with what modesty and dignity! Her words elude my pen as I attempt to put them on paper; and, indeed, it was not so much what she said as her manner; and that I cannot reproduce. Perhaps it was of a piece with the strangeness of this whole business, that she should tacitly acknowledge to a third party the love she feels for a man she has never beheld!

It is past midnight, and I am too sleepy to write more.

Edward Delaney to John Flemming

August 28.

We returned only this morning from Appledore, that enchanted island,—at four dollars per day. I find on my desk three letters from you! Pardon my candor, dear Flemming, but the conviction forces itself upon me that as your leg grows stronger your head becomes weaker.

You say you are able, with the aid of a cane, to walk about your chamber, and that you purpose to come to The Pines the instant Dillon thinks you strong enough to stand the journey. I advise you not to. Do you not see that, every hour you remain away, Marjorie's glamour deepens, and your influence over her deepens? Wait until you are entirely recovered; in any case, do not come without giving me warning.

Miss Daw was evidently glad to see us back again, and gave me both hands in the frankest way. She stopped at the door a moment, this afternoon, in the carriage; she had been over to Rivermouth for her pictures. Unluckily, the photographer had spilt some acid on the plate, and she was obliged to give him another sitting.

Edward Delaney to John Flemming

August 29.

You must not dream of coming to The Pines. Marjorie has told her father everything! I saw her for a few minutes, an hour ago, in the garden; and, as near as I could gather from her confused statement, the facts are these: Lieutenant Bradley—that's the naval officer—has been paying court to Miss Daw for some time past, but not so much to her liking as to that of the colonel, who it seems is an old friend of the young gentleman's father. Yesterday (I knew she was in some trouble when she drove up to our gate) the colonel spoke to Marjorie of Bradley,—urged his suit, I infer. Marjorie expressed her dislike for the lieutenant with characteristic frankness, and finally confessed to her father—well, I really do not know what she confessed. It must have been the vaguest of confessions. At any rate, it exasperated the colonel and he feels bitterly towards me. It is probable that the friendly relations between his house and ours will be broken off.

Colonel Daw is sitting on the piazza looking rather wicked. I have not seen Marjorie since I parted with her in the garden.

Edward Delaney to Thomas Dillon, M.D., Madison Square, New York

August 30.

My dear Doctor: If you have any influence over Flemming, I beg of you to exert it to prevent his coming to this place at present. There are circumstances, which I will explain to you before long, that make it of the first importance that he should not come into this neighborhood. Of course you will not mention my name in this connection. You know me well enough, my dear doctor, to be assured that, in begging your secret cooperation, I have reasons that will meet your entire approval when they are made plain to you. My father and I shall return to town on the 15th of next month. With great esteem, I am etc. etc.

Edward Delaney to John Flemming

August 31.

Your letter, announcing your mad determination to come here, has just reached me. I beseech you to reflect a moment. The step would be fatal to your interests and hers. You would furnish just cause for irritation to R.W.D.: and, though he loves Marjorie tenderly, he is capable of going to any lengths if opposed. You would not like, I am convinced, to be the means of causing him to treat *her* with severity. Trust a little to my sagacity. Wait and see what happens.

Telegrams

September 1.

To Edward Delaney.—Letter received. I think I ought to be on the ground. J.F.

To John Flemming.—Stay where you are. You would only complicate matters. Do not move until you hear from me. E.D.

To Edward Delaney.—My being at The Pines could be kept secret. I must see her. J.F.

To John Flemming.—Do not think of it. It would be useless. R.W.D. has locked M. in her room. You would not be able to effect an interview. E.D.

To Edward Delaney.—Locked her in her room. Good God. That settles it. I shall leave by the twelve-fifteen express. J.F.

On the second of September, 187—, as the dawn express due at 3.40 left the station at Hampton, a young man, leaning on the shoulder of a servant, stepped from the platform into a hack, and requested to be driven to "The Pines." On arriving at the gate of a modest farm-house, a few miles from the station, the young man descended with difficulty from the carriage, and, casting a hasty glance across the road, seemed much impressed by some peculiarity in the landscape. Again leaning on the shoulder of the servant, he walked to the door of the farm-house and inquired for Mr. Edward Delaney. He was informed by the aged man who answered his knock, that Mr. Edward Delaney had gone to Boston the day before, but that Mr. Jonas Delaney was within. This information did not appear satisfactory to the stranger, who inquired if Mr. Edward Delaney had left any message for Mr. John Flemming. There was a letter for Mr. Flemming, if he were that person. After a brief absence the aged man reappeared with a letter.

Edward Delaney to John Flemming

September 1.

I am horror-stricken at what I have done! I tried to make a little romance to interest you, something soothing and idyllic, and, by Jove! I have done it only too well! My father doesn't know a word of this, so don't jar the old gentleman any more than you can help. I fly from the wrath to come—when you arrive! For, O, dear Jack, there isn't any colonial mansion on the other side of the road, there isn't any piazza, there isn't any hammock,—there isn't any Marjorie Daw!

❧❧❧

A friend whom you have been enjoying during your whole life, you ought not to be displeased with in a moment. A stone is many years becoming a ruby; take care that you do not destroy it in an instant against another stone.

—SAADI

❧❧❧

"The only peaceful societies are the societies of the mind . . ."

TRUE SOCIETIES OF THE MIND
Irwin Edman

Perhaps the true societies of the mind and those one remembers best are those that never meet, or that meet only once and by accident, or that emerge suddenly in the midst of casual conversation among a group of friends who transform it into an exchange of ideas clearly perceived and emotions directly felt, giving and catching mutual fire. And sometimes, when one is quite alone, one's imagination is peopled with ideas, those one has just been reading, those to which some reading has recently prompted one, or during or after listening to music alone. The ultimate society of the mind, when the spirit listeth, is a soliloquy, and that isolated heaven is crowded with friends in the form of congenial themes. Later, perhaps, one meets others who have in their solitude lived at some time or another in the same beatitude. I rather think that is what the great mystics, such as St. John of the Cross, meant or felt when they spoke of the loneliness of the journey toward an insight into true being and the finding of others at the end of the journey sharing the same vision. It is as if one had found one's way to a lonely mountain top by oneself on a path where one met no one, but at the peak met others who had come by their own solitary paths to the same final vista.

Instances of such chance meetings and such isolated private peoplings of one's mind must come to everyone. I recall a few. The close of a long desultory evening in a Senior Common Room at Oxford, where I had been invited to dinner at the High Table. The conversation had been, as I found it often to be at Oxford, almost deliberately simple and casual, gossip of the country and the college, of the weather and of food. As the group included so good a talker as H. W. Garrod, the caustic and brilliant former professor of poetry at Oxford, and others not much less gifted than he, I was a little disappointed—and surprised. Over the port and nuts in the Senior Common Room after dinner, nothing much happened. There was a slow fire in the grate, but it was no slower than the conversation. Nobody said much but "Oh, really." Occasionally there was a spark in the fire. There was finally one in the conversation. Somebody mentioned something, I believe it was a church in Southern France. And then gradually, everybody throwing a little coal upon the intellectual fire, there was a blaze of light and warmth, and though God, Freedom, and Immortality were not settled by midnight, the themes had been brought out and illuminated. I cannot remember when I have heard so many people speak with such sincerity and eloquence about their ultimate convictions....

There was an evening (it had been very gay) when a group of people, including a very modernist composer and a pianist, were gathered in the same room on the same mountainside. There had hardly been a serious word all evening. Somebody suggested we play a little music and put on a phonograph the slow movement of the first *Brandenburg Concerto* of Bach. It had that poignancy and depth of feeling that still the mouths of those who treat Bach as if he were simply a highly skilled musical mathematician. Everyone was stilled, even by the second-rate representation on a portable phonograph. There ensued a controversy as intense as if one's ultimate moral convictions were being tested—as perhaps they were—on what were really the unquestionably great moments in music; where and what composers had written passages that had the note of ultimacy and the cadence of absolute musical and imaginative power. The Wagner, anti-Wagner battle broke out again, and there was a pitched battle between those who found Wagner the great rhetorician and those who held him the soaring and impassioned spirit of the love duet of *Tristan,* or of the outburst of sheer musical gladness as in the great quintet of the third act of the *Meistersinger.* The battle broke out over Debussy; whether he was a skillful and esoteric trifler or whether, as some of us thought, there was a note of exquisite pathos and distance and nuance of spirit in him that was unique in musical history. A war was raging in Spain and another one in China, and another might soon be raging in all Europe; and yet even those whom such a haunting nightmare of contemporary disaster preoccupied had forgotten it. When the ultimate questions of human equity shall have been settled, the passions of men may be absorbed by ultimate questions of taste. The arts are the languages of men, and a passionate conflict over a symbol may be as symptomatic as the quarrel over a religious and political creed. But in such matters quarrels become discussions, and the discussions are innocent. Our quarrel over taste divided but educated rather than destroyed us. The same is hardly true of the quarrels of men over politics and morals. The only peaceful societies are the societies of the mind, for in such societies alone, one gains by sharing, and communication is contagion and growth.

"AS TOILSOME I WANDERED VIRGINIA'S WOODS"

Walt Whitman

As toilsome I wandered Virginia's woods,
To the music of rustling leaves kicked by my feet,
    (for 'twas autumn)
I marked at the foot of a tree the grave of a soldier;
Mortally wounded he and buried on the retreat
    (easily all could I understand,)
The halt of a mid-day hour, when up! no time to lose—
    yet this sign left,
On a tablet scrawled and nailed on the tree by the grave,
Bold, cautious, true, and my loving comrade.
Long, long I muse, then on my way go wandering.
Many a changeful season to follow, and many a scene of life,
Yet at times through changeful season and scene, abrupt,
    alone, or in the crowded street,
Comes before me the unknown soldier's grave, comes the
    inscription rude in Virginia's woods,
Bold, cautious, true, and my loving comrade.

"... we met on the porch of our little church ..."

RECONCILIATION

Pierre van Paassen

In the fall of 1921, the Canadian government announced an agricultural settlement scheme for discharged soldiers in the far north: a farm, a house, and a loan of a thousand dollars for every able-bodied veteran who wished to take advantage of the offer. I was seriously considering the proposition when I dropped into the old Union Depot [in Toronto], which was part of my beat, and sat down among the crowds in the waiting room. Presently two priests entered and took a seat beside me. They spoke in French. This was nothing unusual in Canada, of course, but I soon noticed that theirs was not the quaint, almost medieval speech of Quebec. We entered into conversation, when one of the clerics asked me in broken English how much time they had for the Montreal train. I told them the hour, and I added: "But you are from France, *mon Père,* and not from Montreal!"

"*Ah, oui, oui, c'est bien vrai,*" came the answer. "But I have not seen France for twenty-two years."

"Twenty-two years! *Mon Dieu,* that is a long time. You will find the country greatly changed. The whole north is devastated, right down to St. Quentin and Arras."

"Yes, I know," sighed the priest, "but I learned all this but three months ago."

"Three months ago? You heard about the war but three months ago? How is that possible?" I asked. "The war has been over for three years!"

"We learned of the war three months ago, and not that it had finished, but that it had just started," the priest said. "You see," he went on, "we are missionaries, this father and I." He pointed to his companion. "We have been stationed in the interior of Borneo for twenty-two years. Three months ago, a Dutch trading expedition came to our station in the uplands from points still farther inland. From its members we learned that a war had broken out in Europe. Belgium had been invaded, they told us, Louvain destroyed, Rheims bombarded, Paris threatened. What we heard was incredible, ghastly: the massacre of civilians at Namur, the deportation of thousands of Belgians to Germany. To say that we were thunderstruck would be using a mild expression. *Nous fûmes annihilés.* The thought of that war crushed us, each in his own way, for I am a Frenchman, but my colleague here," he pointed again to the other priest, "this father is a German. We were in a most painful situation. For long years we had worked together as brothers, with never a cross word or disagreement between us—and then suddenly that news.

"Yes," he continued, "it was more than painful. It was torture. We dared not look each other in the face. For even if I am a priest, I am a son of France, too. The thought of my country and my people being trod underfoot choked me. My companion was as badly disturbed as I was. Perhaps more so. We could not speak. We could not eat. We could not sleep. We walked around, each with his own thoughts, thoughts of murder at times. Horrible!" He was silent for a while.

"Well," he looked up at the clock, "it is time. We must be going." They rose to leave.

"Permit me to help you down with your baggage," I offered, picking up a couple of their satchels.

As we walked down the stairs to the train, I asked: "And how long did that awful tension between you two last, Father?"

"For two weeks we could not bear the sight of each other. We avoided each other, each going his own way. It was dreadful. Yes, life was ebbing out of me, with sorrow and indignation. Then one day, as we met on the porch of our little church, both of us stretching out our hands to ring the bell for the Angelus, we burst into tears and wept on each other's shoulders."

＊＊＊＊＊＊＊

Friendship is a vase, which, when it is flawed by heat or violence or accident, may as well be broken at once; it can never be trusted after. The more graceful and ornamental it was, the more clearly do we discern the hopelessness of restoring it to its former state. Coarse stones, if they are fractured, may be cemented again; precious ones never.

—WALTER SAVAGE LANDOR

＊＊＊＊＊＊＊

"Which of these three . . . proved neighbor unto him?"

THE GOOD SAMARITAN
St. Luke

And behold, a certain lawyer stood up and tempted him, saying, Master, what shall I do to inherit eternal life? And he said unto him, What is written in the law? how readest thou? And he answering said, Thou shalt love the Lord thy God with all thy heart, and with all thy soul, and with all thy strength, and with all thy mind; and thy neighbor as thyself. And he said unto him, Thou hast answered right: this do, and thou shalt live.

But he, desiring to justify himself, said unto Jesus, And who is my neighbor? Jesus made answer and said, A certain man was going down from Jerusalem to Jericho; and he fell among robbers, which both stripped him and beat him, and departed, leaving him half dead. And by chance a certain priest was going down that way: and when he saw him, he passed by on the other side. And in like manner a Levite also, when he came to the place, and saw him, passed by on the other side. But a certain Samaritan, as he journeyed, came where he was: and when he saw him, he was moved with compassion, and came to him, and bound up his wounds, pouring on them oil and wine; and he set him on his own beast, and brought him to an inn, and took care of him. And on the morrow he took out two pence, and gave them to the host, and said, Take care of him; and whatsoever thou spendeth more, I, when I come back again, will repay thee. Which of these three, thinkest thou, proved neighbor unto him that fell among robbers? And he said, He that sheweth mercy on him. And Jesus said unto him, Go, and do thou likewise.

(*New Testament*)

❧❧❧❧❧

"... that lovable, stubborn old fool ..."

IRWIN S. COBB TELLS THE STORY OF SOME MODERN GOOD SAMARITANS

When I came to know him Morgan Robertson was on the way to be one of the forgotten men of the writing game. In his youth he had been a bucko mate on a Down-East clipper. He sickened of the brutality which harsh fate decreed should be the lot of foremost hands on sailing ships....

Having walked ashore, he learned the watchmaker's trade—he had always been nimble with his fingers—and spent the next few years hunched in the front window of a jeweler's shop in a State of Maine coast town, with a microscope screwed in one puckered eye and a table before him littered with pinions and mainsprings and little cogwheels. On a night he sat with some cronies talking of this and that and drinking in between. He fell to complaining of the mistakes of people who wrote seafaring tales. "I could write a better yarn about life on a windjammer than any of them," he said. "Because I know windjammers and these lubbers don't."

"Well, why don't you, then?" asked one of his hearers.

"By dern, I will!" he said.

And he did. Before he went to bed that night he had whittled out the beginnings of a short story which was destined to be the first of a series dealing with the rude and sometimes violent adventures of a certain "Sinful Peck" and his dissolute friends....

For the next few years Morgan sold his stuff to the magazines as fast as he could turn it out, which was pretty tolerably fast.... He rode a high wave and spent the money as fast as it came in. Even for those frugal times he never got top prices though....

The crest on which he coasted flattened and left him in shoal waters. He lost his vogue. Perhaps he lost the knack, for, sooner or later, does he but live long enough, every fiction writer pumps himself to a musty sterility. He became that most melancholy figure in literature—the spot marked X where a vanished talent was last seen. Considering the quality of the work he had wrought, there was an amazing and a lamentable swiftness in the way Robertson passed out of popular remembrance. One thing about him: When he was done he knew he was done. He quit trying to pump life back into the cold corpse of his creative faculty.

When I first met him he was living somewhere in the festering jungles of Harlem—he and his wife. He used to sit with us of afternoons in the press box at the ball park. None of us seemed to know—perhaps none of us cared—where or after what fashion he spent the rest of his waking hours. He was short, stocky, rather silent even when he'd had a dram too many. He was shabby, but always precise and neat, with the primness of a man who had lived for long in cramped quarters. Regarding his fallen state he was quite philosophic and very gallant. From time to time he borrowed small sums, always suiting his demands to the pocketbook of the other person—a dollar here, two dollars there, rarely as much as five dollars; and although he carefully had entered the date and the amount of the loan in a little grubby notebook which he carried, the creditor figured the transaction was closed forever. He didn't know that to this little aging man these were debts of honor. Sometimes—but not often—Morgan tippled a wee bit too much.

We were living on the West Side then, in One Hundred and Tenth Street. One evening Bozeman Bulger, who newly had graduated out of sports-writing into a free-lancing job, raised me on the telephone.

"How much cash have you got on you?" he asked. His tone was urgent.

"Enough to go along on but not enough to stand much of a touch," I parried. "Why the mad rush, Brother Bones?"

"Keep it intact until I can get down there," he said. (He lived six blocks farther up Riverside Drive.) "A little while ago I got a telephone message from Morgan—with the charge reversed. He didn't even have the nickel to pay for the call. I went to the address he gave—a back room in a crummy old flat building on the edge of the Black Belt. Dam' it to hell, Cobb, that pair literally have been starving to death and too proud to tell anybody about it. They've sold or pledged everything they had, down to their extra clothes and the bed they slept in and the gas stove they cooked on—when they had anything to cook on it—and every stick of plunder that they could raise as much as a thin dime on. They had a pallet on the floor and boxes to sit on and another box for a table and that's about all. There wasn't a bite to eat in the place. And there's a dispossess notice tacked on the door. Unless they can raise rent money by tomorrow the wolves will be throwing those brave hungry old people out on the dirty sidewalk. I had enough spare change to rustle up a market basket of groceries and I got some scraps of necessary furniture out of hock, but we'll need still more money in the morning. I'll be right down."

I remember the next afternoon was a hot, muggy afternoon in July and how Bulger and I sweated as we panhandled north on Broadway from the Flatiron Building to the top borders of the old Tenderloin, as it existed then, then up in the mid Fifties. We tacked back and forth from one side of the street to the other, stalking people from behind, buttonholing people on the sidewalks, invading bars and cafes and other likely coverts. Then we caught the el and rode to the Polo Grounds and canvassed the grandstand and the playing field for likely prey.

Our manner of approach didn't vary much. To each prospective subject we applied the same formula. One of us would say:

Listen, there's a good fellow—and his sweet little wife—in a tough jam through no fault of his own. You probably wouldn't remember him but in his day he gave joy to millions of people. We're organizing a club to give that couple temporary relief until a bunch of us can figure out a way to get 'em back on their feet. This is a club with only two rules: Five dollars pays your initiation fees and your dues for evermore. A candidate can buy only one five-dollar membership, no more and no less. And the other rule is that nobody must ask the name of these people or where they live or any single solitary blamed thing about 'em. Are you in or are you not?"

Out of those we halted and there were close to a hundred of them, and all, we figured, amply able to contribute, just two failed us.... Before sunset we had collected upwards of five hundred dollars. It came from gamblers, actors, actresses, confidence men, ball players, promoters, writers, agents, dramatists, brokers, vaudevillians, businessmen, professional newspapermen, wasters, grafters, theatrical producers, chorus beauties, pugilists, one college professor, and two sporting clergymen—a Catholic monsignor and the rich rector of a swanky Episcopal parish uptown.

The fund didn't last long. It couldn't, seeing the uses to which Morgan put most of it. First, in celebration of his renewed and fortified fortunes, he went on a gentlemanly and restrained tour of various grogshops and had a drink in each one. And then—but I'll tell about it in Bulger's language to me:

"You know what that lovable, stubborn old fool is doing? He's batting around with that funny little account book of his in his hand, hunting up every chap that he's ever touched, and repaying the loan— with interest. If anybody refuses to accept the money he gets mad as the Devil. Well, what are we going to do next?"

From experiences which he made Robertson repeat to him he wrote two articles entitled "I Was a Sailor." I helped a little in the revisions. Lorimer bought both of them for the *Saturday Evening Post* and, being made aware of the circumstances, paid better than customary rates. The checks went to Bulger, but were by him endorsed over to Morgan. The yarns were printed anonymously and made talk.

With funds on deposit, the Robertsons had moved out of the slum into comfortable quarters and Morgan turned up for a World Series wearing a new toppiece in place of the crippled and infirm derby hat which through constant wear had become almost a part of him. But such succor as we had given the two of them was only a makeshift and stopgap. A sort of committee on ways and means was formed, made up of writers and publishers, and the committee set to work on a plan for a permanent and, hopefully, a safe and profitable endowment to be raised in a way which would bring neither unpleasant notoriety nor embarrassment to its beneficiaries.

From the various publishing concerns which had published Morgan's works in book form we obtained releases on copyright assignments held by them....

At actual cost one publishing house printed a uniform edition of Morgan's completed writings. At actual cost another concern, specializing in subscription sales on a premium basis, loaned us the expert services of its corps of canvassers and distributors. On the day before the edition went on sale nearly every daily newspaper of consequence in the United States carried in its literary section or, more commonly, on its sporting page, something—a paragraph, a column, an illustrated special even—telling of the rediscovery of a great American writer and pointing out that his collected stories, now for the first time available, would have an irresistible appeal for all lovers of outdoor adventure and more particularly for those who went down to the sea in ships—or hoped to. The federated baseball writers of the town had conspired together to fire this broadside of publicity—an advertisement which could not have been bought for any imaginable sum of money. Oh yes, each volume carried an eulogistic foreword done by a distinguished author—Tarkington, Ade, Rex Beach, Richard Harding Davis, Charley Van Loan, and so on.

People who never before had heard of Morgan Robertson, or if they had, had forgotten him, fell over themselves to buy his books. People bought them who possibly never read them afterward. But they bought them and they paid for them, which was what counted with the promoters of our scheme. . . .

Through the sales a nourishing sum totaling well up into the thousands was forthcoming. A wealthy Wall Street operator—I wish I could recall his name now and print it here—volunteered to take a considerable part of the proceeds and see whether he couldn't fatten them up by a quick turn in the market, he practically guaranteeing us against any loss. As bread cast on the waters—the waters of speculation—the money came back, heavily buttered with a fifty-per-cent increase. And that Wall Street man had never seen Morgan and knew of him only through what some of us told him.

Next a fund was created, with a bank as trustee to invest and guard and pay out monthly installments for life to Morgan and, if she should survive him, to Mrs. Robertson through the remainder of her days. But so wisely was the money administered that presently the accumulated dividends exceeded the payments and the bank was empowered, in its discretion, to hand over these surpluses to Morgan. However, he would not apply for such extra remittances unless this had the joint approval of Bulger and myself, whom he regarded as his unofficial but—bless his trustful old soul—his competent financial advisers.

In the following year I had a call from Bulger. There was a grin on his homely face—and just a suggestion of moistness in his eye. And his voice was a bit husky.

"Morgan won't come to you direct," he said, "afraid you might laugh at him, I reckon, or think he was being extravagant in his old age. So he sent me to find out how you stand. All his life, he says, he's had an ambition to follow the example of the richest man in the Yankee town where he lived when he was a kid growing up. He's always wanted a fur overcoat, and a gold-headed cane. He thinks he can afford these luxuries now. He won't buy them though unless we give our consent."

Through the good offices of a famous Jewish comedian, a smart merchant who knew the peltry market from the hair roots up, we got, at a sacrificial price, a garment with at least two kinds of dead animal skins on it. One kind, I suspect, was dyed rabbit; it might not have fooled other rabbits but it fooled Morgan. Nevertheless this undoubtedly was a bargain, even though purchased in the middle of an August hot spell when the overcoat market would be seasonably sluggish. The kindly captain of our precinct station house escorted Bulger to the shop of a professional fence masquerading as a pawnbroker and, under police pressure, the proprietor dug out from a stock of what undoubtedly was stolen goods, and sold at a ridiculously low figure, a heavy ebony stick adorned at the handle end with a great clump of scrolled gold. The gold bore some stranger's initials but a handy engraver remedied that small matter and cut the new owner's name into the massy bulb.

I think it was about three weeks after that when Bulger got me on the telephone. He was sniffling and before he finished with what he had to say, was blubbering over the wire:

"Morgan's gone," he said, "but gee, Cobb, what a swell finish! Yesterday he slipped away and went down to Atlantic City all alone and took a room at a cheap hotel on the Boardwalk—a front room so he could see the ocean from his window and hear the waves hitting the beach. They found him there this morning, cold and stiff. He was sitting in a chair at the open window. He had that ratty fur overcoat over his shoulders with the sleeves pulled around him as if they were hugging him and the gold-headed cane was across his knees—and his eyes were staring out at the sea. So the last thing he ever saw in this world was the thing he'd loved most in this world. Gee, Cobb, could you beat it for a finish!"

❦❦❦

TO A DISTANT FRIEND

William Wordsworth

Why art thou silent? Is thy love a plant
  Of such weak fibre that the treacherous air
  Of absence withers what was once so fair?
Is there no debt to pay, no boon to grant?

Yet have my thoughts for thee been vigilant,
  Bound to thy service with unceasing care—
The mind's least generous wish a mendicant
  For nought but what thy happiness could spare.

Speak!—though this soft warm heart, once free to hold
  A thousand tender pleasures, thine and mine,
Be left more desolate, more dreary cold
Than a forsaken bird's-nest fill'd with snow
  Midst its own bush of leafless eglantine—
Speak, that my torturing doubts their end may know!

❦❦❦

"Do not suffer your mind to be disquieted."

THOMAS JEFFERSON TO
JOHN ADAMS

Monticello, October 12, 1823

Dear sir.—I do not write with the ease which your letter of September 18th supposes. Crippled wrists and fingers make writing slow and laborious. Yet while writing you, I lose the sense of these things in the recollection of ancient times, when youth and health made happiness out of everything. I forget for a while the hoary winters of age, when we can think of nothing but how to keep warm, and how to get rid of our heavy hours until the friendly hand of death shall rid us of all at once. Against this tedium vitae [weary life], however, I am fortunately mounted on a hobby, which, indeed, I should have better managed some thirty or forty years ago. . . . This is the establishment of a university [The University of Virginia]. . . .

Putting aside these things, however, for the present, I write this letter as due a friend coeval with our government, and now attempted to be poisoned when too late in life to be replaced by new affections. I had for some time observed in the public papers, dark hints and mysterious innuendos of a correspondence of yours with a friend, to whom you had opened your bosom without reserve, and which was to be made public by that friend or his representative. And now, it is said to be actually published. It has not yet reached us, but extracts have been given, and such as seemed most likely to draw a curtain of separation between you and myself, were there no other motive than that of indignation against the author of this outrage on private confidence, whose shaft seems to have been aimed at yourself more particularly, this would make it the duty of every honorable mind to disappoint that aim, by opposing to its impression a sevenfold shield of apathy and insensibility. With me, however, no such armor is needed. The circumstances of the times in which we have happened to live, and the particular period, placed us in a state of apparent opposition, which some might suppose to be personal also; and there might not be wanting those who wished to make it so, by filling our ears with malignant falsehoods. . . . And if there had been at any time, a moment when we were off our guard, and in a temper let the whispers of these people make us forget what we had known of each other for so many years, and years of so much trial, yet all men . . . who have seen the false colors under which passion sometimes dresses the actions and motives of others, have seen also those passions subsiding with time and reflection, dissipating like mists before the rising sun, and restoring us the sight of all things in their true shape and colors. It would be strange indeed, if, at our years, we were to go back an age to hunt up imaginary or forgotten facts, to disturb the repose of affections so sweetening to the evening of our lives. Be assured, my dear sir, that I am incapable of receiving the slightest impression from the effort now made to plant thorn on the pillow of age, worth and wisdom, and to sow tares between friends who have been such for nearly half a century. Beseeching you, then, not to suffer your mind to be disquieted by this wicked attempt to poison its peace, and praying you to throw it by among the things which have never happened, I add sincere assurances of my unabated and constant attachment, friendship and respect.

THOMAS JEFFERSON

"Friends are true Twins in soul ..."

QUAKER FRIENDSHIP

William Penn

This is the Comfort of Friends, that though they may be said to Die, yet their Friendship and Society are, in the best Sense, ever present, because immortal.

Friendship is the next Pleasure we may hope for: and where we find it not at Home, or have no home to find it in, we may seek it abroad. It is an Union of Spirits, a Marriage of Hearts, and the Bond thereto Vertue.

There can be no Friendship where there is no Freedom. Friendship loves a Free Air, and will not be penned up in straight and narrow Enclosures. It will speak freely, and act so too; and take nothing ill where no ill is meant; nay, where it is, 'twill easily Forgive, and forget too, upon small Acknowledgments.

Friends are true Twins in soul; they sympathize in every thing, and have the same Love and Aversion.

One is not happy without the other, nor can either of them be miserable alone: as if they take their turns in Pain as well as in Pleasure; relieving one another in their most adverse Conditions.

What one enjoys the other cannot Want. Like the Primitive Christians, they have all things in common, no Property but in one another.

A true Friend unbosoms freely, advises justly, assists readily, adventures boldly, takes all patiently, defends courageously.

These being the Qualities of a Friend, we are to find them before we choose one.

AROUND THE CORNER

Charles Hanson Towne

Around the corner I have a friend,
  In this great city that has no end;
Yet days go by and weeks rush on,
  And before I know it a year is gone,
And I never see my old friend's face.
  For life is a *swift and terrible* race.

He knows I like him just as well
  As in the days when I rang his bell
And he rang mine. We were younger then;
  And now we are busy, tired men—
Tired of playing a foolish game;
  Tired with trying to make a name.

"To-morrow," I say, "I will call on Jim,
  Just to show that I'm thinking of him."
But to-morrow comes and to-morrow goes;
  And the distance between us grows and grows.

Around the corner! Yet miles away!
  "Here's a telegram, sir." "Jim died today!"
And that's what we get and deserve in the end—
  Around the corner—a vanished friend.

"The apparition arises of another little friend . . ."

PIERRE LOTI'S CHILDHOOD FRIENDS

"Once upon a time a little girl, opening a great big fruit from the colonies, there came out a beast—a green beast—which stung her—and she died of it."

It was my little friend Antoinette—she six and I seven—who told me this story, apropos to an apricot which we had just divided.

We are sitting at the bottom of her garden, in the sweet month of June, under a thick apricot tree, close together on one stool in a hut as big as a bee-hive, built with our own hands for our private accommodation, out of old planks, covered with West Indian matting which had served to pack coffee imported from the Antilles. Tiny specks of sunlight peep through our roof of coarse woven reeds, and dance on our white pinafores, and our faces, broken by the leaves of the trees which are stirred by a warm breeze.

For at least two summers our favorite amusement was building these Robinson Crusoe huts in corners which we fancied solitary, and sitting in them quite hidden to hold our chat. In the story of the little girl stung by a beast these words alone had plunged me at once into a reverie: "A great big fruit from the colonies." And a vision had come to me of trees, and strange fruits, and forests peopled with wonderful birds....

The colonies! How can I express everything that tried to struggle into being in my brain at the mere ring of the word? A fruit from the colonies, a bird, a shell, were to me forthwith objects almost of enchantment. There were quantities of these colonial treasures at Antoinette's home; a parrot, birds of all colors in a cage, collections of shells and insects. In her mother's drawers I had seen quaint strings of fragrant berries; and in the lofts where we would sometimes rummage together, we found the skins of beasts, queer bags, cases with the names of West Indian places still legible on them; and a vague exotic perfume pervaded the whole house. Her garden was divided from ours by only a very low wall covered with roses and jasmine; and a pomegranate which grew there, a tall and venerable tree, threw its branches over our yard, and in the season shed its coral petals there.

We would often talk behind the scenes, from one house to the other.

"May I go over and play with you, I say? Will your mama let me?"

"No. I have been naughty, I am in disgrace." This was often the case. Then I felt greatly disappointed but less for her sake, I must own, than for the sake of the parrot and the foreign countries.

She herself had been born there in the colonies, this very little Antoinette, and—how strange it seemed, she did not appear to understand the value of the privilege....

I will tell you the game which most amused Antoinette and me during these two delicious summers.

It was this: we were caterpillars; we crawled on the ground, with difficulty, on our hands and stomachs, searching for leaves to eat. Then we made believe that invincible sleep numbed our senses, and we lay down in some corner under the boughs, covering our heads with our white pinafores; we were chrysalises in our cocoons. This state lasted a longer or shorter time, and we so fully entered into our part of insects undergoing metamorphosis that a listener might have overheard such phrases as these spoken in tones of entire conviction:

"Do you think you will soon fly?"

"Oh, it will be very soon this time. I feel them on my shoulders—they are unfolding...." They, of course, were wings.

At last we woke up; stretched ourselves with airs and graces, not speaking a word, but as if we were amazed at the phenomenon of this final transformation. And then suddenly, we began to run about, hither and thither, very lightly in our little thin shoes; with our hands we held the corners of our white pinnies, fluttering them to "make believe" wings—and we ran and ran, flitting after each other in sharp fantastic curves; close to every flower to smell it with the restless hurry of a butterfly, and making a buzzing noise, "Hooooo" with our lips nearly shut and our cheeks puffed out....

The apparition arises of another little friend when I was eleven. She was called Jeanne and belonged to a family of naval officers who had been connected with our own for more than a century. Her elder by two or three years, I had not at first taken any notice of her, thinking her too much of a baby no doubt.

To begin with, she had such a puny kitten-like face; it was impossible to foresee what the too tiny features might become, to say whether she would turn out pretty or ugly; then soon she acquired a certain winning grace, and by the time she was eight or ten years old, had developed into a charming, darling little girl. Very full of fun and as sociable as I was shy; and as she went to many dances and children's parties to which I never went, she seemed to me the acme of fashionable elegance and correctness.

In spite of the intimacy between our two families it was obvious that her parents looked askance at our growing friendship, perhaps not approving of her having a boy for a companion. I was very much hurt at this, and so vivid are our childish impressions, that it took years—indeed I was almost a young man, before I could forgive her father and mother the slights I then felt.

In consequence, I felt a growing desire to be allowed to play with her and she, seeing this, assumed the part of the inaccessible little princess of the fairy tales, laughed mercilessly at my shyness, my awkward way of holding myself, my blundering entrance into the drawing-room; there was a constant passage of arms between us, or an endless exchange of priceless compliments.

When I was invited to pass the day with her, I enjoyed it very much in anticipation, but I had many mortifications afterwards, for I was always doing something stupid in the presence of people who did not understand me....

One day, when she came back from Paris, little Jeanne delighted me with an account of the fairy tale of *Peau d'Ane* (about a princess disguised in an ass's skin) which she had seen acted.

Her time, at any rate, was not thrown away, for *Peau d'Ane* was destined for four or five years to take up many hours, more precious than any I have ever wasted since.

Together we formed the splendid idea of mounting it on a little theatre which I possessed. This undertaking threw us together.— And little by little the project assumed in our heads the most gigantic proportions; it grew and grew, from month to month, as our powers of execution perfected themselves. We painted fantastic scenery, we dressed numberless little dolls for the processions. Indeed, I shall often recur to this fairy tale which was one of the principal features of my childhood.

And even after Jeanne was tired of it, I went on with it alone. . . . All the dreams of enchanted dwellings, and of foreign luxury which I realized more or less, at a later time, in different parts of the globe, had their origin for the first time on the little stage in this fairy tale. . . .

And since I am anticipating the future, I may as well say the final word on the subject: during the last few years, now Jeanne has grown into a beautiful woman, we have twenty times talked of opening together the boxes where our little dead dolls are sleeping—but we have lived so fast in the present day, that we have never yet found time, and never shall.

Our children, perhaps, some day—or who knows, our grandchildren! In some future age when we are forgotten, our unknown successors, rummaging at the bottom of the mysterious cupboards, will make the extraordinary discovery of hosts of little people, nymphs, fairies and genii dressed by our hands.

(*Translated by Mrs. Clara Bell*)

FROM "ADONAIS"

Percy Bysshe Shelley

I weep for Adonais—he is dead!
O weep for Adonais! though our tears
Thaw not the frost which binds so dear a head!
And thou, sad Hour, selected from all years
To mourn our loss, rouse thy obscure compeers,

And teach them thine own sorrow, say: "With me
Died Adonais; till the Future dares
Forget the Past, his fate and fame shall be
An echo and a light unto eternity!"

∿∿∿∿∿∿∿

". . . he was secure of his friend's truth and honour . . ."

DAMON AND PYTHIAS
Charlotte M. Yonge

Most of the best and noblest of the Greeks held what was called the Pythagorean philosophy. This was one of the many systems framed by the great men of heathenism, when by the feeble light of nature they were, as St. Paul says, "seeking after God, if haply they might feel after him," like men groping in the darkness. Pythagoras lived before the time of history, and almost nothing is known about him, though his teaching and his name were never lost....

The Pythagoreans were bound together in a brotherhood, the members of which had rules that are not now understood, but which linked them so as to form a sort of club, with common religious observances and pursuits of science, especially mathematics and music. And they were taught to restrain their passions, especially that of anger, and to endure with patience all kinds of suffering; believing that such self-restraint brought them nearer to the gods, and that death would set them free from the prison of the body. The souls of evil-doers would, they thought, pass into the lower and more degraded animals, while those of good men would be gradually purified, and rise to a higher existence. This, though lamentably deficient, and false in some points, was a real religion, inasmuch as it gave a rule of life, with a motive for striving for wisdom and virtue. Two friends of this Pythagorean sect lived at Syracuse, in the end of the fourth century before the Christian era. Syracuse was a great Greek city, built in Sicily, and full of all kinds of Greek art and learning; but it was a place of danger in their time, for it had fallen under the tyranny of a man of strange and capricious temper, though of great abilities, namely, Dionysius....

Dionysius was an exceedingly able man, and made the city much more rich and powerful, he defeated the Carthaginians, and rendered Syracuse by far the chief city in the island, and he contrived to make every one so much afraid of him that no one durst attempt to overthrow his power. He was a good scholar, and very fond of philosophy and poetry, and he delighted to have learned men around him, and he had naturally a generous spirit; but the sense that he was in a position that did not belong to him, and that every one hated him for assuming it, made him very harsh and suspicious. . . .

Thus Dionysius was in constant dread. He had a wide trench round his bedroom, with a drawbridge that he drew up and put down with his own hands; and he put one barber to death for boasting that he held a razor to the tyrant's throat every morning. After this he made his young daughters shave him; but by-and-by he would not trust them with a razor, and caused them to singe off his beard with hot nut-shells! He was said to have put a man named Antiphon to death for answering him, when he asked what was the best kind of brass, "That of which the statues of Harmodius and Aristogeiton were made." These were the two Athenians who had killed the sons of Pisistratus the tyrant, so that the jest was most offensive, but its boldness might have gained forgiveness for it. One philosopher, named Philoxenus, he sent to a dungeon for finding fault with his poetry, but he afterwards composed another piece, which he thought so superior, that he could not be content without sending for this adverse critic to hear it. When he had finished reading it, he looked to Philoxenus for a compliment; but the philosopher only turned round to the guards, and said dryly, "Carry me back to prison." This time Dionysius had the sense to laugh, and forgive his honesty.

All these stories may not be true; but that they should have been current in the ancient world shows what was the character of the man of whom they were told, how stern and terrible was his anger, and how easily it was incurred. Among those who came under it was a Pythagorean called Pythias, who was sentenced to death, according to the usual fate of those who fell under his suspicion.

Pythias had lands and relations in Greece, and he entreated as a favour to be allowed to return thither and arrange his affairs, engaging to return within a specified time to suffer death. The tyrant laughed his request to scorn. Once safe out of Sicily, who would answer for his return? Pythias made reply that he had a friend, who would become security for his return; and while Dionysius, the miserable man who trusted nobody, was ready to scoff at his simplicity, another Pythagorean, by name Damon, came forward, and offered to become surety for his friend, engaging that, if Pythias did not return according to promise, to suffer death in his stead.

Dionysius, much astonished, consented to let Pythias go, marvelling what would be the issue of the affair. Time went on, and Pythias did not appear. The Syracusans watched Damon, but he showed no uneasiness. He said he was secure of his friend's truth and honour, and that if any accident had caused the delay of his return, he should rejoice in dying to save the life of one so dear to him.

Even to the last day Damon continued serene and content, however it might fall out; nay, even when the very hour drew nigh and still no Pythias. His trust was so perfect, that he did not even grieve at having to die for a faithless friend who had left him to the fate to which he had unwarily pledged himself. It was not Pythias' own will, but the winds and waves, so he still declared, when the decree was brought and the instruments of death made ready. The hour had come, and a few moments more would have ended Damon's life, when Pythias duly presented himself, embraced his friend, and stood forward himself to receive his sentence, calm, resolute, and rejoiced that he had come in time.

Even the dim hope they owned of a future state was enough to make these two brave men keep their word, and confront death for one another without quailing. Dionysius looked on more struck than ever. He felt that neither of such men must die. He reversed the sentence of Pythias, and calling the two to his judgment seat, he entreated them to admit him as a third in their friendship.

OLD FRIENDSHIP

Eunice Tietjens

Beautiful and rich is an old friendship,
Grateful to the touch as ancient ivory,
Smooth as aged wine, or sheen of tapestry
Where light has lingered, intimate and long.

Full of tears and warm is an old friendship.
That asks no longer deeds of gallantry,
Or any deed at all—save that the friend shall be
Alive and breathing somewhere, like a song.

The comfort of having a friend may be taken away, but not that of having had one.

—SENECA

**". . . live in the future with the thought that
sometime I shall embrace you . . ."**

DOSTOEVSKY TO HIS BROTHER

The Peter and Paul Fortress,
December 22, 1849

Mihail Mihailovich Dostoevsky,
    Nevsky Prospect, opposite Gryazny Street,
        in the house of Neslind

Brother, my precious friend! all is settled! I am sentenced to four
years' hard labor in the fortress (I believe, of Orenburg), and after that
to serve as a private. Today, the 22nd of December, we were taken to
the Seminov Drill Ground. There the sentence of death was read to all
of us, we were told to kiss the Cross, our swords were broken over our
heads, and our last toilet was made (white shirts). Then three were tied
to the pillar for execution. I was the sixth. Three at a time were called
out; consequently, I was in the second batch and no more than a minute
was left me to live.

I remembered you, brother, and all yours; during the last minute you,
you alone, were in my mind, only then I realized how I love you, dear
brother mine! I also managed to embrace Plescheyev and Durov who
stood close to me, and to say good-by to them. Finally the retreat was
sounded, and those tied to the pillar were led back, and it was announced to us that His Imperial Majesty granted us our lives. Then
followed the present sentences. Palm alone has been pardoned, and
returns with his old rank to the army.

I was just told, dear brother, that today or tomorrow we are to be
sent off. I asked to see you. But I was told that this was impossible; I
may only write you this letter: make haste and give me a reply as soon
as you can.

I am afraid that you may somehow have got to know of our death
sentence. From the windows of the prison van, when we were taken to
the Seminov Drill Ground, I saw a multitude of people; perhaps the
news reached you, and you suffered for me. Now you will be easier on
my account.

Brother! I have not become downhearted or low-spirited. Life is
everywhere life, life in ourselves, not in what is outside us. There will
be people near me, and to be a man among people and remain a man
for ever, not to be downhearted nor to fall in whatever misfortunes may
befall me—this is life; this is the task of life. I have realized this. This
idea has entered into my flesh and into my blood. . . .

Now, brother, I may perhaps have to march a long distance. Money is needed. My dear brother, when you receive this letter, and if there is any possibility of getting some money, send it to me at once. Money I need now more than air (for one particular purpose). Send me also a few lines. Then if the money from Moscow comes—remember me and do not desert me. Well, that is all! I have debts, but what can I do? ...

Kiss your wife and children. Remind them of me continually; see that they do not forget me. Perhaps, we shall yet meet some time! Brother, take care of yourself and of your family, live quietly and carefully. Think of the future of your children. ...

At the first opportunity I shall let you know about myself. Give the Maikovs my farewell and last greetings. Tell them that I thank them all for their constant interest in my fate. Say a few words for me, as warm as possible, as your heart will prompt you, to Eugenia Petrovna. I wish her much happiness and shall ever remember her with grateful respect. Press the hands of Nikolay Apollonovich, and Apollon Maikov, and also of all the others. Find Yanovsky. Press his hand, thank him. Finally, press the hands of all who have not forgotten me. And those who have forgotten me—remember me to them also. Kiss our brother Kolya. Write a letter to our brother Andrey and let him know about me. Write also to Uncle and Aunt. This I ask you in my own name, and greet them for me. Write to our sisters: I wish them happiness.

And maybe, we shall meet again some time, brother! Take care of yourself, go on living, for the love of God, until we meet. Perhaps some time we shall embrace each other and recall our youth, our golden time that was, our youth and our hopes, which at this very instant I am tearing out from my heart with my blood, to bury them. ...

Write to me more often, write more details, more, more facts. In every letter write about all kinds of family details, of trifles, don't forget. This will give me hope and life. If you knew how your letters revived me here in the fortress! These last two months and a half, when it was forbidden to write or receive a letter, have been very hard on me. I was ill. The fact that you did not send me money now and then worried me on your account; it meant you yourself were in great need! Kiss the children once again; their lovely little faces do not leave my mind. Ah, that they may be happy! Be happy yourself too, brother, be happy!

But do not grieve, for the love of God, do not grieve for me! Do believe that I am not downhearted, do remember that hope has not deserted me. In four years there will be a mitigation of my fate. I shall be a private soldier—no longer a prisoner, and remember that some time I shall embrace you. I was today in the grip of death for three quarters of an hour; I have lived it through with that idea; I was at the last instant and now I live again!

If anyone has bad memories of me, if I have quarreled with anyone, if I have created in anyone an unpleasant impression—tell them they should forget it, if you manage to meet them. There is no gall or spite in my soul; I should dearly love to embrace any one of my former friends at this moment. It is a comfort, I experienced it today when saying good-by to my dear ones before death. I thought at that moment that the news of the execution would kill you. But now be easy, I am still alive and shall live in the future with the thought that sometime I shall embrace you. Only this is now in my mind.

What are you doing? What have you been thinking today? Do you know about us? How cold it was today!

Ah, if only my letter reaches you soon! Otherwise I shall be for four months without news of you. I saw the envelopes in which you sent money during the last two months; the address was written in your hand, and I was glad that you were well. . . .

Good-by, good-by, my brother! When shall I write you again? You will receive from me as detailed an account as possible of my journey. If I can only preserve my health, then everything will be right!

Well, good-by, good-by, brother! I embrace you closely. I kiss you closely. Remember me without pain in your heart. Do not grieve, I pray you, do not grieve for me! In the next letter I shall tell you of how I go on. Remember then what I have told you: plan out your life, do not waste it, arrange your destiny, think of your children. Oh, to see you, to see you! Good-by! Now I tear myself away from everything that was dear; it is painful to leave it! It is painful to break oneself in two, to cut the heart in two. Good-by! Good-by! But I shall see you, I am convinced—I hope; do not change, love me, do not let your memory grow cold, and the thought of your love will be the best part of my life. Good-by, good-by, once more! Good-by to all! Your brother

FYODOR DOSTOEVSKY

(Translated by Koteliansky and Murry)

A LOST FRIEND

John Boyle O'Reilly

My friend he was; my friend from all the rest;
With childish faith he oped to me his breast;
No door was locked on altar, grave, or grief;
No weakness veiled, concealed no disbelief;
The hope, the sorrow, and the wrong were bare,
And, ah, the shadow only showed the fair.

I gave him love for love; but deep within
I magnified each frailty into sin;
Each hill-topped foible in the sunset glowed,
Obscuring vales where rivered virtues flowed.
Reproof became reproach, till common grew
The captious word at every fault I knew.
He smiled upon the censorship, and bore
With patient love the touch that wounded sore;
Until at length, so had my blindness grown,
He knew I judged him by his faults alone.

Alone of all men, I who knew him best,
Refused the gold, to take the dross for test.
Cold strangers honored for the worth they saw;
His friend forgot the diamond in the flaw.

At last it came—the day he stood apart,
When from my eyes he proudly veiled his heart;
When carping judgment and uncertain word
A stern resentment in his bosom stirred;
When in his face I read what I had been,
And with his vision I saw what he had seen.

Too late! too late! Oh, could he then have known,
When his love died, that mine had perfect grown;
That when the veil was drawn, abased, chastised,
The censor stood, and the lost one truly prized.

Too late we learn, a man must hold his friend
Unjudged, accepted, trusted to the end.

"I owe everything to Miss Martha."

MARTHA'S LADY *

Sara Orne Jewett

One day, many years ago, the Old Judge Pyne house wore an unwonted look of gayety and youthfulness. The high-fenced green garden
was bright with June flowers. Under the elms in the large shady front

* Abridged by Editor.

yard you might see some chairs placed near together, as they often used to be when the family were all at home and life was going on gayly with eager talk and pleasure-making; when the elder judge, the grandfather, used to quote that great author, Dr. Johnson, and say to his girls, "Be brisk, be splendid, and be public."

It was evident to every one in town that Miss Harriet Pyne, to use the village phrase, had company. She was the last of her family, and was by no means old; but being the last, and wonted to live with people much older than herself, she had formed all the habits of a serious elderly person. Ladies of her age, something past thirty, often wore discreet caps in those days, especially if they were married, but being single, Miss Harriet clung to youth in this respect, making the one concession of keeping her waving chestnut hair as smooth and stiffly arranged as possible. Now that she was left alone it seemed quite the best thing frankly to accept the fact of age, and to turn more resolutely than ever to the companionship of duty and serious books. She was more serious and given to routine than her elders themselves, as sometimes happened when the daughters of New England gentlefolks were brought up wholly in the society of their elders. At thirty-five she had more reluctance than her mother to face an unforeseen occasion, certainly more than her grandmother, who had preserved some cheerful inheritance of gayety and worldliness from colonial times.

In these days New England life held the necessity of much dignity and discretion of behavior; there was the truest hospitality and good cheer in all occasional festivities, but it was sometimes a self-conscious hospitality, followed by an inexorable return to asceticism both of diet and of behavior. Miss Harriet Pyne belonged to the very dullest days of New England. It was high time for a little leaven to begin its work, in this moment when the great impulses of the war for liberty had died away and those of the coming war for patriotism and a new freedom had hardly yet begun.

The dull interior, the changed life of the old house, whose former activities seemed to have fallen sound asleep, really typified these larger conditions, and a little leaven had made its easily recognized appearance in the shape of a light-hearted girl. She was Miss Harriet's young Boston cousin, Helena Vernon, who, half-amused and half-impatient at the unnecessary sober-mindedness of her hostess and of Ashford in general, had set herself to the difficult task of gayety. Cousin Harriet looked on at a succession of ingenious and, on the whole, innocent attempts at pleasure, as she might have looked on at the frolics of a kitten who easily substitutes a ball of yarn for the uncertainties of a bird or a wind-blown leaf, and who may at any moment ravel the fringe of a sacred curtain-tassel in preference to either.

Helena, with her mischievous appealing eyes, with her enchanting old songs and her guitar, seemed the more delightful and even reasonable because she was so kind to everybody, and because she was a beauty. She had the gift of most charming manners. There was all the unconscious lovely ease and grace that had come with the good breeding of her city home, where many pleasant people came and went; she had no fear, one had almost said no respect, of the individual, and she did not need to think of herself. Cousin Harriet turned cold with apprehension when she saw the minister coming in at the front gate, and wondered in agony if Martha were properly attired to go to the door, and would by any chance hear the knocker; it was Helena who, delighted to have anything happen, ran to the door to welcome the Reverend Mr. Crofton as if he were a congenial friend of her own age. She could behave with more or less propriety during the stately first visit, and even contrive to lighten it with modest mirth, and to extort the confession that the guest had a tenor voice, though sadly out of practice; but when the minister departed a little flattered, and hoping that he had not expressed himself too strongly for a pastor upon the poems of Emerson, and feeling the unusual stir of gallantry in his proper heart, it was Helena who caught the honored hat of the late Judge Pyne from its last resting-place in the hall, and holding it securely in both hands, mimicked the minister's self-conscious entrance. She copied his pompous and anxious expression in the dim parlor in such delicious fashion that Miss Harriet, who could not always extinguish a ready spark of the original sin of humor, laughed aloud.

"My dear!" she exclaimed severely the next moment, "I am ashamed of your being so disrespectful!" and then laughed again, and took the affecting old hat and carried it back to its place.

"I wish I had asked him if he would be so kind as to climb the cherry-tree," said Helena, unbending a little at the discovery that her cousin would consent to laugh no more. "There are all those ripe cherries on the top branches. I can climb as high as he, but I can't reach far enough from the last branch that will bear me. The minister is so long and thin"—

"I don't know what Mr. Crofton would have thought of you; he is a very serious young man," said cousin Harriet, still ashamed of her laughter. "Martha will get the cherries for you, or one of the men. I should not like to have Mr. Crofton think you were frivolous, a young lady of your opportunities"—but Helena had escaped through the hall and out at the garden door at the mention of Martha's name. Miss Harriet Pyne sighed anxiously, and then smiled, in spite of her deep convictions, as she shut the blinds and tried to make the house look solemn again.

The front door might be shut, but the garden door at the other end of the broad hall was wide open upon the large sunshiny garden. It was now late in the afternoon, and the sun was low behind great apple-trees at the garden's end, which threw their shadows over the short turf of the bleaching-green. The cherry-trees stood at one side in full sunshine, and Miss Harriet, who presently came to the garden steps to watch like a hen at the water's edge, saw her cousin's pretty figure in its white dress of India muslin hurrying across the grass. She was accompanied by the tall, ungainly shape of Martha the new maid, who, dull and indifferent to every one else, showed a surprising willingness and allegiance to the young guest.

"Martha ought to be in the dining-room, already, slow as she is; it wants but half an hour of tea-time," said Miss Harriet, as she turned and went into the shaded house. It was Martha's duty to wait at table, and there had been many trying scenes and defeated efforts toward her education. Martha was certainly very clumsy, and she seemed the clumsier because she had replaced her aunt, a most skillful person, who had but lately married a thriving farm and its prosperous owner. It must be confessed that Miss Harriet was a most bewildering instructor, and that her pupil's brain was easily confused and prone to blunders. The coming of Helena had been somewhat dreaded by reason of this incompetent service, but the guest took no notice of frowns or futile gestures at the first tea-table, except to establish friendly relations with Martha on her own account by a reassuring smile. They were about the same age, and next morning, before cousin Harriet came down, Helena showed by a word and a quick touch the right way to do something that had gone wrong and been impossible to understand the night before. A moment later the anxious mistress came in without suspicion, but Martha's eyes were as affectionate as a dog's, and there was a new look of hopefulness on her face; this dreaded guest was a friend after all, and not a foe come from proud Boston to confound her ignorance and patient efforts.

The two young creatures, mistress and maid, were hurrying across the bleaching-green.

"I can't reach the ripest cherries," explained Helena politely, "and I think that Miss Pyne ought to send some to the minister. He has just made us a call. Why, Martha, you haven't been crying again!"

"Yes'm," said Martha sadly. "Miss Pyne always loves to send something to the minister," she acknowledged with interest, as if she did not wish to be asked to explain these latest tears.

"We'll arrange some of the best cherries in a pretty dish. I'll show you how, and you shall carry them over to the parsonage after tea," said Helena cheerfully, and Martha accepted the embassy with pleasure. Life was beginning to hold moments of something like delight in the last few days.

Down came the scarlet fruit like bright rain into the green grass.

"Break some nice twigs with the cherries and leaves together; oh, you're a duck, Martha!" and Martha, flushed with delight, and looking far more like a thin and solemn blue heron, came rustling down to earth again, and gathered the spoils into her clean apron.

That night at tea Miss Harriet announced, as if by way of apology, that she thought Martha was beginning to understand something about her work. "Her aunt was a treasure, she never had to be told anything twice; but Martha has been as clumsy as a calf," said the precise mistress of the house. "I have been afraid sometimes that I never could teach her anything. I was quite ashamed to have you come just now, and find me so unprepared to entertain a visitor."

"Oh, Martha will learn fast enough because she cares so much," said the visitor eagerly. "I think she is a dear good girl. I do hope that she will never go away. I think she does things better every day, cousin Harriet," added Helena pleadingly, with all her kind young heart. The china-closet door was open a little way, and Martha heard every word. From that moment, she not only knew what love was like, but she knew love's dear ambitions. To have come from a stony hill-farm and a bare small wooden house, was like a cave-dweller's coming to make a permanent home in an art museum, such had seemed the elaborate-ness and elegance of Miss Pyne's fashion of life; and Martha's simple brain was slow enough in its processes and recognitions. But with this sympathetic ally and defender, this exquisite Miss Helena who believed in her, all difficulties appeared to vanish.

Later that evening, no longer homesick or hopeless, Martha returned from her polite errand to the minister, and stood with a sort of triumph before the two ladies, who were sitting in the front doorway, as if they were waiting for visitors, Helena still in her white muslin and red ribbons, and Miss Harriet in a thin black silk. Being happily self-forgetful in the greatness of the moment, Martha's manners were perfect, and she looked for once almost pretty and quite as young as she was.

"The minister came to the door himself, and returned his thanks. He said that cherries were always his favorite fruit, and he was much obliged to both Miss Pyne and Miss Vernon. He kept me waiting a few minutes, while he got this book ready to send to you, Miss Helena."

"What are you saying, Martha? I have sent him nothing!" exclaimed Miss Pyne, much astonished. "What does she mean, Helena?"

"Only a few cherries," explained Helena. "I thought Mr. Crofton would like them after his afternoon of parish calls. Martha and I arranged them before tea, and I sent them with our compliments."

"Oh, I am very glad you did," said Miss Harriet, wondering, but much relieved. "I was afraid—"

"No, it was none of my mischief," answered Helena daringly. "I did not think that Martha would be ready to go so soon. I should have shown you how pretty they looked among their green leaves. We put them in one of your best white dishes with the openwork edge. Martha shall show you to-morrow; mamma always likes to have them so." Helena's fingers were busy with the hard knot of a parcel.

"See this, cousin Harriet!" she announced proudly, as Martha disappeared round the corner of the house, beaming with the pleasures of adventure and success. "Look! the minister has sent me a book: Sermons on *what?* Sermons — it is so dark that I can't quite see."

"It must be his 'Sermons on the Seriousness of Life'; they are the only ones he has printed, I believe," said Miss Harriet, with much pleasure. "They are considered very fine discourses. He pays you a great compliment, my dear. I feared that he noticed your girlish levity."

"Do ask the kind gentleman to tea! He needs a little cheering up," begged the siren in India muslin, as she laid the shiny black volume of sermons on the stone doorstep.

"Perhaps I shall, if Martha improves as much as she has within the last day or two," Miss Harriet promised hopefully. "It is something I always dread a little when I am all alone, but I think Mr. Crofton likes to come. He converses so elegantly."

These were the days of long visits. Helena lingered through the pleasant weeks of early summer, and departed unwillingly at last to join her family at the White Hills, where they had gone to pass the month of August out of town. The happy-hearted young guest left many lamenting friends behind her, and promised each that she would come back again next year. Even Miss Harriet Pyne herself had lost some of the unnecessary provincialism and prejudice which had begun to harden a naturally good and open mind and affectionate heart. She was conscious of feeling younger and more free, and not so lonely. Nobody had ever been so gay, so fascinating, or so kind as Helena, so full of social resource, so simple and undemanding in her friendliness.

Martha came into Miss Helena's bedroom that last morning, and it was easy to see that she had been crying; she looked just as she did in that first sad week of homesickness and despair. All for love's sake she had been learning to do many things, and to do them exactly right; her eyes had grown quick to see the smallest chance for personal service. Nobody could be more humble and devoted; she looked years older than Helena, and wore already a touching air of caretaking.

"You spoil me, you dear Martha!" said Helena from the bed. "I don't know what they will say at home, I am so spoiled."

Martha went on opening the blinds to let in the brightness of the summer morning, but she did not speak.

"You are getting on splendidly, aren't you?" continued the little mistress. "You have tried so hard that you make me ashamed of myself. At first you crammed all the flowers together, and now you make them look beautiful. Last night cousin Harriet was so pleased when the table was so charming, and I told her you did everything yourself, every bit. Won't you keep the flowers fresh and pretty in the house until I come back? It's so much pleasanter for Miss Pyne, and you'll feed my little sparrows, won't you? They're growing so tame."

"Oh, yes, Miss Helena!" and Martha looked almost angry for a moment, then she burst into tears and covered her face with her apron. "I couldn't understand a single thing when I first came. I never had been anywhere to see anything, and Miss Pyne frightened me when she talked. It was you made me think I could ever learn. I wanted to keep the place, 'count of mother and the little boys; we're dreadful hard pushed. Hepsy has been good in the kitchen; she said she ought to have patience with me, for she was awkward herself when she first came."

Helena laughed; she looked so pretty under the tasseled white curtains.

"I dare say Hepsy tells the truth," she said. "I wish you had told me about your mother. When I come again, some day we'll drive up country, as you call it, to see her. Martha! I wish you would think of me sometimes after I go away. Won't you promise?" and the bright young face suddenly grew grave. "I have hard times myself; I don't always learn things that I ought to learn, I don't always put things straight. I wish you wouldn't forget me ever, and would just believe in me. I think it does help more than anything."

"I won't forget," said Martha slowly. "I shall think of you every day." She spoke almost with indifference, as if she had been asked to dust a room, but she turned aside quickly and pulled the little mat under the hot water jug quite out of its former straightness; then she hastened away down the long white entry, weeping as she went.

To lose out of sight the friend whom one has loved and lived to please is to lose joy out of life. But if love is true, there comes presently a higher joy of pleasing the ideal, that is to say, the perfect friend. The same old happiness is lifted to a higher level. As for Martha, the girl who stayed behind in Ashford, nobody's life could seem duller to those who could not understand; she was slow of step, and her eyes were almost always downcast as if intent upon incessant toil; but they startled you when she looked up, with their shining light. She was capable of the happiness of holding fast to a great sentiment, the ineffable satisfaction of trying to please one whom she truly loved. She never thought of trying to make other people pleased with herself; all she lived for was to do the best she could for others, and to conform to an ideal, which grew at last to be like a saint's vision, a heavenly figure painted upon the sky.

On Sunday afternoons in summer, Martha sat by the window of her chamber, a low-storied little room, which looked into the side yard and the great branches of an elm-tree. She wore her plain black dress and a clean white apron, and held in her lap a little wooden box, with a brass ring on top for a handle. She was past sixty years of age and looked even older. It seemed like yesterday that Helena Vernon had gone away, and it was more than forty years.

War and peace had brought their changes and great anxieties, the face of the earth was furrowed by floods and fire, the faces of mistress and maid were furrowed by smiles and tears, and in the sky the stars shone on as if nothing had happened. The village of Ashford added a few pages to its unexciting history, the minister preached, the people listened; now and then a funeral crept along the street, and now and then the bright face of a little child rose above the horizon of a family pew. Miss Harriet Pyne lived on in the large white house, which gained more and more distinction because it suffered no changes.

Hardly any great social event had ruffled the easy current of life since Helena Vernon's marriage. To this Miss Pyne had gone, stately in appearance and carrying gifts of some old family silver which bore the Vernon crest. A brilliant English match was not without its attractions to an old-fashioned gentlewoman like Miss Pyne, and Helena herself was amazingly happy; one day there had come a letter to Ashford, in which her very heart seemed to beat with love and self-forgetfulness, to tell cousin Harriet of such new happiness and high hope. "Tell Martha all that I say about my dear Jack," wrote the eager girl; "please show my letter to Martha, and tell her that I shall come home next summer and bring the handsomest and best man in the world to Ashford. I have told him all about the dear house and the dear garden; there never was such a lad to reach for cherries with his six-foot-two." Miss Pyne, wondering a little, gave the letter to Martha, who took it deliberately and as if she wondered too, and went away to read it slowly by herself. Martha cried over it, and felt a strange sense of loss and pain; it hurt her heart a little to read about the cherry-picking. Her idol seemed to be less her own since she had become the idol of a stranger. She never had taken such a letter in her hands before, but love at last prevailed, since Miss Helena was happy, and she kissed the last page where her name was written, feeling overbold, and laid the envelope on Miss Pyne's secretary without a word.

The most generous love cannot but long for reassurance, and Martha had the joy of being remembered. She was not forgotten when the day of the wedding drew near, but she never knew that Miss Helena had asked if cousin Harriet would not bring Martha to town; she should like to have Martha there to see her married. "She would help about the flowers," wrote the happy girl; "I know she will like to come, and I'll ask mamma to plan to have some one take her all about Boston and make her have a pleasant time after the hurry of the great day is over."

Cousin Harriet thought it was very kind and exactly like Helena, but Martha would be out of her element; it was most imprudent and girlish to have thought of such a thing. Helena did not forget to ask if Martha had come, and was astonished by the indifference of the answer. She knew that Martha would have loved to be near, for she could not help understanding in that moment of her own happiness the love that was hidden in another heart. Next day this happy young princess, the bride, cut a piece of a great cake and put it into a pretty box that had held one of her wedding presents. With eager voices calling her, she still lingered and ran to take one or two trifles from her dressing-table, a little mirror and some tiny scissors that Martha would remember, and one of the pretty handkerchiefs marked with her maiden name. These she put in the box too; it was half a girlish freak and fancy, but she could not help trying to share her happiness, and Martha's life was so plain and dull. She whispered a message, and put the little package into cousin Harriet's hand for Martha and she said good-by. If she had known it, as she kissed cousin Harriet good-by, they were never going to see each other again until they were old women. The first step that she took out of her father's house that day, married, and full of hope and joy, was a step that led her away from the green elms of Boston Common and away from her own country and those she loved best, to a brilliant, much-varied foreign life, and to nearly all the sorrows and nearly all the joys that the heart of one woman could hold or know.

On Sunday afternoons Martha used to sit by the window in Ashford and hold the wooden box which a favorite young brother, who afterward died at sea, had made for her, and she used to take out of it the pretty little box with a gilded cover that had held the piece of wedding-cake, and the small scissors, and the blurred bit of a mirror in its silver case; as for the handkerchief with the narrow lace edge, once in two or three years she sprinkled it as if it were a flower, and spread it out in the sun on the old bleaching-green, and sat near by in the shrubbery to watch lest some bold robin or cherry-bird should seize it and fly away.

Miss Harriet Pyne was often congratulated upon the good fortune of having such a helper and friend as Martha. As time went on this tall, gaunt woman, always thin, always slow, gained a dignity of behavior and simple affectionateness of look which suited the charm and dignity of the ancient house. She was unconsciously beautiful like a saint, like the picturesqueness of a lonely tree which lives to shelter unnumbered lives and to stand quietly in its place. There was such rustic homeliness and constancy belonging to her, such beautiful powers of apprehension, such reticence, such gentleness for those who were troubled or sick; all these gifts and graces Martha hid in her heart. She had been educated by a remembrance; Helena's young eyes forever looked at her reassuringly from a gay girlish face. Helena's sweet patience in teaching her own awkwardness could never be forgotten.

"I owe everything to Miss Helena," said Martha, half aloud, as she sat alone by the window; she had said it to herself a thousand times. When she looked in the little keep-sake mirror she always hoped to see some faint reflection of Helena Vernon, but there was only her own brown old New England face to look back at her wonderingly.

Miss Pyne went less and less often to pay visits to her friends in Boston; there were very few friends left to come to Ashford and make long visits in the summer, and life grew more and more monotonous. Now and then there came news from across the sea and messages of remembrance, letters that were closely written on thin sheets of paper, and that spoke of lords and ladies, of great journeys, of the death of little children and the proud successes of boys at school, of the wedding of Helena Dysart's only daughter; but even that had happened years ago. These things seemed far away and vague.

Miss Pyne herself had many fixed habits, but little ideality or imagination, and so at last it was Martha who took thought for her mistress, and gave freedom to her own good taste. After a while, without any one's observing the change, the every-day ways of doing things in the house came to be the stately ways that had once belonged only to the entertainment of guests. Happily both mistress and maid seized all possible chances for hospitality, yet Miss Harriet nearly always sat alone at her exquisitely served table with its fresh flowers, and the beautiful old china which Martha handled so lovingly. And every day, as she had promised, she thought of Miss Helena,—oh, many times in every day: whether this thing would please her, or that be likely to fall in with her fancy or ideas of fitness. As far as was possible the rare news that reached Ashford through an occasional letter or the talk of guests was made part of Martha's own life, the history of her own heart.

One Sunday afternoon in early summer Miss Harriet Pyne came hurrying along the entry that led to Martha's room and called two or three times before its inhabitant could reach the door. Miss Harriet looked unusually cheerful and excited, and she held something in her hand. "Where are you, Martha?" she called again. "Come quick, I have something to tell you!"

"Here I am, Miss Pyne," said Martha, who had only stopped to put her precious box in the drawer, and to shut the geography.

"Who do you think is coming this very night at half-past six? We must have everything as nice as we can; I must see Hannah at once. Do you remember my cousin Helena who has lived abroad so long? Miss Helena Vernon,—the Honorable Mrs. Dysart, she is now."

"Yes, I remember her," answered Martha, turning a little pale.

"I knew that she was in this country, and I had written to ask her to come for a long visit," continued Miss Harriet, who did not often explain things, even to Martha, though she was always conscientious about the kind messages that were sent back by grateful guests. "She telegraphs that she means to anticipate her visit by a few days and come to me at once. The heat is beginning in town, I suppose. I daresay, having been a foreigner so long, she does not mind traveling on Sunday. Do you think Hannah will be prepared? We must have tea a little later."

"Yes, Miss Harriet," said Martha. She wondered that she could speak as usual, there was such a ringing in her ears. "I shall have time to pick some fresh strawberries; Miss Helena is so fond of our strawberries."

"Why I had forgotten," said Miss Pyne, a little puzzled by something quite unusual in Martha's face. "We must expect to find Mrs. Dysart a good deal changed, Martha; it is a great many years since she was here; I have not seen her since her wedding, and she has had a great deal of trouble, poor girl. You had better open the parlor chamber, and make it ready before you go down."

"It is all ready," said Martha. "I can carry some of those little sweet-brier roses upstairs before she comes."

"Yes, you are always thoughtful," said Miss Pyne, with unwonted feeling.

Martha did not answer. She glanced at the telegram wistfully. She had never really suspected before that Miss Pyne knew nothing of the love that had been in her heart all these years; it was half a pain and half a golden joy to keep such a secret; she could hardly bear this moment of surprise.

Presently the news gave wings to her willing feet. When Hannah, the cook, who never had known Miss Helena, went to the parlor an hour later on some errand to her old mistress, she discovered that this stranger guest must be a very important person. She had never seen the tea-table look exactly as it did that night, and in the parlor itself there were fresh blossoming boughs in the Old East India jars, and lilies in the paneled hall, and flowers everywhere, as if there were some high festivity.

Miss Pyne sat by the window watching, in her best dress, looking stately and calm; she seldom went out now, and it was almost time for the carriage. Martha was just coming in from the garden with the strawberries, and with more flowers in her apron. It was a bright cool evening in June, the golden robins sang in the elms, and the sun was going down behind the apple-trees at the foot of the garden. The beautiful old house stood wide open to the long-expected guest.

"I think that I shall go down to the gate," said Miss Pyne, looking at Martha for approval, and Martha nodded and they went together slowly down the broad front walk.

There was a sound of horses and wheels on the roadside turf: Martha could not see at first; she stood back inside the gate behind the white lilac-bushes as the carriage came. Miss Pyne was there; she was holding out both arms and taking a tired, bent little figure in black to her heart. "Oh, my Miss Helena is an old woman like me!" and Martha gave a pitiful sob; she had never dreamed it would be like this; this was the one thing she could not bear.

"Where are you, Martha?" called Miss Pyne. "Martha will bring these in; you have not forgotten my good Martha, Helena?" Then Mrs. Dysart looked up and smiled just as she used to smile in the old days. The young eyes were there still in the changed face, and Miss Helena had come.

That night Martha waited in her lady's room just as she used, humble and silent, and went through with the old unforgotten loving services. The long years seemed like days. At last she lingered a moment trying to think of something else that might be done, then she was going silently away, but Helena called her back. She suddenly knew the whole story and could hardly speak.

"Oh, my dear Martha!" she cried, "won't you kiss me good night? Oh, Martha, have you remembered like this, all these long years!"

Old friends are the great blessing of one's latter years. Half a word conveys one's meaning. They have a memory of the same events, and have the same mode of thinking. I have young relations that may grow upon me, for my nature is affectionate, but can they grow old friends?
—HORACE WALPOLE

There is in friendship something of all relations, and something above them all. It is the golden thread that ties the heart of all the world.
—JOHN EVELYN

"I took my leave forever of my dear old friend . . ."

SAMUEL JOHNSON'S FAREWELL TO HIS MOTHER'S AGED SERVANT

Sunday, October 18, 1767—Yesterday, October 17, at about ten in the morning, I took my leave forever of my dear old friend Catherine Chambers, who came to live with my mother about 1724, and has been but little parted from us since. She buried my father, my brother, and my mother. She is now fifty-eight years old.

I desired all to withdraw, then told her that we were to part forever; that as Christians, we should part with prayer, and that I would, if she was willing, say a short prayer beside her. She expressed great desire to hear me; and held up her poor hands, as she lay in bed, with great fervor while I prayed, kneeling by her, nearly in the following words:—

"Almighty and most merciful Father, whose loving kindness is over all thy works, behold, visit, and relieve this thy servant, who is grieved with sickness. Grant that the sense of her weakness may add strength to her faith, and seriousness to her repentance. And grant that by the help of thy Holy Spirit, after the pains and labors of this short life, we may all obtain everlasting happiness through Jesus Christ our Lord; for whose sake hear our prayers. Amen. Our Father," etc.

I then kissed her. She told me that to part was the greatest pain that she had ever felt, and that she hoped we should meet again in a better place. I expressed, with swelled eyes and great emotion of tenderness, the same hopes. We kissed and parted, I humbly hope to meet again and part no more.

". . . the Greeks honored Achilles . . . because he preferred his friend . . ."

GREEK CONCEPTS OF FRIENDSHIP

Plato

[Phaedrus speaking]

"Among warmly attached friends, a man is especially grieved to be discovered by his friend in any dishonourable act. If, then, by any contrivance, a state or army could be composed of friends bound by strong attachment, it is beyond calculation how excellently they would administer their affairs, refraining from anything base, contending with each other for the acquirement of fame, and exhibiting such valour in battle as that, though few in numbers, they might subdue all mankind. For should one friend desert the ranks or cast away his arms in the presence of the other, he would suffer far acuter shame from that one person's regard, than from the regard of all other men. A thousand times would he prefer to die, rather than desert the object of his attachment, and not succour him in danger....

"Achilles, though informed by his mother that his own death would ensue upon his killing Hector, but that if he refrained from it he might return home and die in old age, yet preferred revenging and honouring his beloved Patroclus; not to die for him merely, but to disdain and reject that life which he had ceased to share. Therefore the Greeks honoured Achilles beyond all other men, because he thus preferred his friend to all things else.

"On this account have the Gods rewarded Achilles more amply than Alcestis; permitting his spirit to inhabit the islands of the blessed. Hence do I assert that Love is the most ancient and venerable of deities, and most powerful to endow mortals with the possession of happiness and virtue, both whilst they live and after they die...."

[*Pausanias speaking*]

"Not only friendship, but philosophy and the practice of the gymnastic exercises, are represented as dishonourable by the tyrannical governments under which the barbarians live. For I imagine it would little conduce to the benefit of the governors, that the governed should be disciplined to lofty thoughts and to the unity and communion of steadfast friendship, of which admirable effects the tyrants of our own country have also learned that Love is the author. For the love of Harmodius and Aristogiton, strengthened into a firm friendship, dissolved the tyranny. Wherever, therefore, it is declared dishonourable in any case to serve and benefit friends, that law is a mark of the depravity of the legislator, the avarice and tyranny of the rulers, and the cowardice of those who are ruled. Wherever it is simply declared to be honourable without distinction of cases, such a declaration denotes dullness and want of subtlety of mind in the authors of the regulation. Here the degrees of praise or blame to be attributed by law are far better regulated; but it is yet difficult to determine the cases to which they should refer....

"It is considered as dishonourable to be inspired with love at once, lest time should be wanting to know and approve the character of the object. It is considered dishonourable to be captivated by the allurements of wealth and power, or terrified through injuries to yield up the affections, or not to despise in the comparison with an unconstrained choice all political influence and personal advantage. For no circumstance is there in wealth or power so invariable and consistent, as that no generous friendship can ever spring up from amongst them....

"Love is the divinity who creates peace among men, and calm upon the sea, the windless silence of storms, repose and sleep in sadness. Love divests us of all alienation from each other, and fills our vacant hearts with overflowing sympathy; he gathers us together in such social meetings as we now delight to celebrate, our guardian and our guide in dances, and sacrifices, and feasts. Yes, Love, who showers benignity upon the world, and before whose presence all harsh passions flee and perish; the author of all soft affections; the destroyer of all ungentle thoughts; merciful, mild; the object of the admiration of the wise, and the delight of gods; possessed by the fortunate, and desired by the unhappy, therefore unhappy because they possess him not; the father of grace, and delicacy, and gentleness, and delight, and persuasion, and desire; the cherisher of all that is good, the abolisher of all evil; our most excellent pilot, defence, saviour and guardian in labour and in fear, in desire and in reason; the ornament and governor of all things human and divine; the best, the loveliest; in whose footsteps every one ought to follow, celebrating him excellently in song, and bearing each his part in that divinest harmony which Love sings to all things which live and are, soothing the troubled minds of Gods and men."

(Translated by Percy Bysshe Shelley)

ORESTES AND PYLADES
Euripides

Pylades: That thou shouldst die, and I behold this light,
Were base: with thee I sailed, with thee to die
Becomes me; else shall I obtain the name
Of a vile coward through the Argive state,
And the deep vales of Phocis. Most will think,
For most think ill, that by betraying thee
I saved myself, home to return alone:
Or haply that I slew thee, and thy death
Contrived, that in the ruin of thy house
Thy empire I might grasp, to me devolved
As wedded to thy sister, now sole heir.
These things I fear, and hold them infamous.
Behooves me then with thee to die, with thee
To bleed a victim, on the pyre with thine

To give my body to the flames; for this
Becomes me as thy friend, who dread reproach.
Orestes: Speak more auspicious words: 'tis mine to bear
Ills that are mine: and single when the woe,
I would not bear it double. What thou sayest
Is vile and infamous, would light on me,
Should I cause thee to die, who in my toils
Hast borne a share: to me, who from the gods
Suffers afflictions which I suffer, death
Is not unwelcome: thou art happy, thine
An unpolluted and a prosperous house;
Mine impious and unblest. If thou art saved,
And from my sister, whom I gave to thee
Betrothed thy bride, are blessed with sons, my name
May yet remain, nor all my father's house
In total ruin sink. Go then, and live;
Dwell in the mansions of thy ancestors.
And when thou comest to Greece, to Argos famed
For warrior-steeds, by this right hand I charge thee
Raise a sepulchral mound, and on it place
A monument to me; and to my tomb
Her tears, her tresses let my sister give:
And say that by an Argive woman's hand
I perished, to the altar's bloody rites
A hallowed victim. Never let thy soul
Betray my sister, for thou seest her state
Of friends how destitute, her father's house
How desolate. Farewell! Of all my friends
Thee have I found most friendly, from my youth
Trained up with me, in all my sylvan sports
Thou dear associate, and through many toils
Thou faithful partner of my miseries....
Pylades: Yes, I will raise thy tomb: thy sister's bed
I never will betray, unhappy youth,
For I will hold thee dearer when thou'rt dead,
Than while thou livest; nor hath yet the voice
Of Phoebus quite destroyed thee, though thou stand
To slaughter nigh: but sometimes mighty woes
Yield mighty changes, so when fortune wills.
Orestes: Forbear: the words of Phoebus nought avail me;
For passing from the shrine the virgin comes.

(Translated by Robert Potter)

"... something human, in passing, had touched me."

THE DRUNKARD

David Grayson (Ray Stannard Baker)

I have had a singular adventure, in which I have made a friend. And I have seen new things which are also true.

My friend is a drunkard—at least so I call him, following the custom of the country. On his way from town he used often to come by my farm. I could hear him singing far off. Beginning at the bridge, where on still days one can hear the rattle of a wagon on the loose boards, he sang in a peculiar high clear voice. I make no further comment on the singing, nor the cause of it; but in the cool of the evening when the air was still—and he usually came in the evening—I often heard the cadences of his song with a thrill of pleasure. Then I saw him come driving by my farm, sitting on the spring seat of his one-horse wagon, and if he chanced to see me in my field, he would take off his hat and make a grandiloquent bow, but never for a moment stop his singing. And so he passed the house and I, with a smile, saw him moving up the hill in the north road, until finally his voice, still singing, died away in the distance.

Once I happened to reach the house just as the singer was passing, and Harriet said: "There goes the drunkard."

It gave me an indescribable shock. Of course I had known as much, and yet I had not directly applied the term. I had not thought of my singer as *that*, for I had often been conscious in spite of myself, alone in my field, of something human and cheerful which had touched me, in passing.

After Harriet applied the name to my singer, I was of two minds concerning him. I struggled with myself: I tried instinctively to discipline my pulses when I heard the sound of his singing. For was he not a drunkard? Lord! how we get our moralities mixed up with our realities!

And then one evening when I saw him coming—I had been a long day alone in my field—I experienced a sudden revulsion of feeling. With an indescribable joyousness of adventure I stepped out toward the fence, and pretended to be hard at work.

"After all," I said to myself, "this is a large world, with room in it for many curious people."

I waited in excitement. When he came near me I straightened up just as though I had seen him for the first time. When he lifted his hat to me, I lifted my hat as grandiloquently as he.

"How are you, neighbor?" I asked.

He paused for a single instant and gave me a smile; then he replaced his hat as though he had far more important business to attend to, and went on up the road.

My next glimpse of him was a complete surprise to me. I saw him in the street in town. Harriet pointed him out, else I should never have recognized him: a quiet, modest man, as different as one could imagine from the singer I had seen so often passing my farm. He wore neat, worn clothes; and his horse stood tied in front of the store. He had brought his honey to town to sell. He was a bee-man.

I stopped and asked him about his honey, and whether the fall flowers had been plenty; I ran my eye over his horse, and said that it seemed to be a good animal. But I could get very little from him, and that little in a rather low voice. I came away with my interest whetted to a still keener edge. How a man has come to what he is—is there any discovery better worth making?

After that day in town I watched for the bee-man, and I saw him often on his way to town, silent, somewhat bent forward in his seat, driving his horse with circumspection, a Dr. Jekyll of propriety; and a few hours later he would come homeward a wholly different person, straight of back, joyous of mien, singing his song in his high clear voice, a very Hyde of recklessness. Even the old horse seemed changed: he held his head higher and stepped with a quicker pace. When the bee-man went toward town he never paused, nor once looked around to see me in my field; but when he came back he watched for me, and when I responded to his bow he would sometimes stop and reply to my greeting.

One day he came from town on foot and when he saw me, even though I was some distance away, he approached the fence and took off his hat, and held out his hand. I walked over toward him. I saw his full face for the first time; a rather handsome face. The hair was thin and curly, the forehead generous and smooth; but the chin was small. His face was slightly flushed and his eyes—his eyes *burned!* I shook his hand.

"I had hoped," I said, "that you would stop sometime as you went by."

"Well, I've wanted to stop—but I'm a busy man. I have important matters almost all the time...."

So he set off down the road, and as he passed my house he began singing in his high voice. I walked away with a feeling of wonder, not unmixed with a sorrow. It was a strange case!

Gradually I became really acquainted with the bee-man, at first with the exuberant, confident, imaginative, home-going bee-man; far more slowly with the shy, reserved, townward-bound bee-man. It was quite an adventure, my first talk with the shy bee-man. I was driving home;

I met him near the lower bridge. I cudgeled my brain to think of some way to get at him. As he passed, I leaned out and said:

"Friend, will you do me a favor? I neglected to stop at the post-office. Would you call and see whether anything has been left for me in the box since the carrier started?"

"Certainly," he said, glancing up at me, but turning his head swiftly aside again.

On his way back he stopped and left me a paper. He told me volubly about the way he would run the post-office if he were "in a place of suitable authority."

"Great things are possible," he said, "to the man of ideas."

At this point began one of the by-plays of my acquaintance with the bee-man. The exuberant bee-man referred disparagingly to the shy bee-man.

"I must have looked pretty seedy and stupid this morning on my way in. I was up half the night; but I feel all right now."

The next time I met the shy bee-man he on his part apologized for the exuberant bee-man—hesitatingly, falteringly, winding up with the words, "I think you will understand." I grasped his hand, and left him with a wan smile on his face. Instinctively I came to treat the two men in a wholly different manner. With the one I was blustering, hail-fellow-well-met, listening with eagerness to his expansive talk; but to the other I said little, feeling my way slowly to his friendship, for I could not help looking upon him as a pathetic figure. He needed a friend. The exuberant bee-man was sufficient unto himself, glorious in his visions, and I had from him no little entertainment. . . .

At last the time came, as things come to him who desires them faithfully enough. One afternoon not long ago, when the trees were glorious on the hills, the Indian summer sun never softer, I was tramping along a wood lane far back of my farm. And at the road side, near the trunk of an oak tree, sat my friend, the bee-man. He was a picture of despondency, one long hand hanging limp between his knees, his head bowed down. When he saw me he straightened up, looked at me, and settled back again. My heart went out to him, and I sat down beside him.

"Have you ever seen a finer afternoon?" I asked.

He glanced up at the sky.

"Fine?" he answered vaguely, as if it had never occurred to him.

I saw instantly what the matter was; the exuberant bee-man was in process of transformation into the shy bee-man. I don't know exactly how it came about, for such things are difficult to explain, but I led him to talk of himself.

"After it is all over," he said, "of course I am ashamed of myself. You don't know, Mr. Grayson, what it all means. I am ashamed of myself, now, and yet I know I shall do it again."

"No," I said, "you will not do it again."

"Yes, I shall. Something inside me argues: Why should you be sorry? Were you not free for a whole afternoon?"

"Free?" I asked.

"Yes—free. You will not understand. But every day I work, work, work. I have friends, but somehow I can't get to them; I can't even get to my wife. It seems as if a wall hemmed me in, as if I were bound to a rock which I couldn't get away from. I am also afraid. When I am sober I know how to do great things, but I can't do them. After a few glasses—I never take more—I not only know I can do great things, but I feel as though I were really doing them."

"But you never do?"

"No, I never do, but I *feel* that I can. All the bonds break and the wall falls down and I am free. I can really touch people. I feel friendly and neighborly."

He was talking eagerly now, trying to explain, for the first time in his life, he said, how it was that he did what he did. He told me how beautiful it made the world, where before it was miserable and friendless, how he thought of great things and made great plans, how his home seemed finer and better to him, and his work more noble. The man had a real gift of imagination and spoke with an eagerness and eloquence that stirred me deeply. I was almost on the point of asking him where his magic liquor was to be found! When he finally gave me an opening, I said:

"I think I understand! Many men I know are in some respect drunkards. They all want some way to escape themselves—to be free of their own limitations."

"That's it! That's it!" he exclaimed eagerly.

We sat for a time side by side, saying nothing. I could not help thinking of that line of Virgil referring to quite another sort of intoxication:

"With voluntary dreams they cheat their minds."

Instead of that beautiful unity of thought and action which makes the finest character, here was this poor tragedy of divided life.... No man can be two men successfully.

So we sat and said nothing. What indeed can any man *say* to another under such circumstances....

I've always felt that the best thing one man can give another is the warm hand of understanding. And yet when I thought of the pathetic, shy bee-man, hemmed in by his sunless walls, I felt that I should also say something. Seeing two men struggling shall I not assist the better? Shall I let the sober one be despoiled by him who is riotous? There are realities, but there are also moralities—separated.

"Most of us," I said finally, "are in some respects drunkards. We don't give it so harsh a name, but we are just that. Drunkenness is not a mere matter of intoxicating liquors; it goes deeper—far deeper. Drunkenness is the failure of a man to control his thoughts."

The bee-man sat silent, gazing out before him. I noted the blue veins in the hand that lay on his knee. It came over me with sudden amusement and I said:

"I often get drunk myself."

"You?"

"Yes—dreadfully drunk."

He looked at me and laughed—for the first time! And I laughed, too. Do you know, there's a lot of human nature in people! And when you think you are deep in Tragedy, behold, humor lurks around the corner! ...

"Sometimes," I said, "when I'm on *my* kind of spree, I try not so much to empty my mind of the thoughts which bother me, but rather to fill my mind with other, stronger thoughts—"

Before I could finish he interrupted: "Haven't I tried that, too: don't I think of other things? I think of bees—and that leads me to honey, doesn't it? And that makes me think of putting the honey in the wagon and taking it to town. Then, of course, I think how it will sell. Instantly, stronger than you can imagine, I see a dime in my hand. Then it appears on the wet bar. I *smell the smell* of the liquor. And there you are!"

We did not talk much more that day. We got up and shook hands and looked each other in the eye. The bee-man turned away, but came back hesitatingly.

"I am glad of this talk, Mr. Grayson. It makes me feel like taking hold again. I have been in hell for years—"

"Of course," I said, "you needed a friend. You and I will come up together."

As I walked toward home that evening, I felt a curious warmth of satisfaction in my soul—and I marvelled at the many strange things that are to be found upon this miraculous earth.

I suppose, if I were writing a story, I should stop at this point; but I am dealing in life. And life does not always respond to our impatience with satisfactory moral conclusions. Life is inconclusive, quite open at the end. I had a vision of a new life for my neighbor, the bee-man—and have it yet, for I have not done with him—but—

Last evening, and that is why I have been prompted to write the whole story, my bee-man came again along the road by my farm; my exuberant bee-man. I heard him singing afar off.

He did not see me as he went by, but as I stood looking out at him, it came over me with a sudden sense of largeness and quietude that the sun shone on him as graciously as it did on me, and that the leaves did not turn aside from him, nor the birds stop singing when he passed.

"He also belongs here," I said.

And I watched him mount the distant hill, until I could no longer hear the high clear cadences of his song. And it seemed to me that something human, in passing, had touched me.

We cannot tell the precise moment when friendship is formed. As in filling a vessel drop by drop, there is at last a drop which makes it run over; so in a series of kindnesses there is at last one which makes the heart run over.

—SAMUEL JOHNSON

THE UNILLUMINED VERGE
To a Friend Dying
Robert Bridges

They tell you that Death's at the turn of the road,
    That under the shade of a cypress you'll find him,
And, struggling on wearily, lashed by the goad
    Of pain, you will enter the black mist behind him.

I can walk with you up to the ridge of the hill,
    And we'll talk of the way we have come through the valley;
Down below there a bird breaks into a trill,
    And a groaning slave bends to the oar of his galley.

You are up on the heights now, you pity the slave—
    "Poor soul, how fate lashes him on at his rowing!
Yet it's joyful to live, and it's hard to be brave
    When you watch the sun sink and the daylight is going."

We are almost there—our last walk on this height—
    I must bid you good-bye at that cross on the mountain.
See the sun glowing red, and the pulsating light
    Fill the valley, and rise like the flood in a fountain.

And it shines in your face and illumines your soul;
  We are comrades as ever, right here at your going;
You may rest if you will within sight of the goal,
  While I must return to my oar and the rowing.

We must part now? Well, here is the hand of a friend;
  I will keep you in sight till the road makes its turning.
Just over the ridge within reach of the end
  Of your arduous trail,—the beginning of learning.

You will call me once from the mist, on the verge,
  "Au revoir!" and "Good night!" while the twilight is creeping
Up luminous peaks, and the pole stars emerge?
  Yes, I hear your faint voice: "This is rest, and like sleeping!"

A TEST

Jalāl-uddīn Rūmī

Once a man came and knocked at the door of his friend.
His friend said, "Who art thou, O faithful one?"
He said, "'Tis I." He answered, "There is no admittance.
There is no room for the raw at my well-cooked feast.
Naught but fire and separation and absence
Can cook the raw one and free him from hypocrisy!
Since thy self has not left thee,
Thou must be burned in fiery flames."

The poor man went away, and for one whole year
Journeyed burning with grief for his friend's absence.
His heart burned till it was cooked; then he went again
And drew near to the house of his friend.
He knocked at the door in fear and trepidation
Lest some careless word should fall from his lips;
His friend shouted, "Who is that at the door?"
He answered, "'Tis thou who art at the door, O beloved!"
The friend said, "Since it is I, let me come in,
There is not room for two I's in one house."

"We relished this mute communion."

FROM THE SHORT STORY, "LETTER TO A HOSTAGE"

Antoine de Saint Exupéry

France, indeed, for me was neither an abstract goddess nor some historian's concept, but well and truly living flesh on which I depended, a net-work of ties which determined my actions, an arrangement of poles which fixed the trends of my heart. I had a need to feel that those whom I needed to give me direction were solider and more enduring than myself. To know where to return. To exist.

In them, my country dwelt in its entirety and lived through them in myself. For him who navigates the seas a continent epitomizes itself in the simple flash of some beacons. A beacon gives no measure of distance. Its light appears to the eye and that is all. Yet all the wonders of the continent dwell in that star.

And so to-day, when France, after the total occupation, with all its cargo, has passed wholly into silence, like a ship steaming without lights, of which no one knows whether or no it survives the perils of the sea, the fate of each of those I love tortures me more than some incurable disease. I find myself menaced to the core by their fragility.

He who, tonight, haunts my memory, is fifty. He is ill. And a Jew. How will he survive the German terror? To imagine he still breathes I must make myself think him unknown to the invader, secretly sheltered behind the fine rampart of silence of the peasants of his village. Then, only, do I believe he lives still. Then only, strolling off into the realm of his friendship, which no frontiers bound, can I let myself feel no emigrant, but a traveller. For the desert is not where one thinks it is. The Sahara is more alive than a metropolis and the city that most swarms with life grows empty if the essential poles of existence are demagnetized.

How then does life build these magnetic lines by which we live? Whence comes the weight that draws me towards the house of this friend? What then are those high moments that made this presence one of the poles I need? With what hidden happenings then must personal affections be moulded, and through them, the love of one's land?

The real miracles, how little noise they make! Cardinal events, how simple they are! Of that moment I wish to relate, so little is there to be said that I have to ponder on it and talk to this friend.

It was on a day before the war, on the banks of the Saône, near Tournus. We had picked a restaurant for lunch whose wooden balcony overhung the river. Our elbows resting on a plain wood table, scored by customers' knives, we had ordered two Pernods. Your doctor had forbidden you spirits, but on big occasions you cheated. This was one. We did not know why, but it was one. What was rejoicing us was more impalpable than the quality of the light. And so, you decided for the Pernod that marked important occasions. And as, a few steps away, two men were unloading a barge, we invited the bargees. We had beckoned them from the balcony. And they came. Perfectly naturally. It seemed so obvious to invite these friends, perhaps because of this invisible heyday we were feeling. They saw it so well that they immediately responded. And so we drank together.

The sun felt good. The poplars on the farther bank, the plain to the very horizon, were bathed in its warm honey. And we went on getting more and more cheerful without knowing why. Everything assured us; the clear sunlight, the river flowing, the meal, the bargees for having responded, the maid who served us with a sort of consummate grace, as though in charge of some eternal feast. We were wholly at peace, tucked well away from all confusion in a finite civilization. We savoured a sort of state of perfection, in which, every wish vouchsafed, nothing remained to reveal to each other. We felt we were pure, upright, lambent, indulgent. We could not have said what truth was thus being manifested. But the dominant feeling was certainly that of assurance. Of an assurance almost proud.

Thus, the universe, through us, showed its kindness. The nebulae condensed, the planets hardened, the first amoeba came into being and life's gigantic labour pains led the amoeba to man in order that all should converge harmoniously, through us, in this quality of pleasure! It was not so bad, as an achievement.

And so we relished this mute communion and these almost religious rites. Lulled by the movements of the hieratic maid, the bargees and ourselves drank together like worshippers of the same religion, though none of us would have said which. One of the bargees was Dutch. The other, German. In the past, he had fled from the Nazis, who had been after him as a Communist, or a Trotskyist, or a Catholic or a Jew. (I have forgotten the label under which the man was outlawed.) But at this moment the bargee was something very different from a label. It was what was inside that counted. The human leaven. He was a friend, pure and simple. And we were agreed, as among friends. You, I, the bargees and the maidservant. Agreed about what? The Pernod? The meaning of life? The mellow sunlight? That too, we could not have said. But this agreement was so complete, so deep rooted, and its whole substance, though impossible to formulate in words, was based so clearly on a faith, that we would willingly have set to fortify the chalet, sustaining a siege and dying behind machine guns to preserve that substance.

What substance? ... And this is just where it is difficult to express what one means! It runs the danger of capturing only the reflections, not the essence. Inadequate words will allow my truth to escape. I should be being obscure if I claim that we would easily have fought to rescue a certain something in the bargees' smile, in your smile, in mine and in the maid's, some miracle of that sun, which, with so much effort, for so many millions of years, had managed to achieve through us the quality of a smile that was pretty satisfactory.

Essentials, most often, are imponderable. The essential here apparently, was but a smile. Often, the essential is a smile. One is paid by a smile. One is repaid by a smile. One is animated by a smile. And the quality of a smile may lead to one's death.... This quality freed us so completely from the anguish of these times, vouchsafed us certitude, hope, peace....

Is not this quality of joy the most precious fruit of the civilization which is ours? A totalitarian tyranny, too, might satisfy us in our material needs. But we are not beasts to be fattened. Prosperity and comfort could never of themselves wholly satisfy our needs. For us, brought up to believe in human respect, simple meetings which sometimes change into wonderful occasions are heavy with meaning.

Human respect! Human respect! ... There is the touchstone! When the Nazi respects only what resembles him, he is respecting nothing but himself. He rejects creative contradictions, shatters all hope of man's ascent, and for a thousand years, in place of man, creates an ant-heap robot. Order for order's sake gelds man of his essential power, which is to transform both the world and himself. Life creates order, but order does not create life.

To me, far otherwise, it seems that our ascent is not completed, that tomorrow's truth feeds on yesterday's error and that the contradictions to be overcome are the very compost of our growth. We recognize as ours those even who differ from us. But what a strange kinship! It is based on the future, not on the past. On the objective, not on origins. We are pilgrims to each other who, along different roads, all toil towards the same rendezvous.

But to-day, human respect, the very condition of our ascent, is in danger. The creakings of the modern world have drawn us into darkness. The problems have no coherence, the solutions are contradictory. Yesterday's truth is dead, to-morrow's still to be erected. There is no valid synthesis perceptible, and each of us holds only a bit of the truth. Lacking proof to make them convincing, the political religions resort to violence. And so, being divided as to methods, we risk no longer realizing that we are hastening towards the same end.

The traveller crossing the mountain, following a star, risks forgetting the star that guides him if too engrossed in pondering ways of reaching the top. If his only reason for action has become action, he will get nowhere. The pew-opener, too keenly pursuing her job, runs the risk of forgetting she serves a god. So, by absorbing myself too closely in some party passion, I risk forgetting that politics are meaningless unless they serve some spiritual truth. In wonderful moments we have savoured a certain quality in human relation: there, for us, is truth.

However urgent action may be, it is forbidden to us to forget, failing which such action must be sterile, that vocation must determine it. We wish to establish human respect. Why should we hate each other inside the same camp? None of us has a monopoly in pure intentions. I may dispute, in favour of my road, the road that someone else has chosen. I may criticize the way his mind works. Minds work erratically. But I ought to respect the man, as far as spirit is concerned, if he toils towards the same star.

Human respect! Human respect! ... If human respect is established in men's hearts, men will certainly end by establishing in return the social, political or economic system that will sanctify this respect. A civilization first establishes itself on matter. It is, at first, in man, the blind desire for a certain warmth. Thereafter, man, from error to error, discovers the road that leads to fire.

And that is why, no doubt, my friend, I so much need your friendship. I thirst for a companion who, superior to the disputations of reason, respects in me the pilgrim of that fire. I must sometimes savour, in advance, the promised warmth and rest, outside myself a little, in that rendezvous that is to be ours.

I am so weary of controversy, of the opinionated, of fanaticism. I can visit you without donning a uniform, without having to recite some Koran, without renouncing anything whatever of my homeland inside. With you, I do not have to exonerate myself, to plead, to prove: I find peace, as at Tournus. Beyond my clumsy words, beyond the reasonings that may lead me astray, you regard in me the Man simply. You honour in me the ambassador of a faith, of customs, of special affections. If I differ from you, far from injuring you, I augment you. You cross-question me as one does a traveller.

I, who, like each of us, feel the need to be recognized, in you I feel pure and I go to you. There is a need in me to go where I am pure. It is not my formulae nor the things I do that ever enlightened you as to the man I am. It is the acceptance of who I am which made you, at need, indulgent to these things as to these formulae. I am grateful to you for accepting me as you find me. What do I want with a friend who judges me? If I welcome a friend to a meal, I ask him to sit down if he limps, and do not ask him to dance.

My friend, I need you as one needs a height on which to breathe! I need to sit close beside you, once again, on the banks of the Saône, at some little gimcrack inn table where we could ask two bargees to drink and where we would all sit together in the peace of a smile at daybreak.

As you say, we don't need soft skies to make friendship a joy to us. What a heavenly thing it is; "World without end," truly. I grow warm thinking of it, and should glow at the thought if all the glaciers of the Alps were heaped over me! Such friends God has given me in this little life of mine!

—CELIA THAXTER

THE FRIEND WHO JUST STANDS BY

B. Y. Williams

When trouble comes your soul to try,
You love the friend who just "stands by."
Perhaps there's nothing he can do—
The thing is strictly up to you;
For there are troubles all your own,
And paths the soul must tread alone;
Times when love cannot smooth the road
Nor friendship lift the heavy load,
But just to know you have a friend
Who will "stand by" until the end,
Whose sympathy through all endures,
Whose warm handclasp is always yours—
It helps, someway, to pull you through,
Although there's nothing he can do.
And so with fervent heart you cry,
"God bless the friend who just 'stands by.'"

When friends ask there is no tomorrow.

—PROVERB

"How sacred is memory."

JOHN BURROUGHS AND WALT WHITMAN

The more I see of Walt, the more I like him.... He is by far the wisest man I have ever met. There is nothing more to be said after he gives his views. It is as if Nature herself has spoken. And so kind, sympathetic, charitable, humane, tolerant a man I did not suppose was possible. He loves everything and everybody.... He appreciates everybody, and no soul will get fuller justice in the next world than it gets at his hands here.

I related to him our Adirondack trip, the deer-shooting, etc., which so pleased him that he said seriously he should make a "leaf of grass" about it. I related to him other country experiences which he relished hugely. In the spring he wants to go out to my home with me to make sugar, and get a taste of that kind of life.... He also wants to go up to the Adirondacks and spend a season at the Upper Iron Works. He says a trip to Europe would be nothing compared to it....

Sept 27 [1883]. Walt Whitman came yesterday and his presence and companionship act like a cordial upon me that nearly turns my head. The great bard on my right hand, and the sea upon my left—the thought of the one equally grand with the suggestions and elemental heave of the other. From any point of view W.W. is impressive. The slope of the back of his head and shoulders and back—how suggestive! You would know that he was an extraordinary man.

Sept. 29. Long autumn days by the sea with Whitman. Much and copious talk. His presence loosens my tongue, that has been so tied since I came here. I feel as if under the effects of some rare tonic or cordial all the time. There is something grainy and saline in him, as in the voice of the sea. Sometimes his talk is choppy and confused, or elliptical and unfinished; again there comes a long splendid roll of thought that bathes one from head to foot, or swings you quite free from your moorings. I leave him and make long loops off down the coast, or back inland, while he moves slowly along the beach, or sits, often with bare head, in some nook sheltered from the wind and sun....

September 30. Perfect days by the sea with W.W. A sort of realization of Homer to me. No man I have ever seen cuts such a figure on the beach as W.W. He looks at home there; is ample for such a setting.

Oct. 1. A last look at the sea with W.W. In the early gray light we stood upon the windy verge and saw the "foamy wreck of the stranded waves cover the shore." Looking down the beach, the scene recalled

November frosts and snows—the waves churned into foam and spume
blown by the winds—the rime of the sea. Great gluffy masses of sea-
foam blew like wool far up the sands. The swells not large, but grand
and full of fury.

February, 1890

Dear Walt:

Here I am back from Poughkeepsie in my little study tonight with a
maple and hickory fire burning in the open fireplace and thinking of
you. How many times have I planted you there in my big chair by the
window, or here in front of the open fire, and talked the old talks with
you. Alas, alas, that I should never see you there in the body as well as
in spirit! ... How sacred is memory. As one grows old, how much he
lives in the past, how trivial and cheap seems the present. A tender and
beautiful light fills my mind when I think of those years in Washington
when we were all there; a light I know that never was on sea or land.
How solemn and pathetic, as well as beautiful, it must seem to you, considering all you passed through there!

With the old love,
JOHN BURROUGHS

A GREETING

Austin Dobson

But once or twice we met, touched hands,
To-day between us both expands
   A waste of tumbling waters wide,—
   A waste by me as yet untried,
Vague with the doubt of unknown lands.

Time like a despot speeds his sands:
A year he blots, a day he brands;
   We walked, we talked by Thamis' side
      But once or twice.

What makes a friend? What filmy strands
Are these that turn to iron bands?
   What knot is this so firmly tied
   That naught but fate can now divide?—
Ah, these are things one understands
      But once or twice.

". . . it is the duty of one friend to guess another's problems."

THE ART OF FRIENDSHIP
André Maurois

The ties of friendship are very different from those which unite the married couple and the family. Intellectual emotions come first in friendship; they dominate the instinctive ones. Why are the latter not sufficient? Does not the family permit each human being to find, with the least possible opposition, the companions needed for the journey through life?

The first answer to this question is that a large number of people live their whole lives in ignorance of marriage. Most of them simply have not considered it; some consciously flee from it. . . .

Even for those who have founded a family, for the husband and wife who love one another truly, for children who have parents with whom they get on well, and for Don Juan too, with his thousand and three mistresses, something besides this is necessary. We frequently find that we cannot speak of what is nearest our hearts to our families or to those with whom we are in love, because family ties are of blood and not of the mind, and because affection is too easily given; and two people in love are always acting parts. Thus in the minds of all— children, father, mother, husband, wife, lover, mistress—are concealed unspoken grievances.

These unspoken things poison the minds of introspective people, as foreign bodies enclosed in a wound poison the tissues. They should talk, open their minds, be themselves in the spiritual sense as well as in the almost purely physical sense of the family circle or of love. Secret and rebellious emotions must be given expression; they must be discussed with intimate friends who, even if they refuse advice, will bring concealed malice and spite out into the open. There is need of another tie than that of love and another group than that of the family. . . .

The birth of friendship is slower. In the early stages it seems such a fragile plant that love, spring up close to its pale, weak stalk, may smother it. La Rochefoucauld says that most women are little given to friendship, because friendship is insipid compared to love. Insipid? No, but cruelly lucid in its early stages. . . . How is the close bond of friendship to be established between two perfectly lucid people who are not physically attracted to one another?

In some cases this close bond is entirely natural, for the very simple reason that the person encountered possesses rare qualities that are recognized as such. There is friendship at first sight as well as love. A word, a smile, a look reveals a kindred spirit. A charming act makes us sure we have discovered a noble personality. So friendship starts with friendship as love starts with love. These sudden friendships are possible even when the chosen friend does not possess high qualities, for all discrimination is relative. One young girl suddenly becomes the confidante and constant companion of another; by still another she is thoroughly disliked. In the first instance, chance has revealed a kind of pre-established harmony and friendship comes into being....

These chance friendships, however, are not necessarily true ones. "We console ourselves with several friends for not having found one real one," says Abel Bonnard. Real friendship takes for granted a surer choice. Montaigne had great respect for La Boëtie, as well as affection. Not all men and women can devote themselves thus to those whom they respect. Some are jealous of superiority and are far more interested in revealing the faults than in imitating the virtues of a noble character. Others fear the opinion of a mind that is too lucid and prefer to be friends with someone less exacting.

"Well fitted for friendship is he whom men have not disgusted with mankind, and who, believing and knowing that there are a few noble men, a few great minds, a few delightful souls scattered through the crowd, never tires of searching for them, and loves them even before he has found them." I should like to add, to these words of Bonnard, that a few amiable weaknesses, added to those high qualities, foster rather than prevent our affection for a person. We do not completely love those at whom we cannot smile. There is something inhuman in absolute perfection which overwhelms the mind and heart, which commands respect but keeps friendship at a distance through discouragement and humiliation. We are always glad when a great man reassures us of his humanity by possessing a few peculiarities.

A chance word or look, then, may reveal similarity in personality and intelligence. Restraint and will power allow this early sympathy to grow and establish itself. Confidences are exchanged and we soon achieve far more intellectual freedom with this comparative stranger than with those to whom we are bound by ties of blood or physical love....

Disinterestedness is a necessary attribute to real friendship and it is the duty of one friend to guess another's problems and render assistance before it is asked. If our friends have needs that we can satisfy, we should relieve them of the necessity of seeking our help. Apart from the satisfaction usually produced by an action, this permanent ability to give pleasure is perhaps the only advantage of wealth and power.

Another essential attribute of friendship is, I believe, mutual admiration. "But," you will say, "I have friends whom I do not admire. I love them just the same, and would tell them frankly that I do not admire them." There is a confusion here and the need to probe more deeply into reality. We all have friends to whom we speak harsh truths, and indeed there can be no true friendship without this kind of sincerity. But if we can endure criticism from a friend, which, coming from another, would anger us, isn't it because we know that he admires us fundamentally? I do not mean that he thinks we possess all the virtues or that he finds us particularly intelligent. It is more complex than that. I mean that he has carefully considered our faults and our good qualities and has chosen us; better still, he has preferred us to others.

It is very important to realize that sincerity is possible only because of this admiration. We accept any criticism from him who loves or admires us because it does not impair the self-confidence without which our life would be unbearable. Great friendships between writers have been made possible by this alone. Louis Bouilhet sincerely criticized Flaubert, but Flaubert did not mind it because he knew that Bouilhet thought him a master. Heaven protect us from the "sincere friend" whose sincerity consists only of depressing us, who carefully warns us of the evil that is being spoken of us and seems to be afflicted with a peculiar deafness regarding the good.

And Heaven protect us also from the easily offended friend who, refusing to understand once and for all that we are fond of him but that life is short and difficult and human beings capricious, watches us unceasingly so that he may interpret every manifestation of impatience or bad humor as an omen. An easily offended person will never make real friends. True friendship implies full confidence which may only be completely given or completely withdrawn. If friendship has continually to be analyzed, nursed, and cured, it will cause more anguish than love itself, without having love's strength and its remedies. And if this confidence is ill-placed? Well—I would rather be betrayed by a false friend than deceive a true one. . . .

I believe that we need only observe life to be convinced that women can be friends. It must be pointed out, however, that friendships between young girls usually amount to veritable passions, more violent than those of boys, and that they contain an element of complicity, of secret alliance against all adversaries: sometimes family; sometimes men, regarded as a hostile race against which the weaker sex feels it must join forces; sometimes other groups of girls. This need for complicity and mutual assistance is due to the greater weakness of the adolescent female and to the stricter restraint to which she has for so long been subjected. In the nineteenth century she could never mention in the family circle the things that were most constantly in her mind. She had to have a confidante.

A successful marriage puts an end to feminine friendships; but if marriage is a failure, the young woman must have others to confide in. Complicity springs up again, not against the family but the husband. Many women remain faithful throughout their lives to the idea of banding together to defend themselves against the dangerous tribe of men. . . .

Families are often extremely jealous of friendships which are too close, and this is easy to understand. A friend is a confidant, as it were, hostile to the family. It has always been said that a woman, upon her marriage, causes discord between a man and his friends. But there is a purely male kind of conversation which will always draw men together, bore all women, and enable friendship to take strange revenges. . . .

It has often been maintained that friendship between men and women can never approach the high level of friendship between men. How, it is objected, could sensuality not be present in such relationships? If it were not present, would not the least coquettish of women feel herself humiliated? It is contrary to every natural impulse for a man to associate with a woman as freely as is usual in friendship without occasionally being conscious of physical desire. . . .

We know of cases in history where pure friendship has existed between men and women. The contradictor will admit this, but he will declare that the cases can be divided into three indistinct and deceptive groups. The first includes lovelorn romantics whose hopeless loves remain in the limbo of emotion. . . .

In the second circle of this sentimental purgatory we find old men who seek refuge in friendship because they are too old for love. Why is old age the most auspicious time for friendship between a man and a woman? Because they have ceased in one sense to be man and woman. Nothing is left but memories of flirting and abstract thoughts of jealousy; but this is enough to lend a certain melancholy charm to an intellectual friendship. Sometimes only one of the two is old, and then the situation becomes more difficult; but it is possible to conceive of agreeable friendships between young cynics and retired coquettes (Byron and Lady Melbourne), between young women and disillusioned old men (Queen Victoria and Lord Melbourne). Nevertheless, the older of the two almost always suffers, because the younger is unresponsive (Walpole and Mme du Deffand). Actually, it is inaccurate to call such relationships by the name of friendship, for there is unhappy love on one side and affectionate indifference on the other.

Finally, in the third circle which has a pleasant atmosphere though it is tinged with a slightly painful monotony, may be put those who, having once been lovers, succeed in passing from love to friendship without quarreling. This is the most natural of all friendships between men and women. Sensuality is appeased, but the memory of a perfect union keeps them from being strangers to one another. Past emotions have immunized them against the dreaded effects of flirting and jealousy, placing their relationship upon an entirely different plane— a more masculine one—while their profound knowledge of one another enables them to achieve a friendship of more than usual intimacy. But here again we find that the relationship is founded upon a confused emotion and that it is quite different from true and simple friendship. . . .

Society of any magnitude must, in order to exist, be made up of couples, and families, which may be regarded as original cells. As, in the human body, there are not only conjunctive and epithelial tissues but also the more complex nerve cells uniting all the others, so I believe we must think of society as made up of families which eventually put forth delicate extensions into several others at once, drawing them together; and we may conceive of friendship and admiration as the more complex nerve cells. So spiritual love weaves among the threads of fleshly love a weaker, more delicate weft, but one without which human society could not exist. Perhaps we can now catch a glimpse of this miraculous fabric of affection, trust, and loyalty which upholds a civilization.

(Translated by James Whitall)

My Dear Liszt: I must say, *You are a friend.* Let me say no more to you, for although I always recognized in friendship between men the noblest and highest relation, it was you who embodied this idea into its fullest reality by letting me no longer imagine, but feel and grasp, what a friend is. I do not thank you, for you alone have the power to thank yourself by your joy in being what you are. It is noble to have a friend, but still nobler to be a friend.

RICHARD WAGNER

FRIENDSHIP

Robert Pollok

Not unremembered is the hour when friends
Met. Friends, but few on earth, and therefore dear;
Sought oft, and sought almost as oft in vain;
Yet always sought, so native to the heart,

So much desired and coveted by all.
Nor wonder thou—thou wonderest not, nor need'st.
Much beautiful, and excellent, and fair
Was seen beneath the sun; but nought was seen
More beautiful, or excellent, or fair
Than face of faithful friend, fairest when seen
In darkest day; and many sounds were sweet,
Most ravishing and pleasant to the ear;
But sweeter none than voice of faithful friend;
Sweet always, sweetest heard in loudest storm.
Some I remember, and will ne'er forget;
My early friends, friends of my evil day;
Friends in my mirth, friends in my misery too;
Friends given by God in mercy and in love;
My counsellors, my comforters, and guides;
My joy in grief, my second bliss in joy;
Companions of my young desires; in doubt,
My oracles, my wings in high pursuit.
Oh, I remember, and will ne'er forget
Our meeting spots, our chosen sacred hours,
Our burning words that uttered all the soul,
Our faces beaming with unearthly love;
Sorrow with sorrow sighing, hope with hope
Exulting, heart embracing heart entire!
As birds of social feather helping each
His fellow's flight, we soared into the skies,
And cast the clouds beneath our feet, and earth,
With all her tardy leaden-footed cares,
And talked the speech, and ate the food of heaven!
These I remember, these selectest men,
And would their names record; but what avails
My mention of their names? Before the throne
They stand illustrious 'mong the loudest harps,
And will receive thee glad, my friend and theirs—
For all are friends in heaven, all faithful friends;
And many friendships in the days of time
Begun, are lasting here, and growing still;
So grows ours evermore, both theirs and mine.

"He only is proved good and faithful before all other friends."

OF THE FAMILIAR FRIENDSHIP OF JESUS

Thomas à Kempis

When our Lord Jesus is present all things are liking, and nothing seemeth hard to do for His love: but when He is absent, all things that are done for His love are painful and hard. When Jesus speaketh not to the soul, there is no faithful consolation: but if He speak one word only, the soul feeleth great inward comfort. Did not Mary Magdalen rise soon from weeping, when Martha shewed her that her Master Christ was nigh and called her? Yes, truly. O that is a happy hour when Jesus calleth us from weeping to joy of spirit! ...

What may this world give thee but through the help of Jesus? To be without Jesus is a pain of hell, and to be with Jesus is a pleasant paradise. If Jesus be with thee there may no enemy grieve thee, and he that findeth Jesus findeth a great treasure, that is best above all other treasures; but he that loseth Jesus loseth very much, and much more than all the world. He is most poor that liveth without Jesus, and he is most rich that is with Jesus. ...

Thou mayest anon drive away thy Lord Jesus and lose His grace, if thou apply thyself to outward things; and if through negligence thou lose Him, what friend shalt thou then have? Without a friend thou mayest not long endure, and if Jesus be not thy friend before all others, thou shalt be very heavy and desolate. ...

Jesus only is to be beloved for Himself, for He only is proved good and faithful before all other friends. In Him and for Him both enemies and friends are to be beloved, and for them all we ought meekly to pray to Him, that so He may be beloved and honored of all His creatures. ...

My son, if thou set thy peace in any person for thine own pleasure or worldly friendship, thou shalt always be unstable, and never shalt thou be contented; but if thou always have recourse to the Truth everlasting, that is God Himself, then the death or going away of thy dearest friend, whatsoever he be, shall little grieve thee. The love of thy friend ought always to be referred to Me; and for Me he is to be beloved, how good and how profitable soever he seem unto thee in this life. Without Me friendship is nought worth, and may not long endure; nor is that love true and clean that is not knit by Me.

(Translated by Richard Whitford)

MY OLD FRIEND

Arthur C. Benson

It seems the world was always bright
  With some divine unclouded weather,
When we, with hearts and footsteps light,
  By lawn and river walked together.

There was no talk of me and you,
  Of theories with facts to bound them,
We were content to be and do,
  And take our fortunes as we found them.

We spoke no wistful words of love,
  No hint of sympathy and dearness,
Only around, beneath, above,
  There ran a swift and subtle nearness.

Each in most thought was known to each
  By some impetuous divination:
We found no need of flattering speech,
  Content with silent admiration.

I think I never touched your hand,
  I took no heed of face or feature,
Only, I thought on sea or land
  Was never such a gracious creature.

It seems I was not hard to please,
  Where'er you led I needs must follow;
For strength you were my Hercules,
  For wit and luster my Apollo.

The years flew onward: stroke by stroke
  They clashed from the impartial steeple,
And we appear to other folk
  A pair of ordinary people.

One word, old friend: though fortune flies,
  If hope should fail—till death shall sever—
In one dim pair of faithful eyes
  You seem as bright, as brave as ever.

". . . touched me to the bottom of my heart."

JUSTICE OLIVER WENDELL HOLMES TO THE U. S. SUPREME COURT WHEN HE RETIRED FROM IT

My Dear Brethren:

You must let me call you so once more. Your more than kind, your generous, letter touched me to the bottom of my heart. The long and intimate association with men who so command my respect and admiration could not but fix my affection as well. For such little time as may be left me I shall treasure it as adding gold to the sunset.

Affectionately yours,
O. W. HOLMES

"I must know him on that higher ground . . ."

WILLIAM HAZLITT'S FRIENDS

I have certain friends whom I visit occasionally, but I commonly part from them early with a certain bitter-sweet sentiment. That which we love is so mixed and entangled with that we hate in one another that we are more grieved and disappointed, aye, and estranged from one another, by meeting than by absence. Some men may be my acquaintances merely, but one whom I have been accustomed to regard, to idealize, to have dreams about as a friend, and mix up intimately with myself, can never degenerate into an acquaintance. I must know him on that higher ground or not know him at all. We do not confess and explain, because we would fain be so intimately related as to understand each other without speech. Our friend must be broad. His must be an atmosphere coextensive with the universe, in which we can expand and breathe. For the most part we are smothered and stifled by one another. I go and see my friend and try his atmosphere. If our atmospheres do not mingle, if we repel each other strongly, it is of no use to stay.

"I owe a great deal to this dear old friend."

LE MARQUIS DE PLOEUC
Anne Douglas Sedgwick *

In the Chateau de Ker-Guelegaan, near Quimper, lived an old friend of my family's, the Marquis de Ploeuc. The chateau was one of the oldest in Finisterre, an immense weather-beaten pile with a moat, a drawbridge, a great crenellated tower, and a turret that, springing from the first story, seemed, with its highpointed roof, to be suspended in the air. Tall, dark trees rose in ordered majesty about the chateau, and before it a wide band of lawn, called a *tapis vert,* ran to the lodge-gates that opened on the highroad. From the upper windows one saw the blue Brittany sea.... The walls were hung with tapestries, at which I used often to gaze with delight. One saw life-sized ladies and gentlemen dancing in stately rounds or laughing under trees and among flowers and butterflies. The great dining-room was paneled with dark wood carved into frames around the portraits of ancestors that were ranged along it. The coffers and the sideboards, where the silver stood, were of the same carved wood. I remember once going down to peep at the kitchen in the basement, and the dark immensity, streaming, as it were, with cooks, servants, kitchen-boys, and maids, so bewildered and almost frightened me that I never ventured there again.

The old marquis was a widower, and his married daughters, the Marquise de L—— and Mme. d'A——, usually lived with him and his unmarried daughter Rosine, who became a nun. He was a splendid old gentleman, tall, with a noble carriage and severe, yet radiant, countenance. In the daytime he dressed always in gray coat and knee-breeches, with gray-and-black striped stockings and buckled shoes. At night his thick white hair was gathered into a *catogan,*—a little square black-silk bag, that is to say, tied with a bow, and he wore a black-silk suit. On festal occasions, Christmas, Easter, or his fete-day he became a magnificent figure in brocaded coat and white-satin waistcoat and knee-breeches; he had diamond shoe- and knee- buckles, diamond buttons on his waistcoat, and gold *aiguillettes* looped across his breast and shoulder.

The diamond buckles he left to me, to be given to me on my first communion, and in his lifetime he had made for me a beautiful missal

---

* The author is giving an old friend's account of her childhood in Brittany about 1850.

bound in white parchment and closed with a diamond and emerald clasp; inside were old illuminations.

In his youth M. de Ploeuc had been an officer of the Chouans, and he was, of course, a passionate royalist. He always wore the Croix de St. Louis, a fleur-de-lis, with the little cross attached by blue ribbon. I asked him once if it was the same sort of decoration as my Grandfather de Rosval's, which, I said, was larger and was tied with red, and I remember the kindly and ironic smile of my old friend as he answered, "Oh, no; that is only the Legion d'honneur."

Brittany had many marquises, some of them also old and distinguished; but he was the *doyen* of them all, and was always called simply *le* marquis. Any disputes or difficulties among the local *noblesse* were always brought to him....

My memories of the place center almost entirely around the figure of my old friend. I was his constant companion. When he rode out after luncheon to visit his farms, I would sit before him on his old horse Pluton. He never let Pluton gallop for fear of tiring him. "Do you see, *ma petite*," he would say, "Pluton is a comrade who has never failed me. He has earned a peaceful old age." We passed, in the wood behind the chateau, a monument of a Templar that frightened and interested me. He lay with his hands crossed over his sword, his feet stayed against a couchant hound, and I could not understand why he wore a knitted coat. My old friend burst out laughing when I questioned him, and said that I was as ignorant as a little carp, and that it was high time I went to the Sacré Coeur. He told me that the knitted coat was a coat of mail, and tried to instil a little history into my mind, telling me of the crusades and St. Louis; but I am afraid that my mind soon wandered away to Pluton's gently pricked ears and to the wonders of the woods that surrounded us. We had walks together, too, and went one day to the sea-shore, where there was a famous grotto often visited by strangers. When we arrived at the black arch among the rocks and I heard it was called the Devil's Grot, I was terrified, clinging to M. de Ploeuc's hand and refusing to enter.

"But why not, Sophie? Why not?" he questioned me. "I am here to take care of you, and there is no danger at all. See, Yann is lighting the torches to show us the way."

"But the devil—the devil will get me," I whispered; "Jeannie told me so."

Jeannie, indeed, was in the habit of punishing or frightening me by tales of the devil and his fork and tail and flames, and of how he would come and carry off disobedient little girls; so it was not to be wondered at that I feared to enter his grot. I imagined that he himself lurked there and would certainly carry me off, for I was well aware that I was often very disobedient. M. de Ploeuc sat down on a rock, took me on his knee, and said:

"It is very wrong of Jeannie to fill your head with such nonsense, my little one. Nothing like her devil exists in the whole world, and you must pay no attention to her stories."

He told me that the cavern was filled with beautiful stalactites, like great clusters of diamonds, and was so gentle and merry and reasonable that the devil was exorcised from my imagination forever, and I consented to enter the grotto.

Yann and the guide, a young farmer of Ker-Guelegaan, led us in with their lighted torches, and I suddenly saw before me, strangely illuminated, a somber, yet gorgeous, fairy-land. Diamonds indeed! Pillars of diamonds rose from the rocky floor to the roof, and pendants hung in long clusters, glittering in inconceivable vistas of splendor. I was so dazzled and amazed that I gave the vaguest attention to M. de Ploeuc's explanation of the way in which the stalactites were formed among the rocks. Indeed, that night I could not sleep, still seeing diamond columns and pillars, and my dear old friend was full of self-reproach next day when he heard that during the night the Devil's Grot had given me a fever.

Sometimes the Marquis de L—— accompanied us on our expeditions, and sometimes I was even left in his charge for an afternoon. I disliked this very much, for he had no amusing stories to tell me and walked very fast, and when my pace flagged, he would pause to look at me reproachfully, tapping his foot on the ground, and crying out, as though I were one of his horses, "Get up! Get up!"

M. de Ploeuc often took me, after lunch, into his little study and played the flute to me. I liked being in the study, but it rather frightened me to see my old friend remove his teeth before beginning to play. Their absence sadly altered his beautiful and stately countenance, and gave, besides, an odd, whistling timbre to his music. Still, I listened attentively, looking away now and then from his rapt, concentrated countenance to the *tapis vert* outside, where the cows were cropping the short grass, or glancing around rather shrinkingly at the headless bust of Marie Antoinette that stood on the mantelpiece. The head lay beside the bust, and there was, even to my childish imagination, a terrible beauty in the proud shoulders thus devastated. This was one of two such busts that had been decapitated by the Revolutionists. The other belonged, I think, later on, to the Empress Eugenie. When the marquis had finished his thin, melancholy airs, it was my turn to perform, and that I liked much better. I saw that he loved to hear the old Breton songs sung in my sweet, piping little voice, and it was especially pleasant, our music over, to be rewarded by being given chocolate pastils from a little enamel box that stood on the writing desk. While I softly crunched the pastils M. de Ploeuc told me about the countries where the plant from which the chocolate came grew. It was not at all common in Brittany at that time, and the pastils much less sweet than our modern bon bons. M. de Ploeuc also carried for his own delectation small violet and peppermint lozenges in a little gold box that he drew from his waistcoat-pocket, and these gave the pleasantest fragrance to his kiss. I often sat on with him in the study, looking at the pictures in the books he gave me while he read or wrote. He wore on the third finger of his right hand an odd black ring that had a tiny magnifying-glass fixed upon it, and while he read his hand moved gently across the page.

I owe a great deal to this dear old friend. He took the deepest interest in my deportment, and *maman* was specially delighted that he should extirpate from my speech provincial words and intonations. He entirely broke me of the bad habits of shrugging my shoulders and biting my nails.

"Only wicked men and women bite their nails," he told me, and pointed out to me as a terrible warning the beautiful and coquettish Mme. de G——, one of his guests, who had bitten her nails to the quick and quite ruined the appearance of her hands.

"And is she so wicked?" I asked. At which he laughed a little, and said that she must become so if she continued to bite her nails. He made me practise coming into and going out of a room until he was satisfied with my ease and grace.

"Do you see, *ma petite Sophie*," he said, "a woman, when she walks well, is a goddess. Walk always as if on clouds, lightly and loftily. Or imagine that you are skimming over fields of wheat, and that not an ear must bend beneath your tread."

TO WHOM IT MAY CONCERN

Christopher Morley, who died March 28, 1957, asked his executors to use this space "to send my unchanged love to many kind and forbearing friends. Our good adventures and absurdities were not forgotten, nor occasions of beauty and moments of disgust. Specially I want to apologize for so many unanswered letters through so many years. Their messages, of whatever sort, were often in mind. I had many reasons for gratitude, and I was grateful."

—*New York Times*, April 1, 1957

THE MONK AND THE PEASANT
Margaret E. Bruner

A peasant once unthinkingly
  Spread tales about a friend;
But later found the rumors false
  And hoped to make amend.

He sought the counsel of a monk,
  A man esteemed and wise,
Who heard the peasant's story through
  And felt he must advise.

The kind monk said: "If you would have
  A mind again at peace,
I have a plan whereby you may
  From trouble find release.

"Go fill a bag with chicken-down
  And to each door-yard go
And lay one fluffy feather where
  The streams of gossip flow."

The peasant did as he was told
  And to the monk returned,
Elated that his penance was
  A thing so quickly earned.

"Not yet," the old monk sternly said,
  "Take up your bag once more
And gather up the feathers that
  Were placed at every door."

The peasant, eager to atone,
  Went hastening to obey;
No feathers met his sight, the wind
  Had blown them all away.

". . . the most valuable of all human possessions . . ."

CICERO'S OPINION

I can only exhort you to look on Friendship as the most valuable of all human possessions, no other being equally suited to the moral nature of man, or so applicable to every state and circumstance, whether of prosperity or adversity, in which he can possibly be placed. But at the same time I lay it down as a fundamental axiom that "true Friendship can only subsist between those who are animated by the strictest principles of honour and virtue. . . ."

But what still farther evinces the strength and efficacy of friendship above all the numberless other social tendencies of the human heart is that, instead of wasting its force upon a multiplicity of divided objects, its whole energy is exerted for the benefit of only two or three persons at the utmost.

Friendship may be shortly defined, "a perfect conformity of opinions upon all religious and civil subjects, united with the highest degree of mutual esteem and affection"; and yet from these simple circumstances results the most desirable blessing (virtue alone excepted) that the gods have bestowed on mankind.

It is virtue, yes, let me repeat it again, it is virtue alone that can give birth, strength, and permanency to friendship. For virtue is a uniform and steady principle ever acting consistently with itself. They whose souls are warmed by its generous flames not only improve their common ardour by communication, but naturally kindle into that pure affection of the heart towards each other which is distinguished by the name of amity, and is wholly unmixed with every kind and degree of selfish considerations. Since man holds all his possessions by a very precarious and uncertain tenure we should endeavour, as our old friends drop off, to repair their loss by new acquisitions, lest one should be so unhappy as to stand in his old age a solitary, unconnected individual, bereaved of every person whom he loves and by whom he is loved. For without a proper and particular object upon which to exercise the kind and benevolent affections, life is destitute of every enjoyment that can render it justly desirable.

(*Translated by W. Melmoth*)

~~~~~~~~

The primary joy of life is acceptance, approval, the sense of appreciation and companionship of our human comrades. Many men do not understand that the need for fellowship is really as deep as the need for food, and so they go throughout life accepting many substitutes for genuine, warm, simple relatedness. The Don Juans eternally seeking some new object of passion, the men and women desperately trying to lose themselves in drink, promiscuity, sensuality—in all of the excess of flesh and power—are, more often than we suspect, lonely children lost and naked in a world that has never woven a garment of love for them and that has relentlessly driven them down the empty corridors of the years, desolate and alone. Penetrate behind the mask of men of ruthlessness and of power, who seem to move from conquest to conquest, and it will often be seen that their soul is really an army in retreat, fleeing from loneliness to loneliness.

—RABBI JOSHUA LOTH LIEBMAN

TO MY FRIEND

Anne Campbell

I have never been rich before,
  But you have poured
Into my heart's high door
  A golden hoard

My wealth is the vision shared,
  The sympathy,
The feast of the soul prepared
  By you for me.

Together we wander through
  The wooded ways.
Old beauties are green and new
  Seen through your gaze.

I look for no greater prize
  Than your soft voice.
The steadiness of your eyes
  Is my heart's choice.

I have never been rich before,
  But divine
Your step on my sunlit floor
  And wealth is mine!

"... we talked in perfect freedom, elbows on the table ..."

ALPHONSE DAUDET RECALLS
DAYS IN PARIS

The time is ten or twelve years ago, the scene Gustave Flaubert's home in the rue Murillo. The coquettish little rooms, hung with Oriental materials, opened upon the Parc Monceau, that trim and aristocratic garden which held up a blind of greenery before the windows. There we met every Sunday, five or six of us, always the same, in a delightful intimacy. Strangers and bores were always rigidly excluded.

One Sunday, when I came as usual to meet the old master and the expected friends, Flaubert seized upon me the moment I entered.

"You do not know Turgenev? There he is."

And without waiting for an answer he pushed me into the drawing-room. On a divan lounged a tall old man with a snow-white beard, who as I entered raised and uncoiled himself like a boa-constrictor with great astonished eyes from the pile of cushions.

It must be owned that we French live in extraordinary ignorance of all foreign literature. Our minds are as stay-at-home as our bodies, and with a horror of travel amid the unknown, we read no better than we colonize, when we are taken out of our own country. As it happened, I knew Turgenev's writings well. I had read with the deepest interest the *Mémoires d'un Seigneur Russe,* and the study of this book had led me on to the knowledge of others. We had a link to bind us together, even before we became personally acquainted, in our common love of cornfields, of forest thickets, of nature, in short—a twin comprehension of its penetrating charm....

It was the steppes of Russia that brought the heart and senses of Turgenev to blossoming point. One becomes good by listening to nature, and those who love her do not lose their interest in mankind. Hence that sympathetic gentleness, sad as a moujik's song, which seems to sob in the background of all Slavic story-tellers' tales. It is the sigh of humanity....

I knew all this when I met Turgenev. For a long time he had reigned in my Olympus on an ivory throne among the ranks of my deities. But far from suspecting his presence in Paris I had never even asked myself whether he were dead or alive. Imagine my astonishment when I found myself face to face with him in a Parisian drawing-room on the third floor looking on to the Parc Monceau.

I told him all this lightly and expressed my admiration for him. I told him, too, how I had read him in the woods of Sénart. There his spirit was so well in unison with the surroundings, and the balmy remembrances of the landscape and of his books were so intermingled that more than one of his stories was represented in my thoughts by the color of a little patch of pink heather already faded by autumn.

Turgenev could not hide his astonishment.

"What! you have really read me?"

Then he gave me some particulars as to the small sale of his books, and the obscurity of his name in France.... It hurt him to live unknown in a country for which he had an affection, and he confessed his mortification a little sadly, but without any bitterness....

It happened on this particular Sunday that there was no one else at Flaubert's, and our tête-à-tête was prolonged. I questioned the writer upon his method of working and expressed surprise that he did not make his own translations, for he spoke excellent French—a shade slowly, to give time for the subtle play of his mind.

He owned to me that the Académie and its Dictionary frightened him. He turned the leaves of that formidable dictionary in fear and trembling, as if it were a code wherein were formulated the laws of words and the penalties incurred for any hardihood of expression....

On this subject, I set forth to Turgenev what I had so much at heart: that the French tongue is not a dead language, to be written with a dictionary of definite expressions, classified as in a Gradus. For myself, I felt it to be instinct with life, a grand river, rolling along with a powerful and scouring current, full to the very brink....

As the day wore on, Turgenev observed, that he must join the "ladies" at the Pasdeloup Concert, and I came away with him. I was delighted to find he loved music. In France, literary men generally have a horror of it.... With Turgenev the taste for music had been part of his Parisian education. He had absorbed it from the surroundings in which he lived.

These surroundings had been formed by an intimacy of thirty years standing, with Madame Viardot, Viardot, the great singer, Viardot-Garcia, sister to Malibran. A bachelor, and very lonely, Turgenev lived for years in the family mansion, 50 rue de Douai.

The "ladies" of whom he had spoken to me at Flaubert's were Madame Viardot and her daughter, whom he loved as his own children. It was in this hospitable dwelling that I visited him....

Upstairs, on the third floor, was a snug little room, crowded as a boudoir, with soft and comfortable furniture. Turgenev had borrowed from his friends their artistic tastes; music from the wife, painting from the husband.

He was lying on a sofa. I sat down by him, and we at once resumed the conversation begun a few days previously....

After this interview our meetings became frequent. Among all the hours we spent together I have a vivid impression of a spring afternoon, a Sunday in the rue Murillo, which stands in my recollections unique and luminous. We had spoken of Goethe, and Turgenev said to us, "You know nothing about him." The following Sunday, he brought *Prometheus and the Satyr,* that Voltairian tale, impious and rebellious, expanded by Goethe into a dramatic poem. From the Parc Monceau came to us the cries and shouts of children, the clear sunshine, the freshness of the well-watered lawns, and we four—Goncourt, Zola, Flaubert and myself—moved by this magnificent improvisation, listened to genius interpreted by genius. This man, who trembled when pen in hand, had, as he stood there, all the splendid audacities of the poet; it was not the misleading translation which curdles and petrifies, but Goethe himself living speaking to us.

Often, too, Turgenev would come to seek me in the heart of the Marais, in the old hotel Henri II, where I then dwelt.... One day, when he arrived—a colossal figure—arm-in-arm with Flaubert, my little boy said to me in a whisper, "Why, they are giants!" Yes, giants they were, excellent giants, with great brains and great hearts proportionate to their appearances. There was a link, an affinity of simple goodness between these two genial natures. It was George Sand who had united them. Flaubert, boaster and fault-finder, a Don Quixote with the voice of a trumpeter of the Guards, and his powerful irony of observation, his manners of a Norman of the Conqueror's time, was certainly the masculine half of this marriage of minds; but who would have guessed that in this other Colossus, with bushy eye-brows and immense flat cheekbones, was the feminine element; the woman of acute delicacy described by Turgenev in his books; that nervous, languid, passionate Russian, sleepy as an Oriental, tragic as a nation in revolt? ...

It was at this late date that the idea of a monthly meeting, at which friends should assemble at a good dinner, occurred to us. It was to be called "the Flaubert dinner," or "dinner of unsuccessful authors." Flaubert was to be admitted, on the strength of a slight check with his *Candidat;* Zola on account of *Bouton de Rose;* Goncourt for *Henriette Maréchal;* myself for my *Arlésienne.* Giradin wished to insinuate into our band, but he was not a literary man, and we refused him admittance. As for Turgenev, he gave us his word of honor he had been damned in Russia, and as it was so far off no one went thither to ascertain the fact. Nothing could be more delightful than these friendly dinners, where we talked in perfect freedom, elbows on the table, our minds thoroughly roused to action. As experienced people should be, we were all *gourmets,* and so there were as many pet dishes as there were temperaments, as many different recipes as there were provinces. Flaubert must have Normandy butter and stewed Rouen ducks; Edmond de Goncourt, exotic and refined, demanded preserved ginger; Zola, sea-urchins and cockles; while Turgenev enjoyed caviare.

Ah! we were not easy to provide for, and the restaurants of Paris no doubt remember us. We often changed our meeting-place.... We were wont to sit down to table at seven o'clock, and at two o'clock we had not finished. Flaubert and Zola dined in their shirt sleeves; Turgenev lounged on the divan; the waiters were turned out—a needless precaution, since Flaubert's "roar" could be heard from roof to cellar of the house—and we talked literature.... We opened our minds to one another without flattery and without any conspiracy of mutual admiration....

I have before me a letter of Turgenev's.... I transcribe it in its entirety, for it well describes the tone of sincerity prevailing among us:

Monday, 24 May '77

My Dear Friend,

If I have not yet spoken to you about your book, it is because I wished to do so at length, and would not content myself with a few commonplace phrases. I postpone it all till our meeting, which will soon take place now, I hope, since Flaubert will soon return and our dinners recommence.

I will confine myself to saying one thing: the *Nabab* is the most remarkable and also the most unequal book you have written. If *Fromont* and *Risler* were represented by a straight line ———, the *Nabab* would have to be figured thus ∕ᴧᴧ and the heights of the zigzags could only be reached by a talent of the first order.

I beg your pardon for expressing myself so geometrically.

When we had done with the books and the chief interest of the moment, the conversation became more general, and we returned to the ever-present themes and ideas of love and death.

The Russian stretched out on his sofa said not a word.

"And you, Turgenev?"

"Oh, I never think about death. In our country no one has any very distinct ideas on the subject; it is a vague, distant notion, enveloped in the Slavonic mist."

After love and death we talked of illnesses, of the slavery which we drag about with us on our wretched bodies, like the convict's cannonball at the end of his chain. The sad confessions in fact of men past their fortieth year! ...

Alas! death of which we were always speaking soon came. First Flaubert was taken. He was the soul, the link which bound us together. Once he was gone our life changed and we met only from time to time, none of us having the courage to resume the meetings so sadly interrupted by mourning.

While I am correcting the proofs of this article, a book of "Souvenirs" is brought to me in which Turgenev, from the other side of the grave, criticizes me without mercy. As an author, I am beneath all criticism; as a man I am the lowest of my kind! My friends were well aware of it and told fine stories about me! What friends did Turgenev allude to, and could they remain my friends if they held such an opinion of me? And himself, that excellent Slav, who obliged him to assume so cordial a manner with me? I can see him at my home, at my table, gentle, affectionate, kissing my children. I have in my possession many exquisite, warm-hearted letters from him. And this was what lay beneath that kindly smile. Good Heavens! how strange life is, and how true that charming word of the Greek language "Eironeia"!

(Translated by Laura Ensor)

I have often thought that as longevity is generally desired, and I believe generally expected, it would be wise to be continually adding to the number of our friends, that the loss of some may be supplied by others. Friendship, "the wine of life," should like a well-stocked cellar, be thus continually renewed; and it is consolatory to think, that although we can seldom add what will equal the generous first-growths, yet friendship becomes insensibly old in much less time than is commonly imagined, and not many years are required to make it very mellow and pleasant. Warmth will, no doubt, make considerable difference. Men of affectionate temper and bright fancy will coalesce a great deal sooner than those who are cold and dull. The proposition which I have now endeavored to illustrate was, at a subsequent period of his life, the opinion of Johnson himself. He said to Sir Joshua Reynolds, "If a man does not make new acquaintances through life, he will soon find himself left alone. A man, Sir, should keep his friendships in constant repair."

—JAMES BOSWELL

Who seeks a friend without a fault remains without one.

—TURKISH PROVERB

"... grant we remain worthy of their love."

A PRAYER FOR FRIENDS
Robert Louis Stevenson

For our absent loved ones we implore Thy loving-kindness. Keep them in life, keep them in growing honor; and for us, grant that we remain worthy of their love. For Christ's sake, let not our beloved blush for us, nor we for them. Grant us but that, and grant us courage to endure lesser ills unshaken, and to accept death, loss, and disappointments as it were straws upon the tide of life.

"A faithful friend is a strong defense ..."

COUNSEL ON FRIENDSHIP FROM THE BOOK OF ECCLESIASTICUS

A sweet word multiplieth friends, and appeaseth enemies, and a gracious tongue in a good man aboundeth.

Be in peace with many, but let one of a thousand be thy counsellor.

If thou wouldst get a friend, try him before thou takest him, and do not credit him easily.

For there is a friend for his own occasion, and he will not abide in the day of thy trouble.

And there is a friend that turneth to enmity; and there is a friend that will disclose hatred and strife and reproaches. And there is a friend a companion at the table, and he will not abide in the day of distress.

A friend if he continue steadfast, shall be to thee as thyself, and shall act with confidence among them of thy household. If he humbles himself before thee, and hide himself from thy face, thou shalt have unanimous friendship for good.

Separate thyself from thy enemies, and take heed of thy friends.

A faithful friend is a strong defense: and he that found him, hath found a treasure. Nothing can be compared to a faithful friend, and no weight of gold and silver is able to countervail the goodness of his fidelity.

A faithful friend is the medicine of life and immortality: and they that fear the Lord, shall find him.

He that feareth God, shall likewise have good friendship: because according to him shall his friend be....

A friend shall not be known in prosperity, and an enemy shall not be hidden in adversity.

In the prosperity of a man, his enemies are grieved: and a friend is known in his adversity.

Never trust thy enemy: for as a brass pot his wickedness rusteth: though he humble himself and go crouching, yet take good heed and beware of him....

He that pricketh the eye, bringeth out tears: and he that pricketh the heart, bringeth forth resentment.

He that flingeth a stone at birds, shall drive them away: so that he that upbraideth his friend, breaketh friendship.

Although thou hast drawn a sword at a friend, despair not: for there may be a returning. To a friend, if thou hast opened a sad mouth, fear not, for there may be a reconciliation: except upbraiding, and reproach, and pride, and disclosing of secrets, or a treacherous wound: for in all these cases a friend will flee away.

Keep fidelity with a friend in his poverty, that in his prosperity also thou mayst rejoice. In the time of his trouble continue faithful to him, that thou mayst also be heir with him in his inheritance.

As the vapors of a chimney, and the smoke of the fire goeth up before the fire: so also injurious words, and reproaches, and threats, before blood.

I will not be ashamed to salute a friend, neither will I hide myself from his face: and if any evil happen to me by him, I will bear it....

Every friend will say: I also am his friend: but there is a friend, that is only a friend in name. Is not this a grief even to death?

But a companion and a friend shall be turned to an enemy. O wicked presumption, whence came thou to cover the earth with thy malice, and deceitfulness?

There is a companion who rejoiceth with his friend in his joys, but in the time of trouble, he will be against him. There is a companion who condoleth with his friend for his belly's sake, and he will take up a shield against the enemy.

Forget not thy friend in thy mind, and be not unmindful of him in thy riches.

(*Old Testament*)

"A long life may be passed without finding a friend . . ."

THE RARITY OF FRIENDS WITH UNDERSTANDING AND JUDGMENT

Samuel Johnson

A long life may be passed without finding a friend in whose understanding and virtue we can equally confide, and whose opinion we can value at once for its justness and sincerity. A weak man, however honest, is not qualified to judge. A man of the world, however penetrating, is not fit to counsel. Friends are often chosen for similitude of manners, and therefore each palliates the other's failings, because they are his own. Friends are tender, and unwilling to give pain, or they are interested, and fearful to offend.

These objections have inclined others to advise, that he who would know himself, should consult his enemies, remember the reproaches that are vented to his face, and listen for the censures that are uttered in private. For his great business is to know his faults, and those malignity will discover, and resentment will reveal. But this precept may be often frustrated; for it seldom happens that rivals or opponents are suffered to come near enough to know our conduct with so much exactness as that conscience should allow and reflect the accusation. The charge of an enemy is often totally false, and commonly so mingled with falsehood, that the mind takes advantage from the failure of one part to discredit the rest, and never suffers any disturbance afterwards from such partial reports.

Anacharsis, coming to Athens, knocked at Solon's door, and told him, that he, being a stranger, was come to be his guest, and contract a friendship with him; and Solon replying, "It is better to make friends at home," Anacharsis replied, "Then you that are at home make friendship with me." Solon, somewhat surprised at the readiness of the repartee, received him kindly, and kept him some time with him.

—Plutarch

AN OLD STORY

Edwin Arlington Robinson

Strange that I did not know him then,
  That friend of mine!
I did not even show him then
  One friendly sign;

But cursed him for the ways he had
  To make me see
My envy of the praise he had
  For praising me.

I would have rid the earth of him
  Once, in my pride....
I never knew the worth of him
  Until he died.

THE NIGHT OF THE STORM

Zona Gale

At one minute the prairie had been empty and white under a low gray sky. At the next minute the air was filled with fine, pelting snow which drove with fury and whirled in a biting wind.

On the main road across the Lewiston Open, a man came riding. He was galloping with the wind, yet in all his haste he stopped at every one of the few scattered houses on the plain and pounded on the door. The women, already busy at supper, answered the summons wondering, or the men came running from stables and cow-sheds, and to these the horseman cried his message, and was off before the gaping fold could stay him with questions.

"Stephen Mine's little girl's lost. She's been gone an hour. 'Nother searchin' party starts off as soon's enough get to Stephen's. Take your lanterns and some rope."

With that he was off—Jake Mullet, on his way to Pillsbury's store in Lewiston to ring for the bucket brigade and to telephone to the few in the neighborhood who had telephones.

"Hannah Mine's girl," said the women. "Which one? Oh, not the baby. It can't be the baby!"

It went up like one cry, all over the Open, while the men made ready to leave and brought rope, and the women filled the lanterns. More than one woman girt her skirts about her and set forth with her man, certain that Hannah Mine needed comforting and, it might be, serving, and unable to wait at home in any case. But when they reached Mine's little house, they found that Hannah had gone with the first searching party, and their glances sweeping the three children huddled by the fire told the truth. The lost child was Hannah Mine's baby. Somewhere out in that storm, already for more than an hour, was Stephen and Hannah Mine's baby, three-year-old Lissa.

Meanwhile Jake Mullet was riding. And when he had done what he could in Lewiston, he took the lower road back, and now he was facing the storm, and its fury was growing with the darkness. When the first farmhouse light showed through the thick white, Jake groaned. She was so little—if night came, or if in two hours they had not found her, who could hope they would be in time?

He continued to call the little houses and to shout his message to any whom he met lumbering through the snow. But when he came to one house, on the forty adjoining Stephen's forty, he did not stop.

"No use wastin' breath on Waldo Rowan," he thought, and galloped. He crossed the cut—a queer, ragged gap in the plain, shallow and rock-filled—and saw a figure fighting its way on foot.

"Turn back to Mine's!" Jake shouted. "His little girl's lost. She's—"

Then he stopped. Here was Waldo Rowan himself, who had not spoken to Stephen and Hannah for ten years, as all the Open knew.

"They wouldn't have my help!" Waldo flung back.

Jake pounded on, carrying coils of rope for the searchers, who were now to spread in a great circle, threading the rope, and so come drawing in. He gave not another thought to the only one on the Open who had failed to answer his appeal. Everybody was used to this feud between Mine and Waldo. Stephen would have done the same if it had been Waldo whose child was lost. But Waldo had no children to lose. In the days when he and Stephen were friends they had loved the same woman, and Stephen had won her—Waldo said, through a lie. She and Stephen had raised their family and seemed happy. Waldo married a girl of the village who had died, with their two-year-old baby, only a year ago. Since then he lived alone, and he was dead to Stephen, as Stephen was to him.

At his own line fence Waldo Rowan left the road and plunged into a grove of dwarf oak and on into a denser stretch of wood. It was evident that this storm was to continue for at least twenty-four hours, and he wanted a look at his traps. He found some empty, one dragged away, and in one something pitiful and struggling helplessly, and moaning, which he dispatched and dropped in his bag. And as he did so, he thought, as he had thought before: "Blowed if I wouldn't druther live on corn bread than do it. Blowed if I never set another trap."

He plunged down into the cut, which was the short way to his cabin. There was another reason for haste besides the weather. He had been out all day, and creeping in his veins came the giddiness and tremor which precede a chill; and with them, too, that curious lightness of head, of body, which presages a possible illness. He must get indoors, build a great fire, heat his kettle of soup, wrap up warmly, and sleep it off.

"I'd ought to had the doctor give me something when I met him this noon," Waldo thought. "What was't he said? He was going sixteen mile north. He won't be back tonight. I guess I can mope it out."

The snow was of a deceiving softness and piled on the rocks of the cut as if billows of foam had rolled in, lapped, and now lay quiet. Here the wind roared through from the northeast, catching the tops of the white pines and making a furious singing. And on that wind Waldo heard a cry.

He heard it for a little before he knew that he heard it—with that strange inner ear which catches sound too light to be less delicately measured. An animal, or a way of the wind, he might have called it and thought no more; but when he was deep in the cut, and before he began the rough ascent, abruptly this cry rose on a single, piercing note, and fell again to its quiet pulsing. He listened.

Still uncertain what he had heard, he turned north and kept along the cut, at every few steps stopping to turn his head to the wind. He was ready to face back, and then it came again. There was no mistaking now, and he broke into a run.

For all his running, he made slow progress, for there was no trail up to the bottom of the cut, and the rocks were rough and huddled. He would have climbed the side and followed the trail on the west of the rim, but he had an instinct that whatever he sought cried from the bottom of the cut. He dared not halloo, for fear if this were, say, a child, he should frighten it. His impulse was to run back to the road and wait for the next passer to help him, but he dared not do that lest the faint cry be swallowed in a ruck of snow and darkness. He kept on, stumbling, scrambling over rocks waist-high. Once the faint voice ceased for so long that he told himself that he had imagined the whole. Then it came again; there was now no mistaking what it was. Then it was silent until he heard it as a deep, sobbing breath behind him, and he had passed it.

He turned, sought on his hands and knees, called softly, whistled, as might be to a little dog. A faint, wailing cry came from the slope just above him. He clambered toward it, his arms sweeping an arc; his hands brushed something yielding, and he was rewarded by a little scream of terror. He gathered the child in his arms.

She was very little and light. As soon as she felt herself on his breast, she yielded to him and snuggled weakly, like a spent puppy. This was an attitude that she knew, and she lay quiet, occasionally drawing a long sobbing breath. She was cloaked and hooded but Waldo, feeling for her hands, found them ice-cold, and one was bare. He unwound the scarf from his neck and wrapped her. All the time, the fact that it was Stephen Mine's child was barely in his consciousness. It was merely a child, terribly near freezing, terribly near death.

To retrace his steps over the rocks with her in his arms was another thing from forcing his own progress. Now he must move slowly and feel each step; he must go round the rock piles now, and not over them. He must get back to the point where the trail crossed the cut and ascended to his cabin. And now the darkness had almost fallen; the wind had its way with him, his neck was bared to the blowing snow, he was cutting his shoes on jagged points and edges of the rocks. When at last he found the up trail, made the ascent of the side, and traversed the distance to his cabin, he was shivering and chattering and hardly able to stand.

The cabin was cold, but he had left the fire ready to light. He laid the child on a quilt before the leaping fire, untied her hood, and chafed her little hands. She was terribly cold and in a perilous drowsiness. Waldo brought in his kettle of soup, hung it on the crane, dipped a little in a tin cup, and held it in the blaze. When he had forced the warmed liquid between her lips, he undressed her feet and rubbed them with snow. Her cheeks were rosy, but he feared for the small white feet.

"How'll I get word to Stephen?" he thought, and in that area in which his sick brain was working there were no thoughts of anything wrong between Stephen and him. All that had dropped away.

"Hannah's little girl," he thought once, and touched her hair wonderingly. He had never seen any of Hannah's children. As he sat there beside the child, hearing her soft breathing, talking to her a little in awkward repetitions, nothing was in his mind save deep thankfulness that he had found her. Occasionally he would rouse her, and she would give her sleepy smile and close her eyes again. Once or twice she yawned, and he was enchanted by the little tasting curl of her lips before she finally closed them.

His chill had now settled upon the man so that he was shaking. He drank a cupful of the soup, and said that it would have to be he who would go to tell Stephen that he had found her. But he could not leave her there alone, and he saw that when she was thoroughly warmed he must wrap her up and take her home. That half mile would not matter to him now—only he must make it soon, soon, before he grew worse. When the baby was warm and rested, they would go.

He sat down in his chair before the hot fire; the strong soup ran in his blood, his weariness preyed upon him, his head sank upon his breast.

He was wakened by a sound which at first he thought came from without—a calling and a trampling. Abruptly this impression changed, and his eyes went to the child in terror. It was she—it was her breathing. That rough, rattling sound was in her little throat, and in a moment Waldo knew. His two years of fatherhood were there to serve him, and he sprang up in that terror which all watchers upon children know.

In the same instant the noise which he had fancied without was sharpened and defined. It was as he had thought—a trampling of feet. He did not see the face outside the cabin window, but there was a leap of feet on to his threshold, and Jake Mullet was there, looking like a snow man. And he whirled and shouted:

"Stephen! Here—she's here!"

There was a rush of cold air across the floor, and Waldo sprang before the child and lifted the quilt to cover her. At the same instant Stephen Mine leaped into the room. "Here!" he cried out in a terrible voice. "Here!"

He strode forward, tore the quilt from Waldo's hand, and looked. The door filled with faces, with figures crusted with snow, and the cruel night air swept in and possessed the cabin. Waldo turned to the throng at the door and shook both fists in the air.

"Get in or get out!" he shouted. "Don't leave the door open on her. She's sick."

They crowded into the room, stamping and breathing loudly, and made way for a woman who came staggering in and threw herself beside the child. It was Hannah Mine, and she dared not touch the baby with her own stiff hands and in her wet garments. She only crouched beside her, and burst into terrible dry sobs. The cabin door was sharply shut, and then the thirty or more men and women who had crowded into the room became conscious of its fearful tension.

Stephen Mine stood with his child at his feet, and he lifted his head and looked at Waldo. Stephen was a huge man, black and thick. Waldo, small, and shaken by his chill, began to tell how all this had come about.

"In the cut, Stephen," he said, "about a quarter mile down the cut, toward Rightsey's. I'd been to look at my traps, and I heard her cry. She was in the bottom of the cut. I found her. I've rubbed snow on her feet —but I'm afraid—"

Stephen Mine came close to Waldo and looked down at him.

"You expect I'm going to believe that?" he said.

The silence in the room was instant and terrifying.

Waldo lifted his face. The matted hair was low on his forehead; he brushed it aside, and his clear eyes met Stephen's; but his shaking hands and his shaking voice gave doubt to his hearers. "Stephen, I swear—" he began, and Stephen laughed.

"I seen you sneaking past my place twice today," he said. "I know you. You found a way to get even at last, and you took it, you dog."

He stooped to the woman.

"Wrap her up, Hannah," he said.

Waldo put out his trembling hands.

"Stephen!" he cried. "The child's sick—she's done. You mustn't take her out. Stay here—you're all more than welcome—and keep care of her. I've got what she needs. Don't take her out into this."

"How do I know," said Stephen Mine, "what it is you mean to give her? Hannah, wrap her up."

The woman, still breathing heavily, put her hand on her husband's knee.

"No, no, Stephen," she said. "He's right. Can't you hear her breathe? Let her stay here—"

"So you and him can take care of her while I go for the doctor—is that it?" he sneered.

She seemed not to hear him.

"It's croup, Stephen," she said. "You can't take her out—" Stephen shook her off impatiently.

"I'll get out—I'll go for the doctor!" Waldo cried. "And I'll keep away. But you and Hannah stay with her, here."

"Wrap her up!" said Stephen Mine.

Two or three of the neighbor women came forward now, protesting, and Jake Mullet cried out:

"Look here, Mine. This ain't no time to remember old scores. You got the kid to think of."

"Wrap her up!" said Stephen Mine.

"Well, wait until one of us gets somewheres for a team," cried one of the men.

"Stephen—leave her here! I can wring out the hot cloths till the doctor comes—"

"I've—I've got the stuff here that was my baby's," Waldo chattered, but now they could hardly understand him.

"Wrap her up!" said Stephen Mine, and strode to the door.

The others gave way before him, and began to file out. Heavily Hannah Mine began drawing on the sick child's wraps, the sobs breaking through again. Some of the women gave of their own wraps, and seeing that one little mitten was missing, they put two or three pairs on the still inert hands.

"You carry her," said Jake Mullet to Stephen, "and I'll go to Lewiston for the doctor."

"I'll carry her—yes," said Stephen Mine. "And then I'll go up yonder and telephone for the doctor. I'll not trouble any of you that'd have me leave her here."

He took the child from the mother and went out the door.

"He's beside himself," they whispered, and they understood that it was the disease of anger, or he would never have let them go away from their task of that night without so much as a word of thanks. Some lingered for a word with Waldo and would have heard more of his adventure, but all that he could say was, "In the cut," and again and again, "In the cut—all alone." They saw that he was a sick man, and they left him with kindly words of advice, and even—though these folk are chary of expression—an outstretched hand or two. But there were some who went out muttering a half-acceptance of Stephen's implication.

Alone, Waldo began moving about the cabin, mechanically folding the quilt on which the child had lain, sweeping away the snow where the trampling feet had been, carrying the kettle back to its place in the lean-to. He felt sore and ill and weak. He felt stunned, as if he had been flung against some great impalpable thing which had struck back at him with living hands. He could no longer save a child from death and be believed. He had turned to evil in Stephen's eyes, so that what he did that was good seemed of evil. The black wall of hate which he and Stephen had builded was round them, and beyond lay now more hate and evil, born of this night.

Waldo began to think, "If the child should die, it would serve Stephen right"—but he could not finish that thought.

He pictured that slow fight through the snow, the child's breathing in the thick, cold air, the heart of the mother following, the neighbors falling off one by one at their own doors and their own waiting firesides. Then Stephen would leave the child with the mother while he went to the upper road for the doctor. Would he be in time? What if the doctor were out—and abruptly, through the blur of images in his mind, came the cheery face of the doctor, whom he had met on the road that noon, "driving sixteen miles north." When Waldo thought of that, it was as if his heart were a sword and smote him.

He ran to a little chest on a shelf and fumbled among its bottles. There it was, tightly corked, just as they had used it once when their baby had had such an illness; and they were alone with her, and had pulled her through. What if Hannah happened to have nothing?

He stood staring at the bottle. Then he began drawing on his mittens and his cap. His coat he had not had off the whole time. His scarf had been bundled up and carried away with the child. He let himself out into the storm.

His chill was passing and was succeeded by the light-headedness and the imperfect correlation of the first stages of fever. To his fancy, wavering out and seizing upon any figment, it was as if, behind the invisible drive of the snow, there was a glow of pale light. Now right, now left, it shone, as if at the back of his eyes; and he turned his head from side to side to find it. But there were only the cutting volleys of the snow in his face; and everywhere the siege of the wind. Then, as he fared on in the thick, impeding drifts, it was again as if he were beating toward and upon that great dark wall; and he kept saying to himself crazily that this was the wall that he and Stephen had raised, and that he must somehow get through it—beat it down, and get to the child to save her. Yet if he broke down the wall, something would rush upon him—Stephen's hatred, Stephen's hatred! And his own hatred for Stephen, for there was rage in his heart when he remembered the man's look and the man's word. But of these he did not think—he thought only of the child, and he set his teeth and charged at the wall of darkness, and would not wonder what lay beyond. He went through the storm to Stephen's house in a maze of darkness and light.

Toward eight o'clock Stephen came struggling back from the house on the upper road. He had heard what Waldo had already heard, of the doctor driving sixteen miles north. And when he called Oxnard, his heart sinking at the thought of the eighteen miles which lay between, there was a delay which sapped his courage—and then the word that the wires must be down, for Oxnard did not answer. He could only leave his message with Central, for to drive the distance on such a night would mean to return too late.

Stephen came down from the upper road, and his strength and his pride were gone. Abruptly now he was empty of anger, empty of malice, empty of all save his terrible despair. It was strange to see the heat and pride shrivel before the terrible fact that the baby might pay the price. "If she dies," he had heard Jake Mullet say, "we'll all know who killed her."

"O God! O God!" Stephen Mine said.

Abruptly, in the midst of the storm, he seemed to feel a lull, a silence. He went on.

It was before his gate that he stumbled over something yielding and mounded in the road. He stopped, touched the man, and with that which now at last is no decision, but merely the second nature of the race, he got him into his arms and to his own door.

At the sound Hannah flung the door open, and from the dark and wind and snow Stephen staggered across the threshold with Waldo in his arms.

Stephen looked down at him as he would have looked at any other man.

"How is she?" was all that his lips formed.

"Alive," said Hannah Mine.

Waldo opened his eyes, and his snow-crusted mitten tried to find its way to his pocket. "I brought something," he said. "We had it left; give it to her—"

At midnight, when, the message having reached him at last, the doctor came, Stephen met him with a smile.

"She's safe," he said. "She's sleeping. But there's a man here—a friend of ours—sick and done for. We got him into bed. Come and have a look at him."

Up some measureless corridor Waldo at last struggled, when many days had passed. And at its far end it seemed to him that Stephen's face was waiting. That was queer, because it had been years since Stephen had waited for him. Yet there he was, only behind him was still that dead wall, which neither of them could pass, and beyond it lay that old hatred and bitterness, accumulated through the years. And then there was the child—he must find the child.

One day he opened his eyes on that corridor and saw it clear. A homely room, now his own, about which Stephen and Hannah were moving, and a neighbor in homely talk beside the stove.

"Honestly, you'll have to move out to make room for the truck they've brought him."

And Stephen's voice—surely Stephen's voice was saying:

"That's all right; he deserved it."

And again the neighbor's voice: "Well, I'll always be proud it was my husband found Lissa's little mitten down the cut."

Then a child came to hang in the doorway, and to stare at the bed where Waldo was lying; and when she saw his eyes looking at her, she smiled and ran away—Stephen's child, safe and well and smiling.

Waldo lay still. But in his heart there was a certain singing. And it was as if he had stood close to that dead wall of hatred which he had feared, but its door swung open, and lo! there was nothing there.

Friendship is like a debt of honor; the moment it is talked of it loses its real name and assumes the more ungrateful form of obligation. From hence we find that those who regularly undertake to cultivate friendship find ingratitude generally repays their efforts.

—OLIVER GOLDSMITH

IN A GARDEN

Algernon Charles Swinburne

I hear of two far hence
   In a garden met,
And the fragrance blown from thence
   Fades not yet.

The one is seven years old,
   And my friend is he:
But the years of the other have told
   Eighty-three.

To hear these twain converse
   Or to see them greet
Were sweeter than softest verse
   May be sweet.

The hoar old gardener there
   With an eye more mild
Perchance than his mild white hair
   Meets the child.

I had rather hear the words
   That the twain exchange
Than the songs of all the birds
   There that range,

Call, chirp, and twitter there
   Through the garden-beds
Where the sun alike sees fair
   Those two heads—

And which may holier be
   Held in heaven of those
Or more worth heart's thanks to see
   No man knows.

"Never was trust more instinctive ..."

FIRST FRIENDS

George Santayana

My school friends were gone; but just beyond school bounds a new friend appeared, Edward Bayley. I was Lieutenant Colonel of the Boston School Regiment, the Colonel that year being from the English High School which, back to back with the Latin School, was housed in the other half of the same new building. In some matter of vital importance to our forces it became necessary to me to consult my superior officer. We met by appointment, and found that the high questions of epaulettes or of buttons were soon disposed of; but that first interview made us fast friends. We happened to live in the same quarter of the town, the Back Bay, about a mile from our schools, and we at once established the custom of waiting, he for me or I for him, at the corner, so as to walk home together. Yet this did not last many weeks, because that winter my mother moved to Roxbury, having at last got rid of the dreadful burden of our Beacon Street house; so that I saw my new friend only occasionally, or by express appointment. But that made no difference. The bond was established, silently of course, but safely. Even the fact that he was not going to College, but directly into some place of business, so that as it actually came about, we never saw each other after that year, and hardly a letter passed between us, made no difference in our friendship, though it entirely separated our lives. Strange enchantment! Even today, the thought of that youthful comradeship, without incidents, without background, and without a sequel, warms the cockles of my heart like a glass of old port.

There is a sort of indifference to time, as there is a sort of silence, which goes with veritable sympathy. It springs from clear possession of that which is, from sureness about it. Those who are jealous, jealous of time, of rivals, of accidents, care for something vague that escapes them now, and that would always escape them; they are haunted souls, hunting for they know not what. Not so those who know what they love and rest in it, asking for nothing more. If circumstances had led Bayley and me to go through life together, we should have stuck to each other against any incidental danger or enemy; there would have been something to tell about our comradeship; but there would have been nothing new in our friendship. Clearness and depth in the heart, as in the intellect, transpose everything into the eternal.

Is that all? What did he do? What did he say? What did he stand
for? I confess that after sixty years I have to invent a theory to account
for this fact. I have to compare that sudden, isolated brief attachment
with other friendships of mine that had something of its quality, but
were circumstantially more describable. We were eighteen years old,
and there was nothing in us except ourselves. Now, in himself, apart
from circumstances, Bayley was like Warwick Potter, only stronger. In
Warwick the same type of character, weaker although at the time of
our intimacy he was much older, was made describable by his social
background and breeding. He had been brought up in the most select
and superior way in which it was then possible to be brought up in
America.... In the early 1890's the rich dreamt of culture rather than
of leadership. Warwick, who was young for his age, was particularly
open to new impressions, plastic, immensely amused, a little passive and
feminine. It was hard to say what he would have turned into if he
had lived. And yet the dominant trait in him, as in Bayley, was clear
goodness, the absence of all contaminations, such as the very young
are sometimes proud of. He was sure, in great things as in little, to
prefer the better to the worse; he delighted in pleasant ways and people,
and he was religious. Love of historic Christianity opened to him a
wonderful world existing before and beyond America. He felt at home
in England and in the Church. He was civilized.

Now, how did it happen that Bayley who had nothing of that breeding and education, nevertheless possessed the same or a deeper intelligence of spiritual things? Why did a strictly Puritan and inward religion
in him, far from producing narrowness or fanaticism, produce charity
and hospitality of mind? Not that he was in the least what was called
liberal, that is, indifferent and vaguely contemptuous towards all definite
doctrines or practices, and without any discipline of his own. On the
contrary he was absolutely loyal to his own tradition, and master of it;
he was made, finished, imposing in the precision of his affections. He
had perfect integrity (where Warwick had only blamelessness), yet he
had sweetness too, affection for what he excluded from his own sphere,
justice to what he renounced, happiness in the joys of others that were
not joys to him, so that his very limitations were turned into admirable
virtues. Here was this manly boy, taller and stronger than I, firmly and
contentedly rooted in his New England Presbyterianism, yet accepting,
respecting and even envying *me* for being everything that he was not
and did not expect to be. There was no shadow of the pathos of distance
in this; it was honest religious comprehension that there are many
vintages in the Lord's vineyard, and many different things that are
beautiful and good. Where did Bayley learn this?

In his spiritual heritage there were doubtless certain naturalistic maxims that may have struck him in sermons or in casual reading. There was Milton with his Latinity and his Italian sonnets; and there was the young Emerson, a sort of Puritan Goethe, the Emerson of *Nature,* before he had slipped into transcendentalism and moralism and complacency in mediocrity. I may be reading ideals of my own into that very young man, in whom nothing of the sort may ever have come to light; but potentially I cannot help thinking that in him there was something more that those great men never possessed: I mean humility and renunciation. A dumb inglorious Milton who was not a prig, an Emerson with warm blood, who was not proud or oracular or cosmographical, and never thought himself the center of the universe. Young Bayley was my first, perhaps my fundamental, model for *The Last Puritan.*

It was doubtless the discovery that we were both—but differently—religious, that made us so quickly sure of each other. Never was trust more instinctive, more complete, or more silent. It has lasted in silence, at least on my side, for sixty years. Not long ago I asked a Boston friend who turned up at Cortina about these very first friends of mine, Warren and Bayley. Did he know them? Were they still living? What had become of them? And I was not surprised to hear the warmest eulogy of both, although my informant was a Lyman of the Lymans and a Lowell of the Lowells, while Warren and Bayley were not descendants of the Boston Brahmins. And I said to myself, "Oh, my prophetic soul!" My earliest friendships were not illusions.

Rupert Brooke in his youthful days was about to sail from Liverpool to New York. When he got on the ship he saw that everybody except himself had someone on the dock to wave them goodbye when the ship sailed. All of a sudden he felt lonesome. He saw a ragged boy on the dock. He went ashore and said to the boy, "What's your name?" "William," said the boy. "Do you want to earn a sixpence?" "Yes." "Then wave to me when the ship sails." With a dirty handkerchief this boy waved enthusiastically to his unknown friend until the ship was out of sight.

—Rufus M. Jones

"... he charged me to take care for the future ..."

THE TRAVELLERS AND THE BEAR
Aesop

Two men being to travel together through the forest, mutually promised to stand by each other in any danger they should meet upon the way. They had not gone far before a Bear came rushing towards them out of a thicket; upon which one, being a light, nimble fellow, got up into a tree; the other falling flat upon his face, and holding his breath, lay while the Bear came up and smelled at him; but that creature, supposing him to be a dead carcass, went back again into the woods, without doing him the least harm. When all was over, the Spark who had climbed the tree came down to his companion, and, with a pleasant smile, asked him what the Bear said to him—"For," says he, "I took notice that he clapt his mouth very close to your ear."—"Why," replies the other, "he charged me to take care for the future not to put any confidence in such cowardly rascals as you are."

(Translator anonymous)

"You are still the center of my gaze ..."

FRIENDLY PASSAGES FROM
WILLIAM JAMES

If you say that... we cannot be in love with everyone at once, I merely point out to you that, as a matter of fact, certain persons do exist with an enormous capacity for friendships and for taking delight in other people's lives; and... such persons know more of truth than if their hearts were not so big.

I composed a letter to you in my mind, whilst lying awake, dwelling in a feeling manner on the fact that human beings are born into this little span of life of which the best thing is its friendships and intimacies, and soon their places will know them no more, and yet they leave their friendships and intimacies with no cultivation, to grow as

they will by the roadside, expecting them to "keep" by force of mere
inertia; they contribute nothing empirical to the relation, treating it as
something transcendental and metaphysical altogether; whereas in
truth it deserves from hour to hour the most active care and nurture
and devotion.

—William James to Frances R. Morse (1899)

I should like to have you opposite me in any mood, whether the
facetiously excursive, the metaphysically discursive, the personally confidential, or the jaded *cursive* and argumentative—so that the oyster
shells which enclose my being might slowly turn open on their rigid
hinges under the radiation, and the critter within loll out his dried-up
gills into the circumfused ichor of life, till they grew *so* fat as not to
know themselves again.

—William James to Oliver Wendell Holmes, Jr. (1868)

I need not say, my dear old boy, how touched I am at your expressions of affection, or how it pleases me to hear that you have missed
me. You are still the center of my gaze, the pole of my mental magnet.
When I write, 'tis with one eye on the page, and one on you. When I
compose my Gifford lectures mentally, 'tis with the design exclusively
of overthrowing your system, and ruining your peace. I lead a parasitic
life upon you, for my highest flight of ambitious ideality is to become
your conqueror, and go down into history as such, you and I rolled
into one another's arms and silent (or rather loquacious still) in one
last death-grapple of an embrace. How then, O my dear Royce, can
I forget you, or be contented out of your close neighborhood? Different
as our minds are, yours has nourished mine, as no other social influence
ever has, and in converse with you I have always felt that my life was
being lived importantly.

—William James to Josiah Royce (1900)

Your letter, so full of the truest sympathy and friendship, gave both
me and my wife acute pleasure. Affectionate recognition by men like
you is surely to be counted among the prizes of life. Friendships of
personal intimacy grow up in youth, through propinquity. A friendship
like ours, based on higher mental affinities and sympathy of character,
is the fruit of years and of work.

—William James to Carl Stumpf (1899)

"Nor doth any one love Caesar . . ."

ON BEING CAESAR'S FRIEND
Epictetus

What then, is this evil thus hurtful, and to be avoided? "Not to be the friend of Caesar," saith one. He is gone, he fails in the adapting, he is embarrassed, he seeks what is nothing to the purpose. For, if he gets to be Caesar's friend, he is nevertheless distant from what he sought. For what is it that every man seeks? To be secure, to be happy, to do what he pleases without restraint and without compulsion. When he becomes the friend of Caesar, then, doth he cease to be restrained? To be compelled? Is he secure? Is he happy? Whom shall we ask? Whom can we better credit than this very man, who hath been his friend? Come forth and tell us whether you sleep more quietly now, or before you were the friend of Caesar? You presently hear him cry, "Leave off, for heaven's sake, and do not insult me. You know not the miseries I suffer; there is no sleep for me; but one comes, and saith that Caesar is already awake; another, that he is just going out. Then follow perturbations, then cares." Well, and when did you use to sup more pleasantly, formerly, or now? Hear what he says about this, too. When he is not invited, he is distracted; and if he is, he sups like a slave with his master, solicitous all the while not to say or do anything foolish. And what think you? Is he afraid of being whipped like a slave? How can he hope to escape so well? No; but as becomes a great man, Caesar's friend, of losing his head.—And when did you bathe more quietly; when did you perform your exercises more at your leisure; in short, which life would you rather wish to live, your present, or the former? I could swear, there is no one so stupid and insensible as not to deplore his miseries, in proportion as he is more the friend of Caesar.

No one fears Caesar himself, but death, banishment, loss of goods, prison, disgrace. Nor doth any one love Caesar, unless he be a person of great worth; but we love riches, the tribunate, the praetorship, the consulship. When we love and hate and fear these things, they who have the disposal of them must necessarily be our masters.

(Translated by Elizabeth Carter)

FROM "IN MEMORIAM"
Alfred, Lord Tennyson

("In Memoriam" was written in memory of Arthur Hallam,
affianced to Tennyson's sister and the poet's dear friend. Hallam's
death in 1833, at age twenty-two, deeply shocked Tennyson.)

Forgive my grief for one removed,
   Thy creature, whom I found so fair.
   I trust he lives in thee, and there
I find him worthier to be loved....

I sometimes hold it half a sin
   To put in words the grief I feel;
   For words, like Nature, half reveal
And half conceal the Soul within....

Fair ship, that from the Italian shore
   Sailest the placid ocean-plains
   With my lost Arthur's loved remains,
Spread thy full wings, and waft him o'er.

So draw him home to those that mourn
   In vain; a favorable speed
   Ruffle thy mirror'd mast, and lead
Thro' prosperous floods his holy urn.

All night no ruder air perplex
   Thy sliding keel, till Phosphor, bright
   As our pure love, thro' early light
Shall glimmer on the dewy decks.

Sphere all your lights around, above;
   Sleep, gentle heavens, before the prow;
   Sleep, gentle winds, as he sleeps now,
My friend, the brother of my love;

My Arthur, whom I shall not see
   Till all my widow'd race be run;
   Dear as the mother to the son,
More than my brothers are to me....

Lo, as a dove when up she springs
    To bear thr' Heaven a tale of woe,
    Some dolorous message knit below
The wild pulsation of her wings;

Like her I go; I cannot stay;
    I leave this mortal ark behind,
    A weight of nerves without a mind,
And leave the cliffs, and haste away

O'er ocean-mirrors rounded large,
    And reach the glow of southern skies,
    And see the sails at distance rise,
And linger weeping on the marge,

And saying, "Comes he thus, my friend?
    Is this the end of all my care?"
    And circle moaning in the air:
"Is this the end? Is this the end? ..."

The paths by which we twain did go,
    Which led by tracts that pleased us well,
    Through four sweet years arose and fell,
From flower to flower, from snow to snow:

And we with singing cheered the way,
    And crowned with all the season lent,
    From April on to April went,
And glad at heart from May to May:

But where the path we walked began
    To slant the fifth autumnal slope,
    As we descended following hope,
There sat the Shadow feared of man;

Who broke our fair companionship,
    And spread his mantle dark and cold;
    And wrapt thee formless in the fold,
And dulled the murmur on thy lip,

And bore thee where I could not see
    Nor follow, though I walk in haste;
    And think that, somewhere in the waste,
The Shadow sits and waits for me....

O yet we trust that somehow good
  Will be the final goal of ill,
  To pangs of nature, sins of will,
Defects of doubt, and taints of blood;

That nothing walks with aimless feet;
  That not one life shall be destroy'd,
  Or cast as rubbish to the void,
When God hath made the pile complete;

That not a worm is cloven in vain;
  That not a moth with vain desire
  Is shrivell'd in a fruitless fire,
Or but subserves another's gain.

Behold, we know not anything;
  I can but trust that good shall fall
  At last—far off—at last, to all,
And every winter change to spring.

So runs my dream: but what am I?
  An infant crying in the night:
  An infant crying for the light:
And with no language but a cry....

Peace; come away: the song of woe
  Is after all an earthly song:
  Peace; come away: we do him wrong
To sing so wildly; let us go.

Come; let us go; your cheeks are pale;
  But half my life I leave behind:
  Methinks my friend is richly shrined;
But I shall pass; my work will fail.

Yet in these ears, till hearing dies,
  One set slow bell will seem to toll
  The passing of the sweetest soul
That ever look'd with human eyes.

I hear it now, and o'er and o'er,
  Eternal greetings to the dead;
  And "Ave, Ave, Ave," said,
"Adieu, adieu," for evermore....

Thy voice is on the rolling air;
I hear thee where the waters run;
Thou standest in the rising sun,
And in the setting thou art fair.

⚜⚜⚜⚜⚜

"... it was to him I owe my entry into politics."

THEODORE ROOSEVELT RECALLS
A POLITICAL FRIEND

It was over thirty-three years ago that I became a member of the Twenty-third District Republican Association in the city of New York.... The big leader was Jake Hess, who treated me with rather distant affability. There were prominent lawyers and business men who belonged, but they took little part in the actual meetings. What they did was done elsewhere. The running of the machine was left to Jake Hess and his captains of tens and of hundreds.

Among these lesser captains I soon struck up a friendship with Joe Murray, a friendship which is as strong now as it was thirty-three years ago. He had been born in Ireland, but brought to New York by his parents when he was three or four years old, and, as he expressed it, "raised as a bare-footed boy on First Avenue." When not eighteen he had enlisted in the Army of the Potomac and taken part in the campaign that closed the Civil War. Then he came back to First Avenue, and, being a fearless, powerful, energetic young fellow, careless and reckless, speedily grew to some prominence as leader of a gang. In that district, and at that time, politics was a rough business, and Tammany Hall held unquestioned sway. The district was overwhelmingly Democratic, and Joe and his friends were Democrats who on election day performed the usual gang work for the local Democratic leader, whose business it was to favor and reward them in return. This same local leader, like many other greater leaders, became puffed up by prosperity, and forgot the instruments through which he had achieved prosperity. After one election he showed a callous indifference to the hard work of the gang and complete disregard of his before-election promises. He counted upon the resentment wearing itself out, as usual, in threats and bluster.

But Joe Murray was not a man who forgot. He explained to his gang his purposes and the necessity of being quiet. Accordingly they waited for their revenge until the next election day. They then, as Joe expressed it, decided "to vote furdest away from the leader"—I am using the language of Joe's youth—and the best way to do this was to vote the Republican ticket. In those days each party had a booth near the polling-place in each election district, where the party representative dispensed the party ballots. This had been a district in which, as a rule, very early in the day the Republican leader had his hat knocked over his eyes and his booth kicked over and his ballots scattered; and then the size of the Democratic majority depended on an elastic appreciation of exactly how much was demanded from headquarters. But on this day things went differently. The gang, with a Roman sense of duty, took an active interest in seeing that the Republican was given his full rights. Moreover, they made the most energetic reprisals on their opponents, and as they were distinctly the tough and fighting element, justice came to her own with a whoop. Would-be repeaters were thrown out on their heads. Every person who could be cajoled or, I fear, intimidated, was given the Republican ticket, and the upshot was that at the end of the day a district which had never hitherto polled more than two or three per cent of its vote Republican broke about even between the two parties.

To Joe it has been merely an act of retribution in so far as it was not simply a spree. But the leaders at the Republican headquarters did not know this, and when they got over their paralyzed astonishment at the returns, they investigated to find out what it meant. Somebody told them that it represented the work of a young man named Joseph Murray. Accordingly they sent for him. The room in which they received him was doubtless some place like Morton Hall, and the men who received him were akin to those who had leadership in Morton Hall; but in Joe's eyes they stood for a higher civilization, for opportunity, for generous recognition of successful effort—in short, for all the things that an eager young man desires. He was received and patted on the back by a man who was a great man to the world in which he lived. He was introduced to the audience as a young man whose achievement was such as to promise much for the future, and moreover he was given a place in the post-office—as I have said, this was long before the day of Civil Service Reform.

Now, to the wrong kind of man all this might have meant nothing at all. But in Joe Murray's case it meant everything. He was by nature as straight a man, as fearless and as stanchly loyal, as any one whom I have ever met, a man to be trusted in any position demanding courage, integrity, and good faith. He did his duty in the public service, and became devotedly attached to the organization which he felt had given him his chance in life. When I knew him he was already making his way up; one of the proofs and evidences of which was that he owned a first-class racing trotter—"Alice Lane"—behind which he gave me more than one spin. During this first winter I grew to like Joe and his particular cronies. But I had no idea that they especially returned the liking, and in the first row we had in the organization (which arose over a movement, that I backed, to stand by a non-partisan method of street-cleaning) Joe and all his friends stood stiffly with the machine, and my side, the reform side, was left with only some half-dozen votes out of three or four hundred. I had expected no other outcome and took it good-humoredly, but without changing my attitude.

Next fall, as the elections drew near, Joe thought he would like to make a drive at Jake Hess, and after considerable planning decided that his best chance lay in the fight for the nomination to the Assembly, the lower house of the Legislature. He picked me as the candidate with whom he would be most likely to win; and win he did. It was not my fight, it was Joe's; and it was to him that I owe my entry into politics. I had at that time neither the reputation nor the ability to have won the nomination for myself, and indeed never would have thought of trying for it.

Jake Hess was entirely good-humored about it. In spite of my being anti-machine, my relations with him had been friendly and human, and when he was beaten he turned to help Joe elect me. At first they thought they would take me on a personal canvass through the saloons along Sixth Avenue. The canvass, however, did not last beyond the first saloon. I was introduced with proper solemnity to the saloon-keeper—a very important personage, for this was before the days when saloon-keepers became merely the mortgaged chattels of the brewers—and he began to cross-examine me, a little too much in the tone of one who was dealing with a suppliant for his favor. He said he expected that I would of course treat the liquor business fairly; to which I answered, none too cordially, that I hoped I should treat all interests fairly. He then said that he regarded the licenses as too high; to which I responded that I believed they were not really high enough, and that I should try to have them made higher. The conversation threatened to become stormy. Messrs. Murray and Hess, on some hastily improvised plea, took me out into the street, and then Joe explained to me that it was not worth my while staying in Sixth Avenue any longer, that I had better go right back to Fifth Avenue and attend to my friends there, and that he would look after my interests on Sixth Avenue. I was triumphantly elected.

Once before Joe had interfered in similar fashion and secured the nomination of an Assemblyman; and shortly after election he had grown to feel toward this Assemblyman that he must have fed on the meat which rendered Caesar proud, as he became inaccessible to the ordinary mortals whose place of resort was Morton Hall. He eyed me warily for a short time to see if I was likely in this respect to follow in my predecessor's footsteps. Finding that I did not, he and all my other friends and supporters assumed toward me the very pleasantest attitude that it was possible to assume. They did not ask me for a thing. They accepted as a matter of course the view that I was absolutely straight and was trying to do the best I could in the Legislature. They desired nothing except that I should make a success, and they supported me with hearty enthusiasm. I am a little at a loss to know quite how to express the quality in my relationship with Joe Murray and my other friends of this period which rendered that relationship so beneficial to me. When I went into politics at this time I was not conscious of going in with the set purpose to benefit other people, but of getting for myself a privilege to which I was entitled in common with other people. So it was in my relationship with these men. If there had lurked in the innermost recesses of my mind anywhere the thought that I was in some way a patron or a benefactor, or was doing something noble by taking part in politics, or that I expected the smallest consideration save what I could earn on my own merits, I am certain that somehow or other the existence of that feeling would have been known and resented. As a matter of fact, there was not the slightest temptation on my part to have any such feeling or any one of such feelings. I no more expected special consideration in politics than I would have expected it in the boxing ring. I wished to act squarely to others, and I wished to be able to show that I could hold my own against others. The attitude of my new friends toward me was first one of polite reserve, and then that of friendly alliance. Afterwards I became admitted to comradship, and then to leadership. I need hardly say how earnestly I believe that men should have a keen and lively sense of their obligations in politics, of their duty to help forward great causes, and to struggle for the betterment of conditions that are unjust to their fellows, the men and women who are less fortunate in life. But in addition to this feeling there must be a feeling of real fellowship with the other men and women engaged in the same task, fellowship of work, with fun to vary the work; for unless there is this feeling of fellowship, of common effort on an equal plane for a common end, it will be difficult to keep the relations wholesome and natural. To be patronized is as offensive as to be insulted. No one of us cares permanently to have some one else conscientiously striving to do him good; what we want is to work with that someone else for the good of both of us—any man will speedily find that other people can benefit him just as much as he can benefit them.

Neither Joe Murray nor I nor any of our associates at that time were alive to social and industrial needs which we now all of us recognize. But we then had very clearly before our minds the need of practically applying certain elemental virtues, the virtues of honesty and efficiency in politics, the virtue of efficiency side by side with honesty in private and public life alike, the virtues of consideration and fair dealing in business as between man and man, and especially as between the man who is an employer and the man who is an employee. On all fundamental questions Joe Murray and I thought alike. We never parted company excepting the question of Civil Service Reform, where he sincerely felt that I showed doctrinaire affinities, that I sided with the pharisees. We got back again into close relations as soon as I became Police Commissioner under Mayor Strong, for Joe was then made Excise Commissioner and was, I believe, the best Excise Commissioner the city of New York ever had. He is now a farmer, his boys have been through Columbia College, and he and I look at the questions, political, social, and industrial, which confront us in 1913 from practically the same standpoint, just as we once looked at the questions that confronted us in 1881.

There are many debts that I owe Joe Murray, and some for which he was only unconsciously responsible. I do not think that a man is fit to do good work in our American democracy unless he is able to have a genuine fellow-feeling for, understanding of, and sympathy with his fellow-Americans, whatever their creed or their birthplace, the section in which they live, or the work they do, provided they possess the only kind of Americanism that really counts, the Americanism of the spirit. It was no small help to me, in the effort to make myself a good citizen and a good American, that the political associate with whom I was on closest and most intimate terms during my early years was a man born in Ireland, by creed a Catholic, with Joe Murray's upbringing.

There is after all something in those trifles that friends bestow upon each other which is an unfailing indication of the place the giver holds in the affections. I would believe that one who preserved a lock of hair, a simple flower, or any trifle of my bestowing, loved me, though no show was made of it; while all the protestations in the world would not win my confidence in one who set no value on such little things.

Trifles they may be; but it is by such that character and disposition are oftenest revealed.

—Washington Irving

"Every friend is good and wise for his friend . . ."

BALTASAR GRACIAN'S
"WORLDLY WISDOM"

Sympathy with Great Minds. It is an heroic quality to agree with heroes. 'Tis like a miracle of nature for mystery and for use. There is a natural kinship of hearts and minds: its effects are such that vulgar ignorance scents witchcraft. Esteem established, goodwill follows, which at times reaches affection. It persuades without words and obtains without earning. This sympathy is sometimes active, sometimes passive, both alike felicific; the more so, the more sublime. 'Tis a great art to recognize, to distinguish and utilize this gift. No amount of energy suffices without that favor of nature.

Have Friends. 'Tis a second existence. Every friend is good and wise for his friend: among them all everything turns to good. Every one is as others wish him; that they may wish him well, he must win their hearts and so their tongues. There is no magic like a good turn, and the way to gain friendly feelings is to do friendly acts. The most and best of us depend on others; we have to live either among friends or among enemies. Seek some one every day to be a well-wisher if not a friend; by and by after trial some of these will become intimate.

Never Have a Companion Who Casts You in the Shade. The more he does so, the less desirable a companion he is. The more he excels in quality the more in repute: he will always play first fiddle and you second. If you get any consideration, it is only his leavings. The moon shines bright alone among the stars: when the sun rises she becomes either invisible or imperceptible. Never join one that eclipses you, but rather one who sets you in a brighter light. By this means the cunning Fabula in Martial was able to appear beautiful and brilliant, owing to the ugliness and disorder of her companions. But one should as little imperil oneself by an evil companion as pay honor to another at the cost of one's own credit. When you are on the way to fortune associate with the eminent; when arrived, with the mediocre.

We Belong to None and None to Us, Entirely. Neither relationship nor friendship nor the most intimate connection is sufficient to effect this. To give one's whole confidence is quite different from giving one's regard. The closest intimacy has its exceptions, without which the laws of friendship would be broken. The friend always keeps one secret to himself, and even the son always hides something from his father. Some things are kept from one that are revealed to another and *vice versa*. In this way one reveals all and conceals all, by making a distinction among the persons with whom we are connected.

(*Translated by Joseph Jacobs*)

"... some good angel bade thee write it."

TO OLIVIA BOWDITCH, THE SMALL DAUGHTER OF A FRIEND OF WHITTIER'S

Amesbury, 28th 1st mo., 1856

My Dear Friend Olivia,—I thank thee for thy kind note; and am sure some good angel bade thee write it. I was very glad to know that my "Mary Garvin" gave thee so much pleasure. I know of no better way of being happy than in making others so. And then too, as an author, I was gratified by thy praise of my verses, because I was sure it was the honest expression of thy feeling. I remember that after Bernardin St. Pierre had written his beautiful story of "Paul and Virginia" (which I hope thou hast not read yet, because in that case there is so much more pleasure in store for thee), he was afraid it was not good enough for publication, and was on the point of laying it aside, when he chanced to read it to a group of children, whose evident delight and tearful sympathy encouraged him to print it, and thus please and sadden the hearts of young and old from that time to this. Following St. Pierre's example, I think I shall print "Mary Garvin" in a book with some other pieces. If my young critics are pleased I can well afford to let the older ones find fault. I thank thee and thy dear father and mother for the invitation, and hope I shall be able to accept it when the spring brings back the green grass, the bright flowers, and these wintry drifts are only a memory.

JOHN GREENLEAF WHITTIER

Old books, old wine, old Nankin blue;—
All things, in short, to which belong
The charm, the grace that Time makes Strong,—
All these I prize, but (*entre nous*)
Old friends are best!

—AUSTIN DOBSON

"There could be no rivalry between them."

MADAME DE STAËL AND MADAME RÉCAMIER

William Rounseville Alger

The first meeting of these celebrated women took place when Madame de Staël was thirty-two years old; Madame Récamier, twenty-one. Among the few existing papers from the pen of the latter is a description of this interview:—

"She came to speak with me for her father, about the purchase of a house. Her toilet was odd. She wore a morning gown, and a little dress bonnet, adorned with flowers. I took her for a stranger in Paris. I was struck with the beauty of her eyes and her look. She said, with a vivid impressive grace, that she was delighted to know me; that her father, M. Necker—at these words, I recognized Madame de Staël. I heard not the rest of her sentence. I blushed; my embarrassment was extreme. I had just come from reading her 'Letters on Rousseau,' and was full of excitement. I expressed what I felt more by my looks than by my words. She at the same time awed and drew me. She fixed her wonderful eyes on me, with a curiosity full of kindness, and complimented me on my figure, in terms which would have seemed exaggerated and too direct if they had not been marked by an obvious sincerity, which made the praise very seductive. She perceived my embarrassment, and expressed a desire to see me often, on her return to Paris; for she was going to Coppet. It was then a mere apparition in my life; but the impression was intense. I thought only of Madame de Staël, so strongly did I return the action of this ardent and forceful nature."

Madame de Staël was a plain, energetic embodiment of the most impassioned genius. Madame Récamier was a dazzling personification of physical loveliness, united with the perfection of mental harmony. She had an enthusiastic admiration for her friend, who, in return, found an unspeakable luxury in her society. Her angelic candor of soul, and the frosty purity which enveloped her as a shield, inspired the tenderest respect; while her happy equipoise calmed and refreshed the restless and expansive imagination of the renowned author. There could be no rivalry between them. Both had lofty and thoroughly sincere characters. . . . "Are you not happy," writes Madame de Staël, "in your magical power of inspiring affection? To be sure of always being loved by those you love, seems to me the highest terrestrial happiness, the greatest conceivable privilege...." And when, years afterward, on the loss of her property, Madame Récamier betook herself to the Abbaye-aux-Bois, in her humble chamber, where she was more sought and admired than ever in her proudest prosperity, the chief articles to be seen, in addition to the indispensable furniture, were, as Chateaubriand has described the scene, a library, a harp, a piano, a magnificent portrait of Madame de Staël by Gerard, and a moonlight view by Coppet. Madame de Staël had once written to her, "Your friendship is like the spring in the desert, that never fails; and it is this which makes it impossible not to love you." Death caused no decay of that sentiment, but raised and sanctified it. Her translated friend now became an object of worship; and she devoted her whole energies to extend and preserve the memory of the illustrious writer.

THE BANQUET

Louise Driscoll

One dwelt in darkness and sang within his dwelling,
　　An old one, a blind one, in a hut beside the way.
The king rode wearily; sad and full of care was he
　　When he heard the cheerful roundelay.

"Oh," sang the blind man, "I have had a good life!
　　Mine has been a merry life, with pleasant things beguiled.
Once a lass kissed me, once I heard a lark sing,
　　Once I found a flower, and once I comforted a child."

Then the king paused suddenly and held his hand for his men to see,
　　Left his horse, and went to the blind man's door.
"Friend," he called, "good-day to thee. May I come and sup with
　　thee?"
"Aye, friend and welcome. Why came thee not before?"

Then sat the great king, the wise king, the sad king,
　　Stroking slow his long beard while the blind man bent his head.
Salt and wet his eyes were on the bread and wine before him.
　　"Thank Thee," said the blind man, "Who has sent me friend and
　　bread."

Then the king rode hurriedly, then the king rode comforted.
   "Oh," sang the blind man, "life goes merrily."
He dwelt in darkness and he sang within his dwelling,
   "I have bread a-plenty, and a friend has supped with me."

～～～～～

". . . now you have become a stranger to me."

THE ESSENCE OF FRIENDSHIP
Henrik Ibsen

(From Act II of the play *John Gabriel Borkman*)

(Vilhelm Foldal comes softly into the room. He is a bent and worn man with mild blue eyes and long, thin grey hair straggling down over his coat collar. He has a portfolio under his arm, a soft felt hat, and large horn spectacles, which he pushes up his forehead.)

Borkman (changes his attitude and looks at Foldal with a half disappointed, half pleased expression). Oh, is it only you?

Foldal. Good evening, John Gabriel. Yes, you see it is me.

Borkman (with a stern glance). I must say you are rather a late visitor.

Foldal. Well, you know, it's a good bit of way, especially when you have to trudge it on foot.

Borkman. But why do you always walk, Vilhelm? The tramway passes your door.

Foldal. It's better for you to walk—and then you always save twopence. Well, has Frida been playing to you lately?

Borkman. She has just this moment gone. Did you not meet her outside?

Foldal. No, I have seen nothing of her for a long time; not since she went to live with this Mrs. Wilton.

Borkman (seating himself on the sofa and motioning toward a chair). You may sit down, Vilhelm.

Foldal (seating himself on the edge of a chair). Many thanks. *(Looks mournfully at him.)* You can't think how lonely I feel since Frida left home.

Borkman. Oh, come—you have plenty left.

Foldal. Yes, God knows I have—five of them. But Frida was the only one who at all understood me. (*Shaking his head sadly.*) The others don't understand me a bit.

Borkman (*gloomily, gazing straight before him, and drumming on the table with his fingers*). No, that's just it. That is the curse we exceptional, chosen people have to bear. The common herd—the average man and woman—they do not understand us, Vilhelm.

Foldal (*with resignation*). If it were only the lack of understanding —with a little patience, one could manage to wait for that awhile yet. (*His voice choked with tears.*) But there is something still bitterer.

Borkman (*vehemently*). There is nothing bitterer than that.

Foldal. Yes, there is, John Gabriel. I have gone through a domestic scene to-night—just before I started.

Borkman. Indeed? What about?

Foldal (*with an outburst*). My people at home—they despise me.

Borkman (*indignantly*). Despise—!

Foldal (*wiping his eyes*). I have long known it; but today it came out unmistakably.

Borkman (*after a short pause*). You made an unwise choice, I fear, when you married.

Foldal. I had practically no choice in the matter. And, you see, one feels a need for companionship as one begins to get on in years. And so crushed as I then was—so utterly broken down—

Borkman (*jumping up in anger*). Is this meant for me? A reproach—!

Foldal (*alarmed*). No, no, for Heaven's sake, John Gabriel—!

Borkman. Yes, you are thinking of the disaster to the bank; I can see you are!

Foldal (*soothingly*). But I don't blame you for that! Heaven forbid!

Borkman (*growling, resumes his seat*). Well, that is a good thing, at any rate.

Foldal. Besides, you mustn't think it is my wife that I complain of. It is true she has not much polish, poor thing; but she is a good sort of woman all the same. No, it's the children.

Borkman. I thought as much.

Foldal. For the children—well, they have more culture, and therefore they expect more of life.

Borkman (*looking at him sympathetically*). And so your children despise you, Vilhelm?

Foldal (*shrugging his shoulders*). I haven't made much of a career, you see—there is no denying that.

Borkman (*moving nearer to him, and laying his hand upon his arm*). Do they not know, then, that in your young days you wrote a tragedy?

Foldal. Yes, of course they know that. But it doesn't seem to make much impression on them.

Borkman. Then they don't understand these things. For your tragedy is good. I am firmly convinced of that.

Foldal (*brightening up*). Yes, don't you think there are some good things in it, John Gabriel? Good God, if I could only manage to get it placed—! (*Opens his portfolio, and begins eagerly turning over the contents.*) Look here. Just let me show you one or two alterations I have made.

Borkman. Have you it with you?

Foldal. Yes, I thought I would bring it. It's so long now since I have read it to you. And I thought perhaps it might amuse you to hear an act or two.

Borkman (*rising, with a negative gesture*). No, no, we will keep that for another time.

Foldal. Well, well, as you please.

(*Borkman paces up and down the room. Foldal puts the manuscript away.*)

Borkman (*stopping in front of him*). You are quite right in what you said just now—you have not made any career. But I promise you this, Vilhelm, that when once the hour of my restoration strikes—

Foldal (*making a movement to rise*). Oh, thanks, thanks!

Borkman (*waving his hand*). No, please be seated. (*With increasing excitement.*) When the hour of my restoration strikes—when they see that they cannot get on without me—when they come to me, here in the gallery, and crawl to my feet, and beseech me to take the reins of the bank again—! The new bank, that they have founded and can't carry on—(*Taking a position beside the writing-table in the same attitude as before, and striking his breast.*) Here I shall stand, and receive them! And it shall be known far and wide, all the country over, what conditions John Gabriel Borkman imposes before he will—(*Stopping suddenly and staring at Foldal.*) You're looking so doubtfully at me! Perhaps you do not believe that they will come? That they must, must, must come to me some day? Do you not believe it?

Foldal. Yes, Heaven knows I do, John Gabriel.

Borkman (*seating himself again on the sofa*). I firmly believe it. I am immovably convinced—I know that they will come. If I had not been certain of that I would have put a bullet through my head long ago.

Foldal (*anxiously*). Oh, no, for Heaven's sake—!

Borkman (*exultantly*). But they will come! They will come sure enough! You shall see! I expect them any day, any moment. And you see, I hold myself in readiness to receive them.

Foldal (*with a sigh*). If only they would come quickly.

Borkman (*restlessly*). Yes, time flies: the years slip away; life—ah, no—I dare not think of it! (*Looking at him.*) Do you know what I sometimes feel like?

Foldal. What?

Borkman. I feel like a Napoleon who has been maimed in his first battle.

Foldal (*placing his hand upon his portfolio*). I have that feeling too.

Borkman. Oh, well, that is on a smaller scale, of course.

Foldal (*quietly*). My little world of poetry is very precious to me, John Gabriel.

Borkman (*vehemently*). Yes, but think of me, who could have created millions! All the mines I should have controlled! New veins innumerable! And the water-falls! and the quarries! and the trade routes, and steamship lines all the wide world over! I would have organised it all—I alone!

Foldal. Yes, I know, I know. There was nothing in the world you would have shrunk from.

Borkman (*clenching his hands together*). And now I have to sit here, like a wounded eagle, and look on while others pass me in the race, and take everything away from me, piece by piece!

Foldal. That is my fate too!

Borkman (*not noticing him*). Only to think of it; so near to the goal as I was! If I had only had another week to look about me! All the deposits would have been covered. All the securities I had dealt with so daringly should have been in their places again as before. Vast companies were within a hair's-breadth of being floated. Not a soul should have lost a half-penny.

Foldal. Yes, yes; you were on the very verge of success.

Borkman (*with suppressed fury*). And then treachery overtook me! Just at the critical moment! (*Looking at him.*) Do you know what I hold to be the most infamous crime a man can be guilty of?

Foldal. No, tell me.

Borkman. It is not murder. It is not robbery or house-breaking. It is not even perjury. For all these things people do to those they hate, or who are indifferent to them, and do not matter.

Foldal. What is the worst of all then, John Gabriel?

Borkman (*with emphasis*). The most infamous of crimes is a friend's betrayal of his friend's confidence.

Foldal (*somewhat doubtfully*). Yes, but you know—

Borkman (*firing up*). What are you going to say? I see it in your face. But it is of no use. The people who had their securities in the bank should have got them all back again—every farthing. No; I tell you the most infamous crime a man can commit is to misuse a friend's letters, to publish to all the world what has been confided to him alone, in the closest secrecy, like a whisper in an empty, dark, double-locked room. The man who can do such things is infected and poisoned in every fibre with the morals of the higher rascality. And such a friend was mine—and it was he who crushed me.

Foldal. I can guess whom you mean.

Borkman. There was not a nook or cranny of my life that I hesitated to lay open to him. And then, when the moment came, he turned against me the weapons I myself had placed in his hands.

Foldal. I have never been able to understand why he— Of course, there were whispers of all sorts at the time.

Borkman. What were the whispers? Tell me. You see I know nothing. For I had to go straight into—into isolation. What did people whisper, Vilhelm?

Foldal. You were to have gone into the Cabinet, they said.

Borkman. I was offered a portfolio, but I refused it.

Foldal. Then it wasn't there you stood in his way?

Borkman. Oh, no; that was not the reason he betrayed me.

Foldal. Then I really can't understand—

Borkman. I may as well tell you, Vilhelm—

Foldal. Well?

Borkman. There was—in fact, there was a woman in the case.

Foldal. A woman in the case? Well, but John Gabriel—

Borkman (interrupting). Well, well—let us say no more of these stupid old stories. After all, neither of us got into the Cabinet, neither he nor I.

Foldal. But he rose high in the world.

Borkman. And I fell into the abyss.

Foldal. Oh, it's a terrible tragedy—

Borkman (nodding to him). Almost as terrible as yours, I fancy, when I come to think of it.

Foldal (naïvely). Yes, at least as terrible.

Borkman (laughing quietly). But looked at from another point of view, it is really a sort of comedy as well.

Foldal. A comedy? The story of your life?

Borkman. Yes, it seems to be taking a turn in that direction. For let me tell you—

Foldal. What?

Borkman. You say you did not meet Frida as you came in?

Foldal. No.

Borkman. At this moment, as we sit here, she is playing waltzes for the guests of the man who betrayed and ruined me.

Foldal. I hadn't the least idea of that.

Borkman. Yes, she took her music, and went straight from me to— to the great house.

Foldal. Well, you see, poor child—

Borkman. And can you guess for whom she is playing—among the rest?

Foldal. No.

Borkman. For my son.

Foldal. What?

Borkman. What do you think of that, Vilhelm? My son is down there in the whirl of the dance this evening. Am I not right in calling it a comedy?

Foldal. But in that case you may be sure he knows nothing about it.

Borkman. What does he not know?

Foldal. You may be sure he doesn't know how he—that man—

Borkman. Do not shrink from his name. I can quite well bear it now.

Foldal. I'm certain your son doesn't know the circumstances, John Gabriel.

Borkman (*gloomily, sitting and striking the table*). Yes, he knows, as surely as I am sitting here.

Foldal. Then how can he possibly be a guest in that house?

Borkman (*shaking his head*). My son probably does not see things with my eyes. I'll take my oath he is on my enemies' side! No doubt he thinks, as they do, that Hinkel only did his confounded duty when he went and betrayed me.

Foldal. But, my dear friend, who can have got him to see things in that light?

Borkman. Who? Do you forget who has brought him up? First his aunt, from the time he was six or seven years old; and now, of late years, his mother!

Foldal. I believe you are doing them an injustice.

Borkman (*firing up*). I never do any one injustice! Both of them have poisoned his mind against me, I tell you!

Foldal (*soothingly*). Well, well, well, I suppose they have.

Borkman (*indignantly*). Oh these women! They wreck and ruin life for us! Play the devil with our whole destiny—our triumphal progress.

Foldal. Not all of them!

Borkman. Indeed? Can you tell me of a single one that is good for anything?

Foldal. No, that is the trouble. The few that I know are good for nothing.

Borkman (*with a snort of scorn*). Well then, what is the good of it? What is the good of such women existing—if you never know them?

Foldal (*warmly*). Yes, John Gabriel, there is good in it, I assure you. It is such a blessed, beneficent thought that here or there in the world, somewhere, far away—the true woman exists after all.

Borkman (*moving impatiently on the sofa*). Oh, do spare me that poetical nonsense!

Foldal (*looks at him, deeply wounded*). Do you call my holiest faith poetical nonsense?

Borkman (*harshly*). Yes I do! That is what has always prevented you from getting on in the world. If you would get all that out of your head, I could still help you on in life—help you to rise.

Foldal (*boiling inwardly*). Oh, you can't do that.

Borkman. I can, when once I come into power again.

Foldal. That won't be for many a day.

Borkman (*vehemently*). Perhaps you think that day will never come? Answer me!

Foldal. I don't know what to answer.

Borkman (*rising, cold and dignified, and waving his hand towards the door*). Then I no longer have any use for you.

Foldal (*starting up*). No use—!

Borkman. Since you don't believe that the tide will turn for me—

Foldal. How can I believe in the teeth of all reason? You would have to be legally rehabilitated—

Borkman. Go on! go on!

Foldal. It's true I never passed my examination; but I have read enough law to know that—

Borkman (*quickly*). It is impossible, you mean?

Foldal. There is no precedent for such a thing.

Borkman. Exceptional men are above precedents.

Foldal. The law knows nothing of such distinctions.

Borkman (*harshly and decisively*). You are no poet, Vilhelm.

Foldal (*unconsciously folding his hands*). Do you say that in sober earnest?

Borkman (*dismissing the subject, without answering*). We are only wasting each other's time. You had better not come here again.

Foldal. Then you really want me to leave you?

Borkman (*without looking at him*). I have no longer any use for you.

Foldal (*softly, taking his portfolio*). No, no, no; I daresay not.

Borkman. Here you have been lying to me all the time.

Foldal (*shaking his head*). Never lying, John Gabriel.

Borkman. Have you not sat here feeding me with hope, and trust, and confidence—that was all a lie?

Foldal. It wasn't a lie so long as you believed in my vocation. So long as you believed in me, I believed in you.

Borkman. Then we have been all the time deceiving each other. And perhaps deceiving ourselves—both of us.

Foldal. But isn't that just the essence of friendship, John Gabriel?

Borkman (*smiling bitterly*). Yes, you are right there. Friendship means—deception. I have learnt that once before.

Foldal (looking at him). I have no poetic vocation! And you could actually say it to me so bluntly.

Borkman (in a gentler tone). Well, you know I don't pretend to know much about these matters.

Foldal. Perhaps you know more than you think.

Borkman. I?

Foldal (softly). Yes, you. For I myself have had my doubts, now and then, I may tell you. The horrible doubt that I may have bungled my life for the sake of a delusion.

Borkman. If you have no faith in yourself, you are on the downward path indeed.

Foldal. That was why I found such comfort in coming here to lean upon your faith in me. (*Taking his hat.*) But now you have become a stranger to me.

Borkman. And you to me.

Foldal. Good night, John Gabriel.

Borkman. Good night, Vilhelm.

(*Foldal goes out to the left.*)

(Translated by William Archer)

"IF I CAN STOP ONE HEART FROM BREAKING"

Emily Dickinson

If I can stop one heart from breaking,
I shall not live in vain;
If I can ease one life the aching,
Or cool one pain,
Or help one fainting robin
Unto his nest again
I shall not live in vain.

Fine as friendship is, there is nothing irrevocable about it. The bonds of friendship are not iron bonds, proof against the strongest of strains and the heaviest of assaults. A man by becoming your friend has not committed himself to all the demands which you may be pleased to make upon him. Foolish people like to test the bonds of their friendships, pulling upon them to see how much strain they will stand. When they snap, it is as if friendship itself had been proved unworthy. But the truth is that good friendships are fragile things and require as much care in handling as any other fragile and precious things. For friendship is an adventure and a romance, and in adventures it is the unexpected that happens. It is the zest of peril that makes the excitement of friendship. All that is unpleasant and unfavorable is foreign to its atmosphere; there is no place in friendship for harsh criticism or fault-finding. We will "take less" from a friend than we will from one who is indifferent to us.

—Randolph S. Bourne

**"Human friendship has limits because
of the real greatness of man."**

FRIENDSHIP'S LIMITATIONS
Hugh Black

Human friendship must have limits, just because it is human. It is subject to loss, and often to some extent the sport of occasion. It lacks permanence; misunderstandings can estrange us: slander can embitter us: death can bereave us. We are left very much the victim of circumstances; for like everything earthly it is open to change and decay. No matter how close and spiritual the intercourse, it is not permanent, and never certain. If nothing else, the shadow of death is always on it. Tennyson describes how he dreamed that he and his friend should pass through the world together, loving and trusting each other, and together pass out into the silence.

> "Arrive at last the blessed goal,
>   And He that died in Holy Land
>   Would reach us out the shining hand,
> And take us as a single soul."

It was a dream at the best. Neither to live together nor to die together could blot out the spiritual limits of friendship. Even in the closest of human relations, when two take each other for better or for worse, for richer for poorer, in sickness and in health, they may be made one flesh, but never one soul. Singleness is the ultimate fact of human life. "The race is run by one and one, and never by two and two."

In religion, in the deepest things of the spirit, these limits we have been considering are perhaps felt most of all. With even a friend who is as one's own soul, we cannot seek to make a spiritual impression, without realizing the constraint of his separate individuality. We cannot break through the barriers of another's distinct existence. If we have ever sought to lead to a higher life another whom we love, we must have been made to feel that it does not all rest with us, that he is a free moral being, and that only by voluntarily yielding his heart and will and life to the King, can he enter the Kingdom. We are forced to respect his personality. We may watch and pray and speak, but we cannot save. There is almost a sort of spiritual indecency in unveiling the naked soul, in attempting to invade the personality of another life. There is sometimes a spiritual vivisection which some attempt in the name of religion, which is immoral. Only holier eyes than ours, only more reverent hands than ours, can deal with the spirit of man. He is a separate individual, with all the rights of an individual. We may have many points of contact with him, the contact of mind on mind, and heart on heart; we may even have rights over him, the rights of love; but he can at will insulate his life from ours. Here also, as elsewhere when we go deep enough into life, it is God and the single human soul.

The lesson of all true living in every sphere is to learn our own limitations. It is the first lesson in art, to work within the essential limitations of the particular art. But in dealing with other lives it is perhaps the hardest of all lessons, to learn, and submit to, our limitations. It is the crowning grace of faith, when we are willing to submit, and leave those we love in the hands of God, as we leave ourselves. Nowhere else is the limit of friendship so deeply cut as here in the things of the spirit.

> "No man can save his brother's soul,
> Nor pay his brother's debt."

Human friendship has limits because of the real greatness of man. We are too big to be quite comprehended by another. There is always something in us left unexplained, and unexplored. We do not even know ourselves, much less can another hope to probe into the recesses of our being. Friendship has a limit, because of the infinite element in the soul. It is hard to kick against the pricks, but they are meant to drive us toward the true end of living. It is hard to be brought up by a limit along any line of life, but it is designed to send us to a deeper and richer development of our life. Man's limitation is God's occasion. Only God can fully satisfy the hungry heart of man.

～～～～～

Rejoice and men will seek you;
　　Grieve, and they turn to go,
They want full measure of all your pleasure,
　　But they do not need your woe.
Be glad, and your friends are many;
　　Be sad, and you lose them all,
There are none to decline your nectar'd wine,
　　But alone you must drink life's gall.
　　　　　　　　　　　　—Ella Wheeler Wilcox

～～～～～

"... you are not to suppose that you have lost me ..."

SAMUEL JOHNSON TO GEORGE STRAHAN

Dear George

To give pain ought always to be painful, and I am sorry that I have been the occasion of any uneasiness in you, to whom I hope never to do any thing but for your benefit or your pleasure. Your uneasiness was without any reason on your part, as you had written with sufficient frequency to me, and I had only neglected to answer then, because as nothing new had been proposed to your study no new direction or incitement could be offered you.... You are not to imagine that my friendship is light enough to be blown away by the first cross blast, or that my regard or kindness hangs by so slender a hair, as to be broken off by the unfelt weight of a petty offense. I love you, and hope to love you long. You have hitherto done nothing to diminish my goodwill, and though you had done much more than you have supposed imputed to you my goodwill would not have been diminished.

I write thus largely on this suspicion which you have suffered to enter your mind, because in youth we are apt to be too rigorous in our expectations, and to suppose that the duties of life are to be performed with unfailing exactness and regularity, but in our progress through life we are forced to abate much of our demands, and to take friends such as we can find them, not as we would make them.

These concessions every wise man is more ready to make to others as he knows how often he fails in the observance or cultivation of his best friends, is willing to suppose that his friends may in their turn neglect him without any intention to offend him.

When therefore it shall happen, as happen it will, that you or I have disappointed the expectation of the other, you are not to suppose that you have lost me or that I intended to lose you; nothing will remain but to repair the fault, and to go on as if it had never been committed,

I am Sir, Your affectionate servant
SAMUEL JOHNSON

Thursday July 14, 1763

"I am utterly ashamed of my friendships."

OSCAR WILDE, IN PRISON, TO ROBERT ROSS (1896)

There is a thorn, however—as bitter as that of St. Paul, though different—that I must pluck out of my flesh in this letter. It is caused by a message you wrote on a piece of paper for me to see. I feel that if I kept it secret it might grow in my mind (as poisonous things grow in the dark) and take its place with other terrible thoughts that gnaw me. ... Thought, to those that sit alone and silent and in bonds, being no "winged living thing," as Plato feigned it, but a thing dead, breeding what is horrible like a slime that shows monsters to the moon.

I mean, of course, what you said about the sympathies of others being estranged from me, or in danger of being so, by the deep bitterness of my feelings: and I believe that my letter was lent and shown to others. ... Now, I don't like my letters shown about as curiosities: it is most distasteful to me. I write to you freely as to one of the dearest friends I have, or have ever had: and, with a few exceptions, the sympathy of others touches me, as far as its loss goes, very little. No man of my position can fall into the mire of life without getting a great deal of pity from his inferiors; and I know that when plays last too long, spectators tire. My tragedy has lasted far too long; its climax is over; its end is mean; and I am quite conscious of the fact that when the end does come I shall return an unwelcome visitant to a world that does not want me; a *revenant,* as the French say, and one whose face is grey with long imprisonment and crooked with pain. Horrible as are the dead when they rise from their tombs, the living who come out from tombs are more horrible still. Of all this I am only too conscious. When one has been for eighteen terrible months in a prison cell, one sees things and people as they really are. The sight turns one to stone. Do not think that I would blame any one for my vices. My friends had as little to do with them as I had with theirs. Nature was in this matter a stepmother to all of us. I blame them for not appreciating the man they ruined. As long as my table was red with wine and roses, what did they care? My genius, my life as an artist, my work, and the quiet I needed for it, were nothing to them. I admit I lost my head. I was bewildered, incapable of judgment. I made the one fatal step. And now I sit here on a bench in a prison cell. In all tragedies there is a grotesque element. You know the grotesque element in mine. Do not think I do not blame myself. I curse myself night and day for my folly in allowing something to dominate my life. If there was an echo in these walls, it would cry "Fool" for ever. I am utterly ashamed of my friendships.... For by their friendships men can be judged. It is a test of every man. And I feel poignant abasement of shame for my friendships... of which you may read a full account in my trial.

It is to me a daily source of mental humiliation. Of some of them I never think. They trouble me not. It is of no importance.... Indeed my entire tragedy seems to be grotesque and nothing else. For as a result of my having suffered myself to be thrust into a trap... in the lowest mire of Malebolge, I sit between Gilles de Retz and the Marquis de Sade. In certain places no one, except those actually insane, is allowed to laugh: and indeed, even in their case, it is against the regulations for conduct: otherwise I think I would laugh at that.... For the rest, do not let any one suppose that I am crediting others with unworthy motives. They really had no motives in life at all. Motives are intellectual things. They had passions merely, and such passions are false gods that will have victims at all costs and in the present case have had one wreathed with bay. Now I have plucked the thorn out— that little scrawled line of yours rankled terribly. I now think merely of your getting quite well again.

**"I think of every single friend who has been
kind to me in my prison life . . ."**

OSCAR WILDE'S TRIBUTE TO FRIENDS
WHEN IN PRISON

When I was brought down from my prison to the Court of Bank-ruptcy, between two policemen, —— waited in the long dreary corridor that, before the whole crowd, whom an action so sweet and simple hushed into silence, he might gravely raise his hat to me, as, hand-cuffed and with bowed head, I passed him by. Men have gone to heaven for smaller things than that. It was in this spirit, and with this mode of love, that the saints knelt down to wash the feet of the poor, or stooped to kiss the leper on the cheek. I have never said one single word to him about what he did. I do not know to the present moment whether he is aware that I was even conscious of his action. It is not a thing for which one can render formal thanks in formal words. I store it in the treasure-house of my heart. I keep it there as a secret debt that I am glad to think I can never possibly repay. It is embalmed and kept sweet by the myrrh and cassia of many tears. When wisdom has been profitless to me, philosophy barren, and the proverbs and phrases of those who have sought to give me consolation as dust and ashes in my mouth, the memory of that little, lovely, silent act of love has unsealed for me all the wells of pity; made the desert blossom like a rose, and brought me out of the bitterness of lonely exile into harmony with the wounded, broken, and great heart of the world. When people are able to understand, not merely how beautiful ——'s action was, but why it meant so much to me, and always will mean so much, then, perhaps, they will realize how and in what spirit they should approach me. . . .

Every twelve weeks R—— writes to me a little budget of literary news. Nothing can be more charming than his letters, in their wit, their clever concentrated criticism, their light touch: they are real letters, they are like a person talking to one; they have the quality of a French *causerie intime:* and in his delicate mode of deference to me, appealing at one time to my judgment, at another to my sense of humour, at another to my instinct for beauty or to my culture, and reminding me in a hundred subtle ways that once I was to many arbiter of style in art; the supreme arbiter to some; he shows how he had the tact of love as well as the tact of literature. His letters have been the messengers between me and that beautiful unreal world of art where once I was King, and would have remained King indeed, had I not let myself be lured into the imperfect world of coarse uncompleted passion, of appetite without distinction, desire without limit, and formless greed. . . .

If after I am free a friend of mine gave a feast, and did not invite me to it, I should not mind a bit. I can be perfectly happy by myself. With freedom, flowers, books, and the moon, who could not be perfectly happy? Besides, feasts are not for me any more. I have given too many to care about them. That side of life is over for me, very fortunately, I dare say. But if after I am free a friend of mine had a sorrow and refused to allow me to share it, I should feel it more bitterly. If he shut the doors of the house of mourning against me, I would come back again and again and beg to be admitted, so that I might share in what I was entitled to share in. If he thought me unworthy, unfit to weep with him, I should feel it as the most poignant humiliation, as the most terrible mode in which disgrace could be inflicted on me. . . .

I can think with gratitude of those who by kindness without stint, devotion without limit, cheerfulness and joy in giving have lightened my black burden for me, have visited me again and again, have written to me beautiful and sympathetic letters, have managed my affairs for me, arranged my future life, and stood by me in the teeth of obloquy, taunt and open sneer, or insult even. I owe everything to them. The very books in my cell are paid for by —— out of his pocket-money; from the same source are to come clothes for me when I am released. I am not ashamed of taking a thing that is given in love and affection; I am proud of it. Yes, I think of my friends, such as More Adey, R——, Robert Sherard, Frank Harris, Arthur Clifton, and what they have been to me, in giving me help, affection, and sympathy. I think of every single person who has been kind to me in my prison life down to the warder who gives me a "Good-morning" and a "Good-night" (not one of his prescribed duties) down to the common policemen who, in their homely, rough way strove to comfort me on my journeys to and fro from Bankruptcy Court under conditions of terrible mental distress—down to the poor thief who recognising me as we tramped round the yard at Wandsworth, whispered to me in the hoarse prison voice men get from long and compulsory silence: "I am sorry for you; it is harder for the likes of you than it is for the likes of us."

A great friend of mine—a friend of ten years' standing—came to see me some time ago, and told me that he did not believe a single word of what was said against me, and wished me to know that he considered me quite innocent, and the victim of a hideous plot. I burst into tears at what he said, and told him that while there was much amongst the definite charges that was quite untrue and transferred to me by revolting malice, still that my life had been full of perverse pleasures, and that unless he accepted that as a fact about me and realised it to the full I could not possibly be friends with him any more, or ever be in his company. It was a terrible shock to him, but we are friends, and I have not got his friendship on false pretences. I have said to you to speak the truth is a painful thing. To be forced to tell lies is much worse.

He laughed derision when his foes
   Against him cast, each man, a stone;
His friend in anger flung a rose—
   And all the city heard him moan.

—ANONYMOUS

"... you's de bes' fren's Jim's ever had ..."

HUCK FINN MEETS HIS TEST OF LOYALTY TO JIM, THE RUNAWAY SLAVE
Mark Twain

[Huckleberry Finn had run away from home, but was believed to have drowned in the Mississippi River. It is while hiding on an island in the river that he encounters Jim, an escaped slave who lived in Huck's town.]

"How do you come to here Jim, and how'd you get here?"

He looked pretty uneasy, and didn't say nothing for a minute. Then he says:

"Maybe I better not tell."

"Why, Jim?"

"Well, dey's reasons. But you wouldn' tell on me ef I 'uz to tell you, would you, Huck?"

"Blamed if I would, Jim."

"Well, I b'lieve you, Huck. I—I *run off.*"

"Jim!"

"But mind, you said you wouldn' tell—you know you said you wouldn' tell, Huck."

"Well, I did. I said I wouldn't, and I'll stick to it. Honest *injun,* I will. People would call me a lowdown Abolitionist and despise me for keeping mum—but that don't make no difference. I ain't a-going to tell, and I ain't a-going back there, anyways. So, now, le's know all about it."

"Well, you see, it 'uz dis way. Ole missus—dat's Miss Watson—she pecks on me all de time, en treats me poorty rough, but she awluz said she wouldn't sell me down to Orleans. But I noticed dey wuz a nigger trader roun' de place considerable lately, en I begin to git oneasy. Well, one night I creeps to de do' poorty late, en de do' warn't quite shet, en I hear old missus tell de widder she gwyne to sell me down to Orleans, but she didn't want to, but she could git eigh hund'd dollars for me, en it 'uz sich a big stack o' money she couldn' resis'. De widder she try to git her to say she wouldn't do it, but I never waited to hear de res'. I lit out mighty quick, I tell you...."

We slept most all day, and started out at night, a little ways behind a monstrous long raft that was as long going by as a procession. She had four long sweeps at each end, so we judged she carried as many as thirty men, likely....

We went drifting down into a big bend, and the night clouded up and got hot. The river was very wide, and was walled with solid timber on both sides; you couldn't see a break in it hardly ever, or a light. We talked about Cairo, and wondered whether we would know it when we got to it. I said likely we wouldn't, because I had heard say there warn't but about a dozen houses there, and if they didn't happen to have them lit up, how was we going to know we was passing a town? Jim said if the two big rivers joined together there, that would show. But I said maybe we might think we was passing the foot of an island and coming into the same old river again. That disturbed Jim—and me too. So the question was, what to do? I said, paddle ashore the first time a light showed, and tell them pap was behind, coming along with a trading-scow, and was a green hand at the business and wanted to know how far it was to Cairo. Jim thought it was a good idea, so we took a smoke on it and waited.

There warn't nothing to do now but to look out sharp for the town, and not pass it without seeing it. He said he'd be mighty sure to see it, because he'd be a free man the minute he seen it, but if he missed it he'd be in slave country again and no more show for freedom. Every little while he jumps up and says:

"Dah she is!"

But it warn't. It was Jack-o'-lanterns, or lightningbugs, so he sat down again, and went to watching, same as before. Jim said it made him all over trembly and feverish to be so close to freedom. Well, I can tell you it made me all over trembly and feverish, too, to hear him, because I begun to get it through my head that he *was* most free—and who was to blame for it? Why, *me*. I couldn't get that out of my conscience, no how nor no way. It got to troubling me so I couldn't rest; I couldn't stay still in one place. It hadn't ever come home to me before, what this thing was that I was doing. But now it did; and it stayed with me, and scorched me more and more. I tried to make out to myself that I warn't to blame, because I didn't run Jim off from his rightful owner; but it warn't no use, conscience up and says, every time, "But you knowed he was running for his freedom, and you could 'a' paddled ashore and told somebody." That was so—I couldn't get around that no way. There was where it pinched. Conscience says to me, "What had poor Miss Watson done to you that you could see her nigger go off right under your eyes and never say one single word! What did that poor old woman do to you that you could treat her so mean? Why, she tried to learn you your book, she tried to learn you your manners, she tried to be good to you every way she knowed how. *That's* what she done."

I got to feeling so mean and so miserable I most wished I was dead. I fidgeted up and down the raft, abusing myself to myself, and Jim was fidgeting up and down past me. We neither of us could keep still. Every time he danced around and says, "Dah's Cairo!" it went through me like a shot, and I thought if it *was* Cairo I reckoned I would die of miserableness....

My conscience got to stirring me up hotter than ever, and at last I says to it, "Let up on me—it ain't too late—I'll paddle ashore at the first light and tell." I felt easy and happy and light as a feather right off. All my troubles was gone. I went to looking out sharp for a light, and sort of singing to myself. By and by one showed. Jim sings out:

"We's safe, Huck, we's safe! Jump up and crack yo' heels! Dat's de good old Cairo at las', I jis knows it!"

"I'll take the canoe and go and see, Jim. It mightn't be, you know."

He jumped up and got the canoe ready, and put his old coat in the bottom for me to set on, and give me the paddle; and as I shoved off, he says:

"Poorty soon I'll be a-shoutin' for joy, en I'll say, it's all on accounts o' Huck; I's a free man, en I couldn't ever ben free ef it hadn't ben for Huck; Huck done it. Jim won't ever forgit you, Huck, you's de bes' fren's Jim's ever had; en you's de *only* fren ole Jim's got now."

I was paddling off, all in a sweat to tell on him; but when he says this, it seemed to kind of take the tuck all out of me. I went along slow then, and I warn't right down certain whether I was glad or whether I warn't. When I was fifty yards off, Jim says:

"Dah you goes, de ole true Huck; de on'y white genlman dat ever kep' his promise to ole Jim."

Well, I just felt sick. But I says, I *got* to do it—I can't get *out* of it. Right then along comes a skiff with two men in it with guns, and they stopped and I stopped. One of them says:

"What's that yonder?"

"A piece of raft," I says.

"Do you belong on it?"

"Yes, sir."

"Any men on it?"

"Only one, sir."

"Well, there's five niggers run off to-night up yonder, above the head of the bed. Is your man white or black?"

I didn't answer up prompt. I tried to, but the words wouldn't come. I tried for a second or two to brace up and out with it, but I warn't man enough—hadn't the spunk of a rabbit. I see I was weakening; so I just give up trying, and up and says:

"He's white."

"I reckon we'll go and see for ourselves."

" I wish you would," I says, "because it's pap that's there, and maybe you'd help me tow the raft ashore where the light is. He's sick—and so is mam and Mary Ann."

"Oh, the devil! we're in a hurry, boy. But I s'pose we've got to. Come, buckle to your paddle, and let's get going."

I buckled to my paddle and they laid to their oars. When we had made a stroke or two, I says:

"Pap 'll be mighty much obleeged to you, and I can tell you. Everybody goes away when I want them to help me tow the raft ashore, and I can't do it myself."

"Well, that's infernal mean. Odd, too. Say, boy, what's the matter with your father?"

"It's the—a—the—well, it ain't anything much."

They stopped pulling. It warn't but a mighty little ways to the raft now. One says:

"Boy, that's a lie. What *is* the matter with your pap? Answer up square now, and it'll be the better for you."

"I will, sir, I will, honest—but don't leave us, please. It's the—the— Gentlemen, if you'll only pull ahead, and let me heave you the head-line, you won't have to come a-near the raft—please do."

"Set her back, John, set her back!" says one. They backed water. "Keep away, boy—keep to looard. Confound it, I just expect the wind has blowed it to us. Your pap's got the smallpox, and you know it precious well. Why didn't you come out and say so? Do you want to spread it all over?"

"Well," says I, a-blubbering, "I've told everybody before, and they just went away and left us."

"Poor devil, there's something in that. We are right down sorry for you, but we—well, hang it, we don't want the smallpox, you see. Look here, I'll tell you what to do. Don't you try to land by yourself, or you'll smash everything to pieces. You float along down about twenty miles, and you'll come to a town on the left-hand side of the river. It will be long after sun-up then, and when you ask for help you tell them your folks are all down with chills and fever. Don't be a fool again, and let people guess what is the matter. Now we're trying to do you a kindness; so you just put twenty miles between us, that's a good boy. It wouldn't do any good to land yonder where the light is—it's only a wood-yard. Say, I reckon your father's poor, and I'm bound to say he's in pretty hard luck. Here, I'll put a twenty dollar gold piece on this board, and you get it when it floats by. I feel mighty mean to leave you; but my kingdom! it won't do to fool with smallpox, don't you see?"

"Hold on, Parker," says the man, "here's a twenty to put on the board for me. Good-by, boy; do as Mr. Parker told you, and you'll be all right."

"That's so, my boy—good-by, good-by. If you see any runaway niggers you get help and nab them, and you can make some money by it."

"Good-by, sir," says I; "I won't let no runaway niggers get by me if I can help it."

They went off and I got aboard the raft, feeling bad and low, because I knowed very well I had done wrong, and I see it warn't no use for me to try to learn to do right; a body that don't get *started* right when he's little ain't got no show—when the pinch comes there ain't nothing to back him up and keep him to his work, and so he gets beat. Then I thought a minute, and says to myself, hold on; s'pose you'd 'a' done right and give Jim up, would you felt better than what you do now? No, says I, I'd feel bad—I'd feel just the same way I do now. Well, then, says I, what's the use you learning to do right when it's troublesome to do right and ain't no trouble to do wrong, and the wages is just th' same? I was stuck. I couldn't answer that. So I reckoned I wouldn't bother no more about it, but after this always do whichever comes handiest at the time.

I went into the wigwam; Jim warn't there. I looked all around; he warn't anywhere. I says:

"Jim!"

"Here I is, Huck. Is dey out o' sight yit? Don't talk loud."

He was in the river under the stern oar, with just his nose out. I told him they were out of sight, so he come aboard. He says:

"I was a-listin' to all de talk, en I slips into de river en was gwyne to shove for sho' if dey come aboard. Den I was gwyne to swim to de raf' agin when dey was gone. But lawsy, how you did fool 'em, Huck! Dat *wuz* de smartes' dodge! I tell you, chile, I 'spec it save' ole Jim—ole Jim ain't going to forgit you for dat, honey."

Then we talked about the money. It was a pretty good raise—twenty dollars apiece. Jim said we could take deck passage on a steamboat now, and the money would last us as far as we wanted to go in the free states.

He said twenty miles more warn't far for the raft to go, but he wished
we was already there.

ACHILLES PLEDGES TO AVENGE
THE DEATH OF PATROCLUS

Homer

My mother! it is true, Olympian Jove
That prayer fulfills; but thence, what joy to me,
Patroclus slain? the friend of all my friends
Whom most I loved, dear to me as my life—
Him I have lost. Slain and despoil'd he lies
By Hector of his glorious armor bright,
The wonder of all eyes, a matchless gift
Given by the Gods to Peleus on that day
When thee they doom'd into a mortal's arms.
Oh that with these thy deathless ocean-nymphs
Dwelling content, thou hadst my father left
To espouse a mortal bride, so hadst thou 'scaped
Pangs numberless which thou must now endure
For thy son's death, whom thou shalt never meet
From Troy return'd, in Peleus' mansion more!
For life I covet not, nor longer wish
To mix with human kind, unless my spear
May find out Hector, and atonement take
By slaying him, for my Patroclus slain.
    To whom, with streaming tears, Thetis replied.
Swift comes thy destiny as thou hast said,
For after Hector's death thine next ensues.
    Then answer, thus, indignant he return'd.
Death, seize me now! since when my friend was slain,
My doom was, not to succor him. He died
From home remote, and wanting me to save him.
Now, therefore, since I neither visit more
My native land, nor, present here, have aught
Avail'd Patroclus or my many friends
Whom noble Hector hath in battle slain,
But here I sit unprofitable grown,
Earth's burden, though of such heroic note,
If not in council foremost (for I yield

That prize to others) yet in feats of arms,
Such as none other in Achaia's host,
May fierce contention from among the Gods
Perish, and from among the human race,
With wrath, which sets the wisest hearts on fire;
Sweeter than dropping honey to the taste,
But in the bosom of mankind, a smoke!
Such was my wrath which Agamemnon roused,
The king of men. But since the past is fled
Irrevocable, howsoe'er distress'd,
Renounce we now vain musings on the past,
Content through sad necessity. I go
In quest of noble Hector, who hath slain
My loved Patroclus, and such death will take
As Jove ordains me and the Powers of Heaven
At their own season, send it when they may.
For neither might the force of Hercules,
Although high-favored of Saturnian Jove,
From death escape, but Fate and the revenge
Restless of Juno vanquish'd even Him.
I also, if a destiny like his
Await me, shall, like him, find rest in death;
But glory calls me now....

Yet, my Patroclus! since the earth expects
Me next, I will not thy funereal rites
Finish, till I shall bring both head and arms
Of that bold Chief who slew thee, to my tent.
I also will smite off, before thy pile,
The heads of twelve illustrious sons of Troy,
Resentful of thy death. Meantime, among
My lofty galleys thou shalt lie, with tears
Mourn'd day and night by Trojan captives fair
And Dardans compassing thy bier around,
Whom we, at price of labor hard, ourselves
With massy spears toiling in battle took
From many an opulent city, now no more.
  So saying, he bade his train surround with fire
A tripod huge, that they might quickly cleanse
Patroclus from all stain of clotted gore.
They on the blazing hearth a tripod placed
Capacious, fill'd with water its wide womb,
And thrust dry wood beneath, till, fierce, the flames
Embraced it round, and warm'd the flood within.

Soon as the water in the singing brass
Simmer'd, they bathed him, and with limpid oil
Anointed; filling, next, his ruddy wounds
With unguent mellow'd by nine circling years,
They stretch'd him on his bed, then cover'd him
From head to feet with linen texture light,
And with a wide unsullied mantle, last.
All night with Myrmidons around the swift
Achilles stood, deploring loud his friend.

(Translated by William Cowper)

The very best thing is good talk, and the thing that helps it most, is *friendship*. How it dissolves the barriers that divide us, and loosens all constraints, and diffuses itself like some fine old cordial through all the veins of life—this feeling that we understand and trust each other, and wish each other heartily well! Everything into which it really comes is good. It transforms letter-writing from a task to a pleasure. It makes music a thousand times more sweet. The people who play and sing not *at us,* but *to us,*—how delightful it is to listen to them! Yes, there is a talkability that can express itself even without words. There is an exchange of thoughts and feeling which is happily alike in speech and in silence. It is quietness pervaded with friendship.

—HENRY VAN DYKE

"Tell me, dearest of friends, is your mind at peace?"

CHARLES LAMB'S FRIENDSHIP WITH SAMUEL TAYLOR COLERIDGE

(as revealed by passages from Lamb's letters)

May 27, 1796

Dear Coleridge—Make yourself perfectly easy about May. I paid his bill when I sent your clothes. I was flush of money, and am so still to all the purposes of a single life; so give yourself no further concern about it. The money would be superfluous to me if I had it.

June, 1796

I have one more favour to beg of you, that you never mention Mr. May's affair in any sort, much less *think* of repaying. Are we not flocci-nauci-what-d'ye-call-'em-ists? ...

I am sorry there should be any difference between you and Southey. "Between you two there should be peace," tho' I must say I have borne him no good will since he spirited you away from among us....

Coleridge, to an idler like myself, to write and receive letters are both very pleasant; but I wish not to break in upon your valuable time by expecting to hear very frequently from you. Reserve that obligation for your moments of lassitude, when you have nothing else to do; for your loco-restive and all your idle propensities, of course, have given way to the duties of providing for a family. The mail is come in, but no parcel; yet this is Tuesday. Farewell, then, till to-morrow; for a niche and a nook I must leave for criticisms. By the way, I hope you do not send your only copy of *Joan of Arc:* I will in that case return it immediately.

Your parcel *is* come: you have been *lavish* of your presents....

My heart bleeds for your accumulated troubles: God send you through 'em with patience. I conjure you, dream not that I will ever think of being repaid; the very word is galling to the ears. I have read all your *Religious Musings* with uninterrupted feelings of profound admiration. You may safely rest your fame on it. The best remaining things are what I have before read, and they lose nothing by my recollection of your manner of reciting 'em, for I too bear in mind "the voice, the look" of absent friends, and can occasionally mimic their manner for the amusement of those who have seen 'em. Your impassioned manner of recitation I can recall at any time to mine own heart and to the ears of the bystanders.

June 10, 1796

Thank you for your frequent letters: you are the only correspondent, and I might add, the only friend I have in the world. I go nowhere, and have no acquaintance. Slow of speech, and reserved of manners, no one seeks or cares for my society; and I am left alone. Allen calls very occasionally, as though it were a duty rather, and seldom stays ten minutes. Then judge how thankful I am for your letters! ...

When you left London I felt a dismal void in my heart. I found myself cut off, at one and the same time, from two most dear to me. "How blest with ye the path could I have trod of quiet life!" In your conversation you had blended so many pleasant fancies that they cheated me of my grief. But in your absence the tide of melancholy rushed in again, and did its worst mischief by overwhelming my reason. I have recovered, but feel a stupor that makes me indifferent to the hopes and fears of this life. I sometimes wish to introduce a religious turn of mind; but habits are strong things, and my religious fervours are confined, alas! to some fleeting moments of occasional solitary devotion. A correspondence, opening with you, has roused me a little from my lethargy, and made me conscious of existence. Indulge me in it: I will not be very troublesome.

June 14, 1796

Thursday.—I am now in high hopes to be able to visit you, if perfectly convenient on your part, by the end of next month—perhaps the last week or fortnight in July. A change of scene and a change of faces would do me good, even if that scene were not to be Bristol, and those faces Coleridge's and his friends. In the words of Terence, a little altered, *Taedet me hujus quotidiani mundi,* I am heartily sick of the every-day scenes of life. I shall half wish you unmarried (don't show this to Mrs. C.) for one evening only, to have the pleasure of smoking with you and drinking egg-hot in some little smoky room in a pot-house, for I know not yet how I shall like you in a decent room and looking quite happy. My best love and respects to Sara notwithstanding.

October 17, 1796

My dearest Friend—I grieve from my very soul to observe you, in your plans of life, veering about from this hope to the other, and settling nowhere. Is it an untoward fatality (speaking humanly) that does this for you—a stubborn, irresistible concurrence of events? or lies the fault, as I fear it does, in your own mind? You seem to be taking up splendid schemes of fortune only to lay them down again; and your fortunes are an *ignis fatuus* that has been conducting you, in thought, from Lancaster Court, Strand, to somewhere near Matlock; then jumping across to Dr. Somebody's, whose son's tutor you were likely to be; and would to God the dancing demon *may* conduct you at last, in peace and comfort, to the "life and labours of a cottager."

October 24, 1796

Coleridge, I feel myself much your debtor for that spirit of confidence and friendship which dictated your last letter. May your soul find peace at last in your cottage life! I only wish you were but settled. Do continue to write to me. I read your letters with my sister, and they give us both abundance of delight. Especially they please us when you talk in a religious strain: not but we are offended occasionally with a certain freedom of expression, a certain air of mysticism, more consonant to the conceits of pagan philosophy than consistent with the humility of genuine piety. To instance now, in your last letter you say, "It is by the press that God hath given finite spirits, both evil and good (I suppose you mean *simply* bad men and good men), a portion as it were of His Omnipresence!" Now, high as the human intellect comparatively will soar, and wide as its influence, malign or salutary, can extend, is there not, Coleridge, a distance between the Divine Mind and it, which makes such language blasphemy? ... Be not angry with me Coleridge: I wish not to cavil; I know I cannot instruct you; I only wish to remind you of that humility which best becometh the Christian character. God, in the New Testament (*our best guide*), is represented to us in the kind, condescending, amiable, familiar light of a *parent;* and in my poor mind 'tis best for us so to consider him, as our *heavenly* father, and our *best friend,* without indulging too bold conceptions of his nature. Let us learn to think humbly of ourselves, and rejoice in the appellation of "dear children," "brethren," and "co-heirs with Christ of the promises," seeking to know no further.

I am not insensible, indeed I am not, of the value of that first letter of yours, and I shall find reason to thank you for it again and again, long after that blemish in it is forgotten. It will be a fine lesson of comfort to us, whenever we read it; and read it we often shall, Mary and I.

Accept our loves and best kind wishes for the welfare of yourself and wife and little one. Nor let me forget to wish you joy on your birthday, so lately past; I thought you had been older. My kind thanks and remembrances to Lloyd.

God love us all!—and may He continue to be the father and the friend of the whole human race!

C. LAMB

November 8, 1796

My brother, my friend,—I am distress'd for you, believe me I am; not so much for your painful, troublesome complaint, which, I trust, is only for a time, as for those anxieties which brought it on, and perhaps even now may be nursing its malignity. Tell me, dearest of my friends, is your mind at peace? or has anything, yet unknown to me, happened to give you fresh disquiet, and steal from you all the pleasant dreams of future rest? Are you still (I fear you are) far from being comfortably settled? Would to God it were in my power to contribute towards the bringing of you into the haven where you would be! But you are too well skilled in the philosophy of consolation to need my humble tribute of advice. In pain, and in sickness, and in all manner of disappointments, I trust you have that within you which shall speak peace to your mind. Make it, I entreat you, one of your puny comforts, that I feel for you, and share all your griefs with you. I feel as if I were troubling you about *little* things, now I am going to resume the subject of our last two letters; but it may divert us both from unpleasanter feelings to make such matters, in a manner, of importance. Without further apology, then, it was not that I did not relish, that I did not in my heart thank you for those little pictures of your feelings which you lately sent me, if I neglected to mention them. You may remember you had said much the same things before to me on the same subject in a former letter, and I considered those last verses as only the identical thoughts better clothed; either way (in prose or verse) such poetry must be welcome to me. I love them as I love the Confessions of Rousseau, and for the same reason: the same frankness, the same openness of heart, the same disclosure of all the most hidden and delicate affections of the mind. They make me proud to be thus esteemed worthy of the place of friend-confessor, brother-confessor, to a man like Coleridge. This last is, I acknowledge, language too high for friendship; but it is also, I declare, too sincere for flattery.

January 10, 1797

Priestley, whom I sin in almost adoring, speaks of "such a choice of company as tends to keep up that right bent and firmness of mind which a necessary intercourse with the world would otherwise warp and relax." "Such fellowship is the true balsam of life; its cement is infinitely more durable than that of the friendships of the world; and it looks for its proper fruit and complete gratification to the life beyond the grave." Is there a possible chance for such an one as I to realise in this world such friendships? Where am I to look for 'em? What testimonials shall I bring of my being worthy of such friendship? Alas! the great and good go together in separate herds, and leave such as I to lag far, far behind in all intellectual, and, far more grievous to say, in all moral accomplishments. Coleridge, I have not one truly elevated character among my acquaintance: not one Christian: not one but undervalues Christianity. Singly what am I to do? Wesley (have you read his life?) was *he* not an elevated character? Wesley has said, "Religion is not a solitary thing." Alas! it necessarily is so with me, or next to solitary. 'Tis true you write to me; but correspondence by letter, and personal intimacy, are very widely different. Do, do write to me, and do some good to my mind, already how much "warped and relaxed" by the world! 'Tis the conclusion of another evening. Good night. God have us all in his keeping!

If you are sufficiently at leisure, oblige me with an account of your plan of life at Stowey—your literary occupations and prospects; in short, make me acquainted with every circumstance which, as relating to you, can be interesting to me.... My letter is full of nothingness. I talk of nothing. But I must talk. I love to write to you. I take a pride in it. It makes me think less meanly of myself. It makes me think myself not totally disconnected from the better part of mankind. I know I am too dissatisfied with the beings around me; but I cannot help occasionally exclaiming, "Woe is me, that I am constrained to dwell with Meshech, and to have my habitation among the tents of Kedar!" I know I am noways better in practice than my neighbours, but I have a taste for religion, an occasional earnest aspiration after perfection, which they have not. I gain nothing by being with such as myself: we encourage one another in mediocrity. I am always longing to be with men more excellent than myself. All this must sound odd to you; but these are my predominant feelings when I sit down to write to you.

April 7, 1797

Your last letter was dated the 10th of February; in it you promised to write again the next day. At least, I did not expect so long, so unfriend-like a silence. There was a time, Col., when a remissness of this sort in a dear friend would have lain very heavy on my mind; but latterly I have been too familiar with neglect to feel much from the semblance of it. Yet, to suspect one's self overlooked, and in the way to oblivion, is a feeling rather humbling; perhaps, as tending to self-mortification, not unfavourable to the spiritual state. Still, as you meant to confer no benefit on the soul of your friend, you do not stand quite clear from the imputation of unkindliness (a word, by which I mean the diminutive of unkindness)....

Now, do answer this. Friendship, and acts of friendship, should be reciprocal, and free as the air. A friend should never be reduced to beg an alms of his fellow; yet I will beg an alms: I entreat you to write, and tell me all about poor Lloyd, and all of you. God love and preserve you all!

June 13, 1797

I stared with wild wonderment to see thy well-known hand again. It revived many a pleasing recollection of an epistolary intercourse, of late strangely suspended, once the pride of my life. Before I even opened thy letter I figured to myself a sort of complacency which my little hoard at home would feel at receiving the newcomer into the little drawer where I keep my treasures of this kind. You have done well in writing to me.

[Late in] July 1797

I am scarcely yet so reconciled to the loss of you, or so subsided into my wonted uniformity of feeling, as to sit calmly down to think of you and write to you. But I reason myself into the belief that those few and pleasant holidays shall not have been spent in vain. I feel improvement in the recollection of many a casual conversation. The names of Tom Poole, of Wordsworth and his good sister, with thine and Sara's, are become "familiar in my mouth as household words." You would make me very happy if you think W. has no objection, by transcribing for me that Inscription of his. I have some scattered sentences ever floating in my memory, teasing me that I cannot remember more of it. You may believe I will make no improper use of it. Believe me I can think now of many subjects on which I had planned gaining information from you; but I forgot my "treasure's worth" while I possessed it. Your leg is now become to me a matter of much more importance; and many a little thing, which when I was present with you seemed scarce to *indent* my notice, now presses painfully on my remembrance.... You will oblige me, too, by sending me my great-coat, which I left behind in the oblivious state the mind is thrown into at parting. Is it not ridiculous that I sometimes envy that great-coat lingering so cunningly behind! At present I have none: so send it to me.... But above all, *that Inscription!* It will recall to me the tones of all your voices, and with them many a remembered kindness to one who could and can repay you all only by the silence of a grateful heart. I could not talk much while I was with you; but my silence was not sullenness, nor I hope from any bad motive; but, in truth, disuse has made me awkward at it. I know I behaved myself, particularly at Tom Poole's and at Cruikshank's, most like a sulky child; but company and converse are strange to me. It was kind in you all to endure me as you did.

January 10, 1820

Dear Coleridge—A letter written in the blood of your poor friend would indeed be of a nature to startle you; but this is nought but harmless red ink, or, as the witty mercantile phrase hath it, clerk's blood. Hang 'em! my brain, skin, flesh, bone, carcase, soul, time is all theirs. The Royal Exchange, Gresham's Folly, hath me body and spirit. I admire some of Lloyd's lines on you, and I admire your postponing reading them. He is a sad tattler; but this is under the rose. Twenty years ago he estranged one friend from me quite, whom I have been regretting, but never could regain since. He almost alienated you also from me, or me from you, I don't know which; but that breach is closed. The "dreary sea" is filled up. He has lately been at work "telling again," as they call it, a most gratuitous piece of mischief, and has caused a coolness betwixt me and (not a friend exactly, but) an intimate acquaintance. I suspect also he saps Manning's faith in me, who am to Manning more than an acquaintance. Still I like his writing verses about you. Will your kind host and hostess give us a dinner next Sunday; and, better still, *not expect us* if the weather is very bad?

June 1, 1826

Dear Coleridge—If I know myself, nobody more detests the display of personal vanity, which is implied in the act of sitting for one's picture, than myself. But the fact is, that the likeness which accompanies this letter was stolen from my person at one of my unguarded moments by some too partial artist, and my friends are pleased to think that he has not much flattered me. Whatever its merits may be, you, who have so great an interest in the original, will have a satisfaction in tracing the features of one that has so long esteemed you. There are times when in a friend's absence these graphic representations of him almost seem to bring back the man himself. The painter, whoever he was, seems to have taken me in one of those disengaged moments, if I may so term them, when the native character is so much more honestly displayed than can be possible in the restraints of an enforced sitting attitude. Perhaps it rather describes me as a thinking man, than a man in the act of thought. Whatever its pretensions, I know it will be dear to you, towards whom I should wish my thoughts to flow in a sort of an undress rather than in the more studied graces of diction.

I am, dear Coleridge, yours sincerely,

C. Lamb

April 14, 1832

My dear Coleridge—Not an unkind thought has passed in my brain about you; but I have been wofully neglectful of you; so that I do not deserve to announce to you, that if I do not hear from you before then, I will set out on Wednesday morning to take you by the hand. I would do it this moment, but an unexpected visit might flurry you. I shall take silence for acquiescence, and come. I am glad you could write so long a letter. Old loves to, and hope of kind looks from, the Gillmans when I come.

Yours, *semper idem,*

C. L.

If you ever thought an offence, much more wrote it, against me, it must have been in the times of Noah, and the great waters swept it away. Mary's most kind love, and maybe a wrong prophet of your bodings!—here she is crying for mere love over your letter. I wring out less, but not sincerer showers.

My direction is simply, Enfield.

～～～～～

CHARLES LAMB WRITES AFTER THE DEATH OF COLERIDGE

(October 21, 1834)

When I heard of the death of Coleridge, it was without grief. It seemed to me that he long had been on the confines of the next world,— that he had a hunger for eternity. I grieved then that I could not grieve. But since, I feel how great he was of me. His great and dear spirit haunts me. I cannot think a thought, I cannot make a criticism on men or books, without an ineffectual turning and reference to him.... He was my fifty-years old friend without a dissension. Never saw I his likeness, nor probably the world can see again. I seem to love the house he died at more passionately than when he lived. I love the faithful Gillmans more than while they exercised their virtues towards him living. What was his mansion is consecrated to me a chapel.

～～～～～

"... the soul of Jonathan was knit with the soul of David ..."

DAVID AND JONATHAN

First Book of Samuel

And when Saul saw David go forth against the Philistine, he said unto Abner, the captain of the host, Abner, whose son is this youth? And Abner said, As thy soul liveth, O king, I cannot tell. And the king said, Inquire thou whose son the stripling is. And as David returned from the slaughter of the Philistine, Abner took him, and brought him before Saul with the head of the Philistine in his hand. And Saul said to him, Whose art thou, thou young man? And David answered, I am the son of thy servant Jesse the Bethlehemite. And it came to pass, when he had made an end of speaking unto Saul, that the soul of Jonathan was knit with the soul of David, and Jonathan loved him as his own soul. And Saul took him that day, and would let him go no more to his father's house. Then Jonathan and David made a covenant, because he loved him as his own soul. And Jonathan stripped himself of the robe that was upon him, and gave it to David, and his apparel, even to his sword, and to his bow, and to his girdle. And David went out whithersoever Saul sent him, and behaved himself wisely: and Saul set him over the men of war, and it was good in the sight of all the people, and also in the sight of Saul's servants.

And it came to pass as they came, when David returned from the slaughter of the Philistine, that the women came out of all the cities of Israel, singing and dancing, to meet king Saul, with timbrels, with joy, and with instruments of music. And the women sang one to another in their play, and said,

> Saul hath slain his thousands,
> And David his ten thousands.

And Saul was very wroth, and this saying displeased him; and he said, They have ascribed unto David ten thousands, and to me they have ascribed but thousands: and what can he have more but the kingdom? And Saul eyed David from that day and forward.

And it came to pass on the morrow, that an evil spirit from God came mightily upon Saul, and he prophesied in the midst of the house: and David played with his hand, as he did day by day: and Saul had his spear in his hand. And Saul cast the spear; for he said, I will smite David even to the wall. And David avoided out of his presence twice. And Saul was afraid of David, because the Lord was with him, and was departed from Saul. Therefore Saul removed him from him, and made him captain over a thousand; and he went out and came in before the people. And David behaved himself wisely in all his ways; and the Lord was with him. And when Saul saw that he behaved himself very wisely, he stood in awe of him. But all Israel and Judah loved David. . . .

And Saul gave him Michal his daughter to wife. And Saul saw and knew that the Lord was with David; and Michal Saul's daughter loved him. And Saul was yet the more afraid of David; and Saul was David's enemy continually. . . .

And Saul spake to Jonathan his son, and to all his servants, that they should slay David. But Jonathan Saul's son delighted much in David. And Jonathan told David, saying, Saul my father seeketh to slay thee: now therefore, I pray thee, take heed to thyself in the morning, and abide in a secret place, and hide thyself: and I will go out and stand beside my father in the field where thou art, and I will commune with my father of thee; and if I see aught, I will tell thee. And Jonathan spake good of David unto Saul his father, and said unto him,

Let not the king sin against his servant, against David: because he hath not sinned against thee, and because his works have been to thee-ward very good: for he put his life in his hand, and smote the Philistine, and the Lord wrought a great victory for all Israel: thou sawest it, and didst rejoice: wherefore then wilt thou sin against innocent blood, to slay David without a cause? And Saul harkened unto the voice of Jonathan: and Saul sware, As the Lord liveth, he shall not be put to death. And Jonathan called David, and Jonathan shewed him all those things. And Jonathan brought David to Saul, and he was in his presence, as beforetime.

And there was war again: and David went out, and fought with the Philistines, and slew them with a great slaughter; and they fled before him. And an evil spirit from the Lord was upon Saul, as he sat in his house with his spear in his hand; and David played with his hand. And Saul sought to smite David even to the wall with the spear; but he slipped away out of Saul's presence, and he smote the spear into the wall: and David fled, and escaped that night....

Now David fled, and escaped, and came to Samuel to Ramah, and told him all that Saul had done to him. And he and Samuel went and dwelt in Naioth. And it was told Saul, saying, Behold, David is at Naioth in Ramah. And Saul sent messengers to take David.... Then went he also to Ramah ... and he went thither to Naioth in Ramah....

And David fled from Naioth in Ramah, and came and said before Jonathan, What have I done? what is mine iniquity? and what is my sin before thy father, that he seeketh my life? And he said unto him, God forbid; thou shalt not die: behold, my father doeth nothing either great or small, but that he discloseth it unto me: and why should my father hide this thing from me? it is not so. And David sware moreover, and said, Thy father knoweth well that I have found grace in thine eyes; and he saith, Let not Jonathan know this, lest he be grieved: but truly as the Lord liveth, and as thy soul liveth, there is but a step between me and death. Then said Jonathan unto David, Whatsoever thy soul desireth, I will even do it for thee. And David said unto Jonathan, Behold, tomorrow is the new moon, and I should not fail to sit with the king at meat: but let me go, that I may hide myself in the field unto the third day at even. If thy father miss me at all, then say, David earnestly asked leave of me that he might run to Bethlehem his city: for it is the yearly sacrifice there for all the family. If he say thus, It is well; thy servant shall have peace: but if he be wroth, then know that evil is determined by him. Therefore deal kindly with thy servant; for thou hast brought thy servant into a covenant of the Lord with thee: but if there be in me iniquity, slay me thyself; for why shouldest thou bring me to thy father? And Jonathan said, Far be it from thee: for if I should at all know that evil were determined by my father to come upon thee, then would I not tell thee? Then said David to Jonathan, Who shall tell me if perchance thy father answer thee roughly? And Jonathan said unto David, Come and let us go out into the field. And they went out both of them into the field.

And Jonathan said unto David, The Lord, the God of Israel, be witness; when I have sounded my father about this time tomorrow, or the third day, behold, if there be good toward David, shall I not then send unto thee, and disclose it unto thee? The Lord do so to Jonathan, and more also, should it please my father to do thee evil, if I disclose it not unto thee, and send thee away, that thou mayest go in peace: and the Lord be with thee, as he hath been with my father. And thou shalt not only while yet I live shew me the kindness of the Lord, that I die not: but also thou shalt not cut off thy kindness from my house for ever: no, not when the Lord hath cut off the enemies of David every one from the face of the earth. So Jonathan made a covenant with the house of David, saying, And the Lord shall require it at the hands of David's enemies. And Jonathan then caused David to swear again, for the love that he had to him: for he loved him as he loved his own soul. Then Jonathan said until him, Tomorrow is the new moon: and thou shalt be missed, because thy seat will be empty. And when thou hast stayed three days, thou shalt go down quickly, and come to the place where thou didst hide thyself when the business was in hand, and shalt remain by the stone Ezel. And I will shoot three arrows to the side thereof, as though I shot at a mark. And, behold, I will send the lad, saying, Go, find the arrows. If I say unto the lad, Behold, the arrows are on this side of thee: take them, and come; for there is peace to thee and no hurt, as the Lord liveth. But if I say thus unto the boy, Behold, the arrows are beyond thee: go thy way; for the Lord hath sent thee away. And as touching the matter which thou and I have spoken of, behold, the Lord is between thee and me for ever.

So David hid himself in the field: and when the new moon was come, and the king sat him down to eat meat. And the king sat upon his seat, as at other times, even upon the seat by the wall; and Jonathan stood up, and Abner sat by Saul's side: but David's place was empty. Nevertheless Saul spake not any thing that day: for he thought, Something hath befallen him, he is not clean; surely he is not clean. And it came to pass on the morrow after the new moon, which was the second day, that David's place was empty: and Saul said unto Jonathan his son, Wherefore cometh not the son of Jesse to meat, neither yesterday, nor today? And Jonathan answered Saul, David earnestly asked leave of me to go to Bethlehem: and he said, Let me go, I pray thee; for our family hath a sacrifice in the city; and my brother, he hath commanded me to be there: and now, if I have found favor in thine eyes, let me get away, I pray thee, and see my brother. Therefore he is not come unto the king's table. Then Saul's anger was kindled against Jonathan, and he said unto him, Thou son of a perverse rebellious woman, do not I know that thou hast chosen the son of Jesse to thine own shame, and unto the shame of thy mother's nakedness? For as long as the son of Jesse liveth upon the ground, thou shalt not be stablished, nor thy kingdom. Wherefore now send and fetch him unto me, for he shall surely die. And Jonathan answered Saul his father, and said unto him, Wherefore should he be put to death? what hath he done? And Saul cast his spear at him to smite him: whereby Jonathan knew that it was determined of his father to put David to death. So Jonathan arose from the table in fierce anger, and did eat no meat the second day of the month: for he was grieved for David, because his father had done him shame.

And it came to pass in the morning, that Jonathan went out into the field at the time appointed with David, and a little lad with him. And he said unto his lad, Run, find now the arrows which I shoot. And as the lad ran, he shot an arrow beyond him. And when the lad was come to the place of the arrow which Jonathan had shot, Jonathan cried after the lad, and said, Is not the arrow beyond thee? And Jonathan cried after the lad, Make speed, haste, stay not. And Jonathan's lad gathered up the arrows, and came to his master. But the lad knew not any thing: only Jonathan and David knew the matter. And Jonathan gave his weapons unto his lad, and said unto him, Go carry them to the city. And as soon as the lad was gone, David arose out of a place toward the South, and fell on his face to the ground, and bowed himself three times: and they kissed one another, and wept one with another, until David exceeded. And Jonathan said to David, Go in peace, forasmuch as we have sworn both of us in the name of the Lord, saying, The Lord shall be between me and thee, and between my seed and thy seed, for ever. And he arose and departed: and Jonathan went into the city....

And David abode in the wilderness in the strong holds, and remained in the hill country in the wilderness of Ziph. And Saul sought him every day, but God delivered him not into his hands. And David saw that Saul was come out to seek his life: and David was in the wilderness of Ziph in the wood. And Jonathan Saul's son arose, and went to David into the wood, and strengthened his hand in God. And he said unto him, Fear not: for the hand of Saul my father shall not find thee; and thou shalt be king over Israel, and I shall be next unto thee; and that also Saul my father knoweth. And they two made a covenant before the Lord: and David abode in the wood, and Jonathan went to his house....

Now the Philistines fought against Israel: and the men of Israel fled from before the Philistines, and fell down slain in mount Gilboa. And the Philistines followed hard upon Saul and upon his sons; and the Philistines slew Jonathan, and Abinadab, and Malchishua, the sons of Saul.... Therefore Saul took his sword, and fell upon it. And when his armor-bearer saw that Saul was dead, he likewise fell upon his sword, and died with him....

Now there was long war between the house of Saul and the house of David: and David waxed stronger and stronger, but the house of Saul waxed weaker and weaker....

Then came all the tribes of Israel to David unto Hebron, and spake, saying, Behold, we are thy bone and thy flesh. In times past, when Saul was king over us, it was thou that leddest out and broughtest in Israel: and the Lord said to thee, Thou shalt feed my people Israel, and thou shalt be prince over Israel. So all the elders came to the king to Hebron; and king David made a covenant with them in Hebron before the Lord: and they anointed David king over Israel....

And David said, Is there yet any that is left of the house of Saul that I may shew him kindness for Jonathan's sake? And there was of the house of Saul a servant whose name was Ziba, and they called him unto David; and the king said unto him, Art thou Ziba? And he said, Thy servant is he. And the king said, Is there not yet any of the house of Saul, that I may shew the kindness of God unto him? And Ziba said unto the king, Jonathan hath yet a son, which is lame on his feet. And the king said unto him, Where is he? And Ziba said unto the king, Behold, he is in the house of Machir the son of Ammiel, from Lodebar. Then king David sent, and fetched him out of the house of Machir the son of Ammiel, from Lodebar. And Mephibosheth, the son of Jonathan, the son of Saul, came unto David, and fell on his face, and did obeisance. And David said, Mephibosheth. And he answered, Behold thy servant! And David said unto him, Fear not: for I will surely shew thee kindness for Jonathan thy father's sake, and will restore thee all the land of Saul thy father; and thou shalt eat bread at my table continually. And he did obeisance, and said, What is thy servant, that thou shouldest look upon such a dead dog as I am? Then the king called to Ziba, Saul's servant, and said unto him, All that pertained to Saul and to all his house have I given unto thy master's son. And thou shalt till the land for him, thou, and thy sons, and thy servants; and thou shalt bring in the fruits, that thy master's son may have bread to eat: but Mephibosheth thy master's son shall eat bread alway at my table. Now Ziba had fifteen sons and twenty servants. Then said Ziba unto the king, According to all that my lord the king commandeth his servant, so shall thy servant do. As for Mephibosheth, said the king, he shall eat at my table, as one of the king's sons. And Mephibosheth had a young son, whose name was Mica. And all that dwelt in the house of Ziba were servants unto Mephibosheth.

So Mephibosheth dwelt in Jerusalem: for he did eat continually at the king's table; and was lame on both his feet.

(Old Testament)

The love of friendship should be gratuitous. You ought not to have or to love a friend for what he will give you. If you love him for the reason that he will supply you with money or some other temporal favor, you love the gift rather than him. A friend should be loved freely for himself, and not for anything else.

—St. Augustine (*Translated by Rev. Hugh Talbot, O. Cist.*)

Ah, friend, let us be true
To one another! For the world which seems
To lie before us like a land of dreams,
So various, so beautiful, so new,
Hath really neither joy, nor love, nor light,
Nor certitude, nor peace, nor help for pain;
And we are here as on a darkling plain
Swept with confused alarms of struggle and flight,
Where ignorant armies clash by night.

—Matthew Arnold

"... I call friendship the most spiritual of the affections ..."

LEIGH HUNT RECALLS HIS MANY FRIENDS

(1791-1799)

If I had reaped no other benefit from Christ's Hospital, the school would be ever dear to me from the recollection of the friendships I formed in it, and of the first heavenly taste it gave me of that most spiritual of the affections. I used the word "heavenly" advisedly; and

I call friendship the most spiritual of the affections, because even one's kindred, in partaking of our flesh and blood, become, in a manner, mixed up with our entire being.... I loved my friend for his gentleness, his candor, his truth, his good repute, his freedom even from my own livelier manner, his calm and reasonable kindness. It was not any particular talent that attracted me to him, or anything striking whatsoever. I should say, in one word, it was his goodness. I doubt whether he ever had a conception of a tithe of the regard and respect I entertained for him; and I smile to think of the perplexity (though he never showed it) which he probably felt sometimes at my enthusiastic expressions; for I thought him a kind of angel.... With the other boys I played antics, and rioted in fantastic jests; but in his society, or whenever I thought of him, I fell into a kind of Sabbath state of bliss; and I am sure I could have died for him....

(1809)

Of James Smith, a fair, stout, fresh-colored man, with round features, I recollect little, except as he used to read to us trim verses, with rhymes as pat as butter.... Mr. Smith would sometimes repeat after dinner, with his brother Horace, an imaginary dialogue, stuffed full of incongruities, that made us roll with laughter....

His brother Horace was delicious.... A finer nature than Horace Smith's, except in the single instance of Shelley, I never met with in man; nor even in that instance, all circumstances considered, have I a right to say that those who knew him as intimately as I did the other, would not have had the same reasons to love him. Shelley himself had the highest regard for Horace Smith....

Horace Smith differed with Shelley on some points; but on others, which all the world agree to praise highly and practice very little, he agreed so entirely, and showed unequivocally that he did agree, that with the exception of one person (Vincent Novello), too diffident to gain such an honor from his friends, they were the only two men I had then met with, from whom I could have received and did receive advice or remonstrance with perfect comfort, because I could be sure of the unmixed motives and entire absence of self-reflection, with which it would come from them. Shelley said to me once, "I know not what Horace Smith must take me for sometimes; I am afraid he must think me a strange fellow; but is it not odd, that the only truly generous person I ever knew, who had money to be generous with, should be a stockbroker? And he writes poetry too," continued Shelley, his voice rising in a fervor of astonishment—"he writes poetry and pastoral dramas, and yet knows how to make money, and does make it, and is still generous!" Shelley had reason to like him. Horace Smith was one of the few men, who, through a cloud of detraction, and through all that difference of conduct from the rest of the world which naturally excites obloquy, discerned the greatness of my friend's character. Indeed, he became a witness to a very unequivocal proof of it, which I shall mention by and by. The mutual esteem was accordingly very great, and arose from circumstances most honorable to both parties. "I believe," said Shelley on another occasion, "that I have only to say to Horace Smith that I want a hundred pounds or two, and he would send it to me without any eye to its being returned; such faith has he that I have something within me beyond what the world supposes, and that I could only ask his money for a good purpose." And Shelley would have sent for it accordingly, if the person for whom it was intended had not said Nay. I will now mention the circumstance which first gave my friend a regard for Horace Smith. It concerns the person just mentioned, who is a man of letters. It came to Mr. Smith's knowledge, many years ago, that this person was suffering under a pecuniary trouble. He knew little of him at the time, but had met him occasionally; and he availed himself of this circumstance to write him a letter as full of delicacy and cordiality as it could hold, making it a matter of grace to accept a bank note of one hundred pounds, which he enclosed. I speak on the best authority, that of the obliged person himself; who adds that he not only did accept the money, but felt as light and happy under the obligation, as he had felt miserable under the very report of being obliged to some; and he says that nothing could induce him to withhold his name, but a reason which the generous, during his lifetime, would think becoming....

(1812)

There was an annual dinner of the Irish on Saint Patrick's Day, at which the Prince of Wales's name used to be the reigning and rapturous toast, as that of the greatest friend they possessed in the United Kingdom. He was held to be the jovial advocate of liberality in all things, and sponsor in particular for concession to Catholic claims. But the Prince of Wales, now become Prince Regent, had retained the Tory ministers of his father; he had broken life-long engagements; had violated his promises, particular as well as general, those to the Catholics among them; and led *in toto* a different political life from what had been expected. The name, therefore, which used to be hailed with rapture, was now, at the dinner in question, received with hisses.

An article appeared on the subject in the *Examiner* [which was owned and edited by Leigh Hunt and his brother]; the attorney-general's eye was swiftly upon the article and the result to the proprietors was two years' imprisonment, with a fine, to each, of five hundred pounds....

I entered prison the 3rd of February, 1813, and removed to my new apartments [two rooms in the prison infirmary, to which Hunt had been removed by order of the prison doctor, who was friendly to Hunt] the 16th of March, to get out of the noise of the chains. . . . A thousand recollections rise within me at every fresh period of my imprisonment, such as I cannot trust myself with dwelling upon.

These rooms, and the visits of my friends, were the bright side of my captivity. I read verses without end, and wrote almost as many. . . .

My friends were allowed to be with me till ten o'clock at night, when the under-turnkey, a young man with his lantern, and much ambitious gentility of deportment, came to see them out. I believe we scattered an urbanity about the prison, till then unknown. Even William Hazlitt, who there first did me the honor of a visit, would stand interchanging amenities at the threshold, which I had great difficulty in making him pass. I know not which kept his hat off with the greater pertinacity of deference, I to the diffident cutter-up of Tory dukes and kings, or he to the amazing prisoner and invalid who issued out of a bower of roses. There came my old friends and school fellows, Pitman, whose wit and animal spirits have still kept him alive; Mitchell, now no more, who translated Aristophanes; and Barnes, gone too, who always reminded me of Fielding. It was he that introduced me to the late Mr. Thomas Alsager, the kindest of neighbors, a man of business, who contrived to be a scholar and a musician. Alsager loved his leisure, and yet would start up at a moment's notice to do the least of a prisoner's bidding!

My now old friend, Cowden Clarke, with his ever young and wise heart, was good enough to be his own introducer, paving his way, like a proper visitor of prisons, with baskets of fruit.

The Lambs [Charles and Mary] came to comfort me in all weathers, hail or sunshine, in daylight and darkness, even in the dreadful frost and snow of the beginning of 1814. . . . Great disappointment and exceeding viciousness may talk as they please of the badness of human nature. For my part, I am now in my seventy-fourth year, and I have seen a good deal of the world, the dark side as well as the light, and I say that human nature is a very good and kindly thing, and capable of all sorts of virtues. Art thou not a refutation of all that can be said against it, excellent Sir John Swinburne: another friend whom I made in prison, and who subsequently cheered some of my greatest passes of adversity. Health, as well as sense and generosity, has blessed him; and he retains a young heart at the age of ninety-four.

To evils I have owed some of my greatest blessings. It was imprisonment that brought me acquainted with my friend of friends, Shelley. I had seen little of him before; but he wrote to me, making me a princely offer, which at that time I stood in no need of. . . .

To some other friends, near and dear, I may not even return thanks in this place for a thousand nameless attentions, which they make it a business of their existence to bestow on those they love. I might as soon thank my own heart. But one or two others, whom I have not seen for years, and who by some possibility (if indeed they ever think it worth their while to fancy anything on the subject) might suppose themselves forgotten, I may be suffered to remind of the pleasure they gave me. M. S. [Michael Slegg?], who afterwards saw us so often near London, has long, I hope, been enjoying the tranquillity he so richly deserved; and so, I trust, is C. S. [Caroline Scott?], whose face, or rather something like it (for it was not easy to match her own), I continually met with afterwards in the land of her ancestors. Her veil, and her baskets of flowers, used to come through the portal, like light. . . .

On the 3rd of February, 1815, I was free. It was thought that I should dart out of my cage like a bird, and feel no end in the delight of ranging. But, partly from ill-health, and partly from habit, the day of my liberation brought a good deal of pain with it. . . . It was very slowly that I recovered anything like a sensation of health. The bitterest evil I suffered was in consequence of having been confined so long in one spot. That habit stuck to me on my return home in a very extraordinary manner; and, I fear, some of my friends thought me ungrateful. . . .

This weakness I outlived; but I have never thoroughly recovered the shock given my constitution. My natural spirits, however, have always struggled hard to see me reasonably treated. Many things give me exquisite pleasure which seem to affect other men in a very minor degree; and I enjoyed, after all, such happy moments with my friends, even in prison, that in the midst of the beautiful climate which I afterwards visited, I was sometimes in doubt whether I would not rather have been in gaol than in Italy. . . .

(1815-1816)

As an instance of Shelley's extraordinary generosity, a friend of his, a man of letters, enjoyed from at that period a pension of a hundred a year, though he had but a thousand of his own; and he continued to enjoy it till fortune rendered it superfluous. But the princeliness of his disposition was seen most in his behavior to another friend, the writer of this memoir, who is proud to relate, that with money raised by an effort, Shelley once made him a present of fourteen hundred pounds, to extricate him from debt. I was not extricated, for I had not yet learned to be careful: but the shame of not being so, after such generosity, and the pain which my friend afterwards underwent when I was in trouble and he was helpless, were the first causes of my thinking of money matters to any purpose. His last sixpence was ever at my service, had I chosen to share it. In a poetical epistle written some years afterwards, and published in a volume of *Posthumous Poems,* Shelley, in

alluding to his friend's circumstances, which for the second time were
then straitened, only made an affectionate lamentation that he himself
was poor; never once hinting that he had already drained his purse
for his friend.

To return to Hampstead.—Shelley often came there to see me, sometimes to stop for several days....

I was returning home one night to Hampstead after the opera. As
I approached the door, I heard strange and alarming shrieks, mixed
with the voice of a man. The next day it was reported by the gossips
that Mr. Shelley, no Christian (for it was he who was there), had
brought some "very strange female" into the house, no better, of course,
than she ought to be. The real Christian had puzzled them. Shelley, in
coming to our house that night, had found a woman lying near the
top of the hill, in fits. It was a fierce winter night, with snow upon
the ground; and the winter loses nothing of its fierceness at Hampstead.
My friend, always the promptest as well as most pitying on these
occasions, knocked at the first houses he could reach, in order to have
the woman taken in. The invariable answer was, that they could not
do it. He asked for an outhouse to put her in, while he went for a
doctor. Impossible! In vain he assured them he was no impostor. They
would not dispute the point with him; but doors were closed, and
windows were shut down. Had he lit upon a worthy Mr. Park, the
philologist, that gentleman would assuredly have come, in spite of his
Calvinism. But he lived too far off. Had he lit upon my friend Armitage
Brown, who lived on another side of the Heath; or on his friend and
neighbor Dilke; they would either of them have jumped up from
amidst their books or their bed-clothes, and have gone out with him.
But the paucity of Christians is astonishing; considering the number
of them. Time flies; the poor woman is in convulsions; her son, a young
man, lamenting over her. At last my friend sees a carriage driving up
to a house at a little distance. The knock is given; the warm door
opens; servants and lights pour forth. Now, thought he, is the time. He
puts on his best address, which anybody might recognize for that of
the highest gentleman as well as of an interesting individual, and
plants himself in the way of an elderly person, who is stepping out of
the carriage with his family. He tells his story. They only press on the
faster. "Will you go and see her?" "No, sir; there's no necessity for that
sort of thing, depend on it. Impostors swarm everywhere; the thing
cannot be done; sir, your conduct is extraordinary." "Sir," cried Shelley,
assuming a very different manner, and forcing the flourishing house-
holder to stop out of astonishment, "I am sorry to say that *your* conduct
is *not* extraordinary; and if my own seems to amaze you, I will tell
you something which may amaze you a little more, and I hope I will
frighten you. It is such men as you who madden the spirits and the

patience of the poor and wretched; and if ever a convulsion comes in this country (which is very probably), recollect what I tell you:— you will have your house, that you refuse to put the miserable woman into, burnt over your head!" "God bless me, sir! Dear me, sir!" exclaimed the poor, frightened man, and fluttered into the mansion. The woman was then brought to our house, which was at some distance, and down a bleak path (it was in the Vale of Health); and Shelley and her son were obliged to hold her till the doctor could arrive. It appeared that she had been attending this son in London, on a criminal charge made against him, the agitation of which had thrown her into the fits on her return. The doctor said that she would have perished, had she laid there a short time longer. The next day my friend sent mother and son comfortably home to Hendon, where they were known, and whence they returned him thanks full of gratitude.

My friends are my estate. Forgive me then the avarice to hoard them. They tell me those who were poor early have different views of gold. I don't know how that is. God is not so wary as we, else He would give us no friends, lest we forget Him.

—EMILY DICKINSON

THE MEETING

Henry Wadsworth Longfellow

After so long an absence
    At last we meet again:
Does the meeting give us pleasure,
    Or does it give us pain?

The tree of life has been shaken,
    And but few of us linger now,
Like the Prophet's two or three berries
    In the top of the uppermost bough.

We cordially greet each other
    In the old, familiar tone;
And we think, though we do not say it,
    How old and gray he is grown!

We speak of a Merry Christmas
  And many a Happy New Year;
But each in his heart is thinking
  Of those that are not here.

We speak of friends and their fortunes,
  And of what they did and said,
Till the dead alone seem living,
  And the living alone seem dead.

And at last we hardly distinguish
  Between the ghosts and the guests;
And a mist and shadow of sadness
  Steals over our merriest jests.

Flowers are lovely; Love is flower-like;
Friendship is a sheltering tree;
O! the joys, that came down shower-like,
Of Friendship, Love, and Liberty.
                    —SAMUEL TAYLOR COLERIDGE

LYING AT A REVEREND FRIEND'S HOUSE ONE NIGHT

The author left the following verses in the
room where he slept

Robert Burns

O Thou dread Pow'r, who reign'st above,
  I know Thou wilt me hear:
When for this scene of peace and love,
  I make my pray'r sincere.

The hoary sire—the mortal stroke,
  Long, long, be pleas'd to spare,
To bless his little filial flock,
  And show what good men are.

She, who her lovely offspring eyes
With tender hopes and fears,
O, bless her with a mother's joys,
But spare a mother's tears!

Their hope, their stay, their darling youth,
In manhood's dawning blush;
Bless him, thou God of love and truth,
Up to a parent's wish.

The beauteous, seraph sister-band,
With earnest tears I pray,
Thou know'st the snares on ev'ry hand,
Guide Thou their steps alway.

When soon or late they reach that coast
O'er life's rough ocean driven,
May they rejoice, no wander'r lost,
A family in Heaven!

**". . . I loved the child because she was
my partner in wretchedness."**

TWO FORLORN FRIENDS OF THOMAS DE QUINCEY *

I continued for seven or eight weeks to live most parsimoniously in lodgings. These lodgings, though barely decent in my eyes, ran away with at least two-thirds of my remaining guineas. At length, whilst it was yet possible to reserve a solitary half-guinea towards the more urgent interest of finding daily food, I gave up my rooms, and stating exactly the circumstances in which I stood, requested permission of Mr. Brunell to make use of his large house as a nightly asylum from the open air. I was delighted when Mr. Brunell not only most readily assented to my request, but begged of me to come that very night, and turn the house to account as fully as I possibly could.

A more killing curse there does not exist for man or woman than that bitter combat between the weariness that prompts sleep and the keen,

* Abridged.

searching cold that forces you from the first access of sleep to start up horror-stricken, and to seek warmth vainly in renewed exercise, though long since fainting under fatigue. However, even without blankets, it was a fine thing to have an asylum from the open air, and to be assured of this asylum as long as I was likely to want it.

Towards nightfall I went down to Greek Street, and found, on taking possession of my new quarters, that the house already contained one single inmate—a poor, friendless child, apparently ten years old; but she seemed hunger-bitten; and sufferings of that sort often make children look older than they are. From this forlorn child I learned that she had slept and lived there alone for some time before I came; and great joy the poor creature expressed when she found that I was in future to be her companion through the hours of darkness. The house could hardly be called large—that is, it was not large on each separate storey; but, having four storeys in all, it was large enough to impress vividly the sense of its echoing loneliness; and from the want of furniture, the noise of the rats made a prodigious uproar on the staircase and hall; so that, amidst the real fleshly ills of cold and hunger, the forsaken child had found leisure to suffer still more from the self-created one of ghosts. Against these enemies I could promise her protection; human companionship was in itself protection; but of other and more needful aid I had, alas! little to offer. We lay upon the floor, with a bundle of law-papers for a pillow, but with no other covering than a large horseman's cloak; afterwards, however, we discovered in a garret an old sofa-cover, a small piece of rug, and some fragments of other articles, which added a little to our comfort. The poor child crept close to me for warmth, and for security against her ghostly enemies. When I was not more than usually ill, I took her into my arms, so that, in general, she was tolerably warm, and often slept when I could not; for, during the last two months of my sufferings I slept much in the day-time, and was apt to fall into transient dozings at all hours.

The poor child was never admitted into Mr. Brunell's study (if I may give that name to his chief depository of parchments, law writings, etc.); that room was to her the Bluebeard room of the house, being regularly locked on his departure to dinner, about six o'clock, which usually was his final departure for the day. Whether this child were an illegitimate daughter of Mr. Brunell, or only a servant, I could not ascertain; she herself did not know; but certainly she was treated altogether as a menial servant. No sooner did Mr. Brunell make his appearance than she went below-stairs, brushed his shoes, coat, etc.; and except when she was summoned to run upon some errand, she never emerged from the dismal Tartarus of the kitchen to the upper air until my welcome knock towards nightfall called up her little trembling footsteps to the front-door. Of her life during the daytime, however, I knew little but what I gathered from her own account at night; for, as soon as the hours of business commenced, I saw that my absence would be acceptable; and, in general, therefore, I went off and sat in the park or elsewhere until the approach of twilight.

Except the Bluebeard room, which the poor child believed permanently haunted, and which, besides, was locked, all others, from the attics to the cellars, were at our service. "The world was before us," and we pitched our tent for the night in any spot we might fancy.

This house I have described as roomy and respectable. It stands in a conspicuous situation, in a well-known part of London. I never fail to visit it when accident draws me to London. About ten o'clock this very night (August 15, 1821), being my birthday, I turned aside from my evening walk along Oxford Street, in order to take a glance at it. It is now in the occupation of some family, apparently respectable. The windows are no longer coated by a paste composed of ancient soot and superannuated rain; and the whole exterior no longer wears an aspect of gloom. By the lights in the front drawing-room, I observed a domestic party, assembled, perhaps at tea, and apparently cheerful and gay— marvellous contrast, in my eyes, to the darkness, cold, silence and desolation, of that same house nineteen years ago, when its nightly occupants were one famished scholar and a poor neglected child. Her, by the bye, in after years, I vainly endeavored to trace. Apart from her situation, she was not what would be called an interesting child. She was neither pretty, nor quick in understanding, nor remarkably pleasing in manners. But, thank God! even in those years I needed not the embellishments of elegant accessories to conciliate my affections. Plain human nature, in its humblest and most homely apparel, was enough for me; and I loved the child because she was my partner in wretchedness. If she is now living, she is probably a mother, with children of her own; but, as I have said, I could never trace her.

This I regret; but another person there was, at that time, whom I have since sought to trace with far deeper earnestness, and with far deeper sorrow at my failure. This person was a young woman, and one of that unhappy class who belongs to the outcasts and pariahs of our female population. I feel no shame, nor have any reason to feel it, in avowing that I was then on familiar and friendly terms with many women in that unfortunate condition. A penniless schoolboy could not be supposed to stand within the range of such temptations. These unhappy women, to me, were simply sisters in calamity; and sisters amongst whom, in as large measure as amongst any other equal number of persons commanding more of the world's respect, were to be found humanity, disinterested generosity, courage that would not falter in defense of the helpless, and fidelity that would have scorned to take bribes for betraying. Being myself, at that time, a peripatetic, or a walker of the streets, I naturally fell in more or less frequently with those female peripatetics who are technically called street walkers. Some of these women had occasionally taken my part against watchmen who wished to drive me off the steps of houses where I was sitting; others had protected me against more serious aggressions. But amongst them— the one on whose account I have at all introduced this subject—yet no! let me not class thee, O noble-minded Ann—with that order of women; let me find, if it be possible, some gentler name to designate the condition of her to whose bounty and compassion—ministering to my necessities when all the world stood aloof from me—I owe it to that at this time I am alive. For many weeks I had walked, at nights, with this poor friendless girl up and down Oxford Street, or had rested with her on steps and under the shelter of porticos.

She could not be so old as myself: she told me, indeed, that she had not completed her sixteenth year. By such questions as my interest about her prompted, I had gradually drawn forth her simple history. Hers was a case of ordinary occurrence (as I have since had reason to think), and one in which, in London beneficence had better adapted its arrangements to meet it, the power of the law might oftener be interposed to protect and to avenge. I saw that part of her injuries might have been redressed; and I urged her often and earnestly to lay her complaint before a magistrate and amply avenge her on the brutal ruffian who had plundered her little property. She promised me often that she would; but she delayed taking the steps I pointed out, from time to time; for she was timid and dejected to a degree which showed how deeply sorrow had taken hold of her young heart. Something, however, would perhaps have been done; for it had been settled between us at length (but, unhappily, on the very last time but one that I was ever to see her) that in a day or two I, accompanied by her, should state her case to a magistrate. This little service it was destined, however, that I should never realize.

Meantime, that which she rendered to me, and which was greater than I could ever have repaid her, was this: One night when we were pacing slowly along Oxford Street, and after a day when I had felt unusually ill and faint, I requested her to turn off with me into Soho Square. Thither we went; and we sat down on the steps of a house. Suddenly, as we sat, I grew much worse. I had been leaning my head against her bosom, and all at once I sank from her arms, and fell backwards on the steps. From the sensations I then had, I felt an inner conviction of the liveliest kind that, without some powerful and reviving stimulus, I should either have died on the spot, or should, at least, have sunk to a point of exhaustion from which all re-ascent, under my friendless circumstances, would soon have become hopeless. Then it was, at this crisis of my fate, that my poor orphan companion, who had herself met with little but injuries in this world, stretched out a saving hand to me. Uttering a cry of terror, but without a moment's delay, she ran off into Oxford Street, and, in less time than could be imagined, returned to me with a glass of port-wine and spices, that acted upon my empty stomach (which at that time would have rejected all solid food) with an instantaneous power of restoration; and for this glass the generous girl, without a murmur, paid out of her own humble purse, at a time, be it remembered, when she had scarcely wherewithal to purchase the bare necessaries of life, and when she could have no reason to expect that I should ever be able to reimburse her. O youthful benefactress! how often in succeeding years, standing in solitary places, and thinking of thee with grief of heart and perfect love—how often have I wished that, as in ancient times the curse of a father was believed to have supernatural power, and to pursue its object with a fatal necessity of self-fulfilment, even so the benediction of a heart oppressed with gratitude might have a like prerogative.

Often when I walk, at this time, in Oxford Street by dreamy lamplight, and hear those airs played on a common street-organ which years ago solaced me and my dear youthful companion, I shed tears, and muse with myself at the mysterious dispensation which so suddenly and so critically separated us for ever. How it happened, the reader will understand from what remains of this introductory narration.

Soon after the period of the last incident I have recorded, I met in Albemarle Street a gentleman of his late Majesty's household. This gentleman had received hospitalities, on different occasions, from my family, and he challenged me upon the strength of my family likeness. I did not attempt any disguise, but answered his questions ingenuously; and on his pledging his word of honor that he would not betray me to my guardians, I gave him my real address in Greek Street. The next day I received from him a ten-pound bank-note.

It never occurred to me to think of literary labors as a source of profit. No mode sufficiently speedy of obtaining money had ever suggested itself but that of borrowing on the strength of my future claims and expectations. This mode I sought by every avenue to compass; and amongst other persons I applied to a Jew named Dell.

To this Jew, and to other advertising money-lenders, I had introduced myself, with an account of my expectations; which account they had little difficulty in ascertaining to be correct. But one question still remained, which the faces of the Jews pretty significantly suggested— was I that person? This doubt had never occurred to me as a possible one. To satisfy their scruples, I took the only course in my power. Whilst I was in Wales, I had received various letters from young friends; these I produced, for I carried them constantly in my pocket. Most of these letters were from the Earl of Altamont, who was at that time, and had been for some years back, amongst my confidential friends. These were dated from Eton. I had also some from the Marquis of Sligo, his father.

On reading the letters, one of my Jewish friends agreed to furnish two or three hundred pounds on my personal security, provided I could persuade the young earl—who was, by the way, not older than myself—to guarantee the payment on our joint coming of age. In pursuance of this proposal on the part of the Jew, about eight or nine days after I had received the ten pounds, I prepared to visit Eton.

These arrangements made, soon after six o'clock, on a dark winter evening, I set off, accompanied by Ann, until we came into Golden Square. There, near the corner of Sherrard Street, we sat down, not wishing to part in the tumult and blaze of Piccadilly. I had told Ann of my plans some time before, and now I assured her again that she should share in my good fortune, if I met with any, and that I would never forsake her, as soon as I had power to protect her.

I had apparently most reason for dejection, because I was leaving the savior of my life; yet I, considering the shock my health had received, was cheerful and full of hope. She, on the contrary, who was parting with one who had little means of serving her, except by kindness and brotherly treatment, was overcome by sorrow, so that, when I kissed her at our final farewell, she put her arms about my neck, and wept, without speaking a word. I hoped to return in a week, at furthest, and I agreed with her that, on the fifth night from that, and every night afterwards, she should wait for me, at six o'clock, near the bottom of Great Titchfield Street; which had formerly been our customary haven of rendezvous, to prevent our missing each other in the great Mediterranean of Oxford Street. This, and other measures of precaution, I took; one, only, I forgot. She had either never told me, or (as a matter of no great interest) I had forgotten, her surname.

I returned to London in a Windsor coach three days after I quitted it. And now I come to the end of my story. What had become of Ann? Where was she? According to our agreement, I sought her daily, and waited for her every night, so long as I stayed in London, at the corner of Titchfield Street; and during the last days of my stay in London I put into activity every means of tracing her that my knowledge of London suggested, and the limited extent of my power made possible. The street where she lodged I knew, but not the house; and I remembered, at last, some account which she had given of ill-treatment from her landlord, which made it probable that she had quitted those lodgings before we parted. She had few acquaintance; most people, besides, thought that earnestness of my inquiries arose from motives which moved their laughter or their slight regard. On the day I left London I put into the hands of the only person who

(I was sure) must know Ann by sight, from having been in company with us once or twice, an address to the priory. Always in vain. To this hour I have never heard a syllable about her. This, amongst such troubles as most men meet in this life, has been my heaviest in affliction. If she lived, doubtless we must have been sometime in search of each other, at the very same moment, through the mighty labyrinths of London; perhaps even within a few feet of each other—a barrier no wider, in a London street, often amounting in the end to a separation for eternity!

> That friendship which from withered love does shoot,
> Like the faint herbage on a rock, wants root;
> Love is a tender amity, refined;
> Grafted on friendship, it exalts the mind;
> But when the graft no longer does remain,
> The dull stock lives, but never bears again.
>
> —John Dryden

"... let your letters spread themselves over many pages."

SYMMACHUS TO AGORIUS, UPON THE LATTER'S RECOVERY FROM AN ILLNESS

I am delighted that you are better, for my dearest wish is to see you well. Now if, by the will of the gods, returning strength has restored you to mental effort, let your letters spread themselves over many pages. I hate stinginess in writing. Brevity in a correspondent is more elegant than friendly. I don't want letters that trickle drop by drop from a narrow-necked bottle; what I want is a torrent that cannot be damned, that flows from the deepest springs of the heart. Laconic brevity, you know, used to be admired. With you, however, I had rather follow the Latin, or if you prefer, the Attic habit, in which there was so much glory in eloquence that I suspect the Laconians chose the opposite direction from fear of comparisons. I adore loquacity, but you have to be goaded. At the same time, I must be careful not to offend you by writing too much. So I will restrain my own disposition, in order to indulge yours. By which you must understand that you have reached such a height of importance and prestige, as to impose brevity on me unless you yourself write at great length. Farewell.

(Translated by Dorothy Brooke)

⟞⟞⟞⟞⟞⟞⟞

"The laws of friendship are great, austere, and eternal . . ."

FRIENDSHIP
Ralph Waldo Emerson

We have a great deal more kindness than is ever spoken. Maugre all the selfishness that chills like east winds the world, the whole human family is bathed with an element of love like a fine ether. How many persons we meet in houses, whom we scarcely speak to, whom yet we honor, and who honor us! How many we see in the street, or sit with in church, whom, though silently, we warmly rejoice to be with! Read the language of these wandering eyebeams. The heart knoweth.

The effect of the indulgence of this human affection is a certain cordial exhilaration. In poetry and in common speech, the emotions of benevolence and complacency which are felt toward others, are likened to the material effects of fire; so swift, or much more swift, more active, more cheering are these fine inward irradiations. From the highest degree of passionate love, to the lowest degree of good will, they make the sweetness of life.

Our intellectual and active powers increase with our affection. The scholar sits down to write, and all his years of meditation do not furnish him with one good thought or happy expression; but it is necessary to write a letter to a friend,—and, forthwith, troops of gentle thoughts invest themselves, on every hand, with chosen words....

Pleasant are these jets of affection which relume a young world for me again. Delicious is a just and firm encounter of two, in a thought, in a feeling. How beautiful, on their approach to this beating heart, the steps and forms of the gifted and the true! The moment we indulge our affections, the earth is metamorphosed: there is no winter, and no night; all tragedies, all ennuis vanish;—all duties even; nothing fills the proceeding eternity but the forms all radiant of beloved persons. Let the soul be assured that somewhere in the universe it should rejoin its friend, and it would be content and cheerful alone for a thousand years.

I awoke this morning with devout thanksgiving for my friends, the old and the new. Shall I not call God, the Beautiful, who daily showeth himself so to me in his gifts? I chide society, I embrace solitude, and yet I am not so ungrateful as not to see the wise, the lovely, and the noble-minded, as from time to time they pass my gate. Who hears me, who understands me becomes mine,—a possession for all time. Nor is nature so poor but she gives me this joy several times, and thus we weave social threads of our own, a new web of relations; and, as many thoughts in succession substantiate themselves, we shall by-and-by stand in a new world of our own creation, and no longer strangers and pilgrims in a traditionary globe. My friends have come to me unsought. The great God gave them to me. By oldest right, by the divine affinity of virtue with itself I find them, or rather, not I, but the Deity in me and in them, both deride and cancel the thick walls of individual character, age, sex and circumstance, at which he usually connives, and now makes many one. High thanks I owe you, excellent lovers, who carry out the world for me to new and noble depths, and enlarge the meaning of all my thoughts. These are not stark and stiffened persons, but the newborn poetry of God,— poetry without stop,—hymn, ode, and epic, poetry still flowing, and not yet caked in dead books with annotation and grammar, but Apollo and the Muses chanting still....

I confess to an extreme tenderness of nature on this point. It is almost dangerous to me to "crush the sweet poison of misused wine" of the affections. A new person is to me always a great event, and hinders me from sleep. I have had such fine fancies lately about two or three persons, as have given me delicious hours; but the joy ends in the day: it yields no fruit. Thought is not born of it; my action is very little modified. I must feel pride in my friend's accomplishments as if they were mine,—wild, delicate, throbbing property in his virtues. I feel as warmly when he is praised, as the lover when he hears applause of his engaged maiden. We overestimate the conscience of our friend. His goodness seems better than our goodness, his nature finer, his temptations less. Everything that is his, his name, his form, his dress, books, and instruments, fancy enhances. Our own thought sounds new and larger from his mouth.

Yet the systole and diastole of the heart are not without their analogy in the ebb and flow of love. Friendship, like the immortality of the soul, is too good to be believed. The lover, beholding his maiden, half knows that she is not verily that which he worships; and in the golden hour of friendship we are surprised with shades of suspicion and unbelief. We doubt that we bestow on our hero the virtues in which he shines, and afterward worship the form to which we have ascribed this divine inhabitation. In strictness, the soul does not respect men as it respects itself. In strict science, all persons underlie the same condition of an infinite remoteness. Shall we fear to cool our love by facing the fact, by mining for the metaphysical foundation of this Elysian temple? Shall I not be as real as the things I see? If I am, I shall not fear to know them for what they are. Their essence is not less beautiful than their appearance, though it needs finer organs for its apprehension. ... Is it not that the soul puts forth friends, as the tree puts forth leaves, and presently, by the germination of new buds, extrudes the old leaf? The law of nature is alternation forevermore. Each electrical state superinduces the opposite. The soul environs itself with friends, that it may enter into a grander self-acquaintance or solitude; and it goes alone, for a season, that it may exalt its conversation or society. This method betrays itself along the whole history of our personal relations. Ever the instinct of affection revives the hope of union with our mates, and ever the returning sense of insulation recalls us from the chase. Thus every man passes his life in the search after friendship, and if he should record his true sentiment, he might write a letter like this, to each new candidate for his love.

Dear Friend:—

If I was sure of thee, sure of thy capacity, sure to match my mood with thine, I should never think again of trifles, in relation to thy comings and goings. I am not very wise: my moods are quite attainable: and I respect thy genius: it is to me as yet unfathomed; yet dare I not presume in thee a perfect intelligence of me, and so thou art to me a delicious torment. Thine ever, or never.

Yet these uneasy pleasures and fine pains are for curiosity, and not for life. They are not to be indulged. This is to weave cobweb, and not cloth. Our friendships hurry to short and poor conclusions, because we have made them a texture of wines and dreams, instead of the tough fibre of the human heart. The laws of friendship are great, austere, and eternal, of one web with the laws of nature and of morals. But we have aimed at a swift and petty benefit, to suck a sudden sweetness. We snatch at the slowest fruit in the whole garden of God, which many summers and many winters must ripen. We seek our friend not sacredly, but with an adulterate passion which would appropriate him to ourselves. In vain. We are armed all over with subtle antagonisms, which as soon as we meet, begin to play, and translate all poetry into stale prose. Almost all people descend to meet. All association must be a compromise, and, what is worst, the very flower and aroma of the flower of each of the beautiful natures disappears as they approach each other. What a perpetual disappointment is actual society, even of the virtuous and gifted! ...

I ought to be equal to every relation. It makes no difference how many friends I have, and what content I can find in conversing with each, if there be one to whom I am not equal. If I have shrunk unequal from one contest, instantly the joy I find in all the rest becomes mean and cowardly. I should hate myself, if then I made my other friends my asylum....

Love, which is the essence of God, is not for levity, but for the total worth of man. Let us not have this childish luxury in our regards; but the austerest worth; let us approach our friend with an audacious trust in the truth of his heart, in the breadth impossible to be over-turned, of his foundations.

The attractions of this subject are not to be resisted, and I leave, for the time, all account of subordinate social benefit, to speak of that select and sacred relation which is a kind of absolute, and which even leaves the language of love suspicious and common, so much is this purer, and nothing is so much divine.

I do not wish to treat friendships daintily, but with roughest courage. When they are real, they are not glass threads or frost-work, but the solidest thing we know. For now, after so many ages of experience, what do we know of nature, or of ourselves? Not one step has man taken toward the solution of the problem of his destiny. In one condemnation of folly stand the whole universe of men. But the sweet sincerity of joy and peace, which I draw from this alliance with my brother's soul, is the nut itself whereof all nature and all thought is but the husk and shell. Happy is the house that shelters a friend! It might well be built, like a festal bower or arch, to entertain him a single day. Happier, if he know the solemnity of that relation, and honor its law! It is no idle band, no holiday engagement. He who offers himself as a candidate for that covenant comes up, like an Olympian, to the great games, where the first-born of the world are the compet-itors. He proposes himself for contests where Time, Want, Danger are in the lists, and he alone is victor who has truth enough in his constitution to preserve the delicacy of his beauty from the wear and tear of all these. The gifts of fortune may be present or absent, but all the hap in that contest depends on intrinsic nobleness, and the con-tempt of trifles. There are two elements that go to the composition of friendship, each so sovereign that I can detect no superiority in either, no reason why either should be first named. One is Truth. A friend is a person with whom I may be sincere. Before him, I may think aloud. I am arrived at last in the presence of a man so real and equal that I may drop even those undermost garments of dissimulation, courtesy, and second thought, which men never put off, and may deal with him with the simplicity and wholeness with which one chemical atom meets another. Sincerity is the luxury allowed, like diadems and authority, only to the highest rank, *that* being permitted to speak truth, as having none above it to court or conform unto. Every man alone is sincere. At the entrance of a second person, hypocrisy begins. We parry and fend the approach of our fellowman by compliments, by gossip, by amusements, by affairs. We cover up our thought from him under a hundred folds. I knew a man who, under a certain religious frenzy, cast off this drapery, and omitting all compliment and commonplace, spoke to the conscience of every person he encountered, and that with great insight and beauty. At first he was resisted, and all men agreed he was mad. But persisting, as indeed he could not help doing, for some time in this course, he attained to the advantage of bringing every man of his acquaintance into true relations with him. No man would think of speaking falsely with him, or of putting him off with any chat of markets or reading-rooms. But every man was constrained by so much sincerity to face him, and what love of nature, what poetry, what symbol of truth he had, he did certainly show him. But to most of us society shows not its face and eye, but its side and its back. To stand in true relations with men in a false age is worth a fit of insanity, is it not? We can seldom go erect. Almost every man we meet requires some civility, requires to be humored;—he has some fame, some talent, some whim of religion or philanthropy in his head that is not to be questioned, and so spoils all conversation with him. But a friend is a sane man who exercises not my ingenuity but me. My friend gives me entertainment without requiring me to stoop, or to lisp, or to mask myself. A friend, therefore, is a sort of paradox in nature. I who alone am, I who see nothing in nature whose existence I can affirm with equal evidence to my own, behold now the semblance of my being in all its height, variety and curiosity, reiterated, in a foreign form; so that a friend may well be reckoned the masterpiece of nature.

The other element of friendship is Tenderness. We are holden to men by every sort of tie, by blood, by pride, by fear, by hope, by lucre, by lust, by hate, by admiration, by every circumstance and badge and trifle, but we can scarce believe that so much character can subsist in another as to draw us by love. Can another be so blessed, and we so pure, that we can offer him tenderness? When a man becomes dear to me, I have touched the goal of fortune. I find very little written directly to the heart of this matter in books. And yet I have one text which I cannot choose but remember. My author says, "I offer myself faintly and bluntly to those whose I effectually am, and tender myself least to him to whom I am the most devoted." I wish that friendship should have feet, as well as eyes and eloquence. It must plant itself on the ground, before it walks over the moon. I wish it to be a little of a citizen, before it is quite a cherub. . . .

I hate the prostitution of the name of friendship to signify modish and worldly alliances. I much prefer the company of plough-boys and tin-peddlers to the silken and perfumed amity which only celebrates its days of encounter by a frivolous display, by rides in a curricle, and dinners at the best taverns. The end of friendship is a commerce the most strict and homely that can be joined; more strict than any of which we have experience. It is for aid and comfort through all the relations and passages of life and death. It is fit for serene days, and graceful gifts, and country rambles, but also for rough roads and hard fare, shipwreck, poverty, and persecution. It keeps company with the sallies of the wit and the trances of religion. We are to dignify to each other the daily needs and offices of man's life, and embellish it by courage, wisdom and unity. It should never fall into something usual and settled, but should be alert and inventive, and add rhyme and reason to what was drudgery.

For perfect friendship it may be said to require natures so rare and costly, so well-tempered each, and so happily adapted, and withal so circumstanced, (for even in that particular, a poet says, love demands that the parties be altogether paired) that very seldom can its satisfaction be realized. It cannot subsist in its perfection, say some of those who are learned in this warm lore of the heart, betwixt more than two. I am not quite so strict in my terms, perhaps because I have never known so high a fellowship as others. I please my imagination more with a circle of god-like men and women variously related to each other, and between whom subsists a lofty intelligence. But I find this law of *one to one* peremptory for conversation, which is the practice and consummation of friendship. Do not mix waters too much. The best mix as ill as good and bad. You shall have very useful and cheering discourse at several times with two several men, but let all three of you come together, and you shall not have one new and hearty word. Two may talk and one may hear, but three cannot take part in a conversation of the most sincere and searching sort. In good company there is never such discourse between two, across the table, as takes place when you leave them alone. In good company, the individuals at once merge their egotism into a social soul exactly co-extensive with the several consciousnesses there present. No partialities of friend to friend, no fondness of brother to sister, of wife to husband, are there pertinent, but quite otherwise. Only he may then speak who can sail on the common thought of the party, and not poorly limited to his own. Now this convention, which good sense demands, destroys the high freedom of great conversation, which requires an absolute running of two souls into one.

No two men but being left alone with each other, enter into simpler relations. Yet it is affinity that determines *which* two shall converse. Unrelated men give little joy to each other; will never suspect the latent powers of each....

Friendship requires that rare mean betwixt likeness and unlikeness, that piques each with the presence of power and of consent in the other party. Let me be alone to the end of the world, rather than that my friend should overstep by a word or a look his real sympathy. I am equally baulked by antagonism and by compliance. Let him not cease an instant to be himself. The only joy I have in his being mine, is that the not mine is mine. It turns the stomach, it blots the daylight; where I looked for a manly furtherance, or at least a manly resistance, to find a mush of concession. Better be a nettle in the side of your friend than his echo. The condition which high friendship demands is ability to do without it. To be capable of that high office, requires great and sublime parts. There must be very two, before there can be very one. Let it be an alliance of two large formidable natures, mutually beheld, mutually feared, before yet they recognize the deep identity which beneath these disparities unites them.

He only is fit for this society who is magnanimous. He must be so, to know its law. He must be one who is sure that greatness and goodness are always economy. He must be one who is not swift to intermeddle with his fortunes. Let him not dare to intermeddle with his. Leave to the diamond its ages to grow, nor expect to accelerate the births of the eternal. Friendship demands a religious treatment. We must not be wilful, we must not provide. We talk of choosing our friends, but friends are self-elected. Reverence is a great part of it. Treat your friend as a spectacle. Of course, if he be a man, he has merits that are not yours, and that you cannot honor, if you must needs hold him close to your person. Stand aside. Give those merits room. Let them mount and expand....

Let us buy our entrance to this guild by a long probation. Why should we desecrate noble and beautiful souls by intruding on them? Why insist on rash personal relations with your friend? Why go to his house, or know his mother and brother and sisters? Why be visited by him at your own? Are these things material to our covenant? Leave this touching and clawing. Let him be to me a spirit. A message, a thought, a sincerity, a glance from him, I want, but not news, nor pottage. I can get politics, and chat, and neighborly conveniences, from cheaper companions. Should not the society of my friend be to me poetic, pure, universal, and great as nature itself? ... To my friend I write a letter, and from him I receive a letter. That seems to you a little. Me it suffices. It is a spiritual gift worthy of him to give and of me to receive. It profanes nobody. In these warm lines the heart will trust itself, as it will not to the tongue, and pour out the prophecy of a godlier existence than all the annals of heroism have yet made good....

What is so great as friendship let us carry with what grandeur of spirit we can. Let us be silent,—so we may hear the whisper of the gods. Let us not interfere. Who set you to cast about what you should say to the select souls, or to say anything to such? No matter how ingenious, no matter how graceful and bland. There are innumerable degrees of folly and wisdom, and for you to say aught is to be frivolous. Wait, and thy soul shall speak. Wait until the necessary and everlasting overpowers you, until day and night avail themselves of your lips. The only money of God is God. He pays never with anything less or anything else. The only reward of virtue, is virtue; the only way to have a friend, is to be one. Vain to hope to come nearer a man by getting into his house. If unlike, his soul only flees the faster from you, and you shall catch never a true glance of his eye....

The higher the style we demand of friendship, of course the less easy to establish it with flesh and blood. We walk alone in the world. Friends, such as we desire, are dreams and fables. But a sublime hope cheers ever the faithful heart, that elsewhere, in other regions of the universal power, souls are now acting, enduring, and daring, which can love us, and which we can love. We may congratulate ourselves that the period of nonage, of follies, of blunders, and of shame, is passed in solitude, and when we are finished men we shall grasp heroic hands in heroic hands. Only be admonished by what you already see, not to strike leagues of friendship with cheap persons, where no friendship can be. Or impatience betrays us into rash and foolish alliances which no God attends. By persisting in your path, though you forfeit the little, you gain the great. You become pronounced. You demonstrate yourself, so as to put yourself out of the reach of false relations, and you draw to you the first-born of the world,—those rare pilgrims whereof only one or two wander in nature at once, and before whom the vulgar great, show as spectres and shadows merely....

I do then with my friends as I do with my books. I would have them where I can find them, but I seldom use them. We must have society on our own terms, and admit or exclude it on the slightest cause. I cannot afford to speak much with my friend. If he is great, he makes me so great that I cannot descend to converse. In the great days, presentiments hover before me, far before me in the firmament. I ought then to dedicate myself to them. I go in that I may seize them, I go out that I may seize them. I fear only that I may lose them receding into the sky in which now they are only a patch of brighter light. Then, though I prize my friends, I cannot afford to talk with them and study their visions, lest I lose my own. It would indeed give me a certain household joy to quit this lofty seeking, this spiritual astronomy, or search of stars, and come down to warm sympathies with you; but then I know well I shall mourn always the vanishing of my mighty gods. It is true, next week I shall have languid times, when I can well afford to occupy myself with foreign objects; then I shall regret the lost literature of your mind, and wish you were by my side again. But if you come, perhaps you will fill my mind only with new visions, not with yourself but with your lustres, and I shall not be able any more than now to converse with you. So I will owe to my friends this evanescent intercourse. I will receive from them not what they have, but what they are. They shall give me that which properly they cannot give me, but which radiates from them. But they shall not hold me by any relations less subtle and pure. We will meet as though we met not, and part as though we parted not.

It has seemed to me lately more possible than I knew, to carry a friendship greatly, on one side, without due correspondence on the other. Why should I cumber myself with the poor fact that the receiver is not capacious? It never troubles the sun that some of his rays fall wide and vain into ungrateful space, and only a small part on the reflecting planet. Let your greatness educate the crude and cold companion. If he is unequal, he will presently pass away, but thou art enlarged by thy own shining.

Don't flatter yourselves that friendship authorizes you to say disagreeable things to your intimates. On the contrary, the nearer you come into a relation with a person, the more necessary do tact and courtesy become. Except in cases of necessity, which are rare, leave your friend to learn unpleasant truths from his enemies; they are ready enough to tell them.

—OLIVER WENDELL HOLMES

THE HOUSE BY THE SIDE OF THE ROAD

Sam Walter Foss

He was a friend to man, and lived in a house by the side of the road.
—Homer

There are hermit souls that live withdrawn
In the peace of their self-content;
There are souls, like stars, that dwell apart,
In a fellowless firmament;

There are pioneer souls that blaze their paths
    Where highways never ran;
But let me live by the side of the road
    And be a friend to man.

Let me live in a house by the side of the road,
    Where the race of men go by—
The men who are good and the men who are bad,
    As good and as bad as I;
I would not sit in the scorner's seat,
    Or hurl the cynic's ban;
Let me live in a house by the side of the road
    And be a friend to man.

I see from my house by the side of the road,
    By the side of the highway of life,
The men who press with the ardor of hope,
    The men who are faint with the strife.
But I turn not away from their smiles nor their tears—
    Both parts of an infinite plan;
Let me live in my house by the side of the road
    And be a friend to man.

I know there are brook-gladdened meadows ahead,
    And mountains of wearisome height,
That the road passes on through the long afternoon
    And stretches away to the night.
But still I rejoice when the travelers rejoice,
    And weep with the strangers that moan,
Nor live in my house by the side of the road
    Like a man who dwells alone.

Let me live in my house by the side of the road
    Where the race of men go by—
They are good, they are bad, they are weak, they are strong,
    Wise, foolish,—so am I.
Then why should I sit in the scorner's seat
    Or hurl the cynic's ban?
Let me live in my house by the side of the road
    And be a friend to man.

"... love one another."

THE COMMANDMENT TO LOVE
St. John

These things have I spoken unto you, that my joy may be in you, and that your joy may be fulfilled. This is my commandment, that ye love one another, even as I have loved you. Greater love hath no man than this, that a man lay down his life for his friends. Ye are my friends, if ye do the things which I command you. No longer do I call you servants; for the servant knoweth not what his lord doeth: but I have called you friends; for all the things that I heard from my Father I have made known unto you. Ye did not choose me, but I chose you, and appointed you, that ye should go and bear fruit, and that your fruit should abide: that whatsoever ye shall ask of the Father in my name, he may give it to you. These things I command you, that ye may love one another.

(New Testament)

BILL AND JOE
Oliver Wendell Holmes

Come dear old comrade, you and I
Will steal an hour from days gone by,
The shining days when life was new,
And all was bright with morning dew,—
The lusty days of long ago,
When you were Bill and I was Joe.

Your name may flaunt a titled trail
Proud as a cockerel's rainbow tail,
And mine as brief appendix wear
As Tam O'Shanter's luckless mare:
Today, old friend, remember still
That I am Joe and you are Bill.

You've won the great world's envied prize,
And grand you look in people's eyes,
With H–O–N. and L–L–D.,
In big brave letters, fair to see:
Your fist, old fellow! off they go!—
How are you, Bill? How are you, Joe?

You've worn the judge's ermined robe;
You've taught your name to half the globe;
You've sung mankind a deathless strain;
You've made the dead past life again:
The world may call you what it will,
But you and I are Joe and Bill.

The chaffing young folks stare, and say,
"See those old buffers, bent and gray,—
They talk like fellows in their teens!
Mad, poor old boys! That's what it means,"
And shake their heads: they little know
The throbbing hearts of Bill and Joe!—

How Bill forgets his hour of pride,
While Joe sits smiling at his side;
How Joe, in spite of time's disguise,
Finds the old schoolmate in his eyes,—
Those calm, stern eyes that melt and fill
As Joe looks fondly up at Bill.

Ah, pensive scholar, what is fame?
A fitful tongue of leaping flame;
A giddy whirlwind's fickle gust,
That lifts a pinch of mortal dust:
A few swift years, and who can show
Which dust was Bill and which was Joe?

The weary idol takes his stand,
Holds out his bruised and aching hand,
While gaping thousands come and go,—
How vain it seems, this empty show!
Till all at once his pulses thrill;—
'Tis poor old Joe's "God bless you, Bill!"

And shall we breathe in happier spheres
The names that pleased our mortal ears,—
In some sweet lull of harp and song
For earth-born spirits none too long,
Just whispering of the world below
Where this was Bill and that was Joe?

No matter: while our home is here
No sounding name is half so dear;
When fades at length our lingering day,
Who cares what pompous tombstones say?
Read on the hearts that love us still,
Hic jacet Joe. *Hic jacet* Bill.

"Our friendship has been all clear sunshine . . ."

BENJAMIN FRANKLIN TO
MRS. HEWSON

Passy, January 27, 1783

The departure of my dearest friend [Mrs. Hewson's mother], which I learn from your last letter, greatly affects me. To meet with her once again in this life was one of the principal motives of my proposing to visit England again before my return to America. The last year carried off my friends Dr. Pringle, and Dr. Fothergill, and Lord Kaimes and Lord Le Despencer; this has begun to take away the rest, and strike the hardest. Thus the ties I had to that country, and indeed to the world in general, are loosened one by one; and I shall soon have no attachment left to make me unwilling to follow. . . .

Spring is coming on, when travelling will be delightful. Can you not, when your children are all at school, make a little party and take a trip hither? I have now a large house, delightfully situated, in which I could accommodate you and two or three friends; and I am but half an hour's drive from Paris.

In looking forward, twenty-five years seems a long period; but, in looking back, how short! Could you imagine that it is now full a quarter of a century since we were first acquainted? It was in 1757. During the greatest part of this time I lived in the same house with my dear deceased friend, your mother; of course you and I saw and conversed with each other much and often. It is all to our honor, that, in all that time, we never had among us the smallest misunderstanding. Our friendship has been all clear sunshine, without any, the least, clouds in its hemisphere. Let me conclude by saying to you, what I have had too frequent occasion to say to my other remaining old friends, *the fewer we become, the more let us love one another.*

Adieu, etc.

PLATONIC

William Rogers Terrett

I had sworn to be a bachelor, she had sworn to be a maid,
For we quite agreed in doubting whether matrimony paid;
Besides, we had our higher loves,—fair science ruled my heart,
And she said her young affections were all wound up in art.

So we laughed at those wise men who say that friendship cannot live
'Twixt man and woman, unless each has something more to give;
We would be friends, and friends true as e'er were man and man;
I'd be a second David, and she Miss Jonathan.

We scorned all sentimental trash,—vows, kisses, tears, and sighs;
High friendship, such as ours, might well such childish arts despise;
We *liked* each other, that was all, quite all there was to say,
So we just shook hands upon it, in a business sort of way.

We shared our secrets and our joys, together hoped and feared,
With common purpose sought the goal that young ambition reared;
We dreamed together of the days, the dream-bright days to come,
We were strictly confidential, and we called each other "chum."

And many a day we wandered together o'er the hills,
I seeking bugs and butterflies, and she, the ruined mills
And rustic bridges and the like, that picture-makers prize
To run in with waterfalls, and groves, and summer skies.

And many a quiet evening, in hours of silent ease,
We floated down the river, or strolled beneath the trees,
And talked in long gradation from the poets to the weather,
While the western skies and my cigar burned slowly out together....

"Well, good-by, chum!" I took her hand, for the time had come to go,
My going meant our parting, when to meet, we did not know.
I had lingered long, and said farewell, with a very heavy heart;
For although we were but *friends,* 'tis hard for honest friends to part.

"Good-by old fellow! don't forget your friends beyond the sea,
And some day, when you've lots of time, drop a line or two to me."
The words came lightly, gayly, but a great sob, just behind,
Welled upward with a story of quite a different kind.

And then she raised her eyes to mine,—great liquid eyes of blue,
Filled to the brim, and running o'er, like violet cups of dew;
One long, long glance, and then I did, what I never did before—
Perhaps the *tears* meant friendship, but I'm sure the *kiss* meant more.

A Boy and an Artist Have a Confidential Chat. . . .

THE ROMAN ROAD
Kenneth Grahame

All the roads of our neighborhood were cheerful and friendly, having
each of them pleasant qualities of their own; but this one seemed
different from the others in its masterful suggestion of a serious
purpose, speeding you along with a strange uplifting of the heart. . . .
"The Knight's Road" we children had named it, from a sort of
feeling that, if from any quarter at all, it would be down this track
that we might some day see Lancelot and his peers come pacing
on their warhorses. . . . "All roads lead to Rome," I had once heard
somebody say; and I had taken the remark very seriously, of course,
and puzzled over it many days. There must have been some mistake,
I concluded at last, but of one road at least I intuitively felt it to
be true. . . .
Rome! It was fascinating to think that it lay at the other end of
this white ribbon that rolled itself off from my feet over the distant
downs. . . . I tried to imagine what it would be like when I got
there. . . . It was easier to go a-building among those dream-cities
where no limitations were imposed, and one was sole architect, with
a free hand. Down a delectable street of cloud-built palaces I was
mentally pacing, when I happened upon the Artist.
He was seated at work by the roadside, at a point whence the cool
large spaces of the downs, juniper-studded, swept grandly westwards.

His attributes proclaimed him of the artist tribe; besides, he wore knickerbockers like myself,—a garb confined, I was aware, to boys and artists. I knew I was not to bother him with questions, nor look over his shoulder and breathe in his ear—they didn't like it, this *genus irritable*. But there was nothing about staring in my code of instructions, the point having somehow been overlooked; so, squatting down on the grass, I devoted myself to the passionate absorbing of every detail. At the end of five minutes there was not a button on him that I could not have passed an examination in; and the wearer himself of that homespun suit was probably less familiar with its pattern and texture than I was. Once he looked up, half held out his tobacco pouch, mechanically as it were, then, returning it to his pocket, resumed his work, and I my mental photography.

After another five minutes or so had passed, he remarked, without looking my way: "Fine afternoon we're having: going far today?"

"No, I'm not going any farther than this," I replied. "I *was* thinking of going on to Rome: but I've put it off."

"Pleasant place, Rome," he muttered; "you'll like it." It was some minutes later that he added: "But I wouldn't go just now, if I were you; too jolly hot."

"*You* haven't been to Rome, have you?" I inquired.

"Rather," he replied briefly; "I live there."

This was too much, and my jaw dropped as I struggled to grasp the fact that I was sitting there talking to a fellow who lived in Rome. Speech was out of the question; besides I had other things to do. Ten solid minutes had I already spent in an examination of him as a mere stranger and artist; and now the whole thing had to be done over again, from the changed point of view. So I began afresh, at the crown of his soft hat, and worked down to his solid British shoes, this time investing everything with the new Roman halo; and at last I managed to get out: "But you don't really live there, do you?" never doubting the fact, but wanting to hear it repeated.

"Well," he said, good-naturedly overlooking the slight rudeness of my query, "I live there as much as I live anywhere. About half the year sometimes. I've got a sort of shanty there. You must come and see it someday."

"But do you live anywhere else as well?" I went on, feeling the forbidden tide of questions surging up within me.

"O yes, all over the place," was his vague reply. "And I've got a diggings somewhere off Piccadilly."

"Where's that?" I inquired.

"Where's what?" said he. "O, Piccadilly! It's in London."

"Have you a large garden?" I asked; "and how many pigs have you got?"

"I've got no garden at all," he replied sadly, "and they don't allow me to keep pigs, though I'd like to, awfully. It's very hard."

"But what do you do all day, then," I cried, "and where do you go and play, without any garden, or pigs, and things?"

"When I want to play," he said gravely, "I have to go and play in the street; but it's poor fun I grant you. There's a goat, though, not far off and sometimes I talk to him when I'm feeling lonely; but he's very proud."

"Goats *are* proud," I admitted. "There's one lives near here, and if you say anything to him at all, he hits you in the wind with his head. You know what it feels like when a fellow hits you in the wind?"

"I do, well," he replied, in a tone of proper melancholy, and painted on.

"And have you been to any other places," I began again presently, "besides Rome and Piccy-what's-his-name?"

"Heaps," he said. "I'm sort of Ulysses—seen men and cities, you know. In fact, about the only place I never got to was Fortunate Island."

I began to like this man. He answered your questions briefly and to the point, and never tried to be funny. I felt I could be confidential with him.

"Wouldn't you like," I inquired, "to find a city without any people in it at all?"

He looked puzzled. "I am afraid I don't quite understand," he said.

"I mean," I went on eagerly, "a city where you walk in at the gates, and the shops are all full of beautiful things, and the houses furnished as grand as can be, and there isn't anybody there whatever! And you go into the shops, and take anything you want—chocolates, and magic-lanterns and injirubber balls and there's nothing to pay; and you choose your own house and live there and do just as you like, and never go to bed unless you want to!"

The artist laid down his brush. "That *would* be a nice city," he said. "Better than Rome. You can't do that sort of thing in Rome—or in Piccadilly either. But I fear it's one of the places I've never been to."

"And you'd ask your friends," I went on, warming to my subject; "only those you really like, of course; and they'd each have a house to themselves—there'd be lots of houses—and there wouldn't be any relations at all, unless they promised they'd be pleasant; and if they weren't they'd have to go."

"So you wouldn't have any relations?" said the artist. "Well, perhaps you're right. We have tastes in common, I see."

"I'd have Harold," I said reflectively, "and Charlotte. They'd like it awfully. The others are getting too old. O, and Martha—I'd have Martha to cook and wash up and do things. You'd like Martha. She's ever so much nicer than Aunt Eliza. She's my idea of a real lady."

"Then I'm sure I should like her," he replied heartily, "and when I come to what you call this city of yours? Nephelo-something, did you say?"

"I—I don't know," I replied timidly. "I'm afraid it hasn't got a name—yet."

The artist gazed out over the downs. "The poet says, 'dear city of Cecrops,' he said softly to himself, " 'and wilt thou not say, dear city of Zeus?' That's from Marcus Aurelius," he went on, turning again to his work. "You don't know him, I suppose; you will some day."

"Who's he?" I inquired.

"O, just another fellow who lived in Rome," he replied dabbing away.

"O, dear!" I cried disconsolately. "What a lot of people seem to live at Rome, and I've never even been there! But I think I'd like *my* city best."

"And so would I," he replied with unction. "But Marcus Aurelius wouldn't, you know."

"Then we won't invite him," I said; "will we?"

"I won't if you won't," said he. And that point being settled we were silent for a while.

"Do you know," he said presently, "I've met one or two fellows from time to time, who have been to a city like yours—perhaps it was the same one. They won't talk about it—only broken hints, now and then; but they've been there sure enough. They don't seem to care about anything in particular—and everything's the same to them, rough or smooth; and sooner or later they slip off and disappear; and you never see them again. Gone back, I suppose."

"Of course," said I. "Don't see what they ever came away for. I wouldn't. To be told you've broken things when you haven't, and stopped having tea with the servants in the kitchen, and not allowed to have a dog to sleep with you. But, *I've* known people, too, who've gone there."

The artist stared, but without incivility.

"Well, there's Lancelot," I went on. "The book says he died, but it never seemed to read right, somehow. He just went away, like Arthur. And Crusoe, when he got tired of wearing clothes and being respectable, and all the nice men in the stories who don't marry the Princess, 'cos only one man ever gets married in a book, you know. They'll all be there."

"And the men who never come off," he said, "who try like the rest, but get knocked out, or somehow miss—or break down or get bowled over in the melee—and get no Princess, nor even a second-class kingdom—some of them'll be there, I hope?"

"Yes, if you like," I replied, not quite understanding him; "if they're friends of yours, we'll ask 'em, of course."

"What a time we shall have!" said the artist reflectively, "and how shocked old Marcus Aurelius will be!"

The shadows had lengthened uncannily, a tide of golden haze was flooding the grey-green surface of the downs, and the artist began to put his traps together, preparatory to a move. I felt very low; we would have to part, it seemed, just as we were getting on so well together. Then he stood up, and he was very straight and tall, and the sunset was in his beard and hair as he stood there, high over me. He took my hand like an equal. "I've enjoyed our conversation very much," he said. "That was an interesting subject you started, and we haven't half exhausted it. We must meet again, I hope?"

"Of course we shall," I replied, surprised that there should be any doubt about it.

"In Rome perhaps?" said he.

"Yes, in Rome," I answered; "or Piccy-the-other-place, or somewhere."

"Or else," said he, "in that other city—when we've found the way there. And I'll look out for you, and you'll sing out as soon as you see me. And we'll go down the street arm-in-arm, and into all the shops, and then I'll choose my house, and you'll choose your house and we'll live there like princes and good fellows."

"O, but you'll stay in my house, won't you?" I cried; "I wouldn't ask everybody; but I'll ask *you.*"

He affected to consider a moment; then "Right!" he said; "I believe you mean it, and I *will* come and stay with you. I won't go to anybody else, if they ask me ever so much. And I'll stay quite a long time, too, and I won't be any trouble."

Upon this compact we parted, and I went down-heartedly from the man who understood me, back to the house where I never could do anything right. How was it that everything seemed natural and sensible to him, which these uncles, vicars, and other grown-up men took for the merest tomfoolery? Well, he would explain this, and many other things, when we met again. The Knight's Road! How it always brought consolation! Was he possibly one of those vanished knights I had been looking for, for so long? Perhaps he would be in armour next time—why not? He would look well in armour, I thought. And I would take care to get there first, and see the sunlight flash and play on his helmet and shield, as he rode up the High Street of the Golden City.

Meantime, there only remained the finding it. An easy matter.

In the hour of distress and misery the eyes of every mortal turns to friendship: in the hour of gladness and conviviality, what is your want? It is friendship. When the heart overflows with gratitude, or with any other sweet and sacred sentiment, what is the word to which it would give utterance? A friend.

—WALTER SAVAGE LANDOR

HELENA'S LAMENT OVER HERMIA'S DISLOYALTY
William Shakespeare

Lo, she is one of this confederacy!
Now I perceive they have conjoin'd all three
To fashion this false sport, in spite of me.
Injurious Hermia! most ungrateful maid!
Have you conspired, have you with these contrived
To bait me with this foul derision?
Is all the counsel that we two have shared,
The sister's vows, the hours that we have spent,
When we have chid the hasty-footed time
For parting us,—O, is all forgot?
All school-days' friendship, childhood innocence?
We, Hermia, like two artificial gods,
Have with our needles created both one flower,
Both on one sampler, sitting on one cushion,
Both warbling of one song, both in one key;
As if our hands, our sides, voices, and minds,
Had been incorporate. So we grew together,
Like to a double cherry, seeming parted,
But yet an union in partition;
Two lovely berries moulded on one stem;
So with two seeming bodies, but one heart;
Two of the first, like coats in heraldry,
Due but to one, and crowned with one crest.
And will you rend our ancient love asunder,
To join with men in scorning your poor friend?
It is not friendly, 'tis not maidenly:
Our sex, as well as I, may chide you for it,
Though I alone do feel the injury.

"... we may as well allow women as men to be friends ..."

WOMEN: "THE PRETTINESS OF FRIENDSHIP"

Jeremy Taylor

I cannot say that women are capable of all those excellencies by which men can oblige the world; and therefore a female friend in some cases is not so good a counsellor as a wise man, and cannot so well defend my honor, nor dispose of reliefs and assistances if she be under the power of another; but a woman can love as passionately, and converse as pleasantly, and retain a secret as faithfully, and be useful in her proper ministries; and she can die for her friend as well as the bravest Roman knight....

A man is the best friend in trouble, but a woman may be equal to him in the days of joy: a woman can as well increase our comforts but cannot so well lessen our sorrows; and therefore we do not carry women with us when we go to fight; but in peaceful cities and times, virtuous women are the beauties of society and the prettiness of friendship. And when we consider that few persons in the world have all those excellencies, by which friendship can be useful and illustrious, we may as well allow women as men to be friends; since they can have all that which can be necessary and essential to friendship.

"... I held out my hand to him."

THE LAST MEETING

Ivan Turgenev

Once we were intimate friends ... but the evil moment came, and we parted enemies.

Many years passed by ... and I came to the city in which he lived, and heard that he was hopelessly ill and wished to see me.

I went to see him and entered his chamber ... our eyes met.

I scarcely knew him. Heaven! how illness had changed him!

Yellow, wizened, not a hair on his head, with a thin, gray beard, there he sat scantily covered.

He could not bear the slightest pressure of any article of clothing. He hastily held out his horribly thin, skinny hand, and whispered with effort a few unintelligible words. Were they a welcome or a reproach?—who can tell? His emaciated breast panted heavily, and from his inflamed eyes—the pupils were contracted with pain—dropped a few slow tears.

My heart bled ... I sat down near him, and, involuntarily letting my eyes fall from this terrible picture of suffering, I held out my hand to him.

But it seemed to me as if it could not be his hand which clasped mine.

It seemed to me as if the tall, still, white form of a woman came between us: a long garment covered her from head to foot; her deep, dull eyes gazed into vacancy; her pale, firm lips were silent.

This woman joined our hands ... she reconciled us forever.

Yes, Death reconciled us.

(Translator anonymous)

Turn him and see his threads; look if he be
Friend to himself who would be friend to thee.
For that is first requir'd, a man be his own;
But he that's too much that is friend to none.
Then rest, and a friend's value understand,
It is a richer purchase than of land.

—BEN JONSON

**"From the day that I lost him ... I have led
only a sorrowful and languishing life ..."**

OF FRIENDSHIP

Michel Eyquem de Montaigne

Estienne de la Boetie [wrote] a discourse that he called Voluntary Servitude, which others have since further baptized Le Contre-Un, a piece written in his younger years, by way of essay, in honour of liberty against tyrants.... It is finely written and as full as any thing can possibly be. Yet I may confidently say it is far short of what he is able to do; and if in that more mature age wherein I knew him, he had taken a design like this of mine, to commit his thoughts to writing, we should have seen a great many rare things,... But he has left nothing behind him save this treatise only... and some observations upon that edict of January, made famous by our civil wars, which also shall elsewhere, peradventure, find a place. These were all I could recover of his remains; I, to whom, with so affectionate a remembrance, upon his death-bed, he by his last will bequeathed his library and papers, the little book of his works only excepted, which I committed to the press. And this particular obligation I have to this treatise of his, that it was the occasion of my first coming acquainted with him; for it was showed to me long before I saw him, and gave me the first knowledge of his name; proving so the first cause and foundation of a friendship which we afterwards improved and maintained so long as God was pleased to continue us together, so perfect, inviolate, and entire, that certainly the like is hardly to be found in story, and amongst the men of this age there is no sign nor trace of any such thing. So many concurrents are required to the building of such a one, that 'tis much if fortune bring it but once to pass in three ages.

There is nothing to which nature seems so much to have inclined us as to society; and Aristotle says that good legislators had more respect to friendship than to justice. Now the most supreme point of its perfection is this: for generally all those that pleasure, profit, public or private interest, create and nourish, are so much the less noble and generous, and so much the less friendships, by how much they mix up another cause and design than friendship itself. Neither do the four ancient kinds, natural, sociable, hospitable, and venerean, either separately or jointly, make up a true and perfect friendship.

That of children to parents is rather respect; friendship being nourished by communication, which cannot, by reason of the great disparity, be betwixt them; but would rather perhaps violate the duties of nature; for neither are all the secret thoughts of fathers fit to be communicated to children, lest it beget an indecent familiarity betwixt them; nor can the advices and reproofs, which is one of the principal offices of friendship, be properly performed by the son to the father.... This name of brother does indeed carry with it an amiable and affectionate sound, and for that reason he and I called one another brothers. But the complication of interests, the division of estates, the raising of the one at the undoing of the other, does strangely weaken and slacken the fraternal tie; and brothers pursuing their fortune and advancement by the same path, 'tis hardly possible but they must of necessity often jostle and hinder one another. Besides, why should the correspondence of manners, parts, and inclinations, which beget true and perfect friendships, always meet and concur in these relations? The father and the son may be of quite contrary humours, and brothers be without any manner of sympathy in their natures. He is my son, he is my father; but he is passionate; ill-natured, or a fool. And moreover, by how much these are friendships that the law and natural obligation impose upon us, so much less is there of our own choice and freewill, which freewill of ours has no creation properly its own than through affection and friendship....

We are not here to bring the love we bear to women, though it be an act of our own choice, into comparison; nor rank it with the others. Its fire, I confess,...is more active, more eager, and more sharp; but, withal, 'tis more precipitous, fickle, moving, and inconstant; a fever subject to intermission and paroxysms, that has hold but on one part of us; whereas, in friendship, 'tis a general and universal fire, but temperate and equal, a constant and steady heat, all easy and smooth, without poignancy or roughness. Moreover, in love, 'tis no other than a frantic desire for that which flies from us....

So soon as ever it enters into the terms of friendship, that is to say, into a concurrence of desires, it vanishes and is gone, fruition destroys it, as having only a fleshly end, subject to satiety. Friendship, on the contrary, is enjoyed proportionably as it is desired, and only grows up, is nourished and improves by enjoyment, as being spiritual, and the soul growing still more perfect by use....

Friendship has no manner of business or traffic with any thing but itself. Moreover, to say truth, the ordinary talent of women is not such as is sufficient to maintain the conference and communication required to the support of this sacred tie; nor do they appear to be endued with firmness of mind to endure the constraint of so hard and durable a knot. Doubtless if there could be such a free and voluntary familiarity contracted, where not only the souls might have this entire fruition, but the bodies also might share in the alliance, and the whole man be engaged in it, the friendship would certainly be more full and perfect; but there is no example that this sex ever arrived at such perfection, and, by the ancient schools, is wholly rejected....

"Those are only to be reputed friendships that are fortified and confirmed by judgment and length of time." For the rest, what we commonly call friends and friendships are nothing but an acquaintance and connection, contracted either by accident or upon some design, by means of which there happens some little intercourse betwixt our souls; but, in the friendship I speak of, they mingle and melt into one piece, with so universal a mixture that there is left no more sign of the seam by which they were first conjoined. If any one should importune me to give a reason why I loved him, I feel it could no otherwise be expressed than by making answer, "Because it was he; because it was I." There is beyond what I am able to say, I know not what inexplicable and inevitable power that brought on this union. We sought one another long before we met, and from the characters we heard of one another which wrought more upon our affections than in reason mere reports should do, and, as I think, by some secret appointment of heaven; we embraced each other in our names; and at our first meeting, which was accidentally at a great city entertainment, we found ourselves so mutually pleased with one another, we became, at once, mutually so endeared, that thenceforward nothing was so near to us as one another. He wrote an excellent Latin satire, which is printed, wherein he excuses and explains the precipitateness of our intimacy, so suddenly come to perfection. Having so short a time to continue, as being begun so late, for we were both full grown men, and he some years the older, there was no time to lose; nor was it tied to conform itself to the example of those slow and regular friendships that require so many precautions of a long preliminary conversation. This has no other idea than that of itself. 'Tis no one particular consideration, nor two, nor three, nor four, nor a thousand. 'Tis I know not what quintessence of all this mixture which, seizing my whole will, carried it to plunge and lose itself in his; and that having seized his whole will, brought it, with equal concurrence and appetite, to plunge and lose itself in mine. I may truly say lose, reserving nothing to ourselves that was either his or mine....

No one action of his, what face soever it might bear, could be presented to me, of which I could not presently, and at first sight, find out the moving cause. Our souls have drawn so unitedly together, and we have, with so mutual a confidence, laid open the very bottom of our hearts to one another's view, that I not only knew his as well as my own, but should, certainly in any concern of mine, have trusted my interest much more willingly with him than with myself. Let no one, therefore, rank common friendship with such a one as this. I have had as much experience of these as another, and of the most perfect of their kind; but I do not advise that any should confound the rules of the one and the other; for they would find themselves much deceived. In ordinary friendships you must walk bridle in hand, with prudence and circumspection, for in them the knot is not so sure that a man may not fully depend upon its not slipping.... The good offices, and benefits, by which other friendships are supported and maintained, do not deserve so much as to be mentioned, and are, by this concurrence of our wills, rendered of no use. As the kindness I have for myself receives no increase, for any thing I relieve myself withal, in time of need, whatever the Stoics say, and as I do not find myself obliged to myself for any service I do myself, so the union of such friends, being really perfect, deprives them of all idea of acknowledgement of such duties, and makes them loathe and banish from their conversation these words implying a difference and distinction, benefit, obligation, entreaty, thanks, and the like. All things, wills, thoughts, opinions, goods, wives, children, honour, and life, being, in effect, common betwixt them, and their condition being no other than one soul in two bodies, according to the very proper definition of Aristotle, they can neither lend nor give any thing to one another.... If, in the friendship of which I speak, one could give to the other, the receiver of the benefit would be the man that obliged his friend; for each of them, above all things, studying how to be useful to the other, he that affords the occasion is the generous man, in giving his friend the satisfaction of doing that which, above all things, he does most desire.... Eudamidas, a Corinthian, had two friends, Charixenus, a Syconian, and Aretheus, a Corinthian; this man coming to die, being poor, and his two friends being rich, he made his will, after this manner: "I bequeathe to Aretheus the maintenance of my mother, to support and provide for her in her old age; and to Charixenus I bequeathe the care of marrying my daughter, and to give her of good a portion as he is able; and in case one of these chances to die, I hereby substitute the survivor in his place." They who first saw this will made themselves very merry at the contents; but the heirs being made acquainted with it, accepted the legacies with very great content; and one of them, Charixenus, dying within five days after, and Aretheus having thus the charge of both developed solely to him, he nourished the old woman with very great care and tenderness, and, of five talents he had, gave two and a half in marriage with an only daughter he had of his own, and two and a half in marriage with the daughter of Eudamidas, and in one and the same day solemnized both their nuptials. This example is very full to the point, if one thing were not to be objected, namely, the multitude of friends; for the perfect friendship I speak of is indivisible; each one gives himself so entirely to his friend that he has nothing left to distribute to others; nay, is sorry that he is not double, treble, or quadruple, and that he has not many souls and many wills to confer them all upon this one object. Common friendships will admit of division, one may love the beauty of this, the good humour of that person, the liberality of a third, the paternal affection of a fourth, the fraternal love of a fifth, and so on. But this friendship that possesses the whole soul, and there rules and sways with an absolute sovereignty, can admit of no rival. If two, at the same time, should call to you for succour, to which of them would you run? Should they require of you contrary offices, how could you serve them both? Should one commit a thing to your secrecy that it were of importance to the other to know, how would you disengage yourself? The one particular friendship disunites and dissolves all other obligations whatsoever. The secret I have sworn not to reveal to any other I may, without perjury, communicate to him who is not another, but myself.... There are effects not to be imagined nor comprehended by such as have no experience of them, and which make me infinitely honour and admire the answer of that young soldier to Cyrus, by whom, being asked how much he would take for a horse, with which he had won the prize of a race, and whether he would exchange him for a kingdom? "No, truly, sir," said he, "but I would give him with all my heart for a true friend, could I find a man worthy of that relation." He did well in saying, *could I find*, for though a man may almost everywhere meet with men sufficiently qualified for a superficial acquaintance, yet, in this, where a man is to deal from the very bottom of his heart, without any manner of reservation, it will be requisite that all the wards and springs be true and plain, and perfectly sure....

As he that was found astride upon a stick, playing with his children, entreated the person who had surprised him in that posture to say nothing of it till he himself came to be a father, supposing that the fondness that would then possess his own soul would render him a more equal judge of such an action, so I also could wish to speak to such as have had experience of what I say; though, knowing how remote a thing such a friendship is from the common practice, and how rarely such is to be found, I despair of meeting with any one qualified to be a judge. For even the discourses left us by antiquity upon this subject seem to me flat and low, in comparison of the sense I have of it, and in this particular the effects surpass the very precepts of philosophy....

> I know no pleasure that can health attend,
> Like the delight of an amusing friend.

Menander of old declared him to be happy that had the good fortune to meet with but the shadow of a friend; and doubtless he had good reason to say so, especially if he spoke by experience; for, in good earnest, if I compare all the rest of my life—though, thanks be to God, I have always passed my time pleasantly enough and at my ease, and, the loss of such a friend excepted, free from any grievous affliction, and in great tranquillity of mind, having been contented with my natural and original conveniences and advantages, without being solicitous after others—If I should compare it all, I say, with the four years I had the happiness to enjoy the sweet society of this excellent man, 'tis nothing but smoke, but an obscure and tedious night. From the day that I lost him, ... I have only led a sorrowful and languishing life; and the very pleasures that present themselves to me, instead of administering any thing of consolation, double my affliction for his loss. We were halves throughout, and to that degree that, methinks, by outliving him I defraud him of his part....

I was so accustomed to be always his second in all places, and in all things, that, methinks, I am no more than half a man, and have but half a being.... There is no act or imagining of mine wherein I do not miss him. For as he surpassed me by infinite degrees in virtue and all other accomplishments, so he also did in all offices of friendship....

> "Why should we stop the flowing tear?
> Why blush to weep for one so dear?"
>
> . . . .
>
> "Ah! brother, what a life did I commence,
> From that sad day when thou wert snatched from hence!
> Those joys are vanished which my heart once knew,
> When in sweet converse all our moments flew:
> With thee departing, my good fortune fled,
> And all my soul is lifeless since thou'rt dead.
> The Muses at thy fun'ral I forsook,
> And of all joy my leave for ever took.
> Dearer than life! am I so wretched then,
> Never to hear or speak to thee again?
> Nor see those lips, now frozen up by death?
> Yet I will love thee to my latest breath!"
> (*Translated by Charles Cotton, revised by William Hazlitt*)

Though Nature maintains, and must prevail, there will always be plenty of people, and good people, who cannot, or think they cannot, see anything in that last, wisest, most envelop'd of proverbs, "Friendship rules the World." Modern society, in its largest vein, is essentially intellectual, infidelistic—secretly admires, and depends most on, pure compulsion or science, its rule and sovereignty—is, in short, in "cultivated" quarters, deeply Napoleonic.

"Friendship," said Bonaparte, in one of his lightning-flashes of candid garrulity, "Friendship is but a name. I love no one—not even my brothers; Joseph perhaps a little. Still, if I do love him, it is from habit, because he is the eldest of us. Duroc? Ay, him, if any one, I love in a sort—but why? He suits me; he is cool, undemonstrative, unfeeling—has no weak affections—never embraces any one—never weeps."

I am not sure but the same analogy is to be applied, in cases, often seen, where with an extra development and acuteness of the intellectual faculties, there is a mark'd absence of the spiritual, affectional, and sometimes, though more rarely, the highest aesthetic and moral elements of cognition.

—WALT WHITMAN

EARLY FRIENDSHIP

Stephen E. Spring-Rice

The half-seen memories of childish days,
When pains and pleasures lightly came and went;
The sympathies of boyhood rashly spent
In fearful wand'rings through forbidden ways;
The vague, but manly wish to tread the maze
Of life to noble ends—whereon intent,
Asking to know for what man here is sent,
The bravest heart must often pause, and gaze,—
The firm resolve to seek the chosen end
Of manhood's judgment, cautious and mature,—
Each of these viewless bonds binds friend to friend
With strength no selfish purpose can secure:
My happy lot is this, that all attend
That friendship which first came, and which shall last endure.

CYNICAL MAXIMS

Duc de la Rochefoucauld

A man is never less sincere than when he asks or gives advice. When he seeks counsel with humble deference to the judgment of his friend, he seeks to commend his own conduct and to make his friend a surety for his acts. Giving advice is but repaying with feigned zeal the confidence of others, and at the same time seeking to further one's own ends by the counsel one gives.

The tribulations of our best friends aroused sentiments in us which are not entirely unpleasant.

(Translated by John Heard)

"I pray you all to love him as you love me."

ARRIUS MEETS, IS SAVED BY AND BEFRIENDS BEN-HUR *

Lew Wallace

The tribune, standing upon the helmsman's deck with the order of the duumvir open in his hand, spoke to the hortator, or chief of the rowers.

"What force hast thou?"

"Of oarsmen, two hundred and fifty-two; ten supernumeraries."

At noon that day the galley was skimming the sea off Paestum. The wind was yet from the west, filling the sail to the master's content. And now the better to study his men, he was seated below in the great cabin.

At the after-end of the cabin there was a platform, reached by several steps. Upon it the chief of the rowers sat; in front of him a sounding-table, upon which, with a gavel, he beat time for the oarsmen; at his right a water-clock, to measure the reliefs and watches. Above him, on a higher platform, well guarded by gilded railing, the tribune had his quarters, overlooking everything, and furnished with a couch, a table, and a cushioned chair.

Thus at ease, lounging in the great chair, swaying with the motion of the vessel, the military cloak half draping his tunic, sword in belt, Arrius kept watchful eye over his command. He saw critically everything in view, but dwelt longest upon the rowers.

Nearly all the nations had sons there, mostly prisoners of war, chosen for their brawn and endurance. In one place a Briton; before him a Libyan; behind him a Crimean. Elsewhere a Scythian, a Gaul, and a Thebasite. Roman convicts cast down to consort with Goths and Longobardi, Jews, Ethiopians, and barbarians.

The reach forward, the pull, the feathering the blade, the dip, were motions most perfect when most automatic. So, as the result of long service, the poor wretches became patient, spiritless, obedient—creatures of vast muscle and exhausted intellects, at last lowered into the semiconscious state wherein misery turns to habit, and the soul takes on incredible endurance.

From right to left, hour after hour, the tribune, swaying in his easy chair, amused himself singling out individuals. With his stylus he

* Abridged.

made note of objections, thinking, if all went well, he would find among the pirates better men for the places.

For convenience, the slaves were usually identified by the numerals painted upon the benches to which they were assigned. As the sharp eyes of the great man moved from seat to seat on either hand, they came at last to number sixty, which had been fixed above the first bench of the first bank. There they rested.

The light glinting through the overhead grating showed the rower like all his fellows, naked, except a cincture above the loins. He was very young, not more than twenty.

Arrius observed that the rower seemed of good height, and that his limbs, upper and nether, were singularly perfect. Altogether there was in the man's action a certain harmony which, besides addressing itself to the tribune's theory, stimulated both his curiosity and general interest.

"By the gods," he said to himself, "the fellow impresses me! He promises well. I will know more of him."

Suddenly the rower turned and looked at him.

"A Jew! And a boy!"

Under the tribune's gaze, the large eyes of the slave grew larger, the blade lingered in his hands. But instantly, with an angry crash, down fell the gavel of the hortator. The rower started, withdrew his face from the inquisitor. When he glanced again at the tribune, he was vastly more astonished—he was met with a kindly smile.

Meantime the galley entered the Straits of Messina, and, skimming past the city, turned eastward, leaving the cloud over Aetna in the sky astern.

Often as Arrius returned to his platform in the cabin he returned to study the rower, and he kept saying to himself, "The fellow hath a spirit. A Jew is not a barbarian. I will know more of him."

The fourth day out, and the Astroea was speeding through the Ionian Sea. The sky was clear, and the wind blew as if bearing the good-will of all the gods.

As it was possible to overtake the fleet before reaching the bay east of the island of Cythera, designated for assemblage, Arrius, somewhat impatient, spent much time on deck. He took note diligently of matters pertaining to his ship, and as a rule was well pleased. In the cabin, swinging in the great chair, his thought continually reverted to the rower.

A relief was going on at the moment.

"Knowest thou the man just come from yon bench?" he asked the hortator.

"As thou knowest," he replied, "the ship is but a month from the maker's, and the men are as new to me as the ship."

"He is a Jew," Arrius remarked, thoughtfully.

"And our best rower," said the other. "I have seen his oar bend almost to breaking."

"Of what disposition is he?"

"He is obedient; further I know not. Once he made request of me to change him alternately from the right to the left."

"Did he give a reason?"

"He had observed that the men who are confined to one side become misshapen. He also said that some day of storm or battle there might be sudden need to change him, and he might then be unserviceable."

"*Perpol!* The idea is new. Have you nothing of his history?"

"Not a word."

"If I should be on deck when his time is up, send him to me. Let him come alone."

About two hours later Arrius stood in the stern; the pilot sat with a hand upon the rope by which the rudder paddles, one on each side of the vessel, were managed. In the shade of the sail some sailors lay asleep, and up on the yard there was a lookout. Lifting his eyes, Arrius beheld the rower approaching.

"The chief called thee the noble Arrius, and said it was thy will that I should seek thee here. I have come."

Arrius surveyed the figure, tall, sinewy, glistening in the sun, and tinted by the rich red blood within—surveyed it admiringly, and with a thought of the arena; yet the manner was not without effect upon him; there was in the voice a suggestion of life at least partly spent under refining influences; the eyes were clear and open, and more curious than defiant.

"The hortator tells me thou art his best rower."

"The hortator is kind," the rower answered.

"Hast thou seen much service?"

"About three years. I cannot recall a day of rest from them."

"The labor is hard; few men bear it a year without breaking, and thou—thou art but a boy."

"The noble Arrius forgets that the spirit hath much to do with endurance. By its help the weak sometimes thrive, when the strong perish."

"From thy speech, thou art a Jew."

"My ancestors further back than the first Roman were Hebrews."

"The stubborn pride of thy race is not lost in thee," said Arrius, observing a flush upon the rower's face.

"Pride is never so loud as when in chains."

"I have not been to Jerusalem," Arrius said; "but I have heard of its princes. I knew one of them. He was a merchant, and sailed the seas. He was fit to have been a king. Of what degree art thou?"

"I must answer thee from the bench of a galley. I am of the degree of slaves. My father was a prince of Jerusalem, and, as a merchant,

he sailed the seas. He was known and honored in the guest-chamber
of the great Augustus."

"His name?"

"Ithamar, of the house of Hur."

The tribune raised his hand in astonishment.

"A son of Hur—thou? What brought thee here?"

Judah looked the tribune in the face. "I was accused of attempting
to assassinate Valerius Gratus, the procurator."

"Thou!" cried Arrius, yet more amazed, and retreating a step. "Thou
that assassin! All Rome rang with the story. I thought the family of
Hur blotted from the earth."

Judah drew nearer Arrius, so near that his hands touched the cloak
where it dropped from the latter's folded arms.

"The horrible day is three years gone," he continued, "and every
hour a whole lifetime in a bottomless pit with death, and no relief
but in labor. And in all that time not a word from my mother or
my sister, not a whisper. I have felt the plague's breath, and the shock
of ships in battle; I have heard the tempest lashing the sea, and
laughed, though others prayed: death would have been a riddance.
Tell me they are dead, if no more. I have heard them call me in the
night; I have seen them walking on the water. And Tirzah—she came
and went in music. And mine was the hand that laid them low! I—"

"Dost thou admit thy guilt?" asked Arrius, sternly.

The change that came upon Ben-Hur was instant and extreme. The
voice sharpened; the hands arose tight-clenched. "Thou hast heard
of the God of my fathers," he said. "By his truth and almightiness, and
by the love with which he hath followed Israel from the beginning, I
swear I am innocent."

The tribune was moved. "Didst thou not have a trial?"

"No!"

The Roman raised his head, surprised. "No trial—no witnesses! Who
passed judgment upon thee?"

"They bound me with cords, and dragged me to a vault in the
Tower. I saw no one. No one spoke to me. Next day soldiers took me
to the seaside. I have been a galley-slave ever since."

"Who was with thee when the blow was struck?"

"Tirzah was at my side...." And Judah went on to recount the
fateful accident and its results.

Arrius brought all his experience with slaves to his aid. If the
feeling shown by this one were assumed, the acting was perfect; on
the other hand, if it were real, the Jew's innocence might not be
doubted. A whole family blotted out to atone an accident! The thought
shocked him.

The tribune could be inexorable, else he had not been fit for his
calling; he could also be just; and to excite his sense of wrong was

to put him in the way to right the wrong. The crews of the ships in which he served came after a time to speak of him as the good tribune.

For once the tribune hesitated. He was monarch of the ship. His prepossessions all moved him to mercy. His faith was won. Yet, in the haste to Cythera the best rower could not be spared; Arrius would at least be sure this was the prince Ben-Hur, and that he was of a right disposition. Ordinarily, slaves were liars.

"It is enough," he said aloud. "Go back to thy place."

Ben-Hur bowed; looked once more into the master's face, but saw nothing for hope. He turned away slowly, looked back, and said,

"If thou dost think of me again, O tribune, let it not be lost in thy mind that I prayed thee only for word of my mother and sister."

He moved on and Arrius followed him with admiring eyes.

"*Perpol!*" he thought. "With teaching, what a man for the arena! What a runner! Ye gods! what an arm for the sword or the cestus!— Stay!" he said aloud.

Ben-Hur stopped, and the tribune went to him. "If thou wert free, what wouldst thou do?"

"The noble Arrius mocks me!" Judah said.

"No; by the gods, no!"

"Then I will answer gladly. I would give myself to duty the first of life. I would know no other. I would know no rest until my mother and Tirzah were restored to home. I would give every day and hour to their happiness. They have lost much, but, by the God of my fathers, I would find them more!"

The answer was unexpected by the Roman. "I spoke to thy ambition. If thy mother and sister were dead, or not to be found, what wouldst thou do?"

A distinct pallor overspread Ben-Hur's face, and he looked over the sea. There was a struggle with some strong feeling; when it was conquered, he turned to the tribune.

"Tribune, only the night before the dreadful day of which I have spoken, I obtained permission to be a soldier. I am of the same mind yet; and, as there is but one school of war, thither I would go."

"The palaestra!" exclaimed Arrius.

"No; a Roman camp."

"But thou must first acquaint thyself with the use of arms."

Now a master may never safely advise a slave. Arrius saw his indiscretion, and, in a breath, chilled his voice and manner. "Go now," he said, "and do not build upon what has passed between us. If thou dost think of it with any hope, choose between the renown of a gladiator and the service of a soldier. The former may come of the favor of the emperor; there is no reward for thee in the latter. Thou art not a Roman. Go!"

A short while after Ben-Hur was upon his bench again.

In the Bay of Antemona, east of Cythera, the hundred galleys assembled. There the tribune gave one day to inspection. He sailed then to Naxos, the largest of the Cyclades, midway between Greece and Asia, like a great stone planted in the centre of a highway, from which he could challenge everything that passed; at the same time, he would be in a position to go after the pirates instantly, whether they were in the Aegean or out on the Mediterranean.

As the fleet, in order, rowed in towards the mountain shores of the island, a galley was sighted coming from the north. She proved to be a transport just from Byzantium, and from her commander he learned the particulars of which he stood in most need.

The pirates were from all the farther shores of the Euxine. Their preparations had been with the greatest secrecy. There were sixty galleys in the squadron, all well manned and supplied.

Where were the pirates now?

After sacking Hephaestia, on the island of Lemnos, they had coursed across to the Thessalian group, and, by last account, disappeared in the gulfs between Euboea and Hellas.

Arrius judged that the robbers might be found somewhere below Thermopylae. He resolved to enclose them north and south, to do which not an hour could be lost; he sailed away without stop or tack until, a little before nightfall, Mount Ocha was seen upreared against the sky, and the pilot reported the Euboean coast.

At a signal the fleet rested upon its oars. When the movement was resumed, Arrius led a division of fifty of the galleys, intending to take them up the channel, while another division, equally strong, turned their prows to the outer or seaward side of the island, with orders to make all haste to the upper inlet, and descend sweeping the waters.

Meantime Ben-Hur kept his bench, relieved every six hours. The rest in the Bay of Antemona had freshened him, so that the oar was not troublesome, and the chief on the platform found no fault.

He had no idea that, following the vessel he was helping to drive, there was a great squadron close at hand and in beautiful order; no more did he know the object of which it was in pursuit. Night fell, and the smell of incense floated down the gangways from the deck.

"The tribune is at the altar," he thought. "Can it be we are going into battle?"

A battle possessed for him and his fellow-slaves an interest unlike that of the sailor and marine; it came, not of the danger encountered but of the fact that defeat, if survived, might bring freedom—at least a change of masters, which might be for the better.

In good times the lanterns were lighted and hung by the stairs, and the tribune came down from the deck. At his word the marines put on their armor. At his word again, the machines were looked to, and spears, javelins, and arrows, in great sheaves, brought and laid upon the floor, together with jars of inflammable oil, and baskets of cotton balls wound loose like the wicking of candles. And when, finally, Ben-Hur saw the tribune mount his platform and don his armor, and get his helmet and shield out, he made ready for the last ignominy of his service.

To every bench, as a fixture, there was a chain with heavy anklets. These the hortator proceeded to lock upon the oarsmen, going from number to number, leaving no choice but to obey, and, in event of disaster, no possibility of escape.

Soon the clanking of the fetters notified him of the progress the chief was making in his round. He would come to him in turn; but would not the tribune interpose for him?

Ben-Hur waited anxiously. The interval seemed like an age. At every turn of the oar he looked towards the tribune, who, his simple preparations made, lay down upon the couch and composed himself to rest; whereupon Ben-Hur laughed grimly, and resolved not to look that way again.

The hortator approached. Now he was at number one—the rattle of the iron links sounded horribly. At last number sixty! Calm from despair, Ben-Hur held his oar at poise, and gave his foot to the officer. Then the tribune stirred—sat up—beckoned to the chief.

The chief went to the tribune, and, smiling, pointed to number sixty.

"What strength!" he said.

"And what spirit!" the tribune answered. "*Perpol!* He is better without the irons. Put them on him no more."

So saying, he stretched himself upon the couch again.

The ship sailed on hour after hour under the oars in water scarcely rippled by the wind. And the people not on duty slept, Arrius in his place, the marines on the floor.

The deeper darkness before the dawn was upon the waters, and all things going well with the Astroea, when a man, descending from the deck, walked swiftly to the platform where the tribune slept, and awoke him. Arrius arose, put on his helmet, sword, and shield, and went to the commander of the marines.

"The pirates are close by. Up and ready!" he said, and passed to the stairs, calm and confident.

Every soul aboard, even the ship, awoke. Officers went to their quarters. The marines took arms, and were led out, looking in all respects like legionaries. Sheaves of arrows and armfuls of javelins were carried on deck. By the central stairs the oiltanks and fire-balls were set ready for use. Additional lanterns were lighted. Buckets were filled with water. The rowers in relief assembled under guard in front of the chief. Ben-Hur was one of the latter. Overhead he heard the muffled noise of the final preparations—of the sailors furling sail, spreading the nettings, unslinging the machines, and hanging the armor of bullhide over the side. Presently quiet settled about the galley again; a stillness filled with vague dread and expectation, which means *ready*.

At a signal passed down from the deck, all at once the oars stopped. What did it mean?

A sound like the rowing of galleys astern attracted Ben-Hur, and the Astroea rocked as if in the midst of countering waves. The idea of a fleet at hand broke upon him—a fleet in manoeuvre—forming probably for attack.

Another order was relayed down from the deck. The oars dipped, and the galley started imperceptibly. No sound from without, none from within, yet each man instinctively poised himself for a shock; the very ship seemed to hold its breath, and go crouched tiger-like.

At last there was a sound of trumpets on deck, full, clear, long blown. The chief beat the sounding-board until it rang; the rowers reached forward full length, and, deepening the dip of their oars, pulled suddenly with all their united force. The galley, quivering in every timber, answered with a leap. Other trumpets joined in the clamor—all from the rear, none forward—from the latter quarter only a rising sound of voices in tumult. There was a mighty blow; the rowers in front of the chief's platform reeled, some of them fell; the ship bounded back, recovered, and rushed on more irresistibly than before.

Forward rushed the Astroea; and, as it went, some sailors ran down, and, plunging the cotton balls into the oil-tanks, tossed them dripping to comrades at the head of the stairs: fire was to be added to other horrors of the combat.

The shouting increased on the right hand and on the left; before, behind, swelled an indescribable clamor. Occasionally there was a crash, followed by sudden peals of fright, telling of the ships ridden down, and their crews drowned in the vortexes.

Nor was the fight all on one side. Now and then a Roman in armor was borne down the hatchway, and laid bleeding, sometimes dying, on the floor.

The Astroea all this time was in motion. Suddenly she stopped. The oars forward were dashed from the hands of the rowers, and the rowers from their benches. On deck, then, a furious trampling, and on the sides a grinding of ships afoul of each other. For the first time the beating of the gavel was lost in the uproar. Men sank on the floor in fear. In the midst of the panic a body was pitched headlong down the hatchway, falling near Ben-Hur. He beheld the half-naked carcass, a mass of hair blackening the face, and under it a shield of bull-hide and wicker-work—a barbarian from the white-skinned nations of the North whom death had robbed of plunder and revenge. The Astroea had been boarded? If so, the Romans must be fighting on their own deck! A chill smote the young Jew: Arrius was hard pressed—he might be defending his own life. If he should be slain! God of Abraham forefend! The hopes and dreams so lately come, were they only hopes and dreams? The tumult thundered above him; he looked around; in the cabin all was confusion—the rowers on the benches paralyzed; men running blindly hither and thither; only the chief on his seat imperturbable, vainly beating the sounding-board, and waiting the order of the tribune—in the red murk illustrating the matchless discipline which had won the world.

The example had a good effect upon Ben-Hur. He controlled himself enough to think. Honor and duty bound the Roman to the platform; but what had Ben-Hur to do with such motives then? The bench was a thing to run from; while, if he were to die a slave, who would be the better of the sacrifice? With him living was duty, if not honor. His life belonged to his mother and sister. He saw them, their arms outstretched; he heard them imploring him. And he would go to them. But a Roman judgment held him in doom. While it endured, escape would be profitless. In all the earth there was no place in which he would be safe from the imperial demand. Whereas he required freedom according to the forms of law, so only could he abide in Judea and execute the purpose to which he would devote himself. But what if his benefactor should now be killed?

Once more Ben-Hur looked around. Upon the deck above the battle still beat; against the sides the hostile vessels crushed and grided. On the benches, the slaves struggled to tear loose from their chains, and, finding their efforts vain, howled like madmen; the guards had gone above; discipline was out, panic in. No, the chief kept his chair, unchanged, calm as ever—except the gavel, weaponless. Vainly with his clangor he filled the lulls in the din. Ben-Hur gave him a last look, then broke away to seek the tribune.

He took it with a leap, and was half-way up the companionway—up far enough to glimpse the sky blood-red with fire, the ships alongside, the sea covered with ships and wrecks, the fight closed in about the pilot's quarter, the assailants many, the defenders few—when suddenly his foothold was knocked away, and he pitched backward. The deck, when he reached it, seemed to be lifting itself and breaking to pieces;

then, in a twinkling, the whole after-part of the hull broke asunder, and the sea, hissing and foaming, leaped in. All became darkness and surging water.

In the act of rising, he clutched something, and held to it. The time he was under seemed an age longer than it really was; at last he gained the top; with a great gasp he filled his lungs afresh, and climbed higher up the plank he held, and looked about him.

Smoke lay upon the sea like a semitransparent fog, through which here and there shone cores of intense brilliance of ships on fire. The battle was yet on; nor could he say who was victor.

About that time he heard oars in quickest movement, and beheld a galley coming down upon him.

He struck out, pushing the plank, which was very broad and unmanageable. Seconds were precious—half a second might save or lose him. In the crisis of the effort, up from the sea, within arm's reach, a helmet shot like a gleam of gold. Next came two hands with fingers extended—large hands were they, and strong—their hold once fixed, might not be loosed. Ben-Hur swerved from them appalled. Up rose the helmet and the head it encased—then two arms, which began to beat the water wildly—the head turned back, and gave the face to the light. The mouth gaping wide; the eyes open, but sightless, and the bloodless pallor of a drowning man. Yet he gave a cry of joy at the sight, and as the face was going under again, he caught the sufferer by the chain chin-strap and drew him to the plank.

The man was Arrius, the tribune.

The water foamed and eddied violently about Ben-Hur, taxing all his strength to hold to the support and at the same time keep the Roman's head above the surface. The galley had passed right through the floating men. A muffled crash, succeeded by a great outcry, made the rescuer look again from his charge. A certain savage pleasure touched his heart—the Astroea was avenged.

After that, the battle moved on. Resistance turned to flight. But who were the victors? He pushed the plank under the tribune until it floated him, after which all his care was to keep him there. Would the dawn bring Romans or pirates?

At last morning broke in full, the air without a breath. Off to the left he saw the land, too far to think of attempting to make it. Here and there men were adrift like himself. In spots the sea was blackened by charred and smoking fragments.

An hour passed. His anxiety increased. If relief came not speedily, Arrius would die. Sometimes Arrius seemed already dead, he lay so still. He took the helmet off, and then, with greater difficulty, the cuirass; the heart he found fluttering. He took hope at the sign, and held on.

There was nothing to do but wait, and, after the manner of his people, pray.

Gradually, painfully, Arrius recovered consciousness. From incoherent questions as to where he was, and by whom and how he had been saved, he reverted to the battle.

"Our rescue, I see, depends upon the result of the fight. I see also what thou hast done for me. To speak fairly thou hast saved my life at the risk of thy own. More than that, if we get out of this peril, I will do thee such favor as becometh a Roman to prove his gratitude. Yet, yet it is to be seen if, with thy good intent, thou hast really done me a kindness; or, rather, I would exact of thee a promise to do me, in a certain event, the greatest favor one can do another—and of that let me have thy pledge now."

"If the thing be not forbidden, I will do it."

Arrius rested again. "Art thou, indeed, a son of Hur?" he next asked.

"It is as I have said."

"I knew thy father. I knew him, and loved him," Arrius continued. There was another pause, during which something diverted the speaker's thought.

"It cannot be," he proceeded, "that thou, a son of his, hast not heard of Cato and Brutus. They were very great men, and never as great as in death. In their dying, they left this law—a Roman may not survive his good-fortune. There is a heavy ring on my hand. Take it now and put it on thine own finger."

Ben-Hur did so.

"The trinket hath its uses," said Arrius next. "I have property and money. I am accounted rich even in Rome. I have no family. Show the ring to my freedman, who hath control in my absence; you will find him in a villa near Misenum. Tell him how it came to thee, and ask anything, or all he may have; he will not refuse the demand. If I live, I will do better by thee. I will make thee free, and restore thee to thy home and people; or thou mayst give thyself to the pursuit that pleaseth thee most. Pledge me to do what I tell thee now, and as I tell thee; I am waiting, let me have thy promise."

"Noble Arrius, I am warned by thy manner to expect something of gravest concern. Tell me thy wish first."

"Wilt thou promise then?"

"That were to give the pledge, and— Blessed be the God of my fathers! Yonder cometh a ship from the north."

"Hath she a flag?"

"I cannot see one."

Arrius remained quiet, apparently in deep reflection. "Nor any other sign?"

"She hath a sail set, and is of three banks, and cometh swiftly—that is all I can say of her."

"A Roman in triumph would have out many flags. She must be an enemy. Hear now," said Arrius, "while yet I may speak. If the galley be a pirate, thy life is safe; they may not give thee freedom; they may put thee to the oar again; but they will not kill thee. On the other hand, I—" The tribune faltered.

"This is what I would have thee do," he continued resolutely. "If the galley prove a pirate, push me from the plank and drown me. Dost thou hear? Swear thou wilt do it."

"I will not swear," said Ben-Hur firmly, "neither will I do the deed. The Law, O tribune, would make me answerable for thy life. Take back the ring"—he took the seal from his finger—"take it back, and all thy promises of favor in the event of delivery from this peril. The judgment which sent me to the oar for life made me a slave, yet I am not a slave; no more am I thy freedman. I am a son of Israel, and this moment my own master. Take back the ring."

Arrius remained silent.

"Thou wilt not?" Judah continued. "Then, to free myself from a hateful obligation, I give thy gift to the sea. See, O tribune!"

Arrius heard the splash where the ring struck and sank.

"Thou hast done a foolish thing," he said. "Life is a thread I can break without thy help; and, if I do, what will become of thee? If the ship be a pirate, I will escape from the world. I am a Roman. Success and honor are all in all. Yet I would have served thee; thou wouldst not. The ring was the only witness of my will available in this situation. We are both lost. I will die regretting the victory and glory wrested from me; thou wilt live to die a little later, mourning the pious duties undone because of your own folly. I pity thee."

Ben-Hur did not falter. "In all my servitude, O tribune, thou wert the first to look upon me kindly. No, there was another." And he saw plainly the face of the boy who helped him to a drink by the old well at Nazareth. "At least," he proceeded, "thou wert the first to ask me who I was; and if, when I reached out and caught thee, blind and sinking the last time, I, too, had thought how thou couldst be useful to me in my wretchedness, still the act was not all selfish; this I pray you to believe. Moreover, as a thing of conscience, I would rather die with thee than be thy slayer."

Both became silent, waiting, and Ben-Hur looked at the coming ship, watchful of the actions of the strangers. "Now the ship stops. Now she moves off," he said.

"Whither?"

"On our right there is a galley I take to be abandoned. The newcomer heads towards it. Now she is alongside. Now she is sending men aboard."

Then Arrius opened his eyes. "Thank thou thy God," he said to Ben-Hur, after a look at the galleys, "thank thou thy God, as I do my many gods. A pirate would sink, not save, yon ship. The victory is mine. We are saved. Wave thy hand—call to them—bring them quickly. I shall be duumvir, and thou—I knew thy father, and loved him. He was a prince indeed. He taught me a Jew was not a barbarian. I will take thee with me. Give thy God thanks, and call the sailors. Haste!"

Judah raised himself upon the plank; at last he drew the attention of the sailors in the small boat, and they were speedily taken up.

When the survivors afloat were all saved and the prize secured, Arrius spread his flag of commandant anew, and sailed swiftly northward to rejoin the fleet. In due time the fifty vessels coming down the channel closed in upon the fugitive pirates, and not one escaped. To swell the tribune's glory, twenty galleys of the enemy were captured.

Upon his return, Arrius had warm welcome on the mole at Misenum. The young man attending him very early attracted the attention of his friends and the tribune told the story of his rescue and introduced the stranger, omitting carefully the latter's previous history. At the end, he called Ben-Hur to him.

"Good friends, this is my son and heir, who, as he is to take my property—if it be the will of the gods that I leave any—shall be known to you by my name. I pray you all to love him as you love me."

The adoption was legally perfected. And in such manner the newly-appointed Roman duumvir kept his faith with Ben-Hur, giving him happy introduction into the imperial world of Rome.

❧❧❧❧❧❧

"... I saw you as you are,—noble and true and frank and generous ..."

FROM LAFCADIO HEARN TO HIS ELDERLY FRIEND, HENRY WATKIN

[August 14, 1878, New Orleans, Louisiana]

My Dear Old Man: I think you had better come here next October and rejoin your naughty raven. It would not do you any harm to reconnoitre. Think of the times we could have,—delightful rooms with five large windows opening on piazzas shaded by banana trees; dining at Chinese restaurants and being served by Manila waitresses, with oblique eyes and skin like gold; visiting sugar-cane plantations; scudding over to Cuba; dying with the mere delight of laziness; laughing at cold and smiling at the news of snowstorms a thousand miles away; eating the cheapest food in the world,—and sinning the sweetest kind of sins. Now you know, good old Dad, nice old Dad,—you know that you are lazy and ought to be still lazier. Come here and be lazy. Let me be the siren voice enticing a Ulysses who does not stuff wax in his ears. Don't go to horrid, dreadful Kansas. Go to some outrageous ruinous land, where the moons are ten times larger than they are there. Or tell me to pull up stakes, and I shall take unto myself the wings of a bird and fly to any place but beastly Cincinnati.

Money can be made here out of the poor. People are so poor here that nothing pays except that which appeals to poverty. But I think you could make things hop around lively. Now one can make thirty milk biscuits for five cents and eight cups of coffee for five cents. Just think of it! ...

Cincinnati is bad; but it's going to be a d———d sight worse. You know that as well as I do. Leave the vile hole and the long catalogue of Horrid Acquaintances behind you, and come down here to your own little man,—good little man. Get you nice room, nice board, nice business. Perhaps we might strike ile in a glorious spec. Why don't you spec.? You'd better spec. pretty soon, or the times will get so bad that you will have to get up and dust. This is a seaport. There are tall ships here. They sail to Europe,—to London, Marseilles, Constantinople, Smyrna. They sail to the West Indies and those seaports where we are going to open a cigar store or something of that kind.

> Oh, I have seven tall ships at sea,
> And seven more at hand;
> And five and twenty jolly, jolly seamen
> Shall be at your command.

May the Immortal Gods preserve you in immortal youth.

[July 7, 1882, New Orleans, Louisiana]

My Dear Old Dad: Your letter lies before me here like a white tablet of stone bearing a dead name; and in my mind there is just such a silence as one feels standing before a tomb,—so that I can press your hand only and say nothing.

I must go North in a few months, by way of Cincinnati, and spend a week or so in the city.

"Were you situated like me,—that is, having no large business or large interest,—I think I should try to coax you to seek the El Dorado of the future, where fortunes will certainly be made by practical men,—Mexico,—where no one ever lights a fire, and where one has only to go in the sun when he is too cold, into the shade when he is too warm. But for the present I will only ask you to come down here when the weather gets healthy and your business will allow it. You will stay with me, of course, and no expense. The trip would be agreeable in the season when the air is sweet with orange blossoms.

The population here is exceedingly queer,—something it is hard to describe, and something which it is possible to learn only after a painful experience of years. At present I may say that all my acquaintances here are limited to about half a dozen, with one or two friends whom I invite to see me occasionally. Yet almost daily I receive letters from people I do not know, asking favors which I never grant. You say you cannot write. I differ with you; but it would certainly be impossible for either of us to write many things we would like to say. Still, you can easily drop a line from time to time, even a postal card, just to let me know you are well. If I do not get up to see you by September, I hope to see you down. I dreamed one night that I heard the ticking of the queer clock,—like the long strides of a man booted and spurred. You know the clock I mean,—the long, weird-faced clock. My eyes are not well, of course,—never will be; but they are better. More about myself I cannot tell you in a letter,—except that I suppose I have changed a little. Less despondent, but less hopeful; wiser a little and more silent; less nervous, but less merry; more systematic and perhaps a good deal more selfish. Not strictly economical, but coming to it steadily; and in leisure hours studying the theories of the East, the poetry of antique India, the teachings of the wise concerning absorption and emanation, the illusions of existence, and happiness as the equivalent of annihilation. Think they were wiser than the wisest of Occidental ecclesiastics.

And still there is in life much sweetness and much pleasure in the accomplishment of a fixed purpose. Existence may be a delusion and desire a snare, but I expect to exist long enough to satisfy my desire to see thee again before entering Nirvana. So, reaching to thee the grasp of friendship across the distance of a thousand miles, I remain in the hope of being always remembered sincerely as your friend.

[1887]

DEAR OLD MAN: A delightful trip brought me safe and sound to New York, where my dear friend Krehbiel was waiting to take me to his cosy home. I cannot tell you how much our little meeting delighted me, or how much I regretted to depart so soon, or how differently I regarded our old friendship from my old way of looking at it. I was too young, too foolish, and too selfish to know you as you are, when we used to be together. Ten years made little exterior change in me, but a great deal of heart-change; and I saw you as you are,—noble and true and frank and generous, and felt I loved you more than I ever did before; felt also how much I owed you, and will always owe you,—and understood how much allowance you had made for all my horrid, foolish ways when I used to be with you. Well, I am sure to see you again. I am having one of the most delightful holidays here I ever had in my life; and I expect to stay a few weeks. If it were not for the terrible winters, I should like to live in New York. Some day I suppose I shall have to spend a good deal of my time here. The houses eleven stories high, that seem trying to climb into the moon,—the tremendous streets and roads,—the cascading thunder of the awful torrent of life,—the sense of wealth-force and mind-power that oppresses the stranger here,—all these form so colossal a contrast with the inert and warmly colored Southern life that I know not how to express my impression. I can only think that I have found superb material for a future story, in which the influence of New York on a Southern mind may be described. Well, new as these things may seem to me, they are, no doubt, old and un-interesting to you,—so that I shall not bore you with my impressions. I will look forward to our next meeting, when during a longer stay in Cin. I can tell you such little experiences of my trip as may please you. I want to get into that dear little shop of yours again. I dreamed of it the other night, and heard the ticking of the old clock like a man's feet treading on pavement far away; and I saw the Sphinx, with the mother and child in her arms, move her monstrous head, and observe: "The sky in New York is grey!"

When I woke up it *was* grey, and it remained grey until today. Even now it is not like our summer blue. It looks higher and paler and colder. We are nearer to God in the South, just as we are nearer to Death in that terrible and splendid heat of the Gulf Coast. When I write God, of course I mean only the World-Soul, the mighty and sweetest life of Nature, the great Blue Ghost, the Holy Ghost which fills planets and hearts with beauty.

Believe me, Dear Old Dad,
Affectionately your son,
LAFCADIO HEARN

[September, 1894, Kumamoto, Japan]

DEAR OLD DAD: It delighted me to get that kindest double letter from yourself and sweet-hearted little daughter,—or rather delighted us. My wife speaks no English, but I translated it for her. She will send a letter in Japanese, which Miss Effie will not be able to read, but which she will keep as a curiosity perhaps. Our love to you both.

How often I have thought of you, and wondered about you, and wished I could pass with you more of the old-fashioned evenings, reading ancient volumes of the *Atlantic Monthly*,—so much better a magazine in those days than in these, when I am regularly advertised as one of its contributors.

I often wonder now at your infinite patience with the extraordinary, superhuman foolishness and wickedness of the worst pet you ever had in your life. When I think of all the naughty, mean, absurd, detestable things I did to vex you and to scandalize you, I can't for the life of me understand why you didn't want to kill me,—as a sacrifice to the Gods. What an idiot I was!—and how could you be so good?—and why do men change so? I think of my old self as of something which ought not to have been allowed to exist on the face of the earth,—and yet, in my present self, I sometimes feel ghostly reminders that the old self was very real indeed. Well, I wish I were near you to love you and make up for all old troubles.

When you hear that I have been able to save between thirty-five hundred and four thousand dollars, you will not think I have made no progress. But I have put all, or all that I could reasonably do, in my wife's name. The future looks very black. The reaction against foreign influence is strong; and I feel more and more every day that I shall have to leave Japan eventually, at least for some years. When I first met you I was—nineteen. I am now forty-four! Well, I suppose I must have lots more trouble before I go to Nirvana.

Effie says you do not see my writings. My book will be out by the time you get this letter,—that is, my first book on Japan. Effie can read bits of it to you. And I figure in the *Atlantic* every few months. Cheap fame;—the amazing fortune I once expected doesn't turn up at all. I have been obliged to learn the fact that I am not a genius, and that I must be content with the crumbs from the table of Dives.

But this is all Egotism. I am guilty of it only because you asked for a small quantity. About yourself and all who love you my letter rather ought to be. Speak always well of me to John Chamberlain [a journalist]. I liked him well. Do you remember the long walks over the Ohio, in the evening, among the fireflies and grasshoppers, to hear lectures upon spiritual things? If I were near you now, I could saturate you with Oriental spiritualism,—Buddhism,—everything you would like, but after a totally novel fashion. When one has lived alone five years in a Buddhist atmosphere, one naturally becomes penetrated by the thoughts that hover in it; my whole thinking, I must acknowledge, has been changed, in spite of my long studies of Spencer and of Schopenhauer. I do not mean that I am a Buddhist, but I mean that the inherited ancestral feelings about the universe—the Occidental ideas every Englishman has—have been totally transformed.

I am almost sure I shall have to seek America again. If that happens, I shall see you or die. All now is doubt and confusion. But in this little house all is love to you. We have your picture; ... we all know you, as if you were an old acquaintance.

I wish we could be together somewhere for a pleasant evening chat, hearing in the intervals the office clock, like the sound of a long-legged walker. I wish we could talk over all the hopes and dreams of ideal societies, and the reasons of the failure to realize them. I wish I could tell you about the ideas of Western civilization which are produced by a long sojourn in the Orient. How pleasant to take country walks again! that is, if there be any country left around Cincinnati. How pleasant to read to you strange stories and theories from the Far East! Still, I have become so accustomed to Japanese life that a return to Western ways would not be altogether easy at first. What a pity I did not reach Japan ten years sooner!

Tell me, if you write again, all pleasant news about old friends. Love to you always, and believe me ever,

Your extremely bad and ungrateful

Grey-headed boy,

LAFCADIO HEARN

It is a mistake to think that one makes a friend because of his or her qualities; it has nothing to do with qualities at all. It is the person that we want, not what he does or says, or does not do or say, but what he is! that is eternally enough. Who shall explain the extraordinary instinct that tells us, perhaps after a single meeting, that this or that particular person in some mysterious way matters to us? I confess that, for myself, I never enter a new company without the hope that I may discover a friend, perhaps *the* friend, sitting there with an expectant smile. That hope survives a thousand disappointments. People who deal with life generously and large-heartedly go on multiplying relationships to the end.

—ARTHUR CHRISTOPHER BENSON

It is better to have bitter foes than friends too sweet.

—CATO

FROM "ELEGY WRITTEN IN A COUNTRY CHURCHYARD"

Thomas Gray

Here rests his head upon the lap of Earth
A Youth, to Fortune and to Fame unknown;
Fair Science frown'd not on his humble birth,
And Melancholy mark'd him for her own.

Large was his bounty, and his soul sincere,
Heav'n did a recompense as largely send:
He gave to Misery all he had, a tear,
He gain'd from Heaven ('twas all he wish'd) a friend.

". . . he made New York into a small town."

FATHER DUFFY

Alexander Woollcott

They buried Father Duffy from St. Patrick's at the end of June in 1932. The huge cathedral might as well have been a tiny chapel for all it could hope to hold those of us who wanted to say good-by to him. As I waited in the cool, candle-lit dusk of the church for the procession to make its way up the sunny avenue, all around me lips were moving in prayer and gnarled fingers were telling their rosaries. But even the heathen could at least count over their hours with him. There were many of us there, outsiders who, without belonging to his outfit, had nevertheless been attached to him for rations—of the spirit. One had only to stop for a moment and speak to him on the street to go on one's way immensely set up, reassured by what he was that there might be a good deal, after all, to this institution called the human race.

While we waited, my own wry thoughts jumped back to that desperate October in 1918 when his regiment, the old 69th of New York, was cut to ribbons in the Argonne. Especially I recalled the black day when Colonel Donovan was carried out of the battle on a blanket—Wild Bill, who was the very apple of the Padre's eye. Father Duffy had always scolded him for his gaudy recklessness, and there he was at

last with his underpinnings shot from under him. As they carried
him into the dressing-station he had just strength enough left to shake
a defiant fist. "Ah there, Father," he said, "you thought you'd have
the pleasure of burying me!" Father Duffy shook a fist in reply. "And
I will yet," he said. But it was not to be that way. For here, fourteen
years later, was Wild Bill and a thousand others of the old regiment
coming up the avenue to bury Father Duffy.

One by one there came back to me all the times our paths had crossed
in France and on the Rhine. He would always have tall tales to tell
of his Irish fighters, who, with death all around them, heard only the
grace of God purring in their hearts. It delighted him that they spoke
of the Ourcq as the O'Rourke, and he enjoyed their wonderment at the
French presumption in dignifying so measly a creek by calling it a
river. He loved the story of one wounded soldier who waved aside a
proffered canteen. "Give it to the Ourcq. It needs it more than I do."
And he loved all stories wherein the uppity were discomfited. On the
Rhine he relished the spectacle of Pershing vainly trying to unbend
a bit and play the little father to his troops. The Commander-in-Chief
paused before one Irish doughboy who had three wound stripes on his
arm. "Well, my lad," asked the great man in benevolent tones, "and
where did you get those?" "From the supply sergeant, Sir," the hero
answered, and Father Duffy grinned from ear to ear.

Most often he would talk not of France and the war at all, but of
New York. He liked nothing better than to sit in a shell-hole with
Clancey and Callahan and Kerrigan and talk about New York. I have
stood beside him ankle-deep in the Argonne mud and, above the noise
of the rain pattering on our helmets, heard him speculate about the
gleam of Fifth Avenue in the October sunshine and say how he would
like to see once more that grand actress who called herself Laurette
Taylor, but who, mind you, was born a Cooney....

For he was the great New Yorker. Born in Canada, Irish as Irish,
schooled in Maynooth, he was surely the first citizen of our town. This
city is too large for most of us. But not for Father Duffy. Not too large,
I mean, for him to invest it with the homeliness of a neighborhood.
When he walked down the street—any street—he was like a *curé*
striding through his own village. Everyone knew him. I have walked
beside him and thought I had never before seen so many *pleased* faces.
The beaming cop would stop all traffic to make a path from curb to
curb for Father Duffy. Both the proud-stomached banker who stopped
to speak with him on the corner and the checkroom boy who took his
hat at the restaurant would grin transcendently at the sight of him.
He would call them both by their first names, and you could see how
proud they were on that account. Father Duffy was of such dimensions
that he made New York into a small town.

No wonder all the sidewalk space as far as one could see was needed for the overflow at his funeral. To my notion, the mute multitude in the June sunlight made the more impressive congregation.... One woman I know saw an unused bit of pavement and asked a huge policeman if she might not stand there. He told her the space was reserved. "But," she explained, as if offering credentials, "I was a personal friend of Father Duffy's." The policeman's answer was an epitaph. "That is true, Ma'am," he said, "of everyone here today."

"REMEMBRANCE OF THINGS PAST"
William Shakespeare

When to the sessions of sweet silent thought
I summon up remembrance of things past,
I sigh the lack of many a thing I sought,
And with old woes new wail my dear time's waste:
Then can I drown an eye, unused to flow,
For precious friends hid in death's dateless night,
And weep afresh love's long since cancell'd woe,
And moan the expense of many a vanish'd sight:
Then can I grieve at grievances foregone,
And heavily from woe to woe tell o'er
The sad account of fore-bemoaned moan,
Which I new pay as if not paid before.
But if the while I think on thee, dear friend,
All losses are restored and sorrows end.

"There is a change ..."

SELF-DISCOVERY
Langdon Elwyn Mitchell

I entered upon a day, at the house of my friend to give him greeting. Then I saw that in the face of my friend there was a change and that he did not look upon me with the same eyes as heretofore. "There is a change," I said.

"There is no change," he said.

So I gave him messages, then, and greetings of gladness, and called him by an old name, and I stayed with him, and we spoke together; but, nevertheless, I saw that a change had come over him.

So I said, "My friend, there is a change come over thee."

And he said, "Nay, no change." So we conversed together again, and the hour came for departure. Then my friend bade me stay, but I saw that even in his bidding there was a change. So I said to him, "There is a change, which thou canst not deny. Wherefore art thou changed?" And my friend said to me, "Farewell!" So I departed and left him.

But my heart within me cried out against that estrangement; and my soul was broken daily, so that I could not live.

Therefore again upon a day I entered the house of him, who was my friend, that I might upbraid him; and my friend moving toward me, I cried out against him as he came, "Wherefore art thou estranged from me?" But my friend, heeding me not at all, said "Wherefore hast thou delayed so long?"

And I looked upon his face and he was sorrowful.

Then was I wroth within my mind and knew not which way to turn.

For I saw that the change that had been was in my own soul.

". . . Wretched is every soul bound by the friendship of perishable things . . ."

THE DEATH OF A DEAR FRIEND

St. Augustine

In those years when I first began to teach rhetoric in my native town, I had made one my friend, but too dear to me, from a community of pursuits, of mine own age, and, as myself, in the first opening flower of youth. He had grown up of a child with me, and we had been both school-fellows, and play-fellows. But he was not yet my friend as afterwards, nor even then, as true friendship is; for true it cannot be, unless in such as Thou cementest together, cleaving unto Thee, by that *love which is shed abroad in our hearts by the Holy Ghost, which is given unto us.* Yet was it but too sweet, ripened by the warmth of kindred studies: for, from the true faith (which he as a youth had not soundly and thoroughly imbibed,) I had warped him also to those superstitious and pernicious fables, for which my mother bewailed me. With me he

now erred in mind, nor could my soul be without him. But behold
Thou wert close on the steps of Thy fugitives, at once *God of vengeance,*
and Fountain of mercies, turning us to Thyself by wonderful means;
Thou tookest that man out of this life, when he had scarce filled up
one whole year of my friendship, sweet to me above all sweetness of
that my life.

Who can recount all Thy praises, which he hath felt in his one self?
What diddest Thou then, my God, and how unsearchable is the *abyss
of Thy judgments?* For long, sore sick of a fever, he lay senseless in a
death-sweat; and his recovery being despaired of, he was baptized,
unknowing; myself meanwhile little regarding, and presuming that his
soul would retain rather what it had received of me, not what was
wrought on his unconscious body. But it proved far otherwise: for he
was refreshed, and restored. Forthwith, as soon as I could speak with
him, (and I could, so soon as he was able, for I never left him, and we
hung but too much upon each other,) I essayed to jest with him as
though he would jest with me at that baptism which he had received,
when utterly absent in mind and feeling, but had now understood that
he had received. But he so shrunk from me, as from an enemy; and
with a wonderful and sudden freedom bade me, as I would continue
his friend, forbear such language to him. I, all astonished and amazed,
suppressed all my emotions till he should grow well, and his health
were strong enough for me to deal with him, as I would. But he was
taken away from my phrensy, that with Thee he might be preserved
for my comfort; a few days after, in my absence, he was attacked again
by the fever, and so departed.

At this grief my heart was utterly darkened; and whatever I beheld
was death. My native country was a torment to me, and my father's
house a strange unhappiness; and whatever I had shared with him,
wanting him, became a distracting torture. Mine eyes sought him everywhere, but he was not granted them; and I hated all places, for that they
had not him; nor could they now tell me, "he is coming," as when he
was alive and absent. I became a great riddle to myself, and I asked my
soul, *why she was so sad, and why she disquieted me sorely:* but she
knew not what to answer me. And if I said, *Trust in God,* she very
rightly obeyed me not; because that most dear friend, whom she had
lost, was, being man, both truer and better, than that phantasm she was
bid to trust in. Only tears were sweet to me, for they succeeded my
friend, in the dearest of my affections.

And now, Lord, these things are passed by, and time hath assuaged
my wound. May I learn from Thee, who are Truth, and approach the
ear of my heart unto Thy mouth, that Thou mayest tell me why weeping is sweet to the miserable? ... And yet unless we mourned in Thine
ears, we should have no hope left. Whence then is sweet fruit gathered

from the bitterness of life, from groaning, tears, sighs, and complaints?
Doth this sweeten it, that we hope thou hearest?...For I neither hoped
he should return to life, nor did I desire this with my tears; but I wept
only and grieved. For I was miserable, and had lost my joy....

Wretched I was; and wretched is every soul bound by the friendship
of perishable things; he is torn asunder when he loses them, and then
he feels the wretchedness, which he had, ere yet he lost them. So was
it then with me; I wept most bitterly, and found my repose in bitterness. Thus was I wretched, and that wretched life I held dearer than
my friend. For though I would willingly have changed it, yet was I
more unwilling to part with it, than with him;...But in me there
had arisen some unexplained feeling, too contrary to this, for at once
I loathed exceedingly to live, and feared to die. I suppose, the more I
loved him, the more did I hate, and fear (as a most cruel enemy)
death, which had bereaved me of him: and I imagined it would speedily
make an end of all men, since it had power over him. Thus was it with
me, I remember....

O madness, which knowest not how to love men, like men! O foolish man that I then was, enduring impatiently the lot of man! I fretted
then, sighed, wept, was distracted; had neither rest nor counsel. For I
bore about a shattered and bleeding soul, impatient of being borne by
me, yet where to repose it, I found not. Not in calm groves, not in games
and music, nor in fragrant spots, nor in curious banquettings, nor in
the pleasures of the bed and the couch; nor (finally) in books or poesy,
found it repose. All things looked ghastly, yea, the very light; whatsoever was not what he was, was revolting and hateful, except groaning
and tears. For in those alone found I a little refreshment. But when
my soul was withdrawn from them, a huge load of misery weighed me
down. To Thee, O Lord, it ought to have been raised, for Thee to
lighten; I knew it; but neither could nor would; the more, since, when
I thought of Thee, Thou wert not to me any solid or substantial thing.
For Thou wert not Thyself, but a mere phantom, and my error was my
God....

Times lose no time; nor do they roll idly by; through our senses they
work strange operations on the mind. Behold, they went and came day
by day, and by coming and going, introduced into my mind other
imaginations, and other remembrances; and little by little patched me
up again with my old kind of delights, unto which that my sorrow gave
way. And yet there succeeded, not indeed other griefs, yet the causes of
other griefs. For whence had that former grief so easily reached my
very inmost soul, but that I had poured out my soul upon the dust, in
loving one that must die, as if he would never die? For what restored
and refreshed me chiefly, was the solaces of other friends, with whom
I did love, what instead of Thee I loved: and this was a great fable,

and protracted lie, by whose adulterous stimulus, our soul, which lay itching in our ears, was being defiled. But that fable would not die to me, so oft as any of my friends died....

Blessed whoso loveth Thee, and his friends in Thee, and his enemy for Thee. For he alone loses none dear to him, to whom all are dear in Him Who cannot be lost. And who is this but our God, the *God that made heaven and earth,* and *filleth them,* because by filling them He created them?

(Translated by E. B. Pusey)

❧❧❧❧❧

My only sketch, profile, of Heaven is a large blue sky, and larger than the biggest I have seen in June—and in it are my friends—all of them—every one of them.

—EMILY DICKINSON

❧❧❧❧❧

FROM "LINES ON A FRIEND"
Samuel Taylor Coleridge

As oft at twilight gloom thy grave I pass,
And sit me down upon its recent grass,
With introverted eye I contemplate
Similitude of soul, perhaps of—Fate!
To me hath Heaven with bounteous hand assigned
Energic Reason and a shaping mind,
The daring ken of Truth, the Patriot's part,
And Pity's sigh, that breathes the gentle heart—
Sloth-jaundiced all! and from my graspless hand
Drop Friendship's precious pearls, like hour-glass sand.
I weep, yet stoop not! the faint anguish flows,
A dreamy pang in Morning's feverish doze.

❧❧❧❧❧

If you lend a friend five dollars and never see him again, it's worth it.

—ANONYMOUS

❧❧❧❧❧

". . . excess of sorrow is as foolish as profuse laughter."

SENECA ON SORROW FOR THE DEATH OF FRIENDS

Next to the encounter of death in our own bodies, the most sensible calamity to an honest man is the death of a friend; and we are not in truth without some generous instances of those who have preferred a friend's life before their own; and yet this affliction, which by nature is so grievous to us, is by virtue and Providence made familiar and easy.

To lament the death of a friend is both natural and just; a sigh or a tear I would allow to his memory: but no profuse or obstinate sorrow. Clamorous and public lamentations are not so much the effects of grief as of vain-glory. He that is sadder in company than alone, shows rather the ambition of his sorrow than the piety of it. . . . If destiny were to be wrought upon by tears, I would allow you to spend your days and nights in sadness and mourning, tearing of your hair, and beating of your breast; but if Fate be inexorable, and death will keep what it has taken, grief is to no purpose. And yet I would not advise insensibility and hardness. . . .

A wise man gives way to tears in some cases, and cannot avoid them in others. When one is struck with the surprise of ill news, as the death of a friend, or the like; or upon the last embrace of an acquaintance under the hand of an executioner, he lies under a natural necessity of weeping and trembling. In another case we may indulge our sorrow, as upon the memory of a dead friend's conversation or kindness, one may let fall tears of generosity and joy. We favor the one, and we are overcome by the other; and this is well; but we are not upon any terms to force them: They may flow of their own sweet accord, without derogating from the dignity of a wise man; who at the same time both preserves his gravity, and obeys nature. Nay, there is a certain *decorum* even in weeping; for excess of sorrow is as foolish as profuse laughter.

(*Translated by Sir Roger L'Estrange, Knt.*)

Short accounts make long friends.

—BALZAC

"... my friend's faults never alienate me ..."

MY HUNDRED FRIENDS

Ben Hecht

What fun living would be if all our friendships survived! If all the chums and partners we had still clamored to see us, and we them! How rich our existence would be were it full of that fine cast of characters with whom we played the many scenes of our lives.

But we must grow old on an emptying stage, and in a corner of it, usually. And if anybody speaks our name we are likely not to know theirs. It is a lucky man who after fifty-five can call anyone "old friend."

Our friends vanish with the events that produce them. I look back on a hundred friends, each of them a fellow who once seemed a vital part of my day and is no part of it now.

This is not as depressing as it sounds. I, for one, have never regretted vanished friendships. They are like money happily spent.

I know men who make a career of not permitting friendships to lapse. They keep telephoning, writing, getting together. But when I look closely at the continued friendships of such men I note that it is with "important" people the friendship is kept going. This is the thing that keeps "celebrities" knowing one another longer than people of no renown. Long after their intimacies have ended, celebrities continue to pool their fame. Being together is no longer friendship for them but something almost as important—good publicity. The cafes of New York and Hollywood are filled nightly with a comradeship more for the camera than the soul.

Obviously when I think of how pleasant life would be if our friendships survived, I am not thinking of my old friends alone, but of my own vanished enthusiasms. It is in their air that my old friends breathed and it is for those heady atmospheres I mourn.

I can see now that any time I loved anything, friends bloomed magically around the thing loved. If it was only walking or playing cards, friends appeared to share and increase my pleasure. They stepped out of limbo and became my fellow dreamers. And there were times when it was not I and my activities that lured partisans. These were times when I loved myself.

Out of many friendships I have learned a few unvarying qualities. Most important is the quality of impermanence. Friendship is the thinnest of cements. A change of job or a move to a different street can break the pleasantest of friendships. Marriage can put an end to a dozen of them without a word being spoken. Success requires us to change our friends, as does failure. Persistent calamity is also fatal.

Loyalty and sacrifice, if called on too much, destroy a friendship quickly. It is possible to love a woman who has only troubles to give us. But a friend with similar impediments ceases to be an equal and thus, automatically, ceases to be a friend.

I have noted that the best and closest friends are those who seldom call on each other for help. In fact, such is almost the finest definition of a friend—a person who does not need us but who is able to enjoy us.

I have seldom suffered over the troubles of a friend. Are his mishaps short of tragedy, I am inclined to chuckle. And he is seldom serious in telling me of his misfortunes. He makes anecdotes out of them, postures comically in their midst and tries to entertain me with them. This is one of the chief values of my friendship, as it is of his. We enable each other to play the strong man superior to his fate. Given a friend to listen, my own disasters change color. I win victories while relating them. Not only have I a friend "on my side" who will believe my version of the battle—and permit me to seem a victor in my communiqués—but I have actually a victory in me. I am able to show my friend my untouched side. My secret superiority to bad events becomes stronger when I can speak and have a friend believe in it.

Another asset a friend has to offer is the fact that he is a soothing fellow—always half a bore. There are no mysteries to him. He may think he has secret characteristics that are hidden from me. But this is literally impossible. Whatever secrets in the way of hidden personality or sex aberration my friend may have, I have guessed at them—for it is the mark of friendship to imagine the worst possible thing about a friend. An enemy is a sealed arsenal of vices, a friend is an open clinic.

In fact, I have thought more downright scandal about friends than about an enemy. The fact that I can see his failings so plainly is one of the things that make him my friend. I note that he lies, drinks, falls down manholes, is a secret bounder and makes a fool of himself over idiotic women. I am daily aware that he brags, forgets, is as blind as a goat toward his own lapses, and I feel often that only a miracle can save him from disintegration.

Yet my friend's faults never alienate me, for I am, somehow, never their victim. In a mysterious way his friendship keeps him from directing his faults at me. He will point them at his wife, his paramour and his enemies. That is why his faults are comic to me. He is Harlequin and never horror.

There are many other qualities to friendship, such as the absence of competitiveness. A friend is a rival whom I wish well, whose success does not irk me but adds almost as much to my importance as to his. There is also the quality of love, an odd, unsensual love, a love without greed or possessiveness, the sort of love one has for liquor or an infant or a book or life itself.

Such brotherhoods, dead and alive, hold in them most of my history. While writing this book I have looked forward to telling the stories of my friends, not alone because I have desired to meet them again but because I hoped to recapture the happy things in my life that produced them.

As you get older, and your world keeps shrinking, you sometimes think with amazement of the times when you trifled away friendships —insensitive in the reckless folly of youth to the wounds you inflicted and indifferent to healing them.

—Johann Wolfgang von Goethe
(*Translated by Herman J. Weigand*)

TO ONE WHO PUBLISHED IN PRINT
What Had Been Entrusted to Him by My Fireside
Samuel Taylor Coleridge

Two things hast thou made known to half the nation,
My secrets and my want of penetration:
For O! far more than all which thou hast penn'd
It shames me to have call'd a wretch, like thee, my friend!

"... a jovial party to all eternity!"

ROBERT BURNS TO RICHARD BROWN

Mauchline, 21st May, 1789

My Dear Friend,
I was in the country by accident, and hearing of your safe arrival, I could not resist the temptation of wishing you joy on your return, wishing you would write to me before you sail again, wishing you would always set me down as your bosom friend, wishing you long life

and prosperity, and that every good thing may attend you, wishing Mrs. Brown and your little ones as free of the evils of this world as is consistent with humanity, wishing you and she were to make two at the ensuing lying-in with which Mrs. B. threatens very soon to favor me, wishing I had longer time to write to you at present, and, finally, wishing that if there is to be another state of existence, Mr. B., Mrs. B., our little ones, and both families, and you and I, in some snug retreat, may make a jovial party to all eternity!

My direction is at Ellisland, near Dumfries.

Yours,
R. B.

"He loved me for my own sake . . ."

THE ATHEIST'S MASS *

Honoré de Balzac

Bianchon, a physician to whom science owes a fine system of theoretical physiology, and who, while still young, made himself a celebrity in the medical school of Paris, that central luminary to which European doctors do homage, practiced surgery for a long time before he took up medicine. His earliest studies were guided by one of the greatest of French surgeons, the illustrious Desplein, who flashed across science like a meteor. By the consensus even of his enemies, he took with him to the tomb an incommunicable method. Like all men of genius, he had no heirs; he carried everything in him, and carried it away with him.

On his tomb there is no proclaiming statue to repeat to posterity the mysteries which genius seeks out at its own cost.

But perhaps Desplein's genius was answerable for his beliefs, and for that reason mortal. He believed neither in the antecedent animal nor the surviving spirit of man. Desplein had no doubts; he was positive. His bold and unqualified atheism was like that of many scientific men, the best men in the world, but invincible atheists—atheists such as religious people declare to be impossible. This man died, it is said, in final impenitence, as do, unfortunately, many noble geniuses whom God may forgive.

The life of this man, great as he was, was marred by many meannesses, to use the expression employed by his enemies, who were anxious

* Abridged by the Editor.

to diminish his glory, but which it would be more proper to call apparent contradictions.

As, in Desplein, his glory and science were invulnerable, his enemies attacked his odd moods and his temper, whereas, in fact, he was simply characterised by what the English call eccentricity. Sometimes very handsomely dressed, like Crebillon the tragical, he would suddenly affect extreme indifference as to what he wore; he was sometimes seen in a carriage and sometimes on foot. By turns rough and kind, harsh and covetous on the surface, but capable of offering his whole fortune to his exiled masters—who did him the honour of accepting it for a few days—no man ever gave rise to such contradictory judgments.

Among the riddles which Desplein's life presents to many of his contemporaries, we have chosen one of the most interesting, because the answer is to be found at the end of the narrative, and will avenge him for some foolish charges.

Of all the students in Desplein's hospital, Horace Bianchon was one of those to whom he most warmly attached himself. Before being a house surgeon at the Hôtel-Dieu, Horace Bianchon had been a medical student lodging in a squalid boarding-house in the Quartier Latin, known as the Maison Vauquer. This poor young man had felt there the gnawing of that burning poverty which is a sort of crucible from which great talents are to emerge as pure and incorruptible as diamonds, which may be subjected to any shock without being crushed.

Horace was an upright young fellow, incapable of tergiversation on a matter of honour, going to the point without waste of words, and as ready to pledge his cloak for a friend as to give him his time and his night hours. Horace, in short, was one of those friends who are never anxious as to what they may get in return for what they give, feeling sure that they will in their turn get more than they give. Most of his friends felt for him that deep-seated respect which is inspired by unostentatious virtue, and many of them dreaded his censure. But Horace made no pedantic display of his qualities. He was neither a puritan nor a preacher.

He carried his poverty with the cheerfulness which is perhaps one of the chief elements of courage, and, like all people who have nothing, he made very few debts. As sober as a camel and active as a stag, he was steadfast in his ideas and his conduct.

The happy phase of Bianchon's life began on the day when the famous surgeon had proof of the qualities and the defects which, these no less than those, make Dr. Horace Bianchon doubly dear to his friends. When a leading clinical practitioner takes a young man to his bosom, that young man has, as they say, his foot in the stirrup. Desplein did not fail to take Bianchon as his assistant to wealthy houses, where some complimentary fee almost always found its way into the student's pocket, and where the mysteries of Paris life were insensibly revealed to the young provincial; he kept him at his side when a consultation was to be held, and gave him occupation; sometimes he would send him to a watering-place with a rich patient; in fact, he was making a practice for him. The consequence was that in the course of time the Tyrant of surgery had a devoted ally. These two men—one at the summit of honour and of his science, enjoying an immense fortune and an immense reputation, the other a humble Omega, having neither fortune nor fame—became intimate friends.

One day Bianchon spoke to Desplein of a poor water-carrier of the Saint-Jacques district, who had a horrible disease caused by fatigue and want; this wretched Auvergnat had had nothing but potatoes to eat during the dreadful winter of 1821. Desplein left all his visits and, at the risk of killing his horse, he rushed off, followed by Bianchon, to the poor man's dwelling, and saw himself to his being removed to a sick house, founded by the famous Dubois in the Faubourg Saint-Denis. Then he went to attend the man, and when he had cured him he gave him the necessary sum to buy a horse and a water-barrel. This Auvergnat distinguished himself by an amusing action. One of his friends fell ill, and he took him at once to Desplein, saying to his benefactor: "I could not have borne to let him go to any one else!" Rough customer as he was, Desplein grasped the water-carrier's hand, and said: "Bring them all to me."

He got the native of Cantal into the Hôtel-Dieu, where he took the greatest care of him. Bianchon had already observed in his chief a predilection for Auvergnats, and especially for water-carriers; but as Desplein took a sort of pride in his cures at the Hôtel-Dieu, the pupil saw nothing very strange in that.

One day, as he crossed the Place Saint-Sulpice, Bianchon caught sight of his master going into the church at about nine in the morning. Desplein, who at that time never went a step without his cab, was on foot, and slipped in by the door in the Rue du Petit-Lion, as if he were stealing into some house of ill fame. The house surgeon, naturally possessed by curiosity, knowing his master's opinions, and being himself a rabid follower of Cabanis, Bianchon stole into the church, and was not a little astonished to see the great Desplein, the atheist, who had no mercy on the angels—who give no work to the lancet, and cannot suffer from fistula or gastritis—in short, this audacious scoffer kneeling humbly, and where? In the Lady Chapel, where he remained through the mass, giving alms for the expenses of the service, alms for the poor, and looking as serious as though he were superintending an operation.

Bianchon did not wish to seem as though he were spying on the head surgeon of the Hôtel-Dieu; he went away. As it happened, Desplein asked him to dine with him that day, not at his own house, but at a restaurant. At dessert Bianchon skillfully contrived to talk of the mass.

"A farce," said Desplein. In short, Desplein was delighted to disport himself in his most atheistical vein; a flow of Voltarian satire, or, to be accurate, a vile imitation of the *Citateur.*

"Hallo! where is my worshipper of this morning?" said Bianchon to himself.

He said nothing; he began to doubt whether he had really seen his chief at Saint-Sulpice. Desplein would not have troubled himself to tell Bianchon a lie, they knew each other too well; they had already exchanged thoughts on quite equally serious subjects, and discussed systems *de natura rerum,* probing or dissecting them with the knife and scalpel of incredulity.

Three months went by. Bianchon did not attempt to follow the matter up, though it remained stamped on his memory. One day that year, one of the physicians of the Hôtel-Dieu took Desplein by the arm, as if to question him, in Bianchon's presence.

"What were you doing at Saint-Sulpice, my dear master?" said he.

"I went to see a priest who had a diseased knee-bone, and to whom the Duchesse d'Angoulême did me the honour to recommend me," said Desplein.

The questioner took this defeat for an answer; not so Bianchon.

"Oh, he goes to see damaged knees in church!—He went to mass," said the young man to himself.

Bianchon resolved to watch Desplein. He remembered the day and hour when he had detected him going into Saint-Sulpice and resolved to be there again next year on the same day and at the same hour, to see if he could find him there again. In that case the periodicity of his devotions would justify a scientific investigation; for in such a man there ought to be no direct antagonism of thought and action.

Next year, on the said day and hour, Bianchon, who had already ceased to be Desplein's house surgeon, saw the great man's cab standing at the corner of the Rue de Tournon and the Rue du Petit-Lion, whence his friend jesuitically crept along by the wall of Saint-Sulpice, and once more attended mass in front of the Virgin's altar. It was Desplein, sure enough! The master-surgeon, the atheist at heart, the worshipper by chance. The mystery was greater than ever; the regularity of the phenomenon complicated it. When Desplein had left, Bianchon went to the sacristan, who took charge of the chapel, and asked him whether the gentleman were a constant worshipper.

"For twenty years that I have been here," replied the man, "M. Desplein has come four times a year to attend this mass. He founded it."

"A mass founded by him!" said Bianchon, as he went away.

Some time elapsed before Dr. Bianchon, though so much his friend, found an opportunity of speaking to Desplein of this incident of his life. Though they met in consultation, or in society, it was difficult to find an hour of confidential solitude. At last seven years later, after the Revolution of 1830, Bianchon once more detected Desplein going into Saint-Sulpice. The doctor followed him and knelt down by him without the slightest notice or demonstration of surprise from his friend. They both attended this mass of his founding.

"Will you tell me, my dear fellow," said Bianchon, as they left the church, "the reason for your fit of monkishness? I have caught you three times going to mass— You! You must account to me for this mystery, explain such a flagrant disagreement between your opinions and your conduct. You do not believe in God, and yet you attend mass? My dear master, you are bound to give me an answer."

"I am like a great many devout people, men who on the surface are deeply religious, but quite as much atheist as you or I can be."

"All that has nothing to do with my question," retorted Bianchon. "I want to know the reason for what you have just been doing, and why you founded this mass."

"Faith! my dear boy," said Desplein, "I am on the verge of the tomb; I may safely tell you about the beginning of my life."

At this moment Bianchon and the great man were in the Rue des Quatre-Vents, one of the worst streets in Paris. Desplein pointed to the sixth floor of one of the houses looking like obelisks, of which the narrow door opens into a passage with a winding staircase at the end, with windows appropriately termed "borrowed lights"—or, in French, *jours de souffrance*. It was a greenish structure; the ground floor occupied by a furniture dealer, while each floor seemed to shelter a different and independent form of misery. Throwing up his arm with a vehement gesture, Desplein exclaimed:

"I lived up there for two years."

"I know; Arthez lived there; I went up there almost every day during my first youth; we used to call it then the pickle-jar of great men! What then?"

"The mass I have just attended is connected with some events which took place at the time when I lived in the garret where you say Arthez lived; the one with the window where the clothes line is hanging with linen over a pot of flowers. My early life was so hard, my dear Bianchon, that I may dispute the palm of Paris suffering with any man living. I have endured everything: hunger and thirst, want of money, want of clothes, of shoes, of linen, every cruelty that penury can inflict. I have blown on my frozen fingers in that pickle-jar of great men, which I should like to see again, now, with you. I worked through the whole winter, seeing my head steam, and perceiving the atmosphere of my own moisture as we see that of horses on a frosty day. I do not know where a man finds the fulcrum that enables him to hold out against such a life.

"I was alone, with no one to help me, no money to buy books or to pay the expenses of my medical training; I had not a friend; my irascible, touchy, restless temper was against me. No one understood that this irritability was the distress and toil of a man who, at the bottom of the social scale, is struggling to reach the surface. Still, I had, as I may say to you, before whom I need wear no draperies, I had that ground-bed of good feeling and keen sensitiveness which must always be the birthright of any man who is strong enough to climb to any height whatsoever, after having long trampled in the bogs of poverty. I could obtain nothing from my family, nor from my home, beyond my inadequate allowance. In short, at that time I breakfasted off a roll which the baker in the Rue du Petit-Lion sold me cheap because it was left from yesterday or the day before, and I crumbled it into milk; thus my morning meal cost me but two sous. I dined only every other day in a boarding-house where the meal cost me sixteen sous. You know as well as I what care I must have taken of my clothes and shoes. I hardly know whether in later life we feel grief so deep when a colleague plays us false, as we have known, you and I, on detecting the mocking smile of a gaping seam in a shoe, or hearing the armhole of a coat split. I drank nothing but water; I regarded a cafe with distant respect. Zoppi's seemed to me a promised land where none but the Lucullus of the *pays Latin* had a right of entry. Shall I ever take a cup of coffee there with milk in it? said I to myself, or play a game of dominoes?

"I threw into my work the fury I felt at my misery. I tried to master positive knowledge so as to acquire the greatest personal value, and merit the position I should hold as soon as I could escape from nothingness. I consumed more oil than bread; the light I burned during these endless nights cost me more than food. It was a long duel, obstinate, with no sort of consolation. I found no sympathy anywhere. To have friends, must we not form connections with young men, have a few sous so as to be able to go tippling with them and meet them where students congregate? And I had nothing! And no one in Paris can understand that nothing means *nothing*. When I even thought of revealing my beggary, I had that nervous contraction of the throat which makes a sick man believe that a ball rises up from the oesophagus into the larynx.

"In later life I have met people born to wealth who, never having wanted for anything, had never even heard this problem in the rule of three: A young man is to crime as a five-franc piece is to *x*.—These gilded idiots say to me: 'Why did you get into debt? Why did you involve yourself in such onerous obligations?' They remind me of the princess who, on hearing that the people lacked bread, said: 'Why do not they buy cakes?' I should like to see one of these rich men, who complain that I charge too much for an operation—yes, I should like to see him alone in Paris without a sou, without a friend, without credit, and forced to work with his five fingers to live at all! What would he do? Where would he go to satisfy his hunger?

"Bianchon, if you have sometimes seen me hard and bitter, it was because I was adding my early sufferings on to the insensibility, the selfishness of which I have seen thousands of instances in the highest circles; or, perhaps, I was thinking of the obstacles which hatred, envy, jealousy, and calumny raised up between me and success. In Paris, when certain people see you ready to set your foot in the stirrup, some pull your coattails, others loosen the buckle of the strap that you may fall and crack your skull; one wrenches off your horse's shoes, another steals your whip, and the least treacherous of them all is the man whom you see coming to fire his pistol at you point blank.

"You, yourself, my dear boy, are clever enough to make acquaintance before long with the odious and incessant warfare waged by mediocrity against the superior man. If you should drop five-and-twenty louis one day, you will be accused of gambling on the next, and your best friends will report that you have lost twenty-five thousand. If you have a headache, you will be considered mad. If you are a little hasty, no one can live with you. If, to make a stand against this armament of pigmies, you collect your best powers, your best friends will cry out that you want to have everything, that you aim at domineering, at tyranny. In short, your good points will become your faults, your faults will be vices, and your virtues crimes.

"If you save a man, you will be said to have killed him; if he re-appears on the scene, it will be positive that you have secured the present at the cost of the future. If he is not dead, he will die. Stumble, and you fall! Invent anything of any kind and claim your rights, you will be crotchety, cunning, ill-disposed to rising younger men.

"So, you see, my dear fellow, if I do not believe in God, I believe still less in man. But do not you know in me another Desplein, altogether different from the Desplein whom every one abuses?—However, we will not stir that mud-heap.

"Well, I was living in that house, I was working hard to pass my first examination, and I had no money at all. You know. I had come to one of those moments of extremity when a man says, I will enlist. I had one hope. I expected from my home a box full of linen, a present from one of those old aunts who, knowing nothing of Paris, think of your shirts, while they imagine that their nephew with thirty francs a month is eating ortolans. The box arrived while I was at the schools; it had cost forty francs for carriage. The porter, a German shoemaker living in a loft, had paid the money and kept the box. I walked up and down the Rue des Fosses-Saint-Germain-des-Prés and the Rue de l'Ecole de Médecine without hitting on any scheme which would release my trunk without the payment of the forty francs, which of course I could pay as soon as I should have sold the linen. My stupidity proved to me that surgery was my only vocation. My good fellow, refined souls, whose powers move in a lofty atmosphere, have none of that spirit of intrigue that is fertile in resource and device; their good genius is chance; they do not invent, things come to them.

"At night I went home, at the very moment when my fellow lodger also came in—a water-carrier named Bourgeat, a native of Saint-Flour. We knew each other as two lodgers do who have rooms off the same landing, and who hear each other sleeping, coughing, dressing, and so at last become used to one another. My neighbour informed me that the landlord, to whom I owed three-quarters' rent, had turned me out; I must clear out next morning. He himself was also turned out on account of his occupation. I spent the most miserable night of my life. Where was I to get a messenger who could carry my few chattels and my books? How could I pay him and the porter? Where was I to go? I repeated these unanswerable questions again and again, in tears, as madmen repeat their tunes. I fell asleep; poverty has for its friend heavenly slumbers full of beautiful dreams.

"Next morning, just as I was swallowing my little bowl of bread soaked in milk, Bourgeat came in and said to me in his vile Auvergne accent:

"'Mouchieur l'Etudiant, I am a poor man, a foundling from the hospital at Saint-Flour, without either father or mother, and not rich enough to marry. You are not fertile in relations either, nor well supplied with the ready? Listen, I have a hand-cart downstairs which I have hired for two sous an hour; it will hold all our goods; if you like, we will try to find lodgings together, since we are both turned out of this. It is not the earthly paradise, when all is said and done.'

"'I know that, my good Bourgeat,' said I. 'But I am in a great fix. I have a trunk downstairs with a hundred francs' worth of linen in it, out of which I could pay the landlord and all I owe to the porter, and I have not a hundred sous.'

"'Pooh! I have a few dibs,' replied Bourgeat joyfully, and he pulled out a greasy old leather purse. 'Keep your linen.'

"Bourgeat paid up my arrears and his own, and settled with the porter. Then he put our furniture and my box of linen in his cart, and pulled it along the streets, stopping in front of every house where there was a notice board. I went up to see whether the rooms to let would suit us. At midday we were still wandering about the neighbourhood without having found anything. The price was the great difficulty.

Bourgeat proposed that we should eat at a wine shop, leaving the cart at the door. Towards evening I discovered, in the Cour de Rohan, Passage du Commerce, at the very top of a house next the roof, two rooms with a staircase between them. Each of us was to pay sixty francs a year. So there we were housed, my humble friend and I. We dined together. Bourgeat, who earned about fifty sous a day, had saved a hundred crowns or so; he would soon be able to gratify his ambition by buying a barrel and a horse. On learning my situation—for he extracted my secrets with a quiet craftiness and good nature, of which the remembrance touches my heart to this day, he gave up for a time the ambition of his whole life; for twenty-two years he had been carrying water in the street, and he now devoted his hundred crowns to my future prospects."

Desplein at these words clutched Bianchon's arm tightly. "He gave me the money for my examination fees! That man, my friend, understood that I had a mission, that the needs of my intellect were greater than his. He looked after me, he called me his boy, he lent me money to buy books, he would come in softly sometimes to watch me at work, and took a mother's care in seeing that I had wholesome and abundant food, instead of the bad and insufficient nourishment I had been condemned to. Bourgeat, a man of about forty, had a homely, mediaeval type of face, a prominent forehead, a head that a painter might have chosen as a model for that of Lycurgus. The poor man's heart was big with affections seeking an object; he had never been loved but by a poodle that had died some time since, of which he would talk to me, asking whether I thought the Church would allow masses to be said for the repose of its soul. His dog, said he, had been a good Christian, who for twelve years had accompanied him to church, never barking, listening to the organ without opening his mouth, and crouching beside him in a way that made it seem as though he were praying too.

"This man centered all his affections in me; he looked upon me as a forlorn and suffering creature, and he became to me the most thoughtful mother, the most considerate benefactor, the ideal of the virtue which rejoices in its own work. When I met him in the street, he would throw me a glance of intelligence full of unutterable dignity; he would affect to walk as though he carried no weight, and seemed happy in seeing me in good health and well dressed. It was, in fact, the devoted affection of the lower classes, the love of a girl of the people transferred to a loftier level. Bourgeat did all my errands, woke me at night at any fixed hour, trimmed my lamp, cleaned our landing; as good as a servant as he was as a father, and as clean as an English girl. He did all the housework. Like Philopoemen, he sawed our wood, and gave to all he did the grace of simplicity while preserving his dignity, for he seemed to understand that the end ennobles every act.

"When I left this good fellow, to be house surgeon at the Hôtel-Dieu, I felt an indescribable, dull pain, knowing that he could no longer live with me; but he comforted himself with the prospect of saving up money enough for me to take my degree, and he made me promise to go to see him whenever I had a day out: Bourgeat was proud of me. He loved me for my own sake, and for his own. If you look up my thesis, you will see that I dedicated it to him.

"During the last year of my residence as house surgeon I earned enough money to repay all I owed to this worthy Auvergnat by buying him a barrel and a horse. He was furious with rage at learning that I had been depriving myself of spending money, and yet he was delighted to see his wishes fulfilled; he laughed and scolded, he looked at his barrel, at his horse, and wiped away a tear, as he said: 'It is too bad. What a splendid barrel! You really ought not. Why, that horse is as strong as an Auvergnat!'

"I never saw a more touching scene. Bourgeat insisted on buying for me the case of instruments mounted in silver which you have seen in my room, and which is to me the most precious thing there. Though enchanted with my first success, never did the least sign, the least word, escape him which might imply: 'This man owes all to me!' And yet but for him I should have died of want; he had eaten bread rubbed with garlic that I might have coffee to enable me to sit up at night.

"He fell ill. As you may suppose, I passed my nights by his bedside, and the first time I pulled him through; but two years after he had a relapse; in spite of the utmost care, in spite of the greatest exertions of science, he succumbed. No king was ever nursed as he was. Yes, Bianchon, to snatch that man from death I tried unheard-of things. I wanted him to live long enough to show him his work accomplished, to realise all his hopes, to give expression to the only need for gratitude that ever filled my heart, to quench a fire that burns in me to this day.

"Bourgeat, my second father, died in my arms," Desplein went on, after a pause, visibly moved. "He left me everything he possessed by a will he had had made by a public scrivener, dating from the year when he had gone to live in the Cour de Rohan.

"This man's faith was perfect; he loved the Holy Virgin as he might have loved his wife. He was an ardent Catholic, but never said a word to me about my want of religion. When he was dying he entreated me to spare no expense that he might have every possible benefit of clergy. I had a mass said for him every day. Often, in the night, he would tell me of his fears as to his future fate; he feared his life had not been saintly enough. Poor man! he was at work from morning till night. For whom, then, is Paradise—if there be a Paradise? He received the last sacrament like the saint that he was, and his death was worthy of his life.

"I alone followed him to the grave. When I had laid my only bene-factor to rest, I looked about to see how I could pay my debt to him; I found he had neither family nor friends, neither wife nor child. But he believed. He had a religious conviction; had I any right to dispute it? He had spoken to me timidly of masses said for the repose of the dead; he would not impress it on me as a duty, thinking that it would be a form of repayment for his services. As soon as I had money enough I paid to Saint-Sulpice the requisite sum for four masses every year. As the only thing I can do for Bourgeat is thus to satisfy his pious wishes, on the days when that mass is said, at the beginning of each season of the year, I go for his sake and say the required prayers; and I say with the good faith of a sceptic: 'Great God, if there is a sphere which Thou hast appointed after death for those who have been perfect, remember good Bourgeat; and if he should have anything to suffer, let me suffer it for him, that he may enter all the sooner into what is called Paradise.'

"That, my dear fellow, is as much as a man who holds my opinions can allow himself. But God must be a good fellow; He cannot owe me any grudge. I swear to you, I would give my whole fortune if faith such as Bourgeat's could enter my brain."

Bianchon, who was with Desplein all through his last illness, dares not affirm to this day that the great surgeon died an atheist. Will not those who believe like to fancy that the humble Auvergnat came to open the gate of heaven to his friend, as he did that of the earthly temple on whose pediment we read the words "A grateful country to its great men."

(Translated by Clara Bell)

❦❦❦❦❦

At one time my dearest friend, you had the same tastes in profane things as I. But as regards sacred matters I am afraid that since I was not virtuous, our friendship did not conform to the more important part of the accepted definition. For our agreement regarded merely human, not divine things, though, of course, there was mutual benevolence and good-will. But now, things are changed. How can I express my joy! How can I put into words the happiness that fills my heart in knowing that he who for a long time was my friend, has now become my true friend? For now we share agreement on sacred things; and you, who formerly led with me a worldly life, have now united with me in the hope of life eternal.

—St. Augustine *(Translated by Rev. Hugh Talbot, O. Cist.)*

❦❦❦❦❦

FRIEND OF A WAYWARD HOUR
James Whitcomb Riley

Friend of a wayward hour, you came
Like some good ghost, and went the same;
And I within the haunted place
Sit smiling on your vanished face,
    And talking with—your name.

But thrice the pressure of your hand—
First hail—congratulations—and
Your last "God bless you!" as the train
That brought you snatched you back again
    Into the unknown land.

"God bless me?" Why, your very prayer
Was answered ere you asked it there,
I know—for when you came to lend
Me your kind hand, and call me friend,
    God blessed me unaware.

~~~~~~~

There is indeed a pernicious destructive sort of flattery wherewith rookers and sharks work their several ends upon such as they can make a prey of, by decoying them into traps and snares beyond recovery; but that which is the effect of folly is of a much different nature; it proceeds from a softness of spirit, and a flexibleness of good humour, and comes far nearer to virtue than that other extreme of friendship, namely, a stiff, sour, dogged moroseness: it refreshes our minds when tired, enlivens them when melancholy, reinforces them when languishing, invigorates them when heavy, recovers them when sick, and pacifies them when rebellious: it puts us in a method how to procure friends, and how to keep them; it entices children to swallow the bitter rudiments of learning; it gives a new ferment to the almost stagnated souls of old men; it both reproves and instructs principles without offence under the mask of commendation: in short, it makes every man fond and indulgent of himself, which is indeed no small part of each man's happiness, and at the same time renders him obliging and complaisant in all company, where it is pleasant to see how the asses rub and scratch one another.

—Desiderius Erasmus

(*Translated by White Kennett*)

FROM "EPIPSYCHIDION"

Percy Bysshe Shelley

It is a sweet thing, friendship, a dear balm,
A happy and auspicious bird of calm,
Which rides o'er life's ever tumultous Ocean;
A God that broods o'er chaos in commotion;
A flower which fresh as Lapland roses are,
Lifts its bold head into the world's frore air,
And blooms most radiantly when others die,
Health, hope, and youth, and brief prosperity;
And with the light and odor of its bloom,
Shining within the dungeon and the tomb;
Whose coming is as light and music are
'Mid dissonance and gloom—a star
Which moves not 'mid the moving heavens alone—
A smile among dark frowns—a gentle tone
Among rude voices, a belovèd light,
A solitude, a refuge, a delight.

"I was an enraptured auditor . . ."

BURTON RASCOE RECALLS SOME FRIENDS OF HIS YOUTH

At the beginning I came under the influence of three men, all of whom took a paternal interest in me and became my guides, friends and tutors.

One of them was a fat and erudite dipsomaniac; another was a cultivated Catholic priest who was more devoted to learning perhaps than to piety; and the other was a ne'er-do-well newspaper man who had studied at Amherst in a vain search for a suitable profession among law, medicine, chemistry and pedagogy and had been a camp cook for cowhands on a ranch in the Southwest and had drifted into the newspaper profession through a natural gift for writing and because it was the easiest job handy.

The fat dipsomaniac was an editorial writer on a newspaper where I had taken employment.... His name was Shannon Mountjoy; he had studied for the ministry; had abandoned theology for medicine and surgery; and had once taught anatomy at an Eastern university. He had written little essays, which had appeared in the back pages of the *Atlantic Monthly,* a few popular treatises on medical subjects which had appeared in the Boston *Transcript,* and had become an editorial writer after a protracted spree which had left him without funds and at the mercy of a newspaper editor who knew him and advanced him money for food and lodging.

He and the priest were drawn together by their interest in Latin literature, over which they had irreconcilable differences of opinion not only as to the merits of its various masterpieces, but also as to its pronunciation. Father Gregory had been instructed in the Italian method with its soft *g* and *c* and its Italianated diphthongs, whereas Mr. Mountjoy pronounced Cicero *Kikero,* Caesar *Kaisar,* and made the *g* in Virgil hard and pronounced the *v* as *w.*

Since both of them professed to find ineffable beauty in Latin verse and both of them had committed to memory whole odes, epodes and cantos of Virgil, Horace and Catullus, their definitions of this ineffable beauty were based upon individual perceptions which were unlike in almost every particular. I listened to these Latin enthusiasts with something like awe and rapture, but I was at the same time being instructed by demonstration in the axiom that beauty exists only in the mind of the auditor or beholder, and that the individual mind has a capacity for creating an illusion of beauty where, to another eye or to another ear, beauty does not exist....

Jerry Rand, the third adult of this triumvirate, which was to encourage in me a love for learning, a taste for poetry and a curiosity concerning the constituents of matter and man's relation to the universe, had an admiration for Greek and a disdain for Latin, which language he was fond of saying was a crude and barbarous dialect fit only for traders and bargainers. "Latin found its highest expression in the Roman laws," he would olympiate. "Law is a rule of trade, and lawyers and auctioneers are bargain makers. Cicero was a shyster."

Father Gregory and Mr. Mountjoy, who thought well of Cicero, particularly of his *De Senectute,* were at a disadvantage in this assault upon a language and literature they cherished; for their knowledge of Greek, while it was passable, was unequal to the challenge of comparisons in syntax, prosody and vocabulary hurled at them by Jerry, who also had a knowledge of Latin comparable to their own.

When Jerry was drunk (which was often, though he drank because he liked to and not, like Mr. Mountjoy, because he could not help himself) he recited Homer, Theocritus and Anacreon. He delighted to tease Father Gregory and Mr. Mountjoy by reciting a passage from Greek and asking them, when he had concluded, "Do you know what that is?" and waiting for them to answer.

Timidly Mr. Mountjoy would sometimes make a bluff at recognition and would attribute a poem in Ionic Greek to a Doric poet. Jerry would set him right elaborately, by showing certain modifications which separated the two poets by time and place.

When Father Gregory and Mr. Mountjoy both confessed ignorance of the poem, Jerry would answer his own question by saying, "That contains at once the most perfect and the most poetic iambic hexameter ever written," or, "That is an exceptionally fine example of the mixolydian mode invented by Sappho."

Mr. Mountjoy and Father Gregory tolerated Jerry's badgering because Jerry had a talent for listening when he did not have an urge to air his knowledge, and his fantastic life in many places had given him a fund of anecdote which they could both comprehend and appreciate.

Their sessions to which I was an enraptured auditor were held over a table in a Greek restaurant on late evenings in the fore part of the week when Father Gregory did not have to hear confessions or say the Mass. Occasionally Jerry, who knew modern as well as classical Greek, drew into the circle the Greek waiter and co-proprietor whose name was Miltiades Pappathakos....

I, unlike Father Gregory and Mr. Mountjoy, enjoyed Jerry's Greek recitations and disputes without comprehending them; and they instilled in me a desire to acquire Greek as well as Latin that I might have the distinction of communing with the minds of Homer and Sappho. I was being taught Latin in school, and I acquired a Greek grammar and a Greek lexicon and devoted evenings of dogged industry to them....

Courtesy forbade the intrusion of theological discussions in the circle; but since the three of them felt a responsibility toward my character and mind, they did not omit from their impromptu curricula a haphazard course in moral instruction, in *education* as the French use the term. The three of them urged upon me the idea of chastity in youth, each for quite different reasons. Father Gregory taught that chastity was commendable to God and a duty to a boy's future wife, if he should live to have one. Mr. Mountjoy said that sexual indulgence drained away from the brain the fluids on which the cortices were nourished and should, therefore, be postponed until the brain had reached its full development. And Jerry warned against numerous entanglements as the shackles of freedom and against casual carnality as full of the danger of venereal infection.

Concerning alcoholic indulgence Mr. Mountjoy and Jerry were unanimous in warning me against it. Mr. Mountjoy, who swigged all day from a bottle, was a vehement Prohibitionist. "Drinking destroys the mind, the body and the character," he said, with the humility of one who is offering himself as a horrible example. "It is a curse. The country will be better off when it is dry. When I can afford it, I shall take the cure. If that is not soon, it will get me someday, stop my heart, and I'll keel over in the street." Jerry, who drank only whisky, was an advocate of the restriction of the sale of alcoholic beverages to light wines and beer, with the proviso that legislation should forbid the sale of alcohol in aqueous solutions of any sort to minors. "My authority is my own experience," he said, "but Plato ordained, in his Second Book of Laws, that boys should not taste wine at all, that up to the age of thirty men should drink wine sparingly, but that after forty men should drink wine at banquets to temper their austerity and make them human. For myself, whom I offer neither as a lesson in iniquity nor in piety, I employ alcohol as a substitute for love and as a consolation in adversity. There is this one thing I would impress upon you: The love of the imagination is more satisfying than the love of the flesh. Helen and Andromache are more real to me than any love of my own past."

I failed to understand how this could be; but as my thirst for learning at that period was more insistent than my sexual curiosity, Jerry's suggestions did not pique my interest. It had flattered me to be drawn into this company, and my docility and enthusiasm had been so eager that each took me as an irregular pupil and undertook to instruct me individually. Mr. Mountjoy came to my house once a week to drill me in the pronunciation of French by causing me to read pages from Renan, Mérimée, Daudet and George Sand. When the drill was concluded he would talk to me about the Palatine anthology and what is known of the lives of Aeschylus, Sophocles, Euripides, Sappho, Anacreon and Theocritus....

Father Gregory was solicitous about my education in painting and architecture and loaned me illustrated books on art from the parish library. "You will do well, my son," said Father Gregory, "not to fill your head with the speculations of philosophers. I saw you carrying about a volume by Schopenhauer the other day. And you have begun to bother your mind too much with questions which can only result in confusion. I do not urge you to give up such reading as vexatious to the soul, for happily I believe you will shortly come to some such conclusion yourself. I have here all the books that are on the Index Expurgatorius and you are welcome to them at any time you choose to read them; but the Church is wise in these matters, and I suggest that you read poetry and acquaint yourself with the masterpieces of painting and let the philosophers alone."

Instead of profiting from this sensible advice, I crammed my head with an enormous amount of lumber, so eager was I in the vain pursuit of the answer to the riddle of life.

One day I had gone to see Father Gregory's paintings (for which he was later to become famous)—portraits of the pope and cardinals, interpretations of episodes in the lives of the saints and landscapes. Father Gregory was being remiss in his compact with Mr. Mountjoy that there should be no proselytizing. But Father Gregory's slight sin was to be condoned, for I was plaguing him with questions. "No theology, Father," Mr. Mountjoy had said, "for you must remember that I studied for the Protestant ministry and my mind is a thesaurus of divine exegesis. We should quarrel inevitably, and the nature of our quarrel would be much more serious than our squabbles over the pronunciation of Latin; for the soul is a rag bag filled with relics and mementos of our early life and of the lives of those who begot us, relics and mementos of no intrinsic value, probably, but for which we have an irrational attachment as to a lock of hair, a tintype portrait, or a seared flower which we cannot remember how we come by. My affection is equal to my admiration for you, and I should hate to see that affection cankered by the acrimony of our separate prejudices. Of the literary merits and of the character of any and all of the writing saints we may speak; but this boy's soul is budding, and we must let it seek the sun as it will. No theology, Father...."

I had not observed that extensive learning and classical scholarship had been of great advantage to Mr. Mountjoy and to Jerry in increasing their ability to earn a living. One day Jerry was discharged; for things had been going badly with the newspaper, and it was found necessary to curtail expenses. He joined the weekly gathering at the Greek cafe and announced that he had found a job in Okmulgee. "I was going to leave tonight," he said, "but I shall have to wait until morning. I went down to the yards to get aboard my private car and somebody was putting hogs in it."

The imminence of Jerry's departure affected me as in the nature of a bereavement; and Father Gregory and Mr. Mountjoy showed by their demeanor that relief from Jerry's flings at their inadequacies in Greek would not be a complete solace in losing him as a companion in their rather pathetic retention of an interest in the things of the mind and spirit.

What an ocean is life! and how our barks get separated in beating through it! One of the greatest comforts of the retirement to which I shall soon withdraw, will be its rejoining me to my earliest and best friends, and acquaintances.

—THOMAS JEFFERSON

ESTRANGEMENT
James Russell Lowell

The path from me to you that led,
  Untrodden long, with grass is grown,
Mute carpet that his lieges spread
  Before the Prince Oblivion
When he goes visiting the dead.

And who are they but who forget?
  You, who my coming could surmise
Ere any hint of me as yet
  Warned other ears and other eyes,
See the path blurred without regret.

But when I traced its windings sweet
  With saddened steps, at every spot
That feels the memory in my feet,
  Each grass-blade turns forget-me-not,
Where murmuring bees your name repeat.

"I love my friend before myself . . ."

SIR THOMAS BROWNE
SPEAKS CANDIDLY

That a man should lay down his life for his Friend, seems strange to vulgar affections, and such as confine themselves within that Worldly principle, *Charity begins at home*. For mine own part I could never remember the relations that I held unto myself, nor the respect that I owe unto my own nature, in the cause of God, my Country, and my Friends. Next to these three, I do embrace myself. I confess I do not observe that order that the Schools ordain our affections, to love our Parents, Wives, Children, and then our Friends; for, excepting the injunctions of Religion, I do not find in myself such a necessary and indissoluble Sympathy to all those of my blood. I hope I do not break the fifth Commandment, if I conceive I may love my friend before the nearest of my blood, even those to whom I owe the principles of life. I never yet cast a true affection on a woman; but I have loved my friend as I do virtue, my soul, my God. From hence methinks I do conceive how God loves man, what happiness there is in the love of God....

There are wonders in true affection: it is a body of *Enigmas,* mysteries, and riddles; wherein two so become one, as they both become two. I love my friend before myself, and yet methinks I do not love him enough: some few months hence my multiplied affection will make me believe I have not loved him at all. When I am from him, I am dead till I be with him; when I am with him, I am not satisfied, but would still be nearer him. United souls are not satisfied with imbraces, but desire to be truly each other; which being impossible, their desires are infinite, and must proceed without a possibility of satisfaction. Another misery there is in affection, that whom we truly love like our own selves, we forget their looks, nor can our memory retain the idea of their faces; and it is no wonder, for they are our selves, and our affection makes their looks our own. This noble affection falls not on vulgar and common constitutions, but on such as are mark'd for virtue; he that can love his friend with this noble ardour, will in a competent degree affect all. Now, if we can bring our affections to look beyond the body, and cast an eye upon the soul, we have found out the true object, not only of friendship, but Charity; and the greatest happiness that we can bequeath the soul, is that wherein we all do place our last felicity, Salvation; which though it be not in our power to bestow, it is in our charity and pious invocations to desire, if not procure and further. I cannot contentedly frame a prayer for myself in particular, without a catalogue for my friends; nor request a happiness, wherein my sociable disposition doth not desire the fellowship of my neighbour. I never hear the Toll of a passing Bell, though in my mirth, without my prayers and best wishes for the departing spirit.

My friend peers in on me with merry
Wise face, and though the sky stays dim,
The very light of day, the very
Sun's self comes in with him.
                    —ALGERNON CHARLES SWINBURNE

"...I am more sensitive than another man..."

JEAN JACQUES ROUSSEAU GIVES MADAME D'EPINAY HIS RULES FOR FRIENDSHIP

I should like to make a declaration to you as to what I require from friendship, and as to what I desire to exhibit in it in my turn.

Blame freely what you find blamable in my rules, but do not expect to find me easily departing from them; for they are drawn from my disposition, which I cannot alter.

In the first place, I wish my friends to be my friends, and not my masters: to advise me without claiming to control me: to enjoy all kinds of rights over my heart, none over my freedom. I consider those persons very singular who, under the name of friends, always claim to interfere in my affairs, without telling me anything about theirs.

Let them always speak to me frankly and freely; they can say anything to me; contempt excepted, I allow them everything. The contempt of a person who is indifferent to me is a matter of indifference; but if I were to endure it from a friend, I should deserve it. If he has the misfortune to despise me, let him avoid telling me, let him leave me; that is what he owes to himself. With that exception, when he remonstrates with me, whatever tone he adopts, he is within his rights; when, after having listened to him, I follow my own inclinations, I am within mine; and I greatly dislike anyone to keep eternally chattering to me about what is over and done with.

Their great anxiety to do a number of services which I do not care about is wearisome to me; it seems to imply a certain air of superiority which is displeasing to me; besides, everyone can do as much. I prefer them to love me and let themselves be loved; that is what friends alone can do. Above all, I am indignant when the first new-comer is able to compensate them for my loss, while I cannot endure anyone's society but theirs in the world. Nothing but their affection makes me endure their kindness, but when once I consent to receive them from them, I wish them to consult my tastes and not their own; for we think so differently upon so many things that often what they consider good appears to me bad.

If a quarrel occurs, I should certainly say that he who is in the wrong ought to apologize first; but that means nothing, for everyone always thinks that he is in the right; right or wrong, it is for him who has begun the quarrel to put an end to it. If I take his censure ill, if I am annoyed without reason, if I put myself in a passion at the wrong moment, he ought not to follow my example; if he does, he certainly does not love me. On the contrary, I would have him treat me with affection; do you understand, Madame? In a word, let him begin by soothing me, which will certainly not take long, for there has never been a fire at the bottom of my heart which a tear could not extinguish. Then, when I am softened, calmed, ashamed, and covered with confusion, let him scold me, let him tell me what I have done, and assuredly he will have no reason to complain of me. If it is a question of a trifling detail, which is not worth clearing up, let him drop it; let the aggressor be the first to hold his tongue, let him not make a foolish point of honor always to have the advantage. That is how I wish my friend to act towards me, as I am always ready to act towards him in a similar case.

On this point, I could mention to you a little instance of which you have no suspicion, although it concerns you; it has to do with a note which I received from you some time ago, in answer to another with which I saw you were not satisfied, and in which, as it seems to me, you had failed to understand what I meant. I answered promptly enough, or at least I thought so; my reply certainly was in the tone of true friendship, but, at the same time, I cannot deny that there was a certain amount of warmth in it, and, reading it again, I was afraid that you would be no better pleased with it than with the first; immediately, I threw my letter in the fire; I cannot tell you how pleased I felt to see my eloquence consumed in the flames; I said nothing more to you about it, and I believe that I gained the honor of being beaten; sometimes it only needs a spark to kindle a conflagration my dear, kind friend. Pythagoras said that one should never poke the fire with a sword; this maxim seems to me the most important and the most sacred law of friendship.

I require from a friend even a great deal more than all I have just told you; even more than he must require from me, and than I should require from him, if he were in my place, and I were in his.

As a recluse, I am more sensitive than another man; if I am wrong in my behavior to a friend, he thinks of it for a moment, and then a thousand distractions cause him to forget it for the rest of the day; but nothing distracts my attention from any wrong done by him to me; I cannot sleep; I think of it the whole night long; when walking by myself, I think of it from sunrise to sunset; my heart has not a moment's respite, and the harshness of a friend causes me, in a single day, years of grief. As an invalid, I have a right to the indulgence which humanity owes to the weakness and temper of a sufferer. Who is the friend, who is the honorable man who ought not to be afraid of grieving an unhappy man tormented by a painful and incurable malady? I am poor, and it seems to me that I deserve considerate treatment on this account still more. All these indulgences that I require you have shown me without mentioning them, and surely it will never be necessary for me to ask them from a true friend. But, my dear friend, let us speak frankly, do you know any friend that I have? On my honor, it has been my good fortune to learn to do without them. I know many persons who would be sorry that I should be under obligation to them, and many to whom in fact I am, but hearts fit to respond to mine—oh! it is enough to know one.

(Translated by J. H. Freese)

~~~~~~~

**". . . leave this dealing in trifles and wrangling
to empty hearts . . ."**

MADAME D'EPINAY'S REPLY
TO ROUSSEAU

I think, my friend, that it is very difficult to lay down hard and fast rules as to friendship, for everyone carries them out, as is only reasonable, according to his own way of thinking. You inform me what you claim from your friends; another of my friends will come who will claim something exactly opposite, so that I, who also have quite a different character, shall find out, ten times a day, the secret of getting myself execrated by my friends, and I, on my part, shall of course send them to the deuce. There are two general points, essential and indispensable in friendship, at which everybody is found to meet—indulgence and freedom. Without them, there are no bonds which will not break; to this, or almost to this, my code of friendship may be reduced. I cannot require my friend to love me with warmth, with delicacy, with thoughtfulness, or an effusive heart, but only to love me to the best of his ability, as far as his natural disposition allows; for all my wishes will never reform him if he is reserved or fickle, grave or gay; and as my thought would incessantly be directed towards that quality which was lacking in him, and which I should persist in wishing to find in him, I should necessarily find him unbearable. One ought to love one's friends, as true lovers of art love pictures; their eyes are continually fixed upon their best parts, and they are unable to see anything else.

If a quarrel breaks out, you say, if my friend does me an injury, etc. etc. But I don't know what a man means when he exclaims: "My friend does me an injury." In friendship I know only one kind of injury; that is mistrust. But when I hear you say: "On such and such a day, he behaved mysteriously to me"; on another, "He preferred such and such a thing to the pleasure of my society, or to an attention which was due to me"; or "He ought to have made such and such a sacrifice for me"; and then comes a fit of sulkiness—come, leave this dealing in trifles and wrangling to empty hearts and heads without ideas; it only suits silly, mean, vulgar lovers who, in the place of that confident security, those delightful outpourings of the heart which in honest and brave souls increase the feeling of love by the exercise of virtue and philosophy, put little false or mean quarrels which narrow the mind, embitter the heart, and make people's characters insipid when they do not make them vicious. Does it become a philosopher, a friend of wisdom, to follow the same career as those faint-hearted and narrow-minded devotees who substitute for the true love of God petty feeble and superstitious practices? Believe me, he who is well acquainted with man readily pardons him for the weaknesses into which he falls, and is infinitely grateful to him for the good he does, which costs him so much.

I think your code of friendship, after your quarrel with Diderot, is not unlike the regulation which the English nation never fails to make, when any crisis causes it to perceive in its laws a vice which upsets the whole state, and which cannot be remedied for the moment, for want of having been foreseen.

As for me, my friend, after laying down, at the commencement of my letter, liberty and indulgence as my first principle, I did not foresee that I should make such use of the one and have such need of the other. Excuse my impertinence for the sake of my sincerity. Good heavens! how many more kind things I could say to you, but I am interrupted every minute! I have only time to confide to you in secret that I defy you, in spite of my mischievous pleasantries, to be angry with me; for notwithstanding your faults, I love you with all my heart.

(Translated by J. H. Freese)

"There is a gallantry of the mind which pervades
all conversation with a lady . . ."

FRIENDSHIP BETWEEN MEN AND WOMEN

George Santayana

Friends are generally of the same sex, for when men and women agree, it is only in their conclusions; their reasons are always different. So that while intellectual harmony between men and women is easily possible, its delightful and magic quality lies precisely in the fact that it does not arise from mutual understanding, but is a conspiracy of alien essences and a kissing, as it were, in the dark. The human Race, in its intellectual life, is organized like the bees: the masculine soul is a worker, sexually atrophied, and essentially dedicated to impersonal and universal arts; the feminine is a queen, infinitely fertile, omnipresent in its brooding industry, but passive and abounding in intuitions without method and passions without justice. Friendship with a woman is therefore apt to be more or less than friendship: less, because there is no intellectual parity; more, because (even when the relation remains wholly dispassionate, as in respect to old ladies) there is something mysterious and oracular about a woman's mind which inspires a certain instinctive deference and puts it out of the question to judge what she says by masculine standards. She has a kind of sibylline intuition and the right to be irrationally *à propos*. There is a gallantry of the mind which pervades all conversation with a lady, as there is a natural courtesy towards children and mystics; but such a habit of respectful attention, marking as it does an intellectual alienation as profound, though not as complete, as that which separates us from the dumb animals, is radically incompatible with friendship.

Friendship betwixt men and women may be perilous, for fair beauty lightly cherishes (easily allures) a frail soul; and temptation soon sets fleshly desire on fire, and ofttimes brings in the sin of the body and soul. And so the company of women with men is wont to happen to the destruction of virtue. And yet, this friendship is not unlawful, but needful: if it be had with good soul, and if it be loved for God, and not for the sweetness of the flesh.

—RICHARD ROLLE

THE THREE SORTS OF FRIENDS

Samuel Taylor Coleridge

Though friendships differ endless *in degree,*
The *sorts,* methinks, may be reduced to three.
*Ac*quaintance many, and *Con*quaintance few;
But for *In*quaintance I know only two—
The friend I've mourned with, and the maid I woo!

Commenting on the above Coleridge wrote:

My Dear Gillman—The ground and *matériel* of this division of one's friends into *ac, con* and *in*quaintance, was given by Hartley Coleridge when he was scarcely five years old. On some one asking him if Anny Seeley (a little girl he went to school with) was an acquaintance of his, he replied, very fervently pressing his right hand on his heart, "No, she is an *in*quaintance!" Well, 'tis a father's tale; and the recollection soothes your old friend and *in*quaintance,

S. T. COLERIDGE

"... watch over the children ..."

EPICURUS, ON HIS DEATHBED, TO IDOMENEUS

On this blissful day, which is also the last of my life, I write this to you. My continual sufferings from strangury and dysentery are so great that nothing could augment them; but over against them all I set gladness of mind at the remembrance of our past conversations. But I would have you, as becomes your lifelong attitude to me and to philosophy, watch over the children of Metrodorus.

(Translated by Cyril Bailey)

A LEGACY
John Greenleaf Whittier

Friend of my many years!
When the great silence falls, at last on me,
Let me not leave, to pain and sadden thee,
    A memory of tears,

But pleasant thoughts alone,
Of one who was thy friendship's honored guest
And drank the wine of consolation pressed
    From sorrows of thy own.

I leave with thee a sense
Of hands upheld and trials rendered less—
The unselfish joy which is to helpfulness
    Its own great recompense;

The knowledge that from thine,
As from the garments of the Master, stole
Calmness and strength, the virtue which makes the whole
    And heals without a sign;

Yea more, the assurance strong
That love, which fails of perfect utterance here,
Lives on to fill the heavenly atmosphere
    With its immortal song.

"A hidden grace . . ."

THE WISDOM OF KINDNESS
William Allen White

Let strong men be mean. Let weaklings be lazy and envious. Let the mediocre man be complacently befuddled. So it has always been. Put them to work side by side—the grasping, the do-less, the bewildered. A hidden grace in each of them—perhaps tolerance or a shamefaced nobility or maybe an innate sense of fairness—amalgamates their baser qualities. A pattern of social conduct emerges, strange and full of friendly purpose. They who seem to be pulling and hauling, jostling and clamoring, have done a day's work that is somehow good. But they only are as competent and wise as they are free. So the wisdom of kindness—let us call it the love of man—comes to bless the labor.

Judge not thy friend until thou standest in his place.
         —Rabbi Hillel

". . . he walked among us, both hands full of gifts . . ."

THE MEMORY OF A DEPARTED FRIEND

Robert Louis Stevenson

The first step for all is to learn to the dregs our own ignoble fallibility. When we have fallen through storey after storey of our vanity and aspiration, and sit rueful among the ruins, then it is that we begin to measure the stature of our friends: how they stand between us and our own contempt, believing in our best; how, linking us with others, and still spreading wide the influential circle, they weave us in and in with the fabric of contemporary life; and to what petty size they dwarf the virtues and the vices that appeared gigantic in our youth. So that at the last, when such a pin falls out—when there vanishes in the least breath of time one of those rich magazines of life on which we drew for our supply—when he who had first dawned upon us as a face among the faces of the city, and, still growing, came to bulk on our regard with those clear features of the loved and living man, falls in a breath to memory and shadow, there falls along with him a whole wing of the palace of our life.

One such face I now remember; one such blank some half a dozen of us labour to dissemble. In his youth he was most beautiful in person, most serene and genial by disposition; full of racy words and quaint thoughts. Laughter attended on his coming. He had the air of a great gentleman, jovial and royal with his equals, and to the poorest student gentle and attentive. Power seemed to reside in him exhaustless; we saw him stoop to play with us, but held him marked for higher destinies; we loved his notice; and I have rarely had my pride more gratified than when he sat at my father's table, my acknowledged friend. So he walked among us, both hands full of gifts, carrying with nonchalance the seeds of a most influential life.

The powers and the ground of friendship is a mystery; but, looking back, I can discern that, in part, we loved the thing he was, for some shadow of what he was to be. For with all his beauty, power, breeding, urbanity, and mirth, there was in those days something soulless in our friend. He would astonish us by sallies, witty, innocent, and inhumane; and by a misapplied Johnsonian pleasantry, demolish honest sentiment. I can still see and hear him, as he went his way along the lamplit streets, *La ci darem la mano* on his lips, a noble figure of a youth, but following vanity and incredulous of good; and sure enough, somewhere on the high seas of life, with his health, his hopes, his patrimony, and his self-respect, miserably went down.

From this disaster, like a spent swimmer, he came desperately ashore, bankrupt of money and consideration; creeping to the family he had deserted; with broken wing, never more to rise. But in his face there was a light of knowledge that was new to it. Of the wounds of his body he was never healed; died of them gradually, with clear-eyed resignation; of his wounded pride, we knew only from his silence. He returned to that city where he had lorded it in his ambitious youth; lived there alone, seeing few; striving to retrieve the irretrievable; at times still grappling with that mortal frailty that had brought him down; still joying in his friends' successes; his laugh still ready but with kindlier music; and over all his thoughts the shadow of that unalterable law which he had disavowed and which had brought him low. Lastly, when his bodily evils had quite disabled him, he lay a great while dying, still without complaint, still finding interests; to his last step gentle, urbane, and with the will to smile.

The tale of this great failure is, to those who remained true to him, the tale of a success. In his youth he took thought for no one but himself; when he came ashore again, his whole armada lost, he seemed to think of none but others. Such was his tenderness for others, such his instinct of fine courtesy and pride, that of that impure passion of remorse he never breathed a syllable; even regret was rare with him, and pointed with a jest. You would not have dreamed, if you had known him then, that this was that great failure, that beacon to young men, over whose fall a whole society had hissed and pointed fingers. Often have we gone to him, red-hot with our own hopeful sorrows, railing on the rose-leaves in our princely bed of life, and he would patiently give ear and wisely counsel; and it was only upon some return of our own thoughts that we were reminded what manner of man this was to whom we disembosomed: a man, by his own fault, ruined; shut out of the garden of his gifts; his whole city of hope both ploughed and salted; silently awaiting the deliverer. Then something took us by the throat; and to see him there, so gentle, patient, brave, and pious, oppressed but not cast down, sorrow was so swallowed up in admiration that we could not dare to pity him. Even if the old fault flashed out again, it but awoke our wonder that, in that lost battle, he should have still the energy to fight. He had gone to ruin with a kind of kingly *abandon,* like one who condescended; but once ruined, with the lights all out, he fought as for a kingdom. Most men, finding themselves the authors of their own disgrace, rail the louder against God or destiny. Most men, when they repent, oblige their friends to share the bitterness of that repentance. But he had held an inquest and passed sentence: *mene, mene;* and condemned himself to smiling silence. He had given trouble enough; he had earned misfortune amply, and foregone the right to murmur.

Thus was our old comrade, like Samson, careless in his days of strength; but on the coming of adversity, and when that strength was gone that had betrayed him—"for our strength is weakness"—he began to blossom and bring forth. Well, now, he is out of the fight: the burden that he bore thrown down before the great deliverer. We

> "in the vast cathedral leave him;
> God accept him,
> Christ receive him!"

If we go now and look on these innumerable epitaphs, the pathos and the irony are strangely fled. They do not stand merely to the dead, these foolish monuments; they are pillars and legends set up to glorify the difficult but not desperate life of man. This ground is hallowed by the heroes of defeat.

I see the indifferent pass before my friend's last resting-place; pause, with a shrug of pity, marvelling that so rich an argosy had sunk. A pity, now that he is done with suffering, a pity most uncalled for, and an ignorant wonder. Before those who loved him, his memory shines like a reproach; they honour him for silent lessons; they cherish his example; and in what remains before them of their toil, fear to be unworthy of the dead. For this proud man was one of those who prospered in the valley of humiliation—of whom Bunyan wrote that, "Though Christian had the hard hap to meet in the valley with Apollyon, yet I must tell you, that in former times men have met with angels here; have found pearls here; and have in this place found the words of life."

~~~~~~

I want some good friends, friends who are as familiar as life itself, friends to whom I need not be polite, and who will tell me all their troubles, matrimonial or otherwise, who can quote Aristophanes and crack some dirty jokes, friends who are spiritually rich and who can talk dirt and philosophy with the same candor, friends who have definite hobbies and opinions about persons and things, who have their private beliefs and respect mine.

—LIN YUTANG

~~~~~~

"Thus are the fondest and firmest friendships dissolved . . ."

FELICIA AND FLORETTA

Samuel Johnson

Felicia and Floretta had been bred up in one house, and shared all the pleasures and endearments of infancy together. They entered upon life at the same time, and continued their confidence and friendship; consulted each other in every change of their dress, and every admission of a new lover; thought every diversion more entertaining whenever it happened that both were present, and when separated justified the conduct, and celebrated the excellencies, of one another. Such was their intimacy, and such their fidelity; till a birth-night approached, when Floretta took one morning an opportunity, as they were consulting upon new clothes, to advise her friend not to dance at the ball, and informed her that her performance the year before had not answered the expectation in which her other accomplishments had raised. Felicia commended her sincerity, and thanked her for the caution; but told her that she danced to please herself, and was very little concerned what the men might take the liberty of saying, but that if her appearance gave her dear Floretta any uneasiness, she would stay away. Floretta had now nothing left but to make new protestations of sincerity and affection, with which Felicia was so well satisfied, that they parted with more than usual fondness. They still continued to visit, with this only difference, that Felicia was more punctual than before, and often declared how high a value she put upon her sincerity, how much she thought that goodness to be esteemed which would venture to admonish a friend of an error, and with what gratitude advice was to be received, even when it might happen to proceed from mistake.

In a few months, Felicia, with great seriousness, told Floretta, that though her beauty was such as gave charm to whatever she did, and her qualifications so extensive, that she could not fail of excellence in any attempt, yet she thought herself obliged by the duties of friendship to inform her that if ever she betrayed want of judgment, it was by too frequent compliance with solicitations to sing, for that her manner was somewhat ungraceful, and her voice had no great compass. It is true, says Floretta, when I sang three nights ago at Lady Sprightly's, I was hoarse with a cold; but I sing for my own satisfaction, and am not in the least pain whether I am liked. However, my dear Felicia's kindness is not the less, and I shall always think myself happy in so true a friend.

From this time they saw each other without mutual professions of esteem, and declarations of confidence, but went soon after into the country to visit their relations. When they came back, they were prevailed on, by the importance of new acquaintance, to take lodgings in different parts of the town, and had frequent occasion, when they met, to bewail the distance at which they were placed, and the uncertainty which each experienced of finding the other at home.

Thus are the fondest and firmest friendships dissolved, by such openness and sincerity as interrupt our enjoyment of our own approbation, or recall us to the remembrance of those failings which we are more willing to indulge than to correct.

"FRIENDSHIP IS LOVE WITHOUT HIS WINGS"

Lord Byron

Why should my anxious breast repine,
   Because my youth is fled?
Days of delight may still be mine;
   Affection is not dead.
In tracing back the years of youth,
One firm record, one lasting truth
   Celestial consolation brings;
Bear it, ye breezes, to the seat
Where first my heart responsive beat.—
   "Friendship is Love without his wings!"

Through few, but chequer'd years,
   What moments have been mine!
Now half obscured by clouds of tears,
   Now bright in rays divine;
Howe'er my future doom be cast,
My soul, enraptured with the past,
   To one idea fondly clings;
Friendship! that thought is all thine own,
Worth worlds of bliss, that thought alone—
   "Friendship is Love without his wings!"

"It has been such a rich holiday for me."

MARK TWAIN TO REV. J. H. TWICHELL

[No date]

Dear Old Joe,—It is actually all over! I was so low-spirited at the station yesterday, and this morning, when I woke, I couldn't seem to accept the dismal truth that you were really gone, and the pleasant tramping and talking at an end. Ah, my boy! it has been such a rich holiday for me, and I feel under such deep and honest obligations to you for coming. I am putting out of my mind all memory of the times when I misbehaved toward you and hurt you: I am resolved to consider it forgiven, and to store up and remember only the charming hours of the journeys and the times when I was not unworthy to be with you and share a companionship which to me stands first after Livy's [Mark Twain's wife]. It is justifiable to do this; for why would I let small infirmities of disposition live and grovel among my mental pictures of the eternal sublimities of the Alps?

Livy can't accept or endure the fact that you are gone. But you *are,* and we cannot get around it. So take our love with you, and bear it also over the sea to Harmony, and God bless you both.

Mark

Life is to be fortified by many friendships. To love, and to be loved, is the greatest happiness. If I lived under the burning sun of the equator, it would be pleasure for me to think that there were many human beings on the other side of the world who regarded and respected me; I could not live if I were alone upon the earth, and cut off from the remembrance of my fellow-creatures. It is not that a man has occasion often to fall back upon the kindness of his friends; perhaps he may never experience the necessity of doing so; but we are governed by our imaginations, and they stand there as a solid and impregnable bulwark against all the evils of life.

—SYDNEY SMITH

". . . without friends no one would choose to live . . ."

ARISTOTLE ANALYZES FRIENDSHIP

Friendship is a kind of virtue or implies virtue. It is also indispensable to life. For without friends no one would choose to live, even though he possessed every other good. It even seems that people who are rich and hold official and powerful positions have the greatest need of friends; for what is the good of this sort of prosperity without some opportunity for generosity, which is never so freely or admirably displayed as toward friends? Or how can prosperity be preserved in safety and security without friends? The greater a person's importance, the more liable it is to disaster. And in poverty and other misfortunes our friends are our only refuge. Again, when we are young, friends are a help to us, in saving us from error, and when we grow old, in taking care of us and doing the things for us we are too feeble to do for ourselves. When we are all in the prime of life, they prompt us to noble actions, as the line runs

"Two going together,"

for two people are better than one both in thought and in action. . . .

The friendship of the young is based apparently on pleasure—for they live by emotion and are inclined to pursue most the pleasure of the moment. But as their age increases, their pleasures alter with it. They are therefore quick at making friendships and quick at abandoning them; for their friendships shift with the object that pleases them, and their pleasure is liable to sudden change. . . .

Perfect friendship is the friendship of people who are good and alike in virtue; for they are alike in wishing each other's good, inasmuch as they are good and good in themselves. Those who wish the good of their friends for their friends' sake are in the truest sense friends, since their friendship is the consequence of their own character, and not an accident. Their friendship therefore lasts as long as their goodness, and goodness is a permanent quality. So each of them is good in an absolute sense, and pleasant to one another. For everybody finds pleasure in actions proper to him and in others like him, and all good people act alike or nearly alike.

Such a friendship is naturally permanent, for it unites in itself all the right conditions of friendship. For the aim of all friendship is good or pleasure, either absolute or relative to the person who feels the affection; and it is founded on a certain similarity. In the friendship of good men all the conditions just described are realized in the friends themselves; other friendships bear only a resemblance to the perfect friendship. That which is good in an absolute sense is pleasant also in an absolute sense. They too are the most lovable objects of affection, and for this reason love and friendship in this highest and best sense are found among such men.

Friendships of this kind are likely to be rare; for such people are few. Such friendships require time and familiarity too; for, as the adage puts it, men cannot know one another until they have eaten salt together; nor can they admit one another to friendship, or be friends at all, until each has been proved lovable and trustworthy by the other. People who are quick to treat one another as friends wish to be friends but are not so really, unless they are lovable and know each other to be so; for the wish to be friends may arise in a minute, but not friendship.

This kind of friendship then is perfect as regards durability and in all other respects; and each friend receives from the other in every way the same or nearly the same treatment as he gives, which is as it ought to be. Friendship based on pleasure has a certain resemblance to it, for the good are pleasant to one another. So also with friendship based on utility, for the good are useful to one another. Here likewise friendships are most permanent when the two persons get the same thing, such as pleasure, from one another; and not only the same thing, but from the same source, as happens between two wits.... But those who give and receive not pleasure but profit are both less true and less constant friends. Friendships based on utility are dissolved as soon as the advantage comes to an end, for in them there is no love of a person, but only a love of profit.

For pleasure or profit it is possible that even bad men may be friends to one another, and good people to bad, and one who is neither good nor bad to any sort of person; but clearly none but the good can be friends for the friend's own sake, since bad people do not delight in one another unless to gain something thereby....

Among austere and elderly people friendship arises less easily, because they are less good-tempered and less fond of society, and those are the qualities that seem to be the principal element in and causes of friendship. That is why the young form friendships quickly, but old men do not, for they do not make friends with anyone who is not delightful to them; nor do austere people. Such people, it is true, wish each other well; they desire one another's good, and help one another as needed. But they are not really friends, since they do not fulfill the principal condition of friendship by spending their time together and delighting in each other's society.

It is as impossible to be friends with a great number of people in the perfect sense of friendship as it is to be in love with a great number of people at once. For perfect friendship is in some sense an excess, and such excess of feeling is natural toward one individual, but it is not easy for a great number of people to give intense pleasure to the same person at the same time, or, I may say, to seem even good to him at all. Friendship too involves experience and familiarity, which are very difficult. But it is possible to find a great number of acquaintances who are simply useful or pleasant or agreeable; for people of this kind are numerous and their services do not take much time.

Among such acquaintanceships one that is based on pleasure more nearly resembles a friendship, when each party renders the same service to the other, and is delighted with the other or with the same things, as they are in friendships of the young; for a generous spirit is especially characteristic of these friendships.

Friendships that rest on utility are for commercial characters. Fortunate people, however, do not want what is useful but what is pleasant....

People in positions of authority can make a distinction between their friends. Some are useful to them, and others pleasant, though the same people are not usually both useful and pleasant. They do not look for friends who are good as well as pleasant, or who will help them to attain noble ends; they want to be pleased and look partly for amusing people and partly for those who are clever at doing what they are told. These qualities are hardly ever combined in the same person....

All forms of friendship... imply association. We may, however, properly distinguish the friendships of kinsmen and of comrades from other friendships. As for the friendships of fellow citizens, fellow tribesmen, fellow sailors and such, they are more like simple friendships of association, since they seem based on a sort of compact. We may class them with the friendship of host and guest....

The characteristics of friendships between brothers are the same as between comrades. They are intensified when brothers are good but exist always in consequence of their likeness; for brothers are more nearly related to each other and love one another naturally from birth. There is the greatest similarity of character among children of the same parents, who are brought up together and receive a similar education; and they have stood the strong and sure test of time. The elements of friendship between other kinsmen are in proportion to the nearness of their kinship....

Complaints and bickerings occur exclusively or most frequently in friendships based on utility, and it is reasonable that this should be so. For where the basis of friendship is virtue, friends are eager to do good to each other as a sign of their goodness and friendship. Where rivalry takes this form, there is no room for complaint or bickering; for nobody finds fault with a person who loves him and treats him well. On the contrary, if he is a man of fine feeling, he returns the other's kindness. Nor will a superior person complain of his friend, for he is getting his desire; in such a friendship each friend desires the other's good.

Again, such quarreling hardly ever arises in a friendship of pleasure; for both parties there get what they want, if they enjoy living together. One would make himself ridiculous if he were to complain of the other for not giving him pleasure, when he has the power to stop living in his company. It is friendship based on utility that gives rise to complaints; for the parties to that in their dealings with each other have an eye out for profit. Each always wants the larger share, and imagines he is getting less than his due, and complains of not getting all he needs or deserves. No benefactor can supply all that such a recipient of his benefaction demands. . . .

Differences occur also in friendships in which one party is superior to the other, when each party claims a larger share of the benefit; but when this occurs, the friendship is dissolved. The better of the two friends thinks he should have more, for his virtue deserves the larger share. So too does the more useful, as admittedly a person who is useless ought not to have so much as the one who is of use. His friendship (he says) ceases to be a friendship and becomes a public service if the proceeds of that friendship are not proportionate to the worth of the benefits he confers. For people think that as in a business firm the larger contributors get more of the returns, so it should be in friendship. But the needy or inferior person takes the opposite view. He argues that it is the part of a good friend to assist the needy; for what (he says) is the use of being a friend of a noble or powerful person if he is to get no benefit from it?

It would seem that each is justified in his claim, and that each ought to get more out of the friendship than the other but not more of the same things. The superior person ought to get more honor, and the needy person more profit, for honor is the reward of virtue and generosity, and money is the relief the needy one wants. . . .

Another question that presents a problem is whether we ought or ought not to break off friendships with people whose character is no longer what it once was. If the motive of the friendship was utility or pleasure, then when the utility or the pleasure comes to an end, there is nothing unreasonable in breaking off the friendship. For it was the utility or the pleasure that we loved, and when they have ceased to exist, it is only reasonable that our love should come to an end too.

But a man would have ground for complaint, if a friend who had loved him for his usefulness or pleasantness had pretended to love him for his character. For, as we said at the outset, differences arise between friends most often when the actual grounds of the friendship are not what they suppose it to be. Now if a person, A, has deceived himself into imagining it was his character which won him his B's affection, although there was nothing in B's conduct to warrant such an idea, he has only himself to blame. But if he was deluded by pretense on B's part, he has a right to complain of him as an impostor and to denounce him more bitterly than he would a man who counterfeits money, inasmuch as this felony affects something more precious than money.

But suppose we take a person into our friendship believing him to be a good man, and he turns out and is recognized as a rascal, is it still our duty to love him? Love, it would seem, is now an impossibility, because not everything, but only the good is lovable. Evil neither can nor ought to be loved; for it is not our duty to love the wicked, or to make ourselves like bad men. We have said already that like loves like. Is it right then in such circumstances to break off the friendship at once? Or, perhaps, if not in all cases, at least where the vice is incurable? If there is any possibility of reforming the friend who has gone wrong, we should indeed come to the help of his character even more than of his property, since character is a better thing than property and enters more closely into friendship. Still a person who breaks off a friendship under these circumstances is not thought to be acting at all unreasonably. He was not a friend of the person as that person is now; therefore, if his friend has altered and it is impossible to reclaim him, he lets him go.

Again, suppose A stays as he was but B becomes better and vastly superior to A in virtue. Ought B then to treat A still as a friend? It is, I think, impossible. The case becomes clearest when the distance is wide between the two friends, as happens with childhood friendships, when one of two friends remains a child in mind and the other is a fully developed man. How can they be friends, when they sympathize with each other neither in their ideas nor in their pleasures and pains? There will be no personal understanding between them, and without understanding it is impossible, as we saw, to be friends, for it is impossible for two people to live together.... Is it right, then, when two friends cease to be sympathetic, for one to treat the other exactly as if he had never been his friend? Surely we must not entirely forget the old intimacy, but even as we think we should oblige friends rather than strangers, so for old friends we should show some consideration for the sake of past friendship, provided that the break in friendship was not caused by some extraordinary wickedness.... Good will resembles friendship, but it is not the same thing; for good will, unlike friendship, we may feel for people unknown to us.... Good will may start in a moment, as when we feel good will towards competitors in games. We wish them well and sympathize with them, but we should not think of doing something for them; for, as we said, good will starts in a moment and implies no more than a superficial regard.

Good will then may be called the germ of friendship.... It is impossible for people to be friends who have felt no good will to each other, but it does not follow that, if they feel good will, they are friends. For to those to whom we feel good will we merely wish well; we should not think of doing something for them or of taking serious trouble in their behalf. It may be said then, figuratively, that good will is unproductive friendship, which in course of time and familiarity may become friendship, but not a friendship based on utility or pleasure; for neither utility nor pleasure is the basis of good will....

Benefactors are thought to be better friends to those they have helped than the latter are to their benefactors. This is a puzzling fact, and people try to account for it. The usual explanation is that benefactors are creditors and the receivers of their kindness debtors. Hence, as in the case of loans, the debtors would be glad if their creditors ceased to exist, whereas the creditors look anxiously to the safety of their debtors....

The true reason, however, seems to lie deeper down in the nature of things. It is not the same reason that makes creditors care for their debtors; for creditors have no affection for their debtors, and if they feel a wish for their safety, it is only in hopes of recovering the debt. But those who have done a kindness to others feel love and friendship for the people they have helped, even if the latter do not and cannot do anything for them....

The question is asked whether we need friends more in prosperity or in adversity, the idea being that while an unfortunate man needs someone to help him, a fortunate man needs someone to do good to. It is, I think, absurd to place the happy man in solitude, as no one would choose to possess the whole world by himself. For man is a social being, and disposed to live with others. It follows that a happy man must live in society, for he possesses all that is by nature good. And clearly it is better to spend one's days with friends and good people than with strangers, who may or may not be good. It follows, therefore, that the happy man has need of friends....

Should we then have as many friends as possible? Or is it with friendship as with hospitality, of which it has been neatly said,

"Give me not many guests, nor give me none."

That is, should a man neither be friendless nor again have an excessive number of friends?

In the case of friends whose friendship we make from motives of utility, the saying is perfectly applicable, for to return to the services of many people is a laborious task and life is not long enough. A larger number of such friends then than one needs for one's own life would be superfluous and an obstacle to noble living. We therefore do not want them. As for friends made because they seem pleasant or sweet to us, a few are enough, as a little sweetening is enough in our diet. . . .

We have yet to ask whether we need friends more in prosperity or in adversity? We need them at both times; for in trouble we need assistance, and in prosperity we need people to live with and to do good to; for presumably we wish to do good. Friendship is more necessary in times of trouble; and in trouble we want friends able to help us; but it is nobler in times of good fortune. So in prosperity we look for good people, since we like better to do them services and to live in their society. For the mere presence of friends is pleasant in good fortune, and also in bad, for our distress is lightened by the sympathy of friends. Accordingly it is a question whether they take part of the burden as it were upon themselves, or whether it is rather the pleasure of their presence and the thought of their sympathy that softens our pain.

(Translated by J. E. C. Welldon)

TO ALISON CUNNINGHAM

From Her Boy
Robert Louis Stevenson

For the long nights you lay awake
And watched for my unworthy sake:
For your most comfortable hand
That led me through the uneven land:
For all the story-books you read:
For all the pains you comforted:
For all you pitied, all you bore,
In sad and happy days of yore:—
My second Mother, my first Wife,
The angel of my infant life—
From the sick child, now well and old,
Take, nurse, the little book you hold!

And grant it, Heaven, that all who read
May find as dear a nurse at need,
And every child who lists my rhyme,
In the bright, fireside, nursery clime,
May hear it in as kind a voice
As made my childish days rejoice!

"THESE FRIENDS DELIGHT ME"
H. L. Mencken

Next to agreeable work as a means of attaining happiness I put what
Huxley called the domestic affections—the day to day intercourse with
friends. My home has seen bitter sorrow, but it has never seen any serious
disputes, and it has never seen poverty. I was completely happy with
my mother and sister, and I am completely happy with my wife. Most
of the men I commonly associate with are friends of very old standing.
I have known some of them for more than thirty years. I seldom see
anyone, intimately, whom I have known less than ten years. These
friends delight me. I turn to them when work is done with unfailing
eagerness. We have the same general tastes, and see the world much
alike. Most of them are interested in music, as I am. It has given me
more pleasure in this life than any other external thing. I love it more
every year.

Give me the avowed, the erect, the manly foe;
Bold I can meet, perhaps turn his blow;
But of all plagues, good Heaven, thy wrath can send,
Save, save, oh! save me from the Candid Friend!
—GEORGE CANNING

No friendship is so cordial or so delicious as that of girl for girl;
no hatred so intense and immovable as that of woman for woman.
—WALTER SAVAGE LANDOR

"Our friendship will and must go on as always."

THE FRIENDSHIP OF FRANKLIN D. ROOSEVELT AND HARRY HOPKINS

Robert E. Sherwood

During the years when Harry Hopkins lived as a guest in the White House, he was generally regarded as a sinister figure, a backstairs intriguer, an Iowan combination of Machiavelli, Svengali and Rasputin....

But the Presidential aide who developed in the war years...was in large measure Roosevelt's own creation. Roosevelt deliberately educated Hopkins in the arts and sciences of politics and of war and then gave him immense powers of decision for no reason other than that he liked him, trusted him and needed him. A welfare worker from the Cornbelt, who tended to regard money (his own as well as other people's) as something to be spent as quickly as possible, a studiously unsuave and often intolerant and tactless reformer, Hopkins was widely different from Roosevelt in birth, breeding and manners. But there were qualities in him, including some of the regrettable ones, which Roosevelt admired and enjoyed, perhaps partly because they were so different. One of the best statements of this relationship was written by the perceptive Raymond Clapper in 1938:

"Many New Dealers have bored Roosevelt with their solemn earnestness. Hopkins never does. He knows instinctively when to ask, when to keep still, when to press, when to hold back; when to approach Roosevelt direct, when to go at him roundabout.... Quick, alert, shrewd, bold, and carrying it off with a bright Hell's bells air, Hopkins is in all respects the inevitable Roosevelt favorite."...

A revealing story of Roosevelt's regard for Hopkins was told by Wendell Willkie, who was not one of the more fervent admirers of either man. It will be remembered that, after his defeat at the polls in November, 1940, Willkie provided a fine example of good citizenship and good sportsmanship in accepting the verdict. Supporting Roosevelt's foreign policy, he felt it would be useful for him to visit Britain which was then fighting alone against Hitler's seemingly all-conquering German war machine and was being bombed night after night with all the fury that the Nazi world conquerors could project by air. Roosevelt readily agreed to Willkie's proposal and invited him to come to the White House on January 19, 1941, the day before the first Third Term Inaugural in American history.

At that time, Hopkins was in England, having gone there to explore the prodigious character of Winston Churchill and to report thereon to Roosevelt; so Roosevelt suggested to Willkie that he must be sure to see Hopkins when he arrived in London. Willkie did not greet this suggestion with much enthusiasm. He probably had more cordial dislike and contempt for Hopkins than for anyone else in the Administration against which he had fought so recently and so bitterly. Indeed, he asked Roosevelt a pointed question: "Why do you keep Hopkins so close to you? You surely must realize that people distrust him and they resent his influence." Willkie quoted Roosevelt as replying: "I can understand that you wonder why I need that half-man around me." (The "half-man" was an allusion to Hopkins' extreme physical frailty.) "But—someday you may well be sitting here where I am now as President of the United States. And when you are, you'll be looking at that door over there and knowing that practically everybody who walks through it wants something out of you. You'll learn what a lonely job this is, and you'll discover the need for somebody like Harry Hopkins who asks for nothing except to serve you...."

In the year before Pearl Harbor, and the years of war that followed, Hopkins made it his job, he made it his religion, to find out just what it was that Roosevelt really wanted and then to see to it that neither hell nor high water, nor even possible vacillation by Roosevelt himself, blocked its achievement. Hopkins never made the mistake of Colonel Edward M. House, which caused the fatal breach with Wilson, of assuming he knew the President's mind better than the President did. Roosevelt could send him on any mission, to the Pentagon Building or to Downing Street, with absolute confidence that Hopkins would not utter one decisive word based on guesswork as to his Chief's policies or purposes. Hopkins ventured on no ground that Roosevelt had not charted. When Hopkins first journeyed to Moscow, in July, 1941, within a month after Hitler's assault on the Soviet Union, Roosevelt sent a message to Joseph Stalin: "I ask you to treat him with the identical confidence you would feel if you were talking directly to me...." What was remarkable about this first contact with Stalin is that Hopkins carried with him no written instructions whatsoever from Roosevelt as to what he should say or do. The President could and did trust him fully....

When Roosevelt contemplated a subject, his mind roamed all around it; he considered it in its relation to past, present and future. Hopkins, contemplating the same subject, was interested only in thrusting straight through to its heart and then acting on it without further palaver. In that respect, Hopkins was remarkably useful to Roosevelt —but Roosevelt was essential to Hopkins....

Roosevelt regarded the mild frivolities of his wayward friend with amusement not unmixed with considerable concern. His attitude was that of an indulgent parent toward an errant son whose wild oats, while forgivable, must be strictly rationed.

Following is a handwritten letter, dated May 21, 1939, during one of the many periods when Hopkins was bedridden with wasting sickness:

Dear Harry—

Good Boy! Teacher says you have gained 2 pounds.

$$2 \text{ Lbs.} = 2\$$$

Keep on gaining and put the reward into your little Savings Bank. But you must not gain more than 50 lbs. because Popper has not got more than 50$.

As ever,
F.D.R.

Clipped to that letter were two one-dollar bills. They are still clipped to it as this is written, eight years later. There was not a great deal more money left in the Hopkins estate.

Another letter of May 18, 1944, when Hopkins was in the Ashford General Hospital:

Dear Harry:—

It is grand to get the reports of how well you are getting on at White Sulphur Springs, and I have had a mighty nice letter from [Dr. Andrews B.] Rivers—couched mostly in medical terms—which, however, I have had translated!

The main things I get from it are two. First, that it is a good thing to connect up the plumbing and put your sewerage system into operating condition. The second is (and this comes from others in authority) that you have got to lead not the life of an invalid but the life of common or garden sense.

I, too, over one hundred years older than you are, have come to the same realization and I have cut my drinks down to one and a half cocktails per evening and nothing else—not one complimentary highball or night cap. Also, I have cut my cigarettes down from twenty or thirty a day to five or six a day. Luckily they still taste rotten but it can be done.

The main gist of this is to plead with you to stay away until the middle of June at the earliest. I don't want you back until then. If you do come back before then you will be extremely unpopular in Washington, with the exception of Cissy Patterson who wants to kill you off as soon as possible—just as she does me.

My plans—my medical laboratory work not being finished—are to be here about three days a week and to spend the other four days a week at Hyde Park, Shangri-la or on the Potomac. For later in the Summer I have various hens sitting but I don't know when they will hatch out.

I had a really grand time down at Bernie's [Baruch]—slept twelve hours out of the twenty-four, sat in the sun, never lost my temper, and decided to let the world go hang. The interesting thing is the world didn't hang.

I am off to Hyde Park, to stay until Tuesday or Wednesday next.

Lots of love to you both. Tell Louise to use the old-fashioned hat-pin if you don't behave!

Affectionately,
F.D.R.

It is of incidental interest to note that the foregoing letter was written two weeks before the Allied Forces were due to land in Normandy, a time when Roosevelt was bearing a formidable weight of responsibility and anxiety....

Hopkins left the Mayo Clinic about New Year's, 1938, and went to Florida to stay at the house of Joseph P. Kennedy. The President then wrote him:

Missy (Marguerite LeHand, the President's trusted secretary for many years) has told me that you telephoned on Saturday night. I am sorry I had not returned from the speech, as it would have been grand to have talked with you.

I hope so much that you are not trying to hurry things up. It seems to me almost incredible that you should be walking around so soon. However, it is, of course, grand news.

Jo Kennedy's sounds like an ideal spot for peace and quiet and recuperation.

We all had great fun with Diana [Hopkins' daughter] at Christmas time. She is a lovely youngster and stole the show that day. As you know, of course, she is now at Jimmy's "political" farm in Massachusetts where Jimmy and Bets say they are all having a grand time.

The figurehead picture is bully and I am really awfully glad to have it. Thank you ever so much.

Do keep us in touch with where you are and how you are, and take good care of yourself....

There is no question that in 1938 Roosevelt did all he could—and that was a very great deal—to aid the Hopkins build-up [for the Demo-

cratic Presidential nomination]. When the President was photographed
at a baseball park or on the back platform of a train, or on a fishing
cruise, he had Hopkins at his elbow. This was not by accident. There
were many people who went along with the President when he appeared in public who did not feature prominently in the news photographs. Indeed, it was a matter of discretion as well as courtesy to make
oneself inconspicuous when the flashbulbs were popping unless the
President distinctly asked one to be with him. It was plain to see that
while Hopkins was receiving this preferred treatment other potential
candidates were not.

Mrs. Roosevelt, who often reflected her husband's views in her column, "My Day," wrote the following significant reference:

"It was good to see Mr. Harry Hopkins yesterday and to have him
spend the night with us. He is one of the few people in the world who
give me the feeling of being entirely absorbed in doing his job well.
...He seems to work because he has an inner conviction that his job
needs to be done and that he must do it. I think he would be that way
about *any job he undertook*. He would not undertake it unless he felt
that he could really accomplish something which needed to be done."
[The italics are mine, R.E.S.] ...

Hopkins and his six-year-old daughter, Diana, were guests in the
White House over the [Christmas, 1938] holidays, and he had a conversation with Mrs. Roosevelt for which he was forever grateful. Solicitous
about Hopkins' health, Mrs. Roosevelt asked him what provision he
had made for Diana if he were to die. It appeared that he had done
nothing about making a new will since the death of his second wife a
year previous; so Mrs. Roosevelt told him he must attend to this immediately and said that she would like to be named guardian of Diana.
Hopkins described this conversation in a letter to his daughter years
later. He said:

"At that time I discussed with her the amount of my insurance and
financial affairs and she said that she would undertake to see that you
got a good education and have a little money when you were through
your schooling.

"Mrs. Roosevelt has always believed that the main business of a
modern education is to teach people not only to live in this world with
other people, but for girls to have the kind of education which would
enable them to earn their own living.

"Mrs. Roosevelt was quite right about my being disturbed about your
care in the event that anything happened to me, and, naturally, I was
greatly relieved at her offer which was made with great sincerity. She
had become very fond of you during the time you had lived at the
White House. I was, naturally, quite overcome by her suggestion, not

only because it was an offer that would relieve my mind, but because I was sure was one that would be very good for you."

Hopkins made out a new will in accordance with Mrs. Roosevelt's warmhearted suggestion and she took care of his small daughter until his marriage to Louise Macy in July, 1942....

At the end of March [1939] he [Hopkins] went to Warm Springs with the President. He wrote a description of this visit:

"We left Washington early in the afternoon of Wednesday, March 29—Mrs. Roosevelt had invited Diana to stay at the White House while I was in Warm Springs—so promising real live ducks for Easter—I kissed my adorable one good-by and for the first time in two weeks stepped out of doors on my all too wobbly feet. I had a room in the President's car and slept the afternoon through—and now more than a week has passed and I am feeling ever so much better.

"There is no one here but Missy—the President and me—so life is simple—ever so informal and altogether pleasant. And why not—I like Missy—the President is the grandest of companions—I read for hours—and sleep ever so well. The food as ever around the W. H. menage is medium to downright bad....

"Lunch has usually been F.D.R. with Missy and me—these are the pleasantest because he is under no restraint and personal and public business is discussed with the utmost frankness. The service incidentally is as bad as the food. There are thousands of men in America who get infinitely better care than the President—this in spite of the fact that he is crippled. I would fire them all.

"He will sleep a bit after lunch—and at three drive over the countryside with a guest—visit his farm—look at the new tree plantings—back around four thirty for an hour's dictation. Then relax till dinner at seven. The ceremonial cocktail with the President doing the honors—gin and grapefruit juice is his current favorite—and a vile drink it is! He makes a first rate 'old fashioned' and a fair Martini—which he should stick to—but his low and uncultivated taste in liquors leads him woefully astray. Missy and I will not be bullied into drinking his concoction which leads him to take three instead of his usual quota of two.

"Dinner therefore is gay—as it should be—and the President reminisces long over the personal experiences of his life—he tells incidents well—tho he has a bad habit of repeating them every year or so. I fancy Missy has heard them all many times but she never flickers an eyebrow.

"After dinner the President retreats to his stamps—magazines and the evening paper. Missy and I will play Chinese checkers—occasionally the three of us played but more often we read—a little conversation—important or not—depending on the mood. George Fox comes in to give him a rub down and the President is in bed by ten...."

On August 22 [1939], Hopkins went again to the Mayo Clinic. On August 25, Roosevelt wrote him:

Your birthday has come and gone and although I had it very much on my mind to send you a ribald radio, things began to pop in Europe and I let the day pass by. This is to send you my congratulations and every kind of good wish for many happy returns of the day.

I am delighted that you are at Mayo's. It was the only wise thing to do.

Why don't you stop off at Hyde Park on your way back if I am there —which means if there is no war in Europe. Things are looking a little brighter today.

Do telephone me to let me know how you are.

As ever yours, F.D.R.

P.S. I am counting on you to help entertain the —— who will be back this Fall if there is no war. However, don't pray for a war! ... [The name deleted was one of two friends of Roosevelt's whom Hopkins found boring. R.E.S.]

On August 31, Hopkins wrote to the President:

It was so good to talk to you the other night. You sounded so cheerful and encouraging in spite of the fact that the world seems to be tumbling around our heads. I think your letter to Hitler was grand and I am sure it is having a very real effect on the present delays. The thing I am disturbed about more than anything else is the danger of another Munich which I think would be fatal to the democracies.

They are not through with my tests here yet and I doubt if they will be for another two or three days but I don't imagine I will be out of here until after Labor Day at least. It looks more and more like a dietary problem. I am sure there is nothing wrong with my stomach.

I will be in touch with you during the next few days and will surely accept your cordial invitation to come to Hyde Park if the doctors here will prescribe it. The place is full of your acquaintances, all of whom ask about you....

On May 10 [1940], the day of the attack on the Low Countries, Hopkins went to his office in the Commerce Department—and, as nearly as I can make out, this was the second time he had appeared there in ten months. That evening he went to dinner at the White House. He was feeling miserable and Roosevelt prevailed on him to stay there overnight. He remained, living in what had been Lincoln's study, for three and a half years. Later Missy LeHand remarked, "It was

Harry Hopkins who gave George S. Kaufman and Moss Hart the idea for that play of theirs, 'The Man Who Came to Dinner.' From then on, his work was done in his room at the White House. After breakfast in the morning and after dinner at night and at odd times during the day he talked with the President about the shocking cables that were coming in from Europe; Hopkins undoubtedly had little real understanding of the full import of this news, but Roosevelt was teaching him. On Sundays they usually went cruising on the yacht, *Potomac*. On June 20, Hopkins went with the President for a four days' stay at Hyde Park, during which the news arrived of France's surrender together with some cables from Churchill. A week after the return to Washington, Hopkins went to Chicago to discuss arrangements for the [Democratic National] Convention with Mayor Edward J. Kelly. Acting without express instructions from Roosevelt, but also without prohibition, Hopkins was now moving to take charge of the third term nomination himself....

The job that Hopkins had to do at this dreadful display of democracy at its tawdriest was disagreeable and thankless. He was under fire from all sides, friend and foe alike. But he had assumed this job on his own initiative because it had to be done and there was no one else who had his courage or perhaps the effrontery to do it without written instructions from the President. He handled it only by dint of supreme toughness and a demonstration of political ruthlessness which must have caused some of the professional politicians to reconsider their estimate of him as an amateur. Hopkins knew, however, that his dilemma in Chicago was only a minor projection of Roosevelt's. In ordinary times, Roosevelt would probably have enjoyed a knock-down-and-drag-out political Donnybrook against such opponents as Farley and Garner and legions of ward heelers and he would have handled it without much perceptible difficulty. But this Convention was staged against a background of world catastrophe, of which the delegates had scant conception, and Roosevelt, in his distaste for the whole vulgar proceeding, displayed none of his customary adroitness in controlling the unruly situation. It was a lucky thing for him and for the country that he had Hopkins there to absorb so much of the hatred that was generated.

After Chicago it became all too clear to Hopkins that he must resign as Secretary of Commerce.... On August 22, he submitted his resignation in a letter which stated his physical inability to perform his duties under the rigorous demands of war....

My Dear Mr. President:

... I wanted to resign last May because it seemed to me that you and the country needed the services of cabinet officers whose strength permitted vigorous and continuous assumption of the duties required of them. You indicated then that I should remain throughout the Summer in the hope that I would completely recover my strength. This recovery I have not fully accomplished, therefore, I feel that I must resign as Secretary of Commerce, the resignation to become effective in the immediate future.

An expression of good-will and appreciation from me to you at this time is unnecessary. My abiding devotion and affection for you and Mrs. Roosevelt cannot be authenticated in any exchange of letters.

Roosevelt replied as follows:

I have your letter of August the twenty-second and I fully understand all that you say and much that you have left unsaid.

In giving me this letter of resignation it is possible only for you to break the official ties that exist between us—not the ties of friendship that have endured so happily through the years. I am accepting your resignation, therefore, to take effect at a date to be determined later and, I repeat, this resignation is accepted only in its official sense.

In other words, you may resign the office—only the office—and nothing else. Our friendship will and must go on as always....

In addition to his formal letter, Hopkins wrote one in longhand to the President which represented one of his rare outpourings of the heart:

A public letter of resignation is almost a vulgar institution. Why don't you abolish it? At any rate I have told you little that is in my mind and heart as I leave the government's service.

I think of the things that have made my years with you the happiest time of my life. The first exciting days—the exaltation of being part of government—our first formal dinner at the White House when I met Cardozo and another [when] Bob Jackson tried to sell me some old underwear—and Cocos Island—did you ever see anything so green? Then there were those cigarettes in my pocket—it seems to me in all decency that you should forget that one.

And one day you went to church with me when the going wasn't so good—and life seemed ever so dark.

Those nine old men—a better fight none of us ever took part in—

And there was always New Year's Eve—and the warm glow of Auld Lang Syne—with champagne. That's about the only time we got champagne around your house. Or am I wrong?

I've always been getting on and off trains—and I saw America and learned to know its people. I like them. Whenever I was with you there were the everlasting Secret Service men—they seemed to be always at a dog trot—how many miles do you suppose they have dog trotted beside your car?

You remember the day we got you up a blind road in Nevada and Mac [Marvin McIntyre] wanted to give up his life if the car rolled over the hill? And people at trains with nice faces that smiled. All of them work hard for a living and are devoted to you.

And one day two nice people came to visit you—he was a king—and I hope will be for a long time and she was a Scotch girl who got to be a Queen. And after dinner that night you and Missy and I talked it all over till 2 A.M.

Then there were picnics! I suppose the Roosevelts have always had picnics—cold weather and nothing to drink.

I never knew there were so many mayors and governors and congressmen and senators and county auditors and school boards and irrigation districts in the world. I have met them all. One of them had me arrested and you thought it was funny and promised to visit me in jail.

I presume Henry Morgenthau will ever go to the bathroom when he gets ahead—and "Dollar Watson" will talk about the Powder River.

The cheese store on 42nd street—and first fish in Iowa—and maps and rivers and forests and Admirals and dams and power plants—funny things that no President ever talked about before.

All these things I think of—and Mac and Steve and Tommy and Ben and Rex and Felix and Sam and Missy—I know they are important because I remember them—and they are good.

This letter is simply to say that I have had an awfully good time—and to thank you very much. And by the way—my weather bureau tells me that it will be fair tomorrow....

During the war years, when Hopkins lived in the White House, he said impatiently to a persistent petitioner: "Why do you keep pestering *me* about this? I'm only the office boy around here!..."

One might say that Hopkins became, by his own earlier definition, the supreme office boy of them all. He was of course a channel of communication between the President and various agencies of the Administration, notably the War Department, and the ready means of informal contact with foreign dignitaries. (A British official once said to me, "We came to think of Hopkins as Roosevelt's own, personal Foreign Office.") He also acted in the capacity of a buffer state. He kept problem-laden officials away from Roosevelt; one of his most frequent statements was, "The President isn't going to be bothered with anything as nonsensical and unimportant as that if I can help it!" It was this function that made many of Roosevelt's most loyal friends agree with his worst enemies that Hopkins was an unmitigated menace. For instance: when, for a period of some ten months, Harold Ickes did not have one private appointment with the President, he blamed it all on the vindictiveness of Hopkins. Whether this was just or unjust, it was certainly a comfort to Roosevelt to have someone around to take the blame. It cannot be said that Hopkins suffered unduly in the performance of this unsympathetic role. His loyalty to Roosevelt in the war years was the supreme justification of his continued existence and he enjoyed every opportunity to exercise it. As Marquis Childs wrote:

"Should the President on a dull day suggest casually to his friend and confidant Harry L. Hopkins, that the national welfare would be served if Mr. Hopkins were to jump off the Washington Monument, the appointed hour would find Mr. Hopkins poised for the plunge. Whether with or without parachute would depend on what the President seemed to have in mind.

"Mr. Hopkins would know about that, for he has made a career of understanding, sensing, divining, often guessing—and usually guessing right—what is in Franklin Roosevelt's mind. It is a career that has taken him from the dull routine of social-service to the upper reaches of diplomacy, where he has had a thrilling preview of the shape of things to come. And, what is more, history may show that he was one of the shapers."

Hopkins did not have to do much sensing, divining or guessing while he lived in the White House. He could traipse down the upstairs hall in his old dressing gown to the President's room and ask what his chief wanted done or not done about any given problem. And then act accordingly, without having to reveal to anyone that he was guided not by his own prejudices or hunches but by Roosevelt's express instructions. . . .

Roosevelt, who was tired out himself, had arranged to appear before the Congress immediately after his return to Washington and deliver a speech on the Yalta Conference. Roosevelt's speech must be prepared on the *Quincy* during the trip across the Atlantic and naturally he expected Hopkins to help in its preparation, but Hopkins sent word through Bohlen that he must leave the ship at Algiers and go to Marrakech for a few days' rest and fly from there back to Washington. Although Roosevelt made no particular attempt to persuade Hopkins to change his mind about this, he was disappointed and even displeased. He was sure that Hopkins could get far better care on the *Quincy* than in Marrakech, and he apparently suspected that the desire to leave the ship was due more to boredom than anything else. It was difficult for Roosevelt to imagine anyone feeling miserable on board a ship. But Hopkins dreaded a nine-day voyage across the Atlantic during which he would probably remain confined to his cabin, with seasickness added to his other ills. So he was glad of a chance to escape, but he had cause later to wish that he had stayed with the ship....

When Hopkins left the *Quincy* to go ashore at Algiers, the President's "good-by" to him was not a very amiable one—a circumstance which it is sad to record, for Hopkins never saw his great friend again....

The morning after Roosevelt's death Hopkins telephoned me from St. Mary's Hospital in Rochester, Minnesota. He just wanted to talk to somebody. There was no sadness in his tone; he talked with a kind of exaltation as though he had suddenly experienced the intimation of immortality. He said "You and I have got something great that we can take with us all the rest of our lives. It's a great realization. Because we know it's *true* what so many people believed about him and what made them love him. The President never let them down. That's what you and I can remember. Oh, we all know he could be exasperating, and he could seem to be temporizing and delaying, and he'd get us all worked up when we thought he was making too many concessions to expediency. But all of that was in the little things, the unimportant things—and he knew exactly how little and how unimportant they really were. But in the big things—all of the things that were of real, permanent importance—he never let the people down."

The next afternoon, Saturday, we went to the funeral service in the East Room of the White House. I was sitting on a little gilt chair at the extreme right of the assemblage when I felt a hand squeeze my shoulder. I looked up and it was Hopkins, who had flown in from Rochester. He himself looked like death, the skin of his face a dreadful cold white with apparently no flesh under it. I believed that he now had nothing left to live for, that his life ended with Roosevelt's.

Was it friend or foe that spread these lies?
Nay, Who but an infant questions in such wise?
'Twas one of my most intimate enemies.
—Dante Gabriel Rossetti

A friend you have to buy won't be worth what you pay for him.
—George D. Prentice

"I, who am a prisoner, send you a little token . . ."

TO MARIE-CATHERINE DE CASTELNAU *

Sheffield, the 26 of January (1584)

My goddaughter, my precious, I have been happy to see, through your letters, the proof of the perfections with which, I have heard, God has endowed you even in your earliest years. Learn, my dear, to recognize and serve Him who has given you so many graces, and He will increase them; for this I pray and also that He may give you His holy blessing. I, who am a prisoner, send you a little token so that you may always remember your godmother. It is a small thing, in itself; but I send it to you as a witness of the friendship which I bear toward you and your family; it was given to me by the late King, my highly honored and good father-in-law, when I was very young indeed, and I have kept it until this very hour. Remember me to my godmother your mother, and continue to love me as the second mother I always wish to be to you.

Your affectionate godmother
MARIE
[Mary Queen of Scots]
(*Translated by Dorothy Connor*)

❧❧❧❧❧❧

As widowers proverbially marry again, so a man with the habit of friendship always finds new friends. . . . My old age judges more charitably and thinks better of mankind than my youth ever did. I discount idealization, I forgive one-sidedness, I see that it is essential to perfection of any kind. And in each person I catch the fleeting suggestion of something beautiful, and swear eternal friendship with that.

—GEORGE SANTAYANA

❧❧❧❧❧❧

* She was born in England, where her father, M. de Mauvissière, was French Ambassador. The "late King" referred to in the letter was Henry II of France.

FROM "LYCIDAS: ELEGY ON A FRIEND DROWNED IN THE ENGLISH CHANNEL"

John Milton

Yet once more, O ye laurels, and once more
Ye myrtles brown, with ivy never sere,
I come to pluck your berries harsh and crude,
And with forced fingers rude,
Shatter your leaves before the mellowing year.
Bitter constraint, and sad occasion dear,
Compels me to disturb your season due:
For Lycidas is dead, dead ere his prime,
Young Lycidas, and hath not left his peer:
Who would not sing for Lycidas? he knew
Himself to sing, and build the lofty rhyme.
He must not float upon his watery bier
Unwept, and welter to the parching wind,
Without the meed of some melodious tear....

Weep no more, woeful shepherds, weep no more,
For Lycidas your sorrow is not dead,
Sunk though he be beneath the watery floor;
So sinks the day-star in the ocean-bed,
And yet anon repairs his drooping head,
And tricks his beams, and with new-spangled ore,
Flames in the forehead of the morning sky:
So Lycidas sunk low, but mounted high,
Through the dear might of Him that walk'd the waves;
Where other groves, and other streams along,
With nectar pure his oozy locks he laves,
And hears the unexpressive nuptial song,
In the blest kingdoms meek of joy and love.
There entertain him all the saints above,
In solemn troops, and sweet societies
That sing, and singing in their glory move,
And wipe the tears for ever from his eyes.
Now, Lycidas the shepherds weep no more:
Henceforth thou art the Genius of the shore,
In thy large recompense, and shalt be good
To all that wander in that perilous flood.

Thus sang the uncouth swain to the oaks and rills,
While the still morn went out with sandals grey;
He touch'd the tender stops of various quills,
With eager thought warbling his Doric lay:
And now the sun had stretch'd out all the hills,
And now was dropt into the western bay:
At last he rose, and twitch'd his mantle blue:
Tomorrow to fresh woods, and pastures new.

"... the best of comrades and staunchest of friends."

CAPTAIN ROBERT FALCON SCOTT'S DYING TRIBUTE TO HIS COMRADES IN DISASTER IN THE ANTARCTIC, 1912

My Dear Mrs. Wilson:—If this letter reaches you Bill and I will have gone out together. We are very near it now and I should like you to know how splendid he was at the end—everlastingly cheerful and ready to sacrifice himself for others, never a word of blame to me for leading him into this mess. He is not suffering, luckily, at least only minor difficulties.

His eyes have a comfortable blue look of hope and his mind is peaceful with the satisfaction of his faith in regarding himself as part of a great scheme of the Almighty. I can do no more to comfort you than to tell you that he died as he lived, a brave, true man—the best of comrades and staunchest of friends.

My whole heart goes out to you in pity.—Yours,

R. SCOTT

My Dear Mrs. Bowers:—I am afraid this will reach you after one of the heaviest blows of your life.

I write when we are very near the end of our journey, and I am finishing it in company with two gallant, noble gentlemen. One of these is your son. He had come to be one of my closest and soundest friends, and I appreciate his wonderful upright nature, his ability and energy. As the troubles have thickened his dauntless spirit ever shone brighter and he has remained cheerful, hopeful, and indomitable to the end.

The ways of Providence are inscrutable, but there must be some reason why such a young, vigorous and promising life is taken.

My whole heart goes out to you in pity for you.—Yours,

R. Scott

To the end he talked of you and his sisters. One sees what a happy home he must have had and perhaps it is well to look back on nothing but happiness.

He remains unselfish, self-reliant and splendidly hopeful to the end, believing in God's mercy to you.

"JIM"

Bret Harte

Say there! Pr'aps
   Some on you chaps
   Might know Jim Wild?
Well,—no offence:
That ain't no sense
   In gittin' riled!

Jim was my chum
   Up on the Bar:
That's why I come
   Down from up yar,
Lookin' for Jim.
Thank ye, sir! *You*
Ain't of that crew,—
   Blest if you are!

Money?—Not much:
   That ain't my kind;
I ain't no such,
   Rum?—I don't mind,
Seein' it's you.

Well, this yer Jim,—
Did you know him?
Jess 'bout your size;
Same kind of eyes,—

Well, that is strange:
 Why, it's two years
 Since he came here,
Sick, for a change.

Well, here's to us:
 Eh?
The h——you say!
 Dead?
That little cuss?

What makes you star,
You over thar?
Can't a man drop
's glass in yer shop
But you must r'ar?
 It wouldn't take
 D—— much to break
You and your bar.
 Dead!
Poor—— little —— Jim!
—— Why, thar was me,
Jones, and Bob Lee,
Harry and Ben,—
No-account men:
Then to take *him!*

Well, thar—Good-by,—
No more, sir,—I—
 Eh?
What's that you say?—
Why, dern it!— sho!—
No? Yes! By Joe!
 Sold!
Sold! Why, you limb,
You ornery,
 Derned old
Long-legged Jim!

"... I cannot confuse gratitude with esteem"

HENRI-FRÉDÉRIC AMIEL'S REFLECTION

December 28, 1880.—There are two modes of classing the people we know: the first is utilitarian—it starts from ourselves, divides our friends from our enemies, and distinguishes those who are antipathetic to us, those who are indifferent, those who can serve or harm us; the second is disinterested—it classes men according to their intrinsic value, their own qualities and defects, apart from the feelings which they have for us, or we for them.

My tendency is to the second kind of classification. I appreciate men less by the special affection which they show to me than by their personal excellence, and I cannot confuse gratitude with esteem. It is a happy thing for us when the two feelings can be combined; and nothing is more painful than to owe gratitude where yet we can feel neither respect nor confidence.

I am not very willing to believe in the permanence of accidental states. The generosity of a miser, the good nature of an egotist, the gentleness of a passionate temperament, the tenderness of a barren nature, the piety of a dull heart, the humility of an excitable self-love, interest me as phenomena—nay, even touch me if I am the object of them, but they inspire me with very little confidence. I foresee the end of them too clearly. Every exception tends to disappear and to return to the rule. All privilege is temporary, and besides, I am less flattered than anxious when I find myself the object of a privilege.

A man's primitive character may be covered over by alluvial deposits of culture and acquisition—none the less is it sure to come to the surface when years have worn away all that is accessory and adventitious. I admit indeed the possibility of great moral crises which sometimes revolutionize the soul, but I dare not reckon on them. It is a possibility —not a probability. In choosing one's friends we must choose those whose qualities are inborn, and their virtues virtues of temperament. To lay the foundations of friendship on borrowed or added virtues is to build on an artificial soil; we run too many risks by it.

Exceptions are snares, and we ought above all to distrust them when they charm our vanity. To catch and fix a fickle heart is a task which tempts all women; and a man finds something intoxicating in the tears of tenderness and joy which he alone has had the power to draw from a proud woman. But attractions of this kind are deceptive. Affinity of nature founded on worship of the same ideal, and perfect in proportion to perfectness of soul, is the only affinity which is worth anything. True love is that which ennobles the personality, fortifies the heart, and sanctifies the existence. And the being we love must not be mysterious and sphinx-like, but clear and limpid as a diamond; so that admiration and attachment may grow with knowledge. . . .

A man may be isolated in his own particular and temporary *milieu*, but every one of our thoughts or feelings finds, has found, and will find, its echo in humanity. Such an echo is immense and far-resounding in the case of those representative men who have been adopted by great fractions of humanity as guides, revealers, and reformers; but it exists for everybody. Every sincere utterance of the soul, every testimony faithfully borne to a personal conviction, is of use to some one and some thing, even when you know it not, and when your mouth is stopped by violence, or the noose tightens round your neck. A word spoken to some one preserves an indestructible influence, just as any movement whatever may be metamorphosed, but not undone. Here, then, is a reason for not mocking, for not being silent, for affirming, for acting. We must have faith in truth; we must seek the true and spread it abroad; we must love men and serve them. . . .

A man who has not got happiness cannot impart it. We can only give what we have. Happiness, grief, gayety, sadness, are by nature contagious. Bring your health and your strength to the weak and sickly, and so you will be of use to them. Give them, not your weakness, but your energy, so you will revive and lift them up. Life alone can rekindle life. What others claim from us is not our thirst and our hunger, but our bread and our gourd.

(Translated by Mrs. Humphry Ward)

"... Uncle Thomas was no older than I was."

MY BEST UNCLE

Robert P. Tristram Coffin

I know, now, what made Uncle Thomas my best uncle. I only guessed why when I was a boy. It was because he was a boy, too.

How Uncle Thomas stayed in short pants, with his two hundred pounds of square muscles and bones, his heavy thighs and wide butts, his cornucopia moustaches—I don't know. But stay he did. You could tell his long pants were short pants by their pockets. They were always full of the junk a boy collects. A sinker, a shell, a piece of twine, a

West Indian bean, a luckybone from a cod's head, a pebble with a moonbeam of mica in it. His pockets were always that way. They added to his width of beam.

It is a sort of natural mysticism that makes a boy bring together in his pants the objects the universe spreads apart, the things other people call parts and fragments. And the heat of the boy and of the boy's enthusiasm fuses them into one living substance, and fuses in the boy, too, with the rest. That's how I say it now. But then, I just naturally accepted it as a fact of kinship. For all his nine-inch moustache, Uncle Thomas was no older than I was. And maybe not always so old. So I made up to him and talked to him and touched him as I would one of my kind. And he made up to me the same way. . . .

For there my Uncle Thomas was, up to his knees in shavings as he whittled a schooner out for me, and I could touch him just as I touched any boy of my age. And he could touch me, and did. He would smack me across the shoulders, or lower down where there were two halves to me, just the way a cousin would when he got affectionate. And a *few* cousins I had did get affectionate, though most of them were a remarkably unaffectionate set of people. . . .

Schooners of both sizes, big and small, were what Uncle Thomas had his hands in all the time. For he had lived his forty-five or fifty years in them, and had sailed them out on the Grand Banks and loaded them down with menhaden and cod and hake and mackerel. He knew the shape of schooners, above water and below, as he knew the shape of his moustache and chin. And the tides and fogs of the Atlantic were like brothers to him. He had kept his five quarts of blood warm out in an Atlantic Winter. He had learned to live by the skin of his teeth and the feel of the night breeze on his cheek. He knew his way around schooners all right.

This was a sea uncle. The best of all my sea uncles. And that was probably another good reason why I liked him best, and that was another reason why he kept on being a boy after he had begotten men. For there is no other so good a thing as the sea to keep anyone young. The days and years a man is away on it, away from women and business, are subtracted from a man's life, not added to it. A man gets younger each time he comes home. I have noticed that. Time does not count on the sea. Years go over you and leave no ripple or wrinkle. Children don't count. Trouble doesn't count. It leaves no scar. Women don't count on the sea. . . .

This man I had for uncle was built of the sea. He had it in his blood and eyes. He had three-diameter eyes. A lot of Maine coast men do. Especially those who live along Penobscot or Casco. They have to have, to live. When I say three-diameter eyes, I mean just that. In case you don't know, Uncle Thomas's eyes could enlarge a thing—any distant thing, not a woman near to or such—three times its apparent size. Such a man as Uncle Thomas has field-glasses for eyes. That is, he can see things better with his bare eyes than anybody else can with a pair of field-glasses....

I think men who look far ahead are what the world needs most now. For it takes men like that to look past the disasters of our time and see the old landmarks and sea signs still out there on the horizons of the future. The landmarks and sea-marks men live by. They are still there. Only men who can look far ahead are happy men. It takes a long sight to make out happiness.

Those men who could look far, like Uncle Thomas, were men who got to looking far ahead of their troubles, too. Farsightedness didn't stop at their eyes, it went right on back into their minds....

Far-away eyes, for all their sadness, are happy eyes, boy's eyes. Uncle Thomas had that kind.

So twenty-five years of fishing in Penobscot, out of North Haven and Vinal Haven, had gone over Uncle Thomas as a light s'utheaster and left him smiling for me. And when the menhaden and mackerel had thinned out in the eastern ocean, Uncle Thomas had pulled up trawl and gone over to the western. He had gone out to Puget Sound, got him a boat and men who knew knots and sails, and whose ancestors had been brought up right in Maine waters, and he went after the fish out there. When they ran low, he went on up to Bering Sea and took the fur-seal there. But some capitalists had got ahead of Uncle Thomas and had claimed all the fur-seal as their own. So the revenue-men took my uncle. They could not understand that it was just a boy in knee pants they had in their net, and so they threw him into the brig for some years. But Uncle Thomas did not age any there. He never even told his second wife where he was. When he got out, the revenuers having his boat for keeps, he came on back to Maine and was persuaded to buy a farm on Casco Bay and become a farmer. So he came into my life. That's how I, on a Casco Bay farm, came to have the best boy in the world as an uncle. It was an accident. But it is the way the stars manage things for boys and uncles....

Uncle Thomas took me with him on fishing trips and told me the things I ought to know. He taught me how to box the compass, tub a trawl, and name all the sails and lines on a full-rigged ship and what each one was for and how a score of men's lives could hang on one single knot. He schooled me in wind and weather, the two oldest and most important studies in the world. He told me how I could tell what winds were coming, by the feel of a spar, the looks of the clouds, or the way my head felt inside. He taught me how to look around a corner of one day into the next. The little streaks a cloud left, no bigger than the hairs on a paint brush, and yet they might mean life or death to you next day. He told me what secrets there were in the moon and how a man would die if he didn't watch her carefully to see what she was up to. He made my eyes stretch out to far headlands and blossoms of surf which meant trouble. He made my ears widen out and take in sounds of a low tune in the lines of the rigging. I learned about the sea and her woman tricks from Uncle Thomas. If she was on your side, you were safe. But you had to know her good side and stay on it. The same way with women.

My uncle taught me how to feel what way the tide was in a fog. He told me about the shooting stars and the Northern Lights. Those things weren't just fireworks for my amusement. They were deep secrets being whispered through an August or October night. If you hearkened to them close, you could make out what the dusking flames of the Northern Lights were saying. They were talking about tremendous changes coming over the ocean. They were fiery cradles of the winds. And vast gales could spring out of those cradles of fire rocking up there and flatten a ship or a man out on the waves. You had to know what the winds and the moon and the stars and the Northern Lights were saying. They were talking in whispers all the time. But they were talking. A good sailor was able to hear what they said.

Sailors had known what those things were saying for thousands of years. Before there were any of the religions we have now, they had known. Uncle Thomas opened up the oldest book in the world to me. And he made me wise, for all my knee pants, and his. And out of my wisdom, and his, I loved him.

Yet there were the whole areas Uncle Thomas knew nothing about. Women. Farming. The way of men ashore. Soldiering. Politics. Especially women. Uncle Thomas was one in one-piece pants held together by a safety-pin, to them. They were uncharted continents. He gave them all, save two, wide berths. The sea was enough for one man to know. So sometimes when my aunt scolded, or men came to collect bills or to take Uncle Thomas to vote, he was like a very small boy trembling at a thunderstorm. Gigantic things he knew nothing about were rolling down the sky around him. Maybe the skies themselves were coming down. He sat small and crumpled up, and his eyes were full of surprise and sadness. Like a small boy with the sudden dark coming up over the world and the trees turning their leaves up white, and new trees that grew suddenly with fiery limbs blazing an instant against the dark.

Sometimes, I think I loved Uncle Thomas best those times. Like the day the mortgage was foreclosed on his farm.

But the last act of Uncle Thomas was his best. His farm's being lost to the mortgage was a sad day for me. But not for him. It gave him a chance to go back living altogether where he wanted to be, in a schooner. Yet sad for me, for that schooner was on the opposite side of our continent. It was in Puget Sound again and in the adjacent Pacific. Uncle Thomas went back to the West. He got him a schooner and helped run down the last of the best fish in that ocean out there. Eventually he earned enough to buy another farm for my aunt and cousin. But Thomas's heart stayed at sea. So he was there when age came upon him and snowed on his hair.

❧❧❧❧❧

"... these two noble persons made so happy by their friendship ..."

PÉLISSON AND MLLE. DE SCUDÉRY
William Rounseville Alger

Pélisson was twenty-nine, and Mademoiselle de Scudéry forty-five, when they first met. Their instant mutual interest deepened, on more thorough acquaintance, into the warmest esteem and affection, and remained unshaken for over forty years. The perfection of their intimacy was known to every one; and every one believed in its entire purity. Cousin says it is touching to see these two noble persons made so happy by their friendship—a friendship which even the coarse and slanderous Tallement respected so much that he refrained from casting a single sneer at it. The story of Pélisson's imprisonment in the Bastille is known to the whole world by the anecdote of the spider. His only companion during those wretched years was a large spider, which he had tamed and was accustomed to feed and play with. One day the brute of a jailer trod on him, and killed him; and Pélisson wept.

His friend employed all her ingenuity during his confinement, in inventing means of communication with him. At times, when he was ready to fall into despair, a few lines would reach him, and bring him comfort. At length his prison was opened, and fortune smiled again. At his death, Mademoiselle de Scudéry, though eighty-six years old, wrote and published a simple and affecting memoir of him, paying a deserved tribute to his character, in which, she said, there reigned a singular and most charming combination of tenderness, delicacy, and generosity.

❧❧❧❧❧

POLONIUS' ADVICE TO HIS SON
William Shakespeare

And these few precepts in thy memory
See thou character. Give thy thoughts no tongue,
Nor any unproportion'd thought his act.
Be thou familiar, but by no means vulgar.
The friends thou hast, and their adoption tried,
Grapple them to thy soul with hoops of steel;
But do not dull thy palm with entertainment
Of each new-hatch'd, unfledged comrade. Beware
Of entrance to a quarrel, but being in,
Bear 't that the opposed may beware of thee.
Give every man thy ear, but few thy voice;
Take each man's censure, but reserve thy judgement.
Costly thy habit as thy purse can buy,
But not express'd in fancy; rich, not gaudy;
For the apparel oft proclaims the man....
Neither a borrower nor a lender be;
For loan oft loses both itself and friend,
And borrowing dulls the edge of husbandry.
This above all: to thine own self be true,
And it must follow, as the night the day,
Thou canst not then be false to any man.

"I have long seen 'friend' in your mind . . ."

CHARLOTTE BRONTË TO
ELLEN NUSSEY

Haworth
June 19th, 1834

My *own* dear Ellen,

I may rightfully and truly call you so *now*. You *have* returned, or are returning from London, from the great city which to me is almost apocryphal as Babylon or Nineveh, or ancient Rome. You are withdrawing from the world (as it is called) and bringing with you, if your letters enable me to form a correct judgment, a heart as unsophisticated, as natural, as true, as that you carried there. I am slow, *very* slow to believe all the protestations of another. I know my own sentiments because I can read my own mind, but the minds of the rest of men and women are to me as sealed volumes, hieroglyphical, which I cannot easily either unseal or decipher. Yet time, careful study, long acquaintance, overcome most difficulties; and in your case I think they have succeeded well in bringing to light and construing that hidden language, whose turnings, windings, inconsistencies, and obscurities, so frequently baffle the researches of the honest observer of human nature. How many after having, as they thought, discovered the word friend in the mental volume, have afterwards found they should have read *false* friend! I have long seen "friend" in your mind, in your words, in your actions, but *now* distinctly visible, and clearly written in characters that cannot be distrusted, I discern *true* friend! I am really grateful for your mindfulness of so obscure a person as myself, and I hope the pleasure is not altogether selfish; I trust it is partly derived from the consciousness that my friend's character is of a higher, a more steadfast order than I was once perfectly aware of. Few girls would have done as you have done—would have beheld the glare and glitter and dazzling display of London, with the dispositions so unchanged, hearts so uncontaminated. I see no affectation in your letter, no trifling, no frivolous contempt of plain, and weak admiration of showy persons and things.

CHARLOTTE BRONTË

Haworth,
July 4th, 1834

Dear Ellen,

In your last you tell me to tell you of your faults and cease flattering you. Now, really, Ellen, how can you be so foolish! I won't tell of your faults, because I don't know them. What creature would that be, who, after receiving an affectionate and kind letter from a beloved friend, would sit down and write a catalogue of defects by way of answer! Imagine me doing so, and then consider what epithets you would bestow on me—conceited, dogmatical, hypocritical, little humbug, I should think would be the mildest. Why, child! I've neither time nor inclination to reflect on your faults when you are so far from me, and when, besides kind letters and presents, and so forth, you are continually bringing forth your goodness in the most prominent light. Then, too, there are friends always around you who can much better discharge that unpleasant office. I have no doubt their advice is completely at your service; why then should I intrude mine? Let us have no more nonsense about flattery, Ellen, if you love me.

"... the greatest American friend we have ever known ..."

WINSTON CHURCHILL PAYS TRIBUTE TO A "DEAR AND CHERISHED FRIENDSHIP"

President Roosevelt died suddenly on Thursday, April 12, 1945, at Warm Springs, Georgia. He was sixty-three. In the afternoon, while he was having his portrait painted, he suddenly collapsed, and died the same evening without regaining consciousness....

It may be said that Roosevelt died at the supreme climax of the war, and at the moment when his authority was most needed to guide the policy of the United States. When I received these tidings early in the morning of Friday, the 13th, I felt as if I had been struck a physical blow. My relations with this shining personality had played so large a part in the long, terrible years we had worked together. Now they had come to an end, and I was overpowered by a sense of deep and irreparable loss. I went down to the House of Commons, which met at eleven o'clock, and in a few sentences proposed that we should pay our respects to the memory of our great friend by immediately adjourning. This unprecedented step on the occasion of the death of the head of a foreign State was in accordance with the unanimous wish of the Members, who filed slowly out of the chamber after a sitting which had lasted only eight minutes....

In my message to Mrs. Roosevelt I said:

Prime Minister to Mrs. Roosevelt   13 Apr. 45

Accept my most profound sympathy in your grievous loss, which is also the loss of the British nation and of the cause of freedom in every land. I feel so deeply for you all. As for myself, I have lost a dear and cherished friendship which was forged in the fire of war. I trust you may find consolation in the magnitude of his work and the glory of his name.

And to Harry Hopkins, who had been my precious link on so many occasions:

Prime Minister to Harry Hopkins   13 Apr. 45

I understand how deep your feelings of grief must be. I feel with you that we have lost one of our greatest friends and one of the most valiant champions of the causes for which we fight. I feel a very painful personal loss, quite apart from the ties of public action which bound us so closely together. I had a true affection for Franklin.

When Parliament met on Tuesday, April 17, I moved an address to the King conveying to His Majesty the deep sorrow of the House and their profound sympathy with Mrs. Roosevelt and with the Government and people of the United States. It is customary for the leaders of all parties to speak in support of such a motion, but there developed a spontaneous feeling that it should be left to me alone to speak for the Commons. I cannot today find words which I prefer to those uttered in the emotion of this melancholy event.

"My friendship," I said, "with the great man to whose work and fame we pay our tribute today began and ripened during this war. I had met him, but only for a few minutes, after the close of the last war, and as soon as I went to the Admiralty in September 1939 he telegraphed inviting me to correspond with him direct on naval or other matters if at any time I felt inclined. Having obtained the permission of the Prime Minister, I did so. Knowing President Roosevelt's keen interest in sea warfare, I furnished him with a stream of information about our naval affairs, and about the various actions, including especially the action of the Plate River, which lighted the first gloomy winter of the war.

When I became Prime Minister, and the war broke out in all its hideous fury, when our own life and survival hung in the balance, I was already in a position to telegraph to the President on terms of an association which had become most intimate, and to me most agreeable. This continued through all the up and down of the world struggle until Thursday last, when I received my last messages from him. These messages showed no falling-off in his accustomed clear vision and vigor upon perplexing and complicated matters. I may mention that this correspondence, which of course was greatly increased after the United States' entry into the war, comprises, to and fro between us, over seventeen hundred messages. Many of these were lengthy messages, and the majority dealt with those more difficult points which come to be discussed upon the level of heads of Governments only after official solutions have not been reached at other stages. To this correspondence there must be added our nine meetings—at Argentia, three in Washington, at Casablanca, at Teheran, two at Quebec, and, last of all, at Yalta—comprising in all about one hundred and twenty days of close personal contact, during a great part of which I stayed with him at the White House or at his home at Hyde Park or in his retreat in the Blue Mountains, which he called Shangri-La.

I conceived an admiration for him as a statesman, a man of affairs, and a war leader, I felt the utmost confidence in his upright, inspiring character and outlook, and a personal regard—affection, I must say—for him beyond my power to express today. His love of his own country, his respect for its constitution, his power of gauging the tides and currents of its mobile public opinion, were always evident, but added to these were the beatings of that generous heart which was always stirred to anger and to action by spectacles of aggression and oppression by the strong against the weak. It is indeed a loss, a bitter loss to humanity, that those heartbeats are stilled for ever....

At Yalta I noticed that the President was ailing. His captivating smile, his gay and charming manner, had not deserted him, but his face had a transparency, an air of purification, and often there was a far-away look in his eyes. When I took my leave of him in Alexandria harbor I must confess that I had an indefinable sense of fear that his health and his strength were on the ebb. But nothing altered his inflexible sense of duty....

He has left behind him a band of resolute and able men handling the numerous inter-related parts of the vast American war machine. He has left a successor who comes forward with firm step and sure conviction to carry on the task to its appointed end. For us it remains only to say that in Franklin Roosevelt there died the greatest American friend we have ever known, and the greatest champion of freedom who has ever brought help and comfort from the New World to the Old.

FROM "CONTENT AND RICH"

Robert Southwell

I wrestle not with rage
  While Fury's flame doth burn;
It is in vain to stop the stream
  Until the tide do turn.

But when the flame is out,
  And ebbing wrath doth end,
I turn a late enraged foe
  Into a quiet friend.

"... You may make whatever use of me you please ..."

ELIZABETH BARRETT BROWNING TO MARY RUSSELL MITFORD

Torquay, Friday, November 13, 1838

You Dearest Miss Mitford, Whenever I forget to notice any kindness of yours, do believe, my beloved friend, that I have, notwithstanding, marked the date of it with a white stone, and also with a heart *not* of stone....

Dearest, dearest, Miss Mitford, never, *never* do tear up any old letters of yours for the sake of sending me a new one. Send old and new together. Postage upon *your* letters never can be thought of, and besides, my correspondents are not like yours, millions in the way of numbers. They in Wimpole Street know my doxy upon such subjects too well to keep your letters back with the seeds. They did not *dare* to wait even a day for papa's coming, but sent it out at once to me, doubtless it was, and *in* a letter of Arabel's own, making a triple; and those "discerning spirits" at the post office marked it (for all the thick paper) a *single letter*—immortal essence not weighing anything....

Is not your "Aaron's Daughter" much admired? It *ought* to be. There is a half playfulness and half sentiment which touch my fancy just where it lies nearest to my heart, besides the practical *good sense* (perhaps my sin may be something less for that) which Mr. Kenyon says "is always to be found in Miss Mitford's writings, in the very midst of their gracefulness." Yes, I have seen some kind opinions of my "Romaunt" in the *Chronicle* and elsewhere. *You* set the fashion by overpraising it; and indeed the stiff-necked critics must have caught fresh cold not to be able to bow their necks to receive a tonic from your hands....

Monday, December 3, 1838

You Dearest Miss Mitford, Today was the day fixed for writing to you, even if I had not heard from you yesterday. I thought I would wait one day more, and then write, and in the meantime went on building my Bastille in the air about your unusual silence. And do you know, dearest Miss Mitford, the truth came to me among my fancies. I fancied some illness, and of one dearest to you, kept you silent. It was such a relief to read the first page of your letter, and such a sad confirmation to turn to the second. Well, the evil has passed now. May the shadow of it be kept from your path for very long. While it is, other shadows will fall lightly, and may be trodden upon by a light, and, some of them, by a very scorning foot.

My scorn, really indignation is too good a word for such a subject, unites itself to yours as closely as all my sympathies do to *you* in regard to every detail of your most interesting letter. I am most astonished. Can "high toned" instruments be strung with such cracked wires? That *you* should pay, and he "seem to pay." Yes! and seem to be a poet besides! Upon which there comes into my head a saying of Plato. I had thought before that it ought to come nowhere, albeit Plato's, *"Poets speak nobly, but understand not what they speak."* I feel sorry. It is disappointing to be thrust aside from our estimation of any person. I have been accustomed to associate certain nobleness with certain intellectualities. And although I never dared quite use the words of your prophecy, "He will be a great poet," on account of the present want of what you call civil-ness, and I the power of conception, both of us referring to the same deficiency, the one to the effect, and the other to the cause. Yet I did see in him a poet, and expect from him more than *this....*

But I am thinking, as I ought and must, most of you, my beloved friend, than of any of those people. I cling to the hope that although Mr. Tilt may be irritated into incivilities towards you, and abominable as it is that he should, he is too wise a man to sacrifice his interests to his ill-humors, and lose your editorship of his annual just for the sake of annoying you. But, however it may be, as you think it worth while to put the question (and, while you put it, I do trust you were quite certain what the answer will be) *you may make whatever use of me you please, as long as I am alive, and able to write at all.* I hope, if he, Mr. Tilt, ventured to dismiss *you,* he would pay me the compliment of forgetting my existence altogether, but, whichever way it is, "foul me fall" as a minstrel, if I serve liege ladye in "Finden's Tableaux" except your own self, therefore do not wrong my fealty....

Torquay, January 5, 1839

You Dearest Miss Mitford, I do thank you, my beloved friend, for your kindness in making me a partaker of your gladness. I wish all happiness to both of you—to you and dear Dr. Mitford [father of Mary R. Mitford]—gratefully responding to your wishes to me on the occasion of this putting on of Day Time's new doublet. They have come true already, for *papa has come.* May mine for you come true as truly— May God keep you both from January to January, and grant that you may have and feel no less occasion to look gladly on each other than we all have to look thankfully up to Him! ...

My beloved friend, how very glad must be your gladness to watch, as I trust you are doing, the return of health to your dear invalid—the dearer for the thought of what "might have been"—day after day, and to feel in the respect and attachment demonstrated so affectingly around you that there is a sympathy for your gladness as well as your fearing grief. But still I am anxious for you; I am anxious lest your past and present fatigues should prove too great for you, and that, when the exultation of joy has subsided, this proving may begin. Do be careful, do not, at any time you have thirty-six letters to write, write a thirty-seventh to *me*. I am very thankful for the frequent accounts you have sent me, yet if they helped to tire you—oh, don't let me tire you ever, dearest Miss Mitford, pray do not.

And this suggests a termination to my letter.

MARY RUSSELL MITFORD TO ELIZABETH BARRETT BROWNING

Three Mile Cross, May 5, 1842

Mr. Kenyon's letter, my beloved love, arrived just soon enough to be answered—that is to say, to have a very long postscript appended to a very brief letter. Some friends of his have come to Silchester, and I shall go to see them to-morrow or next day. Oh, that you could be of the party! Well, in spite of the manner in which the winds have affected *that dear heart,* I will hope that the hour may come when we shall see that lovely scene together. The poem on Silchester just made Mr. Kenyon and me friends and that friendship was the remote cause of one to me still more precious—there is one reason for loving Silchester. But the scene itself is so beautiful! ... Oh, how I should love to stand with you upon Silchester Common! Its floral beauty I have endeavored to describe to you in my scrawl of last night—but the purity of the air, the fragrance of the budding woods, the enormous fir-plantations, the wide expanse of richly-scented, blossomed gorse, the acres of wild hyacinth and of lilies of the valley, defy all description. It must be felt. Oh, that we were there together! I so love Silchester—always loved it. Always a drive to Silchester, or ramble through the woods, was to me joy and delight, health, freedom and happiness; and since I have learnt to think of it as a link in the chain of our friendship, I have loved it more and more. Surely a wish so ardent will one day realize itself. We shall stand together in that lily coppice, where terrace hangs over terrace crossed with its thousand trees, carpeted with its myriad flowers, vocal with the blackbird and the nightingale. Surely, surely, we shall some day go together to Silchester. You will think, my dearest, that I rave....

You are far too good, my most dearest, in what you say of my poor letters. They come from my heart, and therefore go to yours—but that is all their merit—merit to us only—to the lover and the loved. Was there enough of the honey to taste? It seemed so light that it might be all empty. From two other "tastes" of the same "honoring gift" (and who should have it, if not you?) it seems to me strongly myrtle-flavored—tasting exactly like the scent of a bruised myrtle-leaf. The most delicious honey that I ever met with came from the orange groves of Sicily, and had the exact flavor of that delicious perfume....

Heaven bless you! I am tired to death, and I presume that my sleepy letters bear sufficient marks of my condition—thrice happy if it may come in aid of opium, and bring sleep to your eyelids.

Once again, heaven bless you, my most dearest! My father sends his kindest love.

Your faithful,
M. R. MITFORD

ACCEPT MY FULL HEART'S THANKS
Ella Wheeler Wilcox

Your words came just when needed.
  Like a breeze
Blowing and bringing from the wide soft sea
Some cooling spray, to meadow scorched with heat
  And choked with dust and clouds of sifted sand
That hateful whirlwinds, envious of its bloom,
  Had tossed upon it. But the cool sea breeze
Came laden with the odors of the sea
  And damp with spray, that laid the dust and sand,
And brought new life and strength to blade and bloom,
  So words of thine came over miles to me,
  Fresh from the mighty sea, a true friend's heart,
And brought me hope, strength, and swept away
  The dusty webs that human spiders spun
Across my path. Friend—and the word means much—
  So few there are who reach like thee, a hand
Up over all the barking curs of spite
  And give the clasp, when most its need is felt,
Friend, newly found, accept my full heart's thanks.

"... you are to me like a Limb lost and buried in another country."

ALEXANDER POPE TO JONATHAN SWIFT

19 December, 1734

I am truly sorry for any Complaint you have, and it is in regard to the Weakness of your Eyes that I write (as well as print) in Folio. You will think (I know you will, for you have all the Candour of a good Understanding) that the thing which Men of our Age feel the most, is the Friendship of our Equals; and that therefore whatever affects those who are stepped a few Years before us, cannot but sensibly affect us who are to follow. It troubles me to hear you complain of your Memory, and if I am in any part of my Constitution younger than you, it will be in my remembering every thing that has pleased me in you, longer than perhaps you will. The two Summers we passed together dwells always on my Mind, like a Vision which gave me a Glimpse of a better Life and better Company than this World otherwise afforded. I am now an Individual upon whom no other depends, and may go where I will, if the wretched Carcase I am annexed to did not hinder me. I rambled by very easy Journies this Year to Lord *Bathurst* and Lord *Peterborrow,* who, upon every Occasion, commemorate, love, and wish for you. I now pass my Days between *Dawley, London,* and this Place, not studious nor idle, rather polishing old Works than hewing out new. I redeem now and then a Paper that has been abandoned several years; and of this sort you will see one, which I inscribe to our old Friend *Arbuthnot.*

Thus far I had written, and thinking to finish my Letter the same Evening, was prevented by Company, and the next Morning found myself in a Fever, highly disordered, and so continued in Bed for five Days, and in my Chamber till now; but so well recovered as to hope to go abroad To-morrow, even by the advice of Dr. *Arbuthnot.* He himself, poor Man, is much broke, though not worse than for these last two Months he has been. He took extremely kind your Letter. I wish to God we could once more meet again before that Separation, which yet I would be glad to believe, shall re-unite us: But he who made us, not for ours but for his Purposes, knows only whether it be for the better or the worse, that the Affections of this Life should or should not continue into the other; and doubtless it is as it should be. Yet I am sure that while I am here, and the thing that I am, I shall be imperfect without the Communication of such Friends as you; you are to me

like a Limb lost and buried in another Country. Though we seem quite
divided, every accident makes me feel you were once a Part of me.

ALEXANDER POPE

A FRIEND

Nicholas Grimald

Of all the heavenly gifts that mortal men commend,
What trusty treasure in the world can countervail a friend?
Our health is soon decayed; goods, casual, light and vain;
Broke have we seen the force of power, and honor suffer stain.
In body's lust man doth resemble but base brute;
True virtue gets and keeps a friend, good guide of our pursuit.
Whose hearty zeal with ours accords in every case;
No terms of time, no space of place, no storm can it deface.

Sentiments are what unites people, opinions what separates them.
Sentiments are a simple bond that gathers us together; opinions represent the principle of variety that scatters. The friendships of youth are
founded on the former, the cliques of old age are to be blamed on the
latter. If we could only realize this early and arrive at a liberal view
as regards others in cultivating our own attitude of mind, we would
be more conciliatory and try to collect by the bond of sentiment what
opinion has dispersed.

—JOHANN WOLFGANG VON GOETHE
(*Translated by Herman J. Weigand*)

The circumstances of the closing scene of poor Keats' life were not
made known to me until the *Elegy* was ready for the press.... He was
accompanied to Rome, and attended in his last illness by Mr. Severn, a
young artist of the highest promise, who, I have been informed, "almost risked his own life, and sacrificed every prospect to unwearied at-
tendance upon his dying friend." Had I known these circumstances
before the completion of my poem, I should have been tempted to add
my feeble tribute of applause to the more solid recompenses which the
virtuous man finds in the recollection of his own motives. Mr. Severn
can dispense with a reward from "such stuff as dreams are made of."

His conduct is a golden augury of the success of his future career—
may the unextinguished Spirit of his illustrious friend animate the
creations of his pencil, and plead against Oblivion for his name!

—Percy Bysshe Shelley

FRIENDS, OLD FRIENDS

William Ernest Henley

Friends...old friends...
One sees how it ends.
A woman looks
Or a man tells lies
And the pleasant brooks
And the quiet skies,
Ruined with brawling
And caterwauling,—
Enchant no more
As they did before,
And so it ends
With friends.

Friends...old friends—
And what if it ends?
Shall we dare to shirk
What we live to learn?
It has done its work,
It has served its turn;
And forgive and forget
Or hanker and fret,
We can be no more
As we were before.
When it ends, it ends
With friends.

Friends...old friends—
So it breaks, so it ends.
There let it rest!
It has fought and won,
And is still the best
That either has done.

Each as he stands
The work of its hands.
Which shall be more
As he was before? ...
What is its ends
With friends?

"... that would be the perfect friend."

TWO KINDS OF FRIENDSHIP

W. Somerset Maugham

There are two kinds of friendship. The first is a friendship of animal attraction; you like your friend not for any particular qualities or gifts, but simply because you are drawn to him. *"C'est mon ami parce que je l'aime; je l'aime parce que c'est mon ami."* It is unreasoning and unreasonable; and by the irony of things it is probable that you will have this feeling for someone quite unworthy of it. This kind of friendship, though sex has no active part in it, is really akin to love; it arises in the same way, and it is not improbable that it declines in the same way.

The second kind of friendship is intellectual. You are attracted by the gifts of your new acquaintance. His ideas are unfamiliar; he has seen sides of life of which you are ignorant; his experience is impressive. But every well has a bottom and finally your friend will come to the end of what he has to tell you: this is the moment decisive for the continuation of your friendship. If he has nothing more in him than his experience and his reading have taught him, he can no longer interest or amuse you. The well is empty, and when you let the bucket down, nothing comes up. This explains why one so quickly makes warm friendships with new acquaintances and as quickly breaks them; also the dislike one feels for these persons afterwards, for the disappointment one experiences on discovering that one's admiration was misplaced turns into contempt and aversion. Sometimes, for one reason or another, however, you continue to frequent these people. The way to profit by their society then is to make them yield you the advantages of new friends; by seeing them only at sufficiently long intervals to allow them to acquire fresh experiences and new thoughts. Gradually the disappointment you experienced at the discovery of their shallowness will wear off, habit brings with it an indulgence for their defects and you may keep up a pleasant friendship with them for many years. But if, having got to the end of your friend's acquired knowledge, you find that he has something more, character, sensibility and a restless mind, then your friendship will grow stronger, and you will have a relationship as delightful in its way as the other friendship of physical attraction.

It is conceivable that these two friendships should find their object in one and the same person; that would be the perfect friend. But to ask for that is to ask for the moon. On the other hand, when, as sometimes happens, there is an animal attraction on one side and an intellectual one on the other, only discord can ensue.

"I remember feeling I had never known anybody so well . . ."

A LITTLE GIRL MEETS HER LITERARY IDOL

Kate Douglas Wiggin

We never read newspapers save the weekly *Portland Transcript,* so that there was a moment of thrilling excitement when my mother, looking up from the *Portland Press,* told us that Mr. Dickens was coming to America, and that he was even then sailing from England. I remember distinctly that I prayed for him fervently several times during the next week, that the voyage might be a safe one, and that even the pangs of seasickness might be spared so precious a personage. In due time we heard that he had arrived in New York, and had begun the series of readings from his books; then he came to Boston, which was still nearer, and then—day of unspeakable excitement!—we learned that he had been prevailed upon to give one reading in Portland, which was only sixteen miles away from our village.

It chanced that my mother was taking me to Charlestown, Massachusetts, to pay a visit to an uncle on the very day after the one appointed for the great event in Portland. She, therefore, planned to take me into town the night before, and to invite the cousin, at whose house we were to sleep, to attend the reading with her. . . .

My mother and I embarked for Portland on the daily train that dashed hither and thither at the rate of about twelve miles an hour.

When the august night and moment arrived, my mother and her cousin set out for the Place, and the moment they were out of sight I slipped out of the door and followed them, traversing quickly the three or four blocks that separated me from the old City Hall and the Preble House, where Dickens was stopping. I gazed at all the windows and all the entrances of both buildings without beholding any trace of my hero. I watched the throng of happy, excited, lucky people crowding the streets on their way to the hall, and went home in a chastening mood to bed....

The next morning we started on our railroad journey, which I remember as being full of excitement from the beginning, for both men and women were discussing the newspapers with extraordinary interest, the day before having been the one on which the President of the United States had been formally impeached. When the train stopped for two or three minutes at North Berwick, the people on the side of the car next the station suddenly arose and looked eagerly out at some object of apparent interest. I was not, at any age, a person to sit still in her seat when others were looking out of windows, and my small nose was quickly flattened against one of the panes. There on the platform stood the Adored One! It was unbelievable, but there he was in the flesh; standing smiling, breathing, like ordinary human beings. There was no doubt, then, that "angels and ministers of grace," called authors, had bodies and could not only write *David Copperfields,* but could be seen with the naked eye. That face, known to me from many pictures, must have looked in some mysterious way into the face of Dora, of Agnes, of Paul Dombey, of Little Dorrit! My spirit gave a leap and entered a new, an unknown world.

Dickens's hands were plunged deep in his pockets (a favorite gesture), but presently one was removed to wave away laughingly a piece of famous Berwick sponge cake, offered him by Mr. Osgood, of Boston, his traveling companion and friend. I knew him at once!— the smiling, genial, mobile face, rather highly colored, the brilliant eyes, the watch-chain, the red carnation in the buttonhole, and the expressive hands, much given to gesture. It was only a momentary view, for the train started, and Dickens vanished, to resume his place in the car next to ours, where he had been, had I known it, ever since we left Portland.

When my mother was again occupied with her book, I slipped away, and, borne along by some resistless and hitherto unrecognized force, I entered the next car; ... I took a humble, unoccupied seat near the end, close by the much patronized tank of (unsterilized) drinking-water and the train-boy's basket of popcorn balls and molasses candy, and gazed steadily at the famous man, who was chatting busily with Mr. Osgood.... Some family friends espied me, and sent me back to ask my mother to come in and sit with them. I brought her back, and, fortunately, there was not room enough for me with the party, so I gladly resumed my modest seat by the pop-corn boy, where I could watch Dickens, quite unnoticed....

Half an hour passed, perhaps, and one gentleman after another came from here or there to exchange a word of greeting with the famous novelist, so that he was never for a moment alone, thereby inciting in my breast my first, and about my last, experience of the passion of jealousy. Suddenly, however, Mr. Osgood arose, and with an apology went into the smoking-car. I never knew how it happened; I had no plan, no preparation, no intention, certainly no provocation; but invisible ropes pulled me out of my seat, and speeding up the aisle, I planted myself breathlessly and timorously down, an unbidden guest, in the seat of honor. I had a moment to recover my equanimity, for Dickens was looking out the window, but he turned suddenly and said with justifiable surprise:

"God bless my soul, child, where did you come from?"

My heart was in my mouth, but there was still room to exercise my tongue, which was generally the case. I was frightened, but not so completely frightened as if I had been meeting a stranger. You see I knew him, even if he did not know me; so I became immediately autobiographical, although palpitating with nervousness. I had to tell him, I thought, where I came from, who I was, where I was going, or how could I account for myself and my presence beside him in Mr. Osgood's seat? So I began, stammeringly, to answer his question.

"I came from Hollis, Maine, and I'm going to Charlestown to visit my uncle. My mother and her cousin went to your reading last night, but of course three couldn't go from the same family, it was so expensive, so I stayed at home. Nora, that's my little sister, is left behind in Hollis. She's too small to go on a journey, but she wanted to go to the reading dreadfully. There was a lady there who had never heard of Betsey Trotwood, and had only read two of your books!"

"Well, upon my word!" he said; "you do not mean to say that *you* have read them!"

"Of course!" I replied; "every one of them but the two that we are going to buy in Boston, and some of them six times."

"Bless my soul!" he ejaculated again. "Those long thick books, and you such a slip of a thing."

"Of course," I explained conscientiously, "I do skip some of the very dull parts once in a while; not the short dull parts, but the long ones."

He laughed heartily. "Now, that is something that I hear very little about," he said, "I distinctly want to learn more about those very long dull parts."

And, whether to amuse himself, or to amuse me, I do not know, he took out a notebook and pencil from his pocket and proceeded to give me an exhausting and exhaustive examination on this subject; the books in which the dull parts predominated; and the characters and subjects which principally produced them. He chuckled so constantly during this operation that I could hardly help believing myself extraordinarily agreeable, so I continued dealing these infant blows, under the delusion that I was flinging him bouquets.

It was not long before one of my hands was in his, and his arm around my waist, while we talked of many things. They say, I believe, that his hands were "undistinguished" in shape, and that he wore too many rings. Well, those criticisms must come from persons who never felt the warmth of his handclasp! For my part, I am glad that Pullman chair cars had not come into fashion, else I should never have experienced the delicious joy of snuggling up to Genius, and of being distinctly encouraged in the attitude.

I wish I could recall still more of his conversation, but I was too happy, too exhilarated, and too inexperienced to take conscious notes of the interview. I remember feeling that I had never known anybody so well and so intimately, and that I talked with him as one talks under cover of darkness or before the flickering light of a fire. It seems to me, as I look back now, and remember how the little soul of me came out and sat in the sunshine of his presence, that I must have had some premonition that the child, who would come to be one of the least of writers, was then talking with one of the greatest;—talking, too, as it were, of the author's profession and high calling, for were we not discussing books? All the little details of the meeting stand out as clearly as though it had happened yesterday. I can see every article of his clothing and of my own; the other passengers in the car; the landscape through the window; and above all the face of Dickens, deeply lined, with sparkling eyes and an amused, waggish smile that curled the corners of his mouth under his grizzled mustache....

"What book of mine do you like best?" Dickens asked, I remember; and I answered with the definite assurance of childhood, "Oh, I like *David Copperfield* much the best. That is the one I have read six times."

"Six times—good, good!" he replied; "I am glad that you like Davy, so do I;—I like it best, too!" clapping his hands; and that was the only remark he made which attracted the attention of the other passengers, who glanced in our direction now and then, I have been told, smiling at the interview, but preserving its privacy with the utmost friendliness. I had never looked behind to see how my mother was faring. There are great crises in life when even mothers must retire to the background. For the moment I had no mother, family, friends, or acquaintances, no home, no personality; I was a sort of atom floating in space, half conscious that I could not float forever, but must come to earth again.

"I almost said *Great Expectations*," I added presently, "because that comes next in our family. We named our little yellow dog 'Mr. Pip' out of your book. They told Father when they gave him to us that he was part rat terrier, and we were all pleased, because, if he was, he wasn't all mongrel. (That means mixed-up.) Then one day Father showed him a trap with a mouse in it. The mouse wiggled its tail just a little, and Pip was so frightened that he ran under the barn and stayed the rest of the day. That showed that there wasn't enough rat terrier in him to be right, and the neighbors made fun of him and used to call 'Rats!' when he went down the street. We loved him just the same and he had as hard a time as Pip in *Great Expectations*."

Here again my new friend's mirth was delightful to behold, so much so that my embarrassed mother, who had been watching me for half an hour, almost made up her mind to drag me away before the very eyes of our fellow passengers. I had never been thought an amusing child in the family circle; what, then, could I be saying to the most distinguished and popular author in the universe?

Dickens here told me little stories about English dogs, but I remember them too vaguely to repeat them or give them their inimitable mingling of fact and nonsense. "Have you only one dog?" he asked.

"We had another," I answered, "a big curly one called John Brent, out of a novel, but he died, and we take all our names from your books now. We know a dog who stays with us most of the time. He doesn't belong to anybody and he likes to visit Pip, so we named him Mr. Pocket after Mr. Pip's friend. The real Mr. Pip and Mr. Pocket met first in Miss Havisham's garden and they had such a funny fight it always makes Father laugh till he can't read properly! Then they became great friends. Perhaps you remember Mr. Pip and Mr. Pocket?" And Dickens thought he did, which, perhaps, is not strange, considering that he was the author of their respective beings....

"Did you want to go to my reading very much, child?" was another question. Here was a subject that had never once been touched upon in all the past days—a topic that stirred the very depths of my disappointment and sorrow, fairly choking me, and making my lip tremble by its unexpectedness, as I faltered, "Yes, I did, more than tongue can tell! I know how I feel when I read one of the books, but I wanted to hear how it sounded."

I looked up a second later, when I was sure that the tears in my eyes were not going to fall, and to my astonishment saw that Dickens's eyes were in precisely the same state of moisture. That was a never-to-be-forgotten moment, although I was too young to appreciate the full significance of it.

"Do you cry when you read out loud, too?" I asked curiously. "We all do in our family. And we never read about Tiny Tim, or about Steerforth when his body is washed up on the beach, on Saturday nights, for fear our eyes will be too swollen to go to Sunday School."

"Yes, I cry when I read about Steerforth," he answered quietly, and I felt no astonishment. "I cried when I wrote it, too! That is still more foolish!"

"Where do you cry the worst?" I asked. "Our time is when it says, '*All the men who carried him had known him and gone sailing with him and seen him merry and bold*'"; and here I grew tearful and reminiscent.

We were now fast approaching our destination—the station in Boston —and the passengers began to collect their wraps and bundles. Mr. Osgood had two or three times made his appearance, but had been waved away with a smile by Dickens—a smile that seemed to say, "You will excuse me, I know, but this child has the right of way."

"You are not traveling alone?" he asked, as he arose to put on his overcoat.

"Oh! my goodness!" I said, coming down to earth for the first time since I had taken my seat beside him—"certainly not; I had a mother, but I forgot all about her." Whereupon he said, "You are past-mistress of the art of flattery!"

But this remark was told me years afterwards by the old lady who was sitting in the next seat, and who overheard as much of the conversation as she possibly could, so she informed me. Her penciled notes, read to me when we met by chance in South Reading, Massachusetts, have helped me greatly in the minor details of the interview and my own phraseology, which amused her because of its chatterbox fluency and the amazing response it elicited from so great a man.

Dickens took me back to the forgotten mother, and introduced himself, and I, still clinging to his hand, left the car and walked with him down the platform until he disappeared in the carriage with Mr. Osgood, leaving me with the feeling that I must continue my existence somehow in a dull and dreary world.

That was my last glimpse of him, but pictures made in childhood are painted in bright hues, and this one has never faded. The child of today would hardly be able to establish so instantaneous a friendship. She would have heard of celebrity hunters and autograph collectors and be self-conscious, while I followed the dictates of my countrified little heart, and scraped acquaintance confidently with the magician who had glorified my childhood by his art.

∿∿∿∿∿

FROM "THREE FRIENDS OF MINE"
Henry Wadsworth Longfellow

When I remember them, those friends of mine,
Who are no longer here, the noble three,
Who half my life were more than friends to me,
And whose discourse was like a generous wine,
I most of all remember the divine
Something, that shone in them, and made us see
The archetypal man, and what might be
The amplitude of Nature's first design.
In vain I stretch my hands to clasp their hands;
I cannot find them. Nothing now is left
But a majestic memory. They meanwhile
Wander together in Elysian lands,
Perchance remembering me, who am bereft
Of their dear presence, and remembering, smile.

" '. . . that pays him some on account
for what he tried to do for me . . .' "

FRIENDS IN SAN ROSARIO
O. Henry

The west-bound stopped at San Rosario on time at 8:20 A.M. A man with a thick black-leather wallet under his arm left the train and walked rapidly up the main street of the town. There were other passengers who also got off at San Rosario, but they either slouched limberly over to the railroad eating-house or the Silver Dollar saloon, or joined the groups of idlers about the station.

Indecision had no part in the movements of the man with the wallet. He was short in stature, but strongly built, with very light, closely trimmed hair, smooth, determined face, and aggressive, gold-rimmed nose glasses. He was well dressed in the prevailing Eastern style. His air denoted a quiet but conscious reserve force, if not actual authority.

After walking a distance of three squares he came to the center of the town's business area. Here another street of importance crossed the main one, forming the hub of San Rosario's life and commerce. Upon one corner stood the postoffice. Upon another Rubensky's Clothing Emporium. The other two diagonally opposing corners were occupied by the town's two banks, the First National and the Stockmen's National. Into the First National Bank of San Rosario the newcomer walked, never slowing his brisk step until he stood at the cashier's window. The bank opened for business at nine, and the working force was already assembled, each member preparing his department for the day's business. The cashier was examining the mail when he noticed the stranger standing at his window.

"Bank doesn't open 'til nine," he remarked, curtly, but without feeling. He had had to make that statement so often to early birds since San Rosario adopted city banking hours.

"I am well aware of that," said the other man, in cool, brittle tones. "Will you kindly receive my card?"

The cashier drew the small, spotless parallelogram inside the bars of his wicket, and read:

J. F. C. NETTLEWICK
National Bank Examiner

"Oh—er—will you walk around inside, Mr.—er—Nettlewick. Your first visit—didn't know your business, of course. Walk right around, please."

The examiner was quickly inside the sacred precincts of the bank, where he was ponderously introduced to each employee in turn by Mr. Edlinger, the cashier—a middle-aged gentleman of deliberation, discretion, and method.

"I was kind of expecting Sam Turner round again, pretty soon," said Mr. Edlinger. "Sam's been examining us now for about four years. I guess you'll find us all right, though, considering the tightness in business. Not overly much money on hand, but able to stand the storms, sir, stand the storms."

"Mr. Turner and I have been ordered by the Comptroller to exchange districts," said the examiner, in his decisive, formal tones. "He is covering my old territory in southern Illinois and Indiana. I will take the cash first, please."

Perry Dorsey, the teller, was already arranging the cash on the counter for the examiner's inspection. He knew it was right to a cent, and he had nothing to fear, but he was nervous and flustered. So was every man in the bank. There was something so icy and swift, so impersonal and uncompromising about this man that his very presence seemed an accusation. He looked to be a man who would never make nor overlook an error.

Mr. Nettlewick first seized the currency, and with a rapid, almost juggling motion, counted it by packages. Then he spun the sponge cup toward him and verified the count by bills. His thin, white fingers flew like some expert musician's upon the keys of a piano. He dumped the gold upon the counter with a crash, and the coins whined and sang as they skimmed across the marble slab from the tips of his nimble digits. The air was full of fractional currency when he came to the halves and quarters. He counted the last nickel and dime. He had the scales brought, and he weighed every sack of silver in the vault. He questioned Dorsey concerning each of the cash memoranda—certain checks, charge slips, etc., carried over from the previous day's work—with unimpeachable courtesy, yet with something so mysteriously momentous in his frigid manner, that the teller was reduced to pink cheeks and a stammering tongue.

This newly imported examiner was so different from Sam Turner. It had been Sam's way to enter the bank with a shout, pass the cigars, and tell the latest stories he had picked up on his rounds. His customary greeting to Dorsey had been, "Hello, Perry! Haven't skipped out with the boodle yet, I see." Turner's way of counting the cash had been different too. He would finger the packages of bills in a tired kind of way, and then go into the vault and kick over a few sacks of silver, and the thing was done. Halves and quarters and dimes? Not for Sam Turner. "No chicken feed for me," he would say when they were set before him. "I'm not in the agricultural department." But, then, Turner was a Texan, an old friend of the bank's president, and had known Dorsey since he was a baby.

While the examiner was counting the cash, Major Thomas B. Kingman—known to everyone as "Major Tom"—the president of the First National, drove up to the side door with his old dun horse and buggy, and came inside. He saw the examiner busy with the money, and, going into the little "pony corral," as he called it, in which his desk was railed off, he began to look over his letters.

Earlier, a little incident had occurred that even the sharp eyes of the examiner had failed to notice. When he had begun his work at the cash counter, Mr. Edlinger had winked significantly at Roy Wilson, the youthful bank messenger, and nodded his head slightly toward the front door. Roy understood, got his hat and walked leisurely out, with his collector's book under his arm. Once outside, he made a bee-line for the Stockmen's National. That bank was also getting ready to open. No customers had, as yet, presented themselves.

"Say, you people!" cried Roy, with the familiarity of youth and long acquaintance, "you want to get a move on you. There's a new bank examiner over at the First, and he's a stem-winder. He's counting nickels on Perry, and he's got the whole outfit bluffed. Mr. Edlinger gave me the tip to let you know."

Mr. Buckley, president of the Stockmen's National—a stout, elderly man, looking like a farmer dressed for Sunday—heard Roy from his private office at the rear and called him.

"Has Major Kingman come down to the bank yet?" he asked of the boy.

"Yes, sir, he was just driving up as I left," said Roy.

"I want you to take him a note. Put it into his own hands as soon as you get back."

Mr. Buckley sat down and began to write.

Roy returned and handed to Major Kingman the envelope containing the note. The major read it, folded it, and slipped it into his vest pocket. He leaned back in his chair for a few moments as if he were meditating deeply, and then rose and went into the vault. He came out with the bulky, old-fashioned leather note case stamped on the back in gilt letters, "Bills Discounted." In this were the notes due the bank with their attached securities, and the major, in his rough way, dumped the lot upon his desk and began to sort them over.

By this time Nettlewick had finished his count of the cash. His pencil fluttered like a swallow over the sheet of paper on which he had set his figures. He opened his black wallet, which seemed to be also a kind of secret memorandum book, made a few rapid figures in it, wheeled and transfixed Dorsey with the glare of his spectacles. That look seemed to say: "You're safe this time, but—"

"Cash all correct," snapped the examiner. He made a dash for the individual bookkeeper, and, for a few minutes there was a fluttering of ledger leaves and a sailing of balance sheets through the air.

"How often do you balance your pass-books?" he demanded, suddenly.

"Er—once a month," faltered the individual bookkeeper, wondering how many years they would give him.

"All right," said the examiner, turning and charging upon the general bookkeeper, who had the statements of his foreign banks and their reconcilement memoranda ready. Everything there was found to be all right. Then the stub book of the certificates of deposit. Flutter-flutter—zip—zip—check! All right. List of over-drafts, please. Thanks. H'm-m. Unsigned bills of the bank next. All right.

Then came the cashier's turn, and easy-going Mr. Edlinger rubbed his nose and polished his glasses nervously under the quick fire of questions concerning the circulation, undivided profits, bank real estate, and stock ownership.

Presently, Nettlewick was aware of a big man towering above him at his elbow—a man sixty years of age, rugged and hale, with a rough, grizzled beard, a mass of gray hair, and a pair of penetrating blue eyes that confronted the formidable glasses of the examiner without a flicker.

"Er—Major Kingman, our president—er—Mr. Nettlewick," said the cashier.

Two men of very different types shook hands. One was a finished product of the world of straight lines, conventional methods, and formal affairs. The other was something freer, wider, and nearer to nature. Tom Kingman had not been cut to any pattern. He had been mule-driver, cowboy, ranger, soldier, sheriff, prospector and cattleman. Now, when he was bank president, his old comrades from the prairies, of the saddle, tent, and trail, found no change in him. He had made his fortune when Texas cattle were at the high tide of value, and had organized the First National Bank of San Rosario. In spite of his large-ness of heart and sometimes unwise generosity toward his old friends, the bank had prospered, for Major Tom Kingman knew men as well as he knew cattle. Of late years the cattle business had known a de-pression, and the major's bank was one of the few whose losses had not been great.

"And now," said the examiner, briskly, pulling out his watch, "the last thing is the loans. We will take them up now, if you please."

He had gone through the First National at almost record-breaking speed—but thoroughly, as he did everything. The running order of the bank was smooth and clean, and that had facilitated his work. There was but one other bank in the town. He received from the Government a fee of twenty-five dollars for each bank that he examined. He should be able to go over those loans and discounts in half an hour. If so, he could examine the other bank immediately afterward, and catch the 11:45, the only other train that day in the direction he was working. Otherwise, he would have to spend the night and Sunday in this un-interesting Western town. That was why Mr. Nettlewick was rushing matters.

"Come with me, sir," said Major Kingman, in his deep voice, that united the Southern drawl with the rhythmic twang of the West. "We will go over them together. Nobody in the bank knows those notes as I do. Some of 'em are a little wobbly on their legs, and some are mavericks without extra many brands on their backs, but they'll most all pay out at the round-up."

The two sat down at the president's desk. First, the examiner went through the notes at lightning speed, and added up their total, finding it to agree with the amount of loans carried on the book of daily balances. Next, he took up the larger loans, inquiring scrupulously into the condition of their endorsers or securities. The new examiner's mind seemed to course and turn and make unexpected dashes hither and thither like a bloodhound seeking a new trail. Finally he pushed aside all the notes except a few, which he arranged in a neat pile before him, and began a dry, formal little speech.

"I find, sir, the condition of your bank to be very good, considering the poor crops and the depression in the cattle interests of your state. The clerical work seems to be done accurately and punctually. Your past-due paper is moderate in amount, and promises only a small loss. I would recommend the calling in of your large loans, and the making of only sixty and ninety day or call loans until general business revives. And now, there is one thing more, and I will have finished with the bank. Here are six notes aggregating something like $40,000.00. They are secured, according to their faces, by various stocks, bonds, shares, etc., to the value of $70,000.00. Those securities are missing from the notes to which they should be attached. I suppose you have them in the safer vault. You will permit me to examine them."

Major Tom's light-blue eyes turned unflinchingly toward the examiner.

"No, sir," he said, in a low but steady tone: "those securities are neither in the safe nor the vault. I have taken them. You may hold me personally responsible for their absence."

Nettlewick felt a slight thrill. He had not expected this. He had struck a momentous trail when the hunt was drawing to a close.

"Ah!" said the examiner. He waited a moment, and then continued: "May I ask you to explain more definitely?"

"The securities were taken by me," repeated the major. "It was not for my own use, but to save an old friend in trouble. Come in here, sir, and we'll talk it over."

He led the examiner into the bank's private office at the rear, and closed the door. There was a desk, and a table, and half-a-dozen leather covered chairs. On the wall was the mounted head of a Texas steer with horns five feet from tip to tip. Opposite hung the major's old cavalry saber that he had carried at Shiloh and Fort Pillow.

Placing a chair for Nettlewick, the major seated himself by the window, from which he could see the post-office and the carved limestone front of the Stockmen's National. He did not speak at once, and Nettlewick felt, perhaps, that the ice should be broken by something so near its own temperature as the voice of official warning.

"Your statement," he began, "since you have failed to modify it, amounts, as you must know, to a very serious thing. You are aware, also, of what my duty must compel me to do. I shall have to go before the United States Commissioner and make—"

"I know, I know," said Major Tom, with a wave of his hand. "You don't suppose I'd run a bank without being posted on national banking laws and the revised statutes! Do your duty. I'm not asking any favors.

But I spoke of my friend. I did want you to hear me tell you about Bob."

Nettlewick settled himself in his chair. There would be no leaving San Rosario for him that day. He would have to telegraph the Comptroller of the Currency; he would have to swear out a warrant before the United States Commissioner for the arrest of Major Kingman; perhaps he would be ordered to close the bank on account of the loss of the securities. It was not the first crime the examiner had unearthed. Once or twice the terrible upheaval of human emotions that his investigations had loosed had almost caused a ripple in his official calm. He had seen bank men kneel and plead and cry like women for a chance —an hour's time—the overlooking of a single error. One cashier had shot himself at his desk before him. None of them had taken it with the dignity and coolness of this stern old Westerner. Nettlewick felt he owed it to him at least to listen if he wished to talk. With his elbow on the arm of his chair, and his square chin resting upon the fingers of his right hand, the bank examiner waited to hear the confession of the president of the First National Bank of San Rosario.

"When a man's your friend," began Major Tom, somewhat didactically, "for forty years, and tried by water, fire, earth, and cyclones, when you can do him a little favor you feel like doing it."

("Embezzle for him $70,000.00 worth of securities," thought the examiner.)

"We were cowboys together, Bob and I," continued the major, speaking slowly, and deliberately, and musingly, as if his thoughts were rather with the past than the critical present, "and we prospected together for gold and silver over Arizona, New Mexico, and a good part of California. We were both in the war of 'sixty-one, but in different commands. We've fought Indians and horse thieves side by side; we've starved for weeks in a cabin in the Arizona mountains, buried twenty feet deep in snow; we've ridden herd together when the wind blew so hard the lightning couldn't strike—well, Bob and I have been through some rough spells since the first time we met in the branding camp of the old Anchor-Bar ranch. And during that time we've found it necessary more than once to help each other out of tight places. In those days it was expected of a man to stick to his friend, and he didn't ask any credit for it. Probably the next day you'd need him to get at your back and help stand off a band of Apaches, or put a tourniquet on your leg above a rattlesnake bite and ride for whisky. So, after all, it was give and take, and if you didn't stand square with your pardner, why, you might be shy one when you needed him. But Bob was a man who was willing to go further than that. He never played a limit.

"Twenty years ago I was sheriff of this county and I made Bob my chief deputy. That was before the boom in cattle when we both made our stake. I was sheriff and collector, and it was a big thing for me then. I was married, and we had a boy and a girl—a four and a six year old. There was a comfortable house next to the courthouse, furnished by the county, rent free, and I was saving some money. Bob did most of the office work. Both of us had seen rough times and plenty of rustling and danger, and I tell you it was great to hear the rain and the sleet dashing against the windows of nights, and be warm and safe and comfortable, and know you could get up in the morning and be shaved and have folks call you 'mister.' And then, I had the finest wife and kids that ever struck the range, and my old friend with me enjoying the first fruits of prosperity and white shirts, and I guess I was happy. Yes, I was happy about that time."

The major sighed and glanced casually out of the window. The bank examiner changed his position, and leaned his chin upon his other hand.

"One winter," continued the major, "the money for the county taxes came pouring in so fast that I didn't have time to take the stuff to the bank for a week. I just shoved the checks into a cigar box and the money into a sack, and locked them in the big safe that belonged in the sheriff's office.

"I had been overworked that week, and was about sick, anyway. My nerves were out of order, and my sleep at night didn't seem to rest me. The doctor had some scientific name for it, and I was taking medicine. And so, added to the rest, I went to bed at night with that money on my mind. Not that there was much need of being worried, for the safe was a good one, and nobody but Bob and I knew the combination. On Friday night there was about $6,500.00 cash in the bag. On Saturday morning I went to the office as usual. The safe was locked, and Bob was writing at his desk. I opened the safe, and the money was gone. I called Bob, and roused everybody in the courthouse to announce the robbery. It struck me that Bob took it pretty quiet, considering how much it reflected upon both him and me.

"Two days went by and we never got a clew. It couldn't have been burglars, for the safe had been opened by the combination in the proper way. People must have begun to talk, for one afternoon in comes Alice —that's my wife—and the boy and girl, and Alice stamps her foot and her eyes flash, and she cries out, 'The lying wretches—Tom, Tom!' and I catch her in a faint, and bring her 'round little by little, and she lays her head down and cries and cries for the first time since she took Tom Kingman's name and fortunes. And Jack and Zilla—the young-sters—they were always wild as tigers' cubs to rush at Bob and climb all over him whenever they were allowed to come to the courthouse— they stood and kicked their little shoes, and herded together like scared partridges. They were having their first trip down into the shadows of life. Bob was working at his desk, and he got up and went out without a word. The grand jury was in session then, and the next morning Bob went before them and confessed that he had stolen the money. He said he lost it in a poker game. In fifteen minutes they had found a true bill and sent me the warrant to arrest the man with whom I'd been closer than a thousand brothers for many a year.

"I did it, and then I said to Bob, pointing: 'There's my house, and here's my office, and up there's Maine, and out that way is California, and over there is Florida—and that's your range 'til court meets. You're in my charge, and I take the responsibility. You be here when you're wanted.'

"'Thanks, Tom,' he said, kind of carelessly; 'I was sort of hoping you wouldn't lock me up. Court meets next Monday, so, if you don't object, I'll just loaf around the office until then. I've got one favor to ask, if it isn't too much. If you'd let the kids come out in the yard once in a while and have a romp I'd like it.'

"'Why not?' I answered him. 'They're welcome, and so are you. And come to my house the same as ever.' You see, Mr. Nettlewick, you can't make a friend of a thief, but neither can you make a thief of a friend, all at once."

The examiner made no answer. At that moment was heard the shrill whistle of a locomotive pulling into the depot. That was the train on the little, narrow-gauge road that struck into San Rosario from the south. The major cocked his ear and listened for a moment, and looked at his watch. The narrow-gauge was in on time—10:35. The major continued:

"So Bob hung around the office, reading the papers and smoking. I put another deputy to work in his place, and, after a while, the first excitement of the case wore off.

"One day when we were alone in the office Bob came over to where I was sitting. He was looking sort of grim and blue—the same look he used to get when he'd been watching for Indians all night or herd-riding.

"'Tom,' says he, 'it's harder than standing off redskins; it's harder than lying in the lava desert forty miles from water; but I'm going to stick it out to the end. You know that's been my style. But if you'd tip me the smallest kind of sign—if you'd just say, "Bob I understand," why, it would make it lots easier.'

"I was surprised. 'I don't know what you mean, Bob,' I said. 'Of course, you know I'd do anything under the sun to help you that I could. But you've got me guessing.'

"'All right, Tom,' was all he said, and he went back to his newspaper and lit another cigar.

"It was the night before the court met when I found out what he meant. I went to bed that night with the same old, light-headed, nervous feeling come back upon me. I dropped off to sleep about midnight. When I woke I was standing half-dressed in one of the courthouse corridors. Bob was holding one of my arms, our family doctor the other and Alice was shaking me and half crying. She had sent for the doctor without my knowing it, and when he came they had found me out of bed and missing, and had begun a search.

" 'Sleep-walking,' said the doctor.

"All of us went back to the house, and the doctor told us some re-markable stories about the strange things people had done while in that condition. I was feeling rather chilly after my trip out, and, as my wife was out of the room at the time, I pulled open the door of an old wardrobe that stood in the room and dragged out a big quilt I had seen in there. With it tumbled out the bag of money for stealing which Bob was to be tried—and convicted—in the morning.

" 'How the jumping rattlesnakes did that get there?' I yelled, and all hands must have seen how surprised I was. Bob knew in a flash.

" 'You darned old snoozer,' he said, with the old-time look on his face, 'I saw you put it there. I watched you open the safe and take it out, and I followed you. I looked through the window and saw you hide it in that wardrobe.'

" 'Then, you blankety-blank, flop-eared, sheep-headed coyote, what did you say you took it for?'

" 'Because,' said Bob, simply, 'I didn't know you were asleep.'

"I saw him glance toward the door of the room where Jack and Zilla were, and I knew then what it meant to be a man's friend from Bob's point of view."

Major Tom paused, and again directed his glance out of the window. He saw someone in the Stockmen's National Bank reach and draw a yellow shade down the whole length of its plate-glass, big front window, although the position of the sun did not seem to warrant such a de-fensive movement against its rays.

Nettlewick sat up straight in his chair. He had listened patiently, but without consuming interest, to the major's story. It had impressed him as irrelevant to the situation, and it could certainly have no effect upon the consequences. Those Western people, he thought, had an exag-gerated sentimentality. They were not business-like. They needed to be protected from their friends. Evidently the major had concluded. And what he had said amounted to nothing.

"May I ask," said the examiner, "if you have anything further to say that bears directly upon the question of those abstracted securities?"

"Abstracted securities, sir!" Major Tom turned suddenly in his chair, his blue eyes flashing upon the examiner. "What do you mean, sir?"

He drew from his coat pocket a batch of folded papers held together by a rubber band, tossed them into Nettlewick's hands, and rose to his feet.

"You'll find those securities there, sir, every stock, bond, and share of 'em. I took them from the notes while you were counting the cash. Examine and compare them for yourself."

The major led the way back into the banking room. The examiner, astounded, perplexed, nettled, at sea, followed. He felt that he had been made the victim of something that was not exactly a hoax, but that left him in the shoes of one who had been played upon, used, and then discarded, without even an inkling of the game. Perhaps, also, his official position had been irreverently juggled with. But there was nothing he could take hold of. An official report of the matter would be an absurdity. And, somehow, he felt that he would never know anything more about the matter than he did then.

Frigidly, mechanically, Nettlewick examined the securities, found them to tally with the notes, gathered his black wallet, and rose to depart.

"I will say," he protested, turning the indignant glare of his glasses upon Major Kingman, "that your statements—your misleading statements, which you have not condescended to explain—do not appear to be quite the thing, regarded either as business or humor. I do not understand such motives or actions."

Major Tom looked down at him serenely and not unkindly.

"Son," he said, "there are plenty of things in the chaparral, and on the prairies, and up the canyons that you don't understand. But I want to thank you for listening to a garrulous old man's prosy story. We old Texans love to talk about our adventures and our old comrades, and the homefolks have long ago learned to run when we begin with 'Once upon a time,' so we have to spin our yarns to the stranger within our gates."

The major smiled, but the examiner only bowed coldly, and abruptly quitted the bank. They saw him travel diagonally across the street in a straight line and enter the Stockmen's National Bank.

Major Tom sat down at his desk and drew from his vest pocket the note Roy had given him. He had read it once, but hurriedly, and now, with something like a twinkle in his eyes, he read it again. These were the words he read:

DEAR TOM:

I hear there's one of Uncle Sam's greyhounds going through you, and that means that we'll catch him inside a couple of hours, maybe. Now, I want you to do something for me. We've got just $2,200.00 in the bank, and the law requires that we have $20,000.00. I let Ross and Fisher have $18,000.00 late yesterday afternoon to buy up that Gibson bunch of cattle. They'll realize $40,000 in less than thirty days on the transaction, but that won't make my cash on hand look any prettier to that bank examiner. Now, I can't show him those notes, for they're just plain notes of hand without any security in sight, but you know very well that Pink Ross and Jim Fisher are two of the finest white men God ever made, and they'll do the square thing. You remember Jim Fisher—he was the one who shot that faro dealer in El Paso. I wired Sam Bradshaw's bank to send me $20,000.00, and it will get in on the narrow-gauge at 10:35. You can't let a bank examiner in to count $2,200 and close your doors. Tom, you hold that examiner. Hold him. Hold him if you have to rope him and sit on his head. Watch our front window after the narrow gauge gets in, and when we've got the cash inside we'll pull down the shade for a signal. Don't turn him loose till then. I'm counting on you, Tom.

> Your old Pard,
> Bob Buckley,
> Prest. Stockmen's National

The major began to tear the note into small pieces and throw them into his waste basket. He gave a satisfied little chuckle as he did so.

"Confounded old reckless cowpuncher!" he growled, contentedly, "that pays him some on account for what he tried to do for me in the sheriff's office twenty years ago."

". . . she will never again need me in the old way . . ."

MEMORY OF A PICNIC
Winifred Kirkland

Her white house is the same, with a difference. It was always a house fitted to the person like a garment, a friendly house with peace in the corners, a house warm with sun or fire-light; yet I think we always used the house merely as a starting-place for picnics, for running away into the out-of-doors with a well-stocked basket. We are at best only reformed dryads, my friends and I, and I am not even reformed. I think perhaps that it was in like manner that we used our two selves, merely as a starting point for picnics, for the leap into the infinite, the challenging of space and time, the tossing of stars like play-balls from one to the other, always with the joy of the word shaping on the tongue to the gleam in a friend's eye. We are lovers of words, I and she. True we also had talk in the library, dusked with books, dead men's spirits packed shoulder to shoulder on the shelves. There was brave firelight in the library, and quiet candles, and there was also Xerxes. The great gray Persian curled on one corner of the big desk. Even asleep he dominated the home in his sole masculinity. Yet to me he was sexless and sphinxlike except when he forsook his Oriental calm for strange gambols in the white moonlight, a bounding gray shape of a tiger grace. Sometimes Xerxes rose and stretched as if our conversation bored him, sometimes his great purring drowned out the Occidental flippancy of our chat. He was more king than cat, and he always made me a little uncomfortable, that Xerxes. Today he is not dead but deposed. His place on the desk is usurped by a sturdy box of cigars.

However happily we might talk in the library we always knew we were better without a roof, for in the blood of the born picnicker there is something that must always be running, dancing, flying. Out-of-doors, there were the little brooks to chuckle at us if talk delved too deep, and the pine-tops to fill all pauses with quiet music. We were the better picnickers because we lived for the most part in life's school-room. We counted our picnic days and sorted them into due order of excellence, some better, some not quite so merry, yet all very good. But lately I had begun to wonder about the picnics, for the difference in the white hill-girdled house is a husband. When our friends marry we always wonder about the picnics, for sorrow is always a third comrade to hold two friends' hands the tighter, and to keep their feet more closely in step; it is happiness that may sever and un-self people.

This, our first married picnic, dawned as brisk and bright as any. The master is not with us. He departs each morning for a mysterious place called "The Works." That is something I have always noticed in husbands, that tendency to go forth to "The Works." Somehow no matter how hard women may toil for their daily bread, they never seem to belong to "The Works" of the world. The white house bustles with picnic preparations....

The hall rocks to the bouncings and barkings of Mac, for he, too, feels picnic in the air. Mac is a newcomer, so is Peggy, the mare, ready tied beneath a tree to carry us over the hills and far away. When Adam came to this Eden, he brought his animals with him, a method much better than the Scriptural one, for it must have been a strain on any honeymoon, that influx of indiscriminate elephant and dinosaur, cormorant and anteater, and what not. The animals here were carefully chosen, Mac, the shaggy, clumsy, warm-hearted Airedale, and Peggy, high-bred as a lady of the Old South, having all such a lady's charm and grace and fundamental loyalty touched with just the dash of deviltry considered meet to spice the masculine palate. It is with the clatter of Mac's ecstatic barking as he plunges before Peggy's light hoofs that we go driving forth toward the blue, hill-swept horizon....

It is the kind of morning for good wishes both for dogs and men. Knotted old farmers, seeing our picnic faces and picnic basket, grin and twinkle, sharing the May sunshine. The hills are a dim blue against a sky still softer. Boulder-strewn pastures, more brown than green, are starred with bluets. Far off there, below a shaggy stretch of pines, is a field so golden with dandelions that it quivers as if held by midsummer heat.

We don't know where we are going; that is always the charm of our picnics, to follow the will of the road. It carries us past a sawmill in the wood. Its stridency and the tang of fresh sawdust strike sharp across the air fragrant with fern. Then the road is off again across the open, cleaving farms with their broad greening fields. The meadowlarks ring out their calls to us. The bobolinks dart and dive and sing....

Everywhere the cherry trees and pear are snowed over with white, but the apple blossoms are unopened, turning to a deep rose amid the pale-green leaves. The orchards are nearly human in their individuality, whether they form a little battalion of old men, sturdy and gnarled and steadfast, or a band of little budding baby trees toddling up a hill. There are no great waters in this countryside, but many little glinting brooks, pattering downhill beside our wheels, then meandering through meadows beneath their bushy willows. We are minded to follow a brook and let it lead us to perfect picnic. It leads us, of course, up a hill and up, away from all farms, all valleys, into a deep woods road, hushed and strange, and at last beckons us aside from the road itself, with a twinkle of white birch stems, and the swirl of wild water, white and amber.

It takes a long time to tie and blanket Peggy while I sit dreaming in the dappled shade beside the musical rush of water, haunted by my friend's own song that once set all this woodland madness to elfin rhythms. But my mood is interrupted by the thumping down of the stout picnic basket. She is smilingly tolerant of my dryad whimseys, but for herself, nowadays, she wishes to unpack that basket and get settled. It is for me, also, perhaps, to be smilingly tolerant of the other dryad turned domestic; for me, brook water still has power to turn me dizzy and to make my heart stop beating.

It is the same basket we used to carry, but, like the house, it has a difference. There is a great object concealed in ebony leather, and it is called the "wap-eradicator." The term is profoundly masculine, for a "wap" is some evil-eyed foreigner who might disturb our picnic privacy, and his eradicator is a pistol. There is also a marvelous jackknife which I pause in unpacking to examine. It again is no lady's toy, seeing that it has not only all the blades a lady might require, but in addition a screwdriver and a corkscrew, a tack-puller and a can-opener. There is stout enamel ware in the basket, too, whereas we always used to carry china, feminine and fragile. Food, much of that,—but then we always did take food, for I have noticed that poets need a deal of victualing. In fact, roast beef is about the best thing you can do for anybody's imagination. One packet I myself put in for old sake's sake, despite her laughter, a yellow envelope packed with her typed poetry. "We'll never look at it," she said, and she generally knows. She pulls forth now some scribbled tablets, skeleton stories of my own, "Your little deedles," she designates them in genial contempt, and plants the cream jar upon them.

Presently she is off to gather fagots for the fire, admonishing my absent-mindedness, "Don't let Mac eat the food before we do." I note how much handier she has grown in all wood-lore. Today the fire needs no coaxing, also it's a much smaller fire than we used to build. We used to have a scorching splutter for a wee bit of coffee. This fire goes briskly and to the point, showering us now and then with cinders, yet on the whole well-behaved. In other days we toasted our bacon on forked sticks, but there's a fine frying-pan now, with rings to thrust a rod into, tightening it with twigs. Bacon and eggs sizzle merrily, and the coffee-kettle boils its cover off. We sit smut-cheeked and zestful, and exhibit a great capacity for sandwiches. There is much complacency in our manners. Her coffee, she remarks, "has seven kinds of sticks in it, but is perfectly potable." The fire, that low, leaping ruddiness against a gray boulder, is the best fire she "ever personally conducted." As for me, there is plenty of chuckle in me, too, but I am thinking, when shall we begin to talk, for was that not what we always went to the woods for? Somehow, what with building fires, and brewing and frying, with eating and drinking, and giving Mac and Peggy to eat and drink, there has not been time for talking. That will come later, when we have packed away the sandwiches we could not eat, and given Mac his drink from our emptied coffee-pail, and Peggy her two lumps of sugar. Then surely at last we shall talk, about poems and stories, and all things writable, and all things livable. Sometimes I think she guesses what I am waiting for and regards me with a twinkle, while she moves about light-footed, setting away our clutter.

But afterwards she is sleepy, lying stretched in flickering shadow on the brown pine needles; and I, the picnic place has caught me again into its spell. Nowhere does spring come stepping so delicately as in New England. In other places there is more riot and revelry in the carnival of bursting blossoms and leaf. In New England spring has the face of a girl nun. There are white violets in our woods and white birch stems. The very light has a quality soft and rare. The sky is the

Quaker ladies' own color. Across the swirling water that leaps down the rock path, the face of a hill rises high into the sky. ... The beautiful tree shapes are unhidden, gray stems twining with brown. There is a satin sheen in the rod of light that lines each trunkshaft turned to the sun. Just now, sailing from nowhere, across the green-veiled gray of the hill opposite, there fluttered a white butterfly.

After a long time I touch the envelope packed with poetry, and move it tentatively toward my friend's hand. She shoves it quietly aside. Drowsy though she is, she has an eye open to watch Peggy's glossy brown head tossing down there in an amber-lit wood space, and to see that Mac does not wake from his nap, where he lies only half visible against the russet leaves he has chosen to match his coat. Nowadays any soaring talk may be interrupted by a hearty "Whoa, Peggy!" or a "Down, Mac!" It is no poor punctuation, no unworthy anchorage, for people whose feet have often ached from treading the tree-tops.

She has tossed aside her poetry, but will listen to my stories. I am eager to tell her about all the new people in my brain. She brushes the cobwebs from their heads and from mine with all her old acumen, knowing, in all the spacious sanities of the married woman, that I need to write, while I, I know, too, that she need not. If we did not, each of us, understand, could there be any more picnics? But the pauses grow longer, filled with the voice of the water and the wood. The air is warm and drowsy, and at last she is fast asleep, held close to the brown earth, and I, the other one, sit straight, my back to a stout pine, while my thoughts go wandering, gazing in at Eden, at all Edens. Everybody's path skirts so many Edens, of the women friends married, and the men friends married. Passing pilgrim-wise, one garners a walletful of reflections. Looking at my friend lying there asleep on brown pine needles, I know, as every woman must know, that she will never again need me in the old way, and, as every woman must be, I am far too glad to be sorry. The question for each of us, man or woman, outside the fence, is, Will he, will she, still come out sometimes into life's great open and picnic with me? That all depends, does it not? on the newcomer.

I had three chairs in my house: one for solitude, two for friendship, three for society.

—HENRY DAVID THOREAU

SONNET
TO JOHN HAMILTON REYNOLDS
John Keats

O that a week could be an age, and we
Felt parting and warm meeting every week,
Then one poor year a thousand years would be,
   The flush of welcome ever on the cheek:
So could we live long life in little space,
   So time itself would be annihilate,
So a day's journey in oblivious haze
   To serve our joys would lengthen and dilate.
O to arrive each Monday morn from Ind!
   To land each Tuesday from the rich Levant!
In little time a host of joys to bind,
   And keep our souls in one eternal pant!
This morn, my friend, and yester-evening taught
Me how to harbour such a happy thought.

"... sometimes maybe we will have a glass of wine to drink
for friendship's sake."

DANNY AND HIS FRIENDS
John Steinbeck

"No, Pilon. I tell the truth. The viejo died. I am the heir. I, the favorite grandson."

"Thou art the only grandson," said the realist, Pilon. "Where are these houses?"

"You know the viejo's house on Tortilla Flat, Pilon?"

"Here in Monterey?"

"Yes, here in Tortilla Flat."

"Are they any good, these houses?"

Danny sank back, exhausted with emotion. "I do not know. I forgot I owned them."

Pilon sat silent and absorbed. His face grew mournful. He threw a handful of pine needles on the fire, watched the flames climb frantically among them and die. For a long time he looked into Danny's face with deep anxiety, and then Pilon sighed noisily, and again he sighed. "Now it is over," he said sadly. "Now the great times are done. Thy friends will mourn, but nothing will come of their mourning."

Danny put down the bottle, and Pilon picked it up and set it in his own lap.

"Now what is over?" Danny demanded. "What do you mean?"

"It is not the first time," Pilon went on. "When one is poor, one thinks, 'If I had money I would share it with my good friends.' But let the money come and charity flies away. So it is with thee, my once-friend. Thou art lifted above thy friends. Thou art a man of property. Thou wilt forget thy friends who shared everything with thee, even their brandy."

His words upset Danny. "Not I," he cried. "I will never forget thee, Pilon."

"So you think now," said Pilon coldly. "But when you have two houses to sleep in, then you will see. Pilon will be a poor paisano, while you eat with the mayor."

Danny arose unsteadily and held himself upright against a tree. "Pilon, I swear, what I have is thine. While I have a house, thou hast a house. Give me a drink."

"I must see this to believe it," Pilon said in a discouraged voice. "It would be a world of wonder if it were so. Men would come a thousand miles to look upon it. And besides, the bottle is empty...."

When the sun was clear of the pines, and the ground was warm, and the night's dew was drying on the geranium leaves, Danny came out on his porch to sit in the sunshine and to muse warmly of certain happenings. He slipped off his shoes and wriggled his toes on the sun-warmed boards of the porch. He had walked down earlier in the morning and viewed the square black ashes and twisted plumbing which had been his other house. He had indulged in a little conventional anger against careless friends, had mourned for a moment over that transitory quality of earthly property which had made spiritual property so much more valuable. He had thought over the ruin of his status as a man with a house to rent; and, all this clutter of necessary and decent emotion having been satisfied and swept away, he had finally slipped into his true emotion, one of relief that at least one of his burdens was removed.

"If it were still there, I would be covetous of the rent," he thought. "My friends have been cool towards me because they owed me money. Now we can be free and happy again."

But Danny knew he must discipline his friends a little, or they would consider him soft. Therefore, as he sat on his porch, warding off flies with a moving hand which conveyed more warning than threat to the flies, he went over the things he must say to his friends before he allowed them back into the corral of his affection. He must show them that he was not a man to be imposed upon. But he yearned to get it over and to be once more that Danny whom every one loved, that Danny whom people sought out when they had a gallon of wine or a piece of meat. As the owner of two houses he had been considered rich, and he had missed a great many tidbits.

Pilon and Pablo and Jesus Maria Corcoran slept a long time on the pine needles in the forest. It had been a night of terrible excitement, and they were tired. But at length the sun shone into their faces with noonday ardor and the ants walked on them, and two blue jays stood on the ground nearby, calling them all manner of sharp names.

What finished their sleep, though, was a picnic party which settled just on the other side of the bush from them and opened a big lunch basket from which moving smells drifted to Pilon and Pablo and Jesus Maria. They awakened; they sat up; and then the enormity of their situation burst upon them.

"How did the fire start?" asked Pablo plaintively, and no one knew.

"Perhaps," said Jesus Maria, "we had better go to another town for a while—to Watsonville or to Salinas; those are nice towns."

Pilon pulled the brassiere from his pocket and ran his fingers over its pink smoothness. And he held it to the sunlight and looked through it.

"That would only delay matters," he decided. "I think it would be better to go to Danny and confess our fault, like little children to a father. Then he can't say anything without being sorry. And besides, have we not this present for Mrs. Morales?"

His friends nodded agreement. Pilon's eyes strayed through the thick brush to the picnic party, and particularly to that huge lunch basket from which came the penetrating odor of deviled eggs. Pilon's nose wrinkled a little, like a rabbit's. He smiled in a quiet reverie. "I am going to walk, my friends. In a little while I will meet you at the quarry. Do not bring the basket, if you can help it."

They watched sadly as Pilon got up and walked away, through the trees, in a direction at right angles to the picnic and the basket. Pablo and Jesus Maria were not surprised, a few moments later, to hear a dog bark, a rooster crow, high shrill laughter, the snarl of a wild cat, a little short scream and a cry for help; but the picnic party was surprised and fascinated. The two men and two women left their basket and trotted away toward these versatile sounds.

Pablo and Jesus Maria obeyed Pilon. They did not take the basket, but always afterwards their hats and their shirts were stained with deviled eggs.

At about three o'clock in the afternoon the three penitents walked slowly toward Danny's house. Their arms were loaded with offerings of reconciliation: oranges and apples and bananas, bottles of olives and pickles, sandwiches of pressed ham, egg sandwiches, bottles of soda pop, a paper carton of potato salad and a copy of the Saturday Evening Post.

Danny saw them coming, and he stood up and tried to remember the things he had to say. They lined up in front of him and hung their heads.

"Dogs of dogs," Danny called them, and "thieves of decent folk's other house," and "spawn of cuttlefish." He named their mothers cows and their fathers ancient sheep.

Pilon opened the bag he held and exposed the ham sandwiches. And Danny said he had no more trust in friends, that his faith had been frostbitten and his friendship trampled upon. And then he began to have a little trouble remembering, for Pablo had taken two deviled eggs out of his bosom. But Danny went back to the grand generation and criticized the virtue of its women and the potency of its men.

Pilon pulled the pink brassiere from his pocket and let it dangle listlessly from his fingers.

Danny forgot everything then. He sat down on the porch and his friends sat down, and the packages came open. They ate to a point of discomfort. It was an hour later, when they reclined at ease on the porch, giving attention to little besides digestion, when Danny asked casually, as about a far-off subject, "How did the fire start?"

"We don't know," Pilon explained. "We went to sleep, and then it started. Perhaps we have enemies."

"Perhaps," said Pablo devoutly, "perhaps God had a finger in it."

"Who can make the good God act the way He does?" added Jesus Maria.

When Pilon handed over the brassiere and explained how it was a present for Mrs. Morales, Danny was reticent. He eyed the brassiere with some skepticism. His friends, he felt, were flattering Mrs. Morales. "That is not a woman to give presents to," he said finally. "Too often we are tied to women by the silk stockings we give them." He could not explain to his friends the coolness that had come to his relationship with Mrs. Morales since he was the owner of only one house; nor could he, in courtesy to Mrs. Morales, describe his own pleasure at that coolness. "I will put this little thing away," he said. "Some day it may be of use to some one."

When the evening came, and it was dark, they went into the house and built a fire of cones in the air-tight stove. Danny, in proof of his forgiveness, brought out a quart of grappa and shared its fire with his friends.

They settled easily into the new life. "It is too bad Mrs. Morales' chickens are all dead," Pilon observed.

But even here was no bar to happiness. "She is going to buy two dozen new ones on Monday," said Danny.

Pilon smiled contentedly. "Those hens of Mrs. Soto's were no good," he said. "I told Mrs. Soto they needed oyster shells, but she paid no attention to me."

They drank the quart of grappa, and there was just enough to promote the sweetness of comradeship.

"It is good to have friends," said Danny. "How lonely it is in the world if there are no friends to sit with one and to share one's grappa."

"Or one's sandwiches," Pilon added quickly.

Pablo was not quite over his remorse, for he suspected the true state of celestial politics which had caused the burning of the house. "In all the world there are few friends like thee, Danny. It is not given to many to have such solace."

Before Danny sank completely under the waves of his friends, he sounded one warning. "I want all of you to keep out of my bed," he ordered. "That is one thing I must have to myself."

Although no one had mentioned it, each of the four knew they were all going to live in Danny's house.

Pilon sighed with pleasure. Gone was the worry of the rent; gone the responsibility of owing money. No longer was he a tenant, but a guest. In his mind he gave thanks for the burning of the other house.

"We will all be happy here, Danny," he said. "In the evenings we will sit by the fire and our friends will come in to visit. And sometimes maybe we will have a glass of wine to drink for friendship's sake."

Then Jesus Maria, in a frenzy of gratefulness, made a rash promise. It was the grappa that did it, and the night of the fire, and all the deviled eggs. He felt that he had received great gifts, and he wanted to distribute a gift. "It shall be our burden and our duty to see that there is always food in the house for Danny," he declaimed. "Never shall our friend go hungry."

Pilon and Pablo looked up in alarm, but the thing was said; a beautiful and generous thing. No man could with impunity destroy it. Even Jesus Maria understood, after it was said, the magnitude of his statement. They could only hope that Danny would forget it.

"For," Pilon mused to himself, "if this promise were enforced, it would be worse than rent. It would be slavery."

"We swear it, Danny!" he said.

They sat about the stove with tears in their eyes, and their love for one another was almost unbearable.

Pablo wiped his wet eyes with the back of his hand, and he echoed Pilon's remark. "We shall be very happy living here," he said.

A BOTTLE AND A FRIEND
Robert Burns

Here's a bottle and an honest friend!
  What wad ye wish for mair, man?
Wha kens, before his life may end,
  What his share may be o' care, man?
Then catch the moments as they fly,
  And use them as ye ought, man:—
Believe me, happiness is shy,
  And comes not aye when sought, man.

~~~~~~~~~~

"... I'm half afraid you may have taken the opportunity to
'grow up'..."

LEWIS CARROLL TO MARY, AGE 12-15, DAUGHTER OF THE SCOTCH POET AND NOVELIST, GEORGE MAC DONALD

Ch. Ch. Oxford,
Jan. 22, 1866

My Dear Mary,

I am very glad you like the new copy of "Alice's Adventures," and I should like very much to come and see you all again, and "Snowdrop," if I could find the time, which I can't at present. But, by the bye, it's your turn to come and see me now. I'm sure *I* called last. My room is very easy to find when you get there, and as for *distance,* you know— why, Oxford is as near to London as London is to Oxford. If your geography-book doesn't tell you that, it must be a wretched affair, and you'd better get another.

Now I want to know what you *mean* by calling yourself "naughty" for not having written sooner! Naughty, indeed! Stuff and nonsense! Do you think I'd call myself naughty, if I hadn't written to you, say for 50 years? Not a bit! I'd just begin as usual "My dear Mary, 50 years ago, you asked me what to do for your kitten, as it had a tooth-ache, and I have just remembered to write about it. Perhaps the tooth-ache has gone off by this time—if not, wash it carefully in hasty-pudding, and give it 4 pincushions boiled in sealing-wax, and just dip the end of its tail in hot coffee. This remedy has never been known to fail." There! *That's* the proper way to write!—

I want you to tell me the surname of those cousins of yours (I think they were) that I met one evening at your house. Mary and May were their Christian names. Also please tell your Papa I have read Alec Forbes, and am delighted with it, and I very much want to meet Annie Anderson in real life. Where does she live?

With kindest regards to your Papa and Mama and best love to your brothers and sisters, I remain,

Your loving friend,
CHARLES L. DODGSON

Ch. Ch. Oxford,
Nov. 30, 1867

My Dear Mary,

It is so long since I've seen you that I'm half afraid you may have taken the opportunity to "grow up," and that you'll turn up your nose at my letter and cry "a nice impertinent composition." Affectionate uncle indeed! Affectionate fiddle stick! I'll just answer him in the *third person!* "Miss M. MacDonald presents her compliments, and is surprised etc. etc."

I am sending you the new number of "Aunt Judy's Magazine," to put away with your copy of "Alice," because it contains a story by the same writer. So, with kind regards to your Papa and Mama, and love to any brothers and sisters you may happen to have,

I remain,
Your affectionate uncle,
C. L. DODGSON

Ch. Ch.
March 13, 1869

Well, you *are* a cool young lady indeed! After keeping me all these weeks, waiting for an answer, you quietly write on another subject, just as if nothing had happened! I wrote, or have written—(observe, Madam, that I put it in the preterite or past tense; it isn't likely I ever *shall* write again about it) on the 26th of January last, offering you a copy of the German edition of "Alice." Well, the days rolled on—and the nights too (as nearly as I can remember, one between every two days or thereabouts), and no *answer* came. And the weeks rolled on, and the months too, and I got older, and thinner, and sadder, and still NO ANSWER came. And then my friends said—how white my hair was getting, and that I was all skin and bone, and other pleasant remarks —and—but I won't go on, it is too dreadful to relate, except that through all these years and years of waiting and anxiety (all of which have elapsed since the 26th of January last—you see, we live so fast at Oxford) still NO ANSWER ever came from this granite-hearted young person! And then she calmly writes and says, "oh, do come and see the race!" And I answer with a groan, "I do see the race—the human race—it is a race full of ingratitude—and of all that race none is more ungratefuller, more worser—more,—my pen chokes, and I can say no more!"

P.S.—I am afraid I shan't be in town—else I should be glad to come, if only to have the opportunity of saying, "Monster of ingratitude! Avaunt!"

MONEY AND A FRIEND

Anonymous

I once had money and a friend,
    Of either, thought I store.
I lent my money to my friend,
    And took his word therefor.
I sought my money from my friend,
    Which I had wanted long.
I lost my money and my friend;
    Now was that not a wrong?

"... it is a mere and miserable solitude to want true friends ..."

OF FRIENDSHIP

Francis Bacon

It had been hard for him that spake it to have put more truth and untruth together in few words than in that speech, "Whosoever is delighted in solitude is either a wild beast or a god." For it is most true that a natural and secret hatred and aversion toward society in any man hath somewhat of the savage beast; but it is most untrue that

it should have any character at all of the divine nature, except it proceed, not out of a pleasure in solitude, but out of a love and desire
to sequester a man's self for a higher conversation.... But little do
men perceive what solitude is, and how far it extendeth. For a crowd
is not company; and faces are but a gallery of pictures; and talk but a
tinkling cymbal, where there is no love. The Latin adage meeteth with
it a little: *"Magna civitas, magna solitudo";* because in a great town
friends are scattered, so that there is not that fellowship, for the most
part, which is in less neighborhoods. But we may go further, and
affirm most truly that it is a mere and miserable solitude to want true
friends, without which the world is but a wilderness; and even in this
sense also of solitude, whosoever in the frame of his nature and affections is unfit for friendship, he taketh it of the beast, and not from
humanity.

A principal fruit of friendship is the ease and discharge of the full-
ness and swellings of the heart, which passions of all kinds do cause
and induce. We know diseases of stoppings and suffocations are the
most dangerous in the body; and it is not much otherwise in the mind.
You may take sarza to open the liver, steel to open the spleen, flower
of sulphur for the lungs, castoreum for the brain; but no receipt
openeth the heart for a true friend; to whom you may impart griefs,
joys, fears, hopes, suspicions, counsels, and whatsoever lieth upon the
heart to oppress it, in a kind of civil shrift or confession.

It is a strange thing to observe how high a rate great kings and
monarchs do set upon this fruit of friendship whereof we speak; so
great, as they purchase it many times at the hazard of their own safety
and greatness. For princes, in regard of the distance of their fortune
from that of their subjects and servants, cannot gather this fruit, except
(to make themselves capable thereof) they raise some persons to be as
it were companions and almost equals to themselves; which many
times sorteth to inconvenience. The modern languages give unto such
persons the name of favorites, or privadoes; as if it were matter of
grace or conversation. But the Roman name attaineth the true use and
cause thereof, naming them *"participes curarum";* for it is that which
tieth the knot. And we see plainly that this hath been done, not by
weak and passionate princes only, but by the wisest and most politic
that ever reigned; who have oftentimes joined to themselves some of
their servants, whom both themselves have called friends, and allowed
others likewise to call them in the same manner, using the word which
is received between private men....

Certainly, if a man would give it a hard phrase, those that want
friends to open themselves unto are cannibals of their own hearts. But
one thing is most admirable (wherewith I will conclude this first fruit
of friendship), which is, that this communicating of a man's self to

his friend works two contrary effects; for it redoubleth joys, and cutteth griefs in halves. For there is no man that imparteth his joys to his friend, but he joyeth the more; and no man that imparteth his griefs to his friend, but he grieveth the less....

The second fruit of friendship is healthful and sovereign for the understanding, as the first is for the affections. For friendship maketh indeed a fair day in the affections, from storm and tempests, but it maketh daylight in the understanding, out of darkness and confusion of thoughts. Neither is this to be understood only of faithful counsel, which a man receiveth from his friend; but before you come to that, certain it is that whosoever hath his mind fraught with many thoughts, his wits and understanding do clarify and break up in the communicating and discoursing with another; he tosseth his thoughts more easily; he marshaleth them more orderly; he seeth how they look when they are turned into words; finally, he waxeth wiser than himself; and that more by an hour's discourse than by a day's meditation.... Neither is this second fruit of friendship, in opening the understanding, restrained only to such friends as are able to give a man counsel (they indeed are best); but even without that, a man learneth of himself, and bringeth his own thoughts to light, and whetteth his wits as against a stone, which itself cuts not. In a word, a man were better relate himself to a statue or picture, than to suffer his thoughts to pass in smother.

Add now, to make this second fruit of friendship complete, that other point which lieth more open, and falleth within vulgar observation; which is faithful counsel from a friend. Heraclitus saith well in one of his enigmas, "Dry light is ever the best"; and certain it is, that the light that a man receiveth by counsel from another, is drier and purer than that which cometh from his own understanding and judgment; which is ever infused and drenched in his affections and customs. So as there is as much difference between the counsel that a friend giveth, and that a man giveth himself, as there is between the counsel of a friend and of a flatterer; for there is no such flatterer as is a man's self, and there is no such remedy against flattery of a man's self as the liberty of a friend. Counsel is of two sorts: the one concerning manners, the other concerning business. For the first, the best preservative to keep the mind in health is the faithful admonition of a friend. The calling of a man's self to a strict account is a medicine sometimes too piercing and corrosive; reading good books of morality is a little flat and dead; observing our faults in others is sometimes improper for our case: but the best receipt (best I say to work and best to take) is the admonition of a friend. It is a strange thing to behold what gross errors and extreme absurdities many (especially of the greater sort) do commit for want of a friend to tell them of them, to the great damage both of their fame and fortune: for, as St. James saith, they are as men "that look sometimes into a glass, and presently forget their own shape and favor." As for business, a man may think, if he will, that two eyes see no more than one; or, that a gamester seeth always more than a looker-on; or, that a man in anger is as wise as he that hath said over the four-and-twenty letters; or, that a musket may be shot off as well upon the arm as upon a rest; and such other fond and high imaginations, to think himself all in all: but when all is done, the help of good counsel is that which setteth business straight: and if any man think that he will take counsel, but it shall be by pieces; asking counsel in one business of one man, and in another business of another man, it is well (that is to say, better, perhaps, than if he asked none at all); but he runneth two dangers: one, that he shall not be faithfully counseled; for it is a rare thing, except it be from a perfect and entire friend, to have counsel given, but such as shall be bowed and crooked to some ends which he hath that giveth it....

After these two noble fruits of friendship (peace in the affections, and support of the judgment), followeth the last fruit, which is like the pomegranate, full of many kernels; I mean aid, and bearing a part in all actions and occasions. Here the best way to represent to life the manifold use of friendship, is to cast and see how many things there are which a man cannot do himself: and then it will appear that it was a sparing speech of the ancients to say, "that a friend is another himself"; for that a friend is far more than himself. Men have their time, and die many times in desire of some things which they principally take to heart; the bestowing of a child, the finishing of a work, or the like. If a man have a true friend, he may rest almost secure that the care of those things will continue after him; so that a man hath, as it were, two lives in his desires. A man hath a body, and that body is confined to a place; but where friendship is, all offices of life are, as it were, granted to him and his deputy; for he may exercise them by his friend. How many things are there, which a man cannot, with any face or comeliness, say or do himself; a man can scarce allege his own merits with modesty, much less extol them; a man cannot sometimes brook to supplicate, or beg, and a number of the like: but all these things are graceful in a friend's mouth, which are blushing in a man's own. So again, a man's person hath many proper relations which he cannot put off. A man cannot speak to his son but as a father; to his wife but as a husband; to his enemy but upon terms: whereas a friend may speak as the case requires, and not as it sorteth with the person: but to enumerate these things were endless; I have given the rule, where a man cannot fitly play his own part, if he have not a friend he may quit the stage.

When the first time of love is over, there comes a something better still. Then comes that other love; that faithful friendship which never changes, and which will accompany you with its calm light through the whole of life. It is only needful to place yourself so that it may come, and then it comes of itself. And then everything turns and changes itself to the best.

—FREDRIKA BREMER

"... I love everybody that is dear to you ..."

GEORGE WASHINGTON TO GENERAL LAFAYETTE, WHEN HE RETURNED TO FRANCE AND RECEIVED THE HIGHEST HONORS

WEST POINT, September 30, 1779

It gave me infinite pleasure to hear, from yourself, of the favorable reception you met with from your sovereign, and of the joy which your safe arrival in France had diffused among your friends. I had no doubt that this would be the case. To hear it from yourself adds pleasure to the account. And here, my dear friend, let me congratulate you. None can do it with more warmth of affection, or sincere joy than myself. Your forward zeal in the cause of liberty; your singular attachment to this infant world; your ardent and persevering efforts, not only in America, but since your return to France, to serve the United States, your polite attention to Americans, and your strict and uniform friendship for me, have ripened the first impressions of esteem and attachment, which I imbibed for you, into such perfect love and gratitude, as neither time nor absence can impair. This will warrant my assuring you that, whether in the character of an officer at the head of a corps of gallant French (if circumstances should require this), whether as a major-general commanding a division of the American army, or whether, after our swords have given place to the ploughshare and the pruninghook, I see you as a private gentleman, a friend and companion, I shall welcome you with all the warmth of friendship to Columbia's shores; and, in the latter case, to my rural cottage, where homely fare and a cordial reception shall be substituted for delicacies and costly living. This, from past experience, I know you can submit to; and if the lovely partner of your happiness will consent to participate with us in such rural entertainment and amusements, I can undertake, on behalf of Mrs. Washington, that she will do everything in her power to make Virginia agreeable to the Marchioness. My inclination and endeavors to do this cannot be doubted, when I assure you, that I love everybody that is dear to you, and consequently participate in the pleasure you feel in the prospect of again becoming a parent, and do most sincerely congratulate you and your lady on this fresh pledge she is about to give you of her love.

GROWING OLD
Ella Wheeler Wilcox

The days grow shorter, the nights grow longer;
  The headstones thicken along the way;
And life grows sadder, but love grows stronger
  For those who walk with us day by day.

The tears come quicker, the laugh comes slower;
  The courage is lesser to do and dare;
And the tide of joy in the heart falls lower,
  And seldom covers the reefs of care.

But all true things in the world seem truer,
  And the better things of earth seem best,
And friends are dearer, as friends are fewer,
  And love is all as our sun dips west.

Then let us clasp hands as we walk together,
  And let us speak softly in low, sweet tone,
For no man knows on the morrow whether
  We two pass on—or but one alone.

A real friend is one who walks in when the rest of the world walks out.

—WALTER WINCHELL

". . . keep your serious views secret."

LORD CHESTERFIELD TO HIS SON

There is an incontinency of friendship among young fellows, who are associated by their mutual pleasures only, which has, very frequently, bad consequences. A parcel of warm hearts and inexperienced heads, heated by convivial mirth, and possibly a little too much wine, vow, and really mean at the time, eternal friendships to each other, and indiscreetly pour out their whole souls in common, and without the least reserve. These confidences are as indiscreetly repealed as they were made; for new pleasures and new places soon dissolve this ill-cemented connection; and then very ill uses are made of these rash confidences. Bear your part, however, in young companies; nay, excel, if you can, in all the social and convivial joy and festivity that become youth. Trust them with your love tales, if you please; but keep your serious views secret. Trust those only to some tried friend, more experienced than yourself, and who, being in a different walk of life from you, is not likely to become your rival; for I would not advise you to depend so much upon the heroic virtue of mankind, as to hope or believe that your competitor will ever be your friend, as to the object of that competition.

These are reserves and cautions very necessary to have, but very imprudent to show.

"Men . . . never could quarrel with him."

CHARLES LAMB AS A FRIEND
C. T. Winchester

Charles Lamb had a genius for friendship. He could discover something amiable in everybody. He drew about him men who were polar opposites in temperament and bitterly antagonistic in opinion; men like Godwin and Wordsworth, Hunt and Southey, who would never have given a hand to each other save on the common ground of their friendship for Lamb. He stoutly defended them to each other, and appreciated whatever was genuine and human in them all. He made free with their follies, quizzed them on their fads or peculiarities with an imprudence that might have been intolerable in any one else. "M-martin," he stammered over the whist table to Burney, "if d-dirt were trumps, what a hand you'd hold!" When Coleridge talked a stricken hour, wrapped in a cloud of lofty metaphysic, Lamb only remarked dryly, "Coleridge is so full of his fun!" But no one took offense. Indeed, no one could be more quick than Lamb himself to perceive, or more careful to avoid, anything that might wound the feelings of others. Men who, like Hazlitt, quarreled with everybody else, never could quarrel with him. It was Charles and Mary Lamb, and one may say only they, that could keep the friendship of William Hazlitt and Sarah Stoddard, not only before their ill-assorted marriage—at which ceremony Lamb confessed he was convulsed with mistimed laughter—but when, in later days, they were separated from each other and from everybody else. Charles and Mary Lamb would cherish no resentment for any slight, or misunderstanding, or desertion. When Hazlitt lay in his last illness alone and unbefriended, it was Lamb who hastened to visit him, stood by his bedside, and held the hand of the dying man to the end.

But it should be remembered that Lamb's best and closest friends were precisely the best and greatest men of his time. He was surrounded by an oddly assorted company on the Wednesday evenings; but he kept his closest intimacy for two or three—for Coleridge and the Wordsworths. There are few letters in the language like those of Lamb to the Wordsworths, so full of mingled humor and pathos, of the most delicate sympathies. These people really knew each other—which is too uncommon a thing in this world.

PARTED FRIENDS

James Montgomery

Friend after friend departs:
  Who hath not lost a friend?
There is no union here of hearts
  That finds not here an end;
Were this frail world our only rest,
Living or dying, none were blest.

Beyond the flight of time,
  Beyond this vale of death,
There surely is some blessèd clime
  Where life is not a breath,
Nor life's affections transient fire,
Whose sparks fly upward to expire.

There is a world above,
  Where parting is unknown;
A whole eternity of love,
  Formed for the good alone;
And faith beholds the dying here
Translated to that happier sphere.

Thus star by star declines,
  Till all are passed away,
As morning high and higher shines,
  To pure and perfect day;
Nor sink those stars in empty night;
They hide themselves in heaven's own light.

"Rascals are always sociable ..."

A DISSENT BY ARTHUR SCHOPENHAUER

All society necessarily involves, as the first condition of its existence, mutual accommodation and restraint upon the part of its members. This means that the larger it is, the more insipid will be its tone. A man can be *himself* only so long as he is alone; and if he does not love solitude, he will not love freedom; for it is only when he is alone that he is really free. Constraint is always present in society, like a companion of whom there is no riddance; and in proportion to the greatness of a man's individuality, it will be hard for him to bear the sacrifices which all intercourse with others demands....

The worst of what is called good society is not only that it offers us the companionship of people who are unable to win either our praise or our affection, but that it does not allow of our being that which we naturally are; it compels us, for the sake of harmony, to shrivel up, or even alter our shape altogether. Intellectual conversation, whether grave or humorous, is only fit for intellectual society; it is downright abhorrent to ordinary people, to please whom it is absolutely necessary to be commonplace and dull. This demands an act of severe self-denial; we have to forfeit three-fourths of ourselves in order to become like other people....

No man can be in *perfect accord* with any one but himself—not even with a friend or the partner of his life; differences of individuality and temperament are always bringing in some degree of discord, though it may be a very slight one. That genuine, profound peace of mind, that perfect tranquillity of soul, which, next to health, is the highest blessing the earth can give, is to be attained only in solitude, and, as a permanent mood, only in complete retirement; and then, if there is anything great and rich in the man's own self, his way of life is the happiest that may be found in this wretched world.

Let me speak plainly. However close the bond of friendship, love, marriage—a man, ultimately, looks to himself, to his own welfare alone; at most, to his child's too. The less necessity there is for you to come into contact with mankind in general, in the relations whether of business or of personal intimacy, the better off you are. Loneliness and solitude have their evils, it is true; but if you cannot feel them all at once, you can at least see where they lie; on the other hand, society is *insidious* in this respect; as in offering you what appears to be the pastime of pleasing social intercourse, it works great and often irreparable mischief....

People are rendered sociable by their inability to endure solitude, that is to say, their own society. They become sick of themselves. It is this vacuity of soul which drives them to intercourse with others....

Ordinary society is, in this respect, very like the kind of music to be obtained from an orchestra composed solely of Russian horns. Each horn has only one note; and the music is produced by each note coming in just at the right moment. In the monotonous sound of a single horn, you have a precise illustration of the effect of most people's minds. How often there seems to be only one thought there! and no room for any other. It is easy to see why people are so bored; and also why they are sociable, why they like to go about in crowds—why mankind is so *gregarious*....

Those who are fond of society from time to time may profit by this simile, and lay it down as a general rule that deficiency of quality in those we meet may be to some extent compensated by an increase in quantity. One man's company may be quite enough, if he is clever; but where you have only ordinary people to deal with, it is advisable to have a great many of them, so that some advantage may accrue by letting them all work together,—on the analogy of the horns; and may Heaven grant you patience for your task! ...

Rascals are always sociable—more's the pity! and the chief sign that a man has any nobility in his character is the little pleasure he takes in others' company. He prefers solitude more and more, and, in course of time, comes to see that, with few exceptions, the world offers no choice beyond solitude on one side and vulgarity on the other....

It is natural for great minds—the true teachers of humanity—to care little about the constant company of others; just as little as the schoolmaster cares for joining in the gambols of the noisy crowd of boys which surrounds him. The mission of these great minds is to guide mankind over the sea of error to the haven of truth—to draw it forth from the dark abysses of a barbarous vulgarity up into the light of culture and refinement. Men of great intellect live in the world without really belonging to it; and so, from their earliest years, they feel that there is a perceptible difference between them and other people....

From what has been said it is obvious that the love of solitude is not a direct, original impulse in human nature, but rather something secondary and of gradual growth. It is the more distinguishing feature of nobler minds, developed not without some conquest of natural desires, and now and then in actual opposition to the promptings of Mephistopheles....

As the years increase, it always becomes easier to say, Dare to be wise—*sapere aude*. And after sixty, the inclination to be alone grows into a kind of real, natural instinct; for at that age everything combines in favor of it.... The generation to which he belonged has passed away, and a new race has sprung up which looks upon him as essentially outside its sphere of activity. And then the years pass more quickly as we become older, and we want to devote our remaining time to the intellectual rather than to the practical side of life.... A thousand things become clear which were formerly enveloped in obscurity, and results are obtained which give a feeling of difficulties overcome. From long experience of men, we cease to expect much from them; we find that, on the whole, people do not gain by a nearer acquaintance; and that—apart from a few rare and fortunate exceptions—we have come across none but defective specimens of human nature which it is advisable to leave in peace. We are no more subject to the ordinary illusions of life; and as, in individual instances, we soon see what a man is made of, we seldom feel any inclinations to come into closer relations with him....

When you find human society disagreeable and feel yourself justified in flying to solitude, you may be so constituted as to be unable to bear the depression of it for any length of time, which will probably be the case if you are young. Let me advise you, then, to form the habit of taking some of your solitude with you into society, to learn to be to some extent alone even though you are in company; not to say at once what you think, and, on the other hand, not to attach too precise a meaning to what others say; rather, not to expect much of them, either orally or intellectually, and to strengthen yourself in the feeling of indifference to their opinion, which is the surest way of always practicing a praiseworthy toleration. If you do that, you will not live so much with other people, though you may appear to move amongst them: your relation to them will be of a purely objective character. This precaution will keep you from too close contact with society, and therefore secure you against being contaminated or even outraged by it....

Men are like children, in that, if you spoil them, they become naughty.

Therefore it is well not to be too indulgent or charitable with anyone. You may take it as a general rule that you will not lose a friend by refusing him a loan, but that you are very likely to do so by granting it; and, for similar reasons, you will not readily alienate people by being somewhat proud and careless in your behavior; but if you are very kind and complaisant towards them, you will often make them arrogant and intolerable, and so a breach will ensue.

There is one thing that, more than any other, throws people absolutely off their balance—the thought that you are dependent upon them. This is sure to produce an insolent and domineering manner towards you. There are some people, indeed, who become rude if you enter into any kind of relation with them; for instance, if you have occasion to converse with them frequently upon confidential matters, they soon come to fancy that they can take liberties with you, and so they try and transgress the laws of politeness. This is why there are so few with whom you care to become more intimate, and why you should avoid familiarity with vulgar people. If a man comes to think that I am more dependent upon him than he is upon me, he at once feels as though I had stolen something from him; and his endeavor will be to have his vengeance and get it back. The only way to attain superiority in dealing with men, is to let it be seen that you are independent of them.

And in this view it is advisable to let everyone of your acquaintance —whether man or woman—feel now and then that you could very well dispense with their company. This will consolidate friendship. Nay, with most people there will be no harm in occasionally mixing a grain of disdain with your treatment of them; that will make them value your friendship all the more. *Chi non istima vien stimato,* as a subtle Italian proverb has it—to disregard is to win regard. But if we really think very highly of a person, we should conceal it from him like a crime. This is not a very gratifying thing to do, but it is right. Why, a dog will not bear being treated too kindly, let alone a man! ...

To become reconciled to a friend with whom you have broken, is a form of weakness; and you pay the penalty of it when he takes the first opportunity of doing precisely the very thing which brought about the breach; nay, he does it the more boldly, because he is secretly conscious that you cannot get on without him....

True and genuine friendship presupposes a strong sympathy with the weal and woe of another—purely objective in its character and quite disinterested; and this in its turn means an absolute identification of self with the object of friendship. The egoism of human nature is so strongly antagonistic to any such sympathy, that true friendship belongs to that class of things—the sea-serpent, for instance,—with regard to which no one knows whether they are fabulous or really exist somewhere or other.

Still, in many cases, there is a grain of true and genuine friendship in the relations of man to man, though generally, of course, some secret personal interest is at the bottom of them—some one among the many forms that selfishness can take. But in a world where all is imperfect, this grain of true feeling is such an ennobling influence that it gives some warrant for calling those relations by the name of friendship, for they stand far above the ordinary friendships that prevail amongst mankind. The latter are so constituted that, were you to hear how your dear friends speak of you behind your back, you would never say another word to them.

Apart from the case where it would be a real help to you if your friend were to make some great sacrifice to serve you, there is no better means of testing the genuineness of his feelings than the way in which he receives the news of a misfortune that has just happened to you. At that moment the expression of his features will either show that his one thought is that of true and sincere sympathy for you; or else the absolute composure of his countenance, or the passing trace of something other than sympathy.... Indeed, at such a moment, the ordinary so-called friend will find it hard to suppress the signs of a slight smile of pleasure. There are few ways by which you can make more certain of putting people into a good humor than by telling them of some trouble that has recently befallen you, or by unreservedly disclosing some personal weakness of yours. How characteristic this is of humanity!

Distance and long absence are always prejudicial to friendship, however disinclined a man may be to admit it. Our regard for people whom we do not see—even though they be our dearest friends—gradually dries up in the course of years, and they become abstract notions; so that our interest in them grows to be more and more intellectual,—nay, it is kept up only as a kind of tradition; whilst we retain a lively and deep interest in those who are constantly before our eyes, even if they be only pet animals. This shows how much men are limited by their senses....

Friends of the house are very rightly so called; because they are friends of the house rather than of its master; in other words, they are more like cats than dogs.

Your friends will tell you that they are sincere; your enemies are really so. Let your enemies' censure be like a bitter medicine, to be used as a means of self-knowledge.

A friend in need, as the saying goes, is rare. Nay, it is just the contrary; no sooner have you made a friend than he is in need, and asks you for a loan.

(*Translated by T. Bailey Saunders*)

ST. THOMAS MORE TO HIS WIFE, UPON LEARNING THAT HIS BARNS AND SOME OF THE BARNS OF HIS NEIGHBORS HAD BEEN BURNED DOWN

I pray you to make good ensearch what my poor neighbors have lost, and bid them take no thought therefore; for, if I should not leave myself a spoon, there shall be no neighbor of mine bear no loss by any chance happened in my house. I pray you be, with my children and your household, merry in God.

(1528)

"...an eternal example of a noble friendship."

THE FRIENDSHIP OF TWO GREAT MEN
George Henry Lewes

There are few nobler spectacles than the friendship of two great men; and the history of literature presents nothing comparable to the friendship of Goethe and Schiller. The friendship of Montaigne and Étienne de la Boétie was perhaps more passionate and entire: but it was the union of two kindred natures, which from the first moment discovered their affinity; not the union of two rivals, incessantly contrasted by partisans, and originally disposed to hold aloof from each other. Rivals Goethe and Schiller were and are; natures in many respects directly antagonistic; chiefs of opposing camps, and brought into brotherly union only by what was highest in their nature and their aims.

To look on these great rivals was to see at once their profound dissimilarity. Goethe's beautiful head had the calm victorious grandeur of the Greek ideal; Schiller's the earnest beauty of a Christian looking towards the future. The massive brow and large-pupiled eyes,—like those given by Raphael to the infant-Christ, in the matchless Madonna di San Sisto; the strong and well-proportioned features, lined indeed by thought and suffering, which have troubled but not vanquished the strong man; a certain healthy vigor in the brown skin,—make Goethe a striking contrast to Schiller, with his eager eyes, narrow brow, tense and intense; his irregular features, worn by thought and suffering and weakened by sickness. The one *looks,* the other *looks out.* Both are majestic; but one has the majesty of repose, the other of conflict. . . .

In comparing one to a Greek ideal, the other to a Christian ideal, it has already been implied that one was the representative of realism, the other of idealism. Goethe has himself indicated the capital distinction between them: Schiller was animated with the idea of freedom; Goethe, on the contrary, was animated with the idea of nature. This distinction runs through their works: Schiller always pining for something greater than nature, wishing to make men demigods; Goethe always striving to let nature have free development, and produce the highest forms of humanity. . . .

Goethe and Schiller were certainly different natures; but had they been so fundamentally opposed as it is the fashion to consider them, they could never have become so intimately united. . . . It will be unnecessary to instance the obvious points which two such poets must have had in common; the mention of some less obvious will suffice for our present purpose. They were both profoundly convinced that art was no luxury of leisure,—no mere amusement to charm the idle or relax the careworn,—but a mighty influence, serious in its aims although pleasurable in its means; a sister of religion, by whose aid the great world-scheme was wrought into reality. This was with them no mere sonorous phrase. They were thoroughly in earnest. They believed that culture would raise humanity to its full powers; and they, as artists, knew no culture equal to that of art. . . .

At the time, then, that these two men seemed most opposed to each other, and *were* opposed in feeling, they were gradually drawing closer and closer in the very lines of their development, and a firm basis was prepared for solid and enduring union. Goethe was forty-five, Schiller five and thirty. Goethe had much to give which Schiller gratefully accepted; and if he could not in return influence the developed mind of his great friend, nor add to the vast stores of its knowledge and experience, he could give him that which was even more valuable, *sympathy* and *impulse.* He excited Goethe to work. He withdrew him from the engrossing pursuit of science, and restored him once more to poetry. He urged him to finish what was already commenced, and not to leave his works all fragments. They worked together with the same purpose and with the same earnestness; and their union is the most glorious episode in the lives of both, and remains as an eternal example of a noble friendship.

Of all the tributes to Schiller's greatness which an enthusiastic people has pronounced, there is perhaps nothing which carries a greater weight of tenderness and authority than Goethe's noble praise.

"The friendship ... met with no diminution ..."

GEORGE WASHINGTON RESPECTS THE CONTRARY POLITICAL CONVICTIONS OF HIS FRIEND AND NEIGHBOR, BRYAN FAIRFAX, WHO REMAINED A SUPPORTER OF THE BRITISH

VALLEY FORGE, March 1, 1778

The friendship which I ever professed and felt for you, met with no diminution from the difference in our political sentiments. I know the rectitude of my own intentions, and believing in the sincerity of yours, lamented, though I did not condemn, your renunciation of the creed which I had adopted. Nor do I think any person or power ought to do it, whilst your conduct is not opposed to the general interest of the people and the measures they are pursuing; the latter, that is our actions, depending upon ourselves, may be controlled; while the powers of thinking, originating in higher causes cannot always be moulded to our wishes.

"... if any friend desire thee to be his surety ..."

SIR WALTER RALEIGH TO HIS SON

Above all things, be not made an ass to carry the burdens of other men: if any friend desire thee to be his surety, give him a part of what thou hast to spare; if he presses thee further, he is not thy friend at all, for friendship rather chooseth harm to itself than offereth it. If thou be bound for a stranger, thou art a fool; if for a merchant, thou puttest thy estate to learn to swim; if for a churchman, he hath no inheritance;

if for a lawyer, he will find an invasion by a syllable or word to abuse thee; if for a poor man, thou must pay it thyself; if for a rich man, he needs not: therefore from suretyship, as from a manslayer or enchanter, bless thyself; for the best profit and return will be this, that if thou force him for whom thou art bound, to pay it himself, he will become thy enemy; if thou use to pay it thyself, thou wilt be a beggar.

PARTING

Coventry Patmore

If thou dost bid thy friend farewell,
But for one night though that farewell may be,
Press thou his hand in thine.
How canst thou tell how far from thee
Fate or caprice may lead his steps ere that tomorrow comes?
Men have been known to lightly turn the corner of a street,
And days have grown to months, and months to lagging years,
Ere they have looked in loving eyes again.
Parting, at best, is underlaid
With tears and pain.
Therefore, lest sudden death should come between,
Or time, or distance, clasp with pressure firm
The hand of him who goeth forth;
Unseen, Fate goeth too.
Yes, find thou always time to say some earnest word
Between the idle talk,
Lest with thee henceforth,
Night and day, regret should walk.

A slender acquaintance with the world must convince every man that actions, not words, are the true criterion of the attachment of friends; and that the most liberal professions of good-will are very far from being the surest marks of it.

—George Washington

"... a woman friend always desires to be proud of you."

THE VALUE OF A WOMAN'S FRIENDSHIP

Sir Edward Bulwer-Lytton

It is a wonderful advantage to a man, in every pursuit or avocation, to secure an adviser in a sensible woman. In woman there is at once a subtile delicacy of tact, and a plain soundness of judgment, which are rarely combined to an equal degree in man. A woman, if she be really your friend, will have a sensitive regard for your character, honor, repute. She will seldom counsel you to do a shabby thing; for a woman friend always desires to be proud of you. At the same time, her constitutional timidity makes her more cautious than your male friend. She, therefore, seldom counsels you to do an imprudent thing. By friendships, I mean pure friendships,— those in which there is no admixture of the passion of love, except in the married state. A man's best female friend is a wife of good sense and good heart, whom he loves, and who loves him. If he have that, he need not seek elsewhere. But suppose the man to be without such a helpmate, female friendship he must have, or his intellect will be without a garden, and there will be many an unheeded gap even in its strongest fence.

Better and safer, of course, are such friendships, where disparities of years or circumstances put the idea of love out of the question. Middle life has rarely this advantage: youth and age have. Molière's old housekeeper was a great help to his genius; and Montaigne's philosophy takes both a gentler and loftier character of wisdom from the date in which he finds, in Marie de Gournay, an adopted daughter.

"... let my father seek another heir."

ROSALIND AND CELIA

William Shakespeare

CELIA:— I pray thee, sweet my coz, be merry.
ROSALIND:— Dear Celia, I show more mirth than I am mistress of; and would you yet I were merrier? Unless you could teach me to forget

a vanished father, you must not learn me how to remember any extraordinary pleasure.

CELIA:— Herein I see thou lovest me not with the full weight that I love thee. If my uncle, thy vanished father, had banished thy uncle, the Duke my father, so thou hadst been still with me, I could have taught my love to take thy father for mine: so wouldst thou, if the truth of thy love to me were so righteously tempered as mine is to thee.

ROSALIND:— Well, I will forget the condition of my estate, to rejoice in yours.

CELIA:— You know my father hath no child but I, nor none is like to have: and, truly, when he dies, thou shalt be his heir; for what he hath taken away from thy father perforce, I will render thee again in affection; by mine honour, I will; and when I break that oath, let me turn monster: therefore, my sweet Rose, my dear Rose, be merry.

ROSALIND:— From henceforth I will, coz....

DUKE FREDERICK:— Mistress, dispatch you with your safest haste
And get you from my court.

ROSALIND:— Me, uncle?

DUKE FREDERICK:—   You, cousin:
Within these ten days if that thou be'st found
So near the public court as twenty miles,
Thou diest for it....
Let it suffice thee that I trust thee not....

CELIA:— Dear sovereign, hear me speak.

DUKE FREDERICK:— Ay, Celia; we stay'd her for your sake,
Else she had with her father ranged along.

CELIA:— I did not then entreat to have her stay;
It was your pleasure and your own remorse:
I was too young that time to value her;
But now I know her: if she be a traitor,
Why so am I; we still have slept together,
Rose at an instant, learn'd, play'd, eat together,
And whersoe'er we went, like Juno's swans,
Still we went coupled and inseparable.

DUKE FREDERICK:— She is too subtle for thee; and her smoothness,
Her very silence and her patience
Speak to the people, and they pity her.
Thou art a fool: she robs thee of thy name;
And thou wilt show more bright and seem more virtuous
When she is gone. Then open not thy lips:
Firm and irrevocable is my doom
Which I have pass'd upon her; she is vanish'd.

CELIA:— Pronounce that sentence then on me, my liege:

I cannot live out of her company.

DUKE FREDERICK:— You are a fool. You, niece, provide yourself:
If you outstay the time, upon mine honour,
And in the greatness of my word, you die.

CELIA:— O my poor Rosalind, whither wilt thou go?
Wilt thou change fathers? I will give thee mine.
I charge thee, be not thou more grieved than I am.

ROSALIND:— I have more cause.

CELIA:— Thou hast not, cousin;
Prithee, be cheerful: know'st thou not, the Duke
Hath banish'd me, his daughter?

ROSALIND:— That he hath not.

CELIA:— No, hath not? Rosalind lacks then the love
Which teacheth thee that thou and I am one:
Shall we be sunder'd? shall we part, sweet girl?
No: let my father seek another heir.
Therefore devise with me how we may fly,
Whither to go and what to bear with us;
And do not seek to take your change upon you,
To bear your griefs yourself and leave me out;
For, by this heaven, now at our sorrows pale,
Say what thou canst, I'll go along with thee.

"Fill their lives with sweetness."

HONOR YOUR FRIENDS WHILE LIVING

George W. Childs

Do not keep the alabaster box of your love and tenderness sealed up until your friends are dead. Fill their lives with sweetness. Speak approving, cheering words while their ears can hear them, and while their hearts can be thrilled and made happier. The kind things you mean to say when they are gone, say before they go. The flowers you mean to send for their coffin, send to brighten and sweeten their homes before they leave them. If my friends have alabaster boxes laid away, full of fragrant perfumes of sympathy and affection, which they intend to break over my body, I would rather they bring them out in my weary and troubled hours and open them, that I may be refreshed and cheered while I need them. I would rather have a plain coffin without

flowers, a funeral without a eulogy, than a life without the sweetness
and love emanating from sympathy. Let us learn to anoint our friends
while they are yet among the living. Post mortem kindness does not
cheer the burdened heart; flowers on the coffin cast no fragrance over
the weary way.

RETIREMENT

William Cowper

I praise the Frenchman, his remark was shrewd,
How sweet, how passing sweet is solitude!
But grant me still a friend in my retreat,
Whom I may whisper, Solitude is sweet.

"... I shall thank you for giving me the opinion of the world ..."

GEORGE WASHINGTON IS GRATEFUL FOR CRITICISM

*(To Colonel Joseph Reed, who wrote Washington frankly regarding
censures passed upon his generalship.)*

Headquarters, Cambridge
January 14, 1776

The hints you have communicated from time to time not only deserve, but do most sincerely and cordially meet with my thanks. You
cannot render a more acceptable service, nor in my estimation give a
more convincing proof of your friendship, than by a free, open, and
undisguised account of every matter relative to myself or conduct. The
man who wishes to stand well in the opinion of others must do this;
because he is thereby enabled to correct his faults, or remove prejudices
which are imbibed against him. For this reason, I shall thank you for
giving me the opinion of the world upon such points as you know me
to be interested in; for, as I have but one capital object in view, I could
wish to make my conduct coincide with the wishes of mankind, as far
as I can consistently, I mean without departing from that great line of
duty.

ON THE HON. SIMON HARCOURT
Only Son of the Lord Chancellor Harcourt
Alexander Pope

To this sad shrine, whoe'er thou art! draw near;
Here lies the Friend most lov'd, the Son most dear;
Who ne'er knew Joy, but Friendship might divide,
Or gave his Father Grief but when he died.
How vain in Reason, Eloquence how weak!
If *Pope* must tell what HARCOURT cannot speak.
Oh let thy once-lov'd Friend inscribe thy Stone,
And, with a Father's sorrows, mix his own!

＊＊＊＊＊＊＊

"... there must be some solid basis for an abiding interest ..."

REQUISITES FOR HIGH FRIENDSHIP
Henry Churchill King

For a significant friendship, besides integrity and spirit, there must
be breadth of personality. Man is a many-sided creature—marked off
from the animal world, for one thing, by the greater multitude of his
instincts, and the multiplicity of his esthetic and practical interests. It
is both a psychological and physiological commonplace, but its suggestion for friendship is all too little heeded. Any refusal by a man to
recognize this broad complexity of his life must narrow every personal
relation. For the simple fact is, that the man who means to bring a
large, a sane, a free, or an influential personality to his friend must
have breadth of interests; for every one of these qualities depends on
such a wide range of interests, and one must wish the same thing for
his friend as well. There must be room for the most varied inter-play
of mind on mind, if a friendship is to be persistently interesting and
stimulating.

To secure such a store of permanent and valuable interests has been
truly called one of the main aims of education; it is, not less, one of
the largest material factors in a rewarding friendship. The man, therefore, who means to be all a friend should be, will recognize the plain

duty of steady growth. And many friendships break down just at this point. There has been no earnest effort to retain an interesting personality. One needs seriously to ask himself: Am I here making it certain that I deserve this high friendship? For if friendships are to abide, there must be some solid basis for an abiding interest; and few of us have such native gifts as can warrant any neglect of steady culture in some form, that shall insure a breadth of personality that may count in friendship. And then we are to make it count....

Even the most ideal interests, it should be noticed, lose by lack of vision, by any attempted isolation in the spirit of exclusiveness. Our highest aims, including those of friendship, gain by wide and varied application. Only so can they be significant and dominant in the whole life. High intention is not enough. If we wish, therefore, the highest in us greatly to count in our friendship with another, we may not ignore the breadth either of his nature or our own; and we must see that no single finite relationship, however precious, can call us out on every side. And that will mean at once that a narrow and selfish jealousy, that would limit my friend to his sole relationship to me, is the blindest folly for us both. Certain relations, of course, have a unique quality that cannot be shared without spoiling them. But that does not at all shut out other friendships of another kind....

And there must be depth of personality, some sense of the deep and steadily deepening significance of life, through which alone the golden rule grows with the years. For where one's own self has revealed depths unplumbed, and one's own demands upon life have continuously increased, there the recognized debt to the other has grown correspondingly. Character can else hardly gain profoundness at all....

This sense of the meaning of life has no place for that indifferent, falsely tolerant folly that puts all value on a dead level—that knows no high resolves, no burning enthusiasms, no hot indignations.... Nothing makes more impossible a genuinely significant friendship than the lackadaisical indifference that finds no heights and depths anywhere, that returns the same response of spirit to each appeal, trivial or exalted....

It is not enough that my friend should be interested in many things. His breadth must be *discriminating* breadth. He must see how deeply significant certain interests are. He must have power of selection and of emphasis. He must see things in their true proportions and care greatly for the great things, and take on greatly great purposes. He must have worked up to the deep meaning of human life.... And this that I demand from my friend he must demand from me in like manner.

No high friendship is possible on lower terms. It is here that the sometimes broadly educated "man of the world" often so grievously fails. It is simply not in him to give a deep response in friendship. He believes in nothing very much, not much in men, not much in friendship.

Now it is precisely at this point above all that religion has its great contribution to make. The great fundamental conviction that gives undying meaning to life belongs to it. It feels the greatness of man and of his destiny—a destiny that means no less than that in endless development one may share in the life of God Himself. The very possibility of friendship with God transfigures life. The religious convictions, thus, tend inevitably to deepen every human friendship, to make it vastly more significant. And it is difficult to see how, apart from these great religious convictions, a friendship can come to its best. If I cannot believe that my friend has within him "the power of the endless life," and that he is by very nature a child of God, of priceless value in the sight of God, the meaning of my friendship is vastly changed.

TO THOMAS MOORE

Lord Byron

My boat is on the shore,
   And my bark is on the sea;
But, before I go, Tom Moore,
   Here's a double health to thee!

Here's a sigh to those who love me,
   And a smile to those who hate;
And, whatever sky's above me,
   Here's a heart for every fate.

Though the ocean roar around me,
   Yet it still shall bear me on;
Though a desert should surround me,
   It hath springs that may be won.

Were the last drop in the well,
   As I gasp'd upon the brink,
Ere my fainting spirit fell,
   'Tis to thee that I would drink.

With what water, as this wine,
The libation I would pour
Should be—Peace with thine and mine
And a health to thee, Tom Moore.

"It has never been my fortune to meet with him since . . ."

SHELLEY RELATES HIS FIRST FRIENDSHIP

I remember forming an attachment of this kind at school. I cannot recall to my memory the precise epoch at which this took place; but I imagine it must have been at the age of eleven or twelve. The object of these sentiments was a boy about my own age, of a character eminently generous, brave and gentle, and the elements of human feeling seemed to have been, from his birth, genially compounded within him. There was a delicacy and a simplicity in his manners, inexpressibly attractive. It has never been my fortune to meet with him since my schoolboy days; but either I confound my present recollections with the delusions of past feelings, or he is now a source of honor and utility to everyone around him. The tones of his voice were so soft and winning, that every word pierced into my heart; and their pathos was so deep that in listening to him the tears have involuntarily gushed from my eyes. Such was the being for whom I first experienced the sacred sentiments of friendship.

"I've always known I was missing a great deal . . ."

YOU WON'T BE SNUBBED
Henry Morton Robinson

Around me, a bright-mufflered throng of winter-sports enthusiasts loafed in the white Adirondack sunshine. Lean ski jumpers puffed at blunt brown pipes; bobsledders tossed challenges and snowballs at each other; wind-burned debutantes basked in deck chairs. The thin northern air crackled with frost and gaiety; everyone was having fun.

That is, everyone but me. The deck chair beside me was vacant, yet no one sat down in it. For years, no one ever *did* sit down by me voluntarily. For some reason I had always been unable to draw other human beings into warm personal contacts.

But the whole picture changed on that snow-brilliant day when David Jessup sat down in the deck chair beside me. I had particularly observed this man; it was a joy to watch him approach a stranger and melt the icy cellophane that most human beings come wrapped in. I envied him his easy approach to others, yet I would have gone to my grave (so stern were the proprieties of my New England upbringing) before speaking to him or any stranger first.

But evidently my high-fenced reserve was no barrier to Jessup, for he turned his friendly gray eyes on me, and smiled with genuine good nature. There were no inanities about the weather, no self-conscious preliminaries. Like a man imparting news of interest to an old friend, he said without tension or embarrassment: "I saw you watching that bronzed chap mending his snowshoes. He's the Rhodes Scholar from New York. He stroked the Cornell crew last year and was president of the debating club besides. Don't you think he's a splendid type to represent American youth at Oxford?"

Jessup's opening remarks led us at once into a discussion of Cecil Rhodes' dream of cementing Anglo-American friendship. From that take-off, our talk continued through many fields of common interest and special information. When we stopped an hour later we were friends. It was something of a miracle, and I asked Jessup point-blank how he did it.

"Your happy knack of speaking to strangers—how do you manage it? Personally, I'm limited to a small circle of friends, all of the same type. All my life I've wanted to mingle with strangers who could widen my interests and quicken my sense of being alive, yet I've always hung back, afraid of a rebuff. How does one overcome this fear of being snubbed?"

Jessup waved his hand inclusively at the throng around us. "My fear of being snubbed," he said, "completely disappears when I remember that the dearest friends I have were once strangers. If you approach your fellow man with honest sympathy and a desire to be humanly friendly, he is not likely to misread your motive. I have met men of the most formidable self-importance, and found them all responsive, eager to visit with me. Rarely have I encountered even the slightest hint of a snub. No, my friend, you mustn't let fear be the basis of your seclusion. The new, the unusual, is no more dangerous than the familiar, and it has the advantage of being decidedly more exciting."

Subsequent experiences with David Jessup proved how right he was. Wherever he went, he would enter into conversation with all manner of people, and was forever turning up strange new types and odd, stimulating information. On one of our trips together we passed a granite quarry in which a number of men were walking about on tiptoe, carrying red flags and acting like advance messengers of doom. Instead of hurrying past, Jessup spoke to one of the flag-carriers, and in a few moments the man was telling us a hair-curling story. It seems that many years ago engineers had drilled 50 holes in this quarry, packed the holes with dynamite, and wired them for a blast. But some of the wiring was defective, and only half of the dynamite exploded! For 20 years workmen could not be persuaded to go near the quarry; it was now being reopened by men who received double pay because of the attendant danger.

Another time, on the shore of a beautiful lake in a state park, Jessup noticed a man making sketches. Skillfully engaging the man in conversation, Jessup discovered that he was a marine horticulturist with a new idea called "pond-scaping." "On the lakes surrounding the ancient Aztec capital," said the sketcher, "were many floating islands covered with feathery trees and rare flowers. I believe that I have rediscovered how such islands can be constructed and kept in motion, and am now making some sketches to interest the park commission in my idea."

On the way home I remarked, "That was one of the most interesting things that ever happened to me. Both the man and his drawings were fascinating."

Jessup agreed, then added slyly: "And you would never have met him if you had waited for an introduction, would you?"

"Don't rub it in, please. I've always known that I was missing a great deal, but I never knew how to get people started."

"To talk to a stranger," advised Jessup, "begin with a remark that penetrates to the core of his interest. Usually it will be something that applies to his work. Inane general remarks or fussy little questions only irk the busy man. One must be genuinely interested in what the stranger is doing, make an intelligent comment, then wait for him to respond. And he *will* respond, for the simple reason that most human beings are overjoyed when another person shows interest in their work. Take that floating-garden chap: if we had seemed bored he wouldn't even have begun to talk, for no man likes to expose his treasures to the indifferent. But when he saw that we were really deriving pleasure from his conversation, he tried to reward our interest. Why should he do this? Simply because no one has ever yet discovered a keener happiness than giving pleasure to others."

I was always expecting Jessup to be snubbed, but the snub never came. Once a trio of noisy roughs boarded our bus and began to annoy the passengers with a display of downright coarseness. Dignified, serious, Jessup got up and went back to them. "Here," thought I, "my friend is riding for a fall." But I was wrong. What Jessup said to those fellows I never knew, but within five minutes he had engaged them in an earnest discussion of labor conditions throughout the country and their own chances of employment.

I've seen Jessup address women bred in the strictest code of convention, and wondered how he avoided being cut by them. He explained it in this way: "If in speaking to a woman you reveal that you are primarily interested in her personally or as a member of the opposite sex, she will instantly resent it, as she has every right to do. In effect, you are insulting her by the assumption that her attention may be so cheaply won. But speak to her as one human being to another, as one interested in the same scenery, the same music, or the same social problems, and she will extend her ready fellowship. Both men and women love to use their minds, and women especially regard it as a distinct compliment to be met on the intellectual plane common to both sexes."

Since knowing David Jessup, the stranger at my elbow has become the most interesting and approachable thing in life. And I know if I approach him unaffectedly there is no danger of being snubbed.

For ultimately we are not so different from one another. Training and tradition may have cast us in dissimilar molds, but the basic stuff of our humanity is pathetically the same. It is this realization that now makes every stranger accessible to me. He may be a barber or a banknote-engraver, but it is almost certain that he can tell me something that will heighten my mental stature or increase my spiritual gauge. I may like him or I may not; if he bores me, I can be off. But the thing that constantly surprises me is the scarcity of people who are really boresome or offensive. By far the larger part of our human race is composed of interesting and friendly members, all eager to know each other. And I have yet to see the person who did not become more attractive and more alive for laying aside his too-prized reserve and mingling on equal terms with other members of our common, struggling, hungering human family.

MEMORIES

Henry Wadsworth Longfellow

Oft I remember those whom I have known
    In other days, to whom my heart was led
    As by a magnet, and who are not dead,
    But absent, and their memories overgrown

With other thoughts and troubles of my own,
   As graves with grasses are, and at their head
   The stone with moss and lichens so o'erspread,
   Nothing is legible but the name alone.
And is it so with them? After long years,
   Do they remember me in the same way,
   And is the memory pleasant as to me?
I fear to ask; yet wherefore are my fears?
   Pleasures, like flowers, may wither and decay,
   And yet the root perennial may be.

"... we love our friend because he is like ourselves ..."

CHARLES LAMB TO ROBERT LLOYD

October 1798

My dear Robert—Mary is better, and I trust that she will yet be restored to me. I am in good spirits, so do not be anxious about me. I hope
you get reconciled to your situation. The worst in it is that you have
no *friend* to talk to—but wait in patience, and you will in good time
make friends. The having a friend is not indispensably necessary to
virtue or happiness. Religion removes those barriers of sentiment which
partition us from the disinterested love of our brethren—we are commanded to love our enemies, to do good to those that hate us; how
much more is it our duty then to cultivate a forbearance and compla-
cence towards those who only differ from us in dispositions and ways
of thinking? There is always, without very unusual care there must
always be, something of Self in friendship; we love our friend because
he is like ourselves; can consequences altogether unmix'd and pure be
reasonably expected from such a source—do not even the publicans and
sinners the same? Say, that you love a friend for his moral qualities, is
it not rather because those qualities resemble what you fancy your own?
This, then, is not without danger. The only true cement of a valuable
friendship, the only thing that even makes it not sinful, is when two
friends propose to become mutually of benefit to each other in a moral
or religious way. But even this friendship is perpetually liable to the
mixture of something not pure; we love our friend, because he is *ours*
—so we do our money, our wit, our knowledge, our virtue; and wherever this sense of APPROPRIATION and PROPERTY enters, so much is to be
subtracted from the value of that friendship or that virtue. Our duties

are to do good, expecting nothing again; to bear with contrary dispositions; to be candid and forgiving, not to crave and long after a communication of sentiment and feeling, but rather to avoid dwelling upon
those feelings, however good, because they are our own. A man may be
intemperate and selfish who indulges in *good feelings* for the mere
pleasure they give him. I do not wish to deter you from making a friend,
a true friend, and such a friendship, where the parties are not blind to
each other's faults, is very useful and valuable. I perceive a tendency in
you to this error, Robert. I know you have chosen to take up an high
opinion of my moral worth, but I say it before God, and I do not lie,
you are mistaken in me. I could not bear to lay open all my failings to
you, for the sentiment of shame would be too pungent. Let this be as an
example to you. Robert, friends fall off, friends mistake us, they change,
they grow unlike us, they go away, they die; but God is everlasting and
incapable of change, and to Him we may look with cheerful, unpre-
sumptuous hope, while we discharge the duties of life in situations
more untowardly than yours.

FROM "THE COURTSHIP OF MILES STANDISH"

Henry Wadsworth Longfellow

Then John Alden spake, and related the wondrous adventure,
From beginning to end, minutely, just as it happened:
How he had seen Priscilla, and how he had sped in his courtship, .
Only smoothing a little, and softening down her refusal.
But when he came at length to the words Priscilla had spoken,
Words so tender and cruel: "Why don't you speak for yourself, John?"
Up leaped the Captain of Plymouth, and stamped on the floor, till his
 armor
Clanged on the wall, where it hung, with a sound of sinister omen.
All his pent-up wrath burst forth in a sudden explosion,
E'en as a hand-grenade, that scatters destruction around it.
Wildly he shouted, and loud: "John Alden! you have betrayed me!
One of my ancestors ran his sword through the heart of Wat Tyler;
Who shall prevent me from running my own through the heart of a
 traitor?
Yours is the greater treason, for yours is a treason to friendship!
You, who lived under my roof, whom I cherished and loved as a
 brother;

You, who have fed at my board, and drunk at my cup, to whose
    keeping
I have intrusted my honor, my thoughts the most sacred and secret,—
You too, Brutus! ah woe to the name of friendship hereafter!
Brutus was Caesar's friend, and you were mine, but henceforward
Let there be nothing between us save war, and implacable hatred!"

So spake the Captain of Plymouth, and strode about in the chamber,
Chafing and choking with rage; like cords were the veins on his
    temples.
But in the midst of his anger a man appeared at the doorway,
Bringing in uttermost haste a message of urgent importance,
Rumors of danger and war and hostile incursions of Indians!
Straightway the Captain paused, and, without further question or
    parley
Took from the nail on the wall his sword with its scabbard of iron,
Buckled the belt round his waist, and, frowning fiercely, departed....

Mute and amazed was Alden: and listened and looked at Priscilla,
Thinking he never had seen her more fair, more divine in her beauty.
He who but yesterday pleaded so glibly the cause of another,
Stood there embarrassed and silent, and seeking in vain for an answer.
So the maiden went on, and little divined or imagined
What was at work in his heart, that made him so awkward and
    speechless.
"Let us, then, be what we are, and speak what we think, and in all
    things
Keep ourselves loyal to truth, and the sacred professions of friendship.
It is no secret I tell you, nor am I ashamed to declare it:
I have liked to be with you, to see you, to speak with you always.
So I was hurt at your words, and a little affronted to hear you
Urge me to marry your friend, though he were the Captain Miles
    Standish.
For I must tell you the truth: much more to me is your friendship
Than all the love he could give, were he twice the hero you think him."
Then she extended her hand, and Alden, who eagerly grasped it,
Felt all the wounds in his heart, that were aching and bleeding so sorely,
Healed by the touch of that hand, and he said, with a voice full of
    feeling:
"Yes, we must ever be friends; and of all who offer you friendship
Let me ever be the first, the truest, the nearest and dearest! ..."

This was the wedding morn of Priscilla the Puritan maiden.
Friends were assembled together; the Elder and Magistrate also

Graced the scene with their presence, and stood like the Law and the
  Gospel.
One with the sanction of earth and one with the blessing of heaven.
Simple and brief was the wedding, as that of Ruth and of Boaz.
Softly the youth and the maiden repeated the words of betrothal,
Taking each other for husband and wife in the Magistrate's presence,
After the Puritan way, and the laudable custom of Holland.
Fervently then, and devoutly, the excellent Elder of Plymouth
Prayed for the hearth and the home, that were founded that day in
  affection,
Speaking of life and of death, and imploring Divine benedictions.

Lo! when the service was ended, a form appeared on the threshold,
Clad in armor of steel, a sombre and sorrowful figure!
Why does the bridegroom start and stare at the strange apparition?
Why does the bride turn pale, and hide her face on his shoulder?
Is it a phantom of air,—a bodiless, spectral illusion?
Is it a ghost from the grave, that has come to forbid the betrothal?
Long had it stood there unseen, a guest uninvited, unwelcomed;
Over its clouded eyes there had passed at times an expression
Softening the gloom and revealing the warm heart hidden beneath
  them,
As when across the sky the driving rack of the rain-cloud
Grows for a moment thin, and betrays the sun by its brightness.
Once it had lifted its hand, and moved its lips, but was silent,
As if an iron will had mastered the fleeting intention.
But when were ended the troth and the prayer and the last benediction,
Into the room it strode, and the people beheld with amazement
Bodily there in his armor Miles Standish, the Captain of Plymouth!
Grasping the bridegroom's hand, he said with emotion, "Forgive me!
I have been angry and hurt,—too long have I cherished the feeling;
I have been cruel and hard, but now, thank God! it is ended.
Mine is the same hot blood that leaped in the veins of Hugh Standish,
Sensitive, swift to resent, but as swift in atoning for error.
Never so much as now was Miles Standish the friend of John Alden."
Thereupon answered the bridegroom: "Let all be forgotten between
  us,—
All save the dear old friendship, and that shall grow older and dearer!"
Then the Captain advanced, and, bowing, saluted Priscilla,
Gravely, and after the manner of old-fashioned gentry in England,
Something of camp and of court, of town and of country, commingled,
Wishing her joy of her wedding, and loudly lauding her husband.

"... the sense of old fellowship ..."

PRAYER FOR FELLOWSHIP

Robert Louis Stevenson

God, who hast given us the love of women and the friendship of men, keep alive in our hearts the sense of old fellowship and tenderness; make offenses to be forgotten and services remembered; protect those whom we love in all things and follow them with kindnesses, so that they may lead simple and unsuffering lives and in the end die easily with quiet minds.

"May our temporary estrangement be for ever effaced ..."

LUDWIG VAN BEETHOVEN TO STEPHAN V. BRUENING

My dear and much loved Stephan:

May our temporary estrangement be for ever effaced by the portrait I now send. I know that I have rent your heart. The emotion which you cannot fail now to see in mine has sufficiently punished me for it. There was no malice towards you in my heart, for then I should no longer be worthy of your friendship. It was *passion* both on *your* part and on *mine;* but mistrust was rife within me, for people had come between us, unworthy both of *you* and of *me.*

My portrait was long ago intended for you; you knew that it was destined for some one—and to whom could I give it with such warmth of heart, as to you, my faithful, good, and noble Stephan?

Forgive me for having grieved you, but I did not myself suffer less when I no longer saw you near me. I then first keenly felt how dear you were, and ever will be to my heart. Surely you will once more fly to my arms as you formerly did.

MAY AND DEATH
Robert Browning

I wish that when you died last May,
　Charles, there had died along with you
Three parts of Spring's delightful things:
　Ay, and, for me, the fourth part too.

A foolish thought, and worse, perhaps!
　There must be many pairs of friends
Who, arm in arm, deserve the warm
　Moon-births and the long evening-ends.

So, for their sake, be May still May!
　Let their new time, as mine of old,
Do all it did for me: I bid
　Sweet sights and sounds throng manifold,

Only, one little sight, one plant,
　Woods have in May, that starts up green
Save a sole streak which, so to speak,
　Is Spring's blood, split its leaves between,—

That, they might spare; a certain wood
　Might miss the plant; their loss were small:
But I,—whene'er the leaf grows there,
　Its drop comes from my heart, that's all.

"A friend must be a creator and renew us often . . ."

THE RELIGION OF FRIENDSHIP
Bronson Alcott

Friendship is the only religion possible to moderns. Our God is a domestic God, and that fine sentiment which binds persons to each other is the only piety practical and efficient....

We must treat our friends as we do pictures and statuary—survey them from the perspectives of an affectionate idealism, or we get nothing out of this enterprise of friendship. A friend must be a creator and renew us often, to win and keep us.

I know of but one soul that can draw me near and make it necessary, in some sense, to abide in his neighborhood. And this emotion of the mind which I call friendship is the nearest that I have attained as yet to what men call religion, if it be not one with that venerable sentiment of the preference of the Deity. It is only in the ebullience of love and genius that we snatch the new delights and discover first the brilliancy of the dove's neck.... Pure intimacies are illustrious, like the reflection of oceans and of firmaments. Introduce me to him, if you have found him, who casts pearls from his lips as stars ray forth from their centers.

For disputations, crowds; for rumination, woods; closets for thought; and for discourse, a single friend....

We conversed all day and late again on the old themes. Toward night we walked to Walden Water and by Thoreau's hermitage.... Concord is classic land; for here dwell the poets, the Americans *par excellence* and men of the future, whose names shall render Harvard and Yale, with their professors and halls, one day ridiculous. The names of Emerson and Thoreau and Channing and Hawthorne are associated with the fields and forests and lakes and rivers of this township, and here still reside the three first-named of them.... And 'tis at heart my own home. I must draw me closer to its bosom and my friends one day, for the cities cannot detain me long....

I am the richest of all men in this Commonwealth, I sometimes think, in possessing these friends of mine. I esteem them as the victories of my life. They are country and countrymen. They are lives and places and times, and stand for thoughts and things perennial and enduring....

Evening, take tea with Emerson and renew the pleasures of our early fellowship in a free and affectionate conversation, returning at near 11. Such interviews revive past delights and prefigure future ones. Of human fellowships this, opening at a fair period of our lives and continued by choice husbanding of sentiment, meeting only when fellowship was spontaneous and for the most part a surprise to both, is an experience to cherish in the memory and possession forever. Rhetoric fails to celebrate it. Better cherish as a sweet and silent joy, diffusing itself over the countenance and telling better than words can speak of its own preciousness. If religion be other than Personal and one with the purest friendship, I must affirm that it is yet a stranger in my breast and I am without a God to love, reverence, and experience. "When shall we meet again? Where?"—are questions religion never puts to the heart, since friends divinely related never know separation.

A Broadway Friendship Without an Angle

FOR A PAL *
Damon Runyon

For a matter of maybe fifteen years or more, Little Yid and Blind Benny are pals, and this is considered a very good thing for Benny because he is as blind as a bat, and maybe blinder, while Yid can see as good as anybody and sometimes better.

So Little Yid does the seeing for Benny, explaining in his own way to Benny just what he sees, such as a race horse or a baseball game or a prize fight or a play or a moving picture or anything else, for Yid and Benny are great hands for going around and about wherever anything is coming off, no matter what, and up to the time this doll Mary Marble comes into their lives they are as happy as two pups in a basket.

How Benny comes to go blind I do not know, and nobody else along Broadway seems to know either, and in fact nobody cares, although I once hear Regret, the horse player, say it is probably in sympathy with the judges at the race track, Regret being such a guy as claims all these judges are very blind indeed. But of course Regret is sore at these race-track judges because they always call the wrong horse for him in the close finishes.

Little Yid tells me that Blind Benny is once a stick man in a gambling joint in Denver, and a very good stick man, at that, and one night a fire comes off in a flop house on Larimer Street, and Blind Benny, who is not blind at this time, runs into the fire to haul out an old guy who has more smoke in him than somewhat, and a rush of flames burns Benny's eyes so bad he loses his sight.

Well, this may be the true story of how Benny comes to go blind, but I know Little Yid likes Benny so much that he is not going to give Benny the worst of any story he tells about him, and for all anybody knows maybe Benny really goes into the fire to search for the old guy. Personally, I do not believe in taking too much stock in any story you hear on Broadway about anything.

But there is no doubt about Blind Benny being blind. His eyelids are tacked down tight over his eyes, and there is no chance that he is faking, because many guys keep close tabs on him for years and never catch him peeping once. Furthermore, several guys send Benny to eye specialists at different times to see if they can do anything about his eyes,

* From *Blue Blate Special* by Damon Runyon. Copyright 1929, 1930, 1931 by Damon Runyon. Published by J. B. Lippincott Company.

and all these specialists say he is one of the blindest guys they ever examine. Regret says maybe it is a good thing, at that, because Benny is so smart as a blind guy that the chances are if he can see he will be too smart to live.

He is especially smart when it comes to playing such games as pinochle. In fact, Benny is about as good a single-handed pinochle player as there is in town, and there are many first-rate pinochle players in this town, if anybody asks you. Benny punches little holes in the cards so he can tell which is which by feeling of them, and the only way anybody can beat him is to cheat him, and it is considered most discourteous to cheat a blind guy, especially as Benny is always apt to catch a guy at cheating and put up an awful beef.

He is a tall, skinny guy with a thin face, and is by no means bad-looking, while Little Yid is about knee high to a snake, and they look like a father and his little boy as they go along the street with Little Yid hanging onto Blind Benny's arm and giving him the right steer.

Of course it is by no means an uncommon thing on Broadway for citizens to come upon blind guys waiting at a corner for traffic to stop, and for the citizens to steer these blind guys across the street, although if the blind guys have any sense they will keep their dukes on their tin cups while they are being steered, but it is a most unusual proposition in this town for anybody to go steering a blind guy around for fifteen years the way Little Yid steers Blind Benny, as Blind Benny is a guy who takes plenty of steering.

In fact, one time Yid has to be away on business for a week, and he leaves Blind Benny with a committee of guys, and every day one of these guys has to steer Benny around wherever he wishes to go, which is wherever there is anything going on, and Benny wears the whole committee plumb out before Yid gets back, as Benny is certainly a guy who likes to go around and about. Furthermore, he is so unhappy while Yid is away that he becomes a very great nuisance, because it seems that none of the committee can see things as good as Yid for him, or explain them so he can understand them.

Personally, I will not care to have Little Yid do my seeing for me, even if I am blind, because I listen to him, telling what he sees to Blind Benny many times, and it seems to me Little Yid is often somewhat cokeyed in his explanations.

Furthermore, I will hate to be explaining things to Blind Benny, because he is always arguing about what is taking place, and giving you his opinions of it, even though he cannot see. In fact, although he cannot see a lick, Blind Benny is freer with his opinions than guys who can see from here to Europe.

It is a very interesting sight to watch Little Yid and Blind Benny at the race track, for they are both great hands for playing the horses and, in fact, Benny is a better handicapper than a lot of guys who have two good eyes and a pair of spectacles to do their handicapping with.

At night they get the form sheet and sit up in their room with Yid reading off the past performances and the time trials, and all this and that, and with Blind Benny doping the horses from what Yid reads, and picking the ones he figures ought to win the next day. They always have a big argument over each horse, and Yid will tell Blind Benny he is a daffy to be picking whatever horse he picks, and Benny will tell Yid he is out of his mind to think anything else can beat this horse and they will holler and yell at each other for hours.

But they always wind up very friendly, and they always play the horse Benny picks, for Yid has much confidence in Benny's judgment, although he hollers and yells at him more than somewhat when one of his picks loses. They sit up in the grandstand during every race, and Yid will explain to Benny what is going on in the race, and generally he manages to mention that the horse they are betting on is right up there and going easy, even though it may be laying back of the nine ball, for Yid believes in making Benny feel good all the time.

But when a horse they are betting on is really in the running, especially in the stretch, Yid starts to root him home, and Benny roots right along with him as if he can see, and rocks back and forth in his seat, and pounds with his cane, and yells, "Come on with him, jock," the same as anybody with two good eyes.

I am telling you all this about Little Yid and Benny to show you that they are very close friends, indeed. They live together and eat together and argue together, and nobody ever hears of a nicer friendship on Broadway, although naturally some citizens figure for a while that one or the other must have some angle in their friendship, as it is practically uncanny for a friendship to last all these years on Broadway.

Blind Benny has some kind of an income from his people, and Little Yid has a piece of a small factory run by a couple of his brothers over in Hoboken where they make caps as some citizens wear on their heads, and it seems this factory does very well, and the brothers are willing to send Little Yid his piece without him being around the factory very much, as they do not seem to consider him any boost to a cap factory.

So Yid and Blind Benny have all the money they need to go along, what with making a little scratch now and then on the races, and they never seem to care for any company but their own and are very happy and contented with each other. In all the years they are together, Yid is never known to more than say hello to a doll, and of course Blind Benny cannot see dolls, anyway, which many citizens claim is a great break for Benny, so Yid and Benny are carrying no weight in this respect.

Now one night it seems that Ike Jacobs, the ticket spec, has a pair of

Chinee duckets to the opening of a new play by the name of Red Hot Love, a Chinee ducket being a complimentary ducket that is punched full of holes like Chinee money, and which you do not have to pay for, and Ike gives these duckets to Little Yid and Blind Benny, which is considered very large-hearted of Ike, at that.

So when the curtain goes up on Red Hot Love, Yid and Benny are squatted right down in front among many well-known citizens who are all dressed up in evening clothes, because this Red Hot Love has a bunch of swell actors in it, and is expected to be first class.

Naturally, when the play begins, Yid has to give Blind Benny a little information about what is doing, otherwise Benny cannot appreciate the thing. So Yid starts off in a whisper, but any time Yid starts explaining anything to Benny he always winds up getting excited, and talking so loud you can hear him down at the Battery.

Of course Blind Benny can follow a play as good as anybody, if there is plenty of gab on the stage, but he likes to know what actors are doing the gabbing, and what they look like, and what the scenery looks like, and other details that he cannot see, and Little Yid is telling him in such a voice as to cause some of the citizens around to say shush-shush. But Little Yid and Blind Benny are accustomed to being shushed in theaters, so they do not pay much attention.

Well, Red Hot Love is one of these problems plays, and neither Little Yid or Blind Benny can make much of it, although they are no worse off than anybody else around them, at that. But Little Yid tries to explain to Blind Benny what it is all about, and Benny speaks out loud as follows:

"It sounds to me like a rotten play."

"Well," Little Yid says, "maybe the play is not so rotten but the acting is."

There is much shushing from one and all around them, and the actors are giving them the bad eye from the stage, because the actors can hear what they say, and are very indignant, especially over this crack about the acting.

Well the next thing anybody knows down the aisle come a couple of big guys who put the arm on Little Yid and Blind Benny and give them the old heave-o out of the joint, as you are not supposed to speak out loud in a theater about any bad acting that is going on there, no matter how bad it is.

Anyway, as Little Yid and Blind Benny are being prodded up the aisle by the big guys, Blind Benny states as follows:

"I still claim," he says, "that it sounds like a rotten play."

"Well," Little Yid says, "the acting certainly is."

There is much applause as Yid and Benny are getting the heave-o, and many citizens claim it is because the customers are glad to see them heaved, but afterwards it comes out that what many of the customers are really applauding is the statements by Little Yid and Benny.

Well, Yid and Benny do not mind getting the heave-o so much, as they are heaved out of many better theaters than this in their time, but they are very indignant when the box office refuses to give them back their admission price, although of course their duckets do not cost them anything in the first place and they are a little out of line trying to collect.

They are standing on the sidewalk saying what an outrage it is when all of a sudden out of the theater pops this doll by the name of Mary Marble, and her face is very red, and she is also very indignant, because it seems that in the second act of the play there are some very coarse cracks let out on the stage, and it seems that Mary Marble is such a doll as believe that cracks of this nature are only fit for married people to hear, and she is by no means married.

Of course Little Yid and Blind Benny do not know at the time that she is Mary Marble, and in fact they do not know her from Adam's off ox as she marches up to them and speaks as follows:

"Gentlemen," she says, "I wish to compliment you on your judgment of the affair inside. I hear what you say as you are being ejected," she says, "and I wish to state that you are both right. It is a rotten play, and the acting is rotten."

Now off this meeting, what happens but Mary Marble gets to going around with Little Yid and Blind Benny whenever she can spare time from her job, which is managing a little joint on Broadway where they sell stockings such as dolls wear on their legs, except in summer time, although even when they wear these stockings you cannot tell if a doll has anything on her legs unless you pinch them, the stockings that dolls wear nowadays being very thin, indeed. Furthermore, whenever she is with them, it is now Mary Marble who does most of the explaining to Blind Benny of what is going on, because Mary Marble is such a doll as is naturally bound to do all the explaining necessary when she is around.

When it comes to looks, Mary Marble is practically no dice. In fact, if she is not the homeliest doll on Broadway, I will guarantee she is no worse than a dead heat with the homeliest. She has a large beezer and large feet, and her shape is nothing whatever to speak of, and Regret, the horse player, says they never need to be afraid of entering Mary Marble in a claiming race at any price. But of course Regret is such a guy as will not give you a counterfeit dime for any doll no matter what she looks like.

Mary Marble is maybe twenty-five years old—although Regret says he will lay six to five against her being any better than twenty-eight—and about all she has running for her, any way you take her, is a voice that is soft and gentle and very nice, indeed, except that she is fond of using it more than somewhat.

She comes from a little town over in Pennsylvania, and is pretty well educated, and there is no doubt whatever that she is unusually respectable, because such a looking doll as Mary Marble has no excuse for being anything but respectable on Broadway. In fact, Mary Marble is so respectable that many citizens figure there must be an angle, but it is agreed by one and all that she is perfectly safe with Little Yid and Blind Benny, no matter what.

And now at night instead of always doping the horses, Little Yid and Blind Benny will often sit up in their room talking about nothing much but Mary Marble, and Benny asks Yid a million questions over and over again.

"Tell me, Yid," Blind Benny will say, "what does Mary look like?"

"She is beautiful," Yid always says.

Well, of course, this is practically perjury, and many citizens figure that Yid tells Blind Benny this very large lie because he has an idea Benny wishes to hear only the very best about Mary Marble, although it comes out afterwards that Little Yid thinks that Mary Marble is beautiful, at that.

"She is like an angel," he says.

"Yes, yes," Blind Benny says, "tell me more."

And Little Yid keeps on telling him, and if Mary Marble is only one eight as good-looking as Yid tells, Ziegfeld and Georgie White and Earl Carroll will be breaking each other's legs trying to get to her first.

"Well," Blind Benny often says, after Little Yid gets through telling him about Mary Marble, "she is just as I picture her to myself, Yid," he says. "I never care so much about not being able to see until now, and even now all I wish to see is Mary."

The idea seems to be that Blind Benny is in love with Mary Marble, and the way Little Yid is always boosting her it is no wonder. In fact, the chances are a lot of other citizens will be in love with Mary Marble if they listen to Yid telling Blind Benny about her, and never get a gander at her personally.

But Blind Benny does not mention right out that he is in love with Mary Marble, and it may be that he does not really know what is eating him, which is often the case with guys who are in love. All Blind Benny knows is that he likes to be with Mary Marble and to listen to her explaining things to him, and, what is more, Mary Marble seems to like to be with Blind Benny, and to explain things to him, although as far as this goes Mary Marble is such a doll as likes to be explaining things to anybody any time she gets a chance.

Now Little Yid and Blind Benny are still an entry at all times, even when Mary Marble is with them, but many citizens see that Little Yid is getting all sorrowed up, and they figure it is because he feels Blind Benny is gradually drifting away from him after all these years, and everybody sympathizes with Little Yid no little, and there is some talk of getting him another blind guy to steer around in case Blind Benny finally leaves him for good.

Then it comes on a Saturday night when Little Yid says he must go over to Hoboken to see his brothers about the cap business and, as Mary Marble has to work in the stocking joint on Saturday nights, Little Yid asks Blind Benny to go with him.

Of course Blind Benny does not care two cents about the cap business, but Little Yid explains to him that he knows a Dutchman's in Hoboken where there is some very nice real beer, and if there is one thing Blind Benny likes more than somewhat it is nice real beer, especially as it seems since they became acquainted with Mary Marble he seldom gets nice real beer, as Mary Marble is a terrible knocker against such matters as nice real beer.

So they start out for Hoboken, and Little Yid sees his brothers about the cap business, and then he takes Blind Benny to a Dutchman's to get the nice real beer, only it turns out that the beer is not real, and by no means nice, being all needled up with alky, and full of headaches, and one thing and another. But of course Little Yid and Blind Benny are not going around complaining about beer even if it is needled, as, after all, needled beer is better than no beer whatever.

They sit around the Dutchman's quite a while, although it turns out that the Dutchman is nothing but a Polack, and then they nab a late ferryboat for home, as Little Yid says he wishes to ride on a ferryboat to get the breeze. As far as Blind Benny is concerned, he does not care how they go as long as he can get back to New York to meet up with Mary Marble when she is through work.

There are not many citizens on the ferryboat with them, because it is getting on toward midnight, and at such an hour anybody who lives in Jersey is home in bed. In fact, there are not over four or five other passengers on the ferryboat with Little Yid and Blind Benny, and these passengers are all dozing on the benches in the smoking-room with their legs stuck out in front of them.

Now if you know anything about a ferryboat you know that they always hook big gates across each end of such a boat to keep automobiles and trucks and citizens and one thing and another from going off these ends and into the water when the ferryboat is traveling back and forth, as naturally it will be a great nuisance to other boats in the river to have things falling off the ferryboats and clogging up the stream.

Well, Little Yid is away out on the end of the ferryboat up against the gate enjoying the breeze, and Blind Benny is leaning against the rail just outside the smoking-room door where Little Yid plants him when they get on the boat, and Blind Benny is smoking a big heater, that he gets at the Dutchman's and maybe thinking of Mary Marble, when all of a sudden Little Yid yells like this:

"Oh, Benny, come here."

Naturally Benny turns and goes in the direction of the voice and Little Yid's voice comes from the stern, and Blind Benny keeps following his beezer in the direction of the voice, expecting to feel Little Yid's hand stopping him any minute, and the next thing he knows he is walking right off the ferryboat into the river.

Of course Blind Benny cannot continue walking after he hits the water, so he sinks at once, making a sound like glug-glug as he goes down. It is in the fall of the year, and the water is by no means warm, so as Benny comes up for air he naturally lets out a loud squawk, but by this time the ferry boat is quite some jumps away from him, and nobody seems to see him, or even hear him.

Now Blind Benny cannot swim a lick, so he sinks again with a glug-glug. He comes up once more, and this time he does not squawk so loud, but he sings out, very distinct, as follows: "Good-by, Pal Yid."

All of a sudden there is quite a splash in the water near the ferry-boat, and Little Yid is swimming for Blind Benny so fast the chances are he will make a sucker of Johnny Weissmuller if Johnny happens to be around, for Little Yid is a regular goldfish when it comes to water, although he is not much of a hand for going swimming without provocation.

He has to dive for Blind Benny, for by this time Blind Benny is going down for the third time, and everybody knows that a guy is only allowed three downs when he is drowning. In fact, Blind Benny is almost down where the crabs live before Little Yid can get a fistful of his collar. At first Little Yid's idea is to take Blind Benny by the hair, but he remembers that Benny does not have much hair, so he compromises on the collar.

And being a little guy, Yid has quite a job getting Benny to the top and keeping him there. By this time the ferryboat is almost at its dock on the New York side, and nobody seems to realize that it is shy a couple of passengers, although of course the ferryboat company is not going to worry about that as it collects the fares in advance. But it is a pretty lucky break for Little Yid and Blind Benny that a tugboat happens along and picks them up, or Yid may be swimming around the North River to this day with Blind Benny by the nape of the neck going glug-glug.

The captain of the tugboat is a kind old guy with whiskers by the name of Deusenberg, and he is very sorry indeed to see them in such a situation, so after he hauls them on board the tugboat, and spreads them out on bunks to let them dry, he throws a couple of slugs of gin into Little Yid and Blind Benny, it being gin of such a nature that they are half sorry they do not go ahead and drown before they meet up with it.

Then the captain unloads them at Forty-second Street on the New York side, and by this time, between the water and the gin, Blind Benny is very much fagged out, indeed, and in bad shape generally, so Little Yid puts him in a cab and takes him to a hospital.

Well, for several days Blind Benny is no better than even money to get well, because after they get the water out of him they still have to contend with the gin, and Mary Marble is around carrying on quite some, and saying she does not know how Little Yid can be so careless as to let Benny walk off the end of a ferryboat when there are gates to prevent such a thing, or how he can let Benny drink tugboat gin, and many citizens do not see either, especially about the gin.

As for Little Yid, he is looking very sad, and is at the hospital at all times, and finally, one day when Blind Benny is feeling all right again, Little Yid sits down beside his bed, and speaks to him as follows:

"Benny," Little Yid says, "I will now make a confession to you, and I will then go away somewhere and knock myself off. Benny," he says, "I let you fall into the river on purpose. In fact," Little Yid says, "I unhook the gate across the passageway and call you, figuring you will follow the sound of my voice and walk on off the boat into the water.

"I am very sorry about this," Little Yid says, "but Benny," he says, "I love Mary Marble more than somewhat, although I never before mention this to a soul. Not even to Mary Marble, because," Little Yid says, "I know she loves you, as you love her. I love her," Little Yid says, "from the first night we meet, and this love winds up by making me a little daffy.

"I get to thinking," Little Yid says, "that with you out of the way Mary Marble will turn to me and love me instead. But," he says, starting to shed large tears, "when I hear your voice from the water saying 'Good-by, Pal Yid,' my heart begins to break, and I must jump in after you. So now you know, and I will go away and shoot myself through the head if I can find somebody to lend me a Roscoe, because I am no good."

"Why," Blind Benny says, "Pal Yid, what you tell me about leading me into the river is no news to me. In fact," he says, "I know it the minute I hit the water because although I am blind, I see many things as I am going down, and I see very plain that you must do this thing on purpose, because I know you are close enough around to grab me if you wish.

"I know, of course," Blind Benny says, "that there is bound to be a gate across the end of the boat because I often feel it before, and in fact I remember hearing them fix this gate when we are leaving Hoboken. So," he says, "I see that you must unhook this gate. I see that for this reason you wish to knock me off, although I do not see the reason, and the chances are I will never see it unless you tell me now, so I do not put up more of a holler and maybe attract the attention of the other guys on the boat. I am willing to let it all go as it lays."

"My goodness," Little Yid says, "this is most surprising to me, indeed. In fact," he says, "I scarcely know what to say, Benny. In fact," he says, "I cannot figure out why you are willing to go without putting up a very large beef."

"Well, Pal Yid," Benny says, reaching out and taking Little Yid by the hand, "I am so fond of you that I figure if my being dead is going to do you any good, I am willing to die, even though I do not know why. Although," Benny says, "it seems to me you can think up a nicer way of scragging me than by drowning, because you know I loathe and despise water. Now then," he says, "as for Mary Marble, if you—"

But Little Yid never lets Blind Benny finish this, because he cuts in and speaks as follows:

"Benny," he says, "if you are willing to die for me, I can certainly afford to give up a doll for you, especially," he says, "as my people tell me only yesterday that if I marry anybody who is not of my religion, which is slightly Jewish, they will chop me off at the pants pocket. You take Mary Marble," he says, "and I will stake you to my blessing, and maybe a wedding present."

So the upshot of the whole business is Mary Marble is now Mrs. Blind Benny, and Blind Benny seems to be very happy, indeed, although some citizens claim the explanations he gets nowadays of whatever is going on are much shorter than when he is with Little Yid, while Little Yid is over in Hoboken in the cap racket with his brothers, and he never sees Blind Benny any more, as Mary Marble still holds the gin against him.

Personally, I always consider Little Yid's conduct in this very very self-sacrificing and furthermore I consider him a very great hero for rescuing Blind Benny from the river, and I am saying as much only the other day to Regret, the horse player.

"Yes," Regret says, "it sounds very self-sacrificing, indeed, and maybe Little Yid is a hero, at that, but," Regret says, "many citizens are criticizing him no little for sawing off such a crow as Mary Marble on a poor blind guy."

THE LIGHT OF OTHER DAYS
Thomas Moore

Oft, in the stilly night,
  Ere slumber's chain has bound me,
Fond Memory brings the light
  Of other days around me:
    The smiles, the tears
    Of boyhood's years,
The words of love then spoken;
    The eyes that shone,
    Now dimm'd and gone,
The cheerful hearts now broken!
Thus, in the stilly night,
  Ere slumber's chain has bound me,
Sad Memory brings the light,
  Of other days around me.

When I remember all
  The friends, so link'd together,
I've seen around me fall
  Like leaves in wintry weather,
    I feel like one
    Who treads alone
Some banquet-hall deserted,
    Whose lights are fled,
    Whose garlands dead,
    And all but he departed!
Thus, in the stilly night,
  Ere slumber's chain has bound me,
Sad Memory brings the light
  Of other days around me.

Instead of loving your enemies, treat your friends a little better.
          —Edgar W. ("Ed") Howe

"We are born to do benefits ..."

TIMON OF ATHENS ON THE OBLIGATIONS OF FRIENDSHIP

William Shakespeare

FIRST LORD:—Might we but have that happiness, my lord, that you would once use our hearts, whereby we might express some part of our zeals, we should think ourselves for ever perfect.

TIMON:—O, no doubt, my good friends, but the gods themselves have provided that I shall have much help from you: how had you been my friends else? why have you that charitable title from thousands, did not you chiefly belong to my heart? I have told more of you to myself than you can with modesty speak in your own behalf; and thus far I confirm you. O you gods, think I, what need we have any friends, if we should ne'er have need of 'em? they were the most needless creatures living, should we ne'er have use for 'em, and would most resemble sweet instruments hung up in cases, that keep their sounds to themselves. Why, I have often wished myself poorer, that I might come nearer to you. We are born to do benefits: and what better or properer can we call our own than the riches of our friends? O, what a precious comfort 'tis, to have so many, like brothers, commanding one another's fortunes! O joy, e'en made away ere 't can be born! Mine eyes cannot hold out water, methinks: to forget their faults, I drink to you.

"... this mild trust translates me."

HENRY THOREAU TO RALPH WALDO EMERSON

February 12, 1843

Dear Friend,—As the packet still tarries, I will send you some thoughts, which I have lately relearned, as the latest public and private news.

How mean are our relations to one another! Let us pause till they are nobler. A little silence, a little rest, is good. It would be sufficient employment only to cultivate true ones.

The richest gifts we can bestow are the least marketable. We hate the kindness which we understand. A noble person confers no such gift as his whole confidence: none so exalts the giver and the receiver; it produces the truest gratitude. Perhaps it is only essential to friendship that some vital trust should have been reposed by the one in the other. I feel addressed and probed even to the remote parts of my being when one nobly shows, even in trivial things, an implicit faith in me. When such divine commodities are so near and cheap, how strange that it should have to be each day's discovery! A threat or a curse may be forgotten, but this mild trust translates me. I am no more of this earth; it acts dynamically; it changes my very substance. I cannot do what before I did. I cannot be what before I was. Other chains may be broken, but in the darkest night, in the remotest place, I trail this thread. Then things cannot happen. What if God were to confide in us for a moment! Should we not then be gods?

How subtle a thing is this confidence! Nothing sensible passes between; never any consequences are to be apprehended should it be misplaced. Yet something has transpired. A new behavior springs; the ship carries new ballast in her hold. A sufficiently great and generous trust could never be abused. It should be cause to lay down one's life,—which would not be to lose it. Can there be any mistake up there? Don't the gods know where to invest their wealth? Such confidence, too, would be reciprocal. When one confides greatly in you, he will feel the roots of an equal trust fastening themselves in him. When such trust has been received or reposed, we dare not speak, hardly to see each other; our voices sound harsh and untrustworthy. We are as instruments which the Powers have dealt with. Through what straits would we not carry this little burden of a magnanimous trust! Yet no harm could possibly come, but simply faithlessness. Not a feather, not a straw, is intrusted; that packet is empty. It is only committed to us, and, as it were, all things are committed to us.

The kindness I have longest remembered has been of this sort,—the sort unsaid; so far behind the speaker's lips that almost it already lay in my heart. It did not have far to go to be communicated. The gods cannot misunderstand, man cannot explain. We communicate like the burrows of foxes, in silence and darkness, under ground. We are undermined by faith and love. How much more full is Nature where we think the empty space is than where we place the solids!—full of fluid influences. Should we ever communicate but by these? The spirit abhors a vacuum more than Nature. There is a tide which pierces the pores of the air. These aerial rivers, let us not pollute their currents. What meadows do they course through? How many fine mails there are which traverse their routes? He is privileged who gets his letter franked by them.

I believe these things.

HENRY D. THOREAU

TO OUR GUEST
Nancy Byrd Turner

If you come cheerily,
Here shall be jest for you;
If you come wearily,
Here shall be rest for you.

If you come borrowing,
Gladly we'll loan to you;
If you come sorrowing,
Love shall be shown to you.

Under our thatch, friend,
Place shall abide for you;
Touch but the latch, friend,
The door shall swing wide for you!

"My friends are not perfect—no more am I ..."

PERFECTION NOT ESSENTIAL TO FRIENDSHIP
Alexander Smith

When a man glances critically through the circle of his intimate friends, he is obliged to confess that they are far from being perfect. They possess neither the beauty of Apollo, nor the wisdom of Solon, nor the wit of Mercutio, nor the reticence of Napoleon III. If pushed hard he will be constrained to admit that he has known each and all get angry without sufficient occasion, make at times the foolishest remarks, and act as if personal comfort were the highest thing in their estimation. Yet, driven thus to the wall, forced to make such uncomfortable confessions, our supposed man does not like his friends one whit the less; nay, more, he is aware that if they were very superior and faultless persons he would not be conscious of so much kindly feeling towards them. The tide of friendship does not rise high on the bank of perfection. Amiable weaknesses and shortcomings are the food of love. It is from the roughnesses and imperfect breaks in a man that you are able to lay hold of him. If a man be an entire and perfect chrysolite, you slide off him and fall back into ignorance. My friends are not perfect—no more am I—and so we suit each other admirably. Their weaknesses keep mine in countenance, and so save me from humiliation and shame. We give and take, bear and forbear; the stupidity they utter to-day salves the recollection of the stupidity I uttered yesterday; in their want of it I see my own, and so feel satisfied and kindly disposed. It is one of the charitable dispensations of Providence that perfection is not essential to friendship.

JOSEPH RODMAN DRAKE

Fitz-Greene Halleck

Green be the turf above thee,
 Friend of my better days!
None knew thee but to love thee,
 Nor named thee but to praise.

Tears fell, when thou wert dying,
 From eyes unused to weep,
And long, where thou art lying,
 Will tears the cold turf steep.

When hearts, whose truth was proven,
 Like thine, are laid in earth,
There should a wreath be woven
 To tell the world their worth;

And I, who woke each morrow
 To clasp thy hand in mine,
Who shared thy joy and sorrow,
 Whose weal and woe were thine,

It should be mine to braid it
Around thy faded brow,
But I've in vain essayed it,
And feel I cannot now.

While memory bids me weep thee,
Nor thoughts nor words are free,
The grief is fixed too deeply
That mourns a man like thee.

". . . you have been true to your friend."

A SMALL TRAGEDY

Agnes Repplier

I was twelve years old, and very happy in my convent school. I did not particularly mind studying my lessons, and I sometimes persuaded the less experienced nuns to accept a retentive memory as a substitute for intelligent understanding, with which it had nothing to do. I "got along" with other children, and I enjoyed my friends; and of such simple things is the life of a child composed.

Then came a disturbing letter from my mother, a letter which threatened the heart of my content. It was sensible and reasonable, and it said very plainly and very kindly that I had better not make an especial friend of Lilly Milton; "not an exclusive friend," wrote my mother, "not one whom you would expect to see immediately after you leave school."

I knew what all that meant. I was as innocent as a kitten; but divorces were not common in those conservative years, and Mrs. Milton had as many to her credit as if she were living—a highly esteemed and popular lady—today. I regretted my mother's tendency to confuse issues with unimportant details (a mistake which grown-up people often made), and I felt sure that if she knew Lilly—who was also as innocent as a kitten, and was blessed with the sweetest temper that God ever gave a little girl—she would be delighted that I had such an excellent friend. So I went on happily enough until ten days later, when Madame Rayburn, a nun for whom I cherished a very warm affection, was talking to me upon a familiar theme—the diverse ways in which I might improve my classwork and my general behavior. The subject did not interest me deeply,—repetition had staled its vivacity,—until my companion said the one thing that had plainly been uppermost in her mind: "And Agnes, how did you come to tell Lilly Milton that your mother did not want you to go with her? I never thought you could have been so deliberately unkind."

This brought me to my feet with a bound. "Tell Lilly!" I cried. "You could not have believed such a thing. It was Madame Bouron who told her."

A silence followed this revelation. The convent discipline was as strict for the nuns as for the pupils, and it was not their custom to criticize their superiors. Madame Bouron was mistress general, ranking next to the august head, and of infinitely more importance to us. She was a cold, severe, sardonic woman, and the general dislike for her had shaped itself into a cult. I had accepted this cult in simple good faith, having no personal grudge until she did this dreadful thing; and I may add that it was the eminently unwise custom of reading all the letters written to or by the pupils which stood responsible for the trouble. The order of nuns was a French one, and the habit of surveillance, which did not seem amiss in France, was ill-adapted to America. I had never before wasted a thought upon it. My weekly home letter and the less frequent but more communicative epistles from my mother might have been read in the market place for all I cared, until this miserable episode proved that a bad usage may be trusted to produce, sooner or later, bad results.

It was with visible reluctance that Madame Rayburn said after a long pause: "That alters the case. If Madame Bouron told Lilly, she must have had some good reason for doing so."

"There was no good reason," I protested. "There couldn't have been. But it doesn't matter. I told Lilly it wasn't so, and she believed me."

Madame Rayburn stared at me aghast. "You told Lilly it was not so?" she repeated.

I nodded. "I could not find out for two days what was the matter," I explained; "but I got it out of her at last, and I told her that my mother had never written a line to me about her. And she believed me."

"But my dear child," said the nun, "you have told a very grievous lie. What is more, you have borne false witness against your neighbor. When you said to Lilly that your mother had not written that letter, you made her believe that Madame Bouron had lied to her."

"She didn't mind believing that," I observed cheerfully, "and there was nothing else that I could say to make her feel all right."

"But a lie is a lie," protested the nun. "You will have to tell Lilly the truth."

I said nothing, but my silence was not the silence of acquiescence. Madame Rayburn must have recognized this fact, for she took another line of attack. When she spoke next, it was in a low voice and very earnestly. "Listen to me," she said. "Friday is the first of May. You are going to confession on Thursday. You will tell Father O'Harra the whole story just as you have told it to me, and whatever he bids you do, you must do it. Remember that if you go to confession and do not tell this you will commit the very great sin of sacrilege; and if you do not obey your confessor you will commit the sin of open disobedience to the Church."

I was more than a little frightened. It seemed to me that for the first time in my life I was confronted by grown-up iniquities to which I had been a stranger. The thought sobered me for two days. On the third I went to confession, and when I had finished with my customary offenses—which, as they seldom varied, were probably as familiar to the priest as they were to me—I told my serious tale. The silence with which it was received bore witness to its seriousness. No question was asked me; I had been too explicit to render questions needful. But after two minutes (which seemed like two hours) of thinking my confessor said: "A lie is a lie. It must be retracted. Tomorrow you will do one of two things. You will tell your friend the truth, or you will tell Madame Bouron the whole story just as you told it to me. Do you understand?"

"Yes," I said in a faint little voice, no louder than a sigh.

"And you will do as I bid you?"

"Yes," I breathed again.

"Then I will give you absolution, and you may go to Communion. But remember, no later than tomorrow. Believe me, it will get no easier by delay."

Of that I felt tolerably sure, and it was with the courage of desperation that I knocked the next morning at the door of Madame Bouron's office. She gave me a glance of wonderment (I had never before paid her a voluntary call), and without pause or preamble I told my tale, told it with such bald uncompromising verity that it sounded worse than ever. She listened at first in amazement, then in anger. "So Lilly thinks I lied to her," she said at last.

"Yes," I answered.

"And suppose I send for her now and undeceive her."

"You can't do that," I said. "I should tell her again my mother did not write the letter, and she would believe me."

"If you told another such lie, you would be sent from the school."

"If I were sent home, Lilly would believe me. She would believe me all the more."

The anger died out of Madame Bouron's eyes, and a look of bewilderment came into them. I am disposed to think that, despite her wide experience as nun and teacher, she had never before encountered an *idée fixe,* and found out that the pyramids are flexible compared to it. "You know," she said uncertainly, "that sooner or later you will have to do as your mother desires."

I made no answer. The "sooner or later" did not interest me at all. I was living now.

There was another long pause. When Madame Bouron spoke again it was in a grave and low voice. "I wish I had said nothing about your mother's letter," she said. "I thought I could settle matters quickly that way, but I was mistaken, and I must take the consequences of my error. You may go now. I will not speak to Lilly, or to anyone else about this affair."

I did not go. I sat stunned, and asking myself if she knew all that her silence would imply. Children seldom give adults much credit for intelligence. "But," I began feebly—

"But me no buts," she interrupted, rising to her feet. "I know what you are going to say; but I have not been the head of a school for years without bearing more than one injustice."

Now when I heard these words sadly spoken something broke up inside of me. It did not break gently, like the dissolving of a cloud; it broke like the bursting of a dam. Sobs shook my lean little body as though they would have torn it apart. Tears blinded me. With difficulty I gasped out three words. "You are good," I said.

Madame Bouron propelled me gently to the door, which I could not see because of my tears. "I wish I could say as much for you," she answered, "but I cannot. You have been very bad. You have been false to your mother, to whom you owe respect and obedience; you have been false to me; and you have been false to God. But you have been true to your friend."

She put me out of the door, and I stood in the corridor facing the clock. I was still shaken by sobs, but my heart was light as a bird. And, believe it or not, the supreme reason for my happiness was—not that my difficulties were over, though I was glad of that; and not that Lilly was safe from hurt, though I was glad of that; but that Madame Bouron, whom I had thought bad, had proved herself to be, according to the standards of childhood, as good as gold. My joy was like the joy of the blessed saints in Paradise.

" 'It is a burning shame that Howells isn't here.' "

MARK TWAIN TO
WILLIAM DEAN HOWELLS

Farmington Avenue, Hartford, May 29, 1877

Confound you, Joe Twichell and I roamed about Bermuda day and night and never ceased to gabble and enjoy. About half the talk was "It is a burning shame that Howells isn't here." "Nobody could get at the very meat and marrow of this pervading charm and deliciousness like Howells." "How Howells would revel in the quaintness and the simplicity of this people and the Sabbath repose of this land." "What an imperishable sketch Howells would make of Capt. West the whaler, and Capt. Hope with the patient, pathetic face, wanderer in all the oceans for 42 years, lucky in none; coming home defeated once more, now, minus his ship—resigned, uncomplaining, being used to this." "What a rattling chapter Howells would make out of the small boy Alfred, with his alert eye and military brevity and exactness of speech; and out of the old landlady; and her sacred onions; and her daughter; and the visiting clergyman; and the ancient pianos of Hamilton and the venerable music in vogue there—and forty other things which we shall leave untouched or touched but lightly upon, we being not worthy." "Dam Howells for not being here!" (this usually from me, not Twichell.)

O, your insufferable pride, which will have a fall some day! If you had gone with us and let me pay the $50 which the trip and board and the various knickknacks and mementos would cost, I would have picked up enough droppings from your conversation to pay me 500 per cent profit in the way of the *several* magazine articles which I could have written, whereas I can now write only one or two and am therefore largely out of pocket by your proud ways. Ponder these things. Lord, what a perfectly bewitching excursion it was! I traveled under an assumed name and was never molested with a polite attention from anybody.

Love to you all,

MARK

"... trust is a kind of higher shrewdness."

NEW ACQUAINTANCES
Richard Burton

The fact that we are inclined to think so well of persons newly met
is only a phase of humanity's deep-rooted feeling that the impossible
may happen. It is a touching proof of the optimism which, in the face
of all past experience, looks upon each last-made acquaintance as the
Ideal Personality of our dreams. And so, often the one thing needed
to destroy the illusion is—further intimacy....

We are all hoping for the best, clinging, with counter-testimony overwhelmingly to the contrary, to some golden guess, some darling desire.
And half the joy of living, did we but realize it, lies in such an attitude of mind. "I do not wish to live in a fool's Paradise," the saying
runs; yet were you ever happier than before the gates were shut upon
your foolish faith? It is wrong to treat as shallow and silly these fervent
inclinations to seize on the new acquaintance, the companion elect,
within an hour after the first meeting, as if a cheap nature were thus
implied, either in you or the just-found friend. Friends tried and true
are precious, yes; the best of all, if you will. But friendships famed in
history and blazoned in literature have been of another sort: to meet
and know, to look and love, to let the reason wait upon the heart's
pronouncement,—this, too, is wise at times....

In sudden likings or loves there lurks that instinct of the ages which
is Nature's short-cut to knowledge, and a most convenient (if sometimes risky) substitute for the slow, cautious, and self-conscious processes of reason. It is that instinct which is at work in what is called
"woman's intuition"; a power or gift by no means confined to the sex,
although confessedly more often there than among the masculine persuasion. Many a man has opposed one of these intuitive opinions to
his disaster; what he grandiloquently called his common-sense bade
him reject the spontaneous judgment, and in the sequence he regretted
his failure to trust the instant impression....

Those sympathetic to oriental forms of thought boldly declare that,
when two persons display instantly an almost magnetic attraction for
each other, it signifies relationship in an earlier existence; this idea,
or something very like it, crops out again and again in Browning's
poetry. Certainly, most of us have seen, if we have not been partici-
pant in, this kind of instantaneous attachment; and have noted that,
instead of being a flash in the pan, it endured the shocks of the years

as well as connections more sensibly formed and slower in welding. "When Time, that breaks all things, has broken the faith between friends"—Swinburne's sad line—does not seem to apply to such friendships, which to all appearances shine but the brighter with the passing of the years. Literature, past and present, is full of references which point unmistakably to this sentiment, or conviction.

In a current novel I chanced to be reading, "Dawn O'Hara," by Edna Ferber, I ran into this sentence: "We became friends, not step by step, but in one gigantic leap such as sometimes triumphs over the gap between acquaintance and liking." The truth is, mankind is naturally idealistic. We set clouds of glory round the new acquaintance, because we would have him so, and as yet there is not sufficient inconvenient knowledge about him to make it difficult to believe. So, too, if we have a genius for friendship, we idealize our friends by simply assuming in them their highest potentialities, and believing that they will live up to them. And it will happen, with one who is all but a stranger, that we can show more of our deeper self for the very reason that the other is not aware of our weaknesses,—is, on his side, idealizing us as well; and cheered by this confidence, we expose psychic layers lying deeper down than we ever go within the bosom of our families. And to treat this experiece as if it were an amusing example of the double game of bluff, were to do it foul wrong. In one of those thrusts into human psychology which make her a great writer, George Eliot declared that we are always underestimating or overestimating each other; it is only God who can see us as we are. He strikes the balance.

But it is very safe to say that he who assumes the best in another hits nearer to the fact than he who assumes the worst. That first rosy estimate of the new-found friend, so generously taken for granted, so pathetically believed in and trusted, has a solid *raison d'être* in human nature, after all allowances are made; and trust is a kind of higher shrewdness. In our analytic, self-conscious age, it is probable that we depend too little upon the testimony of that larger Self which is outside of the petty little Me I am conscious of: the Self that means the race with its eons of experience working in my blood; the Self that is below the threshold of consciousness, yet potent to push me on to my destiny; the Self that is ancestral, the combined wisdom or foolishness of all my forbears influencing my every act; or the Self, if the materialistic explanation be accepted, which is the result of environment; which, as a French critic has put it, "when placed personally before a question of life or death, obeys no preconceived morality, but laws of equilibrium of a purely physical character as compelling as those of gravity."

We can well afford today, in view of the opening up of the deeper possibilities of personality, to trust this more generously defined Ego of ours, and to have faith in new friends, along with the old. The intuitions are not to be despised in the light of modern science; they are to be the more respected.

FROM "EPISTLE TO DAVIE, A BROTHER POET"

Robert Burns

All hail, ye tender feelings dear!
The smile of love, the friendly tear,
  The sympathetic glow!
Long since, this world's thorny ways
Had number'd out my weary days,
  Had it not been for you!
Fate still has blest me with a friend,
In every care and ill;
And oft a more endearing band,
  A tie more tender still.
    It lightens, it brightens
      The tenebrific scene,
    To meet with, and greet with
      My Davie or my Jean.

"... the time is short ..."

"NOW IS THE DAY"

Phillips Brooks

You who are letting miserable misunderstandings run on from year to year, meaning to clear them up someday; you who are keeping wretched quarrels alive because you cannot quite make up your minds that now is the day to sacrifice your pride and kill them; you who are passing men sullenly upon the street, not speaking to them out of some silly spite, and yet knowing that it would fill you with shame and remorse if you heard that one of those men were dead tomorrow morning; you who are letting your neighbor starve, till you hear that he is dying of starvation; or letting your friend's heart ache for a word of appreciation or sympathy, which you mean to give him someday; if you could only know and see and feel, all of a sudden, that "the time is short," how it would break the spell! How you would go instantly and do the thing which you might never have another chance to do!

THE OLD FAMILIAR FACES
Charles Lamb

I have had playmates, I have had companions,
In my days of childhood, in my joyful school-days,
All, all are gone, the old familiar faces.

I have been laughing, I have been carousing,
Drinking late, sitting late, with my bosom cronies.
All, all are gone, the old familiar faces.

I loved a love once, fairest among women;
Closed are her doors on me, I must not see her—
All, all are gone, the old familiar faces.

I have a friend, a kinder friend has no man;
Like an ingrate, I left my friend abruptly;
Left him, to muse on the old familiar faces.

Ghost-like I paced round the haunts of my childhood.
Earth seemed a desert I was bound to traverse,
Seeking to find the old familiar faces.

Friend of my bosom, thou more than a brother,
Why wert thou not born in my father's dwelling?
So might we talk of the old familiar faces—

How some they have died, and some they have left me,
And some are taken from me; all are departed;
All, all are gone, the old familiar faces.

"I cannae draw upon ye, David."

RECONCILIATION
Robert Louis Stevenson

For the best part of three nights we travelled on eerie mountains and among the well-heads of wild rivers; often buried in mist, almost continually blown and rained upon, and not once cheered by any glimpse of sunshine. By day, we lay and slept in the drenching heather; by night, incessantly clambered upon breakneck hills and among the rude crags. We often wandered; we were often so involved in fog, that we must lie quiet till it lightened. A fire was never to be thought of. Our only food was drammach and a portion of cold meat that we had carried from the Cage; and as for drink, Heaven knows we had no want of water....

During all these horrid wanderings, we had no familiarity, scarcely even that of speech. The truth is that I was sickening for my grave, which is the best excuse. But besides that, I was of an unforgiving disposition from my birth, slow to take offense, slower to forget it, and now incensed both against my companion and myself. For the best part of two days, he was unweariedly kind; silent, indeed, but always ready to help, and always hoping (as I could very well see) that my displeasure would blow by. For the same length of time, I stayed in myself, nursing my anger, roughly refusing his services, and passing him over with my eyes as if he had been a bush or a stone....

All the while, I was growing worse and worse. Once I had fallen, my legs simply doubling under me, and this had struck Alan for the moment; but I was afoot so briskly, and set off again with such a natural manner, that he soon forgot the incident. Flushes of heat went over me, and then spasms of shuddering. The stitch in my side was hardly bearable. At last, I began to feel that I could trail myself no farther; and with that there came on me at once the wish to have it out with Alan, let my anger blaze, and be done with life in a more sudden manner. He had just called me "Whig." I stopped.

"Mr. Stewart," said I, in a voice that quivered like a fiddle-string, "you are older than I am, and should know your manners. Do you think it either very wise or very witty to cast my politics in my teeth? I thought, where folk differed, it was the part of gentlemen to differ civilly; and if I did not, I may tell you I could find a better taunt than some of yours."

Alan had stopped opposite to me, his hat cocked, his hands in his breeches pockets, his head a little to one side. He listened, smiling evilly, as I could see by the starlight; and when I had done he began to whistle a Jacobite air. It was the air made in mockery of General Cope's defeat at Preston Pans:—

"Hey, Johnnie Cope, are ye waukin' yet?
And are your drums a-beatin' yet?"

And it came in my mind that Alan, on the day of that battle, had been engaged upon the royal side

"Why do ye take that air, Mr. Stewart?" said I. "Is that to remind me you have been beaten on both sides?"

The air stopped on Alan's lips. "David!" said he.

"But it's time these manners ceased," I continued; "and I mean you shall henceforth speak civilly of my King and my good friends the Campbells."

"I am a Stewart—" began Alan.

"O!" says I, "I ken ye bear a king's name. But you are to remember, since I have been in the Highlands, I have seen a good many of those that bear it; and the best I can say of them is this, that they would be none the worse of washing."

"Do you know that you insult me?" said Alan, very low.

"I am sorry for that," said I, "for I am not done; and if you distaste the sermon, I doubt the pirliecue will please you as little. You have been chased in the field by the grown men of my party; it seems a poor kind of pleasure to outface a boy. Both the Campbells and the Whigs have beaten you; you have run before them like a hare. It behooves you to speak of them as of your betters."

Alan stood quite still, the tails of his great-coat flapping behind him in the wind.

"This is a pity," he said at last. "There are things said that cannot be passed over."

"I never asked you to," said I. "I am as ready as yourself."

"Ready?" said he.

"Ready," I repeated. "I am no blower and boaster like some I could name. Come on!" And drawing my sword, I fell on guard as Alan himself had taught me.

"David!" he cried. "Are ye daft? I cannae draw upon ye, David. It's fair murder."

"That was your lookout when you insulted me," said I.

"It's the truth!" cried Alan, and he stood for a moment, wringing his mouth in his hand like a man in sore perplexity. "It's the bare truth," he said, and drew his sword. But before I could touch his blade with mine, he had thrown it from him and fallen to the ground. "Na, na," he kept saying, "na, na—I cannae, I cannae."

At this the last of my anger oozed all out of me; and I found myself only sick, and sorry, and blank, and wondering at myself. I would have given the world to take back what I had said; but a word once spoken, who can recapture it? I minded me of all Alan's kindness and courage in the past, how he had helped and cheered and borne with me in our evil days; and then recalled my own insults, and saw that I had lost forever that doughty friend. At the same time, the sickness that hung upon me seemed to redouble, and the pang in my side was like a sword for sharpness. I thought I must have swooned where I stood.

This it was that gave me a thought. No apology could blot out what I had said; it was needless to think of one, none could cover the offense; but where an apology was vain, a mere cry for help might bring Alan back to my side. I put my pride away from me. "Alan," said I, "if you cannot help me, I must die here."

He started up sitting, and looked at me.

"It's true," said I. "I'm by with it. O let me get into the bield of a house—I'll can die there easier." I had no need to pretend; whether I chose or not, I spoke in a weeping voice that would have melted a heart of stone.

"Can ye walk?" asked Alan.

"No," said I, "not without help. This last hour, my legs have been fainting under me; I've a stitch in my side like a red-hot iron; I cannae breathe right. If I die, ye'll can forgive me, Alan? In my heart, I liked ye fine—even when I was the angriest."

"Wheesht, wheesht!" cried Alan. "Dinnae say that! David, man, ye ken——" He shut his mouth upon a sob. "Let me get my arm about ye," he continued; "that's the way! Now lean upon me hard. Gude kens where there's a house! We're in Balwhidder, too; there should be no want of houses, no, nor friends' houses here. Do you gang easier so, David?"

"Aye," said I, "I can be doing this way"; and I pressed his arm with my hand.

Again he came near sobbing. "Davie," said he, "I'm no a right man at all; I have neither sense nor kindness; I couldnae remember ye were just a bairn, I couldnae see ye were dying on your feet; Davie, ye'll have to try and forgive me."

"O man, let's say no more about it!" said I. "We're neither one of us to mend the other—that's the truth! We must bear and forbear, man Alan! O, but my stitch is sore! Is there nae house?"

"I'll find a house to ye, David," he said stoutly. "We'll follow down the burn, where there's bound to be houses. My poor man, will ye no be better on my back?"

"O Alan," says I, "and me a good twelve inches taller?"

"Ye're no such a thing," cried Alan, with a start. "There may be a trifling matter of an inch or two; I'm no saying I'm just exactly what ye would call a tall man, whatever; and I daresay," he added, his voice trailing off in a laughable manner, "now when I come to think of it, I daresay ye'll be just about right. Ay, it'll be a foot or near hand; or maybe even mair!"

It was sweet and laughable to hear Alan eat his words up in the fear of some fresh quarrel. I could have laughed, had not my stitch caught me so hard; but if I had laughed, I think I must have wept, too.

"Alan," cried I, "what makes ye so good to me? what makes ye care for such a thankless fellow?"

"Deed, and I don't know," said Alan. "For just precisely what I thought I liked about ye, was that ye never quarrelled;—and now I like ye better!"

JAFFAR

Leigh Hunt

Jaffar, the Barmecide, the good vizier,
The poor man's hope, the friend without a peer,
Jaffar was dead, slain by a doom unjust;
And guilty Haroun, sullen with mistrust
Of what the good, and e'en the bad, might say,
Ordained that no man living from that day
Should dare to speak his name on pain of death.
All Araby and Persia held their breath;

All but the brave Mondeer: he, proud to show
How far for love a grateful soul could go,
And facing death for very scorn and grief
(For his great heart wanted a great relief),
Stood forth in Bagdad daily, in the square
Where once had stood a happy house, and there
Harangued the tremblers at the scymitar
On all they owed to the divine Jaffar.

"Bring me this man," the caliph cried; the man
Was brought, was gazed upon. The mutes began
To bind his arms. "Welcome, brave cords," cried he;
"From bonds far worse Jaffar delivered me;

From wants, from shames, from loveless household fears;
Made a man's eyes friends with delicious tears;
Restored me, loved me, put me on a par
With his great self. How can I pay Jaffar?"

Haroun, who felt that on a soul like this
The mightiest vengeance could but fall amiss,
Now deigned to smile, as one great lord of fate
Might smile upon another half as great.
He said, "Let worth grow frenzied if it will;
The caliph's judgment shall be master still.
Go, and since gifts so move thee, take this gem,
The richest in the Tartar's diadem,
And hold the giver as thou deemest fit!"
"Gifts!" cried the friend; he took, and holding it
High towards the heavens, as though to meet his star,
Exclaimed, "This, too, I owe to thee, Jaffar!"

"Choose a good disagreeable friend, if you be wise . . ."

THACKERAY GIVES SOME AMUSING ADVICE *

Choice of friends, my dear Robert, is a point upon which every man about town should be instructed, as he should be careful. And as example, they say, is sometimes better than precept, and at the risk even of appearing somewhat ludicrous in your eyes, I will narrate to you an adventure which happened to myself, which is at once ridiculous and melancholy (at least to me), and which will show you how a man, not imprudent or incautious of his own nature, may be made to suffer by the imprudent selection of a friend. Attend then, my dear Bob, to "the History of Rasselas, Prince of Abyssinia."

Sir, in the year 1810 I was a jolly young Bachelor; I had a place in the Tape and Sealing-Wax Office; I had chambers in Pump Court, *au troisième,* and led a not uncomfortable life there. I was a free and gay young fellow in those days and not so particular in my choice of friends as subsequent experience has led me to be.

There lived in the set of chambers opposite to mine a Suffolk gentleman, of good family, whom I shall call Mr. Bludyer. Our boys or

* Abridged by Editor.

clerks first made acquaintance, and did each other mutual kind offices: borrowing for their respective masters' benefit, neither of whom was too richly provided with the world's goods, coals, blacking-brushes, crockery-ware, and the like; and our forks and spoons, if either of us had an entertainment in chambers. As I learned presently that Mr. Bludyer had been educated at Oxford, and heard that his elder brother was a gentleman of good estate and reputation in his county, I could have no objection to make his acquaintance, and accepted finally his invitation to meet a large game-pie which he had brought with him from the country.

Mr. Bludyer was a sporting man: it was the custom in those days with many gentlemen to dress as much like coachmen as possible: in top-boots, huge white coats with capes, Belcher neckerchiefs, and the like adornments; and, at the tables of bachelors of the very first fashion, you would meet with prize-fighters and jockeys, and hear a great deal about the prize-ring, the cock-pit, and the odds.

My acquaintance with Mr. Bludyer ripened into a sort of friendship. He was perfectly good-natured, and not ill-bred; and his jovial spirits and roaring stories amused a man who, though always of a peaceful turn, had no dislike to cheerful companions.

I was at this time (and deservedly so, for I had been very kind to her, and my elder brother, your father, neglected her considerably) the favourite nephew of your grand-aunt, my aunt, Mrs. General Mac-Whirter, who was left a very handsome fortune by the General, and to whom I do not scruple to confess I paid every attention to which her age, her sex, and her large income entitled her. I used to take sweetmeats to her poodle. I went and drank tea with her night after night. I accompanied her Sunday after Sunday to hear the Reverend Rowland Hill, at the Rotunda Chapel, over Blackfriars Bridge, and I used to read many of the tracts with which she liberally supplied me—in fact, do everything to comfort and console a lady of peculiar opinions and habits who had a large jointure.

Well, sir, my dear aunt, Mrs. General MacWhirter, made me her chief confidant. I regulated her money matters for her, and acted with her bankers and lawyers; and as she always spoke of your father as a reprobate, I had every reason to suppose I should inherit the property.

Now it so happened that in June 1811—I recollect the Comet was blazing furiously at the time, and Mrs. MacWhirter was of opinion that the world was at an end—Mr. Bludyer, who was having his chambers in Pump Court painted, asked permission to occupy mine, where he wished to give a lunch to some people whom he was desirous to entertain. Thinking no harm, of course I said yes; and I went to my desk at the Tape and Sealing-Wax Office at my usual hour, giving instructions to my boy to make Mr. Bludyer's friends comfortable.

As ill-luck would have it, on that accursed Friday, Mrs. MacWhirter, who had never been up my staircase before in her life (for your dear grand-aunt was large in person, and the apoplexy which carried her off soon after menaced her always), having some very particular business with her solicitors in Middle Temple Lane, and being anxious to consult me about a mortgage, actually mounted my stairs, and opened the door on which she saw written the name of Mr. Thomas Brown. She was a peculiar woman, I have said, attached to glaring colours in her dress, and from her long residence in India, seldom without a set of costly birds of paradise in her bonnet, and a splendid Cashmere shawl.

Fancy her astonishment then, on entering my apartments at three o'clock in the afternoon, to be assailed in the first place by a strong smell of tobacco-smoke which pervaded the passage, and by a wild and ferocious bulldog which flew at her on entering my sitting-room.

This bulldog, sir, doubtless attracted by the brilliant colours of her costume, seized upon her, and pinned her down, screaming so that her voice drowned that of Bludyer himself, who was sitting on the table bellowing, "A Southerly Wind and a Cloudy Sky proclaim it a Hunting Morning"—or some such ribald trash: and the brutal owner of the dog (who was no other than the famous Mulatto boxer, Norroy, called the "Black Prince" in the odious language of the Fancy, and who was inebriated doubtless at the moment), encouraged his dog in the assault upon this defenceless lady, and laughed at the agonies which she endured.

Mr. Bludyer, the black man, and one or two more, were arranging a fight on Moulsey Hurst, when my poor aunt made her appearance among these vulgar wretches. Although it was but three o'clock, they had sent to a neighbouring tavern for gin-and-water, and the glasses sparkled on the board. It appears that at first all the gentlemen screamed with laughter; some of them called my aunt an "old girl"; and it was not until she had nearly fainted that the filthy Mulatto called the dog off from the flounce of her yellow gown of which he had hold.

When this poor victim of vulgarity asked with a scream—where was her nephew? new roars of laughter broke out from the coarse gin-drinkers. "It's the old woman whom he goes to meeting with," cried out Bludyer. "Come away, boys!" And he led his brutalised crew out of my chambers into his own.

When I came home at my usual hour of half-past three, I found Mrs. MacWhirter in hysterics upon my sofa—the pipes were lying about—the tin dish-covers—the cold kidneys—the tavern cruet-stands, and wretched remnants of the orgy were in disorder on the table-cloth, stained with beer. Seeing her fainting, I wildly bade my boy to open the window, and seizing a glass of water which was on the table, I presented it to her lips.—It was gin-and-water, which I proffered to that poor lady.

She started up with a scream, which terrified me so I upset the glass: and with empurpled features, and a voice quivering and choking with anger, she vowed she would never forgive me. In vain I pleaded that I was ignorant of the whole of these disgraceful transactions. I went down on my knees to her, and begged her to be pacified. Go she did directly to her carriage, which was in waiting in Middle Temple Lane, and to which I followed her with tears in my eyes, amidst a crowd of jeering barristers' boys and Temple porters. But she pulled up the window in my face, and would no more come back to me than Eurydice would to Orpheus.

Your great-aunt left thirty thousand pounds to your family and the remainder to the missionaries.

My wishes, dear Bob, are moderate. Your aunt left me a handsome competency—and, I repeat, I do not grudge my brother George the money. Nor is it probable that such a calamity can happen again to any one of our family—that would be too great a misfortune. But I tell you the tale, because at least it shows you how important good company is, and that a young man about town should beware of his friends as well as of his enemies.

The other day I saw you walking by the Serpentine with young Lord Foozle, of the Windsor Heavies, who nodded to all sorts of suspicious broughams on the ride, while you looked about (you know you did, you young rascal) for acquaintances—as much as to say—"See! here am I, Bob Brown, of Pump Court, walking with a lord."

My dear Bob, I own that to walk with a lord, and to be seen with him, is a pleasant thing. Every man of the middle class likes to know persons of rank. And I would certainly wish that you should associate with your superiors rather than your inferiors. There is no more dangerous or stupefying position for a man in life than to be a cock of small society. I set it down as a maxim that it is good for a man to live where he can meet his betters, intellectual and social.

But if you fancy that getting into Lord Foozle's set will do you good or advance your prospects in life, my dear Bob, you are woefully mistaken.

These fellows are like the flowers, and neither toil nor spin, but are decked out in magnificent apparel: and for some wise and useful purpose, no doubt. It is good that there should be honest, handsome, hard-living, hard-riding, stupid young Windsor Heavies—as that there should be polite young gentlemen in the Temple, or any other variety of our genus.

And it is good that you should go from time to time to the Heavies' mess, if they ask you; and know that worthy set of gentlemen. But beware, O Bob, how you live with them. Remember that your lot in life is to toil, and spin too—and calculate how much time it takes a Heavy or a man of that condition to do nothing. He goes on his routine of pleasure, this young Heavy, as you on yours of duty—one man in London is pretty nearly as busy as another. The company of young "Swells," then, if you will permit me the word, is not for you. Yours is the useful part in life and theirs the splendid—though why speak further on this subject? Since the days of the Frog and the Bull, a desire to cope with Bulls has been known to be fatal to Frogs.

And to know young noblemen, and brilliant and notorious town bucks and leaders of fashion, has this great disadvantage—that if you talk about them or are seen with them much, you offend all your friends of middle life. It makes men angry to see their acquaintances better off than they themselves are. If you live much with great people, others will be sure to say that you are a sneak. I don't know any means by which men hurt themselves more in the estimation of their equals than this of talking of great folks. A man may mean no harm by it— he speaks of the grandees with whom he lives, as you and I do of Jack and Tom who give us dinners. But his old acquaintances do not forgive him his superiority.

I remember laughing at the jocular complaint made by one of this sort, a friend, whom I shall call Main. After Main published his "Travels in the Libyan Desert" four years ago, he became a literary lion, and roared in many of the metropolitan *salons*. He is a good-natured fellow, never in the least puffed up by his literary success; and always said that it would not last. But since Main has gone out of, and other authors have come into, fashion—the poor fellow comically grumbles. "That year of lionisation has ruined me. The people who used to ask me before, don't ask me any more. They are afraid to invite me to Bloomsbury because they fancy I am accustomed to Mayfair, and Mayfair has long since taken up with a new roarer—so that I am quite alone!"

If Fate, then, my dear Bob, should bring you in contact with a lord or two, eat their dinners, enjoy their company, but be mum about them when you go away.

And, though it is a hard and cruel thing to say, I would urge you, my dear Bob, specially to beware of taking pleasant fellows for your friends. Choose a good disagreeable friend, if you be wise—a surly, steady, economical, rigid fellow. All jolly fellows, all delights of Club smoking-rooms and billiard-rooms, all fellows who sing a capital song, and the like, are sure to be poor. As they are free with their own money, so will they be with yours; and their very generosity and goodness of disposition will prevent them from having the means of paying you back.

Eschew jolly fellows then, my boy, as the most dangerous and costly of company.

Let us be very gentle with our neighbours' failings, and forgive our friends their debts, as we hope ourselves to be forgiven. But the best thing of all to do with your debts is to pay them. Make none; and don't live with people who do.

EPITAPH ON A FRIEND

Lord Byron

Oh, Friend! forever loved, forever dear!
What fruitless tears have bathed thy honor'd bier!
What sighs re-echo'd to thy parting breath,
Whilst thou wast struggling in the pangs of death!
Could tears retard the tyrant in his course;
Could sighs avert his dart's relentless force;
Could youth and virtue claim a short delay,
Or beauty charm the spectre from his prey;
Thou still hadst lived to bless my aching sight,
Thy comrade's honor and thy friend's delight.
If yet thy gentle spirit hover nigh
The spot where now thy mouldering ashes lie,
Here wilt thou read, recorded on my heart,
A grief too deep to trust the sculptor's art.
No marble marks thy couch of lowly sleep,
But living statues there are seen to weep;
Affliction's semblance bends not o'er thy tomb,
Affliction's self deplores thy youthful doom.
What though thy sire lament his failing line,
A father's sorrow cannot equal mine!
Though none, like thee, his dying hour will cheer,
Yet other offspring soothe his anguish here;
But who with me shall hold thy former place?
Thine image, what new friendship can efface?
Ah, none!—a father's tears will cease to flow,
Time will assuage an infant brother's woe;
To all, save one, is consolation known,
While solitary friendship sighs alone.

"Harry is alive, isn't he?"

QUIET HEROISM
Lowell Thomas

At Las Vegas, New Mexico, Carl Myers spoke up and said: "The Carnegie Medal? What do I care about the medal? Harry is alive, isn't he?" Yes, Harry Reid was alive, and that was reward enough for Carl Myers.

They were both miners, and they planted eleven charges of dynamite in an eighty-five foot shaft. They cut the fuses long enough so they'd be able to climb up to a higher level, where they'd be safe from the blast. Then they lighted the fuses and ran. Carl scampered up the incline. But before Harry could make it, one charge of dynamite went off prematurely, and hurled him down, unconscious, hundreds of splinters piercing his legs. Carl yelled to him. No response. And there were those other ten charges of dynamite, fuses lighted and sputtering! If they exploded with Harry down there, that would be the end of Harry.

Carl took a jump down the incline. The fuses were burning short, the dynamite might go any minute. Carl picked up his unconscious pal, flung him across his shoulder, and started up the steep twenty-five foot slope. It was a muscle-breaking job—he had to go mighty fast. Just as he got to the top to safety, dumped Harry down and fell exhausted—the dynamite roared.

The mine owners announced that they were going to recommend Carl Myers for the Carnegie Award for Heroism. But Carl just growled:—"Damn the medal, Harry is alive, isn't he?"

HERACLITUS
William Cory

They told me, Heraclitus, they told me you were dead,
They brought me bitter news to hear and bitter tears to shed.
I wept as I remember'd how often you and I
Had tired the sun with talking and sent him down the sky.

And now that thou art lying, my dear old Carian guest,
A handful of grey ashes, long, long ago at rest,
Still are thy pleasant voices, thy nightingales, awake;
For Death, he taketh all away, but them he cannot take.

~~~~~~~~

"... I discovered ... I had made a new friend."

A LITTLE GIRL'S MARK TWAIN
Dorothy Quick

A little girl walked round and round the deck of an ocean liner. On the starboard side she fairly flew along, but when she turned the corner and came to the port side of the vessel, she walked slowly and her feet dragged, her eyes lost in admiration of a man who stood at the rail, talking to another man. Both of them were staring out towards the far horizon line, and didn't see the little girl, whose gaze was riveted on the older of the two, the one with a great shock of snowy white hair and a keen, kindly observant face. He was Mark Twain.

I can still remember the thrill I had when, after walking past him five or six times, he suddenly turned, held out his hand and said in a slow, drawly voice, "Aren't you going to speak to me, Little Girl?" His companion faded away into space, as far as I was concerned, when I took his place. In a few seconds I was at the rail, standing beside the Mark Twain whom only yesterday I had seen walking down the platform of a London station surrounded by literally hundreds of admirers. He hadn't seen me hanging half out of the compartment window to catch a glimpse of him, nor had I at that moment dreamed that the next morning I should be standing beside him on the deck of a steamer bound for New York—standing beside him and actually talking to him.

It was too wonderful; and I shall never forget how proud and happy I was. It wasn't very long before he asked me if I knew who he was. I replied, "Of course, you're Mark Twain, and I've read all your books." This, of course, was, as he said about the report of his own death, slightly exaggerated, but in the main it was true enough. My grandfather had recited Shakespeare and *Tom Sawyer* to me in my cradle, and had read me not only *Tom Sawyer*, *Huckleberry Finn*, but *Innocents Abroad* and *A Tramp Abroad*, as a preparation for the trip from which I was now returning.

I don't think Mark Twain, or Mr. Clemens, as I later preferred to call him, quite believed my elaborate statement, because he began asking me questions. If I hadn't actually read the books, this would soon have proved the fact; however as I had not only read them, but they had been read to me, he soon found (as he laughingly said) that I knew more about his books than he did himself.

We got along famously and the time slipped by completely unnoticed. It wasn't until the luncheon gong sounded that I remembered my family with a guilty start. Mr. Clemens said he wanted to meet my mother very much. So hand in hand we walked along the decks of the *S.S. Minnetonka* until we finally got to the lower deck, where my mother and grandparents had ensconced themselves in a sunlit corner. I began to explain my long absence but Mr. Clemens said it would be better if I did some introducing instead, so the explanations dropped. As I found out later, they weren't necessary. Mother had been worried about me and had gone on a searching tour. When she had seen how utterly absorbed I was, and in what good hands, she had gone contentedly back to the steamer chairs to wait until I came.

Almost before I knew it, Mr. Clemens had arranged to have his steamer chair by ours, and I discovered that without doubt I had made a new friend. That night, as usual, I wore a white sailor suit to dinner. Being only nine, I had my dinner very early, so I didn't see Mr. Clemens; but just as I was getting into bed there was a knock on the door and it was my new friend clad in one of his famous white suits, come to see me in mine! Someone had told him about my costume.

Unfortunately, I was attired in pajamas so I could only promise, as he especially requested, to wear the white sailor suit the next day. Fortunately, I had a large supply of them, for he insisted I wear them throughout the rest of the voyage. So we both appeared each day in white. Mark Twain's were made of white flannel and mine of serge, but everyone assured us that we looked very well together. . . .

We were inseparable for the rest of the voyage; he literally wouldn't let me out of his sight. If I was late in appearance, he would come down to the stateroom to "fetch" me; and whenever I played shuffleboard he would have his chair moved where he could superintend, and put my coat around my shoulders between plays. He was much interested in my skill at shuffleboard or "Horse Billiards" as he called it. And even though I was eliminated from the Junior Tournament quite early in the games, he gave me his book, *Eve's Diary,* with this inscription: "To Dorothy with the affectionate regards of the Author. Prize for good play in Horse Billiards Tournament, July 19, 1907." At the same time he called me to his cabin and told me to pick out whichever photograph of him I liked best from a selection of twenty or so, and when I had made the choice he autographed it for me.

The only time during the day we were separated was at meals, Mr. Clemens, of course, being at the Captain's table. But quite often he would leave his table and come over to sit with us. Then the Captain would send him over a plate of baked potatoes, done in a way of which Mr. Clemens was especially fond, declaring that they were better at his own table than at any other. And Mr. Clemens, who had already ordered a portion at our table, would eat both platefuls and swear they tasted exactly alike, which he considered a good joke on the Captain.

Mr. Clemens laughingly called me his business manager; so when they were getting up the concert program and a group of men approached him to see if he would speak, he said that they would have to ask me. "I never do anything unless my business manager says I may. So you'll have to ask her." I, of course, was only too delighted to give the required permission as I wanted above everything to hear him speak myself, and had already received permission to sit up for the occasion. Imagine my pride and delight when I saw printed on the concert program, which is to this day one of my most prized possessions: "S. L. Clemens (Mark Twain) *by courtesy of Miss Dorothy Quick....*"

It was like Mr. Clemens to take every opportunity of helping a cause in which he was interested. I recollect that I was staying with Mr. Clemens, at 21 Fifth Avenue, on a night when the Pleiades Club was giving a dinner in his honor. He had for some reason refused to go. It was a bitter disappointment to me, because my mother was going to be there, and as I had been visiting Mr. Clemens I hadn't seen her for several days. The dinner was at the Hotel Brevoort, very near Mr. Clemens' house. As the time for the dinner drew nearer I became more and more downcast. Finally Mr. Clemens asked what was the matter. I stammered out something about the dinner. "Did you want to go?" he questioned. I nodded. "Then we'll go!" He began roaring up the stairs for his secretary to telephone the Master of Ceremonies we were coming, and when the secretary said, "I thought you'd decided not to go," he replied simply, "Dorothy wants to go and I've just remembered there's something I wanted to talk about."

I wish I could remember what it was, but the excitement of the evening—sitting next to Mark Twain at the Speakers' table, in a chair he had brought specially for me—was too much for my youthful memory. I know everyone said it was one of the best speeches he'd ever made; but the two things that stand out in my mind, apart from actually getting to the dinner, was my mother waiting at the door for us, as we came into the hotel, and whisking me off to fix my long braids —a small detail which Mr. Clemens and I had completely overlooked, and which kept the whole dinner waiting at least twenty minutes— and then being taken home by Mr. Clemens just as a sweet lady who had made a great fuss over me all evening was about to play the piano. I would much rather have remembered what Mr. Clemens spoke of, but I think it was something about making a collection of compliments instead of autographs, or cats and dogs. Anyway I've taken the idea to heart and collected them ever since, just because Mark Twain said, "The paying of compliments is an art by itself."

But I have strayed away from the ocean voyage. When, after the most thrilling and eventful nine days of my life, we arrived in New York, a swarm of reporters surrounded Mr. Clemens, who refused to be photographed unless I would be taken with him. He sent to ask Mother's permission, and once it was granted we went to the sun-deck and let the cameramen have full sway. Both Mr. Clemens and I had on our white suits, and the next day there wasn't a paper in New York that didn't have one of the pictures in. As it was rather unusual for Mr. Clemens to pose for the newspapers, they made the most of it; and even now they always bring forth the pictures we had taken that day whenever there is a call for pictures of Mark Twain.

Later, *The American* did a special article called, "Me and Mark Twain," in which there was a sketch of Mr. Clemens and myself seated on the bow of an ocean liner, I was very comfortably ensconced in his lap. Mr. Clemens liked this the best of all the things that appeared, and said it had given him a new idea. He'd never traveled on the bow of a ship, but he thought he would like to try it sometimes, if I'd go along.

All the papers made much of our friendship. "Mark Twain Home— Captive of Little Girl" was one of the headlines. And they carried long paragraphs about me. I have them all and with them another souvenir of the trip, a drawing of Buster Brown with sprouting wings looking at the following: "Resolved, that Mark Twain has deserted the entire ship's company for Dorothy Quick. I wish my name was Twain. Buster." This is pasted in my scrap book, next to the concert program.

On the dock, my new friend and I parted. But this was the beginning of a treasured friendship, which was for me a great privilege and joy.

So long as we love, we serve. So long as we are loved by others I would almost say we are indispensable; and no man is useless while he has a friend.

—Robert Louis Stevenson

ON THE DEATH OF MR. WILLIAM HERVEY

Abraham Cowley

It was a dismal and a fearful night:
Scarce could the Morn drive on th' unwilling light,
When sleep, death's image, left my troubled breast
   By something liker death possest.
My eyes with tears did uncommanded flow,
   And on my soul hung the dull weight
   Of some intolerable fate.
What bell was that? Ah me! too much I know!

My sweet companion, and my gentle peer,
Why hast thou left me thus unkindly here,
Thy end for ever, and my life, to moan?
   O thou hast left me all alone!
Thy soul and body, when death's agony
   Besieged around thy noble heart,
   Did not with more reluctance part
Than I, my dearest friend, do part from thee.

Ye field of Cambridge, our dear Cambridge, say,
Have ye not seen us walking every day?
Was there a tree about which did not know
   The love betwixt us two?
Henceforth, ye gentle trees, for ever fade;
   Or your sad branches thicker join
   And into darksome shades combine,
Dark as the grave wherein my friend is laid.

Large was his soul: as large a soul as e'er
Submitted to inform a body here;
High as the place 'twas shortly in Heaven to have,
   But low and humble as his grave;
So high that all the virtues there did come
   As to the chiefest seat
   Conspicuous, and great;
So low that for me too it made a room.

Knowledge he only sought, and so soon caught.
As if for him knowledge had rather sought;
Nor did more learning ever crowded lie
    In such a short mortality.
Whene'er the skilful youth discoursed or writ,
    Still did the notions throng
    About his eloquent tongue;
Nor could his ink flow faster than his wit.

His mirth was the pure spirits of various wit,
Yet never did his God or friends forget;
And when deep talk and wisdom came in view,
    Retired, and gave to them their due.
For the rich help of books he always took,
    Though his own searching mind before
    Was so with notions written o'er,
As if wise Nature had made that her book.

With as much zeal, devotion, piety,
He always lived, as other saints do die.
Still with his soul severe account he kept,
    Weeping all debts out ere he slept.
Then down in peace and innocence he lay,
    Like the sun's laborious light,
    Which still in water sets at night,
Unsullied with his journey of the day.

"... I look upon every injury offered to Attilius as done to myself."

PLINY THE YOUNGER WRITES TO SOME OF HIS FRIENDS

(between A.D. 69 and A.D. 110)

To Septitius Clarus

Ah! you are a pretty fellow! You make an engagement to come to supper and then never appear. Justice shall be exacted;—you shall reimburse me to the very last penny the expense I went to on your account; no small sum, let me tell you. I had prepared, you must know, a lettuce a-piece, three snails, two eggs, and a barley cake, with some sweet wine and snow, (the snow most certainly I shall charge to your account, as a rarity that will not keep.) Olives, beet-root, gourds, onions, and a thousand other dainties equally sumptuous. You should likewise have been entertained either with an interlude, the rehearsal of a poem, or a piece of music, whichever you preferred; or (such was my liberality) with all three. But the oysters, sows'-bellies, sea urchins, and dancers from Cadiz of a certain——I know not who, were, it seems, more to your taste. You shall give satisfaction, how, shall at present be a secret. Oh! you have behaved cruelly, grudging your friend,—I had almost said yourself;—and upon second thoughts I do say so;—in this way: for how agreeably should we have spent the evening, in laughing, trifling, and literary amusements! You may sup, I confess, at many places more splendidly; but nowhere with more unconstrained mirth, simplicity, and freedom: only make the experiment, and if you do not ever after excuse yourself to your other friends, to come to me, always put me off to go to them. Farewell.

To Maximus

I think I may claim a right to ask the same services of you for my friends as I would offer to yours had I the same opportunities. Arrianus Maturius occupies the highest social position among the Altinates. When I say this, I am not speaking with respect to his means (which are very considerable), but in allusion to his purity, integrity, dignity, and wisdom. His counsel guides me in my affairs, and his judgment directs me in my studies; for truth, honour, and knowledge, are the distinguishing traits in his character. He loves me (and I cannot express myself more strongly) as well as you love me. He is without ambition and therefore contented with remaining in the equestrian order, when he might easily have advanced himself into a higher rank. However it is my duty to endeavour that his merit be rewarded as it deserves, and I desire very much, without his either knowing or expecting such a thing, and probably too not wishing it, to contribute something to his honours. I want to obtain for him some dignified but not troublesome post, and I beg, when anything of that kind offers, you would think of him; it will be an obligation which both he and I shall ever remember with the greatest gratitude. For although he does not seek anything of this kind, yet he will receive it as gratefully as if he had desired it. Farewell.

To Priscus

You know Attilius Crescens, and you love him; who is there, indeed, of any rank of worth, that does not? For myself, I profess to have a friendship for him far exceeding ordinary attachments of the world. Our native towns are separated only by a day's journey; and we got to care for each other when we were very young; the season for passionate friendships. Ours improved by years; and so far from being chilled, it was confirmed by our riper judgments, as those who know us best can witness. He takes pleasure in boasting everywhere of my friendship; as I do to let the world know that his reputation, his ease, and his interest are my peculiar concern. Insomuch that upon his expressing to me some apprehension of insolent treatment from a certain person who was entering upon the tribuneship of the people, I could not forbear answering,

> "Long as Achilles breathes this vital air,
> To teach thy head no impious hand shall dare."

What is my object in telling you these things? Why, to show you that I look upon every injury offered to Attilius as done to myself. "But what is the object of all this?" you repeat. You must know then, Valerius Varus, at his death, owed Attilius a sum of money. Though I am on friends terms with Maximus, his heir, yet there is a closer friendship between him and you. I beg therefore, and entreat you by the affection you have for me, to take care that Attilius is not only paid the capital which is due to him, but all the long arrears of interest too. He neither covets the property of others nor neglects the care of his own; and as he is not engaged in any lucrative profession, he has nothing to depend upon but his own frugality: for as to literature, in which he greatly distinguishes himself, he pursues this merely from motives of pleasure and ambition. In such a situation, the slightest loss presses hard upon a man, and the more so because he has no opportunities of repairing any injury done to his fortune. Remove then, I entreat you, our uneasiness, and suffer me still to enjoy the pleasure of his wit and bonhommie; for I cannot bear to see the cheerfulness of my friend overclouded, whose mirth and good-humour dissipates every gloom of melancholy in myself. In short, you know what a pleasant entertaining fellow he is, and I hope you will not suffer any injury to engloom and embitter his disposition. You may judge by the warmth of his affection how severe his resentments would prove; for a generous and great mind can ill brook an injury when coupled with contempt. But though *he* could pass it over, yet cannot I: on the contrary, I shall regard it as a wrong and indignity done to myself, and resent it as one offered to my friend; that is, with double warmth. But, after all, why this air of threatening? rather let me end in the same style in which I began, namely, by begging, entreating you so to act in this affair that neither Attilius may have reason to imagine (which I am exceedingly anxious he should not) that I neglect his interest, nor that I may have occasion to charge you with carelessness of mine: as undoubtedly I shall not if you have the same regard for the latter as I have for the former. Farewell.

To Septitius

You tell me certain persons have blamed me in your company, as being upon all occasions too lavish in the praise I give my friends. I not only acknowledge the charge, but glory in it; for can there be a nobler error than an overflowing benevolence? But still, who are these, let me ask, that are better acquainted with my friends than I am myself? Yet grant there are any such, why will they deny me the satisfaction of so pleasing a mistake? For supposing my friends not to deserve the highest encomiums I give them, yet I am happy in believing they do. Let them recommend then this malignant zeal to those (and their number is not inconsiderable) who imagine they show their judgment when they indulge their censure upon their friends. As for myself, they will never be able to persuade me I can be guilty of an excess in friendship. Farewell.

"Each year she has come back . . ."

MY OLD FRIEND, THE LIZARD

Jesse Stuart

I wondered if something had happened to her this year. I kept looking for my old friend, but she had not returned. She had always come back before now, usually in the warm days of late March. I'd begin to wonder if someone had killed her while I had spent my afternoons in bed. There had been several people in the fields, even around the house, whom I had never seen before.

So far, over the years, I had protected her. I've had many high school youths grab a stick when they visited here and want to kill her. Once I grabbed a boy's arm just in time to save her, my old gray lizard that lives on the rock walls of our outdoor oven. I've had any number of guests who can't understand my attitude toward this lizard. And when one of them asks why I protect a lizard, I have many answers. But I don't have and can't find a single reason why a lizard ought to be killed.

The high school boy who grabbed a stick of fire wood couldn't understand when I roughly caught his arm.

"What?" he said. He was surprised. "You don't want that thing killed?"

"I certainly do not," I told him. "It's a pet!"

Then he laughed! While he laughed I reached down and picked this fat old lizard up. I put her on my shoulder. She crawled all over me and finally rested on top of my head while we built the fire. She was even under my shirt. Often I had gone over the yard with her resting on my shoulder. She had caught flies from my shoulder. If this boy had killed her with that stick, I don't know what I would have done.

Each year she has come back to the furnace from her secret place of hibernation. When she is inside the furnace and I build a fire, she comes up the little chimney and goes down the outside into the grass and scampers over the walls to my writing room. She understands about fires in the furnace. She's seen so many built there she knows when to get out of the way.

Now why was I so happy? She was back. No one had hurt her as I had suspected. She scarcely moved when I went to her in the yard. I welcomed her back and chided her for being late.

And this is what I have told so many people who don't know the value of a lizard. First, the gray lizard is harmless. I've heard that the smooth-skinned red-green lizard is poisonous. I have my doubts about this. But I know gray lizards are as harmless as frogs. Their skin is rough and scaly, and perhaps the people who have fears of these innocent little creatures who like to bask in the sun and catch flies are put off by their rough exteriors.

Watch the gray lizard at work and play and you will find a fascinating creature. My parents taught me, when we used to work in the fields together, never to harm a bird, frog or lizard and never to tear a hornet's nest down. All these are great flycatchers. But among these four, they said, the lizard and the frog are the cleverest of all. After watching a lizard at work, I believe they were right.

The mother lizard lays small soft tough-shelled white eggs in the dirt. Many times when I have snatched grass from around the furnace, I pulled up these small white eggs and put them back in the warm ground and covered them over. Later, I saw little lizards scampering over the furnace walls.

I have used lizards in poems. The second article I ever sold was about lizards and hornets being great flycatchers. I received seven dollars for the article. That was long before I ever sold a short story or poem.

Now I inched over closer to my friend and greeted her affectionately. Finally, I touched her with my hand. It had been so long since I'd touched her that she moved away very slowly through the grass. But she was back in her favorite haunt for another season and so was I. I felt that she must feel warmly toward me, though I haven't had it from her directly.

"I would that I were worthy to be any man's Friend."

THOREAU DISCUSSES THE "MIRACLE"
OF TRUE FRIENDSHIP

No word is oftener on the lips of men than Friendship, and indeed no thought is more familiar to their apparitions. All men are dreaming of it, and its drama, which is always a tragedy, is enacted daily. It is the secret of the universe. You may thread the town, you may wander the country, and none shall ever speak it, yet thought is everywhere busy about it, and the idea of what is possible in this respect affects our behavior toward all new men and women, and a great many old ones.... We are continually acting a part in a more interesting drama than any written. We are dreaming that our friends are our *Friends,* and that we are Friends. Our actual Friends are but distant relations of those to whom we are pledged. We never exchange more than three words with a Friend in our lives on that level to which our thoughts and feelings almost habitually rise. One goes forth prepared to say "Sweet Friends!" and the salutation is "Damn your eyes!" But never mind; faint heart never won true Friend. O my Friend, may it come to pass, once, that when you are my Friend I may be yours.

Of what use the friendliest disposition even, if there are no hours given to Friendship, if it is forever postponed to unimportant duties and relations: Friendship is first, Friendship last. But it is equally impossible to forget our Friends, and to make them answer to our ideal. When they say farewell, then indeed we begin to keep them company. How often we find ourselves turning our backs on our actual Friends, that we may go and meet their ideal cousins. I would that I were worthy to be any man's Friend.

What is commonly honored with the name of Friendship is no very profound or powerful instinct. Men do not, after all, love their Friends greatly. I do not often see the farmers made seers by their friendship for one another. They are not often transfigured and translated by love in each other's presence. I do not observe them purified, refined and elevated by the love of men. If one abates a little the price of his wood, or gives a neighbor his vote at town meeting, or a barrel of apples or lends him his wagon frequently, it is esteeemed a rare instance of Friendship.... To say that a man is your Friend means commonly no more than this, that he is not your enemy. Most contemplate only what would be the accidental and trifling advantages of Friendship, so that the Friend can assist in time of need, by his substance, or his influence, or his counsel, but he who foresees such advantages in this relation proves himself blind to its real advantage, or indeed wholly inexperienced in the relation itself. Such services are particular and menial, compared with the perpetual and all-embracing service which it is. Even the utmost good will and harmony and practical kindness are not sufficient for Friendship, for Friends do not live in harmony merely, as some say, but in melody. We do not wish for Friends to feed and clothe our bodies,—neighbors are kind enough for that,—but to do the like office to our spirits. For this few are rich enough, however well disposed they may be.

Think of the importance of Friendship in the education of men. It will make a man honest; it will make him a hero; it will make him a saint. It is the state of the just dealing with the just, the magnanimous with the magnanimous, the sincere with the sincere, man with man. All the abuses which are the object of reform with the philanthropist, the statesman, the housekeeper, are unconsciously amended in the intercourse of Friends. A Friend is one who incessantly pays us the compliment of expecting from us all the virtues and who can appreciate them in us. It takes two to speak the truth,—one to speak, and another to hear.... In daily intercourse with men, our nobler faculties are dormant and suffered to rust. None will pay us the compliment to expect nobleness from us.... What is commonly called Friendship even is only a little more honor among rogues.

But sometimes we are said to *love* another, that is to stand in a true relation to him, so that we give the best to, and receive the best from, him. Between whom there is hearty truth there is love; and in proportion to our truthfulness and confidence in one another, our lives are divine and miraculous, and answer to our ideal. There are passages of affection in our intercourse with mortal men and women, such as no prophecy had taught us to expect, which transcend our earthly life, and anticipate heaven for us....

Friendship takes place between those who have an affinity for one another, and is a perfectly natural and inevitable result. No professions or advances will avail. Even speech, at first, necessarily has nothing to do with it; but it follows after silence, as the buds in the graft do not put forth into leaves till long after the graft has taken. It is a drama in which the parties have no part to act....

Friendship is never established as an understood relation. Do you demand that I be less your Friend that you may know it? Yet what right have I to think that another cherishes so rare a sentiment for me? It is a miracle which requires constant proofs. It is an exercise of the finest imagination and the rarest faith. It says by a silent but eloquent behavior:—"I will be so related to thee as thou canst imagine; even so thou mayest believe. I will spend truth,—all my wealth on thee," and the Friend responds silently through his nature, and life, and treats his Friend with the same divine courtesy....

The language of Friendship is not words but meaning. It is an intelligence above language. One imagines endless conversations with his Friend, in which the tongue shall be loosed, and thoughts be spoken, without hesitancy, or end; but the experience is commonly far otherwise....

Suppose you go to bid farewell to your Friend who is setting out on a journey; what other outward sign do you know than to shake his hand?... There are some things which a man never speaks of, which are much finer kept silent about. To the highest communications we only lend a silent ear.... In human intercourse the tragedy begins, not when there is misunderstanding about words, but when silence is not understood.

BROKEN FRIENDSHIP
(from "Christabel")
Samuel Taylor Coleridge

Alas! they had been friends in youth;
But whispering tongues can poison truth;
And constancy lives in realms above;
    And life is thorny; and youth is vain:
And to be wroth with one we love,
    Doth work like madness in the brain.
And thus it chanced, as I divine,
With Roland and Sir Leoline.

Each spake words of high disdain
    And insult to his heart's best brother:
They parted—ne'er to meet again!
    But never either found another
To free the hollow heart from paining;
They stood aloof, the scars remaining,
Like cliffs which had been rent asunder:
    A dreary sea now flows between,
But neither heat, nor frost, nor thunder,
    Shall wholly do away, I ween,
    The marks of that which once hath been.

"... we spoke of all that was in our hearts ..."

JEWELS OF RECOLLECTION
Arthur Christopher Benson

The talks that remain in my mind as of preeminent interest are long leisurely tête-a-tête talks, oftenest perhaps of all in the course of a walk, when exercise sends the blood coursing through the brain, when a pleasant countryside times the spirit to a serene harmony of mood, and when the mind, stimulated into a joyful readiness by association with some quiet, just, and perceptive companion, visits its dusty warehouse, and turns over its fantastic stories. Then is the time to penetrate into the inmost labyrinths of a subject, to indulge in pleasing discursiveness, as the fancy leads one, and yet to return again and again with renewed relish to the central theme. Such talks as these make the moments, indeed, to which the mind, in the sad mood which remembers the days that are gone, turns with that sorrowful desolation of which Dante speaks, as to a treasure lightly spent and ungratefully regarded. How such hours rise up before the mind! Even now as I write I think of such a scene, when I walked with a friend, long dead, on the broad yellow sands beside a western sea. I can recall the sharp hiss of the shoreward wind, the wholesome savors of the brine, the brisk clap of small waves, the sand-dunes behind the shore, picked with green tufts of grass, the ship moving slowly on the sea's rim, and the shadowy headland to which we hardly seemed to draw more near, while we spoke of all that was in our hearts, and all that we meant to do and be. That day was a great gift from God, and yet, as I received it, I did not know how fair a jewel of memory it would be. I like to think that there are many such jewels of recollection clasped close in the heart's casket.

⌒⌒⌒⌒⌒⌒

"AS ONE WHO, WALKING IN THE TWILIGHT GLOOM"
Henry Wadsworth Longfellow

As one who, walking in the twilight gloom,
    Hears round about him voices as it darkens,
And seeing not the forms from which they come,
    Pauses from time to time, and turns and hearkens;

So walking here in twilight, O my friends!
  I hear your voices, softened by the distance,
And pause, and turn to listen, as each sends
  His words of friendship, comfort, and assistance.

If any thought of mine, or sung or told,
  Has ever given delight or consolation,
Ye have repaid me back a thousand-fold,
  By every friendly sign and salutation.

Thanks for the sympathies that ye have shown!
  Thanks for each kindly word, each silent token,
That teaches me, when seeming most alone,
  Friends are around us, though no word be spoken.

Kind messages, that pass from land to land;
  Kind letters, that betray the heart's deep history,
In which we feel the pressure of a hand,—
  One touch of fire,—and all the rest is mystery! ...

Perhaps on earth I never shall behold,
  With eyes of sense, your outward form and semblance;
Therefore to me ye never will grow old,
  But live forever young in my remembrance!

Never grow old, nor change, nor pass away!
  Your gentle voices will flow on forever,
When life grows bare and tarnished with decay,
  As through a leafless landscape flows a river.

Not a chance of birth or place has made us friends,
  Being oftentimes of different tongues and nations,
But the endeavor for the selfsame ends,
  With the same hopes, and fears, and aspirations.

Therefore I hope to join your seaside walk,
  Saddened, and mostly silent, with emotion;
Not interrupting with intrusive talk
  The grand, majestic symphonies of ocean.

Therefore I hope, as no unwelcome guest,
  At your warm fireside, when the lamps are lighted,
To have my place reserved among the rest,
  Nor stand as one unsought and uninvited!

"... the light of love shone on me."

HOW I LEARNED THE MEANING OF LOVE

Helen Keller

The most important day I remember in all my life is the one on which my teacher, Anne Mansfield Sullivan, came to me. I am filled with wonder when I consider the immeasurable contrast between the two lives which it connects. It was the third of March, 1887, three months before I was seven years old.

On the afternoon of that eventful day, I stood on the porch, dumb, expectant. I guessed vaguely from my mother's signs and from the hurrying to and fro in the house that something unusual was about to happen, so I went to the door and waited on the steps. The afternoon sun penetrated the mass of honeysuckle that covered the porch, and fell on my upturned face. My fingers lingered almost unconsciously on the familiar leaves and blossoms which had just come forth to greet the sweet southern spring. I did not know what the future held of marvel or surprise for me. Anger and bitterness had preyed upon me continually for weeks. Then a languor had succeeded this passionate struggle.

Have you ever been at sea in a dense fog, when it seemed as if a tangible white darkness shut you in, and the great ship, tense and anxious, groped her way toward the shore with plummet and sounding-line, and you waited with beating heart for something to happen? I was like that ship before my education began, only I was without compass or sounding-line, and had no way of knowing how near the harbor was. "Light! give me light!" was the wordless cry of my soul, and the light of love shone on me.

I felt approaching footsteps. I stretched out my hand as I supposed to my mother. Some one took it, and I was caught up and held close in the arms of her who had come to reveal all things to me, and, more than all things else, to love me.

The morning after my teacher came she led me into her room and gave me a doll. The little blind children at the Perkins Institute had sent it; but I did not know this until afterward. When I had played with it a little while, Miss Sullivan slowly spelled into my hand the word "d-o-l-l." I was at once interested in this finger play and tried to imitate it. When I finally succeeded in making the letters correctly I was flushed with childish pleasure and pride. Running downstairs to my mother I held up my hand and made the letters for doll. I did not know that I was spelling a word or even that words existed; I was simply making my fingers go in monkey-like imitation. In the days that followed I learned to spell in this uncomprehending way a great many words, among them pin, hat, cup and a few verbs like sit, stand, and walk. But my teacher had been with me several weeks before I understood that everything has a name.

One day, while I was playing with my new doll, Miss Sullivan put my big rag doll into my lap also, spelled "d-o-l-l" and tried to make me understand that "d-o-l-l" applied to both. Earlier in the day we had a tussle over the words "m-u-g" and "w-a-t-e-r." Miss Sullivan had tried to impress it upon me that "m-u-g" is mug and that "w-a-t-e-r" is water, but I persisted in confounding the two. In despair she had dropped the subject for the time, only to renew it at the first opportunity. I became impatient at her repeated attempts and, seizing the new doll, I dashed it upon the floor. I was keenly delighted when I felt the fragments of the broken doll at my feet. Neither sorrow nor regret followed my passionate outburst. I had not loved the doll. In the still, dark world in which I lived there was no strong sentiment or tenderness. I felt my teacher sweep the fragments to one side of the hearth, and I had a sense of satisfaction that the cause of my discomfort was removed. She brought me my hat, and I knew I was going out into the warm sunshine. This thought, if a wordless sensation may be called a thought, made me hop and skip with pleasure.

We walked down the path to the well-house, attracted by the fragrance of the honeysuckle with which it was covered. Some one was drawing water and my teacher placed my hand under the spout. As the cool stream gushed over one hand she spelled into the other the word water, first slowly, then rapidly. I stood still, my whole attention fixed upon the motions of her fingers. Suddenly I felt a misty consciousness as of something forgotten—a thrill of returning thought; and somehow the mystery of language was revealed to me. I knew then that "w-a-t-e-r" meant the wonderful cool something that was flowing over my hand. That living word awakened my soul, gave it light, hope, joy, set it free! There were barriers still, it is true, but barriers that could in time be swept away.

I left the well-house eager to learn. Everything had a name, and each name gave birth to a new thought. As we returned to the house every object which I touched seemed to quiver with life. That was because I saw everything with the strange, new sight that had come to me. On entering the door I remembered the doll I had broken. I felt my way to the hearth and picked up the pieces. I tried vainly to put them together. Then my eyes filled with tears; for I realized what I had done, and for the first time I felt repentance and sorrow.

I learned a great many new words that day. I do not remember what they all were; but I do know that mother, father, sister, teacher were among them—words that were to make the world blossom for me, "like Aaron's rod, with flowers." It would have been difficult to find a happier child than I was as I lay in my crib at the close of that eventful day and lived over the joys it had brought me, and for the first time longed for a new day to come.

I had now the key to all language, and I was eager to learn to use it. Children who hear acquire language without any particular effort; the words that fall from others' lips they catch on the wing, as it were, delightedly, while the little deaf child must trap them by a slow and often painful process. But whatever the process, the result is wonderful. Gradually from naming an object we advance step by step until we have traversed the vast distance between our first stammered syllable and the sweep of thought in a line of Shakespeare.

At first, when my teacher told me about a new thing I asked very few questions. My ideas were vague, and my vocabulary was inadequate; but as my knowledge of things grew, and I learned more and more words, my field of inquiry broadened, and I would return again and again to the same subject, eager for further information. Sometimes a new word revived an image that some earlier experience had engraved on my brain.

I remember the morning that I first asked the meaning of the word, "love." This was before I knew many words. I had found a few early violets in the garden and brought them to my teacher. She tried to kiss me; but at that time I did not like to have any one kiss me except my mother. Miss Sullivan put her arm gently around me and spelled into my hand, "I love Helen."

"What is love?" I asked.

She drew me closer to her and said, "It is here," pointing to my heart, whose beats I was conscious of for the first time. Her words puzzled me very much because I did not then understand anything unless I touched it.

I smelt the violets in her hand and asked, half in words, half in signs, a question which meant, "Is love the sweetness of flowers?"

"No," said my teacher.

Again I thought. The warm sun was shining on us.

"Is this not love?" I asked, pointing in the direction from which the heat came. "Is this not love?"

It seemed to me that there could be nothing more beautiful than the sun, whose warmth makes all things grow. But Miss Sullivan shook her head, and I was greatly puzzled and disappointed. I thought it strange that my teacher could not show me love.

A day or two afterward I was stringing beads of different sizes in symmetrical groups—two large beads, three small ones, and so on. I had made many mistakes, and Miss Sullivan had pointed them out again and again with gentle patience. Finally I noticed a very obvious error in the sequence and for an instant I concentrated my attention on the lesson and tried to think how I should have arranged the beads. Miss Sullivan touched my forehead and spelled with decided emphasis, "Think."

In a flash I knew that the word was the name of the process that was going on in my head. This was my first conscious perception of an abstract idea.

For a long time I was still—I was not thinking of the beads in my lap, but trying to find a meaning for "love" in the light of this new idea. The sun had been under a cloud all day, and there had been brief showers; but suddenly the sun broke forth in all its southern splendor.

Again I asked my teacher, "Is this not love?"

"Love is something like the clouds that were in the sky before the sun came out," she replied. Then in simpler words than these, which at that time I could not have understood, she explained: "You cannot touch the clouds, you know, but you feel the rain and know how glad the flowers and the thirsty earth are to have it after a hot day. You cannot touch love either; but you feel the sweetness that it pours into everything. Without love you would not be happy or want to play."

The beautiful truth burst open my mind—I felt that there were invisible lines stretched between my spirit and the spirits of others.

From the beginning of my education Miss Sullivan made it a practice to speak to me as she would speak to any hearing child; the only difference was that she spelled the sentences into my hand instead of speaking them. If I did not know the words and idioms necessary to express my thoughts she supplied them, even suggesting conversation when I was unable to keep up my end of the dialogue.

This process was continued for several years; for the deaf child does not learn in a month, or even in two or three years, the numberless idioms and expressions used in the simplest daily intercourse. The little hearing child learns these from constant repetition and imitation. The conversation he hears in his home stimulates his mind and suggests topics and calls forth the spontaneous expression of his own thoughts. This natural exchange of ideas is denied to the deaf child. My teacher, realizing this, determined to supply the kinds of stimulus I lacked. This she did by repeating to me as far as possible, verbatim, what she heard, and by showing me how I could take part in the conversation. But it was a long time before I ventured to take the initiative and still longer before I could find something appropriate to say at the right time.

The deaf and the blind find it very difficult to acquire the amenities of conversation. How much more this difficulty must be augmented in the case of those who are both deaf and blind! They cannot distinguish the tone of the voice or, without assistance, go up and down the gamut of tones that give significance to words; nor can they watch the expression of the speaker's face, and a look is often the very soul of what one says.

⁂

"... here is a friend who facilitates our thinking ..."

FRIENDS AS "SOLVENTS"

Frances Lester Warner

There are friends who act as "solvents" in our minds. They help us blend the stiff incongruities of experience into something that will not clog our brains. Our ideas flow more easily when they are around. And if we want to know whether, for us, any given person falls into this class, we need only ask ourselves the question about the moment when, in the middle of a busy day, the memory of that friend unexpectedly flashes into mind.

The sudden thought of him: does it, in some characteristic fashion, reassure us?

And does it, no matter how we may happen to be feeling, seem to "go to the spot"?

Here is a highly specialized relationship, beyond anybody's power to instigate or control.

Among all our acquaintances, there are some about whom we worry, some about whom we wonder; some who stir us up or tone us down; some who worry about us and for whose sake we know we ought to tinker up our characters and improve. But here is a friend who facilitates our thinking without interrupting it. He can enter our state of mind like a fortunate remark dropped into a conversation, amazingly apropos.

According to the drama of the moment, he takes his place. If we are feeling benevolent, he gives focus to the warm beam of our approval. If we are critical, he balances aptly on the fine edge of our esteem. If we are upset, we know this will not shock him, for he, too, has the emotional suppleness to stand occasionally upon his head. If our likings are catholic and capacious, he promenades without jealousy or jostlings, all up and down the social terraces of our minds. And if our space reserved for personal likings is limited and hidden, he fits into it with a rare perfection that gives us new confidence in our relations with the world. He is good for us when we are feeling spiritually dead and brittle, like the influenza patient who observed mournfully, "The universe has turned a page on me, and left me pressed between the leaves."

Oh, the persons who are solvents for hard moods! We owe them much. In particular we owe them one rather valuable thing: the assurance that, in just the degree to which we have liked them, we ourselves must be compatible with some phase of the human blend. We could not have liked any human being quite so well if we ourselves were totally fossilized.

"MY FRIEND MUST BE A BIRD"
Emily Dickinson

My friend must be a bird,
　Because it flies!
Mortal my friend must be,
　Because it dies!
Barbs has it, like a bee.
Ah, curious friend,
　Thou puzzlest me!

". . . put not so much in a friend's power that . . . he can do you an injury."

THE WRESTLER
Saadi

A person had become a master in the art of wrestling; he knew three hundred and sixty sleights in this art, and could exhibit a fresh trick for every day throughout the year. Perhaps owing to a liking that a corner of his heart took for the handsome person of one of his scholars, he taught him three hundred and fifty-nine of those feats, but he was putting off the last one, and under some pretence deferring it.

In short, the youth became such a proficient in the art and talent of wrestling that none of his contemporaries had ability to cope with him, till he at length had one day boasted before the reigning sovereign, saying: "To any superiority my master possesses over me, he is beholden to my reverence of his seniority, and in virtue of his tutorage; otherwise I am not inferior in power, and am his equal in skill." This want of respect displeased the king. He ordered a wrestling match to be held, and a spacious field to be fenced in for the occasion. The ministers of state, nobles of the court, and gallant men of the realm were assembled, and the ceremonials of the combat marshalled. Like a huge and lusty elephant, the youth rushed into the ring with such a crash that had a brazen mountain opposed him he would have moved it from its base. The master being aware that the youth was his superior in strength, engaged him in that strange feat of which he had kept him ignorant. The youth was unacquainted with its guard. Advancing, nevertheless, the master seized him with both hands, and lifting him bodily from the ground, raised him above his head and flung him on the earth. The crowd set up a shout. The king ordered them to give the master an honorary dress and handsome largess, and the youth he addressed with reproach and asperity, saying: "You played the traitor with your own patron, and failed in your presumption of opposing him." He replied: "O sire! my master did not overcome me by strength and ability, but one cunning trick in the art of wrestling was left which he was reserved in teaching me, and by that little feat had today the upper hand of me." The master said: "I reserved myself for such a day as this. As the wise have told us, put not so much into a friend's power that, if hostilely disposed, he can do you an injury."

(Translated by James Ross)

A TEMPLE TO FRIENDSHIP

Thomas Moore

"A Temple to Friendship," cried Laura, enchanted,
"I'll build in this garden; the thought is divine."
So the temple was built, and she now only wanted
An image of Friendship, to place on the shrine.

So she flew to the sculptor, who set down before her
An image, the fairest his art could invent;
But so cold, and so dull, that the youthful adorer
Saw plainly this was not the Friendship she meant.

"Oh, never," said she, "could I think of enshrining
An image whose looks are so joyless and dim;
But yon little god upon roses reclining,
We'll make, if you please, sir, a Friendship of him."

So the bargain was struck; with the little god laden,
She joyfully flew to her home in the grove.
"Farewell," said the sculptor, "you're not the first maiden
Who came but for Friendship, and took away Love!"

⁂

"... he saw the greater part of mankind attending to anything
rather than securing friends."

ADVICE FROM SOCRATES
Xenophon

On one occasion I heard Socrates holding a discourse concerning friends, by which, it seems to me, a person might be greatly benefited, both as to the acquisition and use of friends.

He said that he had heard many people observe that a true and honest friend was the most valuable of all possessions, but that he saw the greater part of mankind attending to anything rather than securing friends. He observed them industriously endeavoring to procure houses and lands, cattle, slaves, and furniture; but as for a friend, whom they called the greatest of all blessings, he saw the majority considering neither how to procure one, nor how those whom they had might be retained.

Yet in comparison with what possession, of all others, he asked, would not a good friend appear far more valuable? What sort of house, or yoke of oxen, is so useful as a truly good friend? What other acquisition is so beneficial?

A good friend interests himself in whatever is wanting on the part of his friend, whether in his private affairs, or for the public interests. If he is required to do a service to anyone, he assists him with the means; if any apprehensions alarm him, he lends him his aid, sometimes sharing expenditure with him, sometimes cooperating with him, sometimes joining with him to persuade others, sometimes using force towards others; frequently cheering him when he is successful, and frequently supporting him when he is in danger of failing.

What the hands do, what the eyes foresee, what the ears hear, what the feet accomplish for each individual,—none of such services his friend fails to perform. Oftentimes what a person has not effected for himself, or has not seen, or has not heard, or has not accomplished, a friend has succeeded in executing for his friend. Yet, while people try to foster trees for the sake of their fruit, the greater portion of mankind are heedless and neglectful of that most productive possession which is called a friend.

(Translator anonymous)

"They held out their hands to him."

HIS ONLY FRIEND

Fulton Oursler

In Dublin where he came from, Joe Scriven was known as the man who never trusted anybody. They said that he had been born with a glint of suspicion in his eyes. From his earliest schooldays he had played the part of a lone wolf. He never belonged to a boys' club, never went on church picnics, and had never even had a chum.

What was wrong with Joe Scriven? So many years have passed since Joe was born that one can only imagine his youth. Perhaps all that is known about him is the amazing thing that happened to him when he grew up. But one can surmise these things; can look into the past as into a crystal ball and suppose that some disgruntled elder, soured on life, warned the boy against his fellows, against fate, against the world.

One thing we do know. He became dissatisfied with Dublin and decided to seek his fortunes elsewhere. That was how he found his way to a little town in Canada. Perhaps the newness of his surroundings intensified the loneliness he must often have suffered. At any rate, one thing is certain— the man who was afraid of making friends suddenly fell in love. She was young and lovely, with a fragility unusual in the primitive settlements of those days. To this girl Joe Scriven plighted his troth. Forgetting the distrust in which he had been schooled, he gave her his faith, and counted on her promise to meet him at the altar and become his wife. But that promise was not kept.

She had gone to a town across the bay and was returning with her wedding clothes when, on the night before their marriage day, she was drowned, all hands lost in a sudden storm. Joseph Scriven stood alone again in the world. He who had tried to make sure that life could not hurt him now was plunged into what seemed insupportable anguish. The pain of it was too great to be borne alone, yet to whom could he turn? The only friend he had ever made was gone. In his agony, alone in his room, he fell upon his knees and cried to God. And in the darkness the tears came.

When after long hours of seeking the hand of his Father in Heaven he got back on his feet, he felt weak and dazed. Putting on his hat, he started down the stairs of his boardinghouse, and there in the hall he saw a group of people—the ribbon clerk who had the third floor back, the schoolteacher, the old lady from the library, and the boarding-house mistress. They held out their hands to him. They embraced him. They told him to have courage. And the old clergyman was there; he took him by the arm and led him to the manse. Joe Scriven was amazed to find how much sympathy there was in the world, how much friendliness around him like a cloak in the wind.

Now here is the oddity. No one had ever thought of Joe Scriven as being religious, nor had anyone thought of him as being musical. And certainly no one had ever thought of him as one who would be able to bring comfort and consolation and the vision of a courageous new life literally to millions of grieving people. Yet such were the facts.

Joe Scriven, strengthened and deepened by his loss, gave all his goods to the poor, and spent the rest of his life gratuitously sawing wood and making repairs for poor people. And in the solitude of his room one night he wrote a hymn that is still sung in uncounted churches around this world:

"What a friend we have in Jesus."

"Your friends do not and will not forget you."

HAWTHORNE'S FRIENDS COME TO HIS AID

As a result of politics, Nathaniel Hawthorne lost his post as Surveyor at the Salem, Massachusetts, Custom House. As a consequence, George S. Hillard wrote him as follows:

Boston, January 17, 1850

It occurred to me, and some other of your friends that, in considera-tion of the events of the last year, you might at this time be in need of a little pecuniary aid. I have therefore collected, from some of those who admire your genius and respect your character, the enclosed sum of money, which I send you with my warmest wishes for your health and happiness. I know the sensitive edge of your temperament; but do not speak or think of obligation. It is only paying, in a very imperfect measure, the debt we owe you for what you have done for American literature. Could you know the readiness with which every one to whom I applied contributed to this little offering, and could you have heard the warm expressions with which some accompanied their gift, you would have felt that the bread you had cast on the waters had indeed come back to you. Let no shadow of despondency, my dear friend, steal over you. Your friends do not and will not forget you. You shall be protected against "eating cares," which, I take it, mean cares lest we should not have enough to eat.

Hawthorne's Reply

Salem, January 30, 1850

I read your letter in the vestibule of the Post Office; and it drew—what my troubles never have—the water to my eyes; so that I was glad of the sharply cold west wind that blew into them as I came homeward, and gave them an excuse for being red and bleared.

There was much that was very sweet—and something too that was very bitter—mingled with that same moisture. It is sweet to be remembered and cared for by one's friends—some of whom know me for what I am, while others, perhaps, know me only through a generous faith—sweet to think that they deem me worth upholding in my poor work through life. And it is bitter, nevertheless, to need their support. It is something else besides pride that teaches me that ill-success in life is really and justly a matter of shame. I am ashamed of it, and I ought to be. The fault of a failure is attributable—in a great degree at least—to the man who fails. I should apply this truth in judging of other men; and it behooves me not to shun its point or edge in taking it home to my own heart. Nobody has a right to live in the world unless he be strong and able, and applies his ability to good purpose.

The money, dear Hillard, will smooth my path for a long time to come. The only way in which a man can retain his self-respect, while availing himself of the generosity of his friends, is by making it an incitement to his utmost exertions, so that he may not need their help again. I shall look upon it so—nor will shun any drudgery that my hand shall find to do, if thereby I may win bread.

Four years later, while American Consul at Liverpool, Hawthorne wrote:

Liverpool, December 9, 1853

Dear Hillard:

I herewith send you a draft on Ticknor for the sum (with interest included) which was so kindly given me by unknown friends, through you, about four years ago.

I have always hoped and intended to do this, from the first moment when I made up my mind to accept the money. It would not have been right to speak of this purpose before it was in my power to accomplish it; but it has never been out of my mind for a single day, nor hardly, I think, for a single working hour. I am most happy that this loan (as I may fairly call it, at this moment) can now be repaid without the risk on my part of leaving my wife and children utterly destitute. I should have done it sooner; but I felt that it would be selfish to purchase the great satisfaction for myself, at any fresh risk to them. We are not rich, nor are we ever likely to be; but the miserable pinch is over.

The friends who were so generous to me must not suppose that I have not felt deeply grateful, nor that my delight at relieving myself from this pecuniary obligation is of any ungracious kind. I have been grateful all along, and am more so now than ever. This act of kindness did me an unspeakable amount of good; for it came when I most needed to be assured that anybody thought it worthwhile to keep me from sinking. And it did me even greater good than this, in making me sensible of the need of sterner efforts than my former ones, in order to establish a right for myself to live and be comfortable. For it is my creed (and was so even at that wretched time) that a man has no claim upon his fellow-creatures, beyond bread and water and a grave, unless he can win it by his own strength or skill. But so much the kinder were those unknown friends whom I thank again with all my heart.

"... I'll awa' to Marjorie."

SIR WALTER SCOTT AND MARJORIE FLEMING

Dr. John Brown

Sir Walter sat down in his large green morocco elbow-chair, drew himself close to his table, and glowered and gloomed at his writing apparatus, "a very handsome old box, richly carved, lined with crimson velvet, and containing ink-bottles, taper-stand, etc., in silver, the whole in such order, that it might have come from the silversmith's window half an hour before." He took out his paper, then starting up angrily, said, " 'Go spin, you jade, go spin.' No, d— it, it won't do,—

> " 'My spinnin' wheel is aud and stiff,
> The rock o't wunna stand, sir,
> To keep the temper-pin in tiff
> Employs ower aft my hand, sir.'

I am off the fang. I can make nothing of *Waverly* today; I'll awa' to Marjorie. Come wi' me, Maida, you thief." The great creature rose slowly, and the pair were off, Scott taking a *maud* (a plaid) with him. "White as a frosted plum-cake, by jingo!" said he, when he got to the street. Maida gamboled and whisked among the snow, and her master strode across to Young Street, and through it to 1 North Charlotte Street, to the house of his dear friend, Mrs. William Keith, of Corstorphine Hill, niece of Mrs. Keith, of Ravelston, of whom he said at her death, eight years after, "Much tradition, and that of the best, has died with this excellent old lady, one of the few persons whose spirit and *cleanliness* and freshness of mind and body made old age lovely and desirable."

Sir Walter was in that house almost every day, and had a key, so in he and the hound went, shaking themselves in the lobby. "Marjorie! Marjorie!" shouted her friend, "where are ye my bonnie wee croodlin doo?" In a moment a bright, eager child of seven was in his arms, and he was kissing her all over. Out came Mrs. Keith. "Come yer ways in, Wattie." "No, not now. I am going to take Marjorie wi' me, and you may come to your tea in Duncan Roy's sedan, and bring the bairn home in your lap." "Tak' Marjorie, and it *on-ding o' snaw!*" said Mrs. Keith. He said to himself, "On-ding,—that's odd,—that is the very word." Hoot, awa', look here," and he displayed the corner of his plaid, made to hold lambs (the true shepherd's plaid, consisting of two breadths sewed together, and uncut at one end, making a poke or *cul de sac*). "Tak' yer lamb," said she, laughing at the contrivance, and so the Pet was first well happit up, and then put up, laughing silently, into the plaid neuk, and the shepherd strode off with his lamb,—Maida gamboling through the snow, and running races in her mirth.

Didn't he face "the angry airt" and make her bield his bosom, and into his own room with her, and lock the door, and out with the warm, rosy, little wifie, who took it all with great composure! There the two remained for three or more hours, making the house ring with their laughter; you can fancy the big man's and Maidie's laugh. Having made the fire cheery, he set her down in his ample chair, and standing sheepishly before her, began to say his lesson, which happened to be,— "Zicotty, dicotty, dock, the mouse ran up the clock, the clock struck wan, down the mouse ran, zicotty, dicotty, dock." This done repeatedly till she was pleased, she gave him his new lesson, gravely and slowly, timing it upon her small fingers,—he saying it after her.—

> "Wonery, twoery, tickery, seven;
>   Alibi, crackaby, ten, and eleven;
> Pin, pan, musky, dan;
> Tweedle-um, twoddle-um,
> Twenty-wan; eerie, orie, ourie,
> You are out."

He pretended to great difficulty, and she rebuked him with most comical gravity, treating him as a child. He used to say that when he came to Alibi Crackaby he broke down, and Pin-Pan, Musky-Dan, Tweedle-um, Twoddle-um made him roar with laughter. He said *Musky-Dan* especially was beyond endurance, bringing up an Irishman and his hat fresh from the Spice Islands and odoriferous Ind; she getting quite bitter in her displeasure at his ill-behavior and stupidness.

Then he would read ballads to her in his own glorious way, the two getting wild with excitement over *Gil Morrice* or the *Baron of Smailholm;* and he would take her on his knee, and make her repeat Constance's speeches in *King John,* till he swayed to and fro, sobbing his fill. Fancy the gifted little creature, like one possessed, repeating,—

> "For I am sick, and capable of fears,
> Oppressed with wrong, and therefore full of fears;
> A widow, husbandless, subject to fears;
> A woman, naturally born to fears.
> If thou that bidst me be content, wert grim,
> Ugly and slanderous to thy mother's womb,
> Lame, foolish, crooked, swart, prodigious"—

Or drawing herself up "to the height of her great argument,"—

> "I will instruct my sorrows to be proud,
> For grief is proud, and makes his owner stout.
> Here I and sorrow sit."

Scott used to say that he was amazed at her power over him, saying to Mrs. Keith, "She's the most extraordinary creature I ever met with, and her repeating of Shakespeare overpowers me as nothing else does."

THE ARROW AND THE SONG
Henry Wadsworth Longfellow

I shot an arrow into the air,
It fell to earth, I know not where;
For, so swiftly it flew, the sight
Could not follow it in its flight.

I breathed a song into the air,
It fell to earth, I knew not where;
For who has sight so keen and strong,
That it can follow the flight of song?

Long, long afterward, in an oak
I found the arrow, still unbroke;
And the song, from beginning to end,
I found again in the heart of a friend.

"It was a great, warm, outflowing heart . . ."

PORTRAIT OF A FRIEND—
MARY RUSSELL MITFORD

My Dear Mr. Ruskin,—I thank you from my heart for your more than interesting letter. You have helped me to see that dear friend of ours, as without you I could not have seen her, in those last affecting days of illness, by the window not only of the house in Berkshire, but of the house of the body and of the material world—an open window through which the light shone, thank God. It would be a comfort for me now if I had had the privilege of giving her a very, very little of the great pleasure you certainly gave her (for I know how she enjoyed your visit—she wrote and told me), but I must be satisfied with the thought left to me, that now she regrets nothing, not even great pleasures.

I agree with you in much if not in everything you have written of her. It was a great, warm, outflowing heart, and the head was worthy of the heart. People have observed that she resembled Coleridge in her granite forehead—something, too, in the lower part of the face,—however, unlike Coleridge in mental characteristics, in his tendency to abstract speculation, or indeed his ideality. There might have been, as you suggest, a somewhat different development elsewhere than in Berkshire—not very different, though—souls don't grow out of the ground.

I agree quite with you that she was stronger and wider in her conversation and letters than in her books. Oh, I have said so a hundred times. The heat of human sympathy seemed to bring out her powerful vitality, rustling all over with laces and flowers. She seemed to think and speak stronger, holding a hand—not that she required help or borrowed a word, but that the human magnetism acted on her nature as it does upon men born to speak. Perhaps if she had been a man with a man's opportunities, she would have spoken rather than written a reputation. Who can say? She hated the act of composition. Did you hear that from her ever?

Her letters were always admirable, but I do most deeply regret that what made one of their greatest charms unfits them for the public—I mean their personal details. Mr. Harness sends to me for letters, and when I bring them up, and with the greatest pain force myself to examine them (all those letters she wrote to me in her warm goodness and affectionateness), I find with wonder and sorrow how only a half-page here and there *could* be submitted to general readers,—*could,* with any decency, much less delicacy.

But no, her "judgment" was not "unerring." She was too intensely sympathetical not to err often, and in fact it was singular (or seemed so) what faces struck her as most beautiful, and what books as most excellent. If she loved a person, it was enough. She made mistakes one couldn't help smiling at, till one grew serious to adore her for it. And yet when she read a book, provided it wasn't written by a friend, edited by a friend, lent by a friend, or associated with a friend, her judgment could be fine and discriminating on most subjects, especially upon subjects connected with life and society and manners.

ELIZABETH BARRETT BROWNING

HAMLET TO HORATIO
William Shakespeare

Since my dear soul was mistress of her choice
And could of men distinguish, her election
Hath seal'd thee for herself; for thou hast been
As one, suffering all, that suffers nothing,
A man that fortune's buffets and rewards
Hast ta'en with equal thanks: and blest are those

Whose blood and judgement are so well commingled,
That they are not a pipe for fortune's finger
To sound what stop she please. Give me that man
That is not passion's slave, and I will wear him
In my heart's core, ay, in my heart of heart,
As I do thee.

"...you are the best and oldest friend..."

THACKERAY BEFORE LEAVING ON A TRIP TO THE UNITED STATES WRITES A NOTE TO EDWARD FITZGERALD

October 27, 1852

My Dearest Old Friend,

I mustn't go away without shaking your hand, and saying Farewell and God Bless you. If anything happens to me, you by these presents must get ready the Book of Ballads which you like, and which I had not time to prepare before embarking on this voyage. And I should like my daughters to remember that you are the best and oldest friend their Father ever had, and that you would act as such: as my literary executor and so forth. My Books would yield a something as copyrights; and should anything occur, I have commissioned friends in good place to get a Pension for my poor little wife.... Does not this sound gloomily? Well: who knows what Fate is in store: and I feel not at all downcast, but very grave and solemn just at the brink of a great voyage.

I shall send you a copy of Esmond to-morrow or so which you shall yawn over when you are inclined. But the great comfort I have in thinking about my dear old boy is that recollection of our youth when we loved each other as I do now while I write Farewell.

Laurence has done a capital head of me ordered by Smith the Publisher: and I have ordered a copy and Lord Ashburton another. If Smith gives me this one, I shall send the copy to you. I care for you as you know, and always like to think that I am fondly and affectionately yours

W. M. T.

I sail from Liverpool on Saturday Morning by the *Canada* for Boston.

FRIENDSHIP
Ralph Waldo Emerson

A ruddy drop of manly blood
The surging sea outweighs,
The world uncertain comes and goes;
The lover rooted stays.
I fancied he was fled,—
And, after many a year,
Glowed unexhausted kindliness,
Like daily sunrise there.
My careful heart was free again,
O friend, my bosom said,
Through thee alone the sky is arched,
Through thee the rose is red;
All things through thee take nobler form,
And look beyond the earth,
The mill-round of our fate appears
A sun-path in thy worth.
Me too thy nobleness has taught
To master my despair;
The fountains of my hidden life
Are through thy friendship fair.

"... you wish them equally at the devil!"

THOSE WHO CANNOT MAKE FRIENDS
William Hazlitt

There are persons who cannot make friends. Who are they? Those who cannot be friends. It is not the want of understanding or good nature, of entertaining or useful qualities, that you complain of; on the contrary, they have probably many points of attraction; but they have one that neutralizes all these—they care nothing about you, and are neither the better nor worse for what you think of them. They manifest no joy at your approach; and when you leave them, it is with a feeling that they can do just as well without you. This is not sullenness, nor indifference, but absence of mind; but they are intent solely on their own thoughts, and you are merely one of the subjects they exercise them upon. They live in society as in solitude; and however their brain works, their pulse beats neither faster nor slower for the common accidents of life. There is, therefore, something cold and repulsive in the air about them—like that of marble. In a word, they are modern philosophers; and the modern philosopher is what the pedant was of old—a being who lives in a world of his own, and has no correspondence with this. It is not that such persons have not done you services —you acknowledge it; it is not that they have said severe things of you—you submit to it as a necessary evil; but it is the cool manner in which the whole is done that annoys you—the speculating upon you, as if you were a nobody—the regarding you, with a view to an experiment *in corpore vili*—the principle of dissection—the determination to spare no blemishes—to cut you down to your real standard;—in short, the utter absence of the partiality of friendship, the blind enthusiasm of affection, or the delicacy of common decency, that whether they "knew you as a carcase fit for hounds, or carve you as a dish fit for the gods," the operation on your feelings and your sense of obligation is just the same; and whether they are demons or angels in themselves, you wish them equally at the devil!

Other persons of worth and sense give way to mere violence of temperament (with which the understanding has nothing to do)—are burnt up with a perpetual fury—repel and throw you to a distance by their restless, whirling motion—so that you dare not go near them, or feel uneasy in their company as if you stood on the edge of a volcano. They have their *tempora mollia fandi;* but then what a stir may you not expect the next moment! Nothing is less inviting or less comfortable than this state of uncertainty and apprehension.

Then there are those who never approach you without the most alarming advice or information, telling you that you are in a dying way, or that your affairs are on the point of ruin, by way of disburthening their consciences; and others, who give you to understand much the same thing as a good joke, out of sheer impertinence, constitutional vivacity, and want of something to say. All these, it must be confessed, are disagreeable people; and you repay their over-anxiety or total forgetfulness of you, by a determination to cut them as speedily as possible....

There are a vast number who are disagreeable from meanness of spirit, downright insolence, from slovenliness of dress or disgusting tricks, from folly or ignorance; but these causes are positive moral or physical defects, and I only meant to speak of that repulsiveness of manners which arises from want of tact and sympathy with others.

". . . I did not desert my benefactor . . ."

HEROD THE GREAT TO AUGUSTUS CAESAR, AFTER THE DEATH OF MARK ANTHONY, AS REPORTED BY FLAVIUS JOSEPHUS

Herod sailed to Rhodes to meet Augustus Caesar, and to him Herod said:

"O Caesar, as I was made king of the Jews by Antony, so do profess that I have used my royal authority in the best manner, and entirely for his advantage; nor will I conceal this farther, that thou hadst certainly found me in arms, and an inseparable companion of his, had not the Arabians hindered me. However, I sent him as many auxiliaries as I was able, and many ten thousand [cori] of corn.

"Nay, indeed, I did not desert my benefactor after the blow that was given him at Actium; but I gave him the best advice I was able, when I was no longer able to assist him in the war; and I told him that there was but one way of recovering his affairs, and that was to kill Cleopatra; and I promised him, that if she were once dead, I would afford him money and walls for his security, with an army and myself to assist him in his war against thee: but his affections for Cleopatra stopped his ears, as did God himself also, who hath bestowed the government on thee. I own myself also to be overcome together with him, and with this lost fortune I have laid aside my diadem, and am come hither to thee, having my hopes of safety in thy virtue; and I desire thou wilt first consider how faithful a friend, and not whose friend I have been."

Caesar replied, in part: "Nay, thou shalt not only be in safety, but thou shalt be a king, and that more firmly than thou wert before; for thou art worthy to reign over a great many subjects, by reason of the fastness of thy friendship: and do thou endeavor to be equally in thy friendship to me."

(Translated by William W. Whiston)

"In making friends, consider well . . ."

WILLIAM PENN'S ADVICE TO HIS CHILDREN

Ruin not yourselves by kindness to others; for that exceeds the due bounds of friendship, neither will a true friend expect it....

In making friends, consider well first; and when you are fixed, be true, not wavering by reports, nor deserting in affliction, for that becomes not the good and virtuous. Watch against anger; neither speak nor act in it; for, like drunkenness, it makes a man a beast, and throws people into desperate inconveniences. Avoid flatterers, for they are thieves in disguise; their praise is costly, designing to get by those they bespeak; they are the worst of creatures; they lie to flatter, and flatter to cheat; and which is worse, if you believe them, you cheat yourselves most dangerously. But the virtuous, though poor, love, cherish, and prefer. Remember David, who, asking the Lord: "Who shall abide in thy tabernacle? who shall dwell in thy holy hill?" answers "He that walketh uprightly and worketh righteousness, and speaketh the truth in his heart; in whose eyes a vile person is contemned; but he honoreth them that fear the Lord."

SEARCH
Frank Putnam

The city ways are not my ways, and never
Shall I to its demands be reconciled;
I walk amid its roar and rumble, dreaming,
A cool and careful man in outward seeming,
But in my heart a lost and lonely child.

I wear a mark, as you do and as all do,
To hide what none has time to comprehend;
A mark of settled purpose and of daring,
To hide how very little I am caring
For anything but just to find a friend.

"... what earthquakes of the heart ..."

SCHOOLBOY FRIENDSHIPS
Benjamin Disraeli

At school, friendship is a passion. It entrances the being; it tears the soul. All love of afterlife can never bring its rapture, or its wretchedness; no bliss so absorbing, no pangs of jealousy or despair so crushing and so keen! What tenderness and what devotion; what illimitable confidence, infinite revelations of inmost thoughts; what ecstatic present and romantic future; what bitter estrangements and what melting reconciliations; what scenes of wild recrimination, agitating explanations, passionate correspondence; what insane sensitiveness, and what frantic sensibility; what earthquakes of the heart and whirlwinds of the soul are confined in that simple phrase, a schoolboy's friendship!

SUSPENSE
Emily Dickinson

Elysium is as far as to
  The very nearest room,
If in that room a friend await
  Felicity or doom.

What fortitude the soul contains,
  That it can so endure
The accent of a coming foot,
  The opening of a door.

"Stay" is a charming word in a friend's vocabulary.

—A. B. ALCOTT

"I have loved and valued you ever since I knew you . . ."

DR. FRANCIS ATTERBURY TO ALEXANDER POPE

(The following letter was written from the Tower of London, April 10, 1723, where Dr. Atterbury, an Oxford divine, was confined on a charge of treason. He was subsequently deposed and exiled, living his last years in Belgium and France.)

DEAR SIR—I thank you for all the instances of your friendship, both before and since my misfortunes. A little time will complete them, and separate you and me for ever. But in what part of the world, soever I am, I will live mindful of your sincere kindness to me; and will please myself with the thought that I still live in your esteem and affection as much as ever I did; and that no accident of life, no distance of time or place, will alter you in that respect. It never can me, who have loved and valued you ever since I knew you, and shall not fail to do it when I am not allowed to tell you so, as the case will soon be. Give my faithful services to Dr. Arbuthnot, and thanks for what he has sent me, which was much to the purpose, if anything can be said to be to the purpose in a case that is already determined. Let him know that my defense will be such, that neither my friends need blush for me, nor will my enemies have great occasion to triumph, though sure of the victory. I shall want his advice before I go abroad in many things. But I question whether I shall be permitted to see him or anybody, but such as are absolutely necessary towards the dispatch of my private affairs. If so, God bless you both! and may no part of the ill-fortune that attends me ever pursue either of you. I know not but I may not call upon you at my hearing, to say about my way of spending my time at the deanery, which did not seem calculated towards managing plots and conspiracies. But of that I shall consider. You and I have spent many hours together upon much pleasanter subjects; and that I may preserve the old custom, I shall not part with you now till I have closed this letter with three lines of Milton, which you will, I know, readily, and not without some degree of concern, apply to your ever-affectionate, etc.

> "Some natural tears he dropped, but wiped them soon;
> The world was all before him where to choose
> His place of rest, and Providence his guide."

OLD FRIENDS

Robert Hinckley Messinger

Old Friends to talk!
Ay, bring those chosen few,
The wise, the courtly and the true,
  So rarely found;
Him for my wine, him for my stud,
Him for my easel, distich, bud,
  In mountain walk!
  Bring Walter good,
With soulful Fred, and learned Will,
And thee, my alter ego (dearer still
  For every mood).
These add a bouquet to my wine!
These add sparkle to my pine!
If these I tine,
Can books, or fire, or wine be good?

"Oxen and cows will not fatten by themselves..."

FRIENDSHIP AMONG ANIMALS

Gilbert White

There is a wonderful spirit of sociality in the brute creation, independent of sexual attachment; the congregation of gregarious birds in the winter is a remarkable instance.

Many horses, though quiet with company, will not stay one minute in a field by themselves; the strongest fences cannot restrain them. My neighbor's horse will not only not stay by himself abroad, but he will not bear to be left alone in a strange stable, without discovering the utmost impatience, and endeavoring to break the rack and manger with his fore feet. He has been known to leap out at a stable-window, through which dung was thrown, after company; and yet, in other respects, is remarkably quiet. Oxen and cows will not fatten by themselves; but will neglect the finest pasture that is not recommended by society. It would be needless to instance in sheep, which constantly flock together.

But this propensity seems not to be confined to animals of the same species; for we know a doe, still alive, that was brought up from a little fawn with a dairy of cows; with them it goes a-field, and with them it returns to the yard. The dogs of the house take no notice of this deer, being used to her; but, if strange dogs come by, a chase ensues; while the master smiles to see his favorite securely leading her pursuers over hedge, or gate, or stile, till she returns to the cows, who, with fierce lowings, and menacing horns, drive the assailants quite out of the pasture.

Even great disparity of kind and size does not always prevent social advances and mutual fellowship. For a very intelligent and observant person has assured me, that in the former part of his life, keeping but one horse, he happened also on a time to have but one solitary hen. These two incongruous animals spent much of their time together, in a lonely orchard, where they saw no creature but each other. By degrees, an apparent regard began to take between these two sequestered individuals. The fowl would approach the quadruped with notes of complacency, rubbing herself gently against his legs; while the horse would look down with satisfaction, and move with the greatest caution and circumspection, lest he should trample on his diminutive companion. Thus, by mutual good offices, each seemed to console the vacant hours of the other: so that Milton, when he puts the following sentiment in the mouth of Adam, seems to be somewhat mistaken:

"Much less can bird with beast, or fish with fowl
So well converse, nor with the ox the ape."

Friendship is usually treated by the majority of mankind as a tough and everlasting thing which will survive all manner of bad treatment. But this is an exceedingly great and foolish error; it may die in an hour of a single unwise word.

—OUIDA

"... any amicable conversation ... promotes friendship ..."

GOOD CONVERSATION

Benjamin Jowett

We have heard it said that speech is silver, but silence golden; and of a great man of our own times, who poured himself out in conversation freely, it was wittily said that flashes of silence adorned his eloquence. This is one of the commonplaces often repeated, but which does not rest upon any real experience of life. For the truth is that any amicable conversation, however trivial, about the weather, about the crops, about the lengthening of the days of the year, about shooting or fishing, about buying or selling, is better than none at all, because it promotes friendship and good fellowship. There is nothing so trivial which if said in a certain way—an inquiry about a child, an animal, a flattering word about health or looks—may not be a token and assurance of good-will.

Yet besides the desire to promote conversation, there must also be the materials for it. Every person should have some subject of interest which he can contribute to the common stock. In one society literature, in another science, in another politics, in another business, will be the prevailing topic, and we must have some knowledge of them before we can join in the discussion of them. The temper of some companies will lead them to give or receive information; of others, to argue or dispute. Gaiety and seriousness will alternate with one another. If we cannot furnish a jest we may at any rate possess the cheerfulness and good humour which thankfully appreciates one.

And there must be listeners as well as talkers; these too may give a charm to society. It is not an uncommon reflection that somebody is talking too much, that he has not allowed others to speak, that words have fallen too continuously and uninterruptedly from his lips, and, as happened to the poor man at the pool of Siloam, we feel that he steps before us and unfairly deprives us of our turn. And there are others again who do not say much themselves, but have the art of drawing out their companions; who do not throw the ball but take it up, and will barely let the least word fall to the ground without a response; who are thinking not of themselves or of their own interests, but of the persons who are addressing them, and finding out the subjects which interest them.

These two extremes illustrate very well the true nature of social intercourse. In its higher sense it is not the creation of one mind, but of several; and there are many parts in it; and the humbler parts are within the reach of most of us, if we could only lay aside the weakness that so easily besets us—the consciousness of self. When there is a temper of sympathy in us it hardly matters whether we say little or much to others in company; the friendly smile, the ready attention, the kind pressure of the hand, is enough to make us understood by them, and to make all things known to us.

AN EPITAPH
(From an Ancient Greek monument)

Of our great love, Parthenophil,
This little stone abideth still
   Sole sign and token.
I seek thee yet, and yet shall seek
Though faint my eyes, my spirit weak
   With prayers unspoken.

Meanwhile best friend of friends, do thou,
If this the cruel fates allow,
   By death's dark river,
Among those shadowy people, drink
No drop for me on Lethe's brink!
   Forget me never!

(Translator anonymous)

Good books, like good friends, are few and chosen; the more select the more enjoyable; and like these are approached with diffidence, nor sought too familiarly nor too often, having the precedence only when friends tire. The most mannerly of companions, accessible at all times, in all moods, they frankly declare the author's mind, without giving offense. Like living friends they too have their voice and physiognomies, and their company is prized as old acquaintances. We seek them in our need of counsel or amusement, without impertinence or apology, sure of having our claims allowed. . . . What were days without such fellowship? We were alone in the world without it. . . .

Next to a friend's discourse, no morsel is more delicious than a ripe book, a book whose flavor is as refreshing at the thousandth testing as at the first. Books when friends weary, conversation flags, or nature fails to inspire.

—Amos Bronson Alcott

Reading ends in melancholy;
  Wine breeds vices and diseases;
Wealth is but a care, and love but folly;
  Only friendship truly pleases.
My wealth, my books, my flask, my Molly
  Farewell all, if friendship ceases.
                              —MATTHEW PRIOR

WE HAVE BEEN FRIENDS TOGETHER

Caroline Elizabeth Sarah Norton

We have been friends together
  In sunshine and in shade,
Since first beneath the chestnut-tree
  In infancy we played.
But coldness dwells within thy heart;
  A cloud is on thy brow;
We have been friends together,—
  Shall a light word part us now?

We have been gay together:
  We have laughed at little jests;
For the fount of hope was gushing
  Warm and joyous in our breasts,
But laughter now has fled thy lip,
  And sullen glooms thy brow;
We have been friends together,—
  Shall a light word part us now?

We have been sad together;
  We have wept with bitter tears
O'er the grass-grown graves where slumbered
  The hopes of early years.
The voices which are silent there
  Would bid thee clear thy brow;
We have been sad together,—
  O! what shall part us now?

SAMUEL JOHNSON TO
JAMES BOSWELL

My Dear Sir:
Are you playing the same trick again, and trying who can keep
silence longest? Remember that all tricks are either knavish or childish;
and that it is as foolish to make experiments upon the constancy of a
friend as upon the chastity of a wife.

Streatham, September 9, 1779

"It was the first great wrench of his life . . ."

TOM BROWN LOSES HIS DEAREST
FRIEND
Thomas Hughes

Note: *In the summer of 1842, when the term at Oxford ended, Tom
Brown left immediately with two college friends for a fishing trip in
Scotland. One evening they stopped at a little inn at Kyle Rhea ferry, in
Skye. One of Brown's friends was reading a newspaper:—*

"Hullo, Brown! here's something for you," called out the reading
man next moment. "Why, your old master, Arnold of Rugby, is dead."
Tom's hand stopped halfway in his cast, and his line and flies went
all tangling round and round his rod; you might have knocked him
over with a feather. Neither of his companions took any notice of him,
luckily; and with a violent effort he set to work mechanically to dis-
entangle his line. He felt completely carried off his moral and intellectual legs, as if he had lost his standing-point in the invisible world.
Besides which, the deep, loving loyalty which he felt for his old leader
made the shock intensely painful. It was the first great wrench of his
life, the first gap which the angel Death had made in his circle, and he
felt numbed, and beaten down, and spiritless. Well, well! I believe it
was good for him and for many others in like case; who had to learn
by that loss, that the soul of man cannot stand or lean upon any human

prop, however strong, and wise, and good; but that He upon whom alone it can stand and lean will knock away all such props in His own wise and merciful way, until there is no ground or stay left but Himself, the Rock of Ages, upon whom alone a sure foundation for every soul of man is laid.

As he wearily labored at his line, the thought struck him, "It may all be false, a mere newspaper lie," and he strode up to the recumbent smoker.

"Let me look at the paper," said he.

"Nothing else in it," answered the other, handing it up to him listlessly.—"Hullo, Brown! what's the matter, old fellow—ain't you well?"

"Where is it?" said Tom, turning over the leaves, his hands trembling, and his eyes swimming, so that he could not read.

"What? What are you looking for?" said his friend, jumping up and looking over his shoulder.

"That—about Arnold," said Tom.

"Oh, here," said the other, putting his finger on the paragraph. Tom read it over and over again; there could be no mistake of identity, though the account was short enough.

"Thank you," said he at last, dropping the paper. "I shall go for a walk; don't you and Herbert wait supper for me." And away he strode, up over the moor at the back of the house, to be alone, and master his grief if possible.

His friend looked after him, sympathizing and wondering, and, knocking the ashes out of his pipe, walked over to Herbert. After a short parley, they walked together up to the house.

"I'm afraid that confounded newspaper has spoiled Brown's fun for this trip."

"How odd that he should be so fond of his old master," said Herbert. Yet they also were both public-school men.

The two, however, notwithstanding Tom's prohibition, waited supper for him, and had everything ready when he came back some half an hour afterwards. But he could not join in their cheerful talk, and the party was soon silent, notwithstanding the efforts of all three. One thing only had Tom resolved, and that was, that he couldn't stay in Scotland any longer; he felt an irresistible longing to get to Rugby, and then home, and soon broke it to the others, who had too much tact to oppose.

So by daylight the next morning he was marching through Ross-shire, and in the evening hit the Caledonian canal, took the next steamer, and traveled as fast as boat and railway could carry him to the Rugby station.

As he walked up to the town, he felt shy and afraid of being seen, and took the back streets; why he didn't know, but he followed his instinct. At the school gates he made a dead pause; there was not a soul in the quadrangle—all was lonely, and silent, and sad. So with another effort he strode through the quadrangle, and into the schoolhouse offices.

He found the little matron in her room in deep mourning; shook her hand, tried to talk, and moved nervously about: she was evidently thinking of the same subject as he, but he couldn't begin talking.

"Where shall I find Thomas?" said he at last, getting desperate.

"In the servants' hall, I think, sir. But won't you take anything?" said the matron, looking rather disappointed.

"No, thank you," said he, and strode off again to find the old Verger, who was sitting in his little den as of old, puzzling over his hieroglyphics.

He looked up through his spectacles, as Tom seized his hand and wrung it.

"Ah! you've heard all about it, sir, I see," said he.

Tom nodded, and then sat down on the shoe-board, while the old man told his tale, and wiped his spectacles, and fairly flowed over with quaint, homely, honest sorrow.

By the time he had done, Tom felt much better.

"Where is he buried, Thomas?" said he at last.

"Under the altar in the chapel, sir. You'd like to have the key, I dare say."

"Thank you, Thomas—yes, I should very much." And the old man fumbled among his bunch, and then got up, as though he would go with him; but after a few steps stopped short, and said, "Perhaps you'd like to go by yourself, sir?"

Tom nodded, and the bunch of keys were handed to him, with an injunction to be sure and lock the door after him, and bring them back before eight o'clock.

He walked quickly through the quadrangle and out into the close. The longing which had been upon him and driven him thus far, like the gadfly in the Greek legends, giving him no rest in mind or body, seemed all of a sudden not to be satisfied, but to shrivel up, and pall. "Why should I go on? It's no use," he thought, and threw himself at full length on the turf, and looked vaguely at all the well-known objects.... The thought that his sceptre had departed, and his mark was wearing out, came home to him for the first time, and bitterly enough. He was lying on the very spot where the fights came off; where he himself had fought six years ago his first and last battle. He conjured up the scene till he could almost hear the shouts of the ring, and East's whisper in his ear; and looking across the close to the Doctor's private door, half expected to see it open, and the tall figure in cap and gown come striding under the elm-trees towards him.

No, no! the sight could never be seen again. There was no flag flying on the round tower, the schoolhouse windows were all shuttered up; and when the flag went up again, and the shutters came down, it would be to welcome a stranger. All that was left on earth of him whom he had honored, was lying cold and still under the chapel floor. He would go in and see the place once more, and then leave it once and for all. New men and new methods might do for other people; let those who would, worship the rising star; he at least would be faithful to the sun which had set. And so he got up, and walked to the chapel-door and unlocked it, fancying himself the only mourner in all the broad land, and feeding on his own selfish sorrow.

He passed through the vestibule, and then paused for a moment to glance over the empty benches. His heart was still proud and high, and he walked up to the seat which he had last occupied as a sixth-form boy, and sat himself down there to collect his thoughts.

And, truth to tell, they needed collecting and setting in order not a little. The memories of eight years were all dancing through his brain, while, beneath them all, his heart was throbbing with the dull sense of a loss that could never be made up to him. The rays of the evening sun came solemnly through the painted windows above his head, and fell in gorgeous colors on the opposite wall, and the perfect stillness soothed his spirit by little and little. And he turned to the pulpit, and looked at it, and then, leaning forward with head on his hands, groaned aloud. "If he could only have seen the Doctor again for one five minutes,— have told him all that was in his heart, what he owed to him, how he loved and reverenced him, and would by God's help follow his steps in life and death,—he could have borne it all without a murmur. But that he should have gone away forever without knowing it all, was too much to bear.—But am I sure that he does not know it all?"—the thought made him start—"May he not even now be near me, in this very chapel? If he be, am I sorrowing as he would have me sorrow—as I should wish to have sorrowed when I shall meet him again?"

He raised himself up and looked round; and after a minute rose and walked humbly down to the lowest bench, and sat down on the very seat which he had occupied on his first Sunday at Rugby. And then the old memories rushed back again, but softened and subdued, and soothing him as he let himself be carried away by them. And he looked up at the great painted window above the altar, and remembered how when a little boy he used to try not to look through it at the elm-trees and the rooks, before the painted glass came—and the subscription for the painted glass, and the letter he wrote home for money to give to it. And there, down below, was the very name of the boy who sat on his right hand on that first day, scratched rudely in the oak panelling.

And then came the thought of all his old school-fellows; and form after form of boys, nobler, braver, and purer than he, rose up and seemed to rebuke him. ... Then the grief which he began to share with others became gentle and holy, and he rose up once more, and walked up the steps to the altar; and while the tears flowed freely down his cheeks, knelt down humbly and hopefully, to lay down there his share of a burden which had proved itself too heavy for him to bear in his own strength.

Here let us leave him—where better could we leave him, than at the altar, before which he had first caught a glimpse of the glory of his birthright, and felt the drawing of the bond which links all living souls together in one brotherhood—at the grave beneath the altar of him who had opened his eyes to see that glory, and softened his heart till he could feel that bond?

❦❦❦❦❦❦

". . . friendship between an instructor and a student is impossible."

THE IMPOSSIBILITY OF FRIENDSHIP BETWEEN TEACHER AND STUDENT

Jacques Barzun

Let me say bluntly, as I do not hesitate to do when my students broach the subject, that friendship between an instructor and a student is impossible. This does not mean that the two should remain strangers; there can exist cordial, easy relations, tinged perhaps with a certain kind of affection; but friendship, not. For friendship has strict prerequisites, among them, freedom of choice and equality of status. Neither of these can exist in the teacher-student relation. The absence of equality may horrify the sentimental but it is a fact nevertheless. Consider only a few of the things a teacher must do—he must judge work done, decide passing or failing, order tasks, reprove mistakes, discipline conduct, and *deal impartially with all similar cases*. These, I submit, are not the acts of a friend, even if—as equality would demand—the students were allowed reciprocal privileges.

I shall go further and say that it is not good for a teacher to associate steadily with students. Real reciprocity is here again out of the question; differences of age, temperament, purpose and background, are so many hidden reefs over which even conversation founders. This does not mean that it is not delightful once in a while to accept a dinner invitation from a group of students who are friends among themselves, or to join "the gang" in a sandwich and a glass of beer after a seminar. And the talk over the beer need not be in the least stiff or scholastic. Simple manners go farthest, provided they are genuine, and they best protect the very delicate adjustment between student and teacher on which the latter's efficiency depends.

TO HAYLEY

Thy Friendship oft has made my heart to ache:
Do be my Enemy for Friendship's sake.

—WILLIAM BLAKE

"... I saw him use his fork like any other Christian!"

A SNOB AND HIS FRIEND

William Makepeace Thackeray

I once knew a man who committed before me an act as atrocious as the using the fork in the guise of a toothpick. I once, I say, knew a man who, dining in my company at the "Europa Coffeehouse" (opposite the Grand Opera, and, as everybody knows, the only decent place for dining at Naples), ate peas with the assistance of his knife. He was a person with whose society I was greatly pleased at first—indeed, we had met in the crater of Mount Vesuvius, and were subsequently robbed and held to ransom by brigands in Calabria, which is nothing to the purpose—a man of great powers, excellent heart, and varied information; but I had never before seen him with a dish of peas, and his conduct in regard to them caused me the deepest pain.

After having seen him thus publicly comport himself, but one course was open to me—to cut his acquaintance. I commissioned a mutual friend (the Honourable Poly Anthus) to break the matter to this gentleman as delicately as possible, and to say that painful circumstances—in nowise affecting Mr. Marrowfat's honour, or my esteem for him—had occurred, which obliged me to forego my intimacy with him; and accordingly we met, and gave each other the cut direct that night at the Duchess of Monte Fiasco's ball.

Everybody at Naples remarked the separation of the Damon and Pythias—indeed, Marrowfat had saved my life more than once—but, as an English gentleman, what was I to do? ...

The cause of my quarrel with Marrowfat I never breathed to mortal soul for four years. We met in the halls of the aristocracy—our friends and relatives. We jostled each other in the dance or at the board; but the estrangement continued, and seemed irrevocable, until the fourth of June, last year.

We met at Sir George Golloper's. We were placed, he on the right, your humble servant on the left, of the admirable Lady G. Peas formed part of the banquet—ducks and green peas. I trembled as I saw Marrowfat helped, and turned away sickening, lest I should behold the weapon darting down his horrid jaws.

What was my astonishment, what my delight, when I saw him use his fork like any other Christian! He did not administer the cold steel once. Old times rushed back upon me—the remembrance of old services—his rescuing me from the brigands—his gallant conduct in the affair with the Countess Dei Spinachi—his lending me the £1700. I almost burst into tears with joy—my voice trembled with emotion. "George, my boy!" I exclaimed; "George Marrowfat, my dear fellow! a glass of wine!"

Blushing—deeply moved—almost as tremulous as I was myself, George answered, "Frank, shall it be Hock or Madeira?" I could have hugged him to my heart but for the presence of the company. Little did Lady Golloper know what was the cause of the emotion which sent the duckling I was carving into her Ladyship's pink satin lap. The most good-natured of women pardoned the error, and the butler removed the bird.

We have been the closest friends ever since, nor, of course, has George repeated his odious habit.

❦❦❦❦❦

During the First World War a soldier in the trenches saw his friend out in no-man's land—the ground between our trenches and those of the enemy—stumble and fall in a hail of bullets. He said to his officer, "May I go, sir, and bring him in?" But the officer refused. "No one can live out there," he said. "I should only lose you as well." Disobeying the order, the man went to try and save his friend, for they had been like David and Jonathan throughout the whole war. Somehow he got his friend on to his shoulder and staggered back to the trenches, but he himself lay mortally wounded and his friend was dead. The officer was angry. "I told you not to go," he said. "Now I have lost both of you.

It was not worth it." With his dying breath the man said, "But it was worth it, sir." "Worth it!" said the officer. "How could it be? Your friend is dead and you are mortally wounded." The boy shrank from the reproach, but looking up into his officer's face he said, "It was worth it, sir, because when I got to him, he said, 'Jim, I knew you'd come.'"

—LESLIE D. WEATHERHEAD

FORBEARANCE

Ralph Waldo Emerson

Hast thou named all the birds without a gun;
Loved the wood-rose, and left it on its stalk;
At rich men's tables eaten bread and pulse;
Unarmed, faced danger with a heart of trust;
And loved so well a high behavior
In man or maid that thou from speech refrained,
Nobility more nobly to repay?—
O be my friend, and teach me to be thine!

FRIENDS

E. V. Lucas

You ask me "Why I like him." Nay
  I cannot; nay I would not, say.
I think it vile to pigeonhole
The pros and cons of a kindred soul.

You "wonder he should be my friend."
  But then why should you comprehend?
Thank God for this—a new-surprise:
My eyes, remember, are not your eyes.

Cherish this one small mystery;
And marvel not that love can be
  "In spite of all his many flaws,"
In spite? Supposing I said "Because."

A truce, a truce to questioning:
"We two are friends" tells everything.
Yet if you must know, this is why:
Because he is he, and I am I.

❧❧❧❧❧

Behold, how good and how pleasant it is for brethren to dwell together in unity!
It is like the precious ointment upon the head, that ran down upon the beard, even Aaron's beard; that went down to the skirts of his garments:
As the dew of Hermon, and as the dew that descended upon the mountain of Zion: for there the Lord commanded the blessing, even life for evermore.

(Holy Bible, Psalm 133)

❧❧❧❧❧

Wherein mutual sorrow deepens friendship...

MISS TEMPY'S WATCHERS *

Sara Orne Jewett

The time of year was April; the place was a small farming town in New Hampshire, remote from any railroad. One by one the lights had been blown out in the scattered houses near Miss Tempy Dent's; but as her neighbors took a last look out-of-doors, their eyes turned with instinctive curiosity toward the old house, where a lamp burned steadily. They gave a little sigh. "Poor Miss Tempy!" said more than one bereft acquaintance; for the good woman lay dead in her north chamber, and the light was a watcher's light. The funeral was set for the next day, at one o'clock.

The watchers were two of the oldest friends, Mrs. Crowe and Sarah Ann Binson. They were sitting in the kitchen, because it seemed less awesome than the unused best room, and they beguiled the long hours by steady conversation. One would think that neither topics nor opinions would hold out, at that rate, all through the long spring night; but there was a certain degree of excitement just then, and the two women had risen to an unusual level of expressiveness and confidence. Each

* Abridged.

had already told the other more than one fact that she had determined to keep secret; they were again and again tempted into statements that either would have found impossible by daylight. Mrs. Crowe knew exactly what she was about, however; she was of a much cooler disposition than Sister Binson.

Their faces were interesting,—of the dry, shrewd, quick-witted New England type, with thin hair twisted neatly back out of the way. Mrs. Crowe could look vague and benignant, and Miss Binson was, to quote her neighbors, a little too sharp-set; but the world knew that she had need to be, with the load she must carry of supporting an inefficient widowed sister and six unpromising and unwilling nieces and nephews. Sarah Ann Binson, for all her sharp, anxious aspect, never defended herself, when her sister whined and fretted. She was told every week of her life that the poor children never would have had to lift a finger if their father had lived, and yet she had kept her steadfast way with the little farm, and patiently taught the young people many useful things. However pleasureless her life appeared to outward view, it was brimful of pleasure to herself.

Mrs. Crowe, on the contrary, was well to do, her husband being a rich farmer and an easy-going man. She was a stingy woman, but for all that she looked kindly; and when she gave away anything, or lifted a finger to help anybody, it was thought a great piece of beneficence. Everybody liked to be on good terms with Mrs. Crowe. Socially she stood much higher than Sarah Ann Binson. They were both old schoolmates and friends of Temperance Dent, who had asked them, one day, not long before she died, if they would not come together and look after the house, and manage everything, when she was gone. She may have had some hope that they might become closer friends in this period of intimate partnership, and that the richer woman might better understand the burdens of the poorer.

There was a brook which ran down the hillside very near the house, and the sound of it was much louder than usual. When there was silence in the kitchen, the busy stream had a strange insistence in its wild voice, as if it tried to make the watchers understand something that related to the past.

"I declare, I can't begin to sorrow for Tempy yet. I am so glad to have her at rest," whispered Mrs. Crowe. "It is strange to set here without her, but I can't make it clear that she has gone. I feel as if she had got easy and dropped off to sleep, and I'm more scared about waking her up than knowing any other feeling."

"Yes," said Sarah Ann, "it's just like that, ain't it? But I tell you we are goin' to miss her worse than we expect. She's helped me through many a trial, has Temperance. I ain't the only one who says the same, neither."

These words were spoken as if there were a third person listening; somebody beside Mrs. Crowe. The watchers could not rid their minds of the feeling that they were being watched themselves. The spring wind whistled in the window crack, now and then, and buffeted the little house in a gusty way that had a sort of companionable effect. Yet, on the whole, it was a very still night, and the watchers spoke in a half-whisper.

"She was the freest-handed woman that ever I knew," said Mrs. Crowe, decidedly. "According to her means, she gave away more than anybody. I used to tell her 't wa'n't right. I used really to be afraid that she went without too much, for we have a duty to ourselves."

Sister Binson looked up in a half-amused, unconscious way, and then recollected herself.

Mrs. Crowe met her look with a serious face. "It ain't so easy for me to give as it is for some," she said simply, but with an effort which was made possible only by the occasion. "I should like to say, while Tempy is laying here yet in her own house, that she has been a constant lesson to me. Folks are too kind, and shame me with thanks for what I do. I ain't such a generous woman as poor Tempy was."

Sarah Binson was much moved at this confession, and was even pained and touched by the unexpected humility. "You have a good many calls on you"—she began, and then left her kind little compliment half finished.

"Yes, yes, but I've got means enough. My disposition's more of a cross to me as I grow older, and I made up my mind this morning that Tempy's example should be my pattern henceforth." She began to knit faster than ever.

" 'T ain't no use to get morbid: that's what Tempy used to say herself," said Sarah Ann, after a minute's silence. "Ain't it strange to say 'used to say'?" and her own voice choked a little. "She never did like to hear folks git goin' about themselves."

" 'T was only because they're apt to do it so as other folks will say 't wasn't so, an' praise 'em up," humbly replied Mrs. Crowe, "and that ain't my object. There wa'n't a child but what Tempy set herself to work to see what she could do to please it. One time my brother's folks had been stopping here in the summer, from Massachusetts. The children was all little, and they broke up a sight of toys, and left 'em when they were going away. Tempy come right up after they rode by, to see if she couldn't help me set the house to rights, and she caught me just as I was going to fling some of the clutter into the stove. I was kind of tired out, starting 'em off in season. 'Oh, give me them!' says she, real pleading; and she wropped 'em up and took 'em home with her when she went, and she mended 'em up and stuck 'em together, and made some young one or other happy with every blessed one. You'd thought

I'd done her the biggest favor. 'No thanks to me. I should ha' burnt 'em, Tempy,' says I."

"I can tell you the biggest thing she ever done, and I don't know's there's anybody left but me to tell it. I don't want it forgot," Sarah Binson said, looking up at the clock to see how the night was going. "It was that pretty-looking Trevor girl, who taught the Corners school, and married so well afterwards, out in New York State.

"She was a splendid scholar, folks said, and give the school a great start; but she'd overdone herself getting her education, and working to pay for it, and she all broke down one spring, and Tempy made her come and stop with her a while,—you remember that? Well, she had an uncle, her mother's brother, out in Chicago, who was well off and friendly, and used to write to Lizzie Trevor, and I dare say make her some presents; but he was a lively, driving man, and didn't take time to stop and think about his folks. He hadn't seen her since she was a little girl. Poor Lizzie was so pale and weakly that she just got through the term o' school. She looked as if she was just going straight off in a decline. Tempy, she cosseted her up a while, and then, next thing folks knew, she was tellin' round how Miss Trevor had gone to see her uncle. Now I happened to know that the poor girl was in debt for her schoolin' when she come here, and her last quarter's pay had just squared it off at last, and left her without a cent ahead, hardly. An' I taxed Tempy about the girl's goin' off on such a journey till she owned up, rather'n have Lizzie blamed, that she'd given her sixty dollars, same's if she was rolling in riches, and sent her off to have a good rest and vacation."

"Sixty dollars!" exclaimed Mrs. Crowe. "Tempy only had ninety dollars a year that came in to her; rest of her livin' she got by helpin' about, with what she raised off this little piece o' ground, sand one side an' clay the other."

The women looked at each other in silence; the magnitude of the generous sacrifice was almost too great for their comprehension.

"She was just poor enough to do that!" declared Mrs. Crowe at last, in an abandonment of feeling. "Say what you may, I feel humbled to the dust," and her companion ventured to say nothing. She never had given away sixty dollars at once, but it was simply because she never had it to give.

"Folks say a great deal of generosity, and this one's being public-sperited, and that one free-handed about giving," said Mrs. Crowe, who was a little nervous in the silence. "I suppose we can't tell the sorrow it would be to some folks not to give, same's 't would be to me not to save. I seem kind of made for that, as if 't was what I'd got to do. I should feel sights better about it if I could make it evident what I was savin' for. If I had a child, now, Sarah Ann," and her voice was a little husky,—"if I had a child, I should think I was heapin' of it up because he was the one trained by the Lord to scatter it again for good. But here's Mr. Crowe and me, we can't do anything with money, and both of us like to keep things same's they've always been. I maintain," continued Mrs. Crowe stoutly, "that folks wastes sights o' good money doin' just such foolish things. Tearin' out the insides o' meetin'-houses, and fixin' the pews different; 't was good enough as 't was with mendin'; then times come, an' they want to put it all back same's 't was before."

This touched upon an exciting subject to active members of that parish. Miss Binson and Mrs. Crowe belonged to opposite parties, and had at one time come as near hard feelings as they could, and yet escape them. Each hastened to speak of other things and to show her untouched friendliness.

"I do agree with you," said Sister Binson, "that few of us know what use to make of money, beyond every-day necessities. You've seen more o' the world than I have, and know what's expected. When it comes to taste and judgment about such things, I ought to defer to others"; and with this modest avowal the critical moment passed when there might have been an improper discussion.

In the silence that followed, the fact of their presence in a house of death grew more clear than before. There was something disturbing in the noise of a mouse gnawing at the dry boards of a closet wall near by. Both the watchers looked up anxiously at the clock; it was almost the middle of the night, and the whole world seemed to have left them alone with their solemn duty. Only the brook was awake.

"Perhaps we might give a look up-stairs now," whispered Mrs. Crowe, as if she hoped to hear some reason against their going just then to the chamber of death; but Sister Binson rose, with a serious and yet satisfied countenance, and lifted the small lamp from the table. She was much more used to watching than Mrs. Crowe, and much less affected by it. They opened the door into a small entry with a steep stairway; they climbed the creaking stairs, and entered the cold upper room on tiptoe. Mrs. Crowe's heart began to beat very fast as the lamp was put on a high bureau, and made long, fixed shadows about the walls. She went hesitatingly toward the solemn shape under its white drapery, and felt a sense of remonstrance as Sarah Ann gently, but in a business-like way, turned back the thin sheet.

"Seems to me she looks pleasanter and pleasanter," whispered Sarah Ann Binson impulsively, as they gazed at the white face with its wonderful smile. "To-morrow 't will all have faded out. I do believe they kind of wake up a day or two after they die, and it's then they go." She replaced the light covering, and they both turned quickly away; there was a chill in this upper room.

" 'T is a great thing for anybody to have got through, ain't it?" said

Mrs. Crowe softly, as she began to go down the stairs on tiptoe. The warm air from the kitchen beneath met them with a sense of welcome and shelter.

"I don' know why it is, but I feel as near again to Tempy down here as I do up there," replied Sister Binson. "I feel as if the air was full of her, kind of. I can sense things, now and then, that she seems to say."

Mrs. Crowe preserved a gloomy silence. "'T is a great thing to have got through," she repeated, ignoring definitely all that had last been said. "I suppose you know as well as I that Tempy was one that always feared death. Well, it's all put behind her now; she knows what 't is." Mrs. Crowe gave a little sigh, and Sister Binson's quick sympathies were stirred toward this other old friend, who also dreaded the great change.

"I'd never like to forgit almost those last words Tempy spoke plain to me," she said gently, like the comforter she truly was. "She looked up at me once or twice, that last afternoon after I come to set by her, and let Mis' Owen go home; and I says, 'Can I do anything to ease you, Tempy?' and the tears come into my eyes so I couldn't see what kind of a nod she give me. 'No, Sarah Ann, you can't, dear,' says she; and then she got her breath again, and says she, looking at me real meanin', 'I'm only a-gettin' sleepier and sleepier; that's all there is,' says she, and smiled up at me kind of wishful, and shut her eyes. I knew well enough all she meant. She'd been lookin' out for a chance to tell me, and I don' know's she ever said much afterwards."

Mrs. Crowe was not knitting; she had been listening too eagerly. "Yes, 't will be a comfort to think of that sometimes," she said, in acknowledgment. She had recovered from her feeling of nervous dread, the kitchen was so comfortable with lamplight and firelight; and just then the old clock began to tell the hour of twelve with leisurely whirring strokes.

Sister Binson laid aside her work, and rose quickly and went to the cupboard. "We'd better take a little to eat," she explained. "The night will go fast after this. I want to know if you went and made some o' your nice cupcakes, while you was home to-day?" she asked, in a pleased tone; and Mrs. Crowe acknowledged such a gratifying piece of thoughtfulness for this humble friend who denied herself all luxuries. Sarah Ann brewed a generous cup of tea, and the watchers drew their chairs up to the table presently, and quelled their hunger with good country appetites. Sister Binson put a spoon into a small, old-fashioned glass of preserved quince, and passed it to her friend. She was most familiar with the house, and played the part of hostess. "Spread some o' this on your bread and butter," she said to Mrs. Crowe. "Tempy wanted me to use some three or four times, but I never felt to. I know

she'd like to have us comfortable now, and would urge us to make a good supper, poor dear."

"What excellent preserves she did make!" mourned Mrs. Crowe. "None of us has got her light hand at doin' things tasty. She made the most o' everything, too. Now, she only had that one old quince-tree down in the far corner of the piece, but she'd go out in the spring and tend to it, and look at it so pleasant, and kind of expect the old thorny thing into bloomin'."

"She was just the same with folks," said Sarah Ann. "And she'd never git more'n a little apernful o' quinces, but she'd have every mite o' goodness out o' those, and set the glasses up onto her best-room closet shelf, so pleased."

"She didn't begin to age until two or three years ago, did she?" asked Mrs. Crowe. "I never saw anybody keep her looks as Tempy did. She looked young long after I begun to feel like an old woman. The doctor used to say 't was her young heart, and I don't know but what he was right. How she did do for other folks! There was one spell she wasn't at home a day to a fortnight. She got most of her livin' so, and that made her own potatoes and things last her through. None o' the young folks could get married without her, and all the old ones were disappointed if she wa'n't round when they was down with sickness and had to go. An' cleanin', or tailorin' for boys, or rug-hookin',—there was nothin' but what she could do as handy as most. 'I do love to work,' —ain't you heard her say that twenty times a week?"

Sarah Ann Binson nodded, and began to clear away the empty plates. "We may want a taste o' somethin' more towards mornin'," she said. "There's plenty in the closet here; and in case some comes from a distance to the funeral, we'll have a little table spread after we get back to the house."

"Yes, I was busy all the mornin'. I've cooked up a sight o' things to bring over," said Mrs. Crowe. "I felt 't was the last I could do for her."

They drew their chairs near the stove again, and took up their work. Sister Binson's rocking-chair creaked as she rocked; the brook sounded louder than ever. It was more lonely when nobody spoke, and presently Mrs. Crowe returned to her thoughts of growing old.

"Yes, Tempy aged all of a sudden. I remember I asked her if she felt as well as common, one day, and she laughed at me good."

"How many things we shall be wanting to ask Tempy!" exclaimed Sarah Ann Binson, after a long pause. "I can't make up my mind to doin' without her. I wish folks could come back just once, and tell us how 't is where they've gone. Seems then we could do without 'em better."

The brook hurried on, the wind blew about the house now and then; the house itself was a silent place, and the supper, the warm fire, and an absence of any new topics for conversation made the watchers drowsy. Sister Binson closed her eyes first, to rest them for a minute; and Mrs. Crowe glanced at her compassionately, with a new sympathy for the hard-worked little woman. She made up her mind to let Sarah Ann have a good rest, while she kept watch alone; but in a few minutes her own knitting was dropped, and she, too, fell asleep. Overhead, the pale shape of Tempy Dent, the outworn body of that generous, loving-hearted, simple soul, slept on also in its white raiment. Perhaps Tempy herself stood near, and saw her own life and its surroundings with new understanding. Perhaps she herself was the only watcher.

Later, by some hours, Sarah Ann Binson woke with a start. There was a pale light of dawn outside the small windows. Inside the kitchen, the lamp burned dim. Mrs. Crowe awoke, too.

"I think Tempy'd be the first to say 't was just as well we both had some rest," she said, not without a guilty feeling.

Her companion went to the outer door, and opened it wide. The fresh air was none too cold, and the brook's voice was not nearly so loud as it had been in the midnight darkness. She could see the shapes of the hills, and the great shadows that lay across the lower country. The east was fast growing bright.

" 'T will be a beautiful day for the funeral," she said, and turned again, with a sigh, to follow Mrs. Crowe up the stairs.

❦❦❦❦❦

THE HARE AND MANY FRIENDS

John Gay

Friendship, like love, is but a name,
Unless to one you stint the flame.
The child whom fathers share
Hath seldom known a father's care.
'Tis thus in friendships: who depend
On many, rarely find a friend.

A Hare, who in a civil way
Complied with everything, like Gay,
Was known by all the bestial train
Who haunt the wood or graze the plain.
Her care was, never to offend,
And ev'ry creature was her friend.

As forth she went at early dawn
To taste the dew-besprinkled lawn,
Behind her she hears the hunters' cries,
And from the deep-mouthed thunder flies.
She starts, she stops, she pants for breath;
She hears the near advance of death;
She doubles to mislead the hound,
And measures back her mazy round;
Till fainting in the public way,
Half dead with fear, she gasping lay.

What transport in her bosom grew,
When first the horse appeared in view!
"Let me," says she, "your back ascend,
And owe my safety to a friend.
You know my feet betray my flight;
To friendship every burden's light."

The Horse replied:—"Poor honest Puss,
It grieves my heart to see thee thus:
Be comforted, relief is near;
For all your friends are in the rear."

She next the stately Bull implored:
And thus replied the mighty lord:—
"Since every beast alive can tell
That I sincerely wish you well,
I may, without offense, pretend
To take the freedom of a friend.
Love calls me hence; a favorite cow
Expects me near yon barley-mow:
And when a lady's in the case,
You know all other things give place.
To leave you thus might seem unkind;
But see, the Goat is just behind."

The Goat remarked her pulse was high,
Her languid head, her heavy eye;
"My back," says she, "may do you harm:
The Sheep's at hand, and wool is warm."

The Sheep was feeble, and complained
His sides a load of wool sustained:
Said he was slow, confessed his fears;
For hounds eat Sheep, as well as Hares!

She now the trotting Calf addressed,
To save from death a friend distressed.
"Shall I," says he, "of tender age,
In this important care engage?
Older and abler passed you by;
How strong are those! how weak am I!
Should I presume to bear you hence,
Those friends of mine might take offense.
Excuse me then. You know my heart:
But dearest friends, alas! must part.
How shall we all lament! Adieu!
For see, the hounds are just in view."

"...we must go onward..."

BENJAMIN JOWETT
TO DEAN STANLEY

I earnestly hope that the friendship, which commenced between us many years ago, may be a blessing to last us through life. I feel that if it is to be so we must both go onward, otherwise the tear and wear of life, and the "having traveled over each other's minds," and a thousand accidents will be sufficient to break it off. I have often felt the inability to converse with you, but never for an instant the least alienation. There is no one who would not think me happy in having such a friend.

"...we only begin to know the value of friends when they are lost..."

LADY BLESSINGTON
TO WALTER SAVAGE LANDOR

Gore House, Kensington Gore, March 10, 1836

I write to you from my new residence in what I call the country, being a mile from London. I have not forgotten that your last letter announced the pleasing intelligence that you were to be in London in

April, and I write to request that you will take up your residence at my house.

I have a comfortable room to offer you, and, what is better still, a cordial welcome. Pray bear this in mind, and let me have the pleasure of having you under my roof.

Have you heard of the death of poor Sir William Gell? ... I regret him very much; he was gentle, kind-hearted, and good-tempered.... How much more frequently we think of a friend we have lost than when he lived! I have thought of poor Gell continually since I got Mr. Craven's melancholy letter announcing his demise, yet when he lived I have passed weeks without bestowing a thought on him. Is not this a curious fact in all our natures, that we only begin to know the value of friends when they are lost to us forever? It ought to teach us to turn with increased tenderness to those that remain; and I always feel that my affection for living friends is enlivened by the reflection that they too may pass away.

If we were only half as lenient to the living as we are to the dead, how much happiness might we render them, and from how much vain and bitter remorse might we be spared, when the grave, the all-atoning grave, has closed over them.... Let me hear from you, and, above all, tell me that you will take your abode with me, where quiet and friendship await you.

M. BLESSINGTON

THE FAITHFUL BIRD

William Cowper

The greenhouse is my summer seat;
My shrubs displac'd from that retreat
   Enjoy'd the open air;
Two goldfinches, whose sprightly song
Had been their mutual solace long,
   Liv'd happy pris'ners there.

They sang, as blithe as finches sing,
That flutter loose on golden wing,
   And frolic where they list;
Strangers to liberty, 'tis true,
But that delight they never knew,
   And therefore never miss'd.

But nature works in every breast,
With force not easily suppress'd;
  And Dick felt some desires,
That after many an effort vain,
Instructed him at length to gain
  A pass between his wires.

The open windows seem'd t' invite
The freeman to a farewell flight;
  But Tom was still confin'd;
And Dick, although his way was clear,
Was much too gen'rous and sincere
  To leave his friend behind.

So settling on his cage, by play,
And chirp, and kiss, he seem'd to say,
  You must not live alone—
Nor would he quit that chosen stand
Till I, with slow and cautious hand,
  Return'd him to his own.

O ye who never taste the joys
Of Friendship, satisfied with noise,
  Fandango, ball, and rout!
Blush when I tell you how a bird
A prison with a friend preferr'd
  To liberty without.

"... flatterers are not to be seen near ... scenes of adversity ..."

THE DISTINCTION BETWEEN
A FRIEND AND A FLATTERER
Plutarch

He who is justly reproached with being fond of flattery is also very partial to himself, and through abundance of self-kindness not only wishes to inherit the various perfections which may entitle him to the good opinion of others, but really believes he does; and so though it be laudable enough to encourage the wish, yet we should be very cautious how we indulge in the belief....

If indeed the flatterer, like most other evils, were to attack only or principally the abject and depraved part of mankind, the matter would neither be of great importance nor so difficult to be guarded against; but as worms breed and propagate best in tender and sweet wood, so a generosity of manners, and openness and candor of disposition most easily admit and nourish the flatterer.... Wherefore it is a business of no small moment, nor does it require a little share of forethought, so to investigate its nature that, being detected and brought to light, it may neither injure nor depreciate true friendship. For as vermin forsake the expiring body, the blood by which they were fed being extinguished, so flatterers are not to be seen near the dried and withered scenes of adversity, but stick foot and thrive and prosper amid riches and honors and powers, and the moment a change takes place they are fled.

But it would be imprudent in us to await the experiment, which is not only useless but rather dangerous and hurtful; for surely at a time when we stand most in need of friends it is afflicting to perceive that we are forsaken by those whom we esteemed such, especially when we have it not in our power to substitute a valuable and constant friend in the room of the base and faithless wretch who deserted us. Let us therefore have our friend, as we have our money, well tried and proved before the time of necessity, not convicted in the very act of using him; for it is not enough to feel ourselves injured, but we ought to have so much skill and knowledge of the flatterer that we receive no injury; otherwise we shall stand in the same predicament with those who learn the effects of any poisonous and deadly herb from the sad experience of having first tasted it, thus ruining ourselves in improving our judgment.

And so on the one hand we do not applaud such thoughtless and inconsiderate conduct, so on the other we cannot admire that over nice and cautious disposition, which, measuring friendship only by gravity of deportment and utility, concludes that a pleasant and cheerful companion is instantly to be deemed a parasite: for a friend is not a morose unsociable animal, nor is friendship venerable only in a severe austerity of manners, but its very gravity and venerable deportment are pleasing and desirable; but it increases no less the pleasures and happiness of those who are in prosperity than it diminishes the griefs and sorrows of the afflicted in adversity....

And hence we ought not instantly to suspect those of flattery who praise and commend us, for praise when seasonably applied becomes a true friend no less than censure; nay indeed a perpetually morose and querulous disposition is totally foreign to the pleasing intercourse of real amity; whereas men hear patiently and without murmur the rebuke and admonition of a friend whose benevolence prompts him liberally to bestow on their laudable actions a due degree of commendation, being persuaded that he who is so ready to commend must censure through necessity. It is difficult, then, some one may say, to distinguish between the flatterer and the friend, since they differ neither in the pleasure they give nor in the praises they bestow: nay, in various services and performances, we frequently see friendship outstript by flattery. And why should it not be so, we may answer, if indeed we investigate the character of the real flatterer who handles his business with all art and cunning? ... The man who neither appears to be false nor stands confest a flatterer; whom we cannot find lurking about our kitchen, nor watching the hour of dinner; who will not upon any occasion indulge in the pleasure of the bottle, but is always sober, meddling and inquisitive, wishes to mix in our affairs and be made a partaker of our secrets; and in short rather acts in friendship the grave part of tragedy, than the jocose and cheerful one of comedy. For as Plato says "that it is the summit of injustice to put on the appearance of justice without the substance," so that flattery is to be esteemed most dangerous, which does not act openly but in disguise, which is grave and serious in its deportment, and never relaxes.... But we who by no means approve of the saying "let my friend perish so that my enemy perish with him," but rather wish to separate the flatterers from the friend, connected indeed and entangled with him by too great a similarity, ought to be exceedingly careful that we neither throw away the good with the bad, nor, in our endeavor to preserve the friend, meet by mistake with the enemy....

Now since friendship is the sweetest of all human gratifications and nothing so much delights and exhilarates mankind, on this account the flatterer clothes himself in pleasures and is totally occupied in administering them; and because friendship is constantly attended with mutual acts of kindness and benevolence, therefore the flatterer obtruding himself into our services, strives with the most indefatigable zeal and industry ever to appear attentive to our interests; and since a similarity of pursuits and inclinations constitutes chiefly and supports the origin of friendship, the same aversions and desires first cement and confirm the bonds of amity; the flatterer observing this, and being of a very pliable disposition and easily persuaded to put on any appearance, moulds and conforms himself like matter that will receive any impression, seeking only to adjust and regulate his conduct according to the temper of those against whom his designs are formed.

But the most artful part of his conduct is yet to come; for perceiving that a proper freedom of expostulation is allowed universally to be the very voice and language of real friendship, and as peculiar to it as sound is to any animal; and that timid behavior which dares not boldly deliver its sentiments, is repugnant to that liberal openness and sincerity of heart which becomes a true friend; he has not let even this escape his imitation; but as skillful cooks make use of high seasonings to prevent the stomach being satiated by sweet and luscious meats, so the expostulatory freedom of the flatterer is neither genuine nor useful, but, winking as it were under frowns, tends only to soothe and gratify.

Upon these accounts then the flatterer is difficult to be caught, like some animals which, through the bounty of nature, escape pursuit by assuming the color of the earth or herbage that surrounds them. But since he deceives us by being disguised under the resemblance of a friend, it is our business to expose and deter him....

How then are we to convict this hypocrite, and by what distinctions is he to be detected, since he does not really resemble the friend, but imitates only his likeness? In the first place, we ought to observe the equability and consistency of his life and conduct, whether he delights always in the same objects, and be uniform in his approbations, whether he regulates his behavior according to one rule, and afford a proper example in his own life, for such conduct alone becomes the free and ingenuous admirer of real and true friendship; such only is the friend. But the flatterer having as it were no fixt residence of behavior, nor choosing a life to please himself, but moulding and conforming himself entirely to the will of another, is neither consistent nor uniform, but ever various and changeable, flowing about in every direction, from one shape to another, like water turned out of its course and adopting itself to the soil which receives it.... The flatterer allures and attracts others by imitation, though not all in the same manner; for with one he sings and dances, wrestles and boxes with another, and if he chances to fall into the company of any who are fond of hunting and hounds, he scarcely refrains from crying out in the words of Phaedra:

"Oh how I love to hear the hunter's horn"

and yet he cares not a rush for the stag, his care is only to entrap the hunter. If indeed he be in pursuit of any young man who is fond of literature, instantly he is enveloped in books, his beard hangs down to his feet, his cloak is ragged and threadbare, he is indifferent about every other concern, while the numbers, rectangles and triangles of Plato are perpetually in his mouth. If again any rich, idle debauchee, come his way, his threadbare cloak is thrown away, and his beard is mowed down like an unproductive harvest, while he indulges freely in the bottle and the glass and in ridiculing and scoffing at the philosophers. Thus they say at Syracuse when Plato arrived there and Dionysius was enthusiastic in the study of philosophy, that the whole palace was full of dust and sand on account of the great concourse of Geometricians who described their figures there; but when Plato fell into disgrace, and Dionysius forsaking his philosophy betook himself again to drinking, debauchery, and every species of folly and intemperance, instantly were they all transformed as by the cups of Circe, and unlettered barbarism, stupidity and oblivion overwhelmed them.... Alcibiades, while at Athens, indulged his satire and ridicule, kept a stud of horses, and lived a life of urbanity and freedom; at Sparta shaved himself to the skin, put on a worn cloak, and rigidly used the cold bath; the same man in Thrace did nothing but fight and drink; and when he dwelt in Persia with Tissaphernes, was all effeminacy, voluptuousness, and ostentation, thus by accommodating himself to the various manners and customs of mankind he gained universal popularity and esteem....

Such a man, if you chance to censure any of your friends before him, is ready to say, "You are very late in detecting this fellow, for my part I never once had a good opinion of him." If again you change your sentiments and convert your censure into praise, he will affirm with an oath "that he heartily congratulates with you, gives credit to everything you say of the man, and returns you many thanks for his sake." If you now talk of altering your course of life, for example, to betake yourself from public business to retirement and ease; "we ought long ago," says he, "to have retreated from the tumult and envy of the world." If again you express a wish of coming forward into public life and business; he accords with you and cries out, "Now you think worthy of yourself, this retirement has not its charms, but is unglorious and ignoble."

To such a man you ought instantly to say:

Sure from thy former self thou art vastly changed.

I want not a friend servilely to comply with all my humors and fancies, and ever be obedient to my nod, for my shadow does as much as this, but I want one who will follow me only in obedience to truth, and assist me impartially with his judgment. Such then is one mode of discovery of the flatterer....

As bad painters, who have not skill enough to express the finer touches of beauty, confine their business to wrinkles, spots and scars, so the flatterer imitates your intemperance, superstition, irascibility, harshness to servants, and mistreats your familiars and relations.... Flatterers, being desirous of appearing as well agreeable companions as faithful friends, pretend on account of the violence of their affection to be disgusted not even at your vices but in every respect to labor under the same natural infirmities and passions as yourself....

If they meet with men who are rather deaf or blind they can forsooth neither hear nor see well themselves; thus the parasites of Dionysius, who was afflicted with a dimness of sight, used to stumble upon each other, and throw down the dishes in the midst of dinner. Others indeed, laying siege to the passions, insinuate themselves deeper, and work their way into your most secret concerns by pretending to be fellow-sufferers....

Let us not pass over unnoticed that artifice of the flatterer in his imitation of the friend, wherein, though he imitate some virtue, he takes care always to yield him the superiority. With true friends indeed there is neither envy nor emulation, but whether equal or inferior in doing good the same equanimity and moderation of temper uniformly possesses them. But the flatterer, always bearing in his remembrance the inferior parts which he is acting, will never allow himself to be your equal, but confesses that he is every where vanquisht and outstript except in what is bad.

THE WELCOME

Edward Fitzgerald
(From the *Mantik-Ut-Tair* of Faríd-Uddín Attar)

One night, Shah Mahmúd, who had been of late
Somewhat distempered with Affairs of State,
Stroll'd through the Streets disguised, as wont to do—
And coming to the Baths, there on the Flue
Saw the poor Fellow who the Furnace fed
Sitting beside his Water-jug and Bread.
Mahmúd stept in—sat down—unask'd took up
And tasted of the untasted Loaf and Cup,
Saying within himself, "Grudge but a bit,
And, by the Lord, your Head shall pay for it!"
So having rested, warm'd and satisfied
Himself without a Word on either side,
At last the wayward Sultan rose to go.
And then at last his Host broke silence—"So?—
Art satisfied? Well, Brother, any Day
Or Night, remember, when you come this Way
And want a bit of Provender—why, you
Are welcome, and if not—why, welcome, too."—
The Sultan was so tickled with the whim
Of this quaint Entertainment and of him
Who offer'd it, that many a Night again
Stoker and Shah foregather'd in that vein—
Till, the poor Fellow having stood the Test
Of true Good-fellowship, Mahmúd confess'd
One night the Sultan that had been his Guest:

And in requital of the scanty Dole
The Poor Man offer'd with so large a Soul,
Bid him ask any Largess that he would—
A Throne—if he *would* have it, so he *should*.
The Poor Man kiss'd the Dust, and "All," said he,
"I ask is what and where I am to be;
If but the Shah from time to time will come
As now, and see me in the lowly Home
His presence makes a Palace, and my own
Poor Flue more royal than another's Throne."

The Balonda [tribe in Africa] have a most remarkable custom of cementing friendship. When two men agree to be special friends they go through a singular ceremony. The men sit opposite each other holding hands, and by the side of each is a vessel of beer. Slight cuts are then made on the clasped hands, on the pit of the stomach, on the right cheek and in the forehead. The point of a grassblade is pressed against each of these cuts, so as to take up a little of the blood, and each man washes the grass blade in his own beer. The vessels are then exchanged and the contents drunk, so that each imbibes the blood of the other. The two are thenceforth considered as blood-relations, and are bound to assist each other in every possible manner. While the beer is being drunk, the friends of each of the men beat on the ground with clubs, and bawl out certain sentences as ratification of the treaty. The ceremony is called "Kasendi." After it has been completed, gifts are exchanged, and both parties always give their most precious possessions.

—J. G. WOOD

MAN'S INGRATITUDE TO MAN

William Shakespeare

Blow, blow, thou winter wind,
Thou art not so unkind
  As man's ingratitude;
Thy tooth is not so keen,
Because thou art not seen,
  Although thy breath be rude.
Heigh-ho! sing, heigh-ho! unto the green holly:
Most friendship is feigning, most loving mere folly:
  Then heigh-ho, the holly!
  This life is most jolly.

Freeze, freeze, thou bitter sky,
That dost not bite so nigh
    As benefits forgot:
Though thou the waters warp,
Thy sting is not so sharp
    As friend remembered not.

"If he had only known!"

TWO LITTLE SOLDIERS
Guy de Maupassant

Every Sunday, as soon as they were free, the two little soldiers set off. On leaving the barracks they turned to the right; went through Courbevoie with long quick steps, as though they were on a march; then, having left the houses behind them, they followed at a calmer gait the bare and dusty high-road which leads to Bezons.

Being little and thin, they looked quite lost in their coats, which were too big and too long. The sleeves hung down over their hands, and they were much bothered by their enormous red breeches, which compelled them to walk wide. Under their stiff, high shakos their faces seemed like mere nothings—two poor, hollow Breton faces, simple in an almost animal simplicity, and with blue eyes which were gentle and calm.

During the walk they never spoke. They went straight on, each with the same idea in his head as the other. It stood them in place of conversation, for the fact is that just inside the little wood near Les Champioux they had found a place which reminded them of their own country, and it was only there that they felt happy.

When they came under the trees where the road from Colombes and from Chatou cross, they would take off their heavy shakos and wipe their foreheads.

They always stopped a little while on the Bezons bridge to look at the Seine. They would remain there two or three minutes, bent double, leaning on the parapet. Or sometimes they would gaze out over the great basin of Argenteuil, where the skiffs might be seen scudding, with their white, slanted sails, recalling perhaps the look of the Breton water, the harbor of Vannes, near which they lived, and the fishing-boats standing out across the Morbihan to the open sea.

As soon as they had crossed the Seine they bought their provisions from the sausage merchant, the baker, and the seller of the wine of the country. A piece of blood-pudding, four sous' worth of bread, and a little of "petit bleu" constituted the provisions which they carried off in their handkerchiefs. But after they left this village they now went very slowly forward, and they began to talk.

In front of them a barren plain strewn with clumps of trees led to the wood, to the little wood which had seemed to them to resemble the one at Kermarivan. Grain-fields and hay-fields bordered on the narrow path, which lost itself in this young greenness of the crops, and Jean Kerderen would always say to Luc le Ganidec:

"It looks like it does near Plounivon."

"Yes, exactly."

They went onward, side by side, their spirits suffused with vague memories of their own country, filled with awakened images—images as naïve as the pictures on the colored broadsheets which you buy for a penny. And they kept recognizing, as it were, now a corner of a field, a hedge, a bit of moorland, now a cross-roads, now a granite cross.

Then too, they would always stop beside a certain landmark, a great stone, because it looked something like the cromlech at Locneuven.

On arriving at the first clump of trees Luc le Ganidec every Sunday cut a switch, a hazel switch, and began gently to peel off the bark, thinking meanwhile of the folk there at home.

Jean Kerderen carried the provisions.

From time to time Luc mentioned a name, or recalled some doings of their childhood in a few brief words, which caused long thoughts. And their own country, their dear distant country repossessed them little by little, seized upon them, and sent to them from afar her shapes, her sounds, her well-known prospects, her odors—odors of the green land where the salt sea air was blowing.

They were no longer conscious of the exhalations of the Parisian stables on which the earth of the *banlieu* fattens, but of the perfume of the flowering broom, which the salt breeze of the open sea plucks and bears away. And the sails of the boats, appearing above the river-banks, seemed to them the sails of the coasting vessels perceived beyond the great plain which extended from their homes to the very margin of the waves.

They went with short steps, Luc le Ganidec and Jean Kerderen, content and sad, haunted by a sweet melancholy, by the lingering, penetrating sorrow of a caged animal who remembers.

And by the time that Luc had stripped the slender wand of its bark they arrived at the corner of the wood where every Sunday they took breakfast.

They found the two bricks which they had hidden in the thicket, and they kindled a little fire of branches, over which to roast their blood-pudding at the end of a bayonet.

And when they had breakfasted, eaten their bread to the last crumb, and drunk their wine to the last drop, they remained seated side by side upon the grass, saying nothing, their eyes on the distance, their eyelids dropping, their fingers crossed as at mass, their red legs stretched out beside the poppies of the field. And the leather of their shakos and the brass of their buttons glittered in the ardent sun, and made the larks, which sang and hovered above their heads, stop short.

About mid-day they began to turn their eyes from time to time in the direction of the village of Bezons, because the girl with the cow was coming.

She passed by them every Sunday on her way to milk and change the position of her cow—the only cow of this district which ever went out of the stable to grass. It pastured in a narrow field along the edge of wood a little farther on.

They soon perceived the girl, the only human being who came walking across the land. And they felt themselves rejoiced by the brilliant reflections thrown off by her tin milk-pail under the flame of the sun. They never talked about her. They were simply glad to see her, without understanding why.

She was a great strong wench with red hair, burned by the heat of sunny days, a great sturdy wench of the environs of Paris.

Once, finding them again seated in the same place, she said:

"Good morning. You two are always here, aren't you?"

Luc le Ganidec, the bolder, stammered:

"Yes; we come to rest."

That was all. But the next Sunday she laughed on seeing them, laughed with a protecting benevolence and a feminine keenness which knew well enough that they were bashful. And she asked:

"What are you doing here? Are you trying to see the grass grow?"

Luc was cheered up by this, and smiled likewise: "Maybe we are."

She continued: "*Hein!* That's pretty slow work."

He answered, still laughing: "Well, yes, it is."

She went on. But coming back with a milk-pail full of milk, she stopped again before them, and said:

"Would you like a drop? It will taste like home."

With her instinctive feeling that they were of the same peasant race as she, being herself also far away from home perhaps, she had divined and touched the spot.

They were both touched. Then, with some difficulty, she managed to make a little milk run into the neck of the glass bottle in which they carried their wine. And Luc drank first, with little swallows, stopping every minute to see whether he had drunk more than his half. Then he handed the bottle to Jean.

She stood upright before them, her hands on her hips, her pail on the ground at her feet, glad at the pleasure which she had given.

Then she departed, shouting: "*Allons! Adieu!* Till next Sunday!"

And as long as they could see her at all, they followed with their eyes her tall silhouette, which withdrew itself, growing smaller and smaller, and seeming to sink into the verdure of the fields.

When they were leaving the barracks the next week after, Jean said to Luc:

"Oughtn't we buy her something good?"

And they remained in great embarrassment before the problem of the choice of a delicacy for the girl with the cow.

Luc was of the opinion that a bit of tripe would be the best, but Jean preferred some *berlingots,* because he was fond of sweets. His choice fairly made him enthusiastic, and they bought at a grocer's two sous' worth of candies white and red.

They ate their breakfast more rapidly than usual, being nervous with expectation.

Jean saw her first: "There she is!" said he. Luc continued: "Yes, there she is."

While yet some distance off she laughed at seeing them. She cried:

"Is everything going as you like it?"

They answered together:

"Are you getting on all right?"

Then she conversed, talked to them of simple things in which they felt an interest—of the weather, of the crops, and of her master.

They were afraid to offer her their candies, which were slowly melting away in Jean's pocket.

At last Luc grew bold, and murmured:

"We have brought you something."

She demanded, "What is it? Tell me!"

Then Jean, blushing up to his ears, managed to get at the little paper cornucopia, and held it out.

She began to eat the little pieces of sugar, rolling them from one cheek to the other. And they made lumps beneath her flesh. The two soldiers, seated before her, regarded her with emotion and delight.

Then she went to milk her cow, and once more gave them some milk on coming back.

They thought of her all the week; several times they even spoke of her. The next Sunday she sat down with them for a little longer talk; and all three, seated side by side, their eyes lost in the distance, clasping their knees with their hands, told the small doings, the minute details of their life in the villages where they had been born, while over there the cow, seeing that the milk-maid had stopped on her way, stretched out towards her its heavy head with the dripping nostrils, and gave a long low to call her back.

Soon the girl consented to eat a bit of bread with them and drink a mouthful of wine. She often brought them plums in her pocket; for the season of plums had come. Her presence sharpened the wits of the two little Breton soldiers, and they chattered like two birds.

But, one Tuesday, Luc le Ganidec asked for leave—a thing which had never happened before—and he did not return until ten o'clock at night.

Jean racked his brains uneasily for a reason for his comrade's going out in this way.

The next Thursday Luc, having borrowed ten sous from his bed-fellow, again asked and obtained permission to leave the barracks for several hours.

And when he set off with Jean on their Sunday walk his manner was very queer, quite restless and quite changed. Kerderen did not understand, but he vaguely suspected something without divining what it could be.

They did not say a word to one another until they reached their usual stopping-place, where, from their constant sitting in the same spot, the grass was quite worn away. And they ate their breakfast slowly. Neither of them felt hungry.

Before long the girl appeared. As on every Sunday, they watched her coming. When she was quite near, Luc rose and made two steps forward. She put her milk-pail on the ground and kissed him. She kissed him passionately, throwing her arms about his neck, without noticing Jean, without remembering that he was there, without even seeing him.

And he sat there desperate, he the poor Jean, so desperate that he did not understand, his soul quite overwhelmed, his heart bursting, not yet expressing it all to himself.

Then the girl seated herself beside Luc, and they began to chatter.

Jean did not look at them; he now divined why his comrade had gone out twice during the week, and he felt within him a burning grief, a kind of wound, that sense of rending which is caused by a treason.

Luc and the girl got up together to go and change the position of the cow.

Jean followed them with his eyes. He saw them departing side by side. The red breeches of his comrade made a bright spot on the road. It was Luc who picked up the mallet and hammered down the stake to which they tied the beast.

The girl stooped to milk her, while he stroked the cow's sharp spine with a careless hand. They left the milk-pail on the grass, and they went deep into the wood.

Jean saw nothing more but the wall of leaves where they had entered; and he felt himself so troubled that if he had tried to rise he would certainly have fallen.

He sat motionless, stupefied by astonishment and suffering, by a suffering which was simple but which was deep. He wanted to cry, to run away, to hide himself, never to see anybody any more.

Suddenly he saw them issuing from the thicket. They returned gently, holding each other's hand, as in the villages do those who are promised. It was Luc who carried the pail.

They kissed one another again before they separated, and the girl went off after having thrown Jean a friendly "good-evening" and a smile which was full of meaning. To-day she no longer thought of offering him any milk.

The two little soldiers sat side by side, motionless as usual, silent and calm, their placid faces betraying nothing of all which troubled their hearts. The sun fell on them. Sometimes the cow lowed, looking at them from afar.

At their usual hour they rose to go back.

Luc cut a switch. Jean carried the empty bottle. He returned it to the wine-seller at Bezons. Then they sallied out upon the bridge, and, as they did every Sunday, they stopped several minutes in the middle to watch the water flowing.

Jean leaned, leaned more and more, over the iron railing, as though he saw in the current something which attracted him. Luc said: "Are you trying to drink?" Just as he uttered the last word Jean's head overbalanced his body, his legs described a circle in the air, and the little blue and red soldier fell in a lump, entered the water, and disappeared.

Luc, his throat paralyzed with anguish, tried in vain to shout. Farther down he saw something stir; then the head of his comrade rose to the surface of the river and re-entered it as soon.

Farther still he again perceived a hand, a single hand which issued from the stream and then plunged back. That was all.

The barge-men who ran up did not find the body that day.

Luc returned alone to the barracks, running, his head filled with madness; and he told of the accident, with tears in his eyes and voice, blowing his nose again and again; "He leaned over...he...leaned over...so far...so far that his head turned a somersault; and...and ...so he fell...he fell..."

He was strangled by emotion, he could say no more. If he had only known!

(*Translated by Jonathan Sturges*)

~~~~~~~

AN HONEST FRIEND
Henry Carey

With an honest old friend and a merry old song,
And a flask of old port, let me sit the night long,
And laugh at the malice of those who repine
That they must drink porter whilst I can drink wine.

I envy no mortal though ever so great,
Nor scorn I a wretch for his lowly estate;
But what I abhor, and esteem as a curse,
Is poorness of spirit, not poorness of purse.

Then dare to be generous, dauntless and gay,
Let us merrily pass life's remainder away;
Upheld by our friends, we our foes may despise,
For the more we are envied, the higher we rise.

"True friendship is a plant of slow growth..."

GEORGE WASHINGTON'S ADVICE TO HIS NEPHEW

Be courteous to all, but intimate with few; and let those few be well tried before you give them your confidence. True friendship is a plant of slow growth, and must undergo and withstand the shocks of adversity before it is entitled to the appellation. Let your heart feel for the afflictions and distresses of everyone, and let your hand give in proportion to your purse; remembering always the estimation of the widow's mite, that it is not everyone that asketh that deserveth charity; all, however, are worthy of the inquiry, or the deserving may suffer.

Do not conceive that fine clothes make fine men, any more than fine feathers make fine birds. A plain, genteel dress is more admired, obtains more credit, than lace and embroidery, in the eyes of the judicious and sensible.

He who gets and never gives
Will lose the truest friend that lives;
He who gives and never gets
Will sour his friendships with regrets;
Giving and getting, thus alone
A friendship lives—or dies a-moan.

—ALEXANDER MACLEAN

"That little snatch of conversation was so agreeable . . ."

HORACE WALPOLE AT AGE FOURTEEN WRITES A FRIENDLY LETTER TO CHARLES LYTTELTON

My dearest Charles,

The pleasure that the interview, tho' so very short, that I had with you the night before you left town, gave me, has I think made your absence seem still more insupportable. That little snatch of conversation was so agreeable, that I am continually thinking how happy we should be in a much longer. I can reflect with great joy on the moments we passed together at Eton, and long to talk 'em over, as I think we could recollect a thousand passages, which were something above the common rate of schoolboy diversions. I can remember with no small satisfaction that we did not pass our time in gloriously beating great clowns, who would patiently bear children's thumps for the collections, which I think some of our contemporaries were so wise as to make for them afterwards. We had other amusements which I long to call to mind with you: when shall I be so happy? Let me know, my dear Charles, how far you are from Ragley; I have some thoughts of going down thither this summer, and if it is not too far, I will spend a day with you in Worcestershire. You may assure yourself I am mightily put to it for news, when for want of that, I send you some trifling verses of my own, which have nothing to recommend 'em but the subject. I know you will excuse 'em, when you consider they come from

My dearest Charles,
Yr sincere Friend and Servant
HOR: WALPOLE

"...the greatness and the goodness of the heart..."

CHARLES DICKENS PAYS TRIBUTE TO WILLIAM MAKEPEACE THACKERAY

It has been desired by some of the personal friends of the great English writer who established this magazine [*The Cornhill Magazine*], that its brief record of his having been stricken from among men should be written by the old comrade and brother in arms who pens these lines, and of whom he often wrote himself, and always with the warmest generosity.

I saw him first, nearly twenty-eight years ago, when he proposed to become the illustrator of my earliest book. I saw him last, shortly before Christmas at the Athenaeum Club, when he told me that he had been in bed three days—that, after these attacks, he was troubled with cold shiverings, "which quite took the power of work out of him"—and that he had it in his mind to try a new remedy which he laughingly described. He was very cheerful, and looked very bright. In the night of that day week, he died.

The long interval between those two periods is marked in my remembrance of him by many occasions when he was supremely humorous, when he was irresistibly extravagant, when he was softened and serious, when he was charming with children. But, by none do I recall him more tenderly than by two or three that start out of the crowd, when he unexpectedly presented himself in my room, announcing how that some passage in a certain book had made him cry yesterday, and how he had come to dinner, "because he couldn't help it," and must talk such passage over. No one could have seen him more genial, natural, cordial, fresh, and honestly impulsive, than I have seen him at those times. No one can be surer than I, of the greatness and the goodness of the heart that then disclosed itself....

He had a particular delight in boys, and an excellent way with them. I remember him once asking me with fantastic gravity, when he had been to Eton where my eldest son then was, whether I felt as he did in regard of never seeing a boy without wanting instantly to give him a sovereign! I thought of this when I looked down into his grave, after he was laid there, for I looked down into it over the shoulder of a boy to whom he had been kind.

These are slight remembrances; but it is to the little familiar things suggestive of the voice, look, manner, never, never more to be encountered on this earth, that the mind first turns in a bereavement.

And greater things that are known of him, in the way of his warm affections, his quiet endurance, his unselfish thoughtfulness for others, and his munificent hand, may not be told....

On the table before me, there lies all that he had written of his latest and last story. That it would be very sad to anyone—that it is inexpressibly so to a writer—in its evidences of matured designs never to be accomplished, of intentions begun to be executed and destined never to be completed, of careful preparation for long roads of thought that he was never to traverse, and for shining goals that he was never to reach, will be readily believed. The pain, however, that I have felt in perusing it, has not been deeper than the conviction that he was in the healthiest vigor of his powers when he wrought on this last labor. In respect of earnest feeling, far-seeing purpose, character, incident, and a certain loving picturesqueness blending the whole, I believe it to be much the best of all his works. That he fully meant it to be so, that he had become strongly attached to it, and that he bestowed great pains upon it, I trace on almost every page....

The last line he wrote, and the last proof he corrected, are among these papers through which I have so sorrowfully made my way. The condition of the little pages of manuscript where Death stopped his hand, shows that he had carried them about, and often taken them out of his pocket here and there, for patient revision and interlineation. The last words he corrected in print, were "And my heart throbbed with an exquisite bliss." God grant that on that Christmas Eve when he laid his head back on his pillow and threw up his arms as he had been wont to do, when very weary, some consciousness of duty done and Christian hope throughout life humbly cherished, may have caused his own heart so to throb, when he passed away to his Redeemer's rest!

He was found peacefully lying as above described, composed, undisturbed, and to all appearances asleep, on the twenty-fourth of December, 1863. He was only in his fifty-third year; so young a man, that the mother who blessed him in his first sleep, blessed him in his last.

The holy passion of Friendship is so sweet and steady and loyal and enduring a nature that it will last through a whole lifetime, if not asked to lend money.

—SAMUEL L. CLEMENS

"...like the shadow of the sundial..."

A FASHIONABLE FRIEND
Horace Smith

A fashionable friend is one who will dine with you, game with you, walk or ride out with you, borrow money of you, escort your wife to public places—if she be handsome—stand by to see you fairly shot, if you happen to be engaged in a duel and slink away and see you fairly clapped in a prison, if you experience a reverse of fortune. Such a man is like the shadow of the sundial, which appears in fine weather, and vanishes when there comes a rainy day.

QUA CURSUM VENTUS
Arthur Hugh Clough

As ships, becalmed at eve, that lay
   With canvas drooping, side by side,
Two towers of sail at dawn of day
   Are scarce long leagues apart described;

When fell the night, upsprung the breeze,
   And all the darkling hours they plied,
Nor dreamt but each the self-same seas
   By each was cleaving, side by side;

E'en so—but why the tale reveal
   Of those, whom year by year unchanged,
Brief absence joined anew to feel,
   Astounded, soul from soul estranged?

At dead of night their sails were filled,
   And onward each rejoicing steered—
Ah, neither blame, for neither willed,
   Or wist, what first with dawn appeared!

To veer, how vain! On, onward strain,
　Brave barks! In light, in darkness too,
Through winds and tides one compass guides—
　To that, and your own selves, be true.

But O blithe breeze, and O great seas,
　Though ne'er, that earliest parting past,
On your wide plain they join again,
　Together lead them home at last.

One port, methought, alike they sought,
　One purpose hold where'er they fare,—
O bounding breeze, O rushing seas!
　At last, at last, unite them there!

"Ours are ties ... sent us by providence ..."

JOHN KEATS
TO HIS BROTHER GEORGE

Hampstead, October 13, 1818

I am grieved to say I am not sorry you had not Letters at Philadelphia; you could have had no good news of Tom and I have been withheld on his account from beginning these many days; I could not bring myself to say the truth, that he is no better but much worse—However it must be told; and you must my dear Brother and Sister take example from me and bear up against any Calamity for my sake as I do for yours. Ours are ties which independent of their own Sentiment are sent us by providence to prevent the deleterious effects of one great solitary grief. I have Fanny and I have you—three people whose Happiness to me is sacred—and it does annul that selfish sorrow which I should otherwise fall into, living as I do with poor Tom who looks upon me as his only comfort—the tears will come into your Eyes—let them—and embrace each other—thank heaven for what happiness you have, and after thinking a moment or two that you suffer in common with all Mankind hold it not a sin to regain your cheerfulness—

I will relieve you of one uneasiness of overleaf: I returned I said on account of my health—I am now well from a bad sore throat which came of bog trotting in the Island of Mull—of which you shall hear by the copies I shall make from my Scotch Letters—

Your content in each other is a delight to me which I cannot express—the Moon is now shining full and brilliant—she is the same to me in Matter, what you are to me in Spirit. If you were here my dear Sister I could not pronounce the words which I can write to you from a distance: I have a tenderness for you, and an admiration which I feel to be as great and more chaste than I can have for any woman in the world. You will mention Fanny—her character is not formed, her identity does not press upon me as yours does. I hope from the bottom of my heart that I may one day feel as much for her as I do for you— I know not how it is, but I have never made any acquaintance of my own—nearly all through your medium my dear Brother—through you I know not only a Sister but a glorious human being. And now I am talking of those to whom you have made me known I cannot forbear mentioning Haslam as a most kind and obliging and constant friend. His behaviour to Tom during my absence and since my return has endeared him to me for ever—besides his anxiety about you. Tomorrow I shall call on your Mother and exchange information with her. On Tom's account I have not been able to pass so much time with her as I would otherwise have done—I have seen her but twice— once I dined with her and Charles—She was well, in good spirits, and I kept her laughing at my bad jokes. We went to tea at Mrs. Millar's, and in going were particularly struck with the light and shade through the Gateway at the Horse Guards. I intend to write you such Volumes that it will be impossible for me to keep any order or method in what I write: that will come first which is uppermost in my Mind, not that which is uppermost in my heart.

Hampstead, December 18, 1818

Sometimes I fancy an immense separation, and sometimes as at present, a direct communication of Spirit with you. That will be one of the grandeurs of immortality—There will be no space, and consequently the only commerce between spirits will be their intelligence of each other—when they will completely understand each other, while we in this world merely comprehend each other in different degrees— the higher the degree of good so higher is our Love and friendship. I have been so little used to writing lately that I am afraid you will not smoke my meaning so I will give an example—Suppose Brown or Haslam or any one whom I understand in the next degree to what I do you, were in America, they would be so much the farther from me in proportion as their identity was less impressed upon me. Now the reason why I do not feel at the present moment so far from you is that I remember your Ways and Manners and actions; I know your manner of thinking, your manner of feeling: I know what shape your joy or your sorrow would take; I know the manner of your walking, standing, sauntering, sitting down, laughing, punning, and every action so truly that you seem near to me. You will remember me in the same manner—and the more when I tell you that I shall read a passage of Shakespeare every Sunday at ten o'Clock—you read one at the same time, and we shall be as near each other as blind bodies can be in the same room.

THE UNSEEN PLAYMATE

Robert Louis Stevenson

When children are playing alone on the green,
In comes the playmate that never was seen.
When children are happy and lonely and good,
The Friend of the Children comes out of the wood.

Nobody heard him and nobody saw,
His is a picture you never could draw,
But he's sure to be present, abroad or at home,
When children are happy and playing alone.

He lies in the laurels, he runs on the grass,
He sings when you tinkle the musical glass;
Whene'er you are happy and cannot tell why,
The Friend of the Children is sure to be by!

He loves to be little, he hates to be big,
'Tis he that inhabits the caves that you dig;
'Tis he when you play with your soldiers of tin
That sides with the Frenchman and never can win.

'Tis he, when at night you go off to your bed,
Bids you go to your sleep and not trouble your head;
For wherever they're lying, in cupboard or shelf,
'Tis he will take care of your playthings himself!

"... the patrons of philosophy ... are always at leisure, and in good
humor ... "

THE FRIENDSHIP
OF THE PHILOSOPHERS

Seneca

The felicity of mankind depends upon the counsel of philosophers.
Let us rather consider what nature has made superfluous and what
necessary; how easy our conditions are, and how delicious that life
which is governed by reason rather than opinion. . . .

There are a sort of people that are never well but at theatres, spectacles, and public places, men of business, but it is only in their faces:
for they wander up and down without any design; like pismires, eager
and empty; and every thing they do is only *as it happens*. This is an
humor which a man may call a kind of restless laziness. Others you
shall have that are perpetually in haste, as if they were crying *Fire,* or
running for a midwife, and all this hurry, perhaps, only to salute somebody that has no mind to take notice of them; or some such trivial
errand. At night, when they come home tired and weary, ask them
why they went out? where they have been? and what they have done?
it is a very slender account they are able to give you: and yet the next
day they take the same *jaunt* over again: this is a kind of fantastical
industry, a great deal of pains taken to no purpose at all: twenty
visits made, and nobody at home, (they themselves least of all.) They
that have this vice are commonly hearkeners, talebearers, newsmongers,
meddlers in other people's affairs, and curious after secrets, which a
man can neither safely hear nor report. These men of idle employment,
that run up and down eternally vexing others, and themselves too;
that thrust themselves into all companies; what do they get by it? One
man is asleep, another at supper, a third in company, a fourth in haste,
a fifth gives them the slip; and when their folly has gone the round,
they close up the day with shame and repentance. Whereas Zeno,
Pythagoras, Democritus, Aristotle, Theophrastus, and all the patrons
of *philosophy* and virtue, they are always at leisure, and in good humor;
familiar, profitable: a man never comes away empty-handed from
them, but full of comfort and satisfaction; they make all past ages
present to us, or us their contemporaries. The doors of these men are
open night and day; and in their conversation there is neither danger,
treachery, nor expense; but we are the wiser, the happier, and the
richer for it. How blessedly does a man spend his time in this company, where he may advise in all the difficulties of life! Here is counsel

without reproach, and praise without flattery. We cannot be the choosers of our own parents, but of our friends we may; and adopt ourselves into these noble families.

(*Translated by Sir Roger L'Estrange, Knt.*)

"He devoted his life to helping people."

WHAT IS A MAN PROFITED?
William Allen White

The other day in Emporia, the longest funeral procession that has formed in ten years followed the Rev. John Jones three long miles in the hot July sun out to Dry Creek Cemetery. Now, a funeral procession may mean little or much. When a rich and powerful man dies, the people play politics and attend his funeral for various reasons. But here was the body of a meek, gentle little old man—a man "without purse or scrip." It won't take twenty minutes to settle his estate in probate court. He was a preacher of the gospel—but preachers have been buried before this in Emporia without much show of sorrow.

The reason so many people lined up behind the hearse that held the kind old man's mortality was simple: they loved him. He devoted his life to helping people. In a very simple way, without money or worldly power, he gave of the gentleness of his heart to all around him. We are apt to say that money talks, but it speaks a broken, poverty-stricken language. Hearts talk better, clearer, and with a wider intelligence. This old man with the soft voice and the kindly manners knew the language of the heart and he spoke it where it would give zest to joy. He worked manfully and with a will in his section of the vineyard, and against odds and discouragements he won time and again. He was infinitely patient and brave. He held a simple, old-fashioned faith in God and his loving kindness.

When others gave money—which was of their store—he gave prayers and hard work and an inspiring courage. He helped. In his sphere he was a power. And so when he lay down to sleep hundreds of friends trudged out to bid him good-by with moist eyes and with cramped throats to wish him sweet slumber.

And then they turned back to the world to make money—to make money—what a hollow impotent thing! What is a man profited if he gain the whole world and lose his own soul?

INDEX OF AUTHORS
(With Sources)